Literacy in the Early Grades

A Successful Start for PreK–4 Readers and Writers

Fifth Edition

Gail E. Tompkins
Late of California State University, Fresno

Emily Rodgers
The Ohio State University

Director and Publisher: Kevin Davis
Portfolio Manager: Drew Bennett
Managing Content Producer: Megan Moffo
Content Producer: Yagnesh Jani
Portfolio Management Assistant: Maria Feliberty
Managing Digital Producer: Autumn Benson
Digital Studio Producer: Lauren Carlson
Executive Development Editor: Linda Bishop
Executive Product Marketing Manager: Krista Clark
Procurement Specialist: Deidra Headlee

Cover Design: Pearson CSC, SPi Global
Cover Art: Pearson CSC
Full Service Vendor: Pearson CSC
Full Service Project Management: Pearson CSC, Vanitha Puela
Editorial Project Manager: Pearson CSC, Clara Bartunek
Printer-Binder: LSC Communications
Cover Printer: LSC Communications
Text Font: Palatino LT Pro

Credits and acknowledgments for materials borrowed from other sources and reproduced, with permission, in this textbook appear on the appropriate page within the text.

Every effort has been made to provide accurate and current Internet information in this book. However, the Internet and information posted on it are constantly changing, so it is inevitable that some of the Internet addresses listed in this textbook will change.

Library of Congress Cataloging-in-Publication Data

Names: Tompkins, Gail E; Rodger, Emily, author.
Title: Literacy in the early grades: a successful start for preK-4 readers
   and writers / Gail E. Tompkins.
Description: Fifth edition. | Upper Saddle River, New Jersey : Pearson
   Education, Inc., 2019. | Includes bibliographical references and index.
Identifiers: LCCN 2018041392| ISBN 9780134990569 | ISBN 0134990560
Subjects: LCSH: Language arts (Preschool) | Language arts (Elementary) | Language arts (Early childhood) |
   Children—Language. | Child development.
Classification: LCC LB1576 .T6575 2019 | DDC 372.6/049—dc23 LC record available at https://lccn.loc
   .gov/2018041392

1 18

ISBN-13: 978-013-499056-9
ISBN-10:   013-499056-0

*Pearson Education dedicates this book
to Gail E. Tompkins, one of our most gifted writers.
Her talent was valued not only by Pearson but also by
many literacy and language arts professors who recognized her ability
to make research practical and teaching accessible for their students.
Gail understood the literacy needs of children
and also the essential role teachers play in meeting those needs.
She masterfully wrote and deeply cared about both.*

For my nephew Travis and his wife Andrea;
and for all the other early career teachers who, like them,
are making a difference in the
lives of their students.

Emily Rodgers

Dear Reader,

I was delighted to be invited to co-author this new edition of *Literacy in the Early Grades: A Successful Start for PreK-4 Readers and Writers* with Gail Tompkins. Gail's textbooks for preservice teachers are so well-respected for their depth and detail; as a college professor myself, I leapt at the chance to work alongside her. Sadly, I didn't get a chance to meet Gail; she passed away just as our work together on this text was getting underway. However, after a year immersed in co-authoring this text I feel I know Gail very well. We couldn't collaborate in person or on the phone or via Skype as I was imagining we would, but every time I opened a chapter file to work on, I felt I was in close dialogue with her. Gail's voice is that personal, that caring, about preparing expert literacy teachers of young children.

Like Gail, I was a teacher for several years before undertaking a doctoral degree and eventually going on to earn a position as a professor in a college of education. I started out teaching in a third-grade classroom; it was a beautiful group of young students who taught me so much about the range and variation of strengths, needs, and interests that exist in one class. I can still name all 28 students! (You never forget your first class!)

Though I loved teaching third grade, I became increasingly interested in what the reading specialist was doing with my students when they left my classroom for additional instruction. I realized I really wanted to be the specialist who worked with students who needed something more than classroom instruction. That interest led me to pursue a special education degree in reading, and then I spent several years working with 6th–8th graders who were struggling with classroom instruction.

In my new position as a remedial reading teacher, I learned a lot about assessment, diagnosis, and planning instruction. I also learned something else that led me to a third career change: while studying the records of my 6th–8th grade struggling readers, I realized that nearly every single one of the cumulative records contained teacher comments going as far back as kindergarten identifying reading and writing difficulties. I realized that it was possible to see the trajectory of reading progress going off course at a very early age, and I also realized the importance of early literacy instruction. I also learned that if young students are on a successful track early on, they almost certainly will stay on that track throughout the grades. However, young students who are struggling early on will almost certainly continue to struggle unless they have expert instruction from their teachers to help them catch up.

These realizations about the importance of becoming literate and of closing gaps as soon as they appear spurred me on to study early literacy at a doctoral level. I was fortunate to study at The Ohio State University and to become involved in Reading Recovery at OSU as a trainer of teacher leaders for 15 years. In my role as a faculty member at Ohio State, I have continued to work closely with teachers and young children; I wouldn't have it any other way.

As a teacher of young children, you have in your hands a remarkable opportunity to help beginning readers and writers become literate early on. Know that as a classroom teacher you are your students' first tier of instruction and you are responsible for each and every student in your classroom. Know too that you can make an incredible difference in the lives of young individuals who will soon (perhaps sooner than you can imagine) be college and career ready high school students, due in no small part to your early efforts to set them on a strong path to becoming literate.

This textbook, rich in theory and instruction, will help prepare you for that awesome job. I invite you to dialogue with Gail and me, as you read these chapters. Every word is written with you in mind.

Emily Rodgers
Columbus, Ohio

Brief Contents

Contents

Special Features

Teacher Accountability

Instructional Support

Go Digital!

Literacy Portraits

Diverse Learners

Teaching English Learners

If Students Struggle ...

Developmentally Responsive Practice

PreK Practices

Assessment Resources

Preface

Our goal is for all young students to make a successful start in reading and writing. We believe the key to making that happen is for teachers to use a balanced approach that combines explicit instruction, guided practice, and authentic application. Effective teachers know their students and their individual learning needs, and they use this knowledge—and their understanding of how students develop from emergent to beginning to fluent readers and writers—to guide their teaching. This 5th edition of *Literacy in the Early Grades: A Successful Start for PreK–4 Readers and Writers*, provides the background knowledge, modeling, and application tools that will ensure you are well prepared to meet grade-level standards and lead young students to become fluent readers and writers.

New To This Edition

The value of a new edition of the text are the changes that are made to both improve upon the delivery of content and address any concerns text reviewers and users have had. As a result of that review and a careful look at the previous edition, the following is new to this edition:

A NEW AUTHOR!   New to this edition is author Dr. Emily Rodgers. Dr. Rodgers is a professor at The Ohio State University and a well-respected educator in the Reading and Literacy in Early and Middle Childhood Area of Study where she mentors graduate students and teaches courses related to early literacy. Her research examines the nature of effective scaffolding in early literacy instruction; effective coaching of teachers; and challenges of reforming, implementing, scaling, and sustaining effective literacy intervention practices. Her research has been published in a number of prestigious peer-reviewed journals including The Reading Teacher, Reading Research Quarterly, Journal of Early Childhood Literacy, and The Journal of Reading Recovery. She has also contributed to the writing of numerous books on literacy. You will benefit from the ideas and updated research she shares in the pages of this text. Welcome, Dr. Rodgers!

MYLAB EDUCATION.   One of the most visible changes in the 5th edition—also one of the most significant—is the expansion of the digital learning and assessment resources embedded in the eText and the inclusion of MyLab Education in the text. MyLab Education is an online homework, tutorial, and assessment program designed to work with the text to engage learners and to improve learning. Within its structured environment, learners see key concepts demonstrated through real classroom video footage, practice what they learn, test their understanding, and receive feedback to guide their learning and to ensure their mastery of key learning outcomes. Designed to bring learners more directly into the world of K-12 classrooms and to help them see the real and powerful impact of literacy concepts covered in this book, the online resources in MyLab Education with the Enhanced eText include:

- **Video Examples.**   Several embedded videos per chapter provide illustrations of a literacy teaching principle or concept in action. These video examples most often show students and teachers working in classrooms. Sometimes they portray teachers describing their literacy teaching experiences or identify literacy experts who share their wisdom and guidance. Many new videos are included in every chapter. Be sure to read the captions which will identify why you will find the video informative and respond to the caption question to satisfy your own learning.

- **Self-Checks.**   In each chapter, self-check quizzes help assess how well learners have mastered the content. The self-checks are made up of self-grading multiple-choice items that not only provide feedback on whether questions are answered correctly or incorrectly, but also provide rationales for both correct and incorrect answers.

- **Application Exercises.**   These exercises give learners opportunities to practice applying the content and strategies from the chapters. The questions in these exercises are usually constructed-response. Once learners provide their own answers to the questions, they receive feedback in the form of model answers written by experts.

ADVANCED ROLE OF LEARNING OUTCOMES.   Chapter topics are organized around the major concepts shared in the learning outcomes. New to this edition, however, is the greater import of ensuring that the outcomes are realized by you. A Study Plan has been carefully developed for you based on these outcomes. As you complete reading major chapter sections, check your own understanding of the content through Practice questions and Quiz Me sections as part of the Self-Check quizzes in your MyLab. In addition, the Application Exercises provide you with teaching artifacts and/or videos that engage you in observing authentic practice, reviewing examples of the literacy development of young students, and using teaching artifacts that model those actual classroom teachers use. You will be asked to engage in what teachers do to monitor or measure student literacy development and to make instructional decisions. Our goal is to support your college methods course experience and help prepare you as well as we can for actual classroom teaching.

REORGANIZED CHAPTER 1.   Chapter 1, *Becoming an Effective Teacher of Reading*, contains the latest standards for literacy, reading, and language arts as recently updated by the national Board for Professional Teaching Standards. The chapter also covers the principles that undergird literacy teaching, but these principles are now organized under four umbrella themes—*Learning and Learning to Read, Effective Reading Instruction, Differentiating Instruction to Meet Students' Needs*, and *Linking Assessment to Instruction* which are mapped on to the very latest set of standards from the National Board for Professional Teaching Standards. These new themes required revising the Learning Outcomes and make this chapter more manageable for teacher educators and as accessible as it is critical for your growth as a teacher candidate.

CLARITY OF CONCEPTS ABOUT ASSESSMENT.   Chapter 3, *Assessing Students' Literacy Development*, covers assessment of student literacy development and now identifies the differences between assessment and evaluation while better explaining the use and value of running records. Rather than support the misperception that error analysis is the same as running records, new discussions and featured examples identify how to capture the errors young students may make in their reading and measure them to determine students' reading levels. Application exercises, both in this chapter and throughout the text, provide opportunities to monitor and assess student work including practice in completing running records. You will find that assessment that informs instruction is an idea threaded throughout this text.

CONCEPTS ABOUT PHONOLOGICAL AWARENESS.   Chapter 4 in this text, *Cracking the Alphabetic Code*, has been carefully revised to introduce oral language concepts and phonological awareness before developing an understanding of phonemic awareness and the strategies you need to know to engage students in manipulating sounds. Building a strong foundation for recognizing young students' emergent language skills and phonological awareness will better prepare you for developing phonemic awareness and teaching phonics.

UPDATED RESEARCH.   Wise with each edition is the updating of research where research is new. Those of you who have used this title before will recognize the new citations within chapters and in the chapter end references.

A Focus On Classroom Practice

We have written this text for you. It shares our vision for reading and writing instruction because we know you want to become a successful teacher of reading and writing, capable of using instructional approaches and procedures that unlock the door to reading and writing for young students. Grounding the text in both scientific research and authentic classroom practice, we cover the fundamental components of literacy instruction, illustrate how to teach developmental strategies and skills, and identify how to differentiate instruction to meet the needs of every student in your classroom—students who come to school well prepared for literacy learning and those who struggle with learning to read and write, including students whose first language isn't English. Throughout this text is critical classroom pedagogy organized under five purposeful themes—*teacher accountability, instructional support, developmentally responsive practice, diverse learners,* and *assessment resources.* Text features shared through these themes illustrate the significant roles and responsibilities you'll be expected to undertake in teaching reading and writing to students from PreK through grade 4.

Teacher Accountability

As a teacher, you'll be asked to account for student achievement in reading and writing; your accountability will depend on how you address the Common Core State Standards in your literacy lessons and your successful use of instructional methods. Your knowledge can be significantly advanced through the use of this text and the following distinctive features:

NEW! MY TEACHING TO-DO CHECK-LISTS. Teaching reading and writing requires understanding a number of important components—the processes of reading and writing, literacy assessment, and the strategies and skills for teaching phonemic awareness and phonics, fluency, vocabulary, comprehension, and writing. Along with the instructional knowledge shared in each chapter, we provide *Teaching To-Do Checklists* that will serve as guidelines in your classroom to verify that you've covered key elements for each reading and writing component. You can download these checklists from the eText. Be sure to take them into your classrooms!

MY TEACHING TO-DO CHECKLIST: Comprehension: Reader Factors

- ☐ I teach students to attend to both reader and text factors as they read.
- ☐ I teach comprehension strategies using a combination of explanations, demonstrations, think-alouds, and practice activities.
- ☐ I expect students to apply the strategies they've learned when they're reading independently.
- ☐ I have students apply comprehension strategies in literacy activities as well as in thematic units.
- ☐ I display student-made charts about the strategies in the classroom.
- ☐ I have students read and analyze increasingly complex texts.
- ☐ I have students read grade-appropriate fiction and nonfiction texts.

COMMON CORE STATE STANDARDS. Look for Common Core State Standards boxes that highlight specific English Language Arts Standards you'll be responsible for teaching. These boxes point out how to use grade-level standards to plan concrete and purposeful literacy lessons that align with national and state literacy standards.

Common Core State Standards

Comprehension: Reader Factors

The Common Core State Standards for English Language Arts emphasize that students are expected to read a broad range of high-quality and increasingly challenging texts. Students must understand precisely what authors say and make interpretations based on textual evidence. The Standards specify these comprehension requirements:

- Students determine the central ideas of a text and analyze their development.
- Students make connections with background knowledge and other texts.
- Students draw inferences from the textual evidence.
- Students cite textual evidence that supports an analysis of what the text states explicitly.
- Students comprehend grade-level stories, informational books, and other texts independently and proficiently.

The Standards emphasize that students use reader factors to comprehend increasingly complex fiction and nonfiction texts. To learn more about the Standards, go to http://www.corestandards.org/ELA-Literacy, or check your state's educational standards website.

Teach Kids to Be Strategic!
Comprehension Strategies

Teach students to apply these strategies (presented here in alphabetical order):

- Activate background knowledge
- Connect
- Determine importance
- Draw inferences
- Evaluate
- Monitor
- Predict
- Question
- Repair
- Set a purpose
- Summarize
- Visualize

Students learn to use each strategy and make posters to highlight their new knowledge. They apply strategies as they read and use self-stick notes to record their strategy use. Monitor students' growing use of strategies during independent reading activities, and if they struggle, reteach the strategies, making sure to name them and model their use.

TEACH KIDS TO BE STRATEGIC! This feature will be invaluable to use in the classroom. Specific guidelines list the strategies you need to teach and then explain what to check for to ensure that students are applying them. Utilizing these features will help you and your students meet grade-level standards. Be sure to use them in your classroom!

NEW! ACCOUNTABILITY CHECK Located at the end of each chapter are MyLab: Application Exercises. These self-assessment questions and application activities allow you to test your knowledge of the chapter content. Interactive activities, *Monitoring Literacy Development* and *Assessing Literacy Development,* appear in every chapter, asking you to apply your understanding of students' literacy development and classroom practice and make instructional decisions based on that understanding.

Instructional Support

Balance is critical to teaching reading and writing: balancing the teaching of reading and writing, balancing explicit instruction with practice, and balancing the use of assessment to inform instruction. Knowing how to balance the teaching of reading and writing strategies—when, why, and how—is a significant part of teacher preparation. The following features illustrate explicit instructional procedures, identifying when, why, and how to use them. Many are supported by specific and authentic teaching examples.

First Grade Phonics Instruction

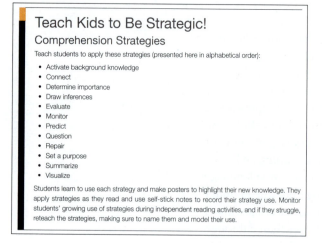

It's 8:10 on Thursday morning, and the 19 first graders in Mrs. Firpo's classroo[m] gathered on the carpet for their 15-minute phonemic awareness lesson. This w[eek's] topic is the short *i* sound and the consonant *x* which sounds like /ks/ like fox; [today] Mrs. Firpo will focus on short *i*. One by one, she holds up cards with pictures repr[esent]-ing the short *i* sound. "Remember," Mrs. Firpo adds, "say the word slowly, just [...]

CHAPTER-OPENING VIGNETTES. As a signature feature of this text, chapter-opening stories describe how effective teachers integrate the teaching of reading and writing to maximize your understanding of classroom practice.

Minilesson

TOPIC: Spelling *-at* Family Words

GRADE: First Grade

TIME: One 10-minute period

Mr. Cheng teaches phonics during guided reading lessons. He introduces, practices, and reviews phonics concepts using words from selections his first graders are reading. The students decode and spell words using letter and word cards, magnetic letters, and small whiteboards and pens.

1. **Introduce the Topic**

   Mr. Cheng holds up a copy of *At Home*, the small paperback Level E book the students read yesterday, and asks them to reread the title. Then he asks the students to identify the first word, *at*. After they read the word, *at*, he hands a card with the word *at* written on it to each of the six students in the guided reading group. "Who can read this word?" he asks. Several students recognize it immediately, and others carefully sound out the two-letter word.

MINILESSONS. Each of these popular step-by-step features models a clear and concise instructional strategy or skill and is meant to serve as a ready tool for your classroom teaching.

BOOKLISTS. Quality books support students' development of literacy and advance their fluency, vocabulary, and comprehension. Booklists appear throughout the chapters to identify grade-appropriate literature for your classroom or point you to literature your students can read independently.

Booklist	Wordplay Books
Type	**Books**
Invented Words	Degan, B. (1985). *Jamberry.* Hutchins, P. (2002). *Don't forget the bacon!* Martin, B., Jr., & Archambault, J. (2009). *Chicka chicka boom boom.* Most, B. (1996). *Cock-a-doodle-moo!* Slate, J. (1996). *Miss Bindergarten gets ready for kindergarten.* Slepian, J., & Seidler, A. (2001). *The hungry thing.*
Repetitive Lines	Deming, A. G. (1994). *Who is tapping at my window?.* Downey, L. (2000). *The flea's sneeze.* Fleming, D. (2007). *In the small, small pond.* Hoberman, M. A. (2003). *The lady with the alligator purse.* Taback, S. (1997). *There was an old lady who swallowed a fly.* Taback, S. (2004). *This is the house that Jack built.* Westcott, N. B. (2003). *I know an old lady who swallowed a fly.* Wilson, K. (2003). *A frog in a bag.*
Rhyming Words	Ehlert, L. (1993). *Eating the alphabet: Fruits and vegetables from A to Z.* McPhail, D. (1996). *Pigs aplenty, pigs galore.* Root, P. (2003). *One duck stuck.* Seuss, Dr. (1963). *Hop on pop.* Shaw, N. (2006). *Sheep in a jeep.*

STUDENT ARTIFACTS. Nothing illustrates connected teaching and learning better than authentic artifacts of students' work. This text is peppered with examples of students' developmental writing performance to help you learn to recognize grade-appropriate writing development.

SCAFFOLDING STUDENTS' READING DEVELOPMENT. Five instructional approaches—*guided reading lessons, basal reading programs, literature focus units, literature circles,* and *reading and writing workshop*—provide concrete means for teaching reading and writing. Chapter 10 reviews these approaches, illustrating organization of your reading and writing instruction including how to plan for and manage each one. You can examine which makes the most sense for your classroom planning in alignment with the requirements of the school district for which you work.

GO DIGITAL! In many schools across the country, teachers engage students in digital learning. Our Go Digital! features provide practical ideas and guidance for using specific programs and products that will benefit you or your students in the use of technology and the development of media skills.

INSTRUCTIONAL PROCEDURES AS POP-UP FEATURES. Throughout this text, **boldface, green** terms identify printable pop-up features that show how to engage in a variety of step-by-step instructional procedures. A fully developed bank of these evidence-based teaching procedures is located in the Compendium at the back of the text. The pop-ups display the step-by-step procedures in brief; the Compendium offers more complete descriptions, including research that supports the use of each procedure.

LITERACY PORTRAITS. Literacy Portraits features draw your attention to five students—Rhiannon, Rakie, Michael, Curt'Lynn, and Jimmy—who are introduced at the beginning of this text as members of Ms. Janusz's second grade class. Direct links to video footage of these five students are available in the eText and allow you to track their reading and writing development through the school year.

Literacy Portraits

Ms. Janusz regularly teaches her second graders about comprehension strategies, including predicting, connecting, visualizing, asking questions, and repairing. She introduces a strategy and demonstrates how to use it in a minilesson; next, she encourages the students to practice using it as she reads books aloud. Then students start using the strategy themselves during guided reading lessons and reading workshop. Ms. Janusz monitors their strategy use as she conferences with them. Listen to Rakie, Rhiannon, and Jimmy talk about comprehension strategies and their ability to use them: Which strategies do they seem most confident about using?

Rakie

Rhiannon

Jimmy

Diverse Learners

No two students in any classroom are alike. Students come to school with different language experiences and literacy opportunities. They also differ in the way they learn and in the languages they speak. This text describes the vast diversity of students and explain what it means to differentiate instruction to meet individual student's literacy needs.

TEACHING ENGLISH LEARNERS. Each expanded chapter section focuses on ways to scaffold students who are learning to read and write at the same time they're learning to speak English. These sections provide in-depth guidance for planning instruction that addresses the needs of culturally and linguistically diverse students.

IF STUDENTS STRUGGLE . . . These text sections describe ways to intervene after an assessment indicates students aren't making adequate progress or meeting a grade-level standard. These suggestions for classroom intervention detail ways to assist struggling readers and writers.

Developmentally Responsive Practice

Effective teaching requires fine-tuning the ability to determine where each child is in his or her literacy development. Features in this text support the development of teaching skills that lead to decision making based on knowledge of students' current level of literacy progress. Many new application exercises, including those at the ends of every chapter, will help you practice developmental decision making.

PREK PRACTICES. PreK Practices draw your attention to the most appropriate instruction for the youngest of literacy learners and especially for four-year-olds.

Developmental Continuum Phonemic Awareness

PreK	K	1	2	3	4
Four-year-olds become aware of words as units of sound as they play with sounds and create rhymes.	Students pronounce sounds and isolate, match, and manipulate them as they learn to blend and segment.	Students use the blending strategy to decode words and the segmenting strategy to spell words.	Second graders continue to use blending and segmenting to decode and spell more challenging words.	Students apply phonemic awareness strategies to decode and spell two- and three-syllable words.	Fourth graders blend and segment sounds as they read and spell multisyllabic words with roots and affixes.

DEVELOPMENTAL CONTINUUM. The Developmental Continuum features typical expectations for students' literacy accomplishments at each grade—prekindergarten through fourth grade—and will help you understand how students grow as readers and writers. Developmental Continuums appear for *reading and writing development*, *phonemic awareness*, *phonics*, *spelling*, *reading and writing fluency*, *vocabulary*, and *comprehension* for both reader and text factors.

Assessment Resources

Assessment requires teachers to plan for, monitor, and evaluate students' literacy progress. Although summative assessment is often a part of a formal all-grade-level or whole-school program, formative assessment measures are typically chosen by and used at the discretion of classroom teachers. Within each chapter, we provide a variety of authentic assessment examples so you can learn how to plan for assessment that measures what's intended, glean ongoing information on student progress, and tailor instruction to meet student needs. Recording assessment data on a frequent basis assists in documenting student progress and achievement.

ASSESSING STUDENTS' LITERACY DEVELOPMENT. Chapter 3 is placed early in the text to lay the groundwork for assessing in line with backward design, ensuring that you know how you're going to measure literacy progress as you set literacy goals. Information in this chapter addresses how to use student performance to inform instructional planning.

INSTRUCTION–ASSESSMENT CYCLE. Effective teachers engage in a four-step cycle that links instructional planning with assessment. The Instruction-Assessment Cycle identifies how teachers plan for, monitor, evaluate, and reflect on instruction that is informed by assessment.

ASSESSMENT TOOLS. Descriptions throughout the text identify well-respected and widely used assessment tools that measure literacy development. Teachers are responsible for knowing about these assessment choices, when it's appropriate to use them, and the kinds of screening or diagnostic information they impart.

Assessment Tools

Comprehension

Teachers use a combination of informal assessment procedures, including story retellings and think-alouds, and commercially available tests to measure students' comprehension. These tests are often used in PreK through fourth grade classrooms:

- **Comprehension Thinking Strategies Assessment**
  The Comprehension Thinking Strategies Assessment (Keene, 2006) examines first through eighth graders' ability to use these strategies to think about fiction and nonfiction texts: activating background knowledge, determining importance, drawing inferences, noticing text structure, questioning, setting a purpose, and visualizing. As students read a passage, they pause and reflect on their strategy use. Teachers score students' responses using a rubric. This 30-minute test can be administered to individuals or to the class, depending on whether students' responses are oral or written. This flexible assessment tool can be used to evaluate students' learning after teaching a strategy, to survey progres... end of the yea...

ASSESSMENT SNAPSHOTS. Chapters include a variety of authentic examples of assessment that portray the literacy performance of various students. Teacher notes are overlaid on each assessment example and illustrate the information teachers gather from assessment and what that information may mean to guide further instruction. You'll have the opportunity to examine assessment samples and draw your own conclusions in many of the *MyLab Application Exercises*.

Assessment Snapshot

Spelling Analysis

I worked hard as a reasearcher. I took my time on pickers and handwriting. I read books too. After that I wrote the facks down on indecks cards. I laid them owt and then numberd them. My favorit part was when I figred owt I was stdying my first choyce.

TEACHER'S NOTE

Tatum spelled 88% of the words correctly, and most errors were representative of the Within-Word Pattern stage. These errors indicate that she's investigating ways to spell complex consonant and vowel sounds. She also wrote 10 two- and three-syllable words and spelled three correctly. Tatum's moving into the Syllables and Affixes stage; her spelling development meets grade-level standards.

Classification of Errors

Letter Name-Alphabetic	Within-Word Pattern	Syllables and Affixes	Derivational Relations
	pickers	reasearcher	
	facks	numberd	
	indecks	favorit	
	owt	figred	
	owt		
	stdying		
	choyce		

Acknowledgements

Many people have contributed in some important way to the production of this new edition. I am grateful to the undergraduate students in my Reading Foundations class at Ohio State for their thoughtful participation in classes; their questions and comments gave me insights in to which topics in this volume would need greater explanation and more examples. I also have enjoyed a special learning relationship with the doctoral students who teach sections of the Reading Foundations course including Jungmin Lee, Rebecca Tang, and Hillary Libnoch.

I want to thank the graduate students who contributed to my thinking about foundations of reading. Thank you to Catie Fisher, Kathleen Warga, and Cameron Carter, all experienced teachers pursuing their master's degrees who gave me insights into what expert reading teachers know and understand how to do. Drs. Sinead Harmey, Robert H. Kelly, and Katherine Brownfield, all former doctoral students, provided me with examples of excellent and caring educators of teachers and children. Virginia Hollatz contributed to our scholarly community for a year while she pursued her master's degree. Current graduate students including Clara Mikita, Rebecca Berenbon, Christa Winkler, Ryan Iaconelli, Tracy Johnson, and Mollie Wright enrich my life daily with their sharp minds about educational research.

Thank you also to my reading colleagues at Ohio State: Drs. Julia Hagge, Michiko Hikida, Barbara Kiefer, Linda Parsons, Shayne Piasta, Adrian Rodgers, Cris Warner and Ian Wilkinson; I am fortunate to have opportunities to discuss reading matters on a regular basis with such smart and kind individuals. I am also deeply grateful to have the opportunity to collaborate with Dr. Jerome D'Agostino—a brilliant mind and a compassionate soul with a passion for fairness and equity that is imbued in his teaching and scholarship. Through our research together, we are learning a lot about reading development and you will find some of those new ideas in these pages.

I also want to thank the professors and teaching professionals who reviewed our text and offered insightful comments that informed development of this revision, among them: Jill Davis, University of Central Oklahoma; Bessie P. Dernikos, Florida Atlantic University; and Sarah Ramsey, Northeastern State University.

I want to express sincere appreciation to the Pearson team for their dedication to perfection and professionalism. Thank you to Drew Bennett, Editor/Portfolios Manager; he invited me to join this project as co-author and then provided guidance and support along the way (always at just the right moments). Thank you also to Yagnesh Jani, Content Producer and Jon Theiss Media Producer, for providing needed videos and pictures on demand, and also to Clara Bartunek, Editorial Project Manager, and Vanitha Puela, Project Manager, who worked together to supervise production of the copyedit and eText. The attractiveness of this volume is due in large part to their efforts. I owe a huge debt of gratitude to Linda Bishop, a talented development editor with whom I have had the good fortune to work with and learn from; know that her voice and touch lie within every page.

Finally, of course, I want to acknowledge Gail Tompkins, long-time author of this volume and many other texts for Pearson. It is indeed an honor to write alongside Gail. I am grateful for her life and for all that she gave to educators and will continue to give in her published works.

Emily Rodgers

Introducing
Ms. Janusz and Her Second Graders

Classrooms are different today; they've become communities of learners. There's a hum as students read together, share their writing, and work in small groups. Students are more culturally and linguistically diverse, and many are English learners. Teachers guide and nurture learning through their instructional programs. Here's what teachers do:

- Balance explicit instruction with authentic application
- Integrate reading and writing
- Teach with trade books as well as textbooks
- Differentiate instruction so every student can succeed
- Link assessments and instruction

To show what literacy looks like in a real classroom, Ms. Janusz and five of her second graders are featured in Literacy Portraits throughout this text. You can track these students' literacy development by reviewing their monthly video clips in the Video Resources located on the navigation bar of the *Pearson eText* and within chapters. Four of these students—Rakie, Rhiannon, Michael, and Curt'Lynn—began second grade not meeting grade-level expectations. Jimmy, however, exemplifies second-grade standards and provides a grade-level comparison. All of the students have shown tremendous growth during the school year, becoming more capable readers and writers.

Rakie

Rakie's favorite color is pink, and she loves her cat, JoJo. She came to America from Africa when she was very young, and she's currently enrolled in the school's pull-out ESL program. Rakie enjoys reading books with friends in the library area. Her favorite book is Doreen Cronin's *Click Clack Moo: Cows That Type* because she appreciates that troublesome duck. Rakie's a fluent reader, but she has difficulty understanding what she reads, mainly because of unfamiliar vocabulary, a common problem for English learners. Rakie's bright, and Ms. Janusz is pleased she is making great strides!

A minte leter I opened the door and JoJo was foze in a ice cobe.

Rhiannon

Rhiannon, the youngest in Ms. Janusz's class, is a charmer. Her gusto for life is contagious! In September, she held books upside down, but she's made tremendous progress since then. Mo Willems is her favorite author; she loves his stories, including *Don't Let the Pigeon Drive the Bus!* She struggles to decode unfamiliar words, usually depending on the "sound it out" strategy. Rhiannon is passionate about writing. She creates inventive stories about her dogs, Taco and Tequila, and gets very animated when sharing them with classmates, but abbreviated spellings make her writing difficult to read.

> I soD it to my DaD. B u D up! So I pot Logr clos onanD pas anD soD It to my DaD. B u D u p!

Michael

Michael is gregarious and loves fun in any size or shape. He takes karate lessons and his Xbox video gaming system is a prized possession. In September, Michael, who is bilingual, was reading below grade level and couldn't stay on task, but after Ms. Janusz encouraged him to choose books that he wanted to read and to identify topics for writing, his motivation began to grow. Now, he is making rapid progress! He's not crazy about reading except for *The Magic Tree House* series of chapter books, but he really enjoys writing. He says that his stories are good because he uses wordplay effectively.

> Beep beep beep beep it was 9:00 am. I new I had to wacke up. I toock my first Step, Slip the flors were frozen Solid.

Jimmy

Jimmy's a big sports fan—he likes the Cleveland Indians and the Ohio State Buckeyes, in particular—but his real passion is World War II. He likes to play Army with his best friend, Sam. Jimmy often chooses nonfiction books on varied topics to read; recently, he read a biography about rock-and-roll idol Elvis Presley. Jimmy's a bright student who achieves at or about grade level in all subjects. He's eager to please and worries about making a mistake when he's sharing his writing or reading aloud. In September, Jimmy had trouble with comprehension, but now he's a confident, strategic reader.

> It was a haunted house! The door creKed opin. "BOO!" said a ghost. And Lady was gone! "AAAA!" said Jim.

Curt'Lynn

Curt'Lynn enjoys playing with her buddies Leah and Audri at recess and spending time with her Granny. Her reading was at early-first grade level at the beginning of second grade. Before second grade, she often "read" books to herself, telling the story through the illustrations. Now Curt'Lynn loves to read Dr. Seuss books because they're funny. Her focus is on decoding words, but she's beginning to think about whether the words she's reading make sense. Curt'Lynn recognizes that her reading has been improving this year because, as she explains, it's becoming easier to get words right.

> When I was just 4 years old, I was a cherLeedre Because I rill wueted to be a cherLeedre.

Chapter 1
Becoming an Effective Teacher of Reading

 ## Learning Outcomes

After studying this chapter, you'll be prepared to:

1.1 Identify key characteristics of four different perspectives about learning.

1.2 Explain what is meant by "a balanced approach" to instruction.

1.3 Explain how and why teachers differentiate instruction.

1.4 Describe how teachers link instruction and assessment.

Effective teachers are the key to ensuring that students learn to read and write successfully. Most researchers agree that teacher quality is the most important factor in determining how well students learn (Vandevoort, Amrein-Beardsley, & Berliner, 2004). Teachers need to be knowledgeable about how students learn to read and write, how to teach literacy, and how to respond to the needs of those learning English as a new language.

Today, teachers are held accountable for their effectiveness. In 2002, the federal No Child Left Behind (NCLB) Act ushered in a new era by holding schools responsible for educating all students to meet mandated standards. Teachers have always been responsible for advancing their students' achievement, but NCLB led to annual standardized tests, beginning in second grade, to measure students' achievement; then the scores were used to determine whether teachers and schools were effective.

President Obama called for "a new culture of accountability"—one that builds on NCLB (Dinan, 2009). He described these components of accountability: better tracking of teachers' performance, higher standards for teachers, and assistance for teachers who aren't effective. He also recommended that exemplary teachers be recognized for their effectiveness and that they be asked to serve as mentors or lead teachers in their schools. Obama's notion of teacher accountability still translates to how well students perform on standardized tests, but new ways of determining teacher effectiveness are on the horizon; one of the most promising involves evaluating teachers against the characteristics of effective teachers.

The National Board for Professional Teaching Standards (National Board for Professional Teaching Standards, 2012) developed a system of standards that represents a national consensus about what makes teachers effective. These 13 standards describe what teachers need to know and do to support students' learning:

Knowledge of Learners.   Accomplished teachers draw on their relationships with students as well as their knowledge of literacy and child development to acquire knowledge of their students as intellectual, social, emotional, cultural, and language learners.

Equity, Fairness, and Diversity.   Accomplished teachers practice equity and fairness; they value diversity and diverse perspectives. They teach all students to know and respect themselves and others and to use literacy practices to promote social justice.

Learning Environment.   Accomplished teachers establish a caring, supportive, inclusive, challenging, democratic, and safe learning community in which students take intellectual, social, and emotional risks while working both independently and collaboratively.

Instruction.   Accomplished teachers employ rich instructional resources and provide instruction that is tailored to the unique needs of students in order to foster inquiry; facilitate learning; and build strategic, independent thinkers who understand the power of language.

Assessment.   Accomplished teachers use a range of ongoing formal and informal assessment methods and strategies to gather data in order to shape and drive instructional decisions, monitor individual student progress, guide student self-assessment, gather information to communicate to various audiences, and engage in ongoing reflection.

Reading.   Accomplished teachers use their knowledge of the reading processes, their students, and the dynamic connections within the other language arts to create effective instruction so that all readers construct meaning and develop an enduring appreciation of reading.

Writing.   Accomplished teachers use their knowledge of writing processes, language acquisition, writing development, and ongoing assessment to provide authentic and relevant instruction that prepares students to write for a variety of purposes and audiences.

Listening and Speaking.   Accomplished teachers know, value, and teach oral language development, listening, and both verbal and nonverbal communication skills as essential components of literacy,. They also provide opportunities for all students to listen and speak for a variety of purposes and audiences.

Viewing and Visual Literacy.   Accomplished teachers know, value, and teach viewing and visual literacy as essential components of literacy instruction in order to prepare students to interpret and interact with an increasingly visual world.

Literacy Across the Curriculum.   Accomplished teachers understand the reciprocal and interrelated nature of the literacy processes of reading, writing, listening, speaking, and viewing and engage students in language arts processes in all disciplines.

Teacher as Learner and Reflective Practitioner.   Accomplished teachers seek to improve their knowledge and practice through a recursive process of learning and reflecting.

Collaboration with Families and Communities.   Accomplished teachers develop positive and mutually supportive relationships with family and community members to achieve common goals for the literacy education of all students.

Professional Responsibility.   Accomplished teachers actively contribute to the improvement of literacy teaching and learning and to the advancement of literacy knowledge and practice for the profession.

To read more about these characteristics, go the National Board for Professional Teaching Standards website (http://www.nbpts.org).

The goal of literacy instruction is to ensure that all students reach their full literacy potential, and in that light, this chapter introduces eight principles of balanced literacy instruction. These principles are stated in terms of what effective teachers do, and they provide the foundation for the chapters that follow. The eight principles are grouped into four themes: *learning and learning to read, effective reading instruction, adjusting instruction to meet the needs of individual learners,* and *linking assessment to instructional planning.*

Theme 1: Learning and Learning to Read

Teaching requires that teachers understand how students learn and theories of learning form a foundation for that understanding. Teachers who are knowledgeable about learning are prepared to create a community of learners—a setting conducive to literacy instruction. And literacy instruction is informed by four cueing systems that serve as the underpinning of language. Effective teachers recognize the role that each of these three principles—knowledge about learning, a community of learners, and language cueing systems—play in the teaching of reading and writing.

Principle 1: Effective Teachers Are Knowledgeable About Learning

Until the 1960s, behaviorism—a teacher-centered theory—was the dominant view; since then, student-centered theories that advocate students' active engagement in authentic literacy activities have become more influential. These student-centered views about learning can be grouped into three distinct approaches: constructivism, sociolinguistics, and information processing. Tracey and Morrow (2006) argue that multiple theoretical perspectives improve the quality of literacy instruction, and the stance advocated in this text is that instruction should represent a realistic balance between teacher-and student-centered theories. Figure 1–1 presents an overview of these theories.

BEHAVIORISM.   Behaviorists focus on the observable and measurable aspects of students' behavior. They believe that behavior can be learned or unlearned as the result of stimulus-and-response actions (O'Donohue & Kitchener, 1998). Reading

Figure 1–1 Learning Theories

ORIENTATION	THEORY	CHARACTERISTICS	APPLICATIONS
Teacher-Centered	Behaviorism	• Focuses on observable changes in behavior • Views the teacher's role as providing information and supervising practice • Describes learning as the result of stimulus–response actions • Uses incentives and rewards for motivation	• Basal readers • Minilessons • Worksheets
Student-Centered	Constructivism	• Describes learning as the active construction of knowledge • Recognizes the importance of background knowledge • Views learners as innately curious • Suggests ways to engage students so they can be successful	• Literature focus units • KWL charts • Thematic units • Word sorts
	Sociolinguistics	• Emphasizes the importance of language and social interaction on learning • Views reading and writing as social and cultural activities • Explains that students learn best through authentic activities • Describes the teacher's role as scaffolding students' learning	• Literature circles • Shared reading • Reading and writing workshop • Author's chair
	Information Processing	• Recommends integrating reading and writing • Views reading and writing as meaning-making processes • Explains that readers' interpretations are individualized • Describes students as strategic readers and writers	• Guided reading • Graphic organizers • Grand conversations • Interactive writing

is viewed as a conditioned response. This theory is described as teacher-centered because it focuses on the teacher's role as a dispenser of knowledge. Skinner (1974) explained that students learn to read by mastering a series of discrete skills and subskills.

Teachers use explicit instruction to teach skills in a planned, sequential order. Information is presented in small steps and reinforced through practice activities until students achieve mastery because each step is built on the previous one. Students practice skills by completing fill-in-the-blank worksheets, and they usually work individually, not in small groups or with a classmate. Behavior modification is another key feature: Teachers control and motivate students through a combination of rewards and punishments.

CONSTRUCTIVISM.   Constructivist theorists describe students as active and engaged learners who construct their own knowledge; learning occurs when students integrate new information with their existing knowledge. This theory is student-centered because teachers engage students with experiences so that they can construct their own knowledge.

Schema Theory.   Knowledge is organized into cognitive structures called **schemas**, and schema theory describes how students learn. Jean Piaget (1969) explained that learning is the modification of schemas as students actively interact with their environment. Imagine that the brain is a mental filing cabinet, and that new information is organized with existing knowledge in the filing system. When students are already familiar with a topic, the new information is added to a mental file, or schema, in a revision process called **assimilation**, but when students study a new topic, they create a new mental file and place the information in it; this more difficult construction process is **accommodation**. Everyone's cognitive structure is different, reflecting knowledge and past experiences.

Inquiry Learning.   John Dewey (1997) advocated an inquiry approach to develop citizens who could participate fully in democracy (Tracey & Morrow, 2006). He theorized that learners are innately curious and actively create their own knowledge. He also concluded that collaboration, not competition, is more conducive to learning. Students collaborate to conduct investigations in which they ask questions, seek information, and create new knowledge to solve problems.

Engagement Theory.   Theorists have examined students' interest in reading and writing and found that engaged learners are intrinsically motivated; they do more reading and writing, enjoy these activities, and reach higher levels of achievement (Guthrie & Wigfield, 2000). Engaged learners have **self-efficacy**, or confidence that they'll reach their goals (Bandura, 1997). Students with high self-efficacy are resilient and persistent, despite obstacles that get in the way of their success. These theorists believe that students are more engaged when they participate in authentic literacy activities in a nurturing classroom community.

SOCIOLINGUISTICS.   Lev Vygotsky (1978, 1986) theorized that language organizes thought and is a learning tool. He recommended that teachers incorporate opportunities for students to talk with classmates as part of the learning process. Vygotsky realized that students can accomplish more challenging tasks in collaboration with adults than they can on their own but that they learn little by performing easy tasks that they can already do independently; he recommended that teachers focus instruction on students' **zone of proximal development**—the level between their actual development and their potential development. As students learn, teachers gradually withdraw their support so that students eventually perform the task independently. Then the cycle begins again.

Sociocultural Theory.   Reading and writing are viewed as social activities that reflect the culture and community students live in (Moll & Gonzales, 2004). Sociocultural theorists explain that students from varied cultures have different expectations about literacy and preferred ways of learning. Teachers apply this theory as they create culturally responsive classrooms that empower everyone—including those from marginalized groups—to become successful readers and writers (Keehne, Sarsona, Kawakami, & Au, 2018). They're respectful of all students and confident in their ability to learn.

Teachers often use powerful multicultural literature to develop students' cross-cultural awareness, including *Goin' Somewhere Special* (McKissack, 2001), about the mistreatment of black students in the segregated South; *Esperanza Rising* (Ryan, 2002), about a Mexican American girl who creates a new future for herself; and *Happy Birthday Mr. Kang* (Roth, 2001), about a Chinese-American grandfather who learns a lesson about freedom. The Booklist presents these and other multicultural books.

Culturally responsive teaching acknowledges the legitimacy of all students' cultures and social customs and teaches students to appreciate their classmates' diverse heritages. This theory emphasizes that teachers must be responsive to their students' instructional needs. When students aren't successful, teachers examine their instructional practices and make changes so that all students become capable readers and writers.

Situated Learning Theory.   Learning takes place as a function of the activity, context, and culture in which it occurs (Lave & Wenger, 1991). Situated learning theory rejects the notion of separating learning to do something from actually doing it and emphasizes the importance of apprenticeship, where beginners move from the edge of a learning community to its center as they develop expertise (Brown, Collins, & Duguid, 1989). Just as chefs learn as they work in restaurants, students learn best through authentic and meaningful activities. They join a community of learners and become more expert readers and writers through interaction with classmates. The teacher serves as an expert model, much like a chef does.

Critical Literacy.   Freire (2000) called for sweeping educational change so that students examine fundamental questions about justice and equity. Critical literacy theorists view language as a means for social action and advocate that students become agents of social change (Johnson & Freedman, 2005). This theory has a

Booklist Multicultural Books

Culture	Books
African American	Bridges, R. (1999). *Through my eyes.* McKissack, P. (2001). *Goin' somewhere special.* Rappaport, D. (2007). *Martin's big words: The life of Dr. Martin Luther King, Jr.* Ringgold, F. (1996). *Tar beach.* Williams, V. B. (1984). *A chair for my mother.* Woodson, J. (2005). *Show way.*
Arab American	Bunting, E. (2006). *One green apple.* Mobin-Uddin, A. (2005). *My name is Bilal.* Nye, N. S. (1997). *Sitti's secrets.* Perkins, M. (2008). *Rickshaw girl.* Wolf, B. (2003). *Coming to America: A Muslim family's story.*
Asian American	Choi, Y. (2003). *The name jar.* Look, L. (2006). *Ruby Lu, brave and true.* Park, L. S. (2008). *Bee-bim bop!* Roth, S. (2001). *Happy birthday Mr. Kang.* Say, A. (2008). *Grandfather's journey.* Yang, B. (2007). *Hannah is my name: A young immigrant's story.*
Hispanic American	Adler, D. A., & Adler, M. S. (2011). *A picture book of Cesar Chavez.* Bunting, E. (1998). *Going home.* Dorros, A. (1997). *Abuela.* Ryan, P. M. (2002). *Esperanza rising.* Soto, G. (1996). *Too many tamales.* Tonatiuh, D. (2010). *Dear Primo: A letter to my cousin.*
Native American	Baylor, B. (1986). *Amigo.* Baylor, B. (1986). *The way to start a day.* Bruchac, J. (1997). *13 moons on a turtle's back.* Martin, B., Jr., & Archambault, J. (1997). *Knots on a counting rope.* McDermott, G. (2001). *Raven: A trickster tale from the Pacific Northwest.*

political agenda, and the increasing social and cultural diversity in American society adds urgency to resolving inequities and injustices. One way that students examine social issues is by reading books such as *Smoky Night* (Bunting, 1999), a Caldecott Medal–winning story about overcoming racism set during the Los

Booklist Books That Foster Critical Literacy

Grades	Books
PreK–K	Boelts, M. (2009). *Those shoes.* DiSalvo-Ryan, D. (1994). *City green.* McBrier, P. (2004). *Beatrice's goat.* Recorvits, H. (2003). *My name is Yoon.* Winter, J. (2008). *Wangari's trees of peace: A true story from Africa.*
1–2	Bunting, E. (1997). *A day's work.* Bunting, E. (2006). *One green apple.* Choi, Y. (2003). *The name jar.* DiSalvo, D. (2001). *A castle on Viola Street.* DiSalvo-Ryan, D. (1997). *Uncle Willie and the soup kitchen.* Golenbock, P. (1992). *Teammates.* Pinkney, A. D. (2003). *Fishing day.* Uchida, Y. (1996). *The bracelet.* Wiles, D. (2005). *Freedom summer.* Woodson, J. (2001). *The other side.*
3–4	Bridges, R. (1999). *Through my eyes.* Bunting, E. (1999). *Smoky night.* Coleman, E. (1999). *White socks only.* Deedy, C. A. (2009). *14 cows for America.* Gunning, M. (2004). *A shelter in our car.* McGovern, A. (1999). *The lady in the box.* Ringgold, F. (2003). *If a bus could talk: The story of Rosa Parks.* Ryan, P. M. (2002). *Esperanza rising.* Tamar, E. (1996). *The garden of happiness.* Weatherford, C. B. (2007). *Freedom on the menu: The Greensboro sit-ins.*

Angeles riots. This story and others presented in this Booklist address injustices that students can discuss and understand (Lewison, Leland, & Harste, 2008).

INFORMATION PROCESSING. Information-processing theory compares the mind to a computer and describes how information moves through a series of processing units—sensory register, short-term memory, and long-term memory—as it's stored (Tracey & Morrow, 2006). There's also a control mechanism that oversees learning. Theorists create models of the reading and writing processes to describe the complicated, interactive workings of the mind (Hayes, 2004; Kintsch, 2013; Rumelhart, 2013). They believe that reading and writing are related, and their models describe a two-way flow of information between what readers and writers know and the words written on the page.

Interactive Models. Reading and writing are interactive meaning-making processes. The interactive model emphasizes that readers focus on comprehension and construct meaning using a combination of reader-based and text-based information. This model also includes an executive monitor that oversees students' attention, determines whether what they're reading makes sense, and takes action when problems arise (Ruddell & Unrau, 2013).

Hayes's (2004) model of writing describes what writers do as they write. It emphasizes that writing is also an interactive, meaning-making process. Students move through a series of stages as they plan, draft, revise, and edit their writing to ensure that readers will understand what they've written. Writers use the same control mechanism that readers do to make plans, select strategies, and solve problems.

Transactional Theory. Rosenblatt's transactional theory (2013) explains how readers create meaning. She describes comprehension as the result of a two-way transaction between the reader and the text. Instead of trying to figure out the author's meaning, readers negotiate an interpretation based on the text and their knowledge about literature and the world. Interpretations are individualized because each student brings different knowledge and experiences to the reading event. Even though interpretations vary, they must be substantiated by the text.

Strategic Behaviors. Students employ strategic or goal-oriented behaviors to direct their thinking. Cognitive strategies, such as visualizing, organizing, and revising, are used to achieve a goal, and metacognitive strategies, such as monitoring and repairing, determine whether that goal is reached (Dean, 2006; Pressley, 2002). The word **metacognition** is often defined as "thinking about your own thinking," but more accurately, it refers to a sophisticated level of thought that people use to control their thinking (Baker, 2008). Metacognition is a control mechanism; it involves both students' awareness and active control of thinking.

Principle 2: Effective Teachers Create a Community of Learners

Classrooms are social settings. Together, students and their teacher create a classroom community, and the environment strongly influences the learning that takes place (Angelillo, 2008; Bullard, 2010). The classroom community should be inviting, supportive, and safe so learners will actively participate in reading and writing experiences. Perhaps the most striking quality is the partnership between the teacher and students: They become a "family" in which all members respect one another and support each other's learning. Students value culturally and linguistically diverse classmates and recognize that everyone makes important contributions.

Think about the differences between renting and owning a home. In a classroom community, students and the teacher are joint "owners" who assume responsibility for

Literacy Portraits

Ms. Janusz spent the first month of the school year creating a community of learners in her classroom. She taught the second graders how to participate in reading and writing workshop, including procedures for choosing books, reading with a buddy, and keeping a writer's notebook. They learned to work cooperatively, take responsibility for their work and behavior, and show respect for their classmates. In the following two videos, respectively, Curt'Lynn interacts with classmates as she shares a story about her family, and Jimmy works with Michael on writing a letter. Which of the characteristics of a community of learners described in the third principle do these video clips demonstrate? Why do you think Ms. Janusz tries to build a community of learners among the students in her classroom?

Curt'Lynn

Jimmy

their behavior and learning, work collaboratively with classmates, complete assignments, and care for the classroom. In traditional classrooms, in contrast, the classroom belongs to the teacher and students are "renters" for the school year. Joint ownership doesn't mean that teachers abdicate their responsibility; on the contrary, they're the guides, instructors, coaches, and evaluators.

CHARACTERISTICS OF A CLASSROOM COMMUNITY.   A successful classroom community has specific, identifiable characteristics that are conducive to learning:

Safety.   The classroom is a safe place that promotes in-depth learning and nurtures students' physical and emotional well-being.

Respect.   Students and the teacher are respectful of each other. Harassment, bullying, and verbal abuse aren't tolerated, and cultural, linguistic, and learning differences are respected so that students feel comfortable and valued.

High Expectations.   Teachers set high expectations and emphasize that all students can be successful. Their expectations promote a positive classroom environment where students behave appropriately and develop self-confidence.

Risk-Taking.   Teachers encourage students to explore new topics, try unfamiliar activities, and develop higher level thinking skills.

Collaboration.   Students work with classmates on literacy activities and other projects. Working together provides scaffolding and enhances their achievement.

Choice.   Students make choices about books they read, topics they write about, and projects they pursue within parameters set by the teacher. When students make choices, they're more motivated to succeed, and they value the activity.

Family Involvement.   Teachers involve parents in classroom activities and develop home–school connections through special programs and regular communication because when parents are involved, students' achievement increases (Edwards, 2004).

These characteristics emphasize the teacher's role in creating an inviting, supportive, and safe classroom climate.

HOW TO CREATE THE CLASSROOM CULTURE.   Teachers are more successful when they take the first several weeks of the school year to establish the classroom climate and their expectations; it's unrealistic to assume that students will instinctively be

Check the Compendium of Instructional Procedures, which follows Chapter 12. These **green** terms also show a brief description of each procedure.

cooperative, responsible, and respectful. Teachers explicitly explain classroom routines, such as how to get supplies out and put them away and how to work with classmates in a small group, and they set the expectation that everyone will adhere to the routines. They demonstrate literacy procedures, including how to choose a book, how to provide feedback about a classmate's writing, and how to participate in a **grand conversation**. Teachers also model ways of interacting with classmates and assisting them with reading and writing projects.

Teachers are the classroom managers: They set expectations and clearly explain to students what's expected of them and what's valued in the classroom. The classroom rules are specific and consistent, and teachers also set limits: Students can talk quietly with classmates when they're working together, for example, but they're not allowed to shout across the classroom, talk when the teacher's talking, or be disruptive when classmates are presenting to the class. Teachers also model classroom rules themselves as they interact with students. This process of socialization at the beginning of the school year is crucial to the success of the literacy program.

Not everything can be accomplished during the first several weeks, however; teachers continue to reinforce classroom routines and literacy procedures. One way is to have student leaders model the desired routines and behaviors; this way, classmates are likely to follow the lead. Teachers also continue to teach additional literacy procedures as students become involved in new activities. The classroom evolves, but the foundation is laid at the beginning of the school year.

The classroom environment is predictable, with familiar routines and literacy procedures. Students feel comfortable, safe, and more willing to take risks in a predictable environment; this is especially true for students from varied cultures, English learners, and struggling readers and writers (Fay & Whaley, 2004).

Principle 3: Effective Teachers Support Use of the Cueing Systems

Language is a complex system for creating meaning through socially shared conventions (Halliday, 1978). English, like other languages, involves four **cueing systems**:

- The phonological, or sound, system
- The syntactic, or structural, system
- The semantic, or meaning, system
- The pragmatic, or social and cultural use, system

Together, these systems make communication possible; students and adults use all four systems simultaneously as they read, write, listen, and talk. The priority people place on the cueing systems varies; however, the phonological system is especially important for beginning readers and writers as it is foundational to learning to use phonics to decode and spell words. An overview of the four cueing systems is presented in Figure 1–2.

THE PHONOLOGICAL SYSTEM. The phonological system is the sound system. There are approximately 44 speech sounds in English; students learn to pronounce these sounds as they learn to talk, and they associate the sounds with letters as they learn to read and write. Sounds are called **phonemes**, and they're represented in print with diagonal lines to differentiate them from **graphemes**, which are letters or letter combinations. For example, the first grapheme in *mother* is *m*, and the phoneme is /m/; the phoneme in *soap* that's represented by the grapheme *oa* is called "long *o*" and is written /ō/.

The phonological system is important for both oral and written language. Regional differences exist in the way people pronounce phonemes; for example, New Yorkers and Texans pronounce sounds differently. English learners learn to pronounce the sounds in

Figure 1–2 The Four Cueing Systems

SYSTEM	TERMS	APPLICATIONS
Phonological System The sound system with approximately 44 sounds and more than 500 ways to spell them	• *Phoneme* (the smallest unit of sound) • *Grapheme* (the written representation of a phoneme using one or more letters) • *Phonological awareness* (knowledge about the sound structure of words) • *Phonemic awareness* (the ability to orally manipulate phonemes in words) • *Phonics* (knowledge about phoneme–grapheme correspondences and rules)	• Decoding words • Using invented spelling • Noticing rhyming words • Dividing words into syllables
Syntactic System The structural system that governs how words are combined into sentences	• *Syntax* (the structure or grammar of a sentence) • *Morpheme* (the smallest meaningful unit of language) • *Free morpheme* (a morpheme that can stand alone as a word) • *Bound morpheme* (a morpheme that must be attached to a free morpheme)	• Forming compound words • Adding prefixes and suffixes to root words • Using capitalization and punctuation • Writing simple, compound, and complex sentences
Semantic System The meaning system that focuses on vocabulary	• *Semantics* (meaning) • *Synonyms* (words that mean the same or nearly the same thing) • *Antonyms* (opposites) • *Homophones* (words that sound alike but are spelled differently)	• Learning that many words have multiple meanings • Studying synonyms, antonyms, and homonyms • Using a dictionary and a thesaurus
Pragmatic System The social and cultural use system that explains how language varies	• *Standard English* (the form of English used in textbooks and by TV newscasters) • *Nonstandard English* (other forms of English)	• Varying language to fit specific purposes • Comparing standard and nonstandard forms of English

English, and, not surprisingly, sounds that differ from those in their native language are harder to learn. For example, because Spanish doesn't have /th/, native Spanish speakers have difficulty pronouncing this sound, often substituting /d/ for /th/ because the sounds are articulated in similar ways. Younger students usually learn to pronounce unfamiliar sounds more easily than older students and adults do.

This system plays a crucial role in early literacy instruction. In a purely phonetic language, a one-to-one correspondence would exist between letters and sounds, and teaching students to decode words would be simple. But English is not a purely phonetic language because there are 26 letters and 44 sounds and many ways to combine the letters to spell some of the sounds, especially vowels. Consider these ways to spell long *e: sea, green, Pete, me,* and *people.* And the patterns used to spell long *e* don't always work—*head* and *great* are examples of exceptions. **Phonics**, which describes the phoneme–grapheme correspondences and related spelling rules, is an important component of reading instruction. Students use phonics to decode words, but it isn't a complete reading program because many common words can't be decoded easily and reading involves more than just decoding.

THE SYNTACTIC SYSTEM. The syntactic system is the structural organization of English. This system is the grammar that regulates how words are combined into sentences; the word **grammar** means the rules governing how words are combined in sentences, not parts of speech. Students use the syntactic system as they combine words to form sentences. Word order is important in English, and English speakers must arrange words into a sequence that makes sense. Young Spanish speakers who are learning English, for example, learn to say "This is my red sweater," not "This is my sweater red," which is the literal translation from Spanish.

Students use their knowledge of the syntactic system as they read. They expect that the words they're reading have been strung together into sentences. When they come to an unfamiliar word, they recognize its role in the sentence even if they don't know the terms for parts of speech. In the sentence "The horses galloped through the gate and out into the field," students may not know the word *through*, but they can easily substitute a reasonable word or phrase, such as *out of* or *past*.

Another component of syntax is word forms. Words such as *dog* and *play* are **morphemes**, the smallest meaningful units in language. Word parts that change the meaning of a word are also morphemes; when the plural marker *-s* is added to *dog* to make *dogs*, for instance, or the past-tense marker *-ed* is added to *play* to make *played*, these words now have two morphemes because the inflectional endings change the meaning of the words. The words *dog* and *play* are free morphemes because they convey meaning while standing alone; the endings *-s* and *-ed* are bound morphemes because they must be attached to free morphemes to convey meaning. **Compound words** are two or more morphemes combined to create a new word: *Birthday*, for example, is a compound word made up of two free morphemes.

THE SEMANTIC SYSTEM.   The semantic system focuses on meaning. Vocabulary is the key component of this system. Researchers estimate that, on average, students have a vocabulary of 5,000 words by the time they enter school, and they continue to acquire 3,000 to 4,000 words each year; by the time they graduate from high school, their vocabularies reach 50,000 words (Stahl & Nagy, 2006)! Students learn some words through instruction, but they acquire many more words informally through reading and through social studies and science units. Their depth of knowledge about words increases, too, from knowing one meaning for a word to knowing how to use it in many ways. The word *fire*, for example, has more than a dozen meanings; the most common are related to combustion, but others deal with an intense feeling, discharging a gun, or dismissing someone.

THE PRAGMATIC SYSTEM.   The pragmatic system deals with the social aspects of language use. People use language for many purposes; how they talk and write varies according to their purpose and audience. Language use also varies among social classes, ethnic groups, and geographic regions; these varieties are known as **dialects**. School is one cultural community, and the language of school is Standard English. This dialect is formal—the one used in textbooks, newspapers, magazines, and by TV newscasters. Other forms, including some spoken in inner cities or in Appalachia, are generally classified as nonstandard English. These nonstandard forms of English are alternatives in which the phonology, syntax, and semantics differ from those of Standard English. They're neither inferior nor substandard; instead, they reflect the communities of the speakers, and the speakers communicate as effectively as those who use Standard

PreK Practices

Why involve prekindergartners with literacy?

Bennett-Armistead, Duke, and Moses (2005) list these reasons to explain why it's important to provide a literacy-rich environment for young students and to involve them in literacy activities:

- Students learn about different uses of literacy.
- Students discover that reading and writing are fun.
- Students acquire knowledge about the world through book experiences.
- Students prepare for kindergarten and the primary grades as they learn the letters of the alphabet and concepts about print.
- Students build their vocabularies and expand the ways they construct sentences.

In this text, you'll read about ways to involve prekindergartners in reading and writing using a combination of embedded instruction that's developmentally appropriate and explicit instruction that builds skills, including phonemic awareness (Casbergue, 2017).

English. The goal is for students to add Standard English to their repertoire of language registers, not to replace their home dialect with Standard English.

Teachers understand that students use all four cueing systems as they read and write. For example, when students correctly read the sentence "Jimmy is playing ball with his father," they're probably using information from all four systems. A student who substitutes *dad* for *father* and reads "Jimmy is playing ball with his dad" might be focusing on the semantic or pragmatic system rather than on the phonological system. When a student substitutes *basketball* for *ball* and reads "Jimmy is playing basketball with his father," he might be relying on an illustration or his own experience. Or, because both *basketball* and *ball* begin with *b*, he might have used the beginning sound as an aid in decoding, but he apparently didn't consider how long the word *basketball* is compared with the word *ball*. A student who changes the syntax, as in "Jimmy, he play ball with his father," may speak a nonstandard dialect. And sometimes a student reads the sentence so that it doesn't make sense, as in "Jump is play boat with his father," In this case, the student chooses words with the correct beginning sound, but there's no comprehension. This becomes a serious problem because the student doesn't understand that what he reads must make sense.

MyLab Education Self-Check 1.1

Theme 2: Effective Reading Instruction

The components of effective reading instruction have been debated over many years as researchers weighed the importance of phonics instruction versus the use of students' literature to teach reading. Many have concluded that a balanced approach benefits most readers and writers. They also have determined that scaffolding literacy instruction as well as the practice of various instructional approaches are critical to meeting the developmental needs of learners.

Principle 4: Effective Teachers Adopt a Balanced Approach to Instruction

A balanced approach to instruction is based on a comprehensive view of literacy that combines explicit instruction, guided practice, collaborative learning, and independent reading and writing. Cunningham and Allington (2011) compare the balanced approach to a multivitamin, suggesting that it brings together the best of teacher- and student-centered learning theories. Even though balanced programs vary, they usually embody these characteristics:

Literacy.   Literacy involves both reading and writing; in fact, linking the two facilitates students' learning.

Explicit Instruction.   Teachers provide explicit instruction to develop students' knowledge about reading and writing according to grade-level standards.

Authentic Application.   Students have regular opportunities to practice what they're learning by reading trade books and writing compositions.

Reading and Writing Strategies.   Students become strategic readers and writers by learning to apply cognitive and metacognitive strategies.

Oral Language.   Opportunities for students to talk and listen are integrated with reading and writing activities.

Tools for Learning.   Students use reading, talking, writing, and technology as tools for content area learning.

MyLab Education

Video Example 1.1

Teaching from a balanced approach to literacy means using a variety of developmentally appropriate strategies and teaching the core elements of reading and writing instruction. What five critical elements of reading instruction does Dr. Tim Shanahan identify?

Creating a balanced literacy program is a "complex process that requires flexibility and artful orchestration of literacy's various contextual and conceptual aspects" (Pearson, Raphael, Benson, & Madda, 2007, p. 33).

PreK through fourth grade balanced literacy instructional programs include these components:

- Reading
- Phonemic awareness and phonics
- Literacy strategies and skills
- Vocabulary
- Comprehension

- Literature
- Content area study
- Oral language
- Writing
- Spelling

These components are described in Figure 1–3. Creating a balance is essential, because when one component is over- or underemphasized, the development of the others suffers. A balanced literacy program integrating these components is recommended for all students, including those in high-poverty urban schools, struggling readers, and English learners (Braunger & Lewis, 2006).

COMMON CORE STATE STANDARDS.　The Common Core State Standards (CCSS) Initiative identified the knowledge students are expected to learn at each grade level, beginning in kindergarten. It was spearheaded by the National Governors' Association and the Council of Chief State School Officers with the goal of ensuring that all students graduate from high school able to succeed in college or the workforce.

The Common Core State Standards for English Language Arts (2010) are a framework for improving teaching and learning with clear and consistent academic benchmarks (Allyn, 2013; Kendall, 2011). They include rigorous content that requires students to use higher level thinking skills as they apply their knowledge. The Standards expectations grow in sophistication from kindergarten through 12th grade, and at each grade level students are required to read and write more complex texts. Reading and writing are integrated across the curriculum, and students are required to conduct research

Figure 1–3　The Balanced Literacy Approach

COMPONENT	DESCRIPTION
Comprehension	Students learn to use reader factors, including comprehension strategies, and text factors, including text structures, to understand what they're reading.
Content Area Study	Students use reading and writing as tools to learn about social studies and science topics in thematic units.
Literacy Strategies and Skills	Students learn to use problem-solving and monitoring behaviors called *strategies* and automatic actions called *skills* as they read and write.
Literature	Students become engaged readers who enjoy literature through reading and responding to books and learning about genres, text structures, and literary features.
Oral Language	Students use talk and listening as they work with classmates, participate in grand conversations, give oral presentations, and listen to the teacher read aloud.
Phonemic Awareness and Phonics	Students learn to manipulate sounds in words and apply the alphabetic principle and phonics rules to decode words.
Reading	Students participate in a variety of reading experiences using picture-book stories and novels, informational books, books of poetry, textbooks, and internet materials.
Spelling	Students apply what they're learning about English orthography to spell words, and their spellings gradually become conventional.
Vocabulary	Students learn the meaning of words through listening to books teachers read aloud and from content area study.
Writing	Students learn to use the writing process to draft and refine stories, poems, reports, and other compositions.

to answer questions and solve problems. The literacy standards are organized into five strands:

Reading Strand.   The Reading strand consists of three sections: Foundational Skills, Literature, and Informational Texts. Young students develop foundational skills—print concepts, phonological awareness, phonics, word recognition, and fluency—as they learn to read. The emphasis in the Literature and Informational Texts sections is on students' comprehension of complex texts: Students read increasingly sophisticated grade-level texts and grow in their ability to make inferences and connections among ideas and between texts.

Writing Strand.   The Writing strand consists of four sections: Text Types and Purposes, Production and Distribution of Writing, Research to Build and Present Knowledge, and Range of Writing. Students in the primary grades learn to use the writing process to compose texts representing a variety of genres, including narratives and informative texts.

Speaking and Listening Strand.   The Speaking and Listening strand consists of two sections: Comprehension and Collaboration, and Presentation of Knowledge and Ideas. Young students gain mastery of oral language skills; they refine their ability to use speaking and listening informally in discussions and more formally in oral presentations.

Language Strand.   The Language strand consists of three sections: Conventions of Standard English, Knowledge of Language, and Vocabulary Acquisition and Use. Students learn to apply vocabulary, grammar, and Standard English conventions to increasingly sophisticated oral and written presentations.

Media and Technology Strand.   The CCSS integrate the critical analysis of media and the creation of multimedia projects within the other strands.

For each topic, Standards clearly specify what students should accomplish at each grade level. Figure 1–4 shows how the Common Core State Standards are addressed in each chapter of this text.

According to the CCSS website, 41 states, 4 territories, and Department of Defense schools had adopted the standards in 2018. In the years since the introduction of the CCSS, much curriculum has been developed for teachers to assist with meeting the new, more rigorous expectations for young students. One such useful resource was developed by teachers—*Common Core Curriculum Maps in English Language Arts, Grades K–5* (2014). This resource presents a sequence of thematic curriculum units that connect the skills in the CCSS with literature and informational texts. It's also a good idea to visit the webpage of your state department of education for curriculum resources aligned with the CCSS.

Principle 5: Effective Teachers Scaffold Students' Reading and Writing

Teachers scaffold students' literacy development as they demonstrate, guide, and teach, and they vary the amount of support they provide according to the instructional purpose and students' needs. Sometimes teachers model how experienced readers read or record students' dictation when the writing's too difficult for them to do on their own. At other times, they guide students as they read a leveled book or proofread their writing. Teachers use five levels of support, moving from more to less as students assume responsibility (Fountas & Pinnell, 2016). Figure 1–5 presents an overview of these levels of support—modeled, shared, interactive, guided, and independent—for literacy activities.

Figure 1–4 The Common Core State Standards

CHAPTER	READING STRAND: LITERATURE	READING STRAND: INFORMATIONAL TEXTS	READING STRAND: FOUNDATIONAL SKILLS	WRITING STRAND	SPEAKING AND LISTENING STRAND	LANGUAGE STRAND
2 Examining students' Literacy Development			•	•		•
3 Assessing students' Literacy Development	•	•	•	•	•	•
4 Cracking the Alphabetic Code			•			
5 Spelling			•			•
6 Developing Fluent Readers and Writers			•	•		
7 Building students' Vocabulary						•
8 Teaching Comprehension: Reader Factors	•	•			•	
9 Facilitating students' Comprehension: Text Factors	•	•		•		
10 Scaffolding students' Reading Development	•	•				
11 Scaffolding students' Writing Development				•		
12 Integrating Literacy Into Thematic Units	•	•		•	•	•

These five levels of support illustrate Pearson and Gallagher's (1983) "gradual release of responsibility" model. As students move from modeled to interactive to independent reading and writing, they do more of the actual reading and writing, and teachers gradually transfer responsibility to them.

MODELED READING AND WRITING.   Teachers provide the greatest amount of support when they model how expert readers read and expert writers write. When teachers read aloud, they're modeling: They read fluently and with expression, and they talk about their thoughts and the strategies they're using. When they model writing, teachers write a composition on chart paper or an interactive whiteboard so that everyone can see what the teacher does and how it's being written. Teachers use this support

Figure 1–5 Levels of Scaffolding

LEVEL	READING	WRITING
Modeled	Teachers read aloud, modeling how good readers read fluently using books that are too difficult for students to read.	Teachers demonstrate how to write a composition, creating the text, doing the writing, and thinking aloud about their use of strategies and skills.
Shared	Teacher and students read books together, with students following as the teacher reads and then repeating familiar refrains.	Teacher and students create the text together; then the teacher does the actual writing. Sometimes students assist by spelling familiar words.
Interactive	Teacher and students read instructional-level texts together and take turns doing the reading. Teachers help students read fluently and with expression.	Teacher and students create the text and share the pen to do the writing. they spell words correctly and add capitalization, punctuation, and other conventions.
Guided	Teachers teach guided reading lessons to small, homogeneous groups using instructional-level books.	Teachers teach lessons on writing strategies, skills, and procedures, and students participate in supervised practice activities.
Independent	Students read self-selected books independently, and teachers conference with them to monitor their progress.	Students use the writing process to write stories, informational books, and other compositions.

level to demonstrate procedures, such as choosing a book to read or doing a **word sort**, and to introduce new writing genres, such as "I Am . . . " poems. Teachers often do a **think-aloud** to share what they're thinking as they read or write, the decisions they make, and the strategies they use. Teachers use modeling to:

- Demonstrate fluent reading and writing
- Explain how to use reading and writing strategies
- Teach the procedure for a literacy activity
- Show how reading and writing conventions and other skills work

SHARED READING AND WRITING.   Teachers "share" reading and writing tasks with students at this level. Probably the best known activity is **shared reading**, which teachers use to read big books with young students. The teacher does most of the reading, but students join in to read familiar and predictable words and phrases. Teachers use the **Language Experience Approach** to write students' dictation on paintings and brainstorm lists of words on the whiteboard, make **KWL charts**, and write **collaborative books**.

Sharing differs from modeling in that students actually participate in the activity rather than simply observing the teacher. In shared reading, students follow along as the teacher reads, and in shared writing, they suggest the words and sentences for the teacher to write. Teachers use shared reading and writing to:

- Involve students in literacy activities they can't do independently
- Create opportunities for students to experience success in reading and writing
- Provide practice before students read and write independently

INTERACTIVE READING AND WRITING.   Students assume an increasingly important role in interactive reading and writing. They no longer observe the teacher reading or writing, repeat familiar words, or suggest words for the teacher to write; instead, they're actively involved in reading and writing. They support classmates by sharing the reading and writing responsibilities, and their teacher provides assistance when needed. **Choral reading** and **readers theatre** are two examples of interactive reading. In **interactive writing**, students and the teacher create a text and write a message together (Williams, 2018; Tompkins & Collom, 2004). Teachers use interactive reading and writing to:

- Provide practice reading and writing high-frequency words
- Encourage students to apply phonics and spelling skills
- Read and write texts that students can't do independently
- Provide opportunities for students to share their literacy expertise with classmates

Figure 1–6 shows a piece of interactive writing done by a group of five-year-olds after reading Eric Carle's repetitive book *Does a Kangaroo Have a Mother, Too?* (2000). The teacher wrote the title and the author's name, and the students created the sentence *Animals have mothers just like me and you.* They took turns writing the letters they knew in red, and the teacher wrote the letters representing unfamiliar sounds in black. The boxes around four of the letters indicate correction tape the teacher placed over an incorrectly formed letter before the student tried again to print the letter conventionally.

GUIDED READING AND WRITING.   Even though teachers continue to provide support, students do the actual reading and writing themselves. **Guided reading** is the best known example. In this instructional procedure, small, homogeneous groups meet with the teacher to read a book at their instructional level. The teacher introduces the book and guides students as they begin reading. Then students continue reading on their own while the teacher supervises them. **Minilessons** are another example:

Figure 1–6 A Kindergarten Interactive Writing Chart

As teachers teach lessons, they provide practice activities and supervise while students apply what they're reading. Teachers scaffold students' writing as they make pages for **collaborative books**. They also provide guidance during conferences with students about their writing.

Teachers choose this level of scaffolding to support students as they actually read and write. They use guided reading and writing to:

- Support students' reading in appropriate instructional-level materials
- Teach literacy strategies and skills
- Involve students in collaborative writing projects
- Teach students to use the writing process—in particular, how to revise and edit

INDEPENDENT READING AND WRITING. Students do the reading and writing themselves at the independent level, applying the strategies and skills they've learned in authentic literacy activities. During independent reading, students usually choose their own books and work at their own pace as they read and respond to books. Similarly, during independent writing, students usually choose their own topics and move at their own pace as they develop and refine their writing. This isn't to suggest, however, that teachers don't play a role in independent-level activities; they continue to monitor students' progress, but they provide much less support at this level.

Through independent reading, students learn how pleasurable reading is and, teachers hope, become lifelong readers. As they write, students come to view themselves as authors. Teachers use activities at this level to:

- Provide opportunities for students to apply the reading and writing strategies and skills they've learned
- Engage students in authentic literacy experiences in which they choose their own topics, purposes, and materials
- Develop lifelong readers and writers

Teachers working with prekindergartners through fourth graders using all of these levels. When a reading strategy is introduced, for instance, its application is modeled by the teacher. And, when students are to practice a strategy that has already been introduced, they are guided through the activity, with a gradually increasing level of responsibility. The purpose of the activity, not the activity itself, determines the level of support.

Principle 6: Effective Teachers Organize for Literacy Instruction

No single instructional program best represents the balanced approach to literacy; instead, teachers organize for instruction by creating their own program that fits their students' needs and their school's grade-level standards. Instructional programs should reflect these principles:

- Teachers create a community of learners in their classroom.
- Teachers incorporate the components of the balanced approach.
- Teachers scaffold students' reading and writing experiences.

Five popular approaches are guided reading, basal reading programs, literature focus units, literature circles, and reading and writing workshop.

GUIDED READING. Teachers use guided reading to personalize instruction and meet students' individual needs. They meet with small groups of students who read at approximately the same proficiency level for teacher-directed lessons (Fountas & Pinnell, 2016). In these 20-minute lessons, teachers teach word-identification and comprehension strategies and have students apply what they're learning as they read books at their instructional level. Teachers emphasize that the goal of reading is comprehension—understanding what they're reading, not just saying all the words correctly. At the same time, teachers are working with one guided reading group, classmates work at literacy centers or pursue other activities that they can complete independently. This instructional approach is often used in kindergarten through third grade, but it can also be adapted to use with older, struggling readers.

BASAL READING PROGRAMS. Commercially produced reading programs are known as basal readers. These programs feature a textbook containing reading selections with accompanying workbooks, supplemental books, and related instructional materials at each grade level, including digital components. Phonics, vocabulary, comprehension, and spelling instruction is coordinated with the reading selections and aligned with grade-level standards. The teacher's guide provides detailed procedures for teaching the selections and related strategies and skills. Instruction is typically presented to the whole class, with reteaching to small groups of struggling students. Testing materials are also included so that teachers can monitor students' progress. Publishers tout basal readers as a complete literacy program, but effective teachers realize that it is important to incorporate other strategies as well.

LITERATURE FOCUS UNITS. Teachers create literature focus units featuring high-quality picture-book stories and novels. The books are usually chosen from a district- or state-approved list of award-winning books that all students are expected to read at a particular grade level. These books include classics such as *The Very Hungry Caterpillar* (Carle, 2002) and *Charlotte's Web* (White, 2006) and award winners such as *Officer Buckle and Gloria* (Rathmann, 1995) and *Don't Let the Pigeon Drive the Bus!* (Willems, 2003). Everyone in the class reads and responds to the same book, and the teacher supports students' learning through a combination of explicit instruction and reading and writing activities. Through these units, teachers teach about literary genres and authors and develop students' interest in literature.

MyLab Education
Video Example 1.2

In this video, teacher educators describe the reading process. What did you learn about teaching reading?

GO DIGITAL! Incorporate Technology Into Your Classroom.

Teachers integrate 21st-century technology into their classrooms at all grade levels. They use digital software, the Internet, and computer technology for many purposes, including these:

- Presenting information to students
- Scaffolding students' reading and writing
- Involving students in activities and projects
- Responding to students' work
- Assessing students' achievement

Teachers often display information on interactive whiteboards as part of whole-class presentations and minilessons, and they teach students to use a variety of digital tools, including ebooks, digital cameras, and software programs. Basal reading programs offer websites with supplemental activities, and several ebook versions of basal readers are now available.

LITERATURE CIRCLES.   Small groups of students get together in **literature circles** or book clubs to read a story or informational book. To begin, teachers select five or six books at varying reading levels. Often, the books are related in some way—representing the same theme or written by the same author, for instance. They collect multiple copies of each book and give a **book talk** to introduce them. Then students choose a book and form a group to read and respond to it. They set a reading and discussion schedule and work independently, although teachers sometimes sit in on the discussions. Through the experience of reading and discussing a book together, students learn more about how to respond to books and develop responsibility for completing assignments.

READING AND WRITING WORKSHOP.   Students do authentic reading and writing in workshop programs. They select books, read independently, and conference with the teacher about their reading. They write books on topics that they choose and conference with the teacher about their writing. Teachers set aside a time for **reading and writing workshop**, and students read and write while the teacher conferences with small groups. Teachers also teach **minilessons** on reading and writing strategies and skills and read books aloud to the whole class. In a workshop program, students read and write more like adults do—making choices, working independently, and developing responsibility.

These five approaches can be divided into authentic and textbook programs. Guided reading, literature focus units, literature circles, and reading and writing workshop are classified as authentic programs because they use trade books and involve students in meaningful activities. Basal readers, not surprisingly, are textbook programs that reflect the behaviorist theory. Teachers generally combine these programs because students learn best through a variety of reading and writing experiences. Sometimes teachers may use guided reading along with literature focus units and writing workshop; they may alternate literature focus units or literature circles with reading and writing workshop and a textbook program; still others may use some components from each approach throughout the school year.

MyLab Education Self-Check 1.2

MyLab Education Application Exercise 1.1: Scaffolding Fluent Reading

Theme 3: Adjusting Instruction to Meet Students' Needs

Effective teachers adjust and personalize their instruction because students vary in their levels of development, academic achievement, and ability. Teachers vary instructional arrangements, choose instructional materials at students' reading levels, and modify assignments to address the core principles of differentiating instruction.

Principle 7: Effective Teachers Differentiate Instruction

Tomlinson (2004) explains that the one-size-fits-all instructional model is obsolete, and teachers respect students by honoring both their similarities and their differences. Differentiation is based on Vygotsky's idea of a **zone of proximal development**. If instruction is either too difficult or too easy, it isn't effective; instead, teachers must provide instruction that meets students' instructional needs.

HOW TO DIFFERENTIATE INSTRUCTION.   Differentiation involves personalizing the content, the process, and the products:

Differentiating the Content.   Teachers identify the information that students need to learn to meet grade-level standards so that every student will be successful. They differentiate the content in these ways:

- Choose instructional materials at students' reading levels
- Consider students' developmental levels as well as their current grade placement in deciding what to teach
- Use assessment tools to determine students' instructional needs

Differentiating the Process.   Teachers vary instruction and application activities to meet students' needs. They differentiate the process in these ways:

- Provide instruction to individuals, small groups, and the whole class
- Scaffold struggling readers and writers with more explicit instruction
- Challenge advanced readers and writers with activities requiring higher level thinking
- Monitor students' learning and adjust instruction when needed

Differentiating the Products.   Teachers also vary how students demonstrate what they've learned. Demonstrations include both the projects that students create and the tests used to measure their academic achievement. Teachers differentiate the products in these ways:

- Have students create projects individually, with partners, or in small groups
- Design projects that engage students with literacy in meaningful ways
- Assess students using a combination of visual, oral, and written formats

As teachers differentiate instruction, they consider the background knowledge and literacy demands of the reading selection, create a text set of related books, design activities with varied grouping patterns, consider students' preferred language modalities and thinking styles, and determine how much support students are likely to need. Figure 1–7 lists some of the ways teachers differentiate instruction.

Figure 1–7 Ways to Differentiate Instruction

COMPONENT	DESCRIPTION	INSTRUCTIONAL PROCEDURES
Content	Teachers identify the information that students need to learn to meet grade-level standards and the instructional materials to be used.	• Choose instructional materials at students' reading levels. • Consider students' developmental levels as well as their grade placement when deciding what to teach. • Use assessment tools to determine students' instructional needs.
Process	Teachers vary instruction and application activities to meet students' needs.	• Provide instruction to individuals, small groups, and the whole class. • Scaffold struggling readers and writers with more explicit instruction. • Challenge advanced learners with activities requiring higher level thinking.
Products	Teachers modify the ways students demonstrate what they've learned.	• Have students create projects individually or with classmates. • Design projects that engage students in meaningful ways. • Assess students using visual, oral, and written formats.

Teaching English Learners
Be Effective Teachers of Reading

Students who come from language backgrounds other than English and aren't yet proficient in English are known as English learners (ELs). Many can converse in English but may struggle with the academic language of school. These students benefit from participating in the same instructional programs that mainstream classmates do, but teachers are required to make adaptations to create learning contexts that respect minority students and meet their needs (Shanahan & Beck, 2006). Learning to read and write is more challenging because they're learning to speak English at the same time. Teachers scaffold ELs' oral language acquisition and literacy development in these ways:

Explicit Instruction.   Teachers present more explicit instruction on literacy strategies and skills because ELs are more at risk (Graves, Schneider & Ringstaff, 2018) (Graves et al., 2018). They also spend more time teaching unfamiliar academic vocabulary (e.g., _homonym, paragraph, revise, summarize_).

Oral Language.   Teachers provide many opportunities each day for students to practice speaking English comfortably and informally with partners and in small groups. Through conversations about topics they're learning, ELs develop both conversational and academic language, which in turn supports their literacy development (Rothenberg & Fisher, 2007).

Small-Group Work.   Teachers provide opportunities for students to work in small groups because social interaction supports their learning (Moses, Ogden & Kelly, 2015). As English learners talk with classmates, they're learning the culture of literacy.

Reading Aloud to Students.   Teachers read aloud a variety of stories, poems, and informational books, including some books that represent students' home cultures (Rothenberg & Fisher, 2007). In the process, teachers model fluent reading, and students build background knowledge as they become more familiar with English vocabulary and written language structures.

Background Knowledge.   Teachers organize instruction into units to build students' world knowledge about grade-appropriate concepts, and they develop ELs' literary knowledge through minilessons and a variety of reading and writing activities (Braunger & Lewis, 2006).

Authentic Literacy Activities.   Teachers provide daily opportunities for students to apply the strategies and skills they're learning as they read and write for authentic purposes (Akhavan, 2006). English learners participate in meaningful literacy activities through literature circles and reading and writing workshop.

These recommendations promote English learners' academic success.

Teachers' attitudes about minority students and their understanding of how people learn a second language play a critical role in the effectiveness of instruction (Martínez, 2018). It's important that teachers understand that ELs have different cultural and linguistic backgrounds and plan instruction accordingly. Most classrooms reflect the European-American middle-class culture, which differs significantly from minority students' backgrounds and how they use language. For example, some students are reluctant to volunteer answers to teachers' questions, and others may not answer if the questions are different from those their parents ask (Peregoy & Boyle, 2013). Teachers who learn about their students' home language and culture and embed what they learn into their instruction are likely to be more successful.

PARTNERING WITH PARENTS. Parents play a crucial role in helping their children become successful readers and writers, and home-literacy activities profoundly influence students' academic success: Students score higher on standardized achievement tests, have better school attendance, and exhibit stronger thinking skills when parents are involved in their education (Merga & Roni, 2018). Most teachers recognize the importance of home-literacy activities and want to become partners with their students' parents. In some communities, parents respond enthusiastically when teachers ask them to listen to their children read aloud or invite them to participate in a home–school writing event, for example, but in other communities there's little or no response.

Teachers' expectations are often based on middle-class parents, who typically see themselves as partners with teachers—reading to their children, playing educational games, going to the public library together, and helping with homework. Other parents view their role differently (Edwards, 2004): Some are willing to attend teacher–parent conferences and support school projects such as bake sales and carnivals, but they expect teachers to do the teaching; others feel inadequate when it comes to helping their children because of their own unsuccessful school experiences or limited ability to read and write in English. Parents' viewpoints are often a reflection of their culture and socioeconomic status (Lareau, 2000): Middle-class parents usually work with teachers to support their children's literacy development; working-class parents often have the belief that teachers are better qualified to teach their students; and poor, minority, and immigrant parents often feel powerless to help their students. Parents' involvement is also related to educational level: Those who didn't graduate from high school are less likely to get involved in their children's education (Paratore, 2001).

Because some parents don't understand the crucial role they play in their children's academic success, it's up to teachers to establish collaborative relationships with parents. Edwards (2004) explains that parent–teacher collaborations need to change in these ways so that teachers can create more empowering classroom cultures:

> **Respect the literacy activities of families.** Nearly all families incorporate reading and writing activities into their daily routines, but these activities may differ from school-based literacy activities. Some students are at risk of failing because they aren't familiar with the literacy activities and language patterns that teachers use. Nieto (2002) urges teachers to value parents' literacy activities, even if they don't match teachers' expectations, and use them in developing a culturally responsive literacy program.

> **Reach out to families in new ways.** Edwards (2004) recommends that teachers create schoolwide programs with a yearlong schedule of activities that address particular literacy goals at each grade level. Effective communication is essential: When teachers demonstrate that they want to listen to parents, giving them opportunities to share insights about their students and ask questions about how students learn to read and write, parents become more willing to work with teachers and support their children's learning.

Build parents' knowledge of literacy procedures. Too often teachers assume that parents know how to support their children's literacy learning, but many parents don't know how to read aloud, respond to their children's writing, or use other literacy procedures. Parents will be more successful when teachers offer specific suggestions and provide clear directions (Edwards, 2004).

When teachers accept that parents view their role in different ways and become more knowledgeable about cultural diversity and how it affects parent–teacher relationships, they're more likely to be successful.

Interventions

Schools use the results of assessments to identify low-achieving students, and they plan intervention programs to remedy students' reading and writing difficulties and accelerate their learning (Cooper, Chard, & Kiger, 2006). These programs are used in addition to regular classroom instruction, not as a replacement for it. The classroom teacher or a specially trained reading teacher meets with struggling students every day; using paraprofessionals is a widespread practice that's not recommended because aides aren't as effective as certified teachers (Allington, 2012). Teachers provide intensive, expert instruction to individuals or very small groups of no more than three students. Interventions take various forms: They can be provided by adding a second lesson during the regular school day, offering extra instruction in an after-school program, or holding extended-school-year programs during the summer. Figure 1–8 summarizes the recommendations for effective intervention programs.

Until recently, most school-based interventions were designed for middle grade students who were already failing; now the focus has changed to early intervention to eliminate the pattern of school failure that begins early and persists throughout some students' lives (Strickland, 2002). Three types of interventions for young students have been developed:

- Preventive programs to create more effective early-childhood programs
- Family-focused programs to develop young students' awareness of literacy, parents' literacy, and parenting skills
- Early interventions to resolve reading and writing problems and accelerate literacy development for low-achieving K–3 students

Teachers are optimistic that earlier and more intensive intervention will solve many of the difficulties that older students exhibit today.

Figure 1–8 High-Quality Interventions

COMPONENT	DESCRIPTION
Scheduling	Interventions take place daily for 30–45 minutes, depending on students' age and instructional needs. Classroom teachers often provide the interventions, but sometimes specially trained reading teachers provide them.
Grouping	Teachers work with students individually or in very small groups; larger groups, even when students exhibit the same reading or writing problems, aren't as effective.
Reading Materials	Teachers match students to books at their instructional level for lessons and to books at their independent level for voluntary reading.
Instruction	Teachers' lessons generally include rereading familiar books, reading new books, teaching phonics and reading strategies, and writing, but the content varies according to students' areas of difficulty.
Reading and Writing Practice	Teachers provide opportunities for students to practice reading and writing.
Assessment	Teachers monitor progress on an ongoing basis by observing students and collecting work samples. they also use diagnostic tests to document students' learning according to grade-level standards.
Home–School Partnerships	Teachers keep parents informed about students' progress and encourage them to support independent reading and writing at home.

FEDERAL EARLY INTERVENTIONS.   To prevent literacy problems and break the cycle of poverty in the United States, the federal government directs two early-intervention programs for economically disadvantaged students and their parents. Head Start promotes the healthy development and school preparedness of young low-income students through a variety of services; it provides education, health, nutrition, and social support to students and their families. This long-running program, administered by the U.S. Department of Health and Human Services, reaches one million students and their families each year through prenatal and infant programs, preschool programs, and other services for students of migrant farm workers, Native Americans, and homeless families. Head Start began in 1965 as part of President Lyndon Johnson's War on Poverty, and now, more than 50 years later, the program remains controversial because studies evaluating its long-term effectiveness have been inconclusive.

The Even Start Family Literacy Program is a newer program for low-income students from birth to age seven that began as part of NCLB. It's designed to improve educational opportunities for low-income families through these related activities:

- An early childhood education program to prepare students for school success
- An adult literacy program to improve parents' reading and writing competencies
- A parent education program to train parents to participate more fully in students' education
- Opportunities for students and their parents to participate in literacy activities together

All four components are required in this unified family literacy program.

RESPONSE TO INTERVENTION.   Response to Intervention (RTI) is a promising schoolwide initiative to identify struggling students quickly, promote effective classroom instruction, provide interventions, and increase the likelihood that students will be successful (Mellard & Johnson, 2008). It involves three tiers:

Tier 1: Screening and Prevention.   Teachers provide high-quality instruction that's supported by scientifically based research, screen students to identify those at risk for academic failure, and monitor their progress. If students don't make adequate progress toward meeting grade-level standards, they move to Tier 2.

Tier 2: Early Intervention.   Trained reading teachers provide enhanced, individualized instruction targeting students' specific areas of difficulty. If students' literacy problems are resolved, they return to Tier 1; if they make some progress but need additional instruction, they remain in Tier 2; and if they don't show improvement, they move to Tier 3, where the intensity of intervention increases.

Tier 3: Intensive Intervention.   Special education teachers provide more intensive intervention to individual students and small groups. They focus on remedying students' problems and teaching compensatory strategies, and they monitor students' progress more frequently.

This schoolwide instruction and assessment program incorporates data-driven decision making, and special education teachers are optimistic that it will be a better way to diagnose learning-disabled students.

Improving classroom instruction, diagnosing students' specific reading and writing difficulties, and implementing intensive intervention programs to remedy students' literacy problems are three important ways that teachers work more effectively with struggling readers and writers. Visit the *What Works Clearinghouse*, an initiative of the U.S. Department of Education's Institute of Education Sciences, to study evidence ratings for many popular reading intervention programs. The website is located at https://ies.ed.gov/ncee/wwc/.

MyLab Education Self-Check 1.3

Theme 4: Linking Assessment to Instructional Planning

Effective teachers monitor students' learning, make adjustments when necessary, and assess learning in multiple ways, not just using paper-and-pencil tests. Principle 8 describes ways to link instruction and assessment so that they inform each other.

Principle 8: Effective Teachers Link Instruction and Assessment

Assessment is an integral and ongoing part of both learning and teaching (Mariotti & Homan, 2005). Sometimes teachers equate standardized high-stakes achievement tests with assessment, but classroom assessment is much more than a once-a-year test. It's a daily part of classroom life: Teachers collect and analyze data from observations, conferences, and classroom tests, and then use the results to make decisions about students' academic achievement (Cunningham & Allington, 2011). Teachers assess students' learning for these purposes:

Determining Reading Levels. Teachers determine students' reading levels so that they can plan appropriate instruction.

Monitoring Progress. Teachers regularly assess students to ensure that they're making expected progress in reading and writing, and when they're not progressing, teachers take action to get them back on track.

Diagnosing Strengths and Weaknesses. Teachers examine students' progress in specific literacy components, including phonics, fluency, comprehension, writing, and spelling, to identify their strengths and weaknesses. Diagnosis is especially important when students are struggling or aren't making expected progress.

Documenting Learning. Teachers use a combination of test results and collections of students' work to provide evidence of their academic achievement and document that they've met grade-level standards.

These purposes highlight the wide range of ongoing assessment activities that effective teachers use. As you plan for instruction and document learning, use **My Teaching To-Do Checklist: Teaching Effectiveness.**

THE INSTRUCTION–ASSESSMENT CYCLE. Assessment is linked to instruction (Snow, Griffin, & Burns, 2005). Teachers do some assessments before they begin to

---

MY TEACHING TO-DO CHECKLIST: Teaching Effectiveness

- ☐ I apply theories about how students learn in my teaching.
- ☐ I support students' use of the cueing systems as they read and write.
- ☐ I've created a community of learners in my classroom.
- ☐ I've adopted a balanced approach to instruction.
- ☐ I scaffold students as they read and write.
- ☐ I organize my literacy program with instruction, practice opportunities, and independent reading and writing projects.
- ☐ I differentiate instruction to meet my students' needs.
- ☐ I link instruction and assessment.
- ☐ I integrate state standards into my instruction.

teach, some while they're teaching, and others afterward. They link instruction and assessment in this four-step cycle:

Step 1: Planning.   Teachers use their knowledge about students' reading levels, their background knowledge, and their strategy and skill competencies to plan appropriate instruction that's neither too easy nor too difficult.

Step 2: Monitoring.   Teachers monitor instruction that's in progress as they observe students, conference with them, and check their work to ensure that their instruction is effective. They make modifications, including reteaching when necessary, to improve the quality of their instruction and meet students' needs.

Step 3: Evaluating.   Teachers evaluate students' learning using rubrics and check lists to assess students' reading and writing projects and administering teacher-made tests. They also collect samples to document students' achievements.

Step 4: Reflecting.   Teachers judge the effectiveness of their instruction by analyzing students' reading and writing projects and test results and consider how they might adapt instruction to improve student learning.

It's easy to blame the students when learning isn't occurring, but teachers need to consider how they can improve their teaching through planning, monitoring, evaluating, and reflecting because it's their responsibility to ensure that their students are successful.

CLASSROOM ASSESSMENT TOOLS.   Teachers use both a variety of informal assessment tools that they create themselves and commercially available tests (McKenna & Stahl, 2009). Informal assessment tools include these activities:

- Observing students' participating in instructional activities.
- Collecting running records of students' oral reading to analyze their ability to solve reading problems
- Examining students' work for signs of growth
- Conferencing with individual students about their reading and writing progress
- Completing checklists to monitor students' progress
- Using rubrics to assess students' writing and other performances

These assessment tools support instruction, and teachers choose which one to use according to the kind of information they need. They administer commercial tests to individuals or the entire class to determine students' overall reading achievement or their proficiency in a particular component—phonemic awareness or comprehension, for example.

STANDARDIZED TESTS.   Beginning in second grade, the results of yearly standardized tests also provide evidence of students' literacy achievement. The usefulness of the data is limited, however, because the tests are usually administered in the spring and the results aren't released until after the school year ends. At the beginning of the next school year, teachers do examine the data and use what they learn in planning for their new class, but the impact isn't as great as it would be for the teachers who worked with those students during the previous year. Another way the results are used is in measuring the effectiveness of teachers' instruction by examining how much students grew since the previous year's test and whether they met grade-level standards.

MyLab Education
Video Example 1.3

In this video, Alejandro is asked to read the story "*Birthday at the Zoo*." His teacher collects a running record of his performance. What might the teacher do with this data?

MyLab Education Self-Check 1.4

Chapter Review

Becoming an Effective Teacher of Reading

- Teachers understand how teacher-centered theory is different from student-centered theory.

- Teachers adopt a balanced approach to literacy instruction.

- Teachers differentiate instruction so all students can be successful.

- Teachers link instruction and assessment.

Accountability Check

Visit the following assessment links to access quiz questions and instructional applications.

MyLab Education Application Exercise 1.2: Understanding Literacy Development

MyLab Education Application Exercise 1.3: Monitoring Literacy Development

MyLab Education Application Exercise 1.4: Measuring Literacy Development

References

Akhavan, N. (2006). *Help! My kids don't all speak English: How to set up a language workshop in your linguistically diverse classroom.* Portsmouth, NH: Heinemann.

Allington, R. L. (2012). *What really matters for struggling readers: Designing research-based programs* (3rd ed.). Boston: Allyn & Bacon/Pearson.

Allyn, P. (2013). *Be core ready: Powerful, effective steps to implementing and achieving the Common Core State Standards.* Boston: Pearson.

Angelillo, J. (2008). *Whole-class teaching: Minilessons and more.* Portsmouth, NH: Heinemann.

Baker, L. (2008). Metacognition in comprehension instruction. In C. C. Block & S. R. Parris (Eds.), *Comprehension instruction: Research-based best practices* (2nd ed., pp. 65–79). New York: Guilford Press.

Bandura, A. (1997). *Self-efficacy: The exercise of control.* New York: W. H. Freeman.

Bennett-Armistead, V. S., Duke, N. K., & Moses, A. M. (2005). *Literacy and the youngest learner: Best practices for educators of students from birth to 5.* New York: Scholastic.

Braunger, J., & Lewis, J. P. (2006). *Building a knowledge base in reading* (2nd ed.). Newark, DE: International Reading Association/National Council of Teachers of English.

Brown, J. S., Collins, A., & Duguid, S. (1989). Situated cognition and the culture of learning. *Educational Researcher, 18*(1), 32–42.

Bullard, J. (2010). *Creating environments for learning: Birth to age eight* (2nd ed.). Boston: Pearson.

Bunting, E. (1999). *Smoky night.* San Diego: Voyager.

Carle, E. (2000). *Does a kangaroo have a mother, too?* New York: HarperCollins.

Carle, E. (2002). *The very hungry caterpillar.* New York: Puffin Books.

Casbergue, R. M. (2017). Ready for kindergarten? Rethinking early literacy in the Common Core era. *The Reading Teacher, 70*(6), 643–648.

Common core curriculum maps in English language arts, grades K–5. (2014). San Francisco: Jossey-Bass.

Common core state standards for English language arts. (2010). Retrieved from http://www.corestandards.org

Cooper, J. D., Chard, D. J., & Kiger, N. D. (2006). *The struggling reader: Interventions that work*. New York: Scholastic.

Cunningham, P. M., & Allington, R. L. (2011). *Classrooms that work: They can all read and write* (5th ed.). Boston: Allyn & Bacon/Pearson.

Dean, D. (2006). *Strategic writing: The writing process and beyond in the secondary English classroom*. Urbana, IL: National Council of Teachers of English.

Dewey, J. (1997). *Experience and education*. New York: Free Press.

Dinan, S. (2009). Obama wants teacher "accountability." Retrieved from http://www .washingtontimes.com/news/2009/mar/10/obama-calls-accountability-education

Edwards, P. A. (2004). *Students' literacy development: Making it happen through school, family, and community involvement*. Boston: Allyn & Bacon/Pearson.

Fay, K., & Whaley, S. (2004). *Becoming one community: Reading and writing with English language learners*. Portland, ME: Stenhouse.

Fountas, I. C., & Pinnell, G. S. (2016). *Guided reading: Good first teaching for all students*. Portsmouth, NH: Heinemann.

Freire, P. (2000). *Pedagogy of the oppressed* (30th anniversary ed.). New York: Continuum.

Graves, M. F., Schneider, S., & Ringstaff, C. (2018). Empowering students with word-learning strategies: Teach a child to fish. *The Reading Teacher, 71*(5), 533–543.

Guthrie, J. T., & Wigfield, A. (2000). Engagement and motivation in reading. In M. L. Kamil, P. B. Mosenthal, P. D. Pearson, & R. Barr (Eds.), *Handbook of reading research* (Vol. 3, pp. 403–422). Mahwah, NJ: Erlbaum.

Halliday, M. A. K. (1978). *Language as social semiotic: The social interpretation of language and meaning*. Baltimore: University Park Press.

Hayes, J. R. (2004). A new framework for understanding cognition and affect in writing. In R. B. Ruddell & N. J. Unrau (Eds.), *Theoretical models and processes of reading* (5th ed., pp. 1399–1430). Newark, DE: International Reading Association.

Johnson, H., & Freedman, L. (2005). *Developing critical awareness at the middle level*. Newark, DE: International Reading Association.

Keehne, C. N., Sarsona, M. W., Kawakami, A. J., & Au, K. H. (2018). Culturally responsive instruction and literacy learning. *Journal of Literacy Research, 50*(2), 141–166.

Kendall, J. (2011). *Understanding Common Core State Standards*. Alexandria, VA: Association for Supervision and Curriculum Development.

Kintsch, W. (2013). Revisiting the construction-integration model and its implications for instruction. In D. E. Alvermann, N. J. Unrau, & R. B. Ruddell (Eds.), *Theoretical models and processes of reading* (6th ed., pp. 807–839). Newark, DE: International Reading Association.

Lareau, A. (2000). *Home advantage: Social class and parental intervention in elementary education* (2nd ed.). Lanham, MD: Rowman & Littlefield.

Lave, J., & Wenger, E. (1991). *Situated learning: Legitimate peripheral participation*. Cambridge: Cambridge University Press.

Lewison, M., Leland, C., & Harste, J. C. (2008). *Creating critical classrooms: K–8 reading and writing with an edge*. New York: Erlbaum.

Mariotti, A. S., & Homan, S. P. (2005). *Linking reading assessment to instruction*. London: Routledge.

Martínez, R. A. (2018). Beyond the English learner label: Recognizing the richness of bi/multilingual students' linguistic repertoires. *The Reading Teacher, 71*(5), 515–522

McKenna, M. C., & Stahl, K. A. D. (2009). *Assessment for reading instruction* (2nd ed.). New York: Guilford Press.

McKissack, P. (2001). *Goin' somewhere special*. New York: Atheneum.

Mellard, D. F., & Johnson, E. (2008). *RTI: A practitioner's guide to implementing Response to Intervention*. Thousand Oaks, CA: Corwin Press and the National Association of Elementary School Principals.

Merga, M. K., & Roni, S. M. (2018). Empowering parents to encourage students to read beyond the early years. *The Reading Teacher, 72*(2), 213-221.

Moll, L. C., & Gonzales, N. (2004). Engaging life: A funds of knowledge approach to multicultural education. In J. A. Banks & C. A. M. Banks (Eds.), *Handbook of research on multicultural education* (2nd ed., pp. 699–715). San Francisco: Jossey-Bass.

Moses, L., Ogden, M., & Beth Kelly, L. (2015). Facilitating meaningful discussion groups in the primary grades. *The Reading Teacher, 69*(2), 233-237.

National Board for Professional Teaching Standards. (2002). *Early and middle childhood literacy: Reading-language arts standards*. Arlington, VA: Author.

Nieto, S. (2002). *Language, culture, and teaching: Critical perspectives for a new century*. Mahwah, NJ: Erlbaum.

O'Donohue, W., & Kitchener, R. F. (Eds.). (1998). *Handbook of behaviorism*. New York: Academic Press.

Paratore, J. R. (2001). *Opening doors, opening opportunities: Family literacy in an urban community*. Boston: Allyn & Bacon.

Pearson, P. D., & Gallagher, M. C. (1983). The instruction of reading comprehension. *Contemporary Educational Psychology 8*(3), 317–344.

Pearson, P. D., Raphael, T. E., Benson, V. L., & Madda, C. L. (2007). Balance in comprehensive literacy instruction: Then and now. In L. B. Gambrell, L. M. Morrow, & M. Pressley (Eds.), *Best practices in literacy instruction* (3rd ed., pp. 31–54). New York: Guilford Press.

Peregoy, S. F., & Boyle, O. F. (2013). *Reading, writing and learning in ESL: A resource book for K–12 teachers* (6th ed.). Boston: Pearson.

Piaget, J. (1969). *The psychology of intelligence.* Paterson, NJ: Littlefield, Adams.

Pressley, M. (2002). Comprehension strategies instruction: A turn-of-the-century status report. In C. C. Block & M. Pressley (Eds.), *Comprehension instruction: Research-based best practices* (pp. 11–27). New York: Guilford Press.

Rathmann, P. (1995). *Officer Buckle and Gloria.* New York: Putnam.

Rosenblatt, L. M. (2013). The transactional theory of reading and writing. In D. E. Alvermann, N. J. Unrau, & R. B. Ruddell (Eds.), *Theoretical models and processes of reading* (6th ed., pp. 923–956). Newark, DE: International Reading Association.

Roth, S. (2001). *Happy birthday Mr. Kang.* Washington, DC: National Geographic Students' Books.

Rothenberg, C., & Fisher, D. (2007). *Teaching English language learners: A differentiated approach.* Upper Saddle River, NJ: Merrill/Prentice Hall.

Ruddell, R. B., & Unrau, N. J. (2013). Reading as a motivated meaning-construction process: The reader, the text, and the teacher. In D. E. Alvermann, N. J. Unrau, & R. B. Ruddell (Eds.), *Theoretical models and processes of reading* (6th ed., pp. 1015–1068). Newark, DE: International Reading Association.

Rumelhart, D. E. (2013). Toward an interactive model of reading. In D. E. Alvermann, N. J. Unrau, & R. B. Ruddell (Eds.), *Theoretical models and processes of reading* (6th ed., pp. 719–747). Newark, DE: International Reading Association.

Ryan, P. M. (2002). *Esperanza rising.* New York: Scholastic/Blue Sky Press.

Shanahan, T., & Beck, I. (2006). Effective literacy teaching for English-language learners. In D. August & T. Shanahan (Eds.), *Developing literacy in second-language learners: Report of the National Literacy Panel on Language-Minority Students and Youth* (pp. 415–488). Mahwah, NJ: Erlbaum.

Skinner, B. F. (1974). *About behaviorism.* New York: Random House.

Snow, C. E., Griffin, P., & Burns, M. S. (Eds.). (2005). *Knowledge to support the teaching of reading: Preparing teachers for a changing world.* San Francisco: Jossey-Bass.

Stahl, S. A., & Nagy, W. E. (2006). *Teaching word meanings.* Mahwah, NJ: Erlbaum.

Strickland, D. S. (2002). The importance of effective early intervention. In A. E. Farstrup & S. J. Samuels (Eds.), *What research has to say about reading instruction* (3rd ed., pp. 261–290). Newark, DE: International Reading Association.

Tomlinson, C. A. (2004). *How to differentiate instruction in mixed-ability classrooms* (2nd ed.). Alexandria, VA: Association for Supervision and Curriculum Development.

Tompkins, G. E., & Collom, S. (Eds.). (2004). *Sharing the pen: Interactive writing with young students.* Upper Saddle River, NJ: Merrill/Prentice Hall.

Tracey, D. H., & Morrow, L. M. (2006). *Lenses on reading: An introduction to theories and models.* New York: Guilford Press.

Vandevoort, L. G., Amrein-Beardsley, A., & Berliner, D. C. (2004). National board certified teachers and their students' achievement. *Education Policy Analysis Archives, 12*(46). Retrieved from http://epaa.asu.edu/epaa/v12n46

Vygotsky, L. S. (1978). *Mind in society.* Cambridge, MA: Harvard University Press.

Vygotsky, L. S. (1986). *Thought and language.* Cambridge, MA: MIT Press.

White, E. B. (2006). *Charlotte's web.* New York: HarperCollins.

Williams, C. (2018). Learning to write with interactive writing instruction. *The Reading Teacher, 71*(5), 523–532.

Willems, M. (2003). *Don't let the pigeon drive the bus!* New York: Hyperion Books.

Chapter 2
Examining Students' Literacy Development

 Learning Outcomes

After studying this chapter, you'll be prepared to:

2.1   Explain how teachers promote young students' oral language development.

2.2   Discuss the ways teachers build students' interest in written language.

2.3   Describe the three stages that students move through as they develop as readers and writers.

Ms. McCloskey's Students Become Readers and Writers

Monkey Business Images/Shutterstock

Kindergarten through third grade students sit on the carpet for a shared reading lesson. They listen intently as Ms. McCloskey prepares to read *Make Way for Ducklings* (McCloskey, 2004), the big-book version of an award-winning story about a family of ducks living in downtown Boston. She reads the title and the author's name, and some students recognize that the author's last name is the same as hers, but she explains that they aren't related. She reads the first page and asks for predictions. During this first reading, Ms. McCloskey reads each page expressively and tracks the text, word by word, with a pointer as she reads. After she finishes, they talk about the story. Some of the English learners are initially hesitant, but others eagerly relate their own experiences to the story.

The next day, Ms. McCloskey rereads *Make Way for Ducklings*. She begins by asking for volunteers to retell the story. Students take turns retelling each page, using the

In this chapter, you'll learn how young students learn to read and write. They move through three developmental levels—emergent, beginning, and fluent—as they become literate. As you read this vignette, notice how Ms. McCloskey teaches young students at each stage in her multigrade classroom by differentiating instruction. She adapts her use of big books, guided reading groups, and literacy centers to address her students' instructional needs.

illustrations as clues. Ms. McCloskey includes this oral language activity because many of her students are English learners. The class is multilingual: Approximately 45% are Asian Americans who speak Hmong, Khmer, or Lao; 45% are Hispanics who speak Spanish or English at home; and the remaining 10% are African American and white students who speak English.

Next, Ms. McCloskey rereads the story, stopping several times to ask the class to think about the characters, draw inferences, and reflect on the theme. Her questions include: Why did the police officer help the ducks? What would have happened to the ducks if the police officer didn't help? Do you think animals should live in cities? What was Robert McCloskey saying to us? On the third day, Ms. McCloskey reads the story again, and the students take turns using the pointer to track the text and join in reading familiar words. After they finish, the students clap because rereading the now familiar story provides a sense of accomplishment.

Ms. McCloskey understands that her students are moving through three developmental stages—emergent, beginning, and fluent—as they learn to read and write. She monitors each student's development to tailor instruction to meet his or her needs. As she reads the big book aloud, she uses a pointer to show the direction of print, from left to right and top to bottom on the page. She also moves the pointer across the lines of text to demonstrate the relationship between the words on the page and the words she's reading. Emergent-stage readers are learning these concepts.

Others are beginning readers who are learning high-frequency words and to decode phonetically regular words. One day after rereading the story, Ms. McCloskey turns to one of the pages and asks these students to identify familiar high-frequency words (e.g., *don't, make*) and decode CVC words (e.g., *run, big*). She also asks students to isolate individual sentences on the page and note the capital letter at the beginning and the punctuation that marks the end of each sentence.

The students in the third group are fluent readers. Ms. McCloskey addresses their needs as she rereads a page from the story: She asks these students to identify adjectives and notice inflectional endings on verbs. She also rereads the last sentence on the page and asks a student to explain why commas are used in it.

The teacher draws the students' attention to the print as a natural part of **shared reading**: She points out letters, words, and punctuation marks; models strategies; and asks questions about which direction to go when they are reading. As they watch Ms. McCloskey and listen to their classmates, the students learn more about letters, words, sentences, and all about the rules of directionality that must be followed when reading.

Ms. McCloskey and her teaching partner, Mrs. Papaleo, share a large classroom and 40 students; despite the number of students, the room feels spacious. Students' desks are arranged in clusters around the open area in the middle where students meet for whole-class activities. An easel to display big books is placed next to the teacher's chair. Several chart racks stand nearby; one rack holds Ms. McCloskey's morning messages, a second one holds charts with poems that the students use for **choral reading**, and a third rack holds a pocket chart with word cards and sentence strips.

On one side of the classroom is the library with books arranged in crates by topic. One crate has frog books, and others have books about the ocean, plants, and the five senses; additional crates contain books by authors who have been featured in author studies, including Eric Carle, Kevin Henkes, and Paula Danziger. Picture books and chapter books are also arranged in the crates. Sets of leveled books are located on a shelf above the students' reach for the teachers to use in guided reading lessons. A child-size sofa, a table and chairs, pillows, and rugs make the area cozy. A listening center is set up at a nearby table with a tape player and headphones that accommodate six students at a time.

A **word wall** with high-frequency words fills a partition separating instructional areas. It's divided into sections for each letter of the alphabet, and nearly 100 words written on small cards cut into the shape of the words are attached to it. The teachers introduce new words each week and post them on the word wall. The students often practice reading and writing the words as a center activity, and they refer to the word wall to spell words.

A bank of computers, several iPads, and a printer are located on another side of the classroom. Everyone uses them, even the youngest students; those who have stronger computer skills assist their classmates. They use word processing to publish their writing during writing workshop and monitor their independent reading practice on the computer or the iPad using various commercially available supplemental reading programs. At other times, they search the Internet to find information related to topics they're studying in science and social studies.

Literacy center materials are stored in a corner. Clear plastic boxes hold magnetic letters, puppets and other props, whiteboards and pens, puzzles and games, flash cards, and other manipulatives. The teachers choose materials to use during **minilessons**, and they also set boxes of materials out for students to use during center time.

Ms. McCloskey spends the morning teaching reading and writing using a variety of teacher-directed and student-choice activities. Her daily schedule is shown here. After shared reading and a minilesson, the students participate in reading and writing workshop.

The students write books during writing workshop. While most of them are working independently, Ms. McCloskey brings together a small group for a special activity: She conducts **interactive writing** lessons with emergent writers and teaches the writing process and revision strategies to more fluent writers. Today she's conferencing with six students who are beginning writers. Because they're writing longer compositions, she has decided to introduce revising. After each student reads his or her rough draft aloud to the group, classmates ask questions and offer compliments, and Ms. McCloskey encourages them to make a change in their writing so that their readers will understand it better. Anthony reads aloud a story about his soccer game, and after a classmate asks a question he realizes that he needs to add more about how he scored a goal; he moves back to his desk to revise. The group continues with students sharing their writing and beginning to make revisions. At the end of writing workshop, the students come together for author's chair. Each day, three students sit in the author's chair to share their "published" writing.

During reading workshop, students read independently or with a partner while Ms. McCloskey and her teaching partner conduct guided reading lessons. The students

Ms. McCloskey's Schedule

Time	Activity	Description
8:10–8:20	Class Meeting	Students participate in opening activities, read their teachers' morning message, and talk about plans for the day.
8:20–8:45	Shared Reading	The teachers read big books and poems copied on charts; this activity often serves as a lead-in to the minilesson.
8:45–9:00	Minilesson	The teachers teach minilessons on literacy procedures, strategies, and skills.
9:00–9:45	Writing Workshop	Students write books while the teachers confer with individual students and small groups. They also participate in interactive writing activities and share their published books from the author's chair.
9:45–10:00	Recess	
10:00–11:00	Reading Workshop	Students read self-selected books independently while the teachers teach guided reading lessons with small groups.
11:00–11:30	Literacy Centers	Students work at literacy centers, participating in reading, writing, listening, and other activities.
11:30–12:10	Lunch	
12:10–12:30	Read-Aloud	The teachers read aloud picture books and chapter books, and students discuss them in grand conversations.

have access to books in the classroom library, including predictable books for emergent readers, little leveled books from various publishers for beginning readers, and easy-to-read chapter books for fluent readers. The students know how to choose books that they can read successfully so they're able to spend their time really reading.

Ms. McCloskey is working with a group of four emergent readers, and today they'll read *Playing* (Prince, 1999), a seven-page predictable book with one line of text on each page that uses the pattern "I like to ____." She begins by asking students what they like to do when they're playing. Der says, "I like to play with my brother," and Ms. McCloskey writes this on a strip of paper. Some students say only a word or two, and she expands the words into a sentence for the student to repeat; then she writes the expanded sentence and reads it with the student. Next, she introduces the book, saying, "Now let's see what the students in this story like to do!" Ms. McCloskey reads the title and the author's name, and then, turning the pages of the story, she talks about the picture and names the activity the student is doing - running, jumping, sliding, and so on. She reviews the "I like to ____" pattern pointing to the words on the first page as she says the words. Then the students read the book independently while Ms. McCloskey supervises and provides assistance as needed. The students eagerly reread the book several times, becoming more confident with each reading.

Ms. McCloskey reviews the high-frequency sight words *I*, *like*, and *to*, and the students point them out on the classroom word wall. They use magnetic letters to spell the words and then write sentences that begin with *I like to . . .* on whiteboards. Then Ms. McCloskey cuts apart their sentence strips for them to sequence; afterward the students put their sentences into envelopes to practice another day. At the end of the lesson, the teacher suggests that the students might want to write "I like to" books during writing workshop the next day.

During the last 30 minutes before lunch, the students work at literacy centers. Ms. McCloskey and Mrs. Papaleo have set out 12 centers, and the students are free to work

Literacy Centers

Center	Description
Bag a Story	Students use objects in a paper bag to create a story. They draw pictures or write sentences to tell the story they've created.
Clip Boards	Students search the classroom for words beginning with a particular letter or featuring a spelling pattern and write them on paper attached to clip boards.
Games	Students play alphabet, phonics, and other literacy card and board games with classmates.
Library	Students read books related to a thematic unit and write or draw about the books in reading logs.
Listening	Students listen to a recording of a story or informational book while they follow along in a copy of the book.
Making Words	Students practice a making words activity that they've previously done together as a class with teacher guidance.
Messages	Students write notes to classmates and the teachers and post them on a special "Message Center" bulletin board.
Poetry Frames	Students arrange word cards on a chart-sized poetry frame to create a poem and then practice reading it.
Reading the Room	Students use pointers to reread big books, charts, signs, and other texts posted in the classroom.
Research	Students use the Internet, informational books, photos, and realia to learn more about topics in literature focus units and thematic units.
Story Reenactment	Students use small props, finger puppets, or flannel board figures to reenact familiar stories with classmates.
Word Sorts	Students categorize high-frequency or thematic word cards displayed in a pocket chart.

at any one they choose. The students are familiar with the routine and know what's expected of them at each center. The two teachers circulate around the classroom, monitoring students' work and taking advantage of teachable moments to clarify misunderstandings, reinforce previous lessons, and extend students' learning.

After lunch, Ms. McCloskey reads aloud from picture books and easy-to-read chapter books. Sometimes she reads books by a particular author, but at other times, she reads books related to a thematic unit. She uses these read-alouds to teach predicting, visualizing, and other comprehension strategies. This week, she's reading award-winning books, and today she reads aloud *The Stray Dog* (Simont, 2001), the story of a homeless dog that's taken in by a loving family. She uses the **interactive read-aloud** procedure to involve students in the book as she reads, and afterward they talk about it in a **grand conversation**. Ms. McCloskey asks them to share their connections to the story, which she records on a chart divided into three sections. Most comments are text-to-self connections, but several students make other types of connections. Rosario says, "I'm thinking of a movie. It was *101 Dalmatians*. It was about dogs, too."; that's a text-to-text connection. Angelo offers a text-to-world connection: "You got to stay away from stray dogs. They can bite you, and they might have this bad disease called rabies—it can kill you."

L iteracy is a process that begins in infancy and continues throughout life. It used to be that five-year-olds came to kindergarten to be "readied" for reading and writing instruction, which formally began in first grade. The implication was that there's a point in students' development when it's time to teach them to read and write; for those not ready, a variety of "readiness" activities would prepare them. Since the 1970s, this view has been discredited because preschoolers have demonstrated that they could recognize signs and other environmental print, retell stories, scribble letters, invent printlike writing, and listen to stories read aloud (Morrow, Tracey, & Del Nero, 2011). Some young students even arrive at school already knowing how to read!

This perspective on how students learn to read and write is known as **emergent literacy**, a term that New Zealand professor Marie Clay coined in her dissertation research. Studies from 1966 on have shaped the current outlook (McGee & Richgels, 2003): Now, researchers are looking at literacy learning from the student's point of view. Literacy development has been broadened to incorporate the cultural and social aspects of language learning, and students' experiences with and understandings about language— including oral language, reading, and writing—are included as part of emergent literacy.

Promoting Students' Oral Language Development

Young students develop oral language through everyday experiences and interactions with parents and others; they learn words at the grocery store, on the playground, during swimming lessons, and at the zoo, for example. Students who go fishing or plant gardens with their caregivers, or collect Thomas trains or Disney princesses learn new words along the way, too. They learn even more words while listening to adults read aloud from picture books and when watching *Blue's Clues*, *Dora the Explorer*, and other TV programs designed for young students.

Through these experiences, students develop expertise in all four language modes:

Phonology.   Preschoolers learn to produce the sounds of English and to manipulate language in playful ways.

Syntax.   Students learn to combine words into different types of sentences and to use irregular verb forms, pronouns, plural markers, and other inflectional endings.

Semantics. Four- and five-year-olds acquire knowledge about the meanings of words and add approximately 2,000 words to their vocabularies each year.

Pragmatics. Students learn to use language socially—to carry on a conversation, tell stories, and use social conventions, including "hello" and "goodbye" and "please" and "thank you."

By age four or five, students have acquired the oral language of their home culture. They learn to converse with individuals and in groups, to tell stories, and to listen to and follow directions, and they acquire vocabulary related to concepts they're learning.

Oral Language Activities

Check the Compendium of Instructional Procedures, which follows Chapter 12. These **green** terms also show a brief description of each procedure.

Students continue to develop oral language competence at school, especially as they participate in literacy activities. Probably the most valuable activity is the instructional procedure teachers use to read stories and other books aloud that's known as **interactive read-alouds**. As they listen, students learn new vocabulary and acquire more sophisticated sentence structures. The Booklist: Books That Develop Oral Language presents popular picture books that introduce new vocabulary and develop young students' talking and listening abilities. Afterward, they talk about the story in **grand conversations** and participate in **story retelling** and activities using **story boards**.

Figure 2–1 lists literacy activities that develop students' oral language; these activities are described in the Compendium of Instructional Procedures, which follows Chapter 12. In addition, whenever students work together in small groups, they have opportunities to use new vocabulary to talk about things they're learning.

English Learners

All young students, by definition, are English learners, but some students come to school learning English as an additional language to the one they have already learned at home. Both processes, learning English as the first or as an additional language, are developmental processes that require both time and opportunity. Young students learn English as an additional language best in a classroom where talk is encouraged and where the teacher and classmates serve as English language models. They hear English spoken in meaningful contexts and associated with physical actions, artifacts, and pictures. Students acquire conversational English, known as **Basic Interpersonal Communicative Skills (BICS)** quickly—in two years or less—but academic English, known as **Cognitive Academic Language Proficiency (CALP)**, can take seven or eight years to

Figure 2–1 Literacy Activities to Develop Oral Language

COMPONENT	PREK–KINDERGARTEN	FIRST–SECOND GRADES	THIRD–FOURTH GRADES
Expanding Oral Language Expressiveness	Grand conversations Interactive read-alouds Interactive writing Language Experience Approach Story boards Story retelling	Book talks Grand conversations Interactive read-alouds Interactive writing Story boards Story retelling	Book talks Grand conversations Hot seat Interactive read-alouds
Playing With Words	Interactive read-alouds Shared reading	Choral reading Interactive read-alouds Shared reading	Choral reading Interactive read-alouds
Increasing Word Knowledge	Interactive read-alouds Interactive writing	Interactive read-alouds KWL charts Semantic feature analysis Word sorts Word walls	Interactive read-alouds KWL charts Semantic feature analysis Word sorts Word walls

acquire (Cummins, 1979). Even though English learners in third or fourth grade may appear fluent in conversational settings, they may still struggle academically because they haven't learned more formal, academic English.

Societal and cultural factors influence language acquisition; students' personalities, the attitudes of their cultural group, and teacher expectations all play a role (Otto, 2014; Samway & McKeon, 2007). Students' level of proficiency in their first language also affects their additional language development: Those who continue to develop their first language proficiency become better English speakers than those who stop learning their native language (Tabors, 2008).

The Link Between Oral Language and Literacy

Developing students' oral language is essential because it provides the foundation for literacy learning (Roskos, Tabors, & Lenhart, 2009). Students who don't develop strong oral language before first grade have difficulty keeping pace with classmates (Hart & Risley, 2003; Snow, Burns, & Griffin, 1998). Researchers have found that vocabulary knowledge is an important predictor of beginning reading success (Roth, Speece, & Cooper, 2002). Interestingly, students' ability to orally define words was found to be an important predictor of how well they'd be able to decode words and comprehend text in the primary grades. Other significant factors, such as phonemic awareness and letter knowledge, are related to students' ability to decode words, but not to their comprehension.

MyLab Education
Video Example 2.1
In this video, professor MaryEllen Vogt discusses the distinguishing features of English learners' literacy needs. How does Dr. Vogt differentiate conversational and academic language?

Booklist Books That Develop Oral Language

GRADE	BOOKS
PreK	Carle, E. (2002). *The very hungry caterpillar*. Cowley, J. (2002). *The hungry giant's soup*. Henkes, K. (2000). *Wemberly worried*. Litwin, E. (2008). *Pete the cat: I love my white shoes*. Martin, B., Jr., & Archambault, J. (2009). *Chicka chicka boom boom*. Willems, M. (2004). *Knuffle bunny: A cautionary tale*.
K	Fleming, D. (2007). *In the small, small pond*. Hoban, T. (2008). *Over, under, and through*. Logue, M. (2012). *Sleep like a tiger*. Root, P. (2004). *Rattletrap car*. Taback, S. (1997). *There was an old lady who swallowed a fly*. Wood, A., & Wood, D. (2000). *The napping house*.
1	Gray, M. (1995). *My mama had a dancing heart*. Most, B. (1996). *Cock-a-doodle-moo!* Rathmann, P. (1995). *Officer Buckle and Gloria*. Reynolds, A. (2012). *Creepy carrots*. Wilson, K. (2002). *Bear snores on*. Seeger, L. V. (2012). *Green*.
2	Bunting, E. (1999). *Smoky night*. Fosberry, J. (2010). *My name is not Isabella*. Fox, M. (1998). *Tough Boris*. Hurd, T. (2003). *Moo cow kaboom*. St. George, J. (2004). *So you want to be president?* Yolen, J. (1987). *Owl moon*.
3	Obama, B. (2010). *Of thee I sing: A letter to my daughters*. Ryan, P. M. (1999). *Amelia and Eleanor go for a ride*. Scieszka, J. (1995). *Math curse*. Steig, W. (2009). *Amos & Boris*. Van Allsburg, C. (1986). *The stranger*. Zelinsky, P. O. (1997). *Rapunzel*.
4	Burleigh, R. (2002). *Pandora*. Floca, B. (2009). *Moonshot: The flight of Apollo 11*. King, M. L., Jr. (1997). *I have a dream*. Polacco, P. (1994). *Pink & Say*. Say, A. (1993). *Grandfather's journey*. Van Allsburg, C. (1991). *The wretched stone*.

Assessing Students' Oral Language

Early childhood education teachers monitor students' oral language development because they understand its importance for academic achievement. They use informal assessment techniques to check that students demonstrate these language skills:

- Speak clearly in complete sentences
- Respond to questions
- Initiate conversations
- Take turns
- Ask questions
- Participate in discussions
- Sing songs and recite fingerplays
- Tell about experiences

MyLab Education
Video Example 2.2
Teachers often notice that language is developmental in some of the four- and five-year olds they work with, and this problem interferes with literacy progress. Why do you think students' language development may interfere with learning emergent literacy concepts?

Teachers use observations, anecdotal notes, checklists, and video clips (Otto, 2014). They also monitor that young students listen during conversations and discussions as well as to stories teachers are reading and that they can follow directions. They notice whether students play with words (e.g., rhyming words and alliterations), connect new words to concepts they're learning, and use new words appropriately as they talk.

Teachers also use classroom tests to evaluate four- and five-year-olds' oral language development, especially when they suspect that a student may have receptive or expressive language difficulties. The Assessment Tools feature describes tests that provide normative data so teachers can compare their student's score against national benchmarks.

Assessment Tools

Oral Language

Teachers use these classroom tests to screen prekindergartners' and kindergartners' oral language development and identify students with possible language problems:

- **Assessment of Literacy and Language (ALL)**
  Preschool, kindergarten, and first grade teachers use ALL to assess students who they believe are at risk for reading difficulties because of an underlying language disorder. It assesses listening comprehension, semantics and syntax, phonological awareness, understanding of the alphabetic principle, and concepts about print. This test is time-consuming, so teachers use it selectively; it's administered individually in 60 minutes or less. ALL is available for purchase from Pearson.

- **Kindergarten Language Screening Test, 2nd Edition (KLST-2)**
  KLST-2 is an individually administered assessment that's used to quickly identify students who may have language problems that will interfere with their reading and writing development. It assesses four- to seven-year-olds' receptive and expressive language—to understand questions, follow directions, repeat sentences, and use spontaneous speech. KLST-2 is available for purchase from Pearson.

- **Teacher Rating of Oral Language and Literacy (TROLL)**
  Prekindergarten teachers use TROLL to assess three-, four-, and five-year-olds' oral language, reading, and writing. This individual assessment is easy to use and can be completed in 5 to 10 minutes. Teachers judge students' language competence using a 25-item rating scale; 8 of the items focus on oral language, including asking questions, sharing personal experiences, and identifying rhyming words. TROLL is available free of charge from the Center for the Improvement of Early Reading Achievement at the University of Michigan (http://www.ciera.org).

These tests provide normative data so teachers can compare students against national benchmarks as well as chart their growth over the school year.

MyLab Education **Self-Check 2.1**

Building Students' Interest in Written Language

Young students' introduction to written language begins at home, long before they come to school. Parents and other caregivers read to them, and they learn to read signs and other environmental print in their community. They experiment with writing and have their parents write messages for them; they also observe adults writing. When young students come to school, their knowledge about written language expands quickly as they learn concepts about print and participate in meaningful experiences with reading and writing. The Common Core State Standards for English Language Arts (2010) emphasize the importance of fostering students' interest in reading and writing and developing their understanding of concepts about written language. Check the Common Core State Standards box: Concepts About Written Language to learn more about the Standards for young readers and writers.

Concepts About Written Language

Through experiences in their homes and communities, young students learn that print carries meaning, that letters and words represent spoken language, and that reading and writing are used for a variety of purposes (Clay, 2017). They notice menus in restaurants; write and receive email messages, texts, and cards to communicate with friends and relatives; and listen to stories read aloud for enjoyment. Students also observe parents and teachers using written language for all these reasons.

Students' understanding about the purposes of reading and writing reflects how written language is used in their community. Although reading and writing are part of daily life for almost every family, families use written language in different ways (Heath, 1983). Young students have a wide range of literacy experiences in both middle-class and working-class families, even though those experiences might not be the same (Taylor & Dorsey-Gaines, 1987). In some communities, written language is used mainly as a tool for practical purposes such as paying bills, and in others, reading and writing are also used for leisure-time activities. In still other communities, written language serves even wider functions, such as debating social and political issues.

Preschool and kindergarten teachers demonstrate the purposes of written language and provide opportunities for students to experiment with reading and writing in these ways:

- Posting signs in the classroom
- Integrating reading and writing materials into literacy play centers
- Exchanging messages with classmates
- Reading and writing stories
- Labeling classroom items
- Drawing and writing in journals
- Writing notes to parents

Through these activities, young students learn the following concepts about how to look at print:

  Book Orientation Concepts.   Students learn how to hold a book and turn pages, and where to start reading on a page. They also understand that the words, not the illustrations, carry the message.

Common Core State Standards

Concepts About Written Language

The Reading: Foundational Skills Standards explain that young students learn concepts of print, the alphabetic principle, and other conventions of the English writing system as part of a comprehensive literacy program. Kindergartners and first graders are expected to develop these written language concepts in preparation for learning to read and spell words:

- Students demonstrate the progression of print, from left to right and top to bottom.
- Students recognize letters, words, and sentences in print.
- Students name the upper- and lowercase letters of the alphabet.

The Standards emphasize that instruction should be differentiated because young students vary in their knowledge about and experiences with reading and writing. To learn more about the Standards, go to http://www.corestandards.org/ELA-Literacy, or check your state's educational standards website.

Directionality Concepts.   Students learn that print is written and read from left to right and from top to bottom on a page. They learn about return sweep; the idea that at the end of a line they have to go all the way over to the left and start again from there. They also learn to match one-to-one, meaning they learn to match the reader's voice to print, pointing word by word to the text as it's read aloud. Students also learn the concepts of "first" and "last."

Letter and Word Concepts.   Students acquire concepts of what a letter is, what a word is, and what a sentence is; with this understanding, they can identify letters, words, and sentences on a page of text. They also develop awareness of capital letters and punctuation marks and why they're used.

As young students develop these concepts, they apply their knowledge in both reading and writing. For instance, they open books and point to where their teachers or parents should begin reading and pick out familiar letters and words that they notice in the text. Preschoolers also begin to make letterlike forms and add them to their pictures as labels.

Concepts About Words

At first, young students have only vague notions of literacy terms, such as *word, letter, sound,* and *sentence,* that teachers use in talking about reading and writing, but students develop an increasingly sophisticated understanding of what they mean. Students learn that words have different appearances: they can be spoken, listened to, read, and written.

Students develop concepts about words through active participation in literacy activities. They watch as teachers point to words in big books during **shared reading**, and they mimic the teacher and point to words as they reread familiar texts. After many shared reading experiences, students notice that word boundaries are marked with spaces, and they pick out familiar words. Their pointing becomes increasingly exact, and they get better at picking out specific words in the text, noticing that words at the beginnings of sentences are marked with capital letters and words at the ends are followed with punctuation marks.

ENVIRONMENTAL PRINT.   Young students begin reading by recognizing logos on fast-food restaurants, department stores, grocery stores, and commonly used household items within familiar contexts (Harste, Woodward, & Burke, 1984). They recognize the golden arches of McDonald's and say "McDonald's," but when they're shown the word

McDonald's written on a sheet of paper without the familiar sign and restaurant setting, they can't read the word. At first, students depend on context to read familiar words and memorized texts, but slowly, they develop relationships linking form and meaning as they gain more reading and writing experience.

LITERACY PLAY CENTERS.   Young students learn about the purposes of reading and writing as they use written language in their play: While constructing block buildings, students write signs and tape them on the buildings; as they play doctor, students write prescriptions on slips of paper; and as they play teacher, students read stories aloud to stuffed animal "students" (McGee, 2007). Young students use these activities to reenact familiar, everyday activities and to pretend to be someone else. Through these literacy play activities, students use reading and writing for a variety of purposes.

Preschool and kindergarten teachers add literacy materials to play centers to enhance their value for literacy learning (Sluss, 2005). Housekeeping centers are probably the most common play centers; they can easily be transformed into grocery stores, post offices, or medical centers by changing the props. They become literacy play centers when reading and writing materials are included: Food packages, price stickers, and play money are props in grocery store centers; letters, stamps, and mailboxes are props in post office centers; and appointment books, prescription pads, and folders for patient records are props in medical centers. Literacy play centers can be set up in classrooms and coordinated with literature focus units and thematic units. Ideas for eight literacy play centers are presented in Figure 2–2; each center includes authentic literacy materials that young students can experiment with to learn more about the purposes of written language.

MyLab Education
Video Example 2.3
Creating a print-rich environment in your classroom can help students become familiar with the purpose of literacy. What are some ways PreK-4 teachers can set up print-rich classroom environments?

Figure 2–2 Literacy Play Centers

CENTER	MATERIALS			
Bank	teller window checks	play money roll papers for coins	deposit slips money bags	signs receipts
Grocery Store	food packages artificial foods	grocery cart cash register	money grocery bags	cents-off coupons advertisements
Hairdresser	hair rollers brush and comb mirror	empty shampoo bottle towel posters of hair styles	wig and wig stand hairdryer (remove cord) curling iron (remove cord)	ribbons, barrettes, clips appointment book open/closed sign
Medical	appointment book white shirt/jacket medical bag	hypodermic syringe (play) thermometer stethoscope	prescription pad folders (for patient records)	bandages prescription bottles and labels
Office	computer calculator paper	stapler file folders in/out boxes	pens and pencils envelopes and stamps telephone	message pad rubber stamps stamp pad
Post Office	mailboxes envelopes stamps (stickers)	pens wrapping paper tape	packages scale package seals	address labels cash register money
Restaurant	tablecloth dishes glasses	silverware napkins menus	tray order pad and pencil apron for waitress	vest for waiter hat and apron for chef
Veterinarian	stuffed animals cages (cardboard boxes) pet information cards	white shirt/jacket medical bag stethoscope	medicine bottles prescription labels bandages	popsicle stick splints hypodermic syringe (play) open/closed sign

Concepts About the Alphabet

Young students also develop concepts about the alphabet and how letters are used to represent phonemes. Pinnell and Fountas (1998) identified these components of letter knowledge:

- The letter's name
- The formation of the upper- and lowercase letter in manuscript handwriting
- The features of the letter that distinguish it from other letters
- The direction the letter must be turned to distinguish it from other letters (e.g., *b* and *d*)
- The use of the letter in known words (e.g., names and common words)
- The sound the letter represents in isolation
- The sound the letter represents in combination with others (e.g., *ch*, *th*)
- The sound the letter represents in the context of a word (e.g., the *c* sounds in *cat*, *city*, and *chair*)

Students use this knowledge to decode unfamiliar words as they read and to create spellings for words as they write.

The most basic information students learn about the alphabet is how to identify and form the letters. They notice letters in environmental print and learn to sing the ABC song. By the time students enter kindergarten, they usually recognize many letters and can name them—especially those letters in their own names, names of family members and pets, and common words. Students also write some of these familiar letters.

Research suggests that students don't learn alphabet letter names in any particular order or by isolating letters from meaningful written language in skill-and-drill activities. McGee and Richgels (2012) conclude that learning letters of the alphabet requires many, many experiences with meaningful written language and recommend that teachers take these steps to encourage alphabet learning:

Capitalize on students' interests. Teachers provide letter activities that students enjoy, and they talk about letters when students are interested in talking about them. Teachers know what features to comment on because they observe students during reading and writing activities to find out which letters or features of letters they're exploring.

Talk about the role of letters in reading and writing. Teachers talk about how letters represent sounds, how letters combine to spell words, and point out capital letters and lowercase letters. They often talk about the role of letters as they write with students.

Provide a variety of opportunities for alphabet learning. Teachers use students' names and environmental print in literacy activities, use **interactive writing**, and allow students to use invented spelling in their own writing, share alphabet books, and play letter games.

Teachers begin teaching letters of the alphabet using two sources of words—students' own names and environmental print. They teach the ABC song to provide students with a strategy for identifying the name of an unknown letter. Students learn to sing this song and point to each letter on an alphabet chart until they reach the unfamiliar one; this is a very useful strategy because it gives them a real sense of independence in identifying letters. Teachers also provide routines, activities, and games for talking about and manipulating letters. During these familiar, predictable activities, teachers and students say letter names, manipulate magnetic letters, and write letters on whiteboards. At first, the teacher structures and guides the activities, but with experience, the students internalize the routine and do it independently, often at a literacy center. Figure 2–3 presents 10 routines to teach the letters of the alphabet; one of the routines involves using alphabet books. The Booklist called Alphabet Books presents a list of these books.

Figure 2–3 Routines to Teach the Letters of the Alphabet

ROUTINE	DESCRIPTION
Environmental Print	Students sort food labels, toy traffic signs, store names cut from advertisements, and other environmental print to find examples of a letter being studied.
Alphabet Books	Teachers read aloud alphabet books to build vocabulary, and later, students reread the books to find words when making books about a letter.
Magnetic Letters	Students pick all examples of one letter from a collection of magnetic letters or match upper- and lowercase letterforms using magnetic letters. They also arrange the letters in alphabetical order and use them to spell familiar words.
Letter Stamps	Students use letter stamps and ink pads to print letters on paper or in booklets. They also use letter-shaped sponges to paint letters and letter-shaped cookie cutters to cut out clay letters.
Alphabet Chart	Students point to letters and pictures on the alphabet chart as they recite the alphabet and say the names of the pictures, such as "A-airplane, B-baby, C-cat," and so on.
Letter Containers	Teachers collect coffee cans or shoe boxes, one for each letter, and place several familiar objects that represent the letter in each container. Teachers use these containers to introduce the letters, and students use them for sorting and matching activities.
Letter Frames	Teachers make circle-shaped letter frames from tagboard, collect large plastic bracelets, or shape pipe cleaners or Wikki-Stix (pipe cleaners covered in wax) into circles for students to use to highlight particular letters on charts or in big books.
Letter Books	Students make letter books with pictures of objects beginning with a particular letter on each page. They add letter stamps, stickers, or pictures cut from magazines.
Posters	Teachers draw a large letterform on a chart and students add pictures, stickers, and letter stamps.
Letter Sorts	Students sort objects and pictures representing two or more letters and place them in containers marked with the specific letters.
Whiteboards	Students practice writing upper- and lowercase forms of a letter and familiar words on whiteboards.

Being able to name the letters of the alphabet is a good predictor of beginning reading achievement, even though knowing the names of the letters doesn't directly affect a student's ability to read (Adams, 1990; Snow, Burns, & Griffin, 1998). A more likely explanation for this relationship is that students who have been actively involved in literacy activities before first grade know the names of the letters, and they're more likely to begin reading quickly. Simply teaching students to name the letters without the accompanying reading and writing experiences doesn't have this effect.

Manuscript Handwriting

Students enter kindergarten with different backgrounds of handwriting experience. Some five-year-olds have never held a pencil, but many others have written cursive-like scribbles or manuscript letterlike lines and circles. Some have learned to print their names and even a few other letters. Handwriting instruction in kindergarten typically includes developing students' ability to hold pencils, refining their fine-motor control, and focusing on letter formation. Some people might argue that kindergartners are too young to learn handwriting skills, but young students should be encouraged to write from the first day of school. They write letters and words on labels, draw and write stories, keep journals, and write other types of messages. The more students write, the greater their need becomes for instruction in handwriting. Instruction is necessary so that students don't learn bad habits that later must be broken.

To teach students how to form letters, many kindergarten and first grade teachers create brief directions for forming letters and sing the directions using a familiar tune. For example, to form a lowercase *a*, expand the direction "All around and make a tail" into a verse and sing it to the tune of "Mary Had a Little Lamb." As teachers sing the directions, they model the formation of the letter in the air or on a whiteboard using

---

Booklist Alphabet Books

GRADE	BOOKS
PreK	Carle, E. (2007). *Eric Carle's ABC.* Dorling Kindersley. (2012). *Touch and feel: ABC.* Hoban, T. (1995). *26 letters and 99 cents.* Jay, A. (2003). *ABC: A child's first alphabet book.* Munari, B. (2006). *Bruno Munari's ABC.* Seuss, Dr. (1996). *Dr. Seuss's ABC: An amazing alphabet book!* Zuckerman, A. (2009). *Creature ABC.*
K	Baker, K. (2010). *LMNOPeas.* Bingham, K. (2012). *Z is for moose.* Ehlert, L. (1993). *Eating the alphabet: Fruits and vegetables from A to Z.* Kontis, A. (2012). *AlphaOops! The day Z went first.* Martin, B., Jr., & Archambault, J. (2009). *Chicka chicka boom boom.* McLeod, B. (2008). *SuperHero ABC.* Sobel, J. (2006). *B is for bulldozer: A construction ABC.* Wood, A. (2001). *Alphabet adventure.* (And others in the series.)
1–2	Bayer, J. E. (1992). *A, my name is Alice.* Elting, M., & Folsom, M. (2005). *Q is for duck.* Pinto, S. (2003). *The alphabet room.* Rose, D. L. (2000). *Into the A, B, sea: An ocean alphabet book.* Shannon, G. (1999). *Tomorrow's alphabet.* Shoulders, M. (2008). *The ABC book of American homes.* Sobel, J. (2009). *Shiver me letters: A pirate ABC.*
3–4	Ernst, L. C. (2004). *The turn-around, upside-down alphabet book.* Grover, M. (1997). *The accidental zucchini: An unexpected alphabet.* Johnson, S. T. (1999). *Alphabet city.* Johnson, S. T. (2008). *A is for art: An abstract alphabet.* Kratter, P. (2006). *The living rain forest: An animal alphabet.* Palotta, J. (2002). *The jet alphabet book.* Van Allsburg, C. (1998). *The Z was zapped: A play in 26 acts.*

---

large arm motions. Then students sing along and practice forming the letter in the air, in a small tray of sand (bright blue aquarium sand is best!), or on the outside of sealed plastic baggies that have been filled with a gel or foam.

Moving models are much more effective than still models in teaching students how to handwrite, so worksheets on the letters aren't very useful because students may not form the letters correctly. It's important that students watch teachers form letters and then practice forming them themselves. Also, teachers supervise students as they write so that they can correct those who form letters incorrectly. Students must learn to write circles counterclockwise, starting from 1:00, and to form most lines from top to bottom and left to right across the page. When students follow these guidelines, they're less likely to tear their paper, and they'll have an easier transition to cursive handwriting.

Teaching Students About Written Language

Teachers develop young students' concepts about written language as they demonstrate how reading and writing work and involve students in shared and interactive reading and writing activities. In addition, teachers often use previously read texts in minilessons about written language concepts because students are already familiar with them.

MORNING MESSAGE. Teachers write a brief friendly letter, called a morning message, each day to share with students (Payne & Schulman, 1999). Before students arrive, they write a message on chart paper about what will happen that day; then they read the message aloud at the beginning of the school day, pointing at each word as they read. Afterward, students reread it and count the letters, words, and sentences in the message. Depending on their developmental level, they also pick out familiar letters and words, words illustrating a particular phonics concept, or capital letters and punctuation marks.

Teachers usually follow a predictable pattern in their messages each day to make it easier for students to read, as these two morning messages show:

Dear Kindergartners,
Today is Monday.
We will plant seeds.
We will make books
about plants.
    Love,
    Ms. Thao

Dear Kindergartners,
Today is Thursday.
We will measure the plants.
We will write about how
plants grow.
    Love,
    Ms. Thao

The morning messages that teachers write for first and second graders become gradually more complex, as this second grade teacher's message demonstrates:

Good Morning!
    Today is Monday, February 5, 2018.
New literature circles begin on Wednesday.
I'll tell you about the new book choices this
morning, and then you can sign up for your
favorite book. Who remembers what a
synonym is? Can you give an example?
    Love,
    Mrs. Salazar

Teachers usually choose students to take the messages home to share with their families, either day by day or at the end of each week.

LANGUAGE EXPERIENCE APPROACH. Teachers demonstrate how written language works in the **Language Experience Approach** (LEA) (Ashton-Warner, 1986). Students dictate sentences about an experience, and the teacher records their dictation on chart paper. As they write, teachers demonstrate how to write from left to right on a page, how to form letters and to space between words, and how to use capital letters and punctuation marks. Then the completed text becomes the reading material; students practice rereading the text and picking out letters and words. Because the language comes from the students and because the content is based on shared experiences, the text can usually be read easily.

Teachers often use LEA to create collaborative books, where each student creates one page to be added to a class book. For example, as part of a unit on bears, a kindergarten class made a collaborative book on bears. Students each chose a fact about bears for their pages; they drew an illustration and dictated the text for their teacher to record. One page from the class book is shown in Figure 2–4. The teacher took the students' dictation because she wanted the book to be written in conventional spelling so that students and their parents could read it.

INTERACTIVE WRITING. Students and the teacher create a text together using **interactive writing** (McCarrier, Pinnell, & Fountas, 2000; Tompkins & Collom, 2004). The students compose the message together, and then the teacher guides them as they write it word by word on chart paper. Students take turns writing known letters and familiar words, adding punctuation marks, and leaving spaces between words. Everyone participates in creating and writing the text on chart paper, and they also write the text on small whiteboards or on paper as it's written on chart paper. Afterward, students read and reread the text together with classmates and on their own.

Figure 2–4 One Page From a Class Book

Polar bears live in ice and snow.

Assessment Tools

Concepts About Written Language

Teachers monitor students' growing awareness of written language as they observe them during shared reading and other literacy activities. The most widely used assessment is Marie Clay's Concepts About Print:

- **Concepts About Print (CAP)**

- CAP (Clay, 2017) assesses young students' understanding of three concepts about written language: book orientation concepts, directionality concepts, and letter and word concepts. The test has 24 items and is administered individually in about 10 minutes. The teacher reads a short book aloud while a student looks on. The student is asked to open the book, turn pages, and point out particular print features as the text is read. Four forms of the CAP booklet are available: *Sand* (Clay, 2015), *Stones* (Clay, 2014), *Follow Me, Moon* (Clay, 2000), and *No Shoes* (Clay, 2016), as well as a Spanish version. Teachers carefully observe students as they respond, and then mark their responses on a scoring sheet. CAP is included with five other literacy assessment tasks in *An Observation Survey of Early Literacy Achievement* (Clay, 2013), or in a stand-alone version called *Concepts About Print* (Clay, 2017) both of which are available for purchase from Heinemann Books.

Instead of using the test booklets, teachers can also assess a student's understandings about print by using books available in the classroom and the scoring sheet in the Assessment Snapshot: Print Awareness.

Assessment Snapshot Print Awareness

Scoring Sheet

Name _____Adele_____ Date _____Jan. 10_____
Title of Book _____First the Egg_____
Check the items that the student demonstrates.

1. Book Orientation Concepts
   - ☑ Shows the front of a book.
   - ☑ Turns to the first page of the story.
   - ☑ Shows where to start reading on a page.

2. Directionality Concepts
   - ☑ Shows the direction of print across a line of text.
   - ☐ Shows the direction of print on a page with more than one line of print.
   - ☐ Points to individual words as the teacher reads.

3. Letter and Word Concepts
   - ☑ Points to any letter on a page.
   - ☐ Points to a particular letter on a page.
   - ☑ Puts fingers around any word on a page.
   - ☐ Puts fingers around a particular word on a page.
   - ☐ Puts fingers around any sentence on a page.
   - ☐ Points to the first and last letters of a word.
   - ☐ Points to a period or other punctuation mark.
   - ☑ Points to a capital letter.

TEACHER'S NOTE
Adele is familiar with books and has book orientation concepts. It's January and she's just reached the point where most of her classmates were in September. She's working on tracking words and needs to learn more about letters, words, and sentences.

Assessing Students' Knowledge About Written Language

Teachers observe students as they look at books and reread familiar ones. They also watch as students do pretend writing and write their names and other familiar words. They notice which concepts students understand and which ones they need to continue to talk about and demonstrate during shared reading.

As students read aloud, teachers ask the student to point out book orientation concepts, directionality concepts, and letter and word concepts. They can use the scoring sheet shown in the Assessment Snapshot: Print Awareness or develop one of their own to monitor students' growing knowledge about these concepts. Keep in mind that older students who are English learners may also need to learn about print concepts in English if they are literate in another language that is written down differently; Arabic, for example, reads from right to left instead of left to right.

MyLab Education Self-Check 2.2

How Students Develop as Readers and Writers

Students move through three stages as they learn to read and write: emergent, beginning, and fluent (Juel, 1991). During the emergent stage, young students gain an understanding of the communicative purpose of print, and they move from pretend reading to reading predictable books and from using scribbles to simulate writing to writing patterned sentences, such as *I see a bird. I see a tree. I see a car*. The focus of the second stage, beginning reading and writing, is on students' growing ability to use phonics to "crack the alphabetic code" in order to decode and spell words. Students also learn to read and write many high-frequency words and write several sentences to develop a story or other composition. In the fluent stage, students are automatic, fluent readers. In writing, they develop good handwriting skills, spell many high-frequency words correctly, and organize their writing into multiple-paragraph compositions. Figure 2–5 presents an overview of students' literacy accomplishments at each stage.

Stage 1: Emergent Reading and Writing

Students gain an understanding of the communicative purpose of print and develop an interest in reading and writing. They notice **environmental print** and develop concepts about print as teachers read and write with them. As students dictate stories for the teacher to record, for example, they learn that their speech can be written down, and they observe how teachers write from left to right and top to bottom.

Students grow in these ways during the first stage:

- Develop an interest in reading and writing
- Acquire concepts about print
- Develop book handling skills
- Identify the letters of the alphabet
- Develop handwriting skills
- Learn to read and write some high-frequency words

Figure 2–5 Students' Literacy Development

STAGE	READING	WRITING
Emergent	Students: • notice environmental print • show interest in books • pretend to read • use picture cues and predictable patterns in books to retell the story • reread familiar books with predictable patterns • identify some letter names • recognize 5–20 familiar or high-frequency words	Students: • distinguish between writing and drawing • write letters and letterlike forms or scribble randomly on the page • develop an understanding of directionality • show interest in writing • write their first and last names • write 5–20 familiar or high-frequency words • use sentence frames to write a sentence
Beginning	Students: • identify letter names and sounds • match spoken words to written words • recognize 20–100 high-frequency words • use beginning, middle, and ending sounds to decode words • apply knowledge of the cueing systems to monitor reading • self-correct while reading • read slowly, word by word • read orally • point to words when reading • make reasonable predictions	Students: • write from left to right • print the upper- and lowercase letters • write one or more sentences • add a title • spell many words phonetically • spell 20–50 high-frequency words correctly • write single-draft compositions • use capital letters to begin sentences • use periods, question marks, and exclamation points to mark the ends of sentences • can reread their writing
Fluent	Students: • identify most words automatically • read with expression • read at a rate of 100 words per minute or more • prefer to read silently • identify unfamiliar words using the cueing systems • recognize 100–300 high-frequency words • use a variety of strategies effectively • often read independently • use knowledge of text structure and genre to support comprehension • make inferences	Students: • use the writing process to write drafts and final copies • write compositions with more than one paragraph • indent paragraphs • spell most of the 100 high-frequency words • use sophisticated and technical vocabulary • apply vowel patterns to spell words • add inflectional endings to words • apply capitalization rules • use commas, quotation marks, and other punctuation marks

Four- and five-year-olds are usually emergent readers and writers, but some students whose parents have read to them every day and provided a variety of literacy experiences do learn how to read before they come to school. Caroline, a five-year-old emergent reader and writer in Ms. McCloskey's classroom, is presented in the Literacy Portraits on the following pages.

READING.   Emergent readers are interested in books and are developing concepts about written language. Students develop book orientation skills as they listen to teachers read aloud, and they imitate the teacher's behavior as they look at books—locating the cover, turning pages, and pretending to read. They learn that text moves from top to bottom on a page and from left to right across a line. At the same time, emergent readers are learning to name the letters of the alphabet and sing the ABC song to identify unfamiliar letters. They can recognize their own name and some classmates' names and, through lots of reading experiences, they can read *Mom, Dad, love, cat, dog,* and a few high-frequency words, including *the, you, I,* and *is.*

WRITING   Young students make scribbles to represent writing. They may appear randomly on a page at first, but with experience, students line up the marks from left to right on a line and from top to bottom on a page. Students also begin to "read," or tell what their writing says (Schickedanz & Casbergue, 2009). At first, they can reread it only immediately after writing, but with experience, they learn to remember what their writing says and, as their writing becomes more conventional, they're able to decipher it more easily.

Portrait of an Emergent Reader and Writer

Five-year-old Caroline is a friendly, eager student who is learning to speak English as she learns to read and write. Her grandparents emigrated from Thailand to the United States; her family speaks Hmong at home, and she speaks English only at school. When Caroline's Hmong-speaking classmates start to talk in their native language, she admonishes them to speak English because "we learn English school."

When she came to kindergarten, Caroline didn't know any letters of the alphabet and had never held a pencil. She had not listened to stories read aloud and had no book handling experience. She spoke very few words of English. The classroom culture and language were very different than those of her home, but Caroline was eager to learn. For the first few days, she stood back, observing her classmates; then she said "I do" and joined them.

Reading

Caroline has shown remarkable growth in five months. She has been reading books with repetitive sentences on each page, but now at level 3 she's beginning to use phonics to sound out unfamiliar words. She knows the names of most letters and the sounds that the letters represent. She can read about 20 high-frequency words. She has developed good book handling skills and follows the line of words on a page. She reads word by word and points at the text as she reads. She's learning consonant and vowel sounds, but she has difficulty decoding words because of her pronunciation of English sounds and low vocabulary.

Caroline demonstrates that she understands the books she reads, and she makes text-to-self connections. Recently, she was reading a book about a child having a birthday, and she pointed to the picture of a young, blonde mother wrapping a child's

---

Emergent Reader and Writer Characteristics that Caroline Exemplifies

READING	WRITING
• Shows great interest in reading	• Shows great interest in writing
• Has developed book handling skills	• Writes from left to right and top to bottom on a page
• Identifies most of the letters of the alphabet	• Prints most of the letters of the alphabet
• Knows some letter sounds	• Writes 20 high-frequency words
• Sounds out a few CVC words	• Leaves spaces between words
• Reads 20 high-frequency words	• Writes sentences
• Rereads familiar books with predictable patterns	• Begins sentences with a capital letter
• Makes text-to-self connections	• Puts periods at the ends of sentences
	• Rereads what she has written immediately afterward

birthday present. She looked up at Ms. McCloskey and said, "She no mom, she sister. This wrong." The woman in the picture looks nothing like her mother.

Writing

Caroline began participating in writing workshop on the first day of school and, for several weeks, she scribbled. Within a month, she learned how to print some letters because she wanted her writing to look like her classmates'. Soon she wrote her own name, copied classmates' names, and wrote words she saw posted in the classroom.

A month ago, Ms. McCloskey gave Caroline a ring for key words. Every few days, Caroline chooses a new word to add to her ring. Ms. McCloskey writes the word on a word card that Caroline puts on her ring. She has 31 words now, including *you* and *birthday*. She flips through the cards to practice reading, and she uses the words when she writes sentences.

After four months of instruction, Caroline began writing sentences. Ms. McCloskey introduced the frame "I see a . . . " and Caroline wrote sentences using familiar words, including some from her key words ring. Then, to make her writing longer, she wrote the same sentence over and over, as shown in the "Apple" writing sample.

Next, she began reading and writing color words, and she expanded her writing to two sentences. Her two-sentence writing sample, "Zebra," also is shown here. Most of the words that Caroline writes are spelled correctly because she uses key words and words she locates in a picture dictionary. Notice that Caroline puts a period at the end of each sentence; but recently she has seen that some of her classmates put a period at the end of each line, so she also added one at the end of each line in the "Zebra" sample. When she draws a picture to accompany a sentence, Caroline can usually read her writing immediately after she has written it, but by the next day she often doesn't remember what she has written.

Caroline has one of the thickest writing folders in the classroom, and she's very proud of her writing. Nearly 100 pages of writing are stuffed into the folder, tracing her development as a writer since the beginning of the school year.

Instructional Implications

Ms. McCloskey explains, "Caroline is an emergent-stage reader and writer. She's making excellent progress because she can read books with repetitive patterns, is learning phonics and high-frequency words, and can write words and craft sentences."

Now Ms. McCloskey is beginning to ask Caroline to read books without repetitive patterns during guided reading; in these books, she has to recognize high-frequency words and use phonics to identify unfamiliar words rather than rely on repetitive sentence patterns. Similarly, during writing workshop, Ms. McCloskey is encouraging Caroline to write books about events in her life without using repetitive patterns. Working without the support the patterns provide is difficult for Caroline because her knowledge of English is limited. Ms. McCloskey concludes, "Even though Caroline is learning to speak English at the same time she's learning to read and write, I'm confident that she's up to the challenge."

Portrait of a Beginning Reader and Writer

Anthony, a first grader with a ready smile, is a beginning reader and writer. He's six years old, and he says that he likes to read and write. He's a well-behaved student who's extremely competitive. He reads at level 12 now, and recently he announced to Ms. McCloskey that he wants to read at level 15. She explained that to do this, Anthony needs to practice reading at home with his mom, so he's been taking several books home each night to practice. Ms. McCloskey predicts that Anthony will be reading at level 18 by the end of the year; level 18 is the school's benchmark for the end of first grade.

Reading

According to Ms. McCloskey's assessment of Anthony's reading at the end of the second quarter, he recognizes 80 of the 100 high-frequency words taught in first grade, and he can decode most one-syllable words with short and long vowel sounds, including words with consonant blends and digraphs, such as *shock, chest,* and *spike.* He's beginning to sound out some of the more complex vowel digraphs and diphthongs (e.g., *loud, boil, soon*) and *r*-controlled vowels (e.g., *chart, snore*), and in the past month, Ms. McCloskey has noticed that Anthony's ability to decode words is growing, and that about two thirds of the time he can identify these words with more complex vowel sounds in the context of a sentence. He is also decoding some two- and three-syllable words, such as *dinner, parents,* and *hospital,* in books he's reading.

Anthony reads orally and points only when he reads challenging texts. He's beginning to chunk words into phrases as he reads, and he notices when something he's reading doesn't make sense. He uses the cross-checking strategy to make corrections and get back on track.

Beginning Reader and Writer Characteristics that Anthony Exemplifies

READING	WRITING
• Likes to read • Reads orally • Points to words when he reads challenging text • Recognizes 80 high-frequency words • Uses phonics knowledge to decode unfamiliar words • Makes good predictions • Uses the cross-checking strategy • Retells what he reads • Makes text-to-self and text-to-world connections	• Likes to write • Writes single-draft compositions • Adds a title • Writes organized compositions on a single topic • Writes more than five sentences in a composition • Has a beginning, middle, and end in his stories • Refers to the word wall to spell high-frequency words • Uses his knowledge of phonics to spell words • Uses capital letters to mark the beginnings of sentences • Uses periods to mark the ends of sentences • Reads his writing to classmates

Anthony has read 17 books this month, according to his reading workshop log. He's increasingly choosing easy-to-read chapter books, including Syd Hoff's *Sammy the Seal* (2000a) and *Oliver* (2000b). After he reads, he often shares his books with his friend Angel, and they reread them together and talk about their favorite parts. He regularly uses the connecting strategy and shares his text-to-self and text-to-world connections with Angel and Ms. McCloskey. When he reads two or more books by the same author, he shares text-to-text comparisons and can explain to his teacher how these comparisons make him a better reader: "Now I think and read at the same time," he explains.

Writing

Anthony likes to write during writing workshop. He identified his "I Got Sick" story as the very best one he's written, and Ms. McCloskey agrees. Anthony tells an interesting and complete story; you can hear his voice clearly in the story. Anthony's story is shown in the box, and here is a translation of it:

I Got Sick

I went outside with no! jacket on and my throat started to hurt. It really hurt and I was getting sick. I went to find my Mom and I told her I was sick. My Mom gave me some medicine and she made Campbell's chicken noodle soup for me to eat. Then I got all better.

> ### I Got Sick
>
> I went out sid with no! Jaket on and my throt started to hrt. It rele hrt and I was geting Sick. I went to finde my Mom and I tolde her I was sick. My Mom gav me some Medisin and she mad Cambell chicken newdl soup for me to eat. Then I got all Betr.

Anthony's spelling errors are characteristic of phonetic spellers. He sounds out the spelling of many words, such as HRT (*hurt*), MEDISIN (*medicine*), and BETR (*better*), and he's experimenting with final *e* markers at the end of TOLDE and FINDE, but ignores them on other words, such as OUT SID (*outside*) and GAV (*gave*). He uses the word wall in the classroom and spells many high-frequency words correctly (e.g., *with, went, have*).

Anthony writes single-draft compositions in paragraph form, and he creates a title for his stories. He writes in sentences and includes simple, compound, and complex sentences in his writing. He correctly uses capital letters to mark the beginnings of sentences and periods to mark the ends, but as his "I Got Sick" story shows, he continues to randomly capitalize words.

Instructional Implications

"Anthony is a very motivated student: He's eager to read because he has a goal in mind," Ms. McCloskey explains. "I'm confident that he'll reach level 18 by the end of the year. I've been encouraging Anthony to read increasingly difficult chapter books and practice using the strategies he's learned when he's reading independently."

Ms. McCloskey plans to teach Anthony about complex vowel patterns and consonant blends and digraphs so he'll be able to decode unfamiliar words while he's reading. She's also noticed that it's time for him to move beyond single-draft compositions and learn to use the writing process to revise and edit his writing.

Portrait of a Fluent Reader and Writer

Shutterstock

Jazmen is a confident and articulate third grader with an easy smile. She's eight years old, and she celebrated her birthday last fall with a family trip to the Magic Mountain amusement park in Southern California. Jazmen is a computer whiz and she often provides assistance to her classmates. When asked about her favorite school activity, Jazmen says that she likes using the computer best of all. In fact, she's interested in learning more about careers that involve computers because she knows that she always wants to work with them.

Ms. McCloskey identified Jazmen for this feature because she's made such remarkable progress this year. This is the second year that Jazmen has been in Ms. McCloskey's class. Last year, she seemed stuck in the beginning stage, not making too much progress, according to Ms. McCloskey, "but this year, it's like a lightbulb has been turned on!" She's now a fluent reader and writer.

Reading

Jazmen likes to read, and she reports that she has a lot of books at home. According to the Accelerated Reader program, she's reading at 3.8 (third grade, eighth month) level, which means she's reading at or slightly above grade level. She enjoys reading the Marvin Redpost (e.g., *Marvin Redpost: A Magic Crystal?* by Louis Sachar, 2000) and Zack Files (e.g., *Never Trust a Cat Who Wears Earrings*, by Dan Greenburg, 1997) series of easy-to-read paperback chapter books. She says she enjoys these books because they're funny.

Currently, she's reading Paula Danziger's series of chapter-book stories about a third grader named Amber Brown who deals with the realities of contemporary life, including adjusting to her parents' divorce. The first book in the series is *Amber Brown Is Not a Crayon* (2006), about Amber and her best friend, Justin, who moves away at the end of the book; other chapter books in the series are *Amber Brown Goes Fourth* (2007), *Amber Brown Is Feeling Blue* (1999), *Amber Brown Sees Red* (1998), and *Amber Brown Is Green With Envy* (2004).

Fluent Reader and Writer Characteristics that Jazmen Exemplifies

READING	WRITING
• Recognizes most words automatically	• Uses the writing process
• Reads with expression	• Has a sense of audience and purpose
• Reads more than 100 words per minute	• Writes a complete story with a beginning, middle, and end
• Reads independently	• Writes in paragraphs
• Uses a variety of strategies	• Indents paragraphs
• Makes connections when reading	• Uses sophisticated language
• Thinks inferentially	• Spells most words correctly
• Applies knowledge of story structure and genre when reading	• Uses capital letters and punctuation to mark sentence boundaries

Jazmen reads fluently. She recognizes words automatically and reads with expression. She says that when you're reading to someone, you have to be interesting, and that's why she reads the way she does. Her most outstanding achievement, according to Ms. McCloskey, is that she thinks inferentially about stories. She can juggle thinking about plot, characters, setting, and theme in order to make thoughtful connections and interpretations. She knows about various genres and literary elements, and she uses this knowledge as she reflects on her reading.

Writing

Jazmen likes to write. She gets her ideas for stories from TV programs. She explains, "When I'm watching TV, I get these ideas and I draw pictures of them and that's how I think of a story." She's currently working on a story entitled "Lucky and the Color Purple," about a princess named Lucky who possesses magical qualities. Why are her stories interesting? Jazmen says, "Most important is that they are creative." She shares her stories with her classmates, and they agree that Jazmen is a good writer.

Jazmen is particularly pleased with her story "The Super Hero Dog," which is shown here. The story is humorous—just imagine a three-pound dog helping an elephant! Ms. McCloskey said that she likes the story because it's complete with a beginning, middle, and an end, and because Jazmen uses dialogue (and quotation marks) effectively. The errors remaining on the final draft of the paper also suggest direction for future instruction. Jazmen spelled 95% of the words in her composition correctly. In particular, she appears ready to learn more about homophones, possessives, and punctuating dialogue.

Instructional Implications

"Jazmen is a fluent reader," says Ms. McCloskey, "so she's ready to tackle more challenging fiction and nonfiction books, both during guided reading lessons and when she's reading independently." When she reads, Jazmen's focus has changed from decoding the words to comprehending the author's message. Ms. McCloskey plans to teach minilessons about asking questions, drawing inferences, and using other reading strategies to encourage Jazmen to think more deeply about the books she's reading.

Jazmen has begun to use the writing process to refine her compositions, but most of her pieces have been stories. Ms. McCloskey is encouraging Jazmen to write nonfiction books, poems, letters, and other genres. After reading *Hate That Cat* (Creech, 2010), a novel written in verse, Jazmen decided to imitate the genre and draft her own novel in verse, expanding on an encounter she had with a squirrel. Ms. McCloskey also plans to carefully monitor Jazmen's progress and teach minilessons on concepts and skills that she's attempting to use, including homophones, possessives, and dialogue.

The Super Hero Dog

Once upon a time a girl named Jazmen owned a dog named Chewbarka. Chewbarka was a Chorkie. Thats a Chiwuawua and Yorkie mix. Even tho Chorkies only way about three pounds, Chewbarka was a super hero! Chewbarka new how to fly and she had super strength. Then one day Jazmen got a call from Dashawna the vet. Dashawna said "There is an elephant named Rosie that needs help quick!" Rosie had a broken leg and could not walk to the vet with her owner. Jazmen told Chewbarka to fly over to where Rosie was pick her up and fly to the vet. Chewbarka did what she was told. The people who saw Chewbarka and Rosie could not beleve their eyes. There was a tiny dog with super strength flying the elephant over to the vets. After Chewbarka got Rosie to the vet, Dashawna started working on Rosie right away. Now her leg is in a big purple cast. Why did she get a purple cast? Its Rosie's favrite color! Rosie thanked the super hero for her help and they became BFFs. Without Chewbarkas help, Rosie would have never been helped.

PreK Practices

How do teachers promote students' literacy development?

The cornerstone of early literacy instruction, according to Vukelich and Christie (2009), is inter-active read-alouds: As teachers share books, students learn literacy strategies and skills and become interested in reading and making their own books. A print-rich classroom environment is another important component because it provides opportunities for students to engage in emergent reading and writing activities. Teachers also include explicit, developmentally appropriate instruction to teach phonological awareness; concepts about print; and alphabet knowledge. In addition, teachers engage students in conversations and expose them to content-related vocabulary words as they develop their content knowledge.

INSTRUCTIONAL PROCEDURES.   Emergent readers and writers participate in a variety of activities ranging from modeled and shared reading and writing, during which they watch as teachers read and write, to independent reading and writing that they do themselves. Ms. McCloskey's students, for example, listened to her read books aloud and read big books using shared reading, and they also participated in reading and writing workshop.

Stage 2: Beginning Reading and Writing

This stage marks students' growing awareness of the **alphabetic principle**—that letters represent sounds. Students learn about phoneme–grapheme correspondences; phonics rules in words such as *run, hand, this, make, day,* and *road*; and word families, including *-ill (fill, hill, will)* and *-ake (bake, make, take)*. They also apply (and misapply) their developing phonics knowledge to spell words. For example, they spell *night* as NIT and *train* as TRANE. At the same time, they're learning to read and write high-frequency words, many of which can't be sounded out, such as *what, are,* and *there*.

Students grow in these ways during the second stage:

- Learn phonics skills
- Recognize 20–100 high-frequency words
- Apply reading strategies, including cross-checking, predicting, and repairing
- Write five or more sentences, sometimes organized into a paragraph
- Spell phonetically
- Spell 20–50 high-frequency words
- Capitalize letters to begin sentences
- Use punctuation marks to indicate the ends of sentences
- Reread their writing

Most first and second graders are beginning readers and writers and, with explicit instruction and daily opportunities to read and write, students move through this stage to reach the fluent stage. Anthony, a six-year-old beginning reader and writer in Ms. McCloskey's classroom, is presented in the Literacy Portraits.

READING.   Students usually read aloud slowly, word by word, stopping often to sound out unfamiliar words. They point at each word as they read but, by the end of this stage, their reading becomes smoother and more fluent, and they point at words only when the text is especially challenging.

Although the emphasis in this stage is on word identification, students also learn that reading involves comprehension. They make predictions to guide their thinking about events in stories they read, and they make connections between what they're reading and their own lives and the world around them as they personalize the reading experience. They monitor their reading to recognize when it doesn't make sense; cross-check using phonological, semantic, syntactic, and pragmatic information in the text to figure out the problem; and repair or self-correct it (Fountas & Pinnell, 1996). They also learn about story structure—particularly that stories have a beginning, middle, and an end, and use this knowledge to guide their reading and retelling.

WRITING.   Students move from writing one or two sentences to developing longer compositions, with five, eight, or more sentences organized into paragraphs. Their writing is better developed because they're acquiring a sense of audience, and they want their classmates to like what they've written. Students continue to write single-draft compositions but begin to make a few revisions and editing corrections as they learn about the writing process.

Students apply what they're learning about phonics in spelling, and they correctly spell many of the high-frequency words that they've learned to read. They know how to spell some high-frequency words and can locate others on **word walls**. They learn to use capital letters to mark the beginnings of sentences and punctuation to mark the ends. Students are more adept at rereading their writing, both immediately afterward and days later, because they're able to read many of the words they've written.

INSTRUCTIONAL PROCEDURES.   Teachers plan activities for students at the beginning stage that range from modeled to independent reading and writing activities, but the emphasis is on interactive and guided activities. Through interactive writing, choral reading, and guided reading, teachers scaffold students as they read and write, and they use minilessons to provide strategy and skill instruction. For example, Ms. McCloskey's students were divided into small, homogeneous groups for guided reading lessons; the students met to read books at their reading levels, and Ms. McCloskey introduced new vocabulary words, taught reading strategies and skills, and assessed their comprehension.

Teachers introduce the writing process to beginning-stage writers once they develop a sense of audience and want to make their writing better. Students don't immediately start writing rough drafts and final copies or doing both revising and editing: They often begin the writing process by rereading their compositions and adding a word or two, correcting a misspelled word, or capitalizing a lowercase letter. These changes are cosmetic, but the idea that the writing process doesn't end after the first draft is established. Next, students show interest in making a final copy that really looks

Teach Kids to Be Strategic!
Beginning Reading Strategies

Introduce these first reading strategies in kindergarten and first grade:

- Cross-check
- Predict
- Connect
- Monitor
- Repair

Students practice them when they participate in shared and guided reading activities as well as interactive read-alouds. Look for students to use these strategies during guided practice and independent reading activities. If they struggle, reteach the strategies, making sure to name them, model their use, and think aloud and talk about their application.

Developmental Continuum LITERACY LEARNING

PreK	K	1	2	3	4
Some children are emergent readers and writers before coming to school, but others enter the stage as a result of school experiences.	Most students are emergent readers and writers during kindergarten, but a few reach the beginning stage during the school year.	Most students are beginning readers and writers, and through instruction, their understanding of the alphabetic principle grows.	Most second graders continue in the beginning stage, but some reach the fluent stage by the end of the school year.	Most students become fluent readers and writers by the end of the school year, but a few still struggle with literacy.	Most fourth graders are fluent readers and writers, but those who continue to struggle need extra instruction in problem areas.

good. They either recopy the composition by hand or use word processing and print out the final copy. Once students understand that writing involves a rough draft and a final copy, they're ready to learn more about revising and editing, and they usually reach this point at about the same time they become fluent writers.

Stage 3: Fluent Reading and Writing

Fluent readers and writers reach the third stage when they accomplish the following:

- Read fluently and with expression
- Recognize most one-syllable words automatically and can decode other words efficiently
- Use decoding and comprehension strategies effectively
- Write well-developed, multiparagraph compositions
- Use the writing process to draft and refine their writing
- Write stories, reports, letters, and other genres
- Spell most high-frequency and other one-syllable words correctly
- Use capital letters and punctuation marks correctly most of the time

Some second graders reach this stage, and all students should be fluent readers and writers by the end of third grade. Reaching this stage is an important milestone because it indicates that students are ready for the increased literacy demands of fourth grade, when they're expected to read longer chapter-book stories, use writing to respond to literature, read content-area textbooks, and write essays and reports. Jazmen, an eight-year-old fluent reader and writer in Ms. McCloskey's classroom, is profiled in the Portrait of a Fluent Reader and Writer in this chapter.

READING. The distinguishing characteristic of fluent readers is that they read words accurately, rapidly, and expressively. Fluent readers automatically recognize many words and can decode unfamiliar words efficiently. Their reading rate has increased to 100 words or more per minute; in addition, they can vary their speed according to the demands of the text they're reading.

Most fluent readers prefer to read silently because they can read more quickly than when they read orally. No longer do they point at words as they read. Students can read many books independently, actively making predictions, visualizing, monitoring their understanding, and making repairs when necessary. They have a range of strategies available and use them to enhance their comprehension.

Fluent readers' comprehension is stronger, and they think more deeply about their reading than emergent and beginning readers do. It's likely that students' comprehension improves at this stage because they have more cognitive energy available for comprehension now; in contrast, beginning readers use much more cognitive energy to decode words. So, as students become fluent, they use less energy for word identification and have more cognitive resources available for comprehending what they read.

Students now read longer, more sophisticated picture books and chapter books, but they generally prefer chapter books because they enjoy really getting into a story or digging deeply when reading an informational book. They learn more about the literary genres, their structural patterns, and literary devices, such as alliteration, personification, and symbolism. They participate in literature focus units featuring an author, genre, or book, in small-group literature circles where students read and discuss a book together, and in author studies where they read and compare several books by the same author and examine that author's writing style. They're able to explain why they liked a particular book and make recommendations to classmates.

WRITING.   Fluent writers understand that writing is a process, and they use the writing process stages—prewriting, drafting, revising, editing, and publishing. They make plans for writing and write both rough drafts and final copies. They reread their rough drafts and make revisions and editing changes that reflect their understanding of writing forms and their purpose for writing. They increasingly share their rough drafts with classmates and turn to them for advice on how to make their writing better.

Students get ideas for writing from books they've read and from TV programs and movies they've viewed. They organize their writing into paragraphs, indent paragraphs, and focus on a single idea in each paragraph. They develop ideas more completely and use more sophisticated vocabulary to express their ideas.

Fluent writers are aware of writing genres and organize their writing into stories, reports, letters, and poems. Their stories have a beginning, middle, and an end, and the reports they write are structured using sequence, comparison, or cause-and-effect structures. Their letters reflect an understanding of the parts of a letter and how they're arranged on a page. Their poems incorporate alliteration, symbolism, rhyme, or other poetic devices to create vivid impressions.

Students' writing looks more conventional. They spell most of the 100 high-frequency words correctly and use phonics to spell other one-syllable words. They add inflectional endings (e.g., *-s, -ed, -ing*) and experiment with spelling two-syllable and longer words. They've learned to capitalize the first word in sentences and names and to use punctuation marks correctly at the ends of sentences, although they're still experimenting with punctuation marks within sentences.

INSTRUCTIONAL PROCEDURES.   At this stage, students can apply the reading and writing processes and are prepared to participate independently in reading and writing workshop. They're learning about genres, text structures, and literary devices and can apply this knowledge to reading and responding to literature in literature circles. Teachers have shifted their focus from teaching students to decode words to comprehending stories and informational books.

Instructional recommendations for each of the three stages of reading and writing development are presented in Figure 2–6.

Figure 2–6 Instructional Recommendations

STAGE	READING	WRITING
Emergent	• Use environmental print. • Include literacy materials in play centers. • Read aloud to students. • Read big books and poems on charts using shared reading. • Introduce the title and author of books before reading. • Teach directionality and letter and word concepts using big books. • Encourage students to make predictions and text-to-self connections. • Have students retell and dramatize stories. • Have students respond to literature through talk and drawing. • Have students manipulate sounds using phonemic awareness activities. • Use alphabet-learning routines. • Take students' dictation using the Language Experience Approach. • Teach 20–24 high-frequency words. • Post words on a word wall.	• Have students use crayons for drawing and pencils for writing. • Encourage students to use scribble writing or write random letters if they can't do more conventional writing. • Teach handwriting skills. • Use interactive writing for whole-class and small-group writing projects. • Have students write their names on sign-in sheets each day. • Have students write their own names and names of classmates. • Have students inventory or make lists of words they know how to write. • Have students "write the classroom" by making lists of familiar words they find in the classroom. • Have students use frames such as "I like ____" and "I see a ____" to write sentences. • Encourage students to remember what they write so they can read it.
Beginning	• Read charts of poems and songs using choral reading. • Read leveled books during guided reading lessons. • Provide daily opportunities to read and reread books independently. • Teach phonics concepts and rules. • Teach students to cross-check using the cueing systems. • Teach the 100 high-frequency words. • Point out whether texts are stories, informational books, or poems. • Teach predicting, connecting, cross-checking, and other strategies. • Teach the elements of story structure, particularly beginning, middle, and end. • Have students write in reading logs and participate in grand conversations. • Have students take books home to read with parents.	• Use interactive writing to teach concepts about written language. • Provide daily opportunities to write for a variety of purposes and using different genres. • Introduce the writing process. • Teach students to develop a single idea in their compositions. • Teach students to proofread their compositions. • Teach students to spell the 100 high-frequency words. • Teach contractions. • Teach capitalization and punctuation skills. • Have students use computers to publish their writing. • Have students share their writing from the author's chair.
Fluent	• Have students participate in literature circles. • Have students participate in reading workshop. • Teach about genres and other text features. • Involve students in author and genre studies. • Teach students to make text-to-self, text-to-world, and text-to-text connections. • Expand students' ability to use comprehension strategies. • Have students respond to books through talk and writing.	• Have students participate in writing workshop. • Teach students to use the writing process. • Teach students to revise and edit their writing. • Teach paragraphing skills. • Teach spelling rules. • Teach synonyms. • Teach homonyms. • Teach root words and affixes. • Teach students to use a dictionary and a thesaurus.

MyLab Education **Self-Check 2.3**
MyLab Education **Application Exercise 2.1:** Is Mrs. Koch's Word Wall Developmentally Appropriate?

Chapter Review

Examining Students' Literacy Development

- Teachers promote students' language development and build their vocabulary.

- Teachers build young students' interest in literacy and teach concepts about written language.

- Teachers understand that students' progress through the emergent, beginning, and fluent stages of literacy development as they become proficient readers and writers.

Accountability Check

Visit the following assessment links to access quiz questions and instructional applications.

Mylab Education Application Exercise 2.2 : Understanding Literacy Development
Mylab Education Application Exercise 2.3 : Understanding Literacy Development
Mylab Education Application Exercise 2.4 : Understanding Literacy Development
Mylab Education Application Exercise 2.5 : Monitoring Literacy Development
Mylab Education Application Exercise 2.6 : Measuring Literacy Development

References

Adams, M. J. (1990). *Beginning to read: Thinking and learning about print*. Cambridge, MA: MIT Press.

Ashton-Warner, S. (1986). *Teacher*. New York: Simon & Schuster.

Clay, M. M. (2017). *Concepts about print: What have students learned about the way we print language?* Portsmouth, NH: Heinemann.

Clay, M. M. (2016). *No shoes*. Portsmouth, NH: Heinemann.

Clay, M. M. (2015). *Sand*. Portsmouth, NH: Heinemann.

Clay, M. M. (2014). *Stones*. Portsmouth, NH: Heinemann.

Clay, M. M. (2013). *An observation survey of early literacy achievement* (rev. ed.). Portsmouth, NH: Heinemann.

Clay, M. M. (2000). *Follow me, moon*. Portsmouth, NH: Heinemann.

Common core state standards for English language arts. (2010). Retrieved from http://www.corestandards.org

Creech, S. (2010). *Hate that cat*. New York: HarperCollins.

Cummins, J. (1979). Linguistic interdependence and the educational development of bilingual students. *Review of Educational Research, 49*, 222–251.

Danziger, P. (1998). *Amber Brown sees red*. New York: Scholastic.

Danziger, P. (1999). *Amber Brown is feeling blue*. New York: Scholastic.

Danziger, P. (2004). *Amber Brown is green with envy*. New York: Scholastic.

Danziger, P. (2006). *Amber Brown is not a crayon*. New York: Scholastic.

Danziger, P. (2007). *Amber Brown goes fourth*. New York: Puffin Books.

Fountas, I. C., & Pinnell, G. S. (1996). *Guided reading: Good first teaching for all students*. Portsmouth, NH: Heinemann.

Greenburg, D. (1997). *Never trust a cat who wears earrings*. New York: Grosset & Dunlap.

Harste, J., Woodward, V., & Burke, C. (1984). *Language stories and literacy lessons*. Portsmouth, NH: Heinemann.

Hart, B., & Risley, T. (2003). The early catastrophe: The 30 million word gap. *American Educator, 27*(1), 4–9.

Heath, S. B. (1983). *Ways with words*. New York: Oxford University Press.

Hoff, S. (2000a). *Oliver*. New York: HarperCollins.

Hoff, S. (2000b). *Sammy the seal*. New York: HarperCollins.

Juel, C. (1991). Beginning reading. In R. Barr, M. L. Kamil, P. Mosenthal, & P. D. Pearson (Eds.), *Handbook of reading research* (Vol. 2, pp. 759–788). New York: Longman.

McCarrier, A., Pinnell, G. S., & Fountas, I. C. (2000). *Interactive writing: How language and literacy come together, K–2*. Portsmouth, NH: Heinemann.

McCloskey, R. (2004). *Make way for ducklings*. New York: Square Fish Books.

McGee, L. M. (2007). *Transforming literacy practices in preschool: Research-based practices that give all students the opportunity to reach their potential as learners*. New York: Scholastic.

McGee, L. M., & Richgels, D. J. (2003). *Designing early literacy programs: Strategies for at-risk preschool and kindergarten students*. New York: Guilford Press.

McGee, L. M., & Richgels, D. J. (2012). *Literacy's beginnings: Supporting young readers and writers* (6th ed.). Boston: Pearson.

Morrow, L. M., Tracey, D. H., & Del Nero, J. R. (2011). Best practices in early literacy development: Preschool, kindergarten, and first grade. In L. M. Morrow & L. B. Gambrell (Eds.), *Best practices in literacy instruction* (4th ed., pp. 67–95). New York: Guilford Press.

Otto, B. (2014). *Language development in early childhood education* (4th ed.). Boston: Pearson.

Payne, C. D., & Schulman, M. B. (1999). *Getting the most out of morning messages and other shared writing lessons*. New York: Scholastic.

Pinnell, G. S., & Fountas, I. C. (1998). *Word matters: Teaching phonics and spelling in the reading/writing classroom*. Portsmouth, NH: Heinemann.

Prince, S. (1999). *Playing*. Littleton, MA: Sundance.

Roskos, K. A., Tabors, P. O., & Lenhart, L. A. (2009). *Oral language and early literacy in preschool* (2nd ed.). Newark, DE: International Reading Association.

Roth, F. P., Speece, D. L., & Cooper, D. H. (2002). A longitudinal analysis of the connection between oral language and early reading. *Journal of Educational Research, 95*, 259–274.

Sachar, L. (2000). *Marvin Redpost: A magic crystal?* New York: Random House.

Samway, K. D., & McKeon, D. (2007). *Myths and realities: Best practices for English language learners* (2nd ed.). Portsmouth, NH: Heinemann.

Schickedanz, J. A., & Casbergue, R. M. (2009). *Writing in preschool: Learning to orchestrate meaning and marks* (2nd ed.). Newark, DE: International Reading Association.

Simont, M. (2001). *The stray dog*. New York: HarperCollins.

Sluss, D. J. (2005). *Supporting play: Birth through age eight*. Clifton Park, NY: Thomson/Delmar Learning.

Snow, C. E., Burns, M. S., & Griffin, P. (Eds.). (1998). *Preventing reading difficulties in young students*. Washington, DC: National Academy Press.

Tabors, P. O. (2008). *One child, two languages: A guide for early childhood educators of students learning English as a second language* (2nd ed.). Baltimore: Paul H. Brookes.

Taylor, D., & Dorsey-Gaines, C. (1987). *Growing up literate: Learning from inner-city families*. Portsmouth, NH: Heinemann.

Tompkins, G. E., & Collom, S. (Eds.). (2004). *Sharing the pen: Interactive writing with young students*. Upper Saddle River, NJ: Merrill/Prentice Hall.

Vukelich, C., & Christie, J. (2009). *Building a foundation for preschool literacy* (2nd ed.). Newark, DE: International Reading Association.

Chapter 3
Assessing Students' Literacy Development

∨	## Learning Outcomes

After studying this chapter, you'll be prepared to:

3.1 Explain how teachers link instruction and assessment.

3.2 Discuss how teachers use diagnostic tests to determine students' reading levels and diagnose their strengths and weaknesses.

3.3 Define high-stakes testing and discuss its role in literacy instruction and assessment.

3.4 Describe how teachers use portfolios to assess students' learning and their progress toward meeting grade-level standards.

Mrs. McNeal's Second-Quarter Assessments

Arvind Balaraman/Shutterstock

The end of the second quarter is approaching, and Mrs. McNeal is assessing her first graders. She collects assessment data about her students' reading, writing, and spelling development, which she uses to document students' achievement, verify that they're meeting state standards, determine report card grades, and make instructional plans for the third quarter.

Today, Mrs. McNeal assesses Ethan, who is six and a half years old. Mrs. McNeal has a collection of Ethan's writing, but she wants to assess his reading level. At the beginning of the school year, Mrs. McNeal considered him an average student, but in the past month, his reading has accelerated.

ASSESSING ETHAN'S INSTRUCTIONAL READING LEVEL. Mrs. McNeal regularly takes running records as she listens to students reread familiar books to monitor their ability to recognize high-frequency words, decode unfamiliar words, and use reading strategies. In addition, she assesses each student's instructional reading level using the Developmental Reading Assessment (DRA)—an assessment kit with 44 leveled books arranged from kindergarten to fifth grade reading levels.

At the beginning of the school year, most of Mrs. McNeal's first graders were reading at level 3 ; by midyear, they should be reading at level 12; and by the end of the school year, they're expected to reach level 20. Ethan was reading at level 3 in August, like many of his classmates, and at the end of the first quarter, he was reading at level 8. Now, nearing the end of the second quarter, Mrs. McNeal decides to test him at level 16 because he's reading a book at that level in his guided reading group.

Ethan reads *The Pot of Gold* (2001), a level 16 book in the *Developmental Reading Assessment* kit. The book recounts an Irish folktale about a man named Grumble who makes an elf show him where his pot of gold is hidden. Grumble marks the spot by tying a scarf around a nearby tree branch and goes to get a shovel with which to dig up the gold. Grumble admonishes the elf not to move the scarf, and he doesn't; instead, the elf ties scarves on nearby trees so that Grumble can't find the gold. Mrs. McNeal takes a **running record** while Ethan reads; a running record will give her an opportunity to assess what Ethan can do independently. Locate Ethan's running record in this chapter before reading on.

As indicated on the running record sheet, Ethan makes 14 errors and, of those, self-corrects just 2; his accuracy rate is high at 95%. Mrs. McNeal analyzes Ethan's running record by asking herself three questions:

1. Did Ethan have any difficulty with high-frequency words?
2. What sources of information does Ethan typically use and neglect?
3. What reading strategies does Ethan use or not use when he encounters difficulty?

Mrs. McNeal thought that Ethan knew *my* and *that* by sight so she was surprised that his self-corrections were on words that should have been ones that he could recognize automatically.

She is pleased to note that many of Ethan's errors fit all three sources of information—*Grumply* for *Grumble*, *or* for *of*, *make* for *mark*, *me* for *my*, *self* for *scarf*, *they* for *that*, *maybe* for *may*—all make sense, sound acceptable, and look like the actual word in the text. On three occasions however, Ethan used only visual information—*safr* and *scafer* for *scarf*, and *sit* for *still*—and neglected meaning and structure.

Mrs. McNeal examines the record for evidence of Ethan's strategy use. She notes with some concern that Ethan showed very few signs of monitoring his errors. In fact, he only seemed to notice on three occasions that he had encountered difficulty: once when he asked for help with the word *always* and twice more when he corrected his errors—*me* for *my*, and *they* for *that*. Mrs. McNeal knows that, unless Ethan notices when he has made an error, he won't have an opportunity to problem solve. Next, Mrs. McNeal thinks about Ethan's comprehension. When Ethan retells the story, he shows that he comprehends the big idea, but his retelling isn't especially strong: He retells the beginning and the end of the story but leaves out important details in the middle.

Mrs. McNeal pulls together all of the information she has collected and evaluates Ethan's progress. She decides that he is within grade level expectations for that time of the year and that he has made consistently good progress since the start of the school year.

The teacher makes notes about Ethan's instructional priorities for the third quarter of the school year so that he will continue to make progress. A priority will be that he notices when he makes an error and then makes an attempt to solve by cross-checking. In guided reading lessons, she'll focus on teaching Ethan to monitor (or notice). If he

In this chapter, you'll learn how to determine students' reading levels and assess their literacy learning. Teachers integrate assessment with instruction through a four-step cycle of classroom assessment—planning, monitoring, evaluating, and reflecting. As you read this vignette, notice how Mrs. McNeal evaluates her first graders' learning at the end of the second quarter. She uses multiple assessment tools to measure their achievement, determine grades, and set goals for the next quarter.

makes an error and doesn't notice, she will say, "Something you just read wasn't quite right. Go back to find and fix it."

Secondly, so that Ethan will have something to try once he notices he has made an error, she will teach him ways to problem-solve words while reading. To teach him to cross-check information, she will prompt him to use information that he is neglecting. For example, if he only uses visual information, she will say, "You are using the letters to try the word. That's good, but it doesn't make sense. Try something else that will make sense *and* look right." Mrs. McNeal knows that Ethan often uses all sources of information, which is great, but she needs to teach him to use additional visual information at those times. For errors such as *maybe* for *may*, or *self* for *scarf*, she will say, "Take a closer look at that word; it doesn't look quite right."

Finally, because Ethan had difficulty with some high-frequency words that he should know by sight, Mrs. McNeil will add some sight word activities. High-frequency words need to be read with automaticity.

ASSESSING ETHAN'S KNOWLEDGE OF HIGH-FREQUENCY WORDS.   Mrs. McNeal's goal is for her first graders to recognize at least 75 of the 100 high-frequency words by the end of the school year. In August, most students could read at least 12 words; Ethan read 16 correctly. Today, Mrs. McNeal asks Ethan to read the list of 100 high-frequency words again. She expects that he'll be able to read 50 to 60 of the words, and when he misses 5 in a row, she'll stop; but Ethan surprises her and reads 65!

ASSESSING ETHAN'S ABILITY TO WRITE WORDS.   Several days ago, Mrs. McNeal administered the "Words I Know" Test to the class: She asked the students to write as many words as they could in 10 minutes without copying from classroom charts. In August, most students could write and spell 15 to 20 words correctly; Mrs. McNeal's goal is for them to write and spell 50 words by the end of the school year. Ethan wrote 22 words in August, and on the recent test, he wrote 50 correctly spelled words, including *the, hat, bat, come, go, going, dog, dogs, God, cat, cowboys, from, fight, night, sun, run, fish, starfish, fin, trees, what,* and *you.* Mrs. McNeal reviews Ethan's list and notices that most are one-syllable words with short vowels, such as *cat* and *fin,* but he's beginning to write words with more complex spellings, such as *what, come,* and *night;* words with inflectional endings, such as *going;* and two-syllable words, such as *cowboys.* She concludes that Ethan is making very good progress, in both the number of words he can write and the complexity of the spelling patterns he's using.

ASSESSING ETHAN'S COMPOSITIONS.   Mrs. McNeal looks through Ethan's journal and chooses several representative samples written in the past three weeks to score; one of the samples is shown in this chapter. Here's the text with conventional spelling and punctuation:

> *I ate pizza for dinner. My dad took me to Round Table. It was half Hawaiian and half pepperoni. We brought the leftovers home.*

Using the school district's six-point rubric, Mrs. McNeal scores the composition as a four. A score of five is considered to be at grade level at the end of the school year, and Mrs. McNeal believes that Ethan will reach that level before then. She notices that he's writing several sentences, even though he sometimes omits a word or two, and often leaves out the punctuation at the ends of sentences. Mrs. McNeal plans to talk to him about rereading his writing to catch omissions, adding punctuation marks, and correcting misspelled words.

ASSESSING ETHAN'S WORD KNOWLEDGE.   The first graders take a dictation test each week. On Monday, they compose two sentences and write them on a chart displayed in the classroom. They practice writing the sentences on small whiteboards each day,

A Running Record Scoring Sheet.

Name _____ Ethan _____   Date _____ Jan. 14 _____

Level _____ 16 _____ Title _____ The Pot of Gold _____   (Easy) Instructional Hard

Running Record	E	SC	E	SC
2 ✓ ✓ ✓ ✓ ✓ ✓ ✓ ✓ grumply| ✓ ✓ ✓ ✓ ✓ ✓ Grumble|T |A ✓ ✓ ✓ ✓ always|T ✓ ✓ ✓ ✓ ✓ ✓ ✓ ✓ ✓ ✓ ✓ ✓	1 1		ⓜⓢⓥ	
3 ✓ ✓ ✓ ✓ ✓ ✓ ✓ ✓ ✓ ✓ ✓ ✓ ✓ ✓ ✓ ✓ did not| ✓ ✓ didn't | ✓ ✓ ✓ ✓ ✓ ✓ ✓ ✓ ✓ ✓ ✓ ✓ ✓ ✓ ✓ ✓ ✓ ✓ ✓	1		ⓜⓢⓥ	
4 ✓ ✓ ✓ ✓ ✓ ✓ ✓ ✓ ✓ ✓ ✓ ✓ ✓ ✓ ✓ ✓ ✓				
5 ✓ ✓ ✓ ✓ ✓ ✓ ✓ ✓ ✓ ✓ ✓ ✓ ✓ ✓ ✓ I | make| ✓ ✓ I'll | mark| ✓ ✓ ✓ ✓ ✓ ✓ ✓ ✓ ✓ safr | ✓ ✓ ✓ ✓ ✓ or| ✓ ✓ scarf| of|	1 1 1 1		ⓜⓢⓥ ⓜⓢⓥ m s ⓥ ⓜⓢⓥ	
6 ✓ ✓ ✓ ✓ ✓ ✓ me| sc self | ✓ ✓ ✓ my| scarf| ✓ ✓ ✓ ✓ ✓ ✓ ✓ ✓ ✓	1	1	ⓜⓢⓥ m s ⓥ ⓜⓢⓥ	
7 ✓ ✓ ✓ ✓ ✓ ✓ ✓ ✓ ✓ ✓ ✓ ✓ ✓ ✓ ✓ ✓ ✓ ✓ ✓ ✓				
8 ✓ ✓ ✓ ✓ ✓ ✓ ✓ ✓ ✓ ✓ ✓ ✓ ✓ ✓ ✓ ✓ ✓ ✓				
9 ✓ ✓ ✓ take| ✓ scafer| ✓ ✓ ✓ taken| scarf| ✓ ✓ ✓ ✓ ✓ ✓ ✓ ✓	1 1		ⓜ s ⓥ m s ⓥ	
10 ✓ ✓ ✓ ✓ ✓ ✓ ✓ ✓ ✓ ✓ they|sc ✓ ✓ ✓ ✓ ✓ ✓ that | maybe| sit | ✓ ✓ ✓ ✓ may | still | ✓ ✓	1 1	1	ⓜⓢⓥ m s ⓥ ⓜⓢⓥ m s ⓥ	

Scoring 12/266 95% accuracy	Picture Walk Gets gist of story
Types of Errors: Ⓜ Ⓢ Ⓥ Needs to monitor and notice errors Needs to use more visual cues.	Oral Reading Reads fluently
Self-correction Rate 1:7	Retelling/Questions Tells BME but middle is brief

and during **minilessons**, Mrs. McNeal draws their attention to high-frequency words, the phonetic features of words, and capitalization and punctuation rules applied in the sentences. Last week's sentences focused on *The Magic School Bus Lost in the Solar System* (Cole, 1993), a book Mrs. McNeal read aloud:

Their bus turned into a rocket ship. They wanted to visit all of the planets.

Ethan's journal

I ate piza for dinr My dad tok me to Ron Tab. It was haf huyan and haf peprone. We bot the lf ors home.

After practicing the sentences all week, Mrs. McNeal dictates them for the students to write on Friday. She tells them to try to spell the words correctly and to write all of the sounds they hear in the words that they don't know how to spell. Ethan wrote:

The bus turd into a rocket ship they wande to vist all of the planis.

Ethan spelled 10 of the 15 words correctly and included 46 of 51 sounds in his writing. He omitted the period at the end of the first sentence, however, and didn't capitalize the first word in the second sentence.

Mrs. McNeal uses this test to check students' phonics knowledge and ability to spell high-frequency words. Ethan spelled most of the high-frequency words correctly, except that he wrote *the* for *their*. His other errors involved the second syllable of the word or an inflectional ending. Mrs. McNeal concludes that Ethan is making good progress in learning to spell high-frequency words and that he's ready to learn more about two-syllable words and inflectional endings.

EVALUATING ETHAN'S LITERACY ACHIEVEMENT. Having collected and analyzed the assessment data, Mrs. McNeal evaluates Ethan's progress. He and his classmates receive separate number grades on their report cards in reading, writing, and spelling, ranging from one—not meeting grade-level standards—to four— exceeding standards. Ethan receives a three in reading, writing, and spelling; a score of three means that he's meeting grade-level standards. Even though his reading level is higher than average, his lack of noticing errors and problem-solving keep him at the third level in reading.

Assessment has become a priority in 21st-century schools. School district, state, and federal education agencies have increased their demands for accountability, and today, most students take annual high-stakes tests to measure their achievement. By linking assessment and instruction, teachers improve students' learning and their teaching. Near the end of this chapter, you will find "My Teaching To-Do Checklist" for the assessment topics you are about to read. You can print the checklist and keep in a place that you can easily access and refer back to, once you are a teacher.

The terms *assessment* and *evaluation* are often considered interchangeable, but they're not. **Assessment** refers to the collection and interpretation of data to inform decision-making. **Evaluation** refers to the decision-making itself about how well the student has progressed.

Assessments can be formative or summative; it all depends on the purpose behind collecting the information. According to the 2017 Position Statement of the International Literacy Association (ILA, 2017), summative assessments are designed to measure achievement at the end of an instructional sequence. Examples of summative assessments can range from the more formal state tests to the more informal teacher-designed quiz at the end of a unit of instruction. A **running record** can be a summative assessment if it is given at the end of an instructional period to determine the students' final instructional level.

The 2017 Position Statement of the International Literacy Association defines formative assessments as ongoing and taking place during instruction. **Formative assessments** are used for screening and monitoring student progress and to inform instruction. Again, a running record can be an example of a formative assessment if it is given to inform teaching and monitor student progress during the instructional period.

Because the purpose of Mrs. McNeil's assessments (the running record, spelling assessment, knowledge of high-frequency words, writing assessment) was to measure student progress at the end of the second quarter, we can refer to them as **summative assessments**. The same assessments would be considered formative if they were given during the term to help make decisions about what to teach next.

A **high-stakes test** refers to any assessment that is used to make an important high-stakes decision, like retaining a student in a grade or raising state standards for achievement. By definition, any assessment can be a high stakes assessment if its results are used to make a high-stakes decision, but in reality, high-stakes assessments are typically formal, summative assessments like a state achievement test. More on high-stakes assessments appears later in this chapter.

It is important to note that we need a variety of assessments in schools because there are so many stakeholders with different concerns and interests in the progress of students, including parents, other educators, the community, the school district, policy makers, and of course, the students themselves. The goal of all assessments, though, ought to be to produce information that is useful in helping students become better readers (Afflerbach, 2016, p. 414).

In contrast, **evaluation** is the decision-making or judgment that is made after analyzing assessment data. In other words, assessments are given to facilitate evaluation.

Classroom Assessment

Classroom assessment drives instruction, ensures that students are making adequate progress, determines the effectiveness of instruction, and assesses students' achievement. Every day, teachers use a combination of assessment tools to collect meaningful information about what students know and do (Afflerbach, 2007a; Kuhs, Johnson, Agruso, & Monrad, 2001). Assessment involves four steps—planning, assessing, evaluating, and reflecting. Each step serves a different purpose, so teachers need to integrate all of the steps into their literacy programs.

Step 1: Planning for Assessment

Teachers plan for assessment at the same time they're designing instruction, but how do we know what it is that we must teach and assess? Afflerbach (2016) refers to this knowledge that teachers need as the "must haves" (p. 413); in other words, teachers must know what it is that students must have at each grade level in order to be considered proficient readers and writers. When we are certain about the "must haves," then we are better able to plan instruction and assessment accordingly. Throughout this volume, and especially in the chapters to come, you will be learning about the "must haves" of early literacy. In this chapter, we focus on ways to assess the "must haves."

Teachers think about these questions and choose the assessment tools they'll use to get answers:

- What is it that students must have learned in this unit of instruction?
- What kinds of formative assessment will I use while teaching that will tell me whether any students are struggling with the "must haves" and falling behind?
- How often will I conduct the formative assessments I choose?
- How will I collect, organize, and display the information that I collect from the formative assessments?
- If I see students are falling behind, how will I adjust my teaching to help them catch up?

By planning for assessment before they begin teaching, teachers are preparing to use assessment tools wisely; otherwise, classroom assessment turns out to be haphazard and impromptu. Tests are a traditional way to assess students' learning, but increasingly teachers prefer to use students' actual reading and writing activities to assess their achievement.

Step 2: Assessing Students' Progress Every Day

Every day, in every literacy lesson, teachers assess student learning. These classroom-based assessments may be less formal from what we traditionally think of as commercially designed "tests," but they are just as important. Indeed, teachers who collect information about student learning on a regular basis in the classroom are able to adjust instruction from one day to the next. In other words, expert teachers not only teach, but they assess as they go along.

The key to assessing student progress every day is to be organized about how you do it. In this section, we describe seven broad categories for assessing student progress in the classroom and we give strategies to help organize the information you collect to best inform your teaching. The next time you are in a classroom, ask the teacher what kinds of ongoing classroom assessment are used; you will probably hear examples from each one of these six categories: observations, keeping anecdotal notes, conducting student conferences, creating and using checklists, examining student work samples, and applying rubrics.

OBSERVATIONS.   Effective teachers are "kid watchers"—a term Professor Yetta Goodman coined to describe the informal observation of students as they participate in reading and writing activities (Owocki & Goodman, 2002). To be effective kid watchers, teachers must focus on what students do as they read and write, not on whether they're behaving properly or working quietly. Of course, little learning can occur in disruptive situations, but during these observations, the focus is on literacy, not behavior. Observations should be planned. Teachers usually observe a specific group each day so that, over the course of a week, they watch everyone in the class.

ANECDOTAL NOTES.   Teachers write brief notes as they observe students. The most useful notes describe specific events, report rather than evaluate, and relate the events to other information about the student. For instance, teachers make notes about the questions students ask and the responses they offer, their interactions with classmates as they work on projects, and the strategies and skills they use fluently and those they don't understand. They often write their notes in notebooks they've divided into sections for each student, or on small self-stick notes that they post in students' folders. These records monitor and document students' growth and pinpoint problem areas to address in future minilessons.

CONFERENCES.   Teachers talk with students in order to monitor their progress in reading and writing as well as to set goals and help them solve problems. They often conduct these types of conferences during the school day:

On-the-Spot Conferences.   The teacher visits with students at their desks to monitor some aspect of their work or to check on progress. These conferences are brief, with the teacher often spending less than a minute with each student.

MyLab Education
Video Example 3.1

Monitoring students' learning and sharing that documentation with parents are important parts of the assessment process. What planning does a teacher need to do to prepare for documenting student learning?

PreK Practices

How do teachers assess young students?

The two best ways to assess prekindergartners' literacy learning are by observing them and collecting samples of their reading and writing (Bennett-Armistead, Duke, & Moses, 2005; Vukelich & Christie, 2009). Teachers focus on one student at a time, carefully observing his or her language use and literacy behaviors, and document their observations by writing brief anecdotal notes. They also collect writing samples over time and compare them to determine growth. Assessment should be anchored in authentic reading and writing activities because young students' learning can't be measured on standardized tests in ways that are useful to inform day-to-day instruction. Paper-and-pencil tests aren't reliable or valid indicators of what young students can do.

Planning Conferences. The teacher and the student make plans for reading or writing: At a prereading conference, they talk about background knowledge or difficult vocabulary words related to the book, or set guidelines for **reading log** entries; and at a prewriting conference, they discuss possible writing topics or narrow a broad topic into a more manageable one.

Revising Conferences. A small group meets with the teacher to share their rough drafts and get specific suggestions about how to revise them.

Book-Discussion Conferences. Students meet with the teacher to discuss the book they've read. They may share reading log entries, discuss plot or characters, or compare the book to others they've read.

Editing Conferences. The teacher reviews students' proofread compositions and helps them correct spelling, punctuation, capitalization, and other mechanical errors.

Evaluation Conferences. The teacher meets with students after they've completed a project to talk about their growth as readers and writers. They also reflect on their accomplishments and set goals.

Often these conferences are brief and impromptu, held at students' desks as the teacher moves around the classroom; at other times, however, the conferences are planned, and students meet with the teacher at a designated conference table.

CHECKLISTS. Checklists simplify assessment and enhance students' learning (Kuhs, Johnson, Agruso, & Monrad, 2001). Teachers identify the evaluation criteria in advance so students understand what's expected of them before they begin working. Grading is easier because teachers have already set the evaluation criteria, and it's fairer, too, because teachers use the same criteria to grade everyone's work. The Assessment Snapshot coming up in this chapter shows a fourth grade checklist for giving **book talks**; the student's grade was B. At the beginning of the school year, the teacher introduced book talks, modeled how to do one, and developed the checklist. The students use the checklist whenever they're preparing to give a book talk, and the teacher uses it as a rating scale to evaluate the effectiveness of their presentations.

Check the Compendium of Instructional Procedures, which follows Chapter 12. These **green** terms also show a brief description of each procedure.

▶ **MyLab Education**
Video Example 3.2

In this video, Ms. Janusz conferences with Caden about his writing. What goals does Ms. Janusz suggest to Caden to help improve his writing?

Assessment Snapshot

Book Talk Checklist

Name _____Jaime_____ Date: _____November 12_____

Title _____Cockroach Cooties_____

Author _____Laurence Yep_____

✓ Hold up the book to show to classmates.

✓ State the title and author's name.

✓ Interest classmates in the book by asking a question, reading an excerpt, or sharing some information.

Summarize the book, without giving away the ending.

✓ Talk loud enough for everyone to hear you.

✓ Look at the audience.

Limit the book talk to 3 minutes.

TEACHER'S NOTE
Jaime's book talk was effective. She showed the book and generated lots of excitement about it, even though she talked for more than five minutes and didn't summarize the story. She was very poised. She engaged the audience, and her classmates really responded!
Grade B

STUDENTS' WORK SAMPLES.   Teachers collect students' work samples, including reading logs, audio files of students reading aloud, photos of projects, videos of puppet shows and oral presentations, flash drives with digital projects, and copies of books they've written in folders. They use this data to celebrate students' learning as well as to document their progress toward meeting grade-level standards and to assign grades. Students also choose some of their best work to document their own learning and accomplishments.

RUBRICS.   Teachers use **rubrics**, or scoring guides, to assess students' performance according to specific criteria and levels of achievement (Afflerbach, 2007b; Stevens, Levi, & Walvoord, 2012). They're similar to checklists because they specify what students are expected to be able to do, but they go beyond because they also describe levels of achievement. Writing rubrics are the most common type, but teachers also use rubrics to assess students' reading, the projects they develop, and their achievement in other curricular areas.

The Assessment Snapshot Book Talk Checklist, shows a narrative writing rubric with five levels. The achievement levels, ranging from one (lowest) to five (highest) are shown

Assessment Snapshot
A Second Grade Writing Rubric

5
- ✓ Writing has an original title.
- Plot, setting, and other story elements are used effectively.
- Writing shows originality, sense of humor, or cleverness.
- Writing is organized effectively into paragraphs.
- Writing contains very few spelling, capitalization, or punctuation errors.

④ (4)
- Writing has an appropriate title.
- ✓ Beginning, middle, and end are well developed.
- ✓ A problem or goal is identified in the story.
- ✓ Writing is organized into paragraphs.
- ✓ Writing contains a few spelling, capitalization, or punctuation errors.

3
- Writing has a title.
- Writing has a beginning, middle, and an end.
- Events are presented sequentially.
- Writing is not organized into paragraphs.
- Spelling, capitalization, or punctuation errors are present but they don't interfere with meaning.

2
- The title is confusing or incomplete.
- Writing includes two of the three parts of a story.
- Writing may show a partial sequence of events.
- Writing is brief and underdeveloped.
- Writing has spelling, capitalization, and punctuation errors that interfere with meaning.

1
- Writing doesn't have a title.
- Writing lacks a sense of story.
- An illustration may suggest a story.
- Writing is brief and may support the illustration.
- Some words may be recognizable, but the writing is difficult to read.

TEACHER'S NOTE
Jeremy's story, "The Biggest, Baddest Dog Ever," is a clever story about Jeremy's pet Boxer named Randy. In the personal narrative, Jeremy recounts an adventure during a camping trip. His narrative is well organized. He breaks his writing into paragraphs and makes only a few mechanical errors. Jeremy's writing rates a four, indicating that he's a grade-level writer.

on the left, and the descriptors for each level are listed on the right. The Snapshot shows Ms. Kweon's scoring of second grade Jeremy's personal narrative, "The Biggest, Baddest Dog," and the teacher reflects on her scoring in the accompanying Teacher's Note.

Students also use rubrics to self-assess their work, and sometimes classmates use rubrics to assess a student's performance. To be successful, students need to analyze anonymous work samples and identify the qualities that demonstrate strong, average, and weak achievement; it's also helpful for teachers to model how to address the qualities at each level in the rubric. Skillings and Ferrell (2000) taught second and third graders to develop the criteria for evaluating their writing, and the students moved from using the rubrics their teachers prepared to creating their own three-point rubrics, which they labeled as the "very best" level, the "okay" level, and the "not so good" level. Perhaps the most important outcome of teaching students to create rubrics, according to Skillings and Ferrell, is that they develop metacognitive strategies and the ability to think about themselves as writers.

Step 3: Evaluating Students' Learning

Evaluating progress means making sense of the information collected from the various assessments. Equipped with a plan for assessment from the outset, and having collected information in various ways to assess student progress, teachers are now ready to evaluate, or make judgements, about how well students are achieving. In our vignette in this chapter for example, we describe how Mrs. McNeal used the assessment data she collected to evaluate Ethan's progress, as well as the other students in her class. Her evaluation of their progress was expressed as separate number grades on their report cards for reading, writing, and spelling, and ranged from one to four in terms of meeting grade level expectations. Mrs. McNeal can feel confident that her evaluation of her students' progress is sound because it is based on a range of assessments that she used each day in her classroom.

How often teachers evaluate achievement will vary. Teachers evaluate at the end of an instructional period; that could be at the end of a unit, or at the end of the term when report cards are due. The important thing to keep in mind is the need to plan ahead of time, before the school year begins, what assessments you will use and to know how you will use that information to make evaluations about student progress.

GO DIGITAL! Creating Rubrics

Teachers can find tools for generating rubrics and blank rubric templates online as well as a collection of rubrics that other teachers have developed at these websites:

RubiStar. RubiStar (http://rubistar.4teachers.org) is a free tool teachers can use to create effective rubrics. Teachers make their own rubrics for oral language, multimedia, reading, and writing projects using the template at the site.

6 +1 Traits. This website (http://educationnorthwest.org) is designed for teachers who are implementing the writing process and teaching the six traits. The five- and six-point rubrics are for beginning writers (K–2) and for more experienced writers. Take a look at the students' writing samples that have been scored using "illustrated rubrics."

TeAch-nology. TeAch-nology (http://www.teach-nology.com) offers a huge collection of premade grade-level rubrics, beginning at the first grade level, plus a rubric maker that teachers can use to create customized rubrics.

These websites offer a wealth of rubrics that teachers can use or adapt to meet the needs of their students.

Figure 3–1 Ways to Assess Students' Learning

Step 1: Planning	Step 2: Monitoring
• Determine children's reading levels using running records and informal reading inventories. • Choose appropriate books for children. • Match children's reading levels to instructional procedures and approaches.	• Observe children as they read and write. • Conference with students. • Make anecdotal notes. • Have children mark checklists and rubrics to track their progress.
Step 3: Evaluating	**Step 4: Reflecting**
• Use checklists and rubrics to evaluate and grade children's work. • Examine collections of student work to determine grades. • Create tests, when necessary, to evaluate children's achievement.	• Have children respond orally and in writing to questions about their work habits and achievement. • Have children place work that highlights their accomplishments in portfolios. • Reflect on your teaching effectiveness by examining the results of children's assessments.

Step 4: Reflecting on Instruction

Teachers reflect on the instruction they've presented to improve their teaching effectiveness. They ask themselves questions about lessons that were successful and those that weren't and how they might adapt instruction to better meet their students' needs. They also analyze students' achievement, because teachers aren't effective if students aren't learning. Danielson (2009) recommends that teachers work with colleagues who can help to solve problems and improve instruction.

Students also reflect on their achievement to develop self-awareness and to learn to take more responsibility for their learning. Self-assessment is metacognitive: Students evaluate their achievement, ways of learning, and work habits. Teachers often provide questions such as these to prompt students' reflections:

What did you learn during this unit?

How can your teacher help you be a better reader? A better writer?

How did you feel at the beginning, middle, and end of the unit?

How did you contribute to our classroom community of learners?

What are your three strengths as a reader? As a writer?

What would you like to get better at?

Teachers ask these questions during conferences, or students write journal entries or letters to their teacher to respond to them.

Each step serves a different purpose, so it's important that teachers choose assessment tools carefully. Researchers recommend that teachers use a combination of assessment tools to improve the fairness and effectiveness of classroom literacy assessment (Kuhs, Johnson, Agruso, & Monrad, 2001). Figure 3–1 highlights the assessments teachers use during each step of assessment.

> **MyLab Education** Self-Check 3.1
> **MyLab Education** Application Exercise 3.1: Analyzing Alejandro's
> Running Record

Diagnostic Tests

Teachers administer commercial diagnostic tests to inform their instruction. In particular, these tests determine students' reading levels and identify students who are struggling. Then teachers use the results to differentiate instruction, make accurate placement decisions, and create meaningful classroom interventions.

Determining Students' Reading Levels

Teachers match students with books at appropriate levels of difficulty because students are more likely to be successful when they're reading books that aren't too easy or too difficult: Books that are too easy don't provide enough challenge, and those that are too difficult frustrate them. Researchers have identified three reading levels that take into account students' ability to recognize words automatically, read fluently, and comprehend what they're reading:

Independent Reading Level.   Students can read books at the **independent reading level** comfortably, on their own. They recognize almost all words; their accuracy rate is 95%–100%. Their reading is fluent, and they comprehend what they're reading. Books at this level are only slightly easier than those at their instructional level, and they still engage students' interest.

Instructional Reading Level.   Students read and understand books at the **instructional reading level** with instruction, but not on their own. They recognize most words; their accuracy rate is 90%–94%. Their reading may be mostly fluent, but sometimes it isn't. With support from the teacher or classmates, students comprehend what they're reading, but if they're reading by themselves, their understanding is limited.

Frustration Reading Level.   Books at the **frustration reading level** are too difficult for students to read successfully, even with assistance. Students don't recognize enough words automatically, and their accuracy is less than 90%. Students' reading is choppy and word-by-word, and it often doesn't make sense. They show little understanding of what they've read.

These reading levels have important implications for instruction. Students read independent-level books for pleasure and instructional-level books when they're participating in **guided reading** or other reading lessons. They shouldn't be expected to read books at their frustration level; when it's essential that they experience grade-appropriate literature or learn content-area information, teachers should read the text aloud.

The Common Core State Standards for English Language Arts (2010) require teachers to plan instruction using grade-level requirements, not students' developmental reading levels. The 10th Standard at grades 2–4 clearly states that students should read and comprehend grade-level narratives and nonfiction books independently and proficiently by the end of the school year, needing support only to succeed with the most challenging texts. Students who read at or above grade level typically meet this Standard, but struggling students who read two or more grades below their grade placement can't. This Standard emphasizes the importance of using grade-level texts with all students, but teachers must consider students' current levels and provide developmentally appropriate instruction, too, to scaffold struggling readers as they become more proficient. For more information, check this Common Core State Standards box.

READABILITY FORMULAS.   For nearly a century, readability formulas have been used to estimate the ease with which reading materials, both trade books and textbooks, can be read. Readability scores serve as rough gauges of text difficulty and are traditionally reported as grade-level scores. If a book has a readability score of third grade, for example, teachers assume that average third graders will be able to read it. Sometimes readability scores are marked on books with *RL* and a grade level, such as *RL 3*.

Readability scores are determined by correlating semantic and syntactic features in a text. Several passages from a text are identified for analysis, and then vocabulary sophistication is measured by counting the syllables in each word, and sentence complexity by counting the words in each sentence. The syllable and word counts from each passage are averaged, and the readability score is calculated by plotting the averages

Common Core State Standards

Assessment

Common Core State Standards don't identify how to assess learning or which evaluation instruments to use; instead, they specify what students should be able to demonstrate at each grade level, and Standard 10 emphasizes that students in grades two and up should be able to read and comprehend challenging grade-appropriate texts. Sample fiction and nonfiction texts are listed for each grade level in the Standards document. To learn more about the literacy Standards, go to http://www.corestandards.org/ELA-Literacy, or check your state's educational standards website.

on a graph. It seems reasonable that texts with shorter words and sentences would be easier to read than those with longer words and sentences; however, readability formulas take into account only two text factors; they can't consider reader factors, including the experience and knowledge that readers bring to reading, their cognitive and linguistic backgrounds, or their motivation for reading.

One quick and simple readability formula is the Fry Readability Graph, developed by Edward Fry (1968); it's available in *The Reading Teacher's Book of Lists* (Fry & Kress, 2006), and online at numerous websites. This graph predicts the grade-level score for texts. Teachers use a readability formula as an aid in evaluating textbook and tradebook selections for classroom use; however, they can't assume that materials rated as appropriate for a particular level will be appropriate for everyone because students within a class typically vary three grade levels or more in their reading levels.

LEVELED BOOKS.   Basal readers have traditionally been leveled according to grade levels, but grade-level designations, especially in kindergarten and first grade, are too broad. Fountas and Pinnell (2006) developed a text gradient, or classification system that arranges books along a continuum from easiest to hardest, to match students to books in grades K–4. Their system is based on these 10 variables that influence reading difficulty:

- Genre and format of the book
- Organization and use of text structures
- Familiarity with and interest level of the content
- Complexity of ideas and themes
- Language and literary features
- Sentence length and complexity
- Sophistication of the vocabulary
- Word length and ease of decoding
- Relationship of illustrations to the text
- Length of the book, its layout, and other text features

Fountas and Pinnell used these criteria to identify 26 levels, labeled A through Z, for their text gradient, which teachers can also use to level books in their classrooms. More than 59,000 books have been leveled according to this text gradient. A sample trade book for each level is shown in the Booklist coming up; other leveled books are listed in *The Fountas and Pinnell Leveled Book List 2013-2015*—available online at https://www.fandpleveledbooks.com/

THE LEXILE FRAMEWORK.   Another approach to matching books to readers is the Lexile Framework. This approach is different because it's used to measure both students' reading levels and the difficulty level of books. Word familiarity and sentence complexity are the two factors used to determine the difficulty level. **Lexile scores**

range from 100 to 1300, representing kindergarten through 12th grade reading levels. The numerical scores have been organized into grade-level bands to coordinate with the Common Core State Standard 10 expectation and recently recalibrated to increase the challenge presented to students so that they'll be better prepared for college and careers after graduating from high school. For example, the difficulty level of the grades 2–3 band increased by more than 100 points! The Booklist: Fountas and Pinnell's Levels presents the updated Lexile grade bands through fifth grade with sample books.

Students' results on high-stakes tests are often linked to the Lexile Framework. Standardized achievement tests, such as the Iowa Test of Basic Skills and the Stanford Achievement Test, report test results as Lexile scores, and a number of standards-based state reading tests, including the California English-Language Arts Standards Test, the North Carolina End-of-Grade Tests, and the Texas Assessment of Knowledge and Skills, do the same. With this information, students, parents, and teachers can match students to books by searching the online Lexile database to locate books at each student's reading level.

The wide range of scores in the Lexile Framework allows teachers to more closely match students with books. Plus, the availability of the online database with more than 100,000 leveled books, 80 million articles, and 60,000 websites that

Booklist Fountas and Pinnell's Levels

Level	Grade	Books
A	K	Burningham, J. (1985). *Colors.*
B	K–1	Carle, E. (1997). *Have you seen my cat?*
C	K–1	Martin, B., Jr. (2010). *Brown bear, brown bear, what do you see?*
D	1	Peek, M. (2006). *Mary wore her red dress.*
E	1	Hill, E. (2005). *Where's Spot?*
F	1	Hutchins, P. (2005). *Rosie's walk.*
G	1	Shaw, N. (2006). *Sheep in a jeep.*
H	1–2	Kraus, R. (2005). *Whose mouse are you?*
I	1–2	Wood, A., & Wood, D. (2010). *The napping house.*
J	2	Rylant, C. (1996). *Henry and Mudge and the bedtime thumps.*
K	2	Heller, R. (1999). *Chickens aren't the only ones.*
L	2–3	Marshall, J. (2000). *The three little pigs.*
M	2–3	Park, B. (2007). *Junie B. Jones and the stupid smelly bus.*
N	3	Danziger, P. (2006). *Amber Brown is not a crayon.*
O	3–4	Cleary, B. (1992). *Ramona Quimby, age 8.*
P	3–4	Mathis, S. B. (2006). *The hundred penny box.*
Q	4	Howe, D., & Howe, J. (2006). *Bunnicula: A rabbit-tale of mystery.*
R	4	Paulsen, G. (2007). *Hatchet.*
S	4–5	Norton, M. (2003). *The borrowers.*
T	4–5	Curtis, C. P. (2004). *Bud, not Buddy.*
U	5	Lowry, L. (2011). *Number the stars.*
V	5–6	Sachar, L. (2008). *Holes.*
W	5–6	Choi, S. N. (1993). *Year of impossible goodbyes.*
X	6–8	Hesse, K. (1999). *Out of the dust.*
Y	6–8	Lowry, L. (2006). *The giver.*
Z	7–8	Hinton, S. E. (2006). *The outsiders.*

Based on Fountas & Pinnell, 2009.

Booklist The Recalibrated Lexile Grade Bands

Grade Band	Level	Books
K–1*	100–449	Allard, H. (1985). *Miss Nelson is missing!* (340)**
		Bridwell, N. (2002). *Clifford the big red dog* (220)
		Henkes, K. (2007). *Chrysanthemum* (410)
		Lobel, A. (1979). *Frog and toad are friends* (400)
		Willems, M. (2003). *Don't let the pigeon drive the bus!* (120)
2–3	450–790	Blume, J. (2007). *Tales of a fourth grade nothing* (470)
		Brown, J. M. (2009). *Flat Stanley* (640)
		Howe, D., & Howe, J. (2006). *Bunnicula: A rabbit-tale of mystery* (710)
		Rathmann, P. (1995). *Officer Buckle and Gloria* (510)
		Steig, W. (2009). *Amos & Boris* (690)
4–5	770–980	Dahl, R. (2007). *Charlie and the chocolate factory* (810)
		Gantos, J. (2011). *Joey Pigza swallowed the key* (970)
		Lewis, C. S. (2005). *The lion, the witch and the wardrobe* (940)
		Naylor, P. (2000). *Shiloh* (890)
		Rowling, J. K. (1999). *Harry Potter and the sorcerer's stone* (880)

* This band isn't included on most Lexile documents because Common Core State Standard 10 for first grade specifies that students work toward reading grade-level books with prompting and support; mastery isn't required. The band is included here to suggest books at the K–1 level.
** Lexile Score

students, parents, and teachers can access makes it a very useful assessment tool; however, matching readers to books is more complicated than determining a numerical score!

The Assessment Tools included in this chapter describes three screening tools to identify students' reading levels.

The search results present useful information about each book, including the title and author, a photo of the book cover, the book's interest and reading levels, the genre, a summary, and a list of topics related to the book. The reading level is expressed as a grade-level equivalent (e.g., *RL 2.3;* or second grade, third month) and according to both Fountas and Pinnell's levels and Lexile scores. Links are also provided to author information and teaching resources.

Diagnosing Students' Strengths and Needs

Teachers use diagnostic assessments to identify students' strengths and needs, examine areas of difficulty in detail, and decide how to adjust instruction to improve students' reading. They use a variety of diagnostic tests to examine students' achievement in

GO DIGITAL! Online Book-Search Systems.

Teachers can consult online databases to locate books at students' reading levels so that they can match readers with appropriate books. One of the most popular resources for teachers is the Teacher Book Wizard http://www.scholastic.com/tbwpromo/tbwhome.htm—a free book-search system at Scholastic's website. Teachers can search the more than 50,000 books in its database to locate books at a student's reading level or check the reading level of a particular book they'd like to use for a literature focus unit or a literature circle using these search tools:

Quick Search. Teachers search for particular books, themed book lists, or books by an author.

Leveled Search. Teachers customize the search by students' interests, reading levels, language (English or Spanish), topic, and genre.

Assessment Tools

Determining Reading Levels

Teachers use screening assessments to determine students' reading levels, monitor their progress, and document achievement through a school year and across grade levels. Here are three screening assessments:

- **Developmental Reading Assessment, 2nd Edition (DRA2)**
  DRA2 is available as two kits—one for grades K–3 and the other for grades 4–8—to assess reading performance using leveled fiction and nonfiction books. The K–3 kit also includes an individualized diagnostic instrument to assess phonemic awareness and phonics knowledge. Teachers use an online system to manage students' scores and group them for instruction.

- **Fountas and Pinnell Benchmark Assessment System**
  The Fountas and Pinnell Benchmark Assessment System is sold as two kits—one for grades K–2 and the other for grades 3–8. Each kit contains 30 leveled fiction and nonfiction books written specifically for the kit and CDs with assessment forms to manage students' scores. Teachers use the books in the kit to match students' reading levels to the Fountas and Pinnell 26-level text gradient.

  For both assessments, teachers test students individually. The teacher selects an appropriate book for the student to read and then introduces it; the student reads the book, and the teacher takes a running record of the student's reading. Then the student retells the text and answers comprehension questions. The teacher scores and analyzes the results, and testing continues until the teacher determines the student's instructional level.

- **Scholastic Reading Inventory (SRI)**
  SRI is a unique computer-adaptive assessment program that reports students' reading levels using Lexile scores. Students take this 20-minute computerized test individually. The student reads a narrative or informational passage on the computer screen and answers multiple-choice comprehension questions. This test is computer adaptive because if the student answers a question correctly, the next one will be more difficult, but if the answer is wrong, the next question will be easier. Students read passages and answer questions until their reading level is determined. They receive a customized take-home letter with their Lexile score and a personalized list of recommended books.

  These assessments are usually administered at the beginning of the school year and periodically during the year to monitor students' progress. The results are also used to group students for guided reading and to identify those who need diagnostic testing.

phonemic awareness, phonics, fluency, vocabulary, comprehension, and other components of reading and writing. The Assessment Tools feature lists diagnostic tests recommended in this text and directs you to the chapter where you can learn more about them.

RUNNING RECORDS. **Running records** were developed by Marie Clay (1972), and have since been adapted by many people, although the essential format remains the same. Running records are authentic assessment tools because students demonstrate how they read aloud using their regular reading materials as teachers make a systematic account of all of their reading behaviors (Clay, 1972; 2007). Teachers take running records of students' oral reading to assess their word solving and reading fluency. Teachers can use any blank sheet of paper to record the student's reading. Standard coding is used so that teachers can read and interpret each other's records from year to year. Check marks are used for words read accurately; other marks are used to indicate words that the student substitutes, repeats, omits, inserts, mispronounces, or doesn't know, as Mrs. McNeal did in the vignette. The Assessment Snapshot shows the analysis of Ethan's errors from the running record in the vignette. Only words that students mispronounce or substitute can be analyzed; insertions and omissions aren't analyzed.

Assessment Tools

Diagnostic Assessments

Component	Tests	Where to Learn More
Comprehension	Comprehension Thinking Strategies Assessment Developmental Reading Assessment Informal reading inventories	Chapter 8, Facilitating Students' Comprehension: Reader Factors
Concepts About Print	Observation Survey of Early Literacy Achievement	Chapter 2, Examining Students' Literacy Development
Fluency	Fluency rubrics Informal reading inventories Running records	Chapter 6, Developing Fluent Readers and Writers
Oral Language	Assessment of Literacy and Language Teacher Rating of Oral Language and Literacy	Chapter 2, Examining Students' Literacy Development
Phonemic Awareness	Phonological Awareness Literacy Screening Yopp-Singer Test of Phonemic Segmentation	Chapter 4, Cracking the Alphabetic Code
Phonics	Dynamic Indicators of Basic Early Literacy Skills Observation Survey The Tile Test	Chapter 4, Cracking the Alphabetic Code
Spelling	Developmental Spelling Analysis Phonological Awareness Literacy Screening Qualitative Spelling Inventory	Chapter 5, Learning to Spell
Vocabulary	Expressive Vocabulary Test-2 Informal reading inventories Peabody Picture Vocabulary Test-4	Chapter 7, Building Students' Word Knowledge
Word Recognition	Developmental Reading Assessment Phonological Awareness Literacy Screening Running records	Chapter 6, Developing Fluent Readers and Writers
Word Identification	High-frequency word lists Observation Survey	Chapter 6, Developing Fluent Readers and Writers
Writing	Rubrics	Chapter 11, Scaffolding Students' Writing Development

INFORMAL READING INVENTORIES. Teachers use commercial tests called **informal reading inventories** (IRIs) to evaluate students' reading performance. They can be used beginning in first grade, but first grade teachers often find that IRIs don't provide as much useful information about beginning readers as running records do. These popular reading tests are often used as a screening instrument to determine whether students are reading at grade level, but they're also a valuable diagnostic tool (Nilsson, 2008). Teachers can use IRIs to identify struggling students' instructional needs, particularly in word identification, oral reading fluency, and comprehension.

These individualized tests consist of two parts: graded word lists and passages ranging from first to eighth grade level. The word lists contain 10 to 20 words at each level, and students read the words until they become too difficult; this indicates an approximate level for students to begin reading the passages. Because students who can't read the words on their grade-level list may have a word identification problem,

Assessment Snapshot

Error Analysis

Student ___Ethan___   Date ___Jan. 14___

Text ___The Pot of Gold (Level 16)___

Words			Meaning	Syntax	Visual
Text	Student	The error was self-corrected	The substitution made sense up to the error.	The substitution sounded grammatically acceptable up to the error.	The substitution has some visual similarity to the word in the text
Grumble	Grumply		✓	✓	✓
always	omitted				
didn't	did not		✓	✓	✓
I'll	I		✓	✓	✓
mark	make		✓	✓	✓
scarf	safr				✓
of	or		✓	✓	✓
my	me	✓	✓	✓	✓
scarf	self		✓	✓	✓
taken	take		✓		✓
scarf	scafer				✓
that	they	✓	✓	✓	✓
may	maybe		✓	✓	✓
still	sit				✓

TEACHER'S NOTE

Ethan fluently read "The Pot of Gold" with 95% accuracy. Level 16 is his current instructional level. The error analysis indicates that Ethan now often uses all three cues when he makes an error (hooray!) but he usually only uses the initial letter or letters. However, he rarely notices his mistakes and, as a result, rarely problem-solves and rarely self-corrects. I need to now teach Ethan to notice visual mismatches beyond the first letters while still using meaning and syntax.

teachers analyze the words students read incorrectly, looking for error patterns and deciding what kind of visual information the student notices and uses (for example, the initial part of the word only, like milk for made; the initial and ending parts, like dad for did; or the initial, middle, and ending parts, like went for want).

The graded reading passages include both narrative and expository texts, presented in order of difficulty. Unlike running records, students have not received prior instruction on these stories; they are read sight unseen. Students read these passages orally or silently and then answer several comprehension questions that are included for that passage. The teacher asks the questions. Students are asked to recall specific information, draw inferences, or explain the meaning of vocabulary words.

When students read the passage orally, teachers assess their fluency. All students should be able to read the independent level passages fluently (the ones that they score at least 95% accuracy); if they can't, they may have a fluency problem. Teachers also examine students' comprehension. If students can't answer the questions after reading the passage at their grade level, they may have a comprehension problem, and teachers check to see if there's a pattern to the types of questions that they miss.

Teachers use scoring sheets to record students' performance data, and they calculate students' independent, instructional, and frustration reading levels. When a student's reading level is below his or her grade-level placement, teachers also check the student's listening capacity—that is, the ability to understand passages that are read aloud to the student. Knowing whether students can understand and learn from grade-level texts that are read aloud is crucial because that's a common way that teachers support struggling readers.

ORAL LANGUAGE ASSESSMENT.   Teachers assess students who speak a language other than English at home to determine their English language proficiency. They typically use commercial oral language tests to determine if students are proficient in English. If they're not, classroom teachers provide the appropriate supports so that all students can participate meaningfully and equally in classroom instruction. Two widely used tests are the Language Assessment Scales, published by CTB/McGraw-Hill, and the IDEA Language Proficiency Test, published by Ballard and Tighe; both tests assess students' oral and written language (listening, speaking, reading, and writing) proficiency in English. Individual states have developed language assessments that are aligned with their English language proficiency standards; for example, the New York State English as a Second Language Achievement Test and the California English Language Development Test.

An authentic assessment tool that many teachers use is the Student Oral Language Observation Matrix (SOLOM), developed by the San Jose (CA) Area Bilingual Consortium. It's not a test per se; rather, the SOLOM is a rating scale to assess students' command of English as teachers observe them talking and listening in real, day-to-day classroom activities. The SOLOM addresses five oral language components:

Listening.   Teachers score students along a continuum from unable to comprehend simple statements to understanding everyday conversations.

Teaching English Learners
English Proficiency Screening

Civil rights law requires school districts to ensure that English learners (ELs) can participate meaningfully and equally in school instruction. In fact, the Equal Educational Opportunities Act, passed in 1974, states that schools and school districts must act to overcome the language barriers that many ELs face in school.

Most school districts use a home language survey when students first enroll to learn what language (or languages) are spoken at home. Students who are identified by these surveys as being potential ELs must then be assessed with screener tests to determine their level of English proficiency in speaking, read, writing, and listening. The results of the screener test are used to provide ELs with the appropriate language assistance. By law, these services must be provided to ELs until they have reached English language proficiency.

While EL programs are provided by teachers who have specialized training, all teachers are responsible for the teaching and learning of ELs in their classrooms. And, because the population of ELs in the U.S. is steadily increasing, chances are very good that you will have at least one EL, if not more, in your classroom (Rowe, In Press).

The first assessment step for ELs is to learn about the students' language background. Find out from the home language survey what language or languages are spoken at home and learn whether your student is literate in any of them. A student who has already learned to read in Arabic or Chinese, for example, will have different challenges learning to read in English than a student who is literate in Spanish.

Classroom teachers assess ELs' developing language proficiency as well as their progress in learning to read and write. It's more challenging to assess ELs than native English speakers, because when students aren't proficient in English, their scores don't accurately reflect what they know (Peregoy & Boyle, 2013). Their cultural and experiential backgrounds also contribute to making it more difficult to assure that assessment tools being used aren't biased.

Literacy Portraits

Ms. Janusz regularly monitors the second graders' reading achievement. Working one-on-one, she introduces a leveled book and asks the student to read the first part aloud while she takes a running record on a separate sheet of paper. Then the student reads the rest of the book silently. She also asks questions after the student finishes reading orally and again after the student reaches the end of the book. In these videos, Ms. Janusz assesses Jimmy's reading in October and again in March. As these video clips play, think about how Jimmy grew as a reader during the school year. Does he decode unfamiliar words, read fluently, and comprehend what he's read orally and silently? Next, reflect on how Ms. Janusz linked instruction and assessment when she took advantage of teachable moments while she assessed his reading.

Jimmy in
October

Jimmy in
March

Fluency.   Teachers score students along a continuum from halting, fragmentary speech to fluent speech, approximating that of native speakers.

Vocabulary.   Teachers score students along a continuum from extremely limited word knowledge to using words and idioms skillfully.

Pronunciation.   Teachers score students along a continuum from virtually unintelligible speech to using pronunciation and intonation proficiently, similar to native speakers.

Grammar.   Teachers score students along a continuum from excessive errors that make speech unintelligible to applying word order, grammar, and usage rules effectively.

Each component has a 5-point range that's scored 1 to 5; the total possible score on the matrix is 25, and a rating of 20 or higher indicates that students are fluent speakers of English. The SOLOM is available free of charge online at http://www.cal.org, at other websites, and in many professional books.

READING ASSESSMENT.   English learners face two challenges: They're learning to speak English at the same time they're learning to read. They learn to read the same way that native English speakers do, but they face additional challenges because their knowledge of English phonology, semantics, syntax, and pragmatics is limited and their background knowledge is different (Peregoy & Boyle, 2013). Some English learners are fluent readers in their home language (Garcia, 2000); these students already have substantial funds of knowledge about how written language works and about the reading process that they build on as they learn to read in English (Moll, 1994). Having this knowledge gives them a head start, but students also have to learn what transfers to English reading and what doesn't.

Teachers use the same assessments that they use for native English speakers to identify English learners' reading levels, monitor their growth, and document their learning. Peregoy and Boyle (2013) recommend using data from running records or informal reading inventories along with classroom-based informal assessments, such as observing and conferencing with students.

Because many English learners have less background knowledge about topics in books they're reading, it's important that teachers assess ELs' background knowledge before instruction so they can modify their teaching to meet students' needs. One of the best ways to accomplish this is with a **KWL chart**. As they work with students to complete the first two sections of the chart, teachers learn what students know about a topic and have an opportunity to build additional background knowledge and introduce related vocabulary. Later, when students complete the KWL chart, teachers get a clear picture of what they've learned and which vocabulary words they can use.

Another way teachers learn about ELs' development is by asking them to assess themselves as readers. Teachers ask students, for example, what they do when they come to an unfamiliar word, what differences they've noticed between narrative and expository texts, which reading strategies they use, and what types of books they prefer. These quick assessments, commonly done during conferences at the end of a grading period, shed light on students' growth in a way that other assessments can't.

WRITING ASSESSMENT.   English learners' writing develops as their oral language grows and as they become more fluent readers (Riches & Genesee, 2006). For beginning writers, fluency is the first priority. They move from writing strings of familiar words to grouping words into short sentences that often follow a pattern, much like young native English speakers do. As they develop some writing fluency, ELs begin to stick to a single focus, often repeating words and sentences to make their writing longer. Once they become fluent writers, ELs are usually able to organize their ideas more effectively and group them into paragraphs. They incorporate more specific vocabulary and expand the length and variety of sentences. Their mechanical errors become less serious, and their writing is much easier to read. At this point, teachers begin teaching the writer's craft and choosing writing strategies and skills to teach based on the errors that students make.

Peregoy and Boyle (2013) explain that ELs' writing involves fluency, form, and correctness, and that teachers' assessment of students' writing should reflect these components:

- Teachers monitor students' ability to write quickly, easily, and comfortably.
- Teachers assess students' ability to apply writing genres, develop their topics, organize the presentation of ideas, and use sophisticated vocabulary and a variety of sentence structures.
- Teachers check that students control Standard English grammar and usage, spell most words correctly, and use capitalization and punctuation conventions appropriately.

Teachers use rubrics to assess ELs' writing, and the rubrics address fluency, form, and correctness as well as the six traits that teachers have taught. They also conference with students about their writing and provide quick **minilessons**, as needed. To learn about students as writers, teachers observe them as they write, noticing how they move through the writing process, interact in writing groups, and share their writing from the author's chair. In addition, students document writing development by placing their best writing in portfolios.

ALTERNATIVE ASSESSMENTS.   Because of the difficulties inherent in assessing English learners, it's important to use varied types of assessment that involve different language and literacy tasks and ways of demonstrating proficiency (Huerta-Macías, 1995). In addition to commercial tests, O'Malley and Pierce (1996) urge teachers to use authentic assessment tools, including oral performances, story retellings, oral interviews, writing samples, illustrations, diagrams, and projects.

Assessment is especially important for students who are learning to speak English at the same time they're learning to read and write in English. Teachers use many of the same assessment tools that they use for their native English speakers, but they also depend on alternative, more authentic assessments because it's difficult to accurately measure these students' growth. Assessment results must be valid because teachers use them to make placement decisions, modify instruction, and document learning.

MyLab Education Self-Check 3.2

High-Stakes Testing

A high-stakes test is any test that is used to make a high-stakes decision. A test that is used to decide whether a student should be promoted or retained, for example, is a high-stakes test. Annual high-stakes testing is emphasized in American schools with the goal of improving reading instruction. These tests are designed to objectively measure students' knowledge according to grade-level standards. The current emphasis on testing and grade-level standards are reform efforts that began in response to The National Commission on Excellence in Education report *A Nation at Risk* (1983), which argued that American schools were failing miserably. The report stated that American students' test scores were dropping, comparing unfavorably with students' scores in other industrialized countries, and it concluded that the United States was in jeopardy of losing its global superiority. The No Child Left Behind Act (2001), which promoted an increased focus on reading instruction to improve students' reading performance and narrow the racial and ethnic gaps in achievement, reinforced the call for annual standardized testing.

Researchers have repeatedly refuted these arguments (Bracey, 2004; McQuillan, 1998). Allington (2012) explains that average test scores have remained stable for more than 30 years, despite the dramatic increases in federal funding over the past decade. He goes on to explain that reporting average scores obscures important findings because it's necessary to examine subgroup data to discover that most students from middle-class families read well and that many students from low-income families lag behind. He also notes that, although significant progress has been made in closing the achievement gap between white and minority students, the number of minority students has grown tremendously. Finally, he points out that grade-level standards of achievement have increased in the last 50 years so that what was considered third grade level is now second grade level, and older readability formulas have been renormed to reflect today's higher grade-level standards. Nonetheless, the public's perception that schools are failing persists.

High-stakes testing is different from classroom assessment. The test scores typically provide little information for making day-to-day instructional decisions; nevertheless, students, teachers, administrators, and schools are judged and held accountable by the results. The scores are used to make important educational decisions—to determine school placement, for example. These scores influence administrators' evaluations of teachers' effectiveness and even their salaries in some states, and they result in rewards or sanctions for administrators, schools, and school districts.

Standardized tests are comprehensive, with batteries of subtests covering decoding, vocabulary, comprehension, writing mechanics, and spelling. Most tests use multiple-choice test items, although a few are introducing open-ended questions that require students to write responses. Beginning in second grade, classroom teachers administer the tests to their students, typically in the spring. Most require multiple testing periods to administer all of the subtests.

Problems With High-Stakes Testing

A number of problems are associated with high-stakes testing (ILA,1999). Students feel the pressure of these tests, and researchers have confirmed what many teachers have noticed: Students don't try harder because of them (Hoffman, Assaf, & Paris, 2005). Teachers complain that they feel compelled to improve students' test scores at any price, and that they lose valuable instructional time for test-taking and practice sessions (Hollingworth, 2007). Overemphasizing the test often leads teachers to abandon the balanced approach to instruction; sometimes students spend more time completing practice tests than reading books and writing compositions. One of the most insidious side effects is that teachers are often directed to focus on certain groups of students, especially those scoring just below a cutoff point, in hopes of improving test scores.

Preparing for Standardized Tests

Standardized tests are a unique text genre, and they require readers and writers to do different things than they would normally, so teachers can't assume that students already know how to take reading tests. It's essential that they prepare students to take high-stakes tests without abandoning a balanced approach to instruction that's aligned to state standards. Greene and Melton (2007) agree; they maintain that teachers must prepare students for high-stakes tests without sacrificing their instructional program. Unfortunately, with the pressure to raise test scores, some teachers are having students take more multiple-choice tests while creating fewer projects.

Hollingworth (2007) recommends these five ways to prepare for high-stakes tests without sacrificing the instructional program:

- Teachers check that their instructional program aligns with their state's curriculum standards and make any needed adjustments to ensure that they're teaching what's going to be on the test.

- Teachers set goals with students and use informal assessments to regularly monitor their progress.

- Teachers actively engage students in authentic literacy activities so they become capable readers and writers.

- Teachers explain the purpose of the tests and how the results will be used, without making students anxious.

- Teachers stick with a balanced approach that combines explicit instruction and authentic application.

Other researchers advise that, in addition to these recommendations, teachers prepare students to take standardized tests by teaching them how to read and answer test items and having them take practice tests to hone their test-taking strategies (McCabe, 2003). Preparing for tests involves explaining their purpose, examining the genre and format of multiple-choice tests, teaching the formal language of tests and test-taking strategies, and providing opportunities for students to take practice tests; but these lessons should be folded into the existing instructional program, not replace it. Greene and Melton (2007) organized test preparation into **minilessons** that they taught as part of reading workshop.

THE GENRE OF STANDARDIZED TESTS.   Students need opportunities to examine old test forms to learn about the genre of standardized tests and how test questions are formatted. They'll notice that tests look different from other texts they've read; they're typically printed in black and white, the text is dense, and few illustrations are included. Sometimes words, phrases, and lines in the text are numbered, bolded, or underlined. Through this exploration, students begin to think about what makes one type of text harder to read than others, and with practice, they get used to how tests are formatted so that they're better able to read them.

THE LANGUAGE OF TESTING.   Standardized reading tests use formal language that's unfamiliar to many students. For example, some tests use the word *passage* instead of *text* and *author's intent* instead of *big idea*. Test makers also use *locate, except, inform, in order to, provide suspense,* and other words that students may not understand. Greene and Melton (2007) call the language of testing "test talk" and explain that students won't be successful on standardized reading tests unless they can decipher test talk. Students need help understanding test talk so that high-stakes tests really measure what they know and can do.

TEST-TAKING STRATEGIES.   Students vary the test-taking strategies they use according to the type of test they're taking. Most standardized tests employ multiple-choice questions, and successful test-takers use these strategies to answer multiple-choice questions:

Read the entire question first.   Students read the entire question first to make sure they understand what it's asking. For questions about a reading passage, students read the questions first to guide their reading.

Look for key words in the question.   Students identify key words in the question, such as compare, except, and author's intent, that will guide them to choose the correct answer.

Read all answer choices before choosing the correct one.   After students read the question, they stop and think about the answer before reading all of the possible answers. Then they eliminate the unlikely answer choices and identify the correct answer.

Answer easier questions first.   Students answer the questions they know, skipping the difficult ones, and then they go back and answer the questions they skipped.

Make smart guesses.   When students don't know the answer to a question, they make a smart guess, unless there's a penalty for guessing. To make a smart guess, they eliminate the answer choices they're sure are wrong, think about what they know about the topic, and then pick the best remaining answer choice. The correct answer is often the longest one.

Stick with your first answer.   Students shouldn't second-guess themselves; their first answer is probably right. They shouldn't change an answer unless they're certain that their first answer was wrong.

Pace yourself.   Students budget their time so they'll be able to finish the test. They don't spend too much time on any one question.

Check your work carefully.   Students check that they've answered every question if they finish early.

Students use these test-taking strategies along with reading strategies, including determining importance, questioning, and rereading, when they're taking standardized tests.

Test preparation should be embedded in literacy activities and not take up a great deal of instructional time. Teachers often teach test-taking strategies through minilessons where they explain the strategy, model its use, and provide opportunities for guided practice and discussion. Greene and Melton (2007) recommend also teaching minilessons on the genre of tests, test formats, and the language of tests as part of reading workshop. They reported that their students, many of whom are English learners, became more confident and empowered test-takers through test-preparation minilessons, and their test scores improved!

PRACTICE TESTS.   Teachers design practice tests with the same types of items found on the standardized tests students will take. They use easy-to-read materials for practice tests so students can focus on practicing test-taking strategies without being challenged by the difficulty level of the text or the questions. They include a combination of unrelated narrative, poetic, and expository passages on the tests because all three types of texts appear on high-stakes tests. Teachers also provide answer sheets similar to those found on the standardized test so that students gain experience using them. So that students will be familiar with the testing conditions, teachers simulate them in the classroom or take students to where the test will be administered for practice sessions. Through these practice tests, students develop both confidence in their test-taking abilities and the stamina to persist through long tests.

Preparation for reading tests is especially important, because when students aren't familiar with multiple-choice tests, they'll score lower than they otherwise would. Don't confuse test preparation with teaching to the test; preparing for a test involves teaching students how to take a test, but "teaching to the test" is the unethical practice of drilling students on actual questions from old tests. The term is also used in a less pejorative way to describe how teachers tailor instruction to meet state-mandated standards.

The Politics of High-Stakes Testing

The debate over high-stakes testing is a politically charged issue (Casbarro, 2005). Test scores are being used as a means to reform schools, and although improving the quality of instruction and ensuring that all students have equal access to educational opportunities are essential, there are unwanted consequences for both students and teachers. Proponents claim that schools are being reformed, but although some gains in test scores for minority groups have been reported, many teachers believe that the improvement is the result of "teaching to the test." So far, no results indicate that students have actually become better readers and writers because of standardized achievement tests.

Teach Kids to Be Strategic!
Test-Taking Strategies

Beginning in second grade, teach students how to use these test-taking strategies to answer multiple-choice questions on standardized tests:

- Read the entire question first.
- Look for key words in the question.
- Read all answer choices before choosing the correct one.
- Answer easier questions first.
- Make smart guesses.
- Stick with your first answer.
- Pace yourself.
- Check your work carefully.

Students learn to use these strategies through test-prep lessons and practice tests.

MyLab Education Self-Check 3.3

Portfolio Assessment

Students collect their work in portfolios and use them to evaluate their progress and showcase their best work (Afflerbach, 2007b). These systematic and meaningful collections of artifacts document students' literacy development over a period of time (Hebert, 2001). As students select the pieces to be placed in their portfolios, they learn to establish criteria for their selections. Because of students' involvement in developing their portfolios and reflecting on them, portfolio assessment respects students and their abilities.

Portfolios help students, teachers, and parents see patterns of growth from one literacy milestone to another in ways that aren't possible with other types of assessment. There are other benefits, too:

- Students feel ownership of their work.
- Students become more responsible about their work.
- Students provide "windows" on the strategies they use through their work samples.
- Students set goals and are motivated to work toward accomplishing them.
- Students make connections between learning and assessing.

Teachers use portfolios in parent conferences and to supplement the information provided on report cards. In schools where portfolios are used schoolwide, students overwhelmingly report that, by using portfolios, they're better able to show their parents what they're learning and better able to set goals for themselves (Kuhs, Johnson, Agruso, & Monrad, 2001).

Collecting Work in Portfolios

Portfolios are folders, large envelopes, or boxes that hold students' work. Teachers often have students label and decorate large folders and then store them in plastic crates or cardboard boxes. Students date and label items as they place them in their portfolios, and they often attach notes to the items to explain the context for the activity and why they selected a particular item. Portfolios are stored in a readily accessible place in the classroom because students like to review them periodically and add new pieces. Today, many teachers are turning to ePortfolios, where artifacts are stored digitally (Light, Chen, & Ittelson, 2012). Online portfolios incorporate a hierarchical organization, make searching for and retrieving items easier, and can be displayed for audiences to view. They're practical, too, because they don't take up space on bookshelves or in teachers' file cabinets.

Students choose the items to place in their portfolios within the guidelines the teacher provides. Some students submit the original piece of work; others want to keep the original, so they scan it or place a copy in the portfolio instead. In addition to writing samples, students' record oral language and drama samples on audiotapes or video clips, artwork is photographed, and multigenre projects are compiled on flash drives. When students create ePortfolios, they also learn to use scanners, digital cameras, and other technology tools.

Many teachers collect students' work in folders, and they assume that portfolios are basically the same thing; however, the two types of collections differ in several important ways. Perhaps the most important difference is that portfolios are student oriented, but work folders are usually teachers' collections—students choose which samples will be placed in portfolios, but teachers often place all completed assignments in work folders. Next, portfolios focus on students' strengths, not their weaknesses. Because students select items for portfolios, they choose samples that best represent their literacy development. Another difference is that portfolios involve reflection (D'Aoust, 1992); through reflection, students pause and become aware of their strengths as readers and writers.

Involving Students in Self-Assessment

Portfolios are a tool for engaging students in self-assessment and goal setting. Students learn to reflect on and assess their own reading and writing activities and their development as readers and writers (Stires, 1991). Teachers begin by asking students to do **think-alouds** about their reading and writing in terms of contrasts. For reading, students identify the books they've read that they liked most and least, and they ask themselves what these choices suggest about them as readers. They also identify what they do well in reading and what they need to improve. In writing, students make similar contrasts; they identify their best compositions and others that weren't as good, and they think about what they do well when they write and what to improve. By making these comparisons, students begin to reflect on their literacy development.

Teachers use **minilessons** and conferences to teach about the characteristics of good readers and writers. In particular, they discuss these topics:

- What fluent reading is
- Which reading strategies students use
- How students demonstrate their comprehension
- What makes a good project to apply reading knowledge
- What makes an effective piece of writing
- Which writing strategies are most effective
- How to use writing rubrics
- Why correcting mechanical errors is a courtesy to readers

MyLab Education
Video Example 3.3

In this video, a first grade teacher describes why she believes portfolios are most helpful in assessing students' literacy development. How do portfolios help students self-assess their learning?

As students learn about what it means to be effective readers and writers, they acquire the tools they need to reflect on and evaluate their own reading and writing. They learn how to think about themselves as readers and writers and acquire the vocabulary to use in their reflections, such as *goal, strategy,* and *rubric.*

Students write notes on items they put into their portfolios. In these self-assessments, students explain the reasons for their choices and identify strengths and accomplishments in their work. In some classrooms, students write their reflections and other comments on index cards, and in others, they design special comment sheets that they attach to the items in their portfolios.

Teachers usually collect baseline reading and writing samples at the beginning of the school year and then conduct portfolio review conferences with students at the end of each grading period. At these conferences, the teacher and the student talk about the items being placed in the portfolio and the student's self-assessments. Students also talk about what they want to improve or what they want to accomplish during the next grading period.

Showcasing Students' Portfolios

At the end of the school year, many teachers organize "Portfolio Share Days" to celebrate students' accomplishments and to provide an opportunity for them to share their portfolios with classmates and the wider community. Family members, local businesspeople, school administrators, college students, and others are invited to attend. Students and visitors form small groups, and students share their portfolios, pointing out their accomplishments and strengths. This activity is especially useful for involving community members in the school and showing them how students are becoming effective readers and writers.

These sharing days also help students accept responsibility for their own learning—especially those who haven't been as motivated as their classmates. When less motivated students listen to their classmates talk about their work and how they've grown as readers and writers, they often decide to work harder the next year.

Use **My Teaching To-Do Checklist: Assessment** to remind you of your responsibilities in the classroom with regard to planning for and using assessment data to inform instruction.

MY TEACHING TO-DO CHECKLIST: Assessment

- ☐ I determine my students' independent, instructional, and frustration reading levels.
- ☐ I consider the reading level of my instructional materials.
- ☐ I make plans for assessment as I plan for instruction.
- ☐ I monitor my students' progress during instruction.
- ☐ I choose authentic assessment activities as well as tests to measure my students' achievement.
- ☐ I use checklists and rubrics to assess my students' work.
- ☐ I have my students self-assess their work and reflect on their achievement.
- ☐ I teach my students how to take high-stakes tests in grades 2–4.
- ☐ My students keep portfolios to highlight their literacy achievements and milestones.
- ☐ I integrate state standards into my instruction.

MyLab Education **Self-Check 3.4**

Chapter Review

Literacy Assessment

- Teachers link classroom assessment with instruction using four steps: planning for assessment, assessing progress, evaluating students' learning, and reflecting on teaching and learning.

- Teachers use diagnostic assessments to identify students' progress in concepts about written language,

phonemic awareness, phonics, comprehension, and other components of literacy.

- Teachers prepare students to take high-stakes tests without sacrificing their instructional programs.

- Teachers have students document their learning in portfolios.

Accountability Check

Visit the following assessment links to access quiz questions and instructional applications.

MyLab Education Application Exercise 3.2: Understanding Literacy Development
MyLab Education Application Exercise 3.3: Monitoring Literacy Development
MyLab Education Application Exercise 3.4: Measuring Literacy Development

References

Afflerbach, P. (2007a). Best practices in literacy assessment. In L. B. Gambrell, L. M. Morrow, & M. Pressley (Eds.), *Best practices in literacy instruction* (3rd ed., pp. 264–282). New York: Guilford Press.

Afflerbach, P. (2007b). *Understanding and using reading assessment*, K–12. Newark, DE: International Reading Association.

Afflerbach, P. (2016). Reading assessment. *The Reading Teacher*, 69(4), 413-419.

Allington, R. L. (2012). *What really matters for struggling readers: Designing research-based programs* (3rd ed.). Boston: Allyn & Bacon/Pearson.

Bennett-Armistead, V. S., Duke, N. K., & Moses, A. M. (2005). *Literacy and the youngest learner: Best practices for educators of children from birth to 5*. New York: Scholastic.

Blume, J. (2007). *Tales of a fourth grade nothing*. New York: Puffin Books.

Bracey, G. W. (2004). *Setting the record straight: Responses to misconceptions about public education in the United States*. Portsmouth, NH: Heinemann.

Braunger, J., & Lewis, J. P. (2006). *Building a knowledge base in reading* (2nd ed.). Newark, DE: International Reading Association/National Council of Teachers of English.

Casbarro, J. (2005, February). The politics of high-stakes testing. *Education Digest*, 70(6), 20–23.

Clay, M. M. (2007). *An observation survey of early literacy achievement* (rev. ed.). Portsmouth, NH: Heinemann.

Clay, M. M. (1972). The early detection of reading difficulties: *A diagnostic survey*. Auckland, NZ: Heinemann.

Cole, J. (1993). *The Magic School Bus: lost in the solar system*. New York: Scholastic.

Common core state standards for English language arts. (2010). Retrieved from http://www.corestandards.org

Common Core State Standards Initiative. (2010). Common Core State Standards for English language arts & literacy in history/social studies, science, and technical subjects. Retrieved from http://www.corestandards.org/assets/CCSSI_ELA%20Standards.pdf

Danielson, L. M. (2009, February). Fostering reflection. *Educational Leadership*, 66(5). Retrieved from http://www.ascd.org/publications/educational-leadership/feb09/vol66/num05/Fostering-Reflection.aspx

D'Aoust, C. (1992). Portfolios: Process for students and teachers. In K. B. Yancy (Ed.), *Portfolios in the writing classroom* (pp. 39–48). Urbana, IL: National Council of Teachers of English.

Fountas, I. C., & Pinnell, G. S. (2006). *Leveled books, K–8: Matching texts to readers for effective teaching*. Portsmouth, NH: Heinemann.

Fountas, I. C., & Pinnell, G. S. (2009). *The Fountas and Pinnell leveled book list, K–8* (2010–2012 ed.). Portsmouth, NH: Heinemann.

Fry, E. (1968). A readability formula that saves time. *Journal of Reading, 11,* 587.

Fry, E. B., & Kress, J. E. (2006). *The reading teacher's book of lists: Grades K–12* (5th ed.). San Francisco: Jossey-Bass.

Garcia, G. E. (2000). Bilingual children's reading. In M. Kamil, P. Mosenthal, P. D. Pearson, & R. Barr (Eds.), *Handbook of reading research* (Vol. 3, pp. 813–834). Newark, DE: International Reading Association.

Greene, A. H., & Melton, G. D. (2007). *Test talk: Integrating test preparation into reading workshop*. Portsmouth, ME: Stenhouse.

Hebert, E. A. (2001). *The power of portfolios: What children can teach us about learning and assessment*. San Francisco: Jossey-Bass.

Hoffman, J. V., Assaf, L. C., & Paris, S. G. (2005). High-stakes testing in reading: Today in Texas, tomorrow? In S. J. Barrentine & S. M. Stokes (Eds.), *Reading assessment: Principles and practices for elementary teachers* (2nd ed., pp. 108–120). Newark, DE: International Reading Association.

Hollingworth, L. (2007). Five ways to prepare for standardized tests without sacrificing best practice. *The Reading Teacher, 61,* 339–342.

Howe, D., & Howe, J. (2006). *Bunnicula: A rabbit-tale of mystery*. New York: Aladdin Books.

Huerta-Macías, A. (1995). Alternative assessment: Responses to commonly asked questions. TESOL *Journal, 5,* 8–10.

International Reading Association (IRA). (1999). *High-stakes assessments in reading: A position statement*. Newark, DE: Author.

International Literacy Association. (2017). Literacy assessment: What everyone needs to know [Literacy leadership brief]. Newark, DE: Author.

Kame'enui, E., Simmons, D., & Cornachione, C. (2000). *A practical guide to reading assessments*. Newark, DE: International Reading Association.

Kuhs, T. M., Johnson, R. L., Agruso, S. A., & Monrad, D. M. (2001). *Put to the test: Tools and techniques for classroom assessment*. Portsmouth, NH: Heinemann.

Light, T. P., Chen, H. L., & Ittelson, J. C. (2012). *Documenting learning with ePortfolios*. San Francisco: Jossey-Bass.

Mathis, S. B. (2006). *The hundred penny box*. New York: Puffin Books.

McCabe, P. P. (2003). Enhancing self-efficacy for high-stakes reading tests. *The Reading Teacher, 57,* 12–20.

McQuillan, J. (1998). *The literacy crisis: False claims, real solutions*. Portsmouth, NH: Heinemann.

Moll, L. (1994). Literacy research in community and classrooms: A sociocultural approach. In R. R. Ruddell, M. R. Ruddell, & H. Singer (Eds.), *Theoretical models and processes of reading* (4th ed., pp. 197–207). Newark, DE: International Reading Association.

National Commission on Excellence in Education. (1983). *A nation at risk: The imperative for educational reform*. Washington, DC: U.S. Government Printing Office.

Nilsson, N. L. (2008). A critical analysis of eight informal reading inventories. *The Reading Teacher, 61,* 526–536.

O'Malley, J. M., & Pierce, L. V. (1996). *Authentic assessment for English language learners: Practical approaches for teachers*. Boston: Addison-Wesley.

Owocki, G., & Goodman, Y. M. (2002). *Kidwatching: Documenting children's literacy development*. Portsmouth, NH: Heinemann.

Peregoy, S. F., & Boyle, O. F. (2013). *Reading, writing and learning in ESL: A resource book for K–12 teachers* (6th ed.). Boston: Allyn & Bacon/Pearson.

Peverini S. (2009). The value of teacher expertise and good judgment: Recent inspiring reading about assessment. *Language Arts, 86,* 44–47.

Riches, C., & Genesee, F. (2006). Literacy: Crosslinguistic and crossmodal issues. In F. Genesee, K. Lindholm-Leary, W. M. Saunders, & D. Christian (Eds.), *Educating English language learners: A synthesis of research evidence* (pp. 64–108). New York: Cambridge University Press.

Risko, V. J., & Walker-Dalhouse, D. (2010). Making the most of assessments to inform instruction. *The Reading Teacher, 62,* 420–422.

Rowe, L.W. (In press). Say it in your language: Supporting translanguaging in multilingual classes. *The Reading Teacher,* DOI: 10.1002/trtr.167.

Skillings, M. J., & Ferrell, R. (2000). Student-generated rubrics: Bringing children into the assessment process. *The Reading Teacher, 53,* 452–455.

Stevens, D. D., Levi, A. J., & Walvoord, B. E. (2012). *Introduction to rubrics: An assessment tool to save grading time, convey effective feedback, and promote student learning* (2nd ed.) Sterling, VA: Stylus Publications.

Stires, S. (1991). Thinking through the process: Self-evaluation in writing. In B. M. Power & R. Hubbard (Eds.), *Literacy in process: The Heinemann reader* (pp. 295–310). Portsmouth, NH: Heinemann.

The pot of gold (an Irish folk tale). (2001). Upper Saddle River, NJ: Celebration Press/Pearson.

Vukelich, C., & Christie, J. (2009). *Building a foundation for preschool literacy* (2nd ed.). Newark, DE: International Reading Association.

Winograd, P., & Arrington, H. J. (1999). Best practices in literacy assessment. In L. B. Gambrell, L. M. Morrow, S. B. Neuman, & M. Pressley (Eds.), *Best practices in literacy instruction* (pp. 210–241). New York: Guilford Press.

Chapter 4
Cracking the Alphabetic Code

Learning Outcomes

After studying this chapter, you'll be prepared to:

4.1 Define the alphabetic principle and discuss its importance in learning to read.

4.2 Identify five phonemic awareness strategies that students use to decode and spell words.

4.3 Define *phonics*.

4.4 Describe what is meant by the assessment-instruction cycle and how it can be used to plan instruction.

First Grade Phonics Instruction

Beatrice Mihaela/Shutterstock

It's 8:10 on Thursday morning, and the 19 first graders in Mrs. Firpo's classroom are gathered on the carpet for their 15-minute phonemic awareness lesson. This week's topic is the short *i* sound and the consonant *x* which sounds like /ks/ like fox; today Mrs. Firpo will focus on short *i*. One by one, she holds up cards with pictures representing the short *i* sound. "Remember," Mrs. Firpo adds, "say the word slowly, just like a turtle!" Saleena goes first. She looks at the picture of a wig and says, "It's a wig, /w/ /i/ /g/." "Yes," says Mrs. Firpo as Saleena says the word slowly, pausing longer on the short *i* sound to emphasize it. "That's the sound of short *i* that you hear in the middle, /w/ /i/ /g/." Holding up a picture of a pig, she says, "See if you can hear the same sound in this one." Vincent shouts, "It's a pig!" He slowly articulates, "/p/ /i/ /g/." Mrs. Firpo then says, "Yes, that's right! Now, listen. They sound the same in the middle, don't they?" Mrs. Firpo says both words slowly, "/w/ /i/ /g/ and /p/ /i/ /g/. Let's

In this chapter, you'll learn about the alphabetic code and how students develop phonological awareness by manipulating sounds in words, matching letters and sounds to decode words, and representing sounds using letters as they spell words. As you read this vignette, notice how Mrs. Firpo teaches phonemic awareness and phonics: She engages her students in a combination of oral and written activities as they develop phonemic awareness and phonics knowledge.

try one more." Mrs. Firpo holds up a card with a picture of the number six. "What's this called?" Gabi calls out excitedly, "It's a six!" "You're right," Mrs. Firpo says, "now say it slowly and listen carefully for the short *i* sound." Gabi says the word six slowly. "Good," says Mrs. Firpo, "and you said it slowly so you could hear all the sounds, just like a turtle would!"

Next, Mrs. Firpo reminds the class that last week they learned the sound of short *a*. After a quick review with a couple of short *a* cards, Mrs. Firpo has the first graders sort the picture cards according to the short *i* or *a* sound and place them in one of two columns in a nearby pocket chart. They add labels to the columns: *Short i and Short a*. Then Austin uses the pointer to point to each picture card in the pocket chart for the class to read aloud.

Mrs. Firpo begins her phonics lessons with an oral activity because she knows it's important to integrate phonemic awareness with phonics. In the oral activities, students focus on orally segmenting and blending the sounds they hear in words, without worrying about phoneme–grapheme correspondences.

Mrs. Firpo's Focus Wall is shown here. Each week, the teacher posts the strategies and skills she'll be teaching, and the vocabulary words and spelling words are listed there, too. The vocabulary words are written on cards and displayed in a pocket chart attached to the Focus Wall so that they can be rearranged and used for various activities. The reason she posts these topics is to emphasize what she's teaching and what students are learning. In addition, Mrs. Firpo has her state's reading and writing standards for first grade listed on a chart next to the wall.

Mrs. Firpo uses *Reading Street* (Afflerbach et al., 2013), a basal reading textbook series; each week's themes are identified for her in the teacher's edition. Mrs. Firpo's students spend three and a half hours each morning involved in literacy instruction. Most of the goals, activities, and instructional materials come from the basal reading program, but Mrs. Firpo adapts some activities to meet the first graders' varied instructional needs.

MRS. FIRPO'S FOCUS WALL	
Theme: Who Helps Animals?　　Week: 1　　　　Unit: 2	
PHONICS FOCUS: Introduce: Short i, x /KS/ Review: Short a	**COMPREHENSION:** Plot Summarize **WRITING GENRE:** Fantasy

ORAL VOCABULARY WORDS

career	scrub
tool	exercise
sloppy	comfort
service	search

HIGH FREQUENCY WORDS

she	take
up	what

SPELLING WORDS

1. six	6. did
2. lip	7. mix
3. in	8. sit
4. wig	9. pin
5. it	10. fix

Today is Day One, Week Two of the planner provided by the series for each week of instruction and the theme is "Who Helps Animals?" She tells the students to turn to pages 40-41 of their edition—a two-page picture spread in their book showing a busy village downtown scene. "What animal is going to the vet?" she asks. "A pig!" exclaims Jordan. Mrs. Firpo praises Jordan's correct response and then asks students to find other items in the illustration that also contain the short *i* sound. Students examine the illustration carefully. Their responses come a little slowly at first but gradually pick up speed as they catch on to the short *i* sound. "I see a dish!" "Fish!" "There's a stick!" "They look like twins," another says excitedly. "Doesn't twins have a short *i* sound like fish and pig?" Mrs. Firpo guides the students to say each word slowly and listen to the sound of short *i*.

Next Mrs. Firpo moves from a phonemic awareness focus to a phonics one. For the first time this morning, letters and words are introduced in the lesson. Because Mrs. Firpo has only just introduced the sound of /i/ for the first time today, she makes sure to provide a lot of support to the students as they move in to the phonics portion of the lesson. She shows the students pages 48 and 49 of the story, Pig in a Wig. She reads aloud page 48 and writes the word pig on the board. Mrs. Firpo says the word *pig* slowly, like a turtle might, and tells the students that the letter *i* stands for the sound of /i/ that they have been practicing. Mrs. Firpo invites the students to find other words in the sentence that have the same sound. She writes the words on the board as the students identify them: *wig, big.* Now that Mrs. Firpo has modeled that the letter *i* stands for the sound of /i/, she moves to group practice, having students continue to segment and blend words in the story with the sound of /i/ with her.

They take turns using their letter-sound knowledge to sound out these words: *sip, lit, tin, fit, sick, tick,* and *rib.* Then the teacher asks the students to suggest other words with a short *i* sound. Fernando names *pick,* Crystal says *hit,* and Joel adds *win.* Then Mrs. Firpo writes these words on small cards and adds them to the pocket chart in the short *i* column.

During the last 40 minutes of the reading period, Mrs. Firpo conducts guided reading lessons. Her students' reading levels range from beginning first grade to the middle of second grade, with about half of them reading at grade level. She's grouped the first graders into four guided reading groups and meets with two groups each day. Students reading below grade level read leveled books, and those reading at and above grade level read easy-to-read chapter books, including Barbara Park's series of funny stories about a girl named Junie B. Jones (e.g., *Junie B., First Grader: Boss of Lunch* 2003) and Mary Pope Osborne's Magic Tree House series of adventure stories (e.g., *High Tide in Hawaii* 2003). Mrs. Firpo calls this period "differentiated instruction" because students participate in a variety of activities, based on their achievement levels.

While Mrs. Firpo does guided reading with one group, the others participate in seatwork and center activities. The first graders practice their short *i* spelling words using magnetic letters at the spelling center, practice the phonics focus and word pattern using letter cards and flip books at the phonics center, make books at the writing center, listen to the take-home books read aloud at the listening center, and read electronic books interactively at the computer center. The centers are arranged around the perimeter of the classroom; students know how to work at centers and understand what they're expected to do at each one.

After a 15-minute recess, the students spend the last 55 minutes of literacy instruction in writing workshop. Each week, the class focuses on the genre specified in the basal reading program; this week's focus is on personal letters. First, Mrs. Firpo teaches a **minilesson** and guides students as they complete more pages in their workbooks. Today, she reviews how to use commas in a friendly letter. The students examine several letters hanging in the classroom that the class wrote earlier in the school year using

---

ANGELICA'S LETTER

April 29, 2014

Dear Nanna Isabel,

I am writting you a letter. My birthday is in 35 days! Did you no that? I wud like to get a present. I want you to come to my party. It will be very funny.

Love,

Angelica

---

interactive writing. After the class rereads the letters, Mrs. Firpo asks the students to highlight the commas used in each one; Crystal points out that commas are used in the date; Saleena notices that a comma is used at the end of the greeting; and Luis marks the comma used after the closing. Next, students practice adding commas in the sample friendly letters in their workbooks.

Then students spend the remaining 35 minutes of writing workshop working on the letters they're writing to their families. Mrs. Firpo works with five students on their letters while the others work independently. At the end of the writing time, Joel and Angelica sit in the author's chair to read their letters aloud to their classmates. Angelica's letter to her grandmother is shown here.

The Alphabetic Principle

English is an alphabetic language, and students crack this code when they learn *the alphabetic principle*–very simply, all that means is that they realize that the sounds (phonemes) they hear in oral language can be represented by letters (graphemes) in print and vice versa—that letters represent sounds. Before students grasp this idea, they usually represent words by pictures when they write. Once students grasp the alphabetic principle, they begin to develop their knowledge about **graphophonemic** (letter–sound) relationships.

How do we know when students have acquired the alphabetic principle? A student who begins to use letters in writing instead of pictures to represent words (writing a big letter M, for example, instead of drawing a face to write the word Mom), or who excitedly points to the letter D on a car's gearshift and exclaims, "That's my name! It says David" is showing a grasp of the alphabetic principle. It's an exciting and important development in a young student's life, and for the student's caregivers and educators!

However, even before students can acquire the alphabetic principle, there is a foundational awareness that must come first, and that is an awareness of sounds themselves in oral language; that awareness is called **phonological awareness**. By third grade, most students have figured out the alphabetic code, and older students apply what they've learned to decode and spell multisyllabic words. You may think of all of this as phonics, but students actually develop three separate but related types of knowledge about the alphabetic code: phonological awareness, phonics, and orthographic awareness.

Common Core State Standards

Phonological Awareness

The Reading Standards: Foundational Skills and the Language Standards CCSS, (2010) focus on developing students' phonological awareness in kindergarten and first grade. The Standards specify several ways for students to demonstrate their understanding of spoken words, syllables, and phonemes.

By the end of fourth grade, students must be able to use their knowledge of letter–sound correspondences and syllabication patterns to decode unfamiliar multisyllabic words. To learn more about the Standards, go to http://www.corestandards.org/ELA-Literacy/, or check your state's educational standards website.

Phonological Awareness

Phonological awareness is an umbrella term that refers to an awareness of the different units of sounds in oral language. There are three units of sounds in English; from the largest to smallest they are syllables, rimes, and phonemes. Students learn to notice and manipulate the different units of sounds as they notice rhyming words, segment words into syllables and individual sounds, and invent silly words by playing with sounds.

SYLLABLES. The largest units of sound within words are syllables. If students cannot hear these bigger sound breaks, they likely will have a difficult time hearing phonemes—the smallest parts. To assess whether students are sensitive to syllables, show them simple pictures of objects, such as a table, a chair, a house, or animals, like a tiger, a giraffe, or an elephant. Invite the student to name the object in the picture and then to clap its name. (Don't say the name yourself.) Whatever the student labels the object will be fine; the important question is, does the student clap the right number of syllables for the name? One clap for words that have more than one syllable is a definite sign that the student does not yet have syllable awareness.

It won't take too long for students to show they hear syllable breaks; in fact, after a few days of clapping the names of objects in the classroom (make a game of it), the student will soon be able to clap the correct number of times. One last bit of advice: there is no need for the student to count the number of syllables or tell you the number of syllables; that's a different cognitive task. What matters is that the student can clap the right number of syllables. Don't make it too hard; one to three syllables is quite enough.

ONSET-RIME. The next smaller unit of sound is called onset-rime. Single syllables usually contain onset-rime sounds. The rime is the part that comes after the consonant and starts with a vowel. The part that comes before is called the onset. The words "stack," "slack," and "back," for example, all contain the same rime: -ack. They contain these different onsets: st, sl, and b. Students who can be heard playing with rhyming words, even sometimes making up words so they rhyme, have developed a sensitivity to rimes, a medium size unit of sound that occurs in spoken language.

PHONEMES. The very smallest units of sounds in spoken language are called phonemes. They are the smallest sounds of oral language and are the most difficult to distinguish. In fact, even though we try, we cannot actually voice a phoneme by itself. Students who are phonemically aware understand that spoken words are made up of these smallest units of sounds, and they demonstrate their awareness by being able to segment and blend sounds in spoken words.

Developing phonological awareness, particularly an awareness of phonemes, is critical because it is foundational to developing an understanding that letters represent sounds in language and vice versa—that sounds are represented by letters. However, we cannot stop at phonemic awareness when teaching young students to read; we also have to teach phonics and orthographic awareness.

Phonics

Students learn to convert letters into sounds and blend them to recognize words. Those who can apply phonics concepts understand that there are predictable sound–symbol correspondences in English, and they can use decoding strategies to figure out unfamiliar written words.

There are 44 phonemes in the English language. This creates a challenge when learning to read English because there are only 26 letters to represent 44 sounds. Think about the many ways that the sound of long *u* can be represented with letters in the English language: few and dew (but not sew), cube (but not cub), and too (and even to).

Orthographic Awareness

The mismatch between the number of phonemes and number of letters in English is the reason why English is said to have a deep orthography. Other languages, like Spanish, Italian, and Greek are said to have transparent orthographies because of the more consistent match between the sounds in the language and the letters which represent them. As students begin to use letters to write their messages, they soon come to realize that, many times, words are not written exactly the way they sound. The word "play," for example, has a "y" on the end! If they are to spell words correctly, students have to develop orthographic awareness—an awareness of the spelling patterns in English. Students who shift from writing how words sound to thinking about how to make them look right, are developing orthographic awareness.

In the vignette, Mrs. Firpo incorporated all three components into her literacy program. She began the word work lesson on the short *i* sound with an oral phonemic awareness activity; next, she moved to a phonics activity where students read words that had a short *i* sound and categorized them on a pocket chart. Later, they practiced spelling words with short *i* on whiteboards.

Teaching these graphophonemic relationships isn't a complete reading program, but phonemic awareness, phonics, and spelling are integral to effective literacy instruction, especially for students in kindergarten through third grade (National Reading Panel, 2000). However, because of the important foundational role that phonemic awareness is known to play in developing the alphabetic principle, and thus developing phonic knowledge and orthographic awareness, much of this chapter will be devoted to learning about phonemic awareness strategies that students learn to use and strategies that you can teach.

The Common Core State Standards for English Language Arts (2010) address all three types of knowledge about the alphabetic code that students learn and apply to reading and writing during the primary grades. The box presents an overview of the phonemic awareness, phonics, and spelling Standards.

MyLab Education Self-Check 4.1

Developing Phonemic Awareness

Phonemic awareness is a student's basic understanding that speech is composed of a series of individual sounds, and it provides the foundation for phonics and spelling (Armbruster, Lehr, & Osborn, 2001). When students can choose a duck as the animal whose name begins with /d/ from a collection of toy animals, identify *duck* and *luck* as rhyming words in a song, and blend the sounds /d//ŭ//k/ to pronounce *duck*, they are phonemically aware. Cunningham and Allington (2011) describe phonemic awareness as students' ability to break words apart and reassemble them, and to make other changes as well. The emphasis is on the sounds of spoken words, not on reading letters or pronouncing letter names. Developing phonemic awareness enables students to use sound–symbol correspondences to read and spell words (Gillon, 2004).

Developmental Continuum Phonemic Awareness

PreK	K	1	2	3	4
Four-year-olds become aware of words as units of sound as they play with sounds and create rhymes.	Students pronounce sounds and isolate, match, and manipulate them as they learn to blend and segment.	Students use the blending strategy to decode words and the segmenting strategy to spell words.	Second graders continue to use blending and segmenting to decode and spell more challenging words.	Students apply phonemic awareness strategies to decode and spell two- and three-syllable words.	Fourth graders blend and segment sounds as they read and spell multisyllabic words with roots and affixes.

Phonemes are the smallest units of speech, and they're written as **graphemes**, or letters of the alphabet. In this book, phonemes are marked using diagonal lines (e.g., /d/) and graphemes are italicized (e.g., *d*). Sometimes phonemes (e.g., /k/ in *duck*) are spelled with two graphemes (*ck*).

Why Is Phonemic Awareness Important?

A clear connection exists between phonemic awareness and progress in learning to read; researchers have concluded that phonemic awareness is a prerequisite for learning to read. As they become phonemically aware, students recognize that speech can be segmented into smaller units; this knowledge is very useful as they learn about sound–symbol correspondences and spelling patterns (Cunningham, 2011).

Moreover, phonemic awareness has been shown to be the most powerful predictor of later reading achievement. Klesius, Griffith, and Zielonka (1991) found that students who began first grade with strong phonemic awareness were successful regardless of the kind of reading instruction they received, and no particular type of instruction was better for students with limited phonemic awareness at the beginning of first grade.

Understanding that words are composed of smaller sounds—phonemes—is a significant achievement for young students because phonemes are abstract language units. Phonemes carry no meaning, and students think of words according to their meanings, not their linguistic characteristics (Griffith & Olson, 1992). When students think about ducks, for example, they think of feathered animals that swim in ponds, fly through the air, and make noises we describe as "quacks"; they don't think of "duck" as a word with three phonemes or four graphemes, or as a word beginning with /d/ and rhyming with *luck*. Phonemic awareness requires that students treat speech as an object, to shift their attention away from the meaning of words to examine the linguistic features of speech. This focus on phonemes is even more complicated because phonemes aren't discrete units in speech; often they're slurred or clipped in speech—think about the blended initial sound in *tree* and the last sound in *eating*.

Using Phonemic Awareness Strategies

Students become phonemically aware by manipulating spoken language. They apply their phonemic awareness to decode words or to help spell them. Here are some strategies students use to help themselves.

Identifying Sounds.   Students identify a word that begins or ends with a particular sound. For example, when shown a brush, a car, and a doll, they identify *doll* as the word that ends with /l/.

Categorizing Sounds in Words.   Students recognize the "odd" word in a set of three words; for example, when the teacher says, (like a turtle!) *ring, rabbit,* and *sun,* they recognize that *sun* doesn't belong. Remember, do not say "ruh-uh-ing-guh"! Say "riiiinnnnngggg." Otherwise, you will distort the sounds and the student will hear syllables and not phonemes.

Substituting Sounds.   Students remove a sound from a word and substitute a different sound. Sometimes they substitute the beginning sound, changing *bar* to *car,* for example. Or, they change the middle sound, making *tip* from *top,* or substitute the ending sound, changing *gate* to *game.*

Blending Sounds.   Students blend two, three, or four individual sounds to form a word; the teacher says /b//ĭ//g/, for example, and the students say the sounds slowly, blending them to form the word *big.*

Segmenting Sounds.   Students can say words slowly and hear the beginning, middle, and ending sounds. For example, students segment the word *feet* into /f//ē//t/ and *go* into /g//ō/ by saying the words slowly, like a turtle!

Students use these strategies, especially blending and segmenting, to decode and spell words. When they use phonics to sound out a word, for example, they say the sounds represented by each letter and blend them to read the word. Similarly, to spell a word, students say the word slowly, segmenting the sounds.

Teaching Phonemic Awareness Strategies

Students can be explicitly taught to segment and blend speech, and those who receive approximately 20 hours of training in phonemic awareness do better in both reading and spelling (Juel, Griffith, & Gough, 1986). Phonemic awareness is also nurtured in spontaneous ways by providing students with language-rich environments and emphasizing wordplay as teachers read books aloud and engage students in singing songs, chanting poems, and telling riddles.

Teachers promote students' phonemic awareness through the language-rich environments they create in the classroom. As they sing songs, chant rhymes, read aloud

PreK Practices

How do teachers promote 4-year-olds' phonemic awareness?

Prekindergarten teachers develop their students' attention to the sounds in oral language through these developmentally appropriate activities:

- Singing songs
- Reciting nursery rhymes
- Sharing wordplay books
- Playing word games

Through these activities, students tune in to the sounds of words and develop an understanding of rhyme. They recognize and generate rhyming words, segment words into syllables, isolate beginning or ending sounds in words, substitute sounds to create new words, blend sounds into words, and segment words into sounds.

Acquiring these oral language strategies is crucial, according to Strickland and Schickedanz (2009), because students apply them as they learn phonics. Teachers typically spend 20 hours teaching phonemic awareness strategies, but they recognize that students develop phonemic awareness at different rates and that some will need more or less instruction.

wordplay books, and play games, students have many opportunities to orally match, isolate, blend, and substitute sounds and to segment words into sounds (Griffith & Olson, 1992). Teachers often incorporate phonemic awareness into other oral language and literacy activities, but it's also important to teach lessons that focus specifically on the phonemic awareness strategies.

Phonemic awareness instruction should meet three criteria. First, the activities should be appropriate for 4-, 5-, and 6-year-old students. Activities involving songs, nursery rhymes, riddles, and wordplay books are good choices because they encourage students' playful experimentation with oral language. Second, the instruction should be planned and purposeful, not just incidental: Teachers choose instructional materials and plan activities that focus students' attention on the sound structure of oral language. Third, phonemic awareness activities should be integrated with other components of a balanced literacy program. It's crucial that students perceive the connection between oral and written language (Yopp & Yopp, 2000).

Many wordplay books are available for young students. The Booklist presents a collection of wordplay books that teachers often share with students. Books such as *Cock-a-Doodle-Moo!* (Most, 1996) and *Rattletrap Car* (Root, 2004) stimulate students to experiment with sounds and to create nonsense words. Teachers often read wordplay books more than once. During the first reading, students focus on comprehension and what interests them in the book; in a second reading, however, students' attention shifts to the wordplay elements, and teachers ask questions about the way the author manipulated words and sounds. For example, they ask, "Did you notice that and rhyme?" They encourage students to make similar comments, too.

Teachers often incorporate wordplay books, songs, and games into the **minilessons** they teach. The minilesson feature presents a kindergarten teacher's minilesson on blending sounds. The teacher reread Dr. Seuss's *Fox in Socks* (1965) and then asked students to identify words from the book that she pronounced sound by sound. This book is rich in wordplay: rhyming (e.g., *do, you, goo, chew*), initial consonant substitution (e.g., *trick, quick, slick*), vowel substitution (e.g., *blabber, blibber, blubber*), and alliteration (e.g., *Luke Luck likes lakes*).

SOUND MATCHING.   Students choose one of several words beginning with a particular sound or say a word that begins with a particular sound (Yopp, 1992). For these games, teachers use familiar objects (e.g., feather, toothbrush, book) and toys (e.g., small plastic animals, toy trucks, artificial fruits and vegetables), as well as pictures of familiar objects.

Teachers play a sound-matching guessing game (Lewkowicz, 1994) for which they collect two boxes and pairs of objects to place in them (e.g., forks, mittens, erasers, combs, and books); one item from each pair is placed in each box. After the teacher shows the students the objects in the boxes and they name them together, two students play the game. Two students sit back to back. One student selects an object, holds it up, and pronounces the initial (or middle or final) sound; whichever sound has been agreed upon for the game. The second student listens to the sound and chooses an object from the second box that the student thinks the other is holding up. Classmates check to see if the two players are holding the same object.

Students also identify rhyming words as part of sound-matching activities: They name a word that rhymes with a given word and identify rhyming words from familiar songs and stories. As students listen to parents and teachers read Dr. Seuss books, such as *Fox in Socks* (1965), *Hop on Pop* (1963), and other wordplay books, they refine their understanding of rhyme.

SOUND ISOLATION.   Teachers say a word and then students identify the sounds at the beginning, middle, or end of the word, or teachers and students isolate sounds as they sing familiar songs. Yopp (1992) created these verses to the tune of "Old MacDonald Had a Farm":

Check the Compendium of Instructional Procedures, which follows Chapter 12. These **green** terms also show a brief description of each procedure.

MyLab Education
Video Example 4.1
These kindergarteners are working in a learning center on a phonemic awareness activity. How does the activity they are engaged in support the development of phonemic awareness?

What's the sound that starts these words:
Chicken, chin, and cheek?
(wait for response)
/ch/ is the sound that starts these words:
Chicken, chin, and cheek.
With a /ch/, /ch/ here, and a /ch/, /ch/ there,
Here a /ch/, there a /ch/, everywhere a /ch/, /ch/.
/ch/ is the sound that starts these words:
Chicken, chin, and cheek. (p. 700)

Teachers change the question at the beginning of the verse to focus on medial and final sounds. For example:

What's the sound in the middle of these words?
Whale, game, and rain. (p. 700)

And for final sounds:

What's the sound at the end of these words?
Leaf, cough, and beef. (p. 700)

Teachers also set out trays of objects and ask students to choose the one that doesn't belong because it begins with a different sound. For example, from a tray with a toy pig, a puppet, a teddy bear, and a pen, the teddy bear doesn't belong.

SOUND BLENDING. Students blend sounds to combine them and form a word. For example, students blend the sounds /d//ŭ//k/ to form the word *duck*. Teachers play the "What am I thinking of?" game with students by identifying several characteristics of the item and then saying its name, articulating each sound slowly and separately

---

Booklist Wordplay Books

Type	Books
Invented Words	Degan, B. (1985). *Jamberry.* Hutchins, P. (2002). *Don't forget the bacon!* Martin, B., Jr., & Archambault, J. (2009). *Chicka chicka boom boom.* Most, B. (1996). *Cock-a-doodle-moo!* Slate, J. (1996). *Miss Bindergarten gets ready for kindergarten.* Slepian, J., & Seidler, A. (2001). *The hungry thing.*
Repetitive Lines	Deming, A. G. (1994). *Who is tapping at my window?.* Downey, L. (2000). *The flea's sneeze.* Fleming, D. (2007). *In the small, small pond.* Hoberman, M. A. (2003). *The lady with the alligator purse.* Taback, S. (1997). *There was an old lady who swallowed a fly.* Taback, S. (2004). *This is the house that Jack built.* Westcott, N. B. (2003). *I know an old lady who swallowed a fly.* Wilson, K. (2003). *A frog in a bag.*
Rhyming Words	Ehlert, L. (1993). *Eating the alphabet: Fruits and vegetables from A to Z.* McPhail, D. (1996). *Pigs aplenty, pigs galore.* Root, P. (2003). *One duck stuck.* Seuss, Dr. (1963). *Hop on pop.* Shaw, N. (2006). *Sheep in a jeep.*
Songs and Verse	Crebbin, J. (1998). *Cows in the kitchen.* Gollub, M. (2000). *The jazz fly.* Hillenbrand, W. (2002). *Fiddle-i-fee.* Hoberman, M. A. (2004). *The eensy-weensy spider.* Prelutsky, J. (1989). *The baby uggs are hatching.* Raffi. (1988). *Down by the bay.* Raffi. (1990). *The wheels on the bus.*
Sounds	Ehlert, L. (2011). *RRRalph.* Most, B. (1991). *A dinosaur named after me.* Most, B. (2003). *The cow that went oink.* Seuss, Dr. (1974). *There's a wocket in my pocket.*

Minilesson

TOPIC: Blending Sounds Into Words
GRADE: Kindergarten
TIME: One 20-minute period

Ms. Lewis regularly includes a 20-minute lesson on phonemic awareness in her literacy block. She usually rereads a familiar wordplay book and plays a phonemic awareness game with the kindergartners that emphasizes one of the phonemic awareness strategies.

1. **Introduce the Topic**
   Ms. Lewis brings her 19 kindergartners together on the rug and explains that she's going to reread Dr. Seuss's *Fox in Socks* (1965). It's one of their favorite books, and they clap with pleasure. She explains that afterward they're going to play a word game.

2. **Share Examples**
   Ms. Lewis reads aloud *Fox in Socks,* showing the pictures on each page as she reads. She encourages the students to read along. Sometimes, she stops and invites the students to fill in the last rhyming word in a sentence or to echo read (repeating after her like an echo) the alliterative sentences. After they finish reading, she asks what they like best about the book. Pearl replies, "It's just a really funny book. That's why it's so good." "What makes it funny?" Ms. Lewis asks. Teri explains, "The words are funny. They make my tongue laugh. You know—*fox–socks–box–Knox*. That's funny on my tongue!" "Oh," Ms. Lewis clarifies, "your tongue likes to say rhyming words. I like to say them, too." Other students recall these rhyming words from the book: *clocks–tocks–blocks–box, noodle–poodle,* and *new–do–blue–goo*.

3. **Provide Information**
   "Let me tell you about our game," Ms. Lewis explains. "I'm going to say some of the words from the book, but I'll say them sound by sound, and I want you to blend the sounds together and guess the word." "Are they rhyming words?" Teri asks. "Sure," the teacher agrees. "I'll say two words that rhyme, sound by sound, for you to guess." She says the sounds /f//ŏ//ks/ and /b//ŏ//ks/ and the students correctly blend the sounds and say the words *fox* and *box*. She repeats the procedure for *clock–tock, come–dumb, big–pig, new–blue, rose–hose, game–lame,* and *slow–crow*. Ms. Lewis stops and talks about how to "bump" or blend the sounds to figure out the words. She models how she blends the sounds to form the word. "Make the words harder," several students say, and Ms. Lewis offers several more difficult pairs of rhyming words, including *chick–trick* and *beetle–tweedle*.

4. **Guide Practice**
   Ms. Lewis continues playing the guessing game, but now she segments individual words. As each student correctly identifies a word, that student leaves the group and goes to work with the aide. Finally, six students remain who need additional practice. They continue blending *do, new,* and other two-sound words and some of the easier three-sound words, including *box, come,* and *like*.

5. **Assess Learning**
   Through the guided practice part of the lesson, Ms. Lewis informally checks to see which students need more practice blending sounds into words and provides additional practice for them.

Teach Kids to Be Strategic!

Phonemic Awareness Strategies

Introduce these two strategies as students manipulate sounds orally:

- Blend
- Segment

Students practice these strategies orally as they play with words, identify rhyming words, and invent nonsense words. Look for students to apply the strategies to written language when they decode and spell words. If students struggle, reteach the strategies, making sure to name them, model their use with both oral and written language, and talk about their application in reading and writing.

(Yopp, 1992). Then students blend the sounds to identify the word, using the phonological and semantic information that the teacher provided. For example:

> *I'm thinking of a small animal that lives in a pond when it's young, but when it's an adult, it lives on land. It's a /f/ /r/ /ŏ/ /g/. What is it?*

The students blend the sounds to pronounce the word *frog*. Then the teacher sets out magnetic letters for students to arrange to spell and read the word *frog*. In this example, the teacher connects the game with the thematic unit to make it more meaningful.

SOUND ADDITION AND SUBSTITUTION. Students play with words and create nonsense words as they add or substitute sounds in words in songs they sing or in books that are read aloud to them. Teachers read wordplay books such as Pat Hutchins's *Don't Forget the Bacon!* (2002), in which a boy leaves for the store with a mental list of four items to buy. As he walks, he repeats his list, substituting words each time: "A cake for tea" changes to "a cape for me" and then to "a rake for leaves." Students suggest other substitutions, such as "a game for a bee."

Students substitute sounds in refrains of songs (Yopp, 1992). For example, they can change the "Ee-igh, ee-igh, oh!" refrain in "Old MacDonald Had a Farm" to "Bee-bigh, bee-bigh, boh!" to focus on the initial /b/ sound. Teachers can choose one sound, such as /sh/, and have students substitute it for the beginning sound in their names and in words for objects in the classroom. For example, *Jimmy* becomes *Shimmy*, *José* becomes *Shosé*, and *clock* becomes *shock*.

SOUND SEGMENTATION. One of the more difficult phonemic awareness activities is *segmentation*, in which students isolate the sounds in a spoken word (Yopp, 1988). An introductory segmentation activity is to draw out the beginning sound in words. Students enjoy exaggerating the initial sound in their own names and other familiar words. A pet guinea pig named Popsicle lives in Mrs. Firpo's classroom, for instance, and the students exaggerate the beginning sound of her name so that it's pronounced as "P-P-P-Popsicle." Students also pick up objects or pictures of objects and identify the initial sound; a student who picks up a toy truck says, "This is a truck and it starts with /t/."

From that beginning, students move to identifying all the sounds in a word. Using a toy truck again, the student would say, "This is a truck, /t/ /r/ /ŭ/ /k/." Yopp (1992) suggests singing a song to the tune of "Twinkle, Twinkle, Little Star" in which students segment entire words. Here is one example:

> *Listen, listen to my word*
> *Then tell me all the sounds you heard: coat*
> *(slowly)*
> */k/ is one sound*

/ō/ is two
/t/ is last in coat
It's true. (p. 702)

After several repetitions of the verse segmenting other words, the song ends this way:

Thanks for listening to my words
And telling all the sounds you heard! (p. 702)

Teachers also use **Elkonin boxes** to teach students to segment words; this activity comes from the work of Russian psychologist D. B. Elkonin (Clay, 2005). As seen in Figure 4–1, the teacher shows an object or a picture of an object and draws a row of boxes, with one box for each sound in the name of the object. Then the teacher or a student moves a marker into each box as the sound is pronounced. Students can move small markers onto cards on their desks, or the teacher can draw the boxes on the whiteboard and use tape or magnets to hold the larger markers in place. Elkonin boxes can also be used for spelling activities: When a student is trying to spell a word, such as *duck*, the teacher can draw three boxes, do the segmentation activity, and then have the student write the letters representing each sound in the boxes.

Students are experimenting with oral language in these activities, which stimulates their interest in language and provides valuable experiences with books and words. Effective teachers recognize the importance of building this foundation as students are beginning to read and write. Use the "**My Teaching To-Do Checklist: Phonemic Awareness**" to assess the effectiveness of your phonemic awareness instruction.

MyLab Education
Video Example 4.2
Karla Palamino, a first grade teacher works with her English learners to develop phonemic awareness. What strategies do you observe in this video?

Figure 4–1 Elkonin Boxes

Type	Goals	Steps in the Activity
Phonemic Awareness	Segmenting sounds in a one-syllable word	1. Show students an object or a picture of an object with a one-syllable name, such as a duck, game, bee, or cup. 2. On a whiteboard or on chart paper, draw a row of boxes, side by side, corresponding to the number of sounds heard in the object's name. For example, draw two boxes to represent the two sounds in *bee* or three boxes for the three sounds in *duck*. 3. Distribute coins, checkers, or other small items to use as markers. 4. Say the name of the object slowly, moving a marker into each box as the sound is pronounced. Then have students repeat the procedure.
	Segmenting syllables in a multisyllabic word	1. Show students an object or a picture of an object with a multisyllabic name, such as a butterfly, alligator, cowboy, or umbrella. 2. Draw a row of boxes corresponding to the number of syllables in the object's name. For example, draw four boxes to represent the four syllables in *alligator*. 3. Distribute markers. 4. Say the name of the object slowly, moving a marker into each box as the syllable is pronounced. Then have students repeat the procedure.
Spelling	Representing sounds with letters	1. Draw a row of boxes corresponding to the number of sounds heard in a word. For example, draw two boxes for *go*, three boxes for *ship*, and four boxes for *frog*. 2. Pronounce the word, pointing to each box as the corresponding sound is said. 3. Have the student write the letter or letters representing the sound in each box.
	Applying spelling patterns	1. Draw a row of boxes corresponding to the number of sounds heard in a word. For example, draw three boxes for the word *duck*, *game*, or *light*. 2. Pronounce the word, pointing to each box as the corresponding sound is said. 3. Have the student write the letter or letters representing the sound in each box. 4. Pronounce the word again and examine how each sound is spelled. Insert unpronounced letters to complete the spelling patterns.

MY TEACHING TO-DO LIST: Phonemic Awareness

☐ I begin with oral activities, using objects and pictures, but after students learn to identify the letters of the alphabet, I add reading and writing components.

☐ I emphasize experimentation as my students sing songs and play word games.

☐ I read and reread wordplay books, and encourage my students to experiment with rhyming words, alliteration, and other wordplay activities.

☐ I teach minilessons on manipulating words, moving from easier to more complex levels.

☐ I emphasize the blending and segmenting strategies.

☐ I use small-group activities so students can be more actively involved in manipulating language.

☐ I teach phonemic awareness in the context of authentic reading and writing activities.

☐ I spend approximately 20 hours teaching phonemic awareness strategies.

☐ I integrate state standards into my instruction.

Teaching English Learners

Phonemic Awareness

It's more difficult to develop English learners' phonemic awareness than native English speakers' because they're just learning to speak English; however, this training is worthwhile as long as familiar and meaningful words are used (Riches & Genesee, 2006). Teachers create a rich literacy environment and begin by reading books and poems aloud and singing songs so students can learn to recognize and pronounce English sound patterns.

To plan effective phonemic awareness instruction, teachers need to be familiar with English learners' home languages and understand how they differ from English (Peregoy & Boyle, 2013). Instruction should begin with sounds that students can pronounce easily and that don't conflict with those in their home language. Sounds that aren't present in students' home languages or those that they don't perceive as unique, such as /ch/–/sh/ or /eˇ/–/ĭ/ for Spanish speakers, are more difficult. Students may need more time to practice producing and manipulating these difficult sounds.

Researchers recommend explicit instruction on phonemic awareness and practice opportunities for English learners (Snow, Burns, & Griffin, 1998). They sing familiar songs and play language games like native speakers do, but teachers also draw ELs' attention to pronouncing English sounds and words. Teachers often integrate phonemic awareness training, vocabulary instruction, and reading and writing activities to show how oral language sounds are represented by letters in written words.

Phonemic awareness is a common underlying linguistic ability that transfers from one language to another (Riches & Genesee, 2006). Students who have learned to read in their home language—if it's alphabetic—are already phonemically aware, and this knowledge supports their reading and writing development in English.

MyLab Education
Video Example 4.3

Teachers assess first grader's knowledge of phonemic awareness. What do you observe about the teacher's ability to give this assessment and the student's responses?

Assessing Students' Phonemic Awareness

Students need to learn to manipulate words orally before they begin phonics instruction, so assessing their knowledge is crucial. Teachers often administer a screening test to determine the level of students' knowledge about phonemic awareness before instruction, and they use the instruction–assessment cycle to manage assessment during and after instruction. Linking assessment with phonemic awareness instruction is especially important because the instruction should be targeted to students' instructional needs, and it should move to manipulating written words once students can use phonemic awareness strategies orally.

SCREENING TESTS. Teachers administer one of several readily available phonemic awareness tests to screen students' ability to use phonemic awareness strategies, monitor their progress, and document their learning. Four phonemic awareness tests are described in this Assessment Tools feature.

Assessment Tools

Phonemic Awareness

Kindergarten and first grade teachers monitor students' learning by observing them during classroom activities, and they screen, monitor, diagnose, and document their growing phonemic awareness by administering these tests:

- **Dynamic Indicators of Basic Early Literacy Skills (DIBELS): Phoneme Segmentation Fluency Subtest**
  This individually administered DIBELS subtest assesses students' ability to segment words with two and three phonemes. Multiple forms are available so that this test can be used periodically to monitor students' progress. The test is available free of charge on the DIBELS website, but there's a fee for analyzing and reporting the test results.

- **Phonological Awareness Literacy Screening (PALS) System: Rhyme Awareness and Beginning Sound Subtests**
  The kindergarten level of PALS includes brief subtests to assess young students' phonemic awareness. Students look at pictures and supply rhyming words or produce the beginning sounds for picture names. The grades 1–3 tests also include phonemic awareness subtests for students who score below grade level on other tests. PALS is available from the University of Virginia; it's free for Virginia teachers, but teachers in other states must pay for it.

- **Test of Phonological Awareness (TPA)**
  This group test is designed to measure students' ability to isolate individual sounds in spoken words and understand the relationship between letters and phonemes. The TPA is administered in 40 minutes, and it's available from LinguiSystems.

- **Yopp-Singer Test of Phonemic Segmentation**
  This individually administered oral test for kindergartners measures their ability to segment the phonemes in words; it contains 22 items and is administered in less than 10 minutes. The test is free; it can be found in the September 1995 issue of *The Reading Teacher* or online. A Spanish version is also available.

Information gained from classroom observations and these assessments is used to identify students who aren't yet phonemically aware, plan appropriate instruction, and monitor their progress.

THE INSTRUCTION-ASSESSMENT CYCLE.   Teachers use the four-step instruction-assessment cycle to integrate assessment with instruction, and they also address the Common Core State Standards in their instruction and assessment.

Step 1: Planning.   As teachers plan developmentally appropriate instruction based on their understanding about their students' ability to manipulate words and the Common Core State Standards they're expected to teach, they make plans for assessment during and after instruction.

Step 2: Monitoring.   Teachers informally observe students' performance as they read wordplay books, teach **minilessons**, and play phonemic awareness games, such as sorting picture cards according to beginning sounds or identify rhyming words in a familiar song. Based on their observations, teachers modify instruction or teach additional minilessons and play more word and sound games according to students' instructional needs.

Step 3: Evaluating.   Teachers often use checklists to track students' growth in the ability to manipulate words and, in particular, apply the segmenting, blending, and substituting strategies. Through a combination of informal monitoring and one-on-one oral assessments, teachers check that their students are meeting grade-level expectations.

Step 4: Reflecting.   Both teachers and students participate in this step. Teachers use their evaluation of students' learning to judge the effectiveness of their instruction and decide how to adapt instruction to better serve struggling learners. In addition, students reflect on their developing ability to manipulate sounds.

If Students Struggle . . .

Some five-year-olds can't think of a word that rhymes with *pig* or *make*, can't clap the syllables in their names or in common words (e.g., *apple, umbrella*), and aren't interested in wordplay activities; it's likely that these students aren't developing the phonemic awareness knowledge that they need to learn to read and write successfully. If the results of phonemic awareness tests indicate that students are struggling, teachers must act quickly because students with lower levels of phonemic awareness are more likely to experience reading difficulties (Snow, Burns, & Griffin, 1998).

Teachers provide interventions for struggling students that focus on the sounds of oral language, especially during the second half of kindergarten. They work with individual students and small groups using developmentally appropriate activities that emphasize oral language but also make links to reading and writing.

The sequence in learning phonemic awareness moves from recognizing the order of sounds in words to manipulating these sounds. First, students identify and match initial and final sounds in words. Next, they count the phonemes in words, often using Elkonin boxes. Finally, students manipulate sounds in four ways—segmenting, blending, deleting, and substituting. Teachers identify the specific phonemic awareness concepts that students haven't developed and teach lessons to address these topics in order of difficulty.

Students with extremely limited understanding of phonemic awareness may lack knowledge in one or more of these prerequisite concepts:

Environmental Sounds.   Do students notice sounds in their environment? Can they recognize specific sounds, such as a bird chirping, a person coughing, a car horn honking, or a door squeaking? If students are unaware of environmental sounds, teachers develop their awareness by teaching them to identify sounds and classify them according to loudness and pitch.

Concept of "Rhyme."   Do students understand what rhyming words are? Can they break words into onsets and rimes? If not, teachers help students understand that words rhyme when their rimes sound alike (e.g., *go–throw, snail–whale*) and have them identify rhyming words in poems, songs, and books.

Concept of "Word."   Do students understand what a word is? Can they recognize individual words in speech? If students haven't developed this concept, teachers emphasize individual words as they speak and read aloud, and they ask students to listen for specific words.

Concept of "Syllable."   Do students understand what a syllable is? Can they demonstrate how to count the syllables in a word? If students can't, teachers accentuate the syllables in individual words, beginning with students' names, common words (e.g., *baby, pizza, together*), and compound words (e.g., *birthday, airplane*). They also teach students to clap the syllables as they say a word aloud; for example, as they pronounce the word *elephant*, they clap three times.

If students haven't developed these basic understandings, teachers begin their intervention here; however, if students can demonstrate their understanding of these concepts, teachers focus on identifying and manipulating sounds.

Literacy Portraits

Ms. Janusz

Rakie

Curt'Lynn

Rhiannon

Beginning readers and writers usually depend on the "sound it out" strategy to decode and spell words. It's effective for phonetically regular words, such as *bus* and *feet*, but not for figuring out *chair, now,* or *said*. Recall that Ms. Janusz teaches the second graders about other ways to decode and spell words in her minilesson on the "think it out" strategy. (Play the video for her **"think it out" strategy** again if you want a reminder.)

Also, check my interviews with Rakie, Curt'Lynn, and Rhiannon. These students still rely on the "sound it out" strategy; they describe reading as a process of decoding words and emphasize that good writers spell words correctly. Think about the phonics concepts presented in this chapter. How do you expect these students' views to change once they become fluent readers and writers?

MyLab Education Self-Check 4.2
MyLab Education Application Exercise 4.1: Using Phonemic Awareness Strategies

Phonics

Phonics is the set of relationships between **phonology**, the sounds in speech, and **orthography**, the spelling system. The emphasis is on spelling patterns, not individual letters, because there isn't a one-to-one correspondence between phonemes and graphemes in English. Sounds are spelled in different ways, and several reasons explain this inconsistency. One reason is that sounds, especially vowels, vary according to their location in a word (e.g., *go–got*). Adjacent letters often influence how letters are pronounced (e.g., *bed–bead*), as do vowel markers such as the final *e* (e.g., *bit–bite*) (Shefelbine, 1995).

Etymology, or language origin, of words also influences their pronunciation. For example, the *ch* digraph is pronounced in several ways; the three most common are /ch/ as in *chain* (English), /sh/ as in *chauffeur* (French), and /k/ as in *chaos* (Greek). Neither the location of the digraph within the word nor adjacent letters account for these pronunciation differences: In all three words, the *ch* digraph is at the beginning of the word and is followed by two vowels, the first of which is *a*. Some letters aren't pronounced, either. In words such as *write*, the *w* isn't pronounced, even though it probably was at one time. The same is true for the *k* in *knight*, *know*, and *knee*. Silent letters in words such as *sign* and *bomb* reflect their parent words, *signature* and *bombard*, and have been retained for semantic, not phonological, reasons (Venezky, 1999).

Phonics Concepts

Phonics explains the relationships between phonemes and graphemes. There are 44 phonemes in English, which are represented by the 26 letters. The alphabetic principle suggests that there should be a one-to-one correspondence between phonemes and graphemes, so that each sound is consistently represented by one letter. English, however, is an imperfect phonetic language, and there are more than 500 ways to represent the 44 phonemes using single letters or combinations of letters. Think about the word *day*: The two phonemes, /d/ and /ā/, are represented by three letters. The *d* is a consonant, and *a* and *y* are vowels. Interestingly, *y* isn't always a vowel; it's a consonant at the beginning of a word and a vowel at the end. When two vowels

DEVELOPMENTAL CONTINUUM Phonics

PreK	K	1	2	3	4
Young children play with sounds and rhymes, recite the alphabet, and identify some letters, including those in their names.	Kindergartners identify the letters of the alphabet and the sounds they represent, and they decode short-vowel words.	Students blend consonant and short vowel sounds to read CVC words and use phonics rules to decode long-vowel words.	Second graders use consonant blends and digraphs and vowel digraphs and diphthongs to decode more challenging one-syllable words.	Third graders break unfamiliar two- and three-syllable words into syllables and apply phonics to decode these words.	Most fourth graders know how to use phonics to effectively decode and spell one-syllable and longer unfamiliar words.

are side by side at the end of a word, they represent a long vowel sound; in *day*, the vowel sound is long *a*. Primary grade students learn these phonics concepts to decode unfamiliar words.

CONSONANTS. Phonemes are classified as either consonants or vowels. The **consonants** are *b, c, d, f, g, h, j, k, l, m, n, p, q, r, s, t, v, w, x, y*, and *z*. Most consonants represent a single sound consistently, but there are some exceptions. *C*, for example, doesn't represent a sound of its own: When it's followed by *a, o,* or *u*, it's pronounced /k/ (e.g., *cat, coffee, cut*), and when it's followed by *e, i,* or *y*, it's pronounced /s/, as in *city*. *G* represents two sounds, as the word *garbage* illustrates: It's usually pronounced /g/ (e.g., *gate, go, guppy*), but when *g* is followed by *e, i,* or *y*, it's pronounced /j/, as in *giant*. *X* is also pronounced differently according to its location in a word. At the beginning of a word, it's often pronounced /z/, as in *xylophone*, but sometimes the letter name is used, as in *x-ray*. At the end of a word, *x* is pronounced /ks/, as in *box*. The letters *w* and *y* are particularly interesting: At the beginning of a word or a syllable, they're consonants (e.g., *wind, yard*), but when they're in the middle or at the end, they're vowels (e.g., *saw, flown, day, by*).

Two kinds of combination consonants are blends and digraphs. **Consonant blends** occur when two or three consonants appear next to each other in words and their individual sounds are "blended" together, as in *grass, belt,* and *spring*. **Consonant digraphs** are letter combinations representing single sounds that aren't represented by either letter; the four most common are *ch* as in *chair* and *each, sh* as in *shell* and *wish, th* as in *father* and *both,* and *wh* as in *whale*. Another consonant digraph is *ph*, as in *photo* and *graph*.

VOWELS. The remaining five letters—*a, e, i, o,* and *u*—represent vowels, and *w* and *y* are **vowels** when used in the middle and at the end of a syllable or word. Vowels often represent several sounds. The two most common are short and long vowels. Short vowels marked with the symbol ˘, called a *breve*, and long vowels are marked with the symbol ¯, called a *macron*. The short vowel sounds are /ă/ as in *cat*, /ĕ/ as in *bed*, /ĭ/ as in *win*, /ŏ/ as in *hot*, and /ŭ/ as in *cup*. The long vowel sounds—/ā/, /ē/, /ī/, /ō/, and /ŭ/—are pronounced the same as their letter names, and they're illustrated in the words *make, feet, bike, coal,* and *rule*. Long vowel sounds are usually spelled with two vowels, except when the long vowel is at the end of a one-syllable word or a syllable, as in *she* or *secret* and *try* or *tribal*. When *y* is a vowel by itself at the end of a word, it's pronounced as long *e* or long *i*, depending on the length of the word: In one-syllable words such as *by* and *cry*, the *y* is pronounced as long *i*, but in longer words such as *baby* and *happy*, the *y* is usually pronounced as long *e*.

Vowel sounds are more complicated than consonant sounds, and there are many vowel combinations representing long vowels and other vowel sounds. Consider these combinations:

ai as in *nail*	*oa* as in *soap*
au as in *laugh* and *caught*	*oi* as in *oil*
aw as in *saw*	*oo* as in *cook* and *moon*
ea as in *peach* and *bread*	*ou* as in *house* and *through*
ew as in *sew* and *few*	*ow* as in *now* and *snow*
ia as in *dial*	*oy* as in *toy*
ie as in *cookie*	

Most vowel combinations are vowel digraphs or diphthongs: When two vowels represent a single sound, the combination is a **vowel digraph** (e.g., *nail*, *snow*), and when the two vowels represent a glide from one sound to another, the combination is a **diphthong**. Two vowel combinations that are consistently diphthongs are *oi* and *oy*, but other combinations, such as *ou* as in *house* (but not in *through*) and *ow* as in *now* (but not in *snow*), are diphthongs because they represent a glided sound. In *through*, the *ou* represents the /ū/ sound as in *moon*, and in *snow*, the *ow* represents the /ō/ sound.

When one or more vowels in a word are followed by an *r*, it's called an *r-controlled vowel* because the *r* influences the pronunciation of the vowel sound. For example, say these words: *award, nerve, squirt, horse, surf, square, stairs, pearl, cheer, where, pier, board, floor, scored, fourth,* and *cure*. Some words have a single vowel plus *r*, others have two vowels plus *r*, while still others have the *r* in between the vowels. Single vowels with *r* are more predictable than the other types. The most consistent *r*-controlled vowels are *ar* as in *shark* and *or* as in *born*. The remaining single vowel + *r* combinations—*er, ir,* and *ur*—are difficult to spell because they're often pronounced /ûr/ in words, including *herd, father, girls, first, burn,* and *nurse*.

Three-letter spellings of *r*-controlled vowels are more complicated; they include *-are* (*care*), *-ear* (*fear*), *-ere* (*here*), *-oar* (*roar*), and *-our* (*your*). Consider these *-ear* words, in which the vowel sound is pronounced four ways: *bears, beard, cleared, early, earth, hear, heard, heart, learner, pear, pearls, spear, wearing, yearly,* and *yearn*. The most common pronunciation for *ear* is /ûr/, as in *earth, learner,* and *pearls*; this pronunciation is used when *ear* is followed by a consonant, except in *heart* and *beard*. The next most common pronunciation is found in *cleared* and *spear*, where the vowel sounds the same as in the word *ear*. In several words, including *bear* and *wearing*, the vowel sound is pronounced as in the word *air*. Finally, in *heart*, *ear* is pronounced as in *car*. Teachers usually introduce the more predictable ways to decode *r*-controlled vowels, but students learn words with less common pronunciations, including *award, courage, flour, heart, here, very,* and *work*, in other ways.

The vowels in the unaccented syllables of multisyllabic words are often softened and pronounced "uh," as in the first syllable of *about* and *machine*, and the final syllable of *pencil, tunnel, zebra,* and *selection*. This vowel sound is called *schwa* and is represented in dictionaries with, which looks like an inverted *e*.

BLENDING INTO WORDS.   Readers blend or combine sounds to decode words. Even though students may identify each sound, one by one, they must also be able to blend them together. For example, to read the short-vowel word *best*, students identify /b//ĕ/ /s//t/ and then combine them to form the word. For long-vowel words, students identify the vowel pattern as well as the surrounding letters. In *pancake*, for example, students identify /p//ă//n//k//ā//k/ and recognize that the *e* at the end of the word is silent and marks the preceding vowel as long. Shefelbine (1995) emphasizes the importance of blending and explains that students who have difficulty decoding words usually know the sound-symbol correspondences but can't blend the sounds into recognizable words. Blending is a phonemic awareness strategy, and students who haven't had practice blending speech sounds into words are likely to have trouble decoding unfamiliar words.

PHONOGRAMS.   One-syllable words and syllables in longer words can be divided into two parts—the onset and the rime. The **onset** is the consonant sound, if any, that precedes the vowel, and the **rime** is the vowel and any consonant sounds that follow it. For example, in *show, sh* is the onset and *ow* is the rime, and in *ball, b* is the onset and *all* is the rime. For *at* and *up*, there is no onset; the entire word is the rime. Research has shown that students make more errors decoding and spelling the rime than the onset and more errors on vowels than on consonants (Caldwell & Leslie, 2013). In fact, rimes may provide an important key to word identification.

Wylie and Durrell (1970) identified 37 rimes, including *-ay, -ing, -oke,* and *-ump,* that are found in nearly 500 common words; these rimes and some words using each one are presented in Figure 4–2. Knowing these rimes and recognizing common words made from them are very helpful for beginning readers because they can use the words to decode other words (Cunningham, 2013). For example, when students know the *-ay* rime and recognize *say,* they use this knowledge to pronounce *clay*: They identify the *-ay* rime and blend *cl* with *ay* to decode the word. This strategy is called *decoding by analogy,* which you'll read more about in Chapter 6, "Developing Fluent Readers and Writers."

Teachers refer to rimes as **phonograms,** or word families, when they teach them, even though *phonogram* is a misnomer; by definition, a *phonogram* is a letter or group of letters that represent a single sound. Two of the rimes, *-aw* and *-ay,* represent single sounds, but the other 35 don't.

Figure 4–2 The 37 Rimes and Common Words Using Them

Rime	Examples	Rime	Examples
-ack	black, pack, quack, stack	-ide	bride, hide, ride, side
-ail	mail, nail, sail, tail	-ight	bright, fight, light, might
-ain	brain, chain, plain, rain	-ill	fill, hill, kill, will
-ake	cake, shake, take, wake	-in	chin, grin, pin, win
-ale	male, sale, tale, whale	-ine	fine, line, mine, nine
-ame	came, flame, game, name	-ing	king, sing, thing, wing
-an	can, man, pan, than	-ink	pink, sink, think, wink
-ank	bank, drank, sank, thank	-ip	drip, hip, lip, ship
-ap	cap, clap, map, slap	-it	bit, flit, quit, sit
-ash	cash, dash, flash, trash	-ock	block, clock, knock, sock
-at	bat, cat, rat, that	-oke	choke, joke, poke, woke
-ate	gate, hate, late, plate	-op	chop, drop, hop, shop
-aw	claw, draw, jaw, saw	-ore	chore, more, shore, store
-ay	day, play, say, way	-ot	dot, got, knot, trot
-eat	beat, heat, meat, wheat	-uck	duck, luck, suck, truck
-ell	bell, sell, shell, well	-ug	bug, drug, hug, rug
-est	best, chest, nest, west	-ump	bump, dump, hump, lump
-ice	mice, nice, rice, slice	-unk	bunk, dunk, junk, sunk
-ick	brick, pick, sick, thick		

Figure 4–3 Excerpt From a Word Wall of Phonograms

-ock		-oke		-old	
block	lock	broke	poke	bold	hold
clock	rock	Coke	smoke	cold	sold
dock	sock	choke	woke	fold	told
flock		joke		gold	
		*soak			

-op		-ore		-ot	
cop	pop	more	store	dot	lot
chop	plop	sore	tore	got	not
drop	shop	shore	wore	hot	shot
hop	stop	snore		knot	spot
mop	top				
		*door *pour *soar			
		*floor *your *war			

* = exceptions

Beginning readers often read and write words using each phonogram. Second graders can read and write these words made using the *-ain* rime: *brain, chain, drain, grain, main, pain, plain, rain, sprain, stain,* and *train.* Students must be familiar with consonant blends and digraphs to read and spell these words. Teachers often post lists of words students create using phonograms on a **word wall**, as shown in Figure 4–3. Each phonogram and the words made using it are written in a separate section. Teachers use the words on the word wall for a variety of phonics activities, and students refer to it to spell words when they're writing.

Phonics Rules

Because English has an imperfect correspondence between sounds and letters, linguists have created rules to clarify English spelling patterns. One rule is that *q* is followed by *u* and pronounced /kw/, as in *queen, quick,* and *earthquake; Iraq, Qantas,* and other names are exceptions. Another rule that has few exceptions relates to *r*-controlled vowels: *r* influences the preceding vowels so that they're neither long nor short. Examples are *car, wear,* and *four.* There are exceptions, however; one is *fire.*

Many rules aren't very useful because there are more exceptions than words that conform (Clymer, 1963). A good example is this long-vowel rule: When there are two adjacent vowels, the long vowel sound of the first one is pronounced and the second is silent; teachers sometimes call this the "when two vowels go walking, the first one does the talking" rule. Examples of conforming words are *meat, soap,* and *each.* There are many more exceptions, however, including *food, said, head, chief, bread, look, soup, does, too,* and *again.*

Students should learn the rules that work most of the time because they're the most useful (Adams, 1990). Eight useful rules are listed in Figure 4–4. Even though they're fairly reliable, very few of them approach 100% utility. The rule about *r*-controlled vowels just mentioned has been calculated to be useful in 78% of words in which the letter *r* follows the vowel (Adams, 1990). Other commonly taught rules have even lower percentages of utility. The CVC pattern rule—which says that when a one-syllable word has only one vowel and the vowel comes between two consonants, it's usually short, as in *bat, land,* and *cup*—is estimated to work only 62% of the time. Exceptions include *told, fall, fork,* and *birth.* The CVCe pattern rule—which says that when there are two vowels in a one-syllable word and one vowel is an *e* at the end of the word, the first vowel is long and the final *e* is silent—is estimated to work in 63% of CVCe words. Examples of conforming words are *came, hole,* and *pipe;* but three very common words—*have, come,* and *love*—are exceptions.

Figure 4–4 The Most Useful Phonics Rules

Pattern	Description	Examples	
Two sounds of c	The letter c can be pronounced /k/ or /s/. When c is followed by a, o, or u, it's pronounced /k/—the hard c sound. When c is followed by e, i, or y, it's pronounced /s/—the soft c sound.	cat cough cut	cent city cycle
Two sounds of g	The sound associated with g depends on the letter following it. When g is followed by a, o, or u, it's pronounced /g/—the hard g sound. When g is followed by e, i, or y, it's usually pronounced /j/—the soft g sound. Exceptions include get and give.	gate go guess	gentle giant gypsy
CVC pattern	When a one-syllable word has only one vowel and the vowel comes between two consonants, it's usually short. One exception is told.	bat cup land	
Final e or CVCe pattern	When there are two vowels in a one-syllable word and one is an e at the end of the word, the first vowel is long and the final e is silent. Three exceptions are have, come, and love.	home safe tune	
CV pattern	When a vowel follows a consonant in a one-syllable word, the vowel is long. Exceptions include the, to, and do.	go she	
r-controlled vowels	Vowels that are followed by r are overpowered and are neither short nor long. One exception is fire.	car dear	birth pair
-igh	When gh follows i, the i is long and the gh is silent. One exception is neighbor.	high night	
kn- and wr-	In words beginning with kn- and wr-, the first letter isn't pronounced.	knee write	

MyLab Education **Self-Check 4.3**

Teaching Phonics

The best way to teach phonics is through a combination of explicit instruction and authentic application activities. The National Reading Panel (2000) reviewed the research about phonics instruction and concluded that the most effective programs were systematic; that is, the most useful phonics skills are taught in a predetermined sequence. Most teachers begin with consonants and then introduce the short vowels so that students can read and spell consonant-vowel-consonant or CVC-pattern words, such as *dig* and *cup*. Then students learn about consonant blends, digraphs, and long vowels so that they can read and spell consonant-vowel-consonant-*e* or CVCe-pattern

Teach Kids to Be Strategic!

Phonics Strategies

Teach students to use these strategies to decode words:

- Sound it out
- Decode by analogy
- Apply phonics rules

They practice the strategies as they participate in guided reading, word wall activities, and other reading activities. Look for students to apply them during reading workshop and other types of independent reading. If they struggle, reteach the developmentally appropriate strategy, making sure to name it, model its use, and talk about its application.

Figure 4–5 Sequence of Phonics Instruction

Grade	Skills	Description	Examples
K	More common consonants	Students identify consonant sounds, match sounds to letters, and substitute sounds in words.	/b/, /d/, /f/, /m/, /n/, /p/, /s/, /t/
K–1	Less common consonants	Students identify consonant sounds, match sounds to letters, and substitute sounds in words.	/g/, /h/, /j/, /k/, /l/, /q/, /v/, /w/, /x/, /y/, /z/
	Short vowels	Students identify the five short vowel sounds and match them to letters.	/ă/ = cat, /ĕ/ = bed, /ĭ/ = pig, /ŏ/ = hot, /ŭ/ = cut
	CVC pattern	Students read and spell CVC-pattern words.	dad, men, sit, hop, but
1	Consonant blends	Students identify and blend consonant sounds at the beginnings and ends of words.	/pl/ = plant /str/ = string
	Phonograms	Students break CVC words into onsets and rimes and use phonograms to form new words.	not: dot, shot, spot will: still, fill, drill
	Consonant digraphs	Students identify consonant digraphs, match sounds to letters, and read and spell words with consonant digraphs.	/ch/ = chop /sh/ = dash /th/ = with /wh/ = when
	Long vowel sounds	Students identify the five long vowel sounds and match them to letters.	/ā/= name, /ē/ = bee, /ī/ = ice, /ō/ = soap, /ū/ = tune
	CVCe pattern	Students read and spell CVCe-pattern words.	game, ride, stone
	Common long vowel digraphs	Students identify the vowel sound represented by common long vowel digraphs and read and spell words using them.	/ā/ = ai (rain), ay (day) /ē/ = ea (reach), ee (sweet) /ō/ = oa (soap), ow (know)
1–2	w and y	Students recognize when w and y are consonants and when they're vowels, and identify the sounds they represent.	window, yesterday y = /ī/ (by) y = /ē/ (baby)
	Phonograms	Students divide long vowel words into onsets and rimes and use phonograms to form new words.	woke: joke, broke, smoke day: gray, day, stay
	Hard and soft consonant sounds	Students identify the hard and soft sounds represented by c and g, and read and spell words using them.	g = girl (*hard*), gem (*soft*) c = cat (*hard*), city (*soft*)
2–3	Less common vowel digraphs	Students identify the sounds of less common vowel digraphs and read and spell words using them.	/ô/ = al (walk), au (caught), aw (saw), ou (bought) /ā/ = ei (weigh) /ē/ = ey (key), ie (chief) /ī/ = ie (pie) /o͞o/ = oo (good), ou (could) /ū/ = oo (moon), ew (new), ue (blue), ui (fruit)
	Vowel diphthongs	Students identify the vowel diphthongs and read and write words using them.	/oi/ = oi (boil), oy (toy) /ou/ = ou (cloud), ow (down)
	Less common consonant digraphs	Students identify the sounds of less common consonant digraphs and read and write words using them.	ph = phone ng = sing gh = laugh tch = match
	r-controlled vowels	Students identify r-controlled vowel patterns and read and spell words using them.	/âr/ = hair, care, bear, there, their /ar/ = heart, star /er/ = clear, deer, here /or/ = born, more, warm /ûr/ = learn, first, work, burn

words, such as *broke* and *white*, and consonant-vowel-vowel-consonant (CVVC)-patterned words, such as *clean, wheel*, and *snail*. Finally, students learn about the less common vowel digraphs and diphthongs, such as *claw, bought, shook*, and *boil*, and r-controlled vowels, including *square, hard, four*, and *year*. Figure 4–5 details this instructional sequence of phonics skills.

Students also learn strategies to use in identifying unfamiliar words (Mesmer & Griffith, 2005). Three of the most useful strategies are sounding out words, decoding by analogy, and applying phonics rules. When students sound out words, they convert letters and patterns of letters into sounds and blend them to pronounce the word; it's most effective when students are reading regular one-syllable words phonetically. In the second strategy, decoding by analogy, students apply their knowledge of phonograms

> **MY TEACHING TO-DO CHECKLIST: Cracking the Alphabetic Code!**
> ☐ I teach the high-utility phonics concepts that are most useful for reading unfamiliar words.
> ☐ I follow a developmental continuum for systematic phonics instruction, beginning with rhyming and ending with phonics rules.
> ☐ I provide explicit instruction to teach phonics strategies and skills.
> ☐ I provide opportunities for students to apply what they're learning about phonics through word sorts, making words, interactive writing, and other literacy activities.
> ☐ I take advantage of teachable moments to clarify misunderstandings and infuse phonics instruction into literacy activities.
> ☐ I use oral activities to reinforce phonemic awareness strategies as students blend and segment written words during phonics and spelling instruction.
> ☐ I review phonics as part of spelling, when necessary, in the upper grades.
> ☐ I integrate state standards into my instruction.

to analyze the structure of an unfamiliar word (White, 2005); they use known words to recognize unfamiliar ones. For example, if students are familiar with *will*, they can use it to identify *grill*. They also apply phonics rules to identify unfamiliar words, such as *while* and *clean*. These strategies are especially useful when students don't recognize many words, but they become less important as readers gain more experience and can recognize most words automatically.

The second component of phonics instruction is daily opportunities for students to apply the phonics strategies and skills they're learning in authentic reading and writing activities (National Reading Panel, 2000). Cunningham and Cunningham (2002) estimate that the ratio of time spent on real reading and writing to time spent on phonics instruction should be 3 to 1. Without this meaningful application of what they're learning, phonics instruction is often ineffective (Dahl, Scharer, Lawson, & Grogan, 2001).

Phonics instruction begins in kindergarten when students learn to connect consonant and short vowel sounds to the letters, and it's completed by third grade because older students rarely benefit from it (Ivey & Baker, 2004; National Reading Panel, 2000). Use **My Teaching To-Do Checklist: Cracking the Alphabetic Code!** to evaluate your teaching effectiveness.

EXPLICIT INSTRUCTION. Teachers present **minilessons** on phonics concepts to the whole class or to small groups of students, depending on their instructional needs. They follow the minilesson format, explicitly presenting information about a phonics strategy or skill, demonstrating how to use it, and presenting words for students to use in guided practice, as Mrs. Firpo did in the vignette at the beginning of the chapter. During the minilesson, teachers use these activities to provide guided practice opportunities for students to manipulate sounds and read and write words:

MyLab Education
Video Example 4.4
In this video, Dr. Timothy Shanahan discusses the importance of literacy development in the early grades. What is the significance of intervention for young students who struggle?

- Sort objects, pictures, and word cards according to a phonics concept.
- Write letters or words on small whiteboards.
- Arrange magnetic letters or letter cards to spell words.
- Make class charts of words representing phonics concepts, such as the two sounds of *g* or the -*ore* phonogram.
- Make a poster or book of words representing a phonics concept.
- Locate other words exemplifying the spelling pattern in books the students are reading.

The Minilesson shows how a first grade teacher teaches a minilesson on reading and spelling CVC-pattern words using final consonant blends.

Minilesson

TOPIC: Decoding CVC Words With Final Consonant Blends
GRADE: First Grade
TIME: One 30-minute period

Mrs. Nazir is teaching her first graders about consonant blends. She introduced initial consonant blends to the class, and students practiced reading and spelling words, such as *club, drop,* and *swim,* that were chosen from the selection they were reading in their basal readers. Then, in small groups, they completed workbook pages and made words using plastic tiles with onsets and rimes printed on them. For example, using the *-ip* phonogram, they made *clip, drip, flip, skip,* and *trip.* This is the fifth whole-class lesson in the series. Today, Mrs. Nazir is introducing final consonant blends.

1. **Introduce the Topic**
   Mrs. Nazir explains that blends are also used at the ends of words. She writes these words on the whiteboard: *best, rang, hand, pink,* and *bump.* Together the students sound them out: They pronounce the initial consonant sound, the short vowel sound, and the final consonants. They blend the final consonants and then blend the entire word and say it aloud. Students use the words in sentences to ensure that everyone understands them. Dillon, T.J., Pauline, Cody, and Brittany circle the blends in the words on the whiteboard. The teacher points out that *st* is a familiar blend also used at the beginnings of words, but that the other blends are used only at the ends.

2. **Share Examples**
   Mrs. Nazir says these words: *must, wing, test, band, hang, sink, bend,* and *bump.* The first graders repeat each word, isolate the blend, and identify it. Carson says, "The word is *must*—/m/ /ŭ/ /s/ /t/—and the blend is *st* at the end." Bryan points out that Ng is his last name, and everyone claps because his name is so special. Several students volunteer additional words: Dillon suggests *blast,* and Henry adds *dump* and *string.* Then the teacher passes out word cards and students read the words, including *just, lamp, went,* and *hang.* They sound out each word carefully, pronouncing the initial consonant, the short vowel, and the final consonant blend. Then they blend the sounds and say the word.

3. **Provide Information**
   Mrs. Nazir posts a piece of chart paper and labels it "The *-ink* Word Family." The students brainstorm these words with the *-ink* phonogram: *blink, sink, pink, rink, mink, stink,* and *wink,* and they take turns writing the words on the chart. They also suggest *twinkle* and *wrinkle,* and Mrs. Nazir adds them to the chart.

4. **Guide Practice**
   Students create other word family charts using *-and, -ang, -ank, -end, -ent, -est, -ing, -ump,* and *-ust.* Each group brainstorms at least five words and writes them on the chart. Mrs. Nazir monitors students' work and helps them think of additional words and correct spelling errors. Then students post their word family charts and share them with the class.

5. **Assess Learning**
   Mrs. Nazir observes the first graders as they brainstorm words, blend sounds, and spell the words. She notices several students who need more practice and will call them together for a follow-up lesson.

APPLICATION ACTIVITIES. Students apply the phonics concepts they're learning as they read and write and participate in teacher-directed activities. In **interactive writing**, for example, students segment words into sounds and take turns writing letters and sometimes whole words on the chart (McCarrier, Pinnell, & Fountas, 2000; Tompkins & Collom, 2004). Teachers help students correct any errors, and they take advantage of teachable moments to review consonant and vowel sounds, spelling patterns, handwriting skills, and rules for capitalization and punctuation. Teachers use activities such as **making words**, **word ladders**, and **word sorts** to provide opportunities for students to practice what they're learning about **phoneme–grapheme correspondences**, word families, and phonics rules.

Assessing Students' Phonics Knowledge

Teachers assess students' developing phonics knowledge using a combination of tests, observation, and reading and writing samples. They often use a test to screen students at the beginning of the school year, monitor their progress at midyear, and document their achievement at the end of the year. When students aren't making expected progress, teachers administer a test to diagnose the problem and plan for instruction. Three tests that assess students' phonics knowledge are described in this Assessment Tools feature.

THE INSTRUCTION–ASSESSMENT CYCLE. Teachers use the four-step instruction–assessment cycle to plan, teach, and evaluate students' learning and the effectiveness of their instruction.

Step 1: Planning. Teachers plan developmentally appropriate instruction using their knowledge about students' current stage of phonics development, and they

Assessment Tools

Phonics

Teachers screen students' phonics knowledge by administering these tests before planning for instruction:

- **Observation Survey of Early Literacy Achievement (OS): Word Reading and Hearing and Recording Sounds in Words Subtests**
  The OS (Clay, 2013) consists of six subtests. The Word Reading and the Hearing and Recording Sounds in Words subtests are used to assess students' ability to apply phonics concepts to decode and spell words. The subtests are administered individually, and students' scores for each subtest can be standardized and converted to stanines. The OS is published by Heinemann Books.

- **Dynamic Indicators of Basic Early Literacy Skills (DIBELS): Nonsense Word Fluency Subtest**
  This individually administered subtest assesses students' ability to apply phonics concepts to read two-and three-letter nonsense words (e.g., *ap*, *jid*). Multiple forms are available, so this test can be used to monitor students' progress during kindergarten and first grade. The test is available at the DIBELS website free of charge, but there's a fee for scoring tests and reporting scores.

- **The Tile Test**
  This individually administered test (Norman & Calfee, 2004) assesses students' knowledge of phonics. Students manipulate letter tiles to make words, and teachers also arrange tiles to spell words for them to read. The Tile Test can easily be administered in 10 to 15 minutes. It's available online and free of charge.

These tests are useful tools for assessing entire classes or individual students who are struggling.

identify Common Core State Standards they're expected to teach. The two most important considerations are that the instruction is developmentally appropriate and reflects grade-level Standards, and that the assessment will accurately measure the specific concepts and strategies that teachers will teach.

Step 2: Monitoring.   Teachers observe students as they participate in phonics activities and while reading and writing to see how well they're applying the phonics strategies and skills they're learning. When students use magnetic letters to write words with the *-at* phonogram, such as *bat, cat, hat, mat, rat,* and *sat,* for example, they're demonstrating their phonics knowledge. They also show what they've learned during interactive writing, making words, and word sort activities. Similarly, as teachers listen to students read aloud or read students' writing, they analyze their errors to determine which phonics concepts students are confusing or those they don't yet understand.

Step 3: Evaluating.   The best way that students demonstrate their newly learned phonics knowledge is by reading and writing unfamiliar words. Having them apply their knowledge through authentic reading and writing activities is important, but teachers can also ask them to demonstrate their knowledge by sorting packs of word cards, using magnetic letters to spell words, and playing phonics games.

Step 4: Reflecting.   Students often reflect on their achievement by highlighting how many more words they now know how to read and spell. Teachers also reflect on the effectiveness of their instruction, considering how well students learned the concepts and strategies and thinking about how they can improve their effectiveness.

If Students Struggle . . .

Phonics is only one component of a balanced literacy program for young students, but it's an essential part so teachers quickly take steps to assist beginning readers in overcoming their difficulties. Most students learn phoneme–grapheme correspondences (e.g., /m/ is represented in print by the letter *m*) without too many difficulties; it's more likely that they're having trouble blending sounds into words and applying phonics rules. Too often students guess at words based on the first letter or they sound out the letters, one by one, without blending the sounds or thinking about phonics patterns.

The first step is to identify the specific problem, and teachers usually analyze test results to determine students' instructional needs. Next, teachers prepare lessons to reteach the phonics concepts that students haven't learned. They provide explicit instruction, and then students have opportunities to apply what they're learning, first in guided practice activities and then in authentic reading and writing activities. During their lessons, teachers provide information and involve students in hands-on reading and writing activities where they build words using foam letters, read books at their instructional level, highlight words in a text they've read, sort words according to vowel patterns, and spell words on whiteboards. Struggling readers and writers often need extended guided practice before they're ready to apply the concepts and strategies independently.

What's the Role of Phonics in a Balanced Literacy Program?

Phonics is a controversial topic. Some parents and politicians, and even a few teachers, believe that most of our educational ills could be solved if students were taught to read using phonics. A few people still argue that phonics is a complete reading program, but that view ignores what we know about the interrelatedness of the four cueing systems. Reading is a complex process, and the phonological system works in conjunction with the semantic, syntactic, and pragmatic systems, not in isolation.

The controversy now centers on the best way to teach phonics. Marilyn Adams (1990), in her landmark review of the research on phonics instruction, recommends that phonics be taught within a balanced approach that integrates instruction in reading strategies and skills with meaningful opportunities for reading and writing. She emphasizes that phonics instruction should focus on the most useful information for identifying words, that it should be systematic and intensive, and that it should be completed by third grade.

> **MyLab Education** Self-Check 4.4

Chapter Review

Cracking the Alphabetic Code

- Teachers understand that phonological awareness includes three kinds of sound awareness; in order from largest to smallest, they are syllables, onset-rime, and phonemes.

- Teachers teach students to "crack the code" through phonemic awareness and phonics instruction.

- Teachers understand that phonemic awareness is the foundation for phonics instruction.

- Teachers teach high-quality phonics concepts, rules, and phonograms.

- Teachers regularly assess students' growing knowledge of phonics and their ability to apply what they've learned during reading and writing.

Accountability Check

Visit the following assessment links to access quiz questions and instructional applications.

> **MyLab Education** Application Exercise 4.2: Understanding Literacy Development
> **MyLab Education** Application Exercise 4.3: Understanding Literacy Development
> **MyLab Education** Application Exercise 4.4: Understanding Literacy Development
> **MyLab Education** Application Exercise 4.5: Monitoring Literacy Development
> **MyLab Education** Application Exercise 4.6: Measuring Literacy Development

References

Adams, M. J. (1990). *Beginning to read: Thinking and learning about print.* Cambridge, MA: MIT Press.

Afflerbach, P., Blachowicz, C. L. Z., Boyd, C. D., Cheyney, W., Juel, C., Kame'enui, E. J., et al. (2013). *Reading street.* Glenview, IL: Scott Foresman.

Armbruster, B. B., Lehr, F., & Osborn, J. (2001). *Put reading first: The research building blocks for teaching children to read.* Urbana, IL: Center for the Improvement of Early Reading Achievement.

Caldwell, J. S., & Leslie, L. (2013). *Intervention strategies to follow informal reading inventory assessment: So what do I do now?* (3rd ed.). Boston: Pearson.

Clay, M. M. (2005). *Literacy lessons: Designed for individuals (Part 1: Why? When? And how?).* Portsmouth, NH: Heinemann.

Clay, M. M. (2013). *An observation survey of early literacy achievement* (rev. ed.). Portsmouth, NH: Heinemann.

Clymer, T. (1963). The utility of phonic generalizations in the primary grades. *The Reading Teacher, 16,* 252–258.

Common core state standards for English language arts. (2010). Retrieved from http://www.corestandards.org

Cunningham, P. M. (2011). Best practices in teaching phonological awareness and phonics. In L. M. Morrow & L. B. Gambrell (Eds.), *Best practices in literacy instruction* (4th ed., pp. 199–223). New York: Guilford Press.

Cunningham, P. M. (2013). *Phonics they use: Words for reading and writing* (6th ed.). Boston: Pearson.

Cunningham, P. M., & Allington, R. L. (2011). *Classrooms that work: They can all read and write* (5th ed.). Boston: Allyn & Bacon/Pearson.

Cunningham, P. M., & Cunningham, J. W. (2002). What we know about how to teach phonics. In A. E. Farstrup & S. J. Samuels (Eds.), *What research has to say about reading instruction* (3rd ed., pp. 87–109). Newark, DE: International Reading Association.

Dahl, K. L., Scharer, P. L., Lawson, L. L., & Grogan, P. R. (2001). *Rethinking phonics: Making the best teaching decisions.* Portsmouth, NH: Heinemann.

Gillon, G. T. (2004). *Phonological awareness: From research to practice.* New York: Guilford Press.

Griffith, F., & Olson, M. (1992). Phonemic awareness helps beginning readers break the code. *The Reading Teacher, 45,* 516–523.

Hutchins, P. (2002). *Don't forget the bacon!* New York: Red Fox Books.

Ivey, G., & Baker, M. I. (2004). Phonics instruction for older students? Just say no. *Educational Leadership, 61*(6), 35–39.

Juel, C., Griffith, P. L., & Gough, P. B. (1986). Acquisition of literacy: A longitudinal study of children in first and second grade. *Journal of Educational Psychology, 78,* 243–255.

Klesius, J. P., Griffith, P. L., & Zielonka, P. (1991). A whole language and traditional instruction comparison: Overall effectiveness and development of the alphabetic principle. *Reading Research and Instruction, 30,* 47–61.

Lewkowicz, N. K. (1994). The bag game: An activity to heighten phonemic awareness. *The Reading Teacher, 47,* 508–509.

McCarrier, A., Pinnell, G. S., & Fountas, I. C. (2000). *Interactive writing: How language and literacy come together, K–2.* Portsmouth, NH: Heinemann.

Mesmer, H. A. E., & Griffith, P. L. (2005). Everybody's selling it—but just what is explicit, systematic phonics instruction? *The Reading Teacher, 59,* 366–376.

Most, B. (1996). *Cock-a-doodle-moo!* San Diego: Harcourt Brace.

National Reading Panel. (2000). *Teaching children to read: An evidence-based assessment of the scientific research literature on reading and its implications for reading instruction.* Washington, DC: National Institute of Child Health and Human Development.

Norman, K. A., & Calfee, R. C. (2004). Tile Test: A hands-on approach for assessing phonics in the early grades. *The Reading Teacher, 58,* 42–52.

Osborne, M. P. (2003). *High tide in Hawaii.* New York: Random House.

Park, B. (2003). *Junie B., first grader: Boss of lunch.* New York: Random House.

Peregoy, S. F., & Boyle, O. F. (2013). *Reading, writing and learning in ESL: A resource book for K–12 teachers* (6th ed.). Boston: Pearson.

Riches, C., & Genesee, F. (2006). Literacy: Cross-linguistic and crossmodal issues. In F. Genesee, K. Lindholm-Leary, W. M. Saunders, & D. Christian (Eds.), *Educating English language learners: A synthesis of research evidence* (pp. 64–108). New York: Cambridge University Press.

Root, P. (2004). *Rattletrap car.* Cambridge, MA: Candlewick Press.

Seuss, Dr. (1963). *Hop on pop.* New York: Random House.

Seuss, Dr. (1965). *Fox in socks.* New York: Random House.

Shefelbine, J. (1995). *Learning and using phonics in beginning reading* (Literacy research paper; volume 10). New York: Scholastic.

Snow, C. E., Burns, M. S., & Griffin, P. (Eds.). (1998). *Preventing reading difficulties in young children.* Washington, DC: National Academy Press.

Strickland, D. S., & Schickedanz, J. A. (2009). *Learning about print in preschool* (2nd ed.). Newark, DE: International Reading Association.

Tompkins, G. E., & Collom, S. (Eds.). (2004). *Sharing the pen: Interactive writing with young children.* Upper Saddle River, NJ: Merrill/Prentice Hall.

Venezky, R. L. (1999). *The American way of spelling: The structure and origins of American English orthography.* New York: Guilford Press.

White, T. G. (2005). Effects of systematic and strategic analogy-based phonics on grade 2 students' word reading and reading comprehension. *Reading Research Quarterly, 40,* 234–255.

Wylie, R. E., & Durrell, D. D. (1970). Teaching vowels through phonograms. *Elementary English, 47,* 787–791.

Yopp, H. K. (1988). The validity and reliability of phonemic awareness tests. *Reading Research Quarterly, 23,* 159–177.

Yopp, H. K. (1992). Developing phonemic awareness in young children. *The Reading Teacher, 45,* 696–703.

Yopp, H. K., & Yopp, R. H. (2000). Supporting phonemic awareness development in the classroom. *The Reading Teacher, 54,* 130–143.

Chapter 5
Learning to Spell

Learning Outcomes

After studying this chapter, you'll be prepared to:

5.1 Describe the stages of spelling development that students move through as they learn to spell words conventionally.

5.2 List the components of a complete spelling program.

5.3 Describe how teachers assess students' spelling development.

Differentiating Spelling Instruction

Iofoto/Shutterstock

The 21 third graders in Mrs. Zumwalt's class have different spelling needs because they're working at varying levels of spelling development. During the first week of the school year, Mrs. Zumwalt collected writing samples, analyzed students' misspelling errors, and determined each student's stage of spelling development. She continues to analyze their spelling at the end of each quarter and regroup them for instruction. According to her most recent assessment, five students are Within-Word Pattern spellers: They're confusing more complex consonant and vowel patterns. Nick spells *headache* as HEDAKKE, *soap* as SOPE, and *heart* as HART; Jovana spells *wild* as WILDE, *ears* as ERARS, and *found* as FOEUND. Thirteen others spell at the Syllables and Affixes stage: They spell most one-syllable words correctly; their errors involve inflectional endings and the schwa sound in unaccented syllables. Maribel spells *coming* as COMEING; Raziel spells *uncle* as UNKOL and *believed* as BEELEVED. Three others are more sophisticated spellers; Aaron, for example, spells *actor* as ACTER, *collection* as CULECTION, and *pneumonia* as NEWMONIA. These students are beginning the transition into the Derivational Relations stage, where they'll learn Latin and Greek root words and affixes.

Mrs. Zumwalt spends 30 minutes every morning on spelling. On Monday, she administers the pretest for the textbook spelling program that her school uses, and on Friday, she administers the final test. On Tuesdays, Wednesdays, and Thursdays, while

In this chapter, you'll learn that students develop knowledge about spelling as they progress through a series of five stages: Emergent spelling, Letter Name-Alphabetic spelling, Within-Word Pattern spelling, Syllables and Affixes spelling, and Derivational Relations spelling. Teachers plan instruction based on students' developmental levels as well as to meet grade-level standards. As you read this vignette, notice how Mrs. Zumwalt targets her instruction to her students' developmental levels.

students practice the spelling words independently, she teaches **minilessons** to small groups. The topics she chooses for the lessons address her students' needs and the third grade Common Core State Standards.

One day, Mrs. Zumwalt teaches a minilesson to half of the class comparing plurals and possessives because the Syllables and Affixes stage spellers are misusing apostrophes in plurals. For example, one student writes:

The boy's rode their bike's up the biggest hill in town to Chavez Park.

Afterward, the third graders review their journals, locate three interesting sentences using either plurals or possessives, and copy them onto sentence strips. During a follow-up minilesson, they share their sentences, identify the plurals or possessives, and correct any errors. Mrs. Zumwalt notices that several students are still confused about plurals and possessives, so she'll continue to work with them.

Another day, as the students are making **learning logs** for a unit on astronomy, several ask Mrs. Zumwalt why there's an unnecessary *c* following the *s* in the word *science*. She explains that *science* is a Latin word and that a few very special words that have come to English from Latin are spelled with both *s* and *c*. From that exchange, Mrs. Zumwalt decides to teach a minilesson about the ways to spell /s/. To begin, the third graders collect words with the /s/ sound from books they're reading, words posted in the classroom, and other words they know. After a day of collecting words, the students each write the five most interesting words they've found on small cards. Mrs. Zumwalt sorts the words and places them in rows on a pocket chart. Most of the words are spelled with *s* or *ss*, but several students found words using *c* or *ce* to spell /s/. Mrs. Zumwalt adds several other word cards with *se* and *sc* spellings. The students examine the Third Graders' Chart of Ways to Spell /S/ and draw some conclusions about how to spell the *s* sound.

Mrs. Zumwalt is teaching her third graders that good spellers think out the spellings of words; they don't just sound them out. She hung a "how to spell long words" chart in the classroom, and through a series of minilessons, the class develops these rules for spelling unfamiliar words:

1. Break the word into syllables.
2. Say each syllable to yourself.
3. Sound out the spelling of each syllable.
4. Think about rules for spelling vowels and endings.
5. Check to see that the word looks right.
6. Check the dictionary if you're not sure.
7. Ask a friend for help.

Mrs. Zumwalt frequently reviews this strategy chart with the students who are learning to spell two-syllable words. During the **minilesson**, she reads the steps and models each one using the word *welcome*. She breaks the word into two syllables, *well—come*, and writes it on chart paper, spelling it this way: WELLCOME. Then she looks at the word and asks the students to look, too. She says, "I've written *well* and *come*, but the word doesn't look right, does it? I think it looks wrong in the middle. Maybe there's only one *l* in *welcome*." She writes *welcome* under *wellcome* and asks the students if *welcome* looks better. They agree that it does, and Mrs. Zumwalt asks a student to check the spelling in the dictionary.

Then she chooses another word—*market*—and asks a student in the group to guide her through the steps. She follows the student's direction to divide *market* into two syllables—*mark—ket*—and writes the word on chart paper, spelling it *markket*. She looks at the word and tells the student that she thinks it looks correct, but the student disagrees, as do others. So, Mrs. Zumwalt looks at the word again and asks for help. The student explains that only one *k* is needed. Then Mrs. Zumwalt writes the word correctly on chart paper.

Third Graders' Chart of Ways To Spell /S/

Spelling	Examples	Nonexamples	Rules
s	said monsters sister misbehave taste	shop wish	*S* is the most common spelling, but *sh* does not make the *s* sound. *Sh* has a special sound.
c	cent bicycle city decide cereal mice circle face		When *c* is followed by *e*, *i*, or *y*, it makes the s sound.
ce	office dance sentence prince science fence voice juice	cent cement	*ce* is used only at the end of a word.
ss	class guessed kiss blossom fossil lesson		*Ss* is used in the middle and at the end of a word.
sc	scissors science scent	scare rascal	This spelling is unusual. It isn't a blend.
se	else house		This spelling is used only at the end of a word.

Mrs. Zumwalt passes out whiteboards and pens for students to use to practice spelling two-syllable words. First, they practice the strategy of breaking words into syllables with *turkey*. They follow the steps that Mrs. Zumwalt used, and she checks their spelling. Then they continue to practice the strategy using these words: *disturb, problem, number, garden, person,* and *orbit.* The group is very successful, so they ask Mrs. Zumwalt for more difficult words. They try these three-syllable words: *remember, hamburger, banana,* and *populate.*

The next day, Mrs. Zumwalt works with the group of students spelling at the Within-Word Pattern stage. These students still confuse long- and short-vowel words, so Mrs. Zumwalt has prepared a sorting game with similar words, including *rid—ride, hop—hope, cub—cube, slid—slide, cut—cute, pet—Pete, hat—hate, not—note,* and *mad—made.* She passes out envelopes with cards on which the words have been printed. The students sort their cards, matching up the related long- and short-vowel words. They practice reading the words and then write them on whiteboards. Finally, Mrs. Zumwalt asks the students to clarify the difference between the two groups of words; they've been asked this question before, but it's a hard question. The difference, they explain, is that the three-letter words have short vowels and the four-letter words have a final *e* and they're long-vowel words.

While Mrs. Zumwalt works with one group, the other students practice their spelling words. For each word, they spell it in their minds, write the word, and check the spelling using the procedure that Mrs. Zumwalt taught them earlier in the school year.

After they practice their spelling words, students choose spelling games to play. Some play the students' version of Boggle, and others play computer spelling games, explore the Franklin Spelling Ace, or work at the spelling center in the classroom. The spelling center has three packets of activities. One packet has 15 plastic bags with magnetic letters, which students use to spell the 15 spelling words. The second packet has word cards with inflectional endings for students to sort and arrange on the pocket chart hanging next to the center; the word cards include *bunnies, walked, cars, running, hopped, foxes,* and *sleeping*. Several weeks ago, Mrs. Zumwalt taught a series of minilessons about inflectional endings, and now these cards are at the spelling center for extra practice and review. The third packet contains plastic letters for a **making words** activity. This week's word is *grandfather*. Students work in small groups to spell as many words as possible: They manipulate the letters and arrange them to spell one-, two-, three-, four-, five-, and six-letter words. A completed sheet with 30 words made using the letters in *grandfather* is shown here.

On Friday, Mrs. Zumwalt administers the weekly spelling test. She reads the 15 words aloud, and students write them on their papers. Then she asks them to go back and look at each of the words and put a checkmark next to it if it looks right or circle the word if it doesn't. Some of her third graders—especially those at the Within-Word Pattern stage—haven't developed a visual sense of when words "look" right, and through this proofreading exercise, Mrs. Zumwalt is helping them learn to identify misspelled words in their writing. She finds that her more advanced spellers can accurately predict whether their spellings "look" right, but the others can't. As she grades their spelling tests, Mrs. Zumwalt gives extra credit to those students who accurately predict whether their words are spelled correctly.

Words Made Using The Letters In Grandfather

MAKING WORDS							
This week's word is: g r a n d f a t h e r							
1	2	3	4	5	6	7	8
a	at	and	hear	grand	father		
	he	the	hate	great			
	an	her	date	after			
		are	gate				
		hat	hare				
		eat	near				
		ate	tear				
		ear	gear				
		fat	then				
		ran	than				
		fan	hand				

Young students apply what they're learning about phonemic awareness and phonics when they spell words. When beginning writers want to write a word, they say the word slowly, segmenting the sounds; segmenting is a phonemic awareness strategy that writers use to spell words. Then they choose letters to represent the sounds they hear to spell the word. The letters students choose to represent sounds

Common Core State Standards

Spelling

The Common Core State Standards expect students to spell grade-appropriate words correctly. Younger students apply their phonics knowledge to spell phonetically regular words, and older students use additional spelling strategies. The Standards emphasize these points:

- Students apply phonics rules and spelling patterns to spell words conventionally.
- Students spell high frequency words conventionally.
- Students add inflectional suffixes (-*ed*, -*ing*, -*s*) to words correctly.
- Students use homonyms (e.g., *to, too, two*) conventionally.
- Students consult dictionaries to check and correct spelling errors.

To learn more about the spelling Standards, go to http://www.corestandards.org/ELA-Literacy, or check your state's educational standards website.

reflect what they've learned about phonics and spelling patterns. As is to be expected, many spellings are incorrect. Sometimes the spellings are very abbreviated or they're strictly phonetic and ignore spelling patterns. At other times, letters are reversed. These incorrect spellings are clear demonstrations of students' **phonological awareness**. As students' knowledge of English orthography—the spelling system—grows, their spellings increasingly approximate conventional spelling.

Consider the ways young students might spell the word *fairy*. A four-year-old might use scribbles or random letters to write the word or, perhaps, recognize the beginning sound of the word and use the letter *F* to represent the word. A kindergartner or first grader with well-developed phonemic awareness strategies could segment the word into its three sounds—/f //âr//ē/—and spell it FRE, using one letter to represent each sound. By second grade, a student with more knowledge of English spelling patterns might spell the word as FARIEY. This student also segments the word into its three sounds, hears the *r*-controlled vowel pattern, and correctly identifies the three letters used to spell the sound but reverses their order when writing them so that *air* is spelled ARI. The letters *ey* are used to spell the /ē/ sound, perhaps by analogy to the word *money*. Through more experiences reading and writing the word *fairy* and other words with the same sounds, third and fourth graders will learn to spell the word conventionally.

Amazingly, the majority of students move from spelling most words phonetically to spelling most words conventionally in less than four years! In Mrs. Zumwalt's classroom, for instance, most of her third graders correctly spell more than 90% of the words they write. Their understanding of the alphabetic principle—that letters represent sounds—matures through a combination of many, many opportunities to read and write combined with explicit spelling instruction. In the past, weekly spelling tests were the main instructional approach, but now they're only one part of a comprehensive spelling program.

The Common Core State Standards (2010) view spelling as a language tool and address the need for all students to become conventional spellers who can spell grade-appropriate words correctly. Students are expected to learn to spell high frequency words and to be strategic as they attempt to spell unfamiliar words. The Standards don't specify which instructional procedures to use to teach spelling, but this text recommends a comprehensive spelling program using the instructional procedures described in this chapter. This approach is more effective because students receive instruction and practice opportunities, and then they apply what they're learning in authentic and meaningful writing activities. The Common Core State Standards box presents additional information.

Stages Of Spelling Development

As young students begin to write, they create unique spellings based on their knowledge of **phonology** (Read, 1975). The students in Read's studies used letter names to spell words, such as U (*you*) and R (*are*), and they used consonant sounds rather consistently: GRL (*girl*), TIGR (*tiger*), and NIT (*night*). They used several unusual but phonetically based spelling patterns to represent affricates; for example, they replaced *tr* with *chr* (e.g., CHRIBLES for *troubles*) and *dr* with *jr* (e.g., JRAGIN for *dragon*). Words with long vowels were spelled using letter names: MI (*my*), LADE (*lady*), and FEL (*feel*). The students used several ingenious strategies to spell words with short vowels: The preschoolers selected letters to represent short vowels on the basis of place of articulation in the mouth. Short *i* was represented with *e*, as in FES (*fish*); short *e* with *a*, as in LAFFT (*left*); and short *o* with *i*, as in CLIK (*clock*). These spellings may seem odd to adults, but they reflect phonetic relationships.

Based on examinations of students' spellings, researchers have identified five stages that students move through on their way to becoming conventional spellers (Bear, Invernizzi, Templeton, & Johnston, 2016). At each stage, students use different strategies and focus on particular aspects of spelling that often reflect what they're learning about literacy. The characteristics of the five stages are summarized in Figure 5–1.

Stage 1: Emergent Spelling

Young students, typically three to five years old, are Emergent spellers. They make a variety of marks to represent writing, and over time they string scribbles, letters, and letterlike forms together; however, they don't associate the marks they make with any specific phonemes. Spelling at this stage represents a natural, early expression of the alphabet and other written language concepts. Students may write from left to right, right to left, top to bottom, or randomly across the page, but by the end of the stage, they have an understanding of directionality. Some Emergent spellers have a large repertoire of letterforms to use in writing, but others repeat a small number of letters over and over. Although they use both upper- and lowercase letters, they show a distinct preference for uppercase letters. During this stage, students learn these concepts:

Figure 5–1 Stages of Spelling Development

STAGE	DESCRIPTION	GRADES
Emergent	Students string scribbles, letters, and letterlike forms together, but they don't associate the marks they make with any specific phonemes.	PreK–K
Letter Name-Alphabetic	Students learn to represent phonemes in words with letters. At first, their spellings are quite abbreviated, but they learn to use consonant blends and digraphs and short-vowel patterns to spell many words.	K–1
Within-Word Pattern	Students learn long-vowel patterns and *r*-controlled vowels, but they may confuse spelling patterns and spell *meet* as METE, and they reverse the order of letters, such as FORM for *from* and GRIL for *girl*.	1–2
Syllables and Affixes	Students apply what they've learned about one-syllable words to spell longer words and learn to break words into syllables. They also learn to add inflectional endings (e.g., *-es, -ed, -ing*) and to differentiate between homonyms, such as *your-you're*.	2–4
Derivational relations	Students explore the relationship between spelling and meaning and learn that words with related meanings are often related in spelling despite changes in pronunciation (e.g., *wise-wisdom, sign-signal, nation-national*). They also learn about Latin and greek root words and derivational affixes (e.g., *amphi-, pre-, -able, -tion*).	5+

Based on Bear, Invernizzi, Templeton, & Johnston, 2016.

- The distinction between drawing and writing
- How to make letters
- The direction of writing on a page
- Some letter–sound matches

Toward the end of the Emergent stage, students are beginning to discover how spelling works and that letters represent sounds in words.

Stage 2: Letter Name-Alphabetic Spelling

Letter Name-Alphabetic spellers are typically five to seven years old. These students learn to represent **phonemes** in words with letters because there's a link between letters and sounds, known as the **alphabetic principle**. At first, the spellings are quite abbreviated and represent only the most prominent features in words. Students use only several letters of the alphabet to represent an entire word. Examples of early Stage 2 spelling are D (*dog*) and KE (*cookie*), and students prefer to use capital letters. They slowly pronounce the word they want to spell, listening for familiar letter names and sounds. During this stage, students learn to use most beginning and ending consonants and usually include a vowel in syllables, but they spell *like* as LIK and *bed* as BAD. Their writing can be difficult to decode unless teachers are familiar with the ways these spellers represent sounds in writing. Letter Name-Alphabetic spellers learn these concepts:

- The alphabetic principle
- Consonant sounds
- Short vowel sounds
- Consonant blends and digraphs

By the end of the stage, they use consonant blends, digraphs, and short-vowel patterns to spell many words correctly, such as *hat, get,* and *win.* But some students still make errors spelling words with more difficult sounds; for example, they may spell *ship* as SEP. These students can also correctly spell some common CVCe words correctly, such as *name.*

Stage 3: Within-Word Pattern Spelling

Students, typically seven- to nine-year-olds, begin the Within-Word Pattern stage when they can spell most one-syllable, short-vowel words conventionally, and during this stage, they learn to spell long-vowel words and words with *r*-controlled vowels. They experiment with long-vowel patterns and learn that words such as *come* and *bread* are exceptions to the vowel patterns. Students may confuse spelling patterns and spell *meet* as METE, and they reverse the order of letters, such as FORM for *from* and GRIL for *girl.* They also learn about complex consonant sounds, including *-tch* (*match*) and *-dge* (*judge*), and less frequent vowel patterns, such as *oi/oy* (*boy*), *au* (*caught*), *aw* (*saw*), *ew* (*sew, few*), *ou* (*house*), and *ow* (*cow*). Students also compare long- and short-vowel combinations (*hope—hop*) as they experiment with vowel patterns. Spellers at this stage learn these concepts:

- Long-vowel spelling patterns
- *r*-controlled vowels
- More complex consonant patterns
- Diphthongs and other less common vowel patterns

By the end of the Within-Word Pattern stage, students spell most one-syllable words correctly.

MyLab Education
Video Example 5.1
The kindergartners in this video are sorting words into word families. What spelling pattern are students learning?

Stage 4: Syllables and Affixes Spelling

Students, generally third and fourth graders, apply what they've learned about one-syllable words to longer words, such as *explore, freedom, grandmother, around, laughed,* and *poison,* during the Syllables and Affixes stage. They learn about adding **inflectional endings** to nouns and verbs (*-s, -es, -ed,* and *-ing*); comparative and superlative endings to adjectives (*-er* and *-est*); and applying rules about consonant doubling, changing the final *y* to *i,* or dropping the final *e* before adding an inflectional ending to spell these words: *bus—buses, walk—walked, hot—hotter, buy—buying,* and *come—coming.* Students also learn some of the more common **prefixes,** such as *dis-, re-,* and *-un,* and **suffixes,** such as *-able, -ful/fully, -ly,* and *-tion,* to spell multisyllabic words, including *suddenly, cheerful, disagreeable, rebuild, combination,* and *unfair.*

Students also learn to differentiate between **homophones,** such as *see—sea, right—write, pair—pear, to—too—two,* and *there—they're—their.* Even though most homophones are one-syllable words, this is the stage when students who already know how to spell the words can attend to differences in meaning to use the correct word. They learn these concepts during the Syllables and Affixes stage:

- Inflectional endings
- Compound words
- Syllabication
- Affixes
- Homophones

By the end of this stage, Syllables and Affixes spellers can spell most two-syllable words and some longer words, including *follower, handle, painfully, shadow, rainbow, giggles,* and *reflection,* and choose the correct homophone when they're writing.

Stage 5: Derivational Relations Spelling

Students, beginning at about age 11 or 12, explore the relationship between spelling and meaning during the Derivational Relations stage. They learn that words with related meanings are often related in spelling despite changes in vowel and consonant sounds (e.g., *conclude—conclusion, metal—metallic, nation—national*). Changes in consonant sounds are known as *consonant alternations*; for example, *soft—soften, moist—moisten, muscle—muscular.* Changes in vowel sounds are known as *vowel alternations*; for example, *cave—cavity, invite—invitation, volcano—volcanic.*

The focus in this stage is on **morphemes,** and students learn about Greek and Latin root words and affixes. They also begin to examine word histories and the role of history in shaping how words are spelled. For example, some words developed from people's names, such as *maverick* and *sandwich*; they're called *eponyms.* Students learn these concepts during the Derivational Relations stage.

- Consonant alternations
- Vowel alternations
- Greek and Latin root words and affixes
- Etymologies

This is the final stage of spelling development, and many of older students' spelling errors demonstrate their lack of knowledge about consonant and vowel alternations and Greek and Latin root words and affixes.

Primary grade teachers may think that they don't need to know about this stage, but young students who spell phonetically begin to notice consonant and vowel alternations. For instance, when they're sounding out the spelling of *sign,* they're confused about the unpronounced *g* and ask why the word is spelled this way.

Developmental Continuum Spelling

PreK	K	1	2	3	4
Emergent spellers print their names and use scribbles, letterlike forms, letters, and letter strings to write messages.	Students become Letter Name-Alphabetic spellers. They learn letter-sound matches and begin to sound out words.	First graders learn to spell many high-frequency words, short-vowel words, and words with long-vowel patterns.	Students are Within-Word Pattern spellers who can spell one-syllable words with more complex consonant and vowel patterns.	Students reach the Syllables and Affixes stage and spell longer words, including words with inflectional endings.	Fourth graders recognize homonyms and use knowledge about root words and affixes to spell multisyllabic words.

Teachers need to be able to explain that *sign* is a shortened word developed from *signature*. Another shortened word with an unpronounced letter is *bomb*; it developed from *bombard*. Similarly, many second and third graders spell *nation* correctly, but when they try to spell *national*, they apply vowel rules and spell the word this way: NATTIONAL. Once students move beyond spelling phonetically, they're ready for teachers to begin pointing out some of the more sophisticated principles underlying our spelling system.

Students' spelling provides evidence of their growing understanding of English **orthography**. The words they spell correctly show which phonics concepts, spelling patterns, and other language features they've learned to apply, and the words they invent spellings for and misspell show what they're still learning to use as well as those features of spelling that they haven't noticed or learned about. **Invented spelling** is sometimes criticized because it appears that students are learning bad habits by misspelling words, but researchers have confirmed that students grow more quickly in phonemic awareness, phonics, and spelling when they're encouraged to use invented spelling, as long as they're also receiving spelling instruction (Snow, Burns, & Griffin, 1998). As students learn more about spelling, their spellings become more sophisticated to reflect their new knowledge, even if the words are still spelled incorrectly and, increasingly, students spell more and more words correctly as they move through the stages of spelling development.

Teaching English Learners
Spelling

English learners move through the same five developmental stages that native English speakers do, but they move more slowly because they're less familiar with the letter—sound correspondences, spelling patterns, and grammar of English (Helman, Bear, Templeton, Invernizzi, & Johnston, 2012). Students' spelling development reflects their reading achievement, but it lags behind: When ELs learn a word, they begin by learning its meaning and how to pronounce it. Almost immediately, they're introduced to the word's written form, and with practice, they learn to recognize and read it. Soon they're writing the word, too. At first, their spellings reflect what they know about the English spelling system, but with spelling instruction and reading and writing practice, they learn to spell words correctly. Because spelling is more demanding than reading, it's not surprising that students' knowledge about spelling grows this way.

It's essential that teachers learn about English learners' home language, especially about the ways it differs from English They need to explicitly teach students about the contrasts because they're harder to learn than the similarities (Helman et al., 2012). Consider these written language differences, for example: Chinese uses syllable-length characters instead of letters; Arabic is written from right to left, and the way letters are formed varies according to their location within a word; and vowels aren't used in Croatian and Czech. Some languages, including Arabic, Spanish, Kiswahili (Swahili), and Russian, are more phonetically consistent than English; students who speak these languages are often confused by the number of ways a sound can be spelled in English. There are phonological differences, too: Many languages, including Korean, don't have the /th/ sound; there's no /p/ in Arabic, so Arabic speakers often substitute /b/ in English; and /l/ and /r/ sound alike to speakers of Asian languages. Vowels are particularly difficult for English learners because they're often pronounced differently in their home language. For example, Russian speakers don't differentiate between short and long vowels, and Spanish speakers often substitute /ĕ/ for /ā/ and /ō/ for /ŏ/. Many African and Asian languages, including Kiswahili, Punjabi, Chinese, and Thai, as well as Navajo—a Native American language—are tonal; in these languages, pitch, not spelling differences, is used to distinguish between words. In addition, there are syntactic differences that affect spelling: Hmong speakers don't add plural markers to nouns; Korean speakers add grammatical information to the end of verbs instead of using auxiliary verbs; and Chinese speakers aren't familiar with prefixes or suffixes because they're not used in their language.

Teachers base their instruction on English learners' stage of spelling development, and they emphasize the contrasts between students' home languages and English. According to Helman and her colleagues (2012), at each developmental stage, teachers focus their instruction on concepts that confuse English learners:

Emergent Stage. Students learn English letters, sounds, and words, and they learn that English is written from left to right and top to bottom, with spaces between words. Developing this awareness is more difficult for students whose home languages aren't alphabetic.

Letter Name-Alphabetic Stage. Students learn that letters represent sounds, and the sounds that are the same in ELs' home languages and English are the easiest to learn. They learn both consonant and vowel sounds. Those consonant sounds that are more difficult include /d/, /j/, /r/, /sh/, and /th/. English learners often have difficulty pronouncing and spelling final consonant blends (e.g., -st as in *fast*, -ng as in *king*, -mp as in *stomp*, and -rd as in *board*). Long and short vowel sounds are especially hard because they're often pronounced differently than in students' home languages.

Within-Word Pattern Stage. Students move from representing individual sounds in words to using vowel spelling patterns. They practice the CVCe and CVVC patterns and exceptions to these rules (e.g., *lake, have, come, mail, head*); r-controlled vowels are especially tricky because they're found in so many common words, and pronunciation often doesn't predict spelling (e.g., *bear/care/hair, word/heard/fern/burst*). They also learn to spell contractions (e.g., *I will = I'll, cannot = can't, will not = won't*).

Syllables and Affixes Stage. Students learn spelling and grammar concepts together as they investigate verb forms (e.g., *talk—talked, take—took—taken, think—thought*), change adjectives to adverbs (e.g., *quick—quickly*), and add inflectional endings (e.g., *walks—walked—walking*), comparatives, and superlatives (e.g., *sunny—sunnier—sunniest*). During this stage, English learners also learn to pronounce accented and unaccented syllables differently, to use the schwa sound in unaccented syllables, and to differentiate between homophones (e.g., *wear—where, to—too—two*).

Derivational Relations Stage.   Students learn about consonant and vowel alternations in related words (e.g., *crumb—crumble, define—definition*). Some ELs use tonal
changes to signal these relationships in their home languages, but they must learn
that related words in English are signaled by similar spelling and changes in how
the vowels are pronounced. They also learn about Latin and Greek root words and
affixes and use this knowledge as an aid in understanding the meanings of words
and spelling the words.

Spelling instruction for English learners is similar to that for native speakers: Teachers
use a combination of explicit instruction, **word sorts** and other practice activities, and
authentic reading and writing activities. The biggest difference is that ELs need more
instruction on the English spelling concepts that confuse them, often because these
features aren't used in their home languages.

MyLab Education
Video Example 5.2

These educators are engaging young
students in concept sorts. How do
concept sorts prepare students for
word sorts?

MyLab Education **Self-Check 5.1**

Teaching Spelling

Perhaps the best known way to teach spelling is through weekly spelling tests, but tests
should never be considered a complete spelling program. To become good spellers, students
need to learn about the English orthographic system and move through the stages of spelling development. They need to know strategies for spelling unknown words, participate in
a variety of daily reading and writing activities, and gain experience in using dictionaries
and other resources. A complete spelling program includes these components:

Check the Compendium of
Instructional Procedures, which
follows Chapter 12. These **green**
terms also show a brief description
of each procedure.

- Teaching spelling strategies
- Matching instruction to students' levels of spelling development
- Providing daily reading and writing opportunities
- Teaching students to spell high frequency words

A complete spelling program is an important component of a balanced approach to
literacy instruction. Use this Teacher Checklist to determine whether your spelling
program is complete and to assess your ability to teach spelling effectively.

SPELLING STRATEGIES.   Students learn strategies to figure out how to spell unfamiliar words. As they move through the stages of spelling development, they become

PreK Practices

How do I teach spelling to four-year-olds?

Spelling begins as preschoolers learn to identify and print the letters in their names. Soon
these letters and others appear in their drawings. Researchers have identified this sequence in
preschoolers' spelling development:

- Scribbling
- Adding letters and letterlike forms to scribbles
- Using random strings of letters to represent writing
- Copying environmental print (e.g., *M for Mcdonalds)*
- Writing one or more letters that represent obvious sounds in a word (e.g., K = *cat,* APL =
  apple)
- Spelling names and phrases such as "I love you" correctly (Ray & Glover, 2008; Schicke-
  danz & Casbergue, 2009)

As students move along this sequence, it's easy to see what they understand about the alphabet, environmental print, and words.

increasingly more sophisticated in their use of phonological, semantic, and historical knowledge to spell words; that is, they become more strategic. They learn to use these spelling strategies:

- Segmenting the word and spelling each sound, often called "sound it out"
- Spelling unknown words by analogy to familiar words
- Applying affixes to root words
- Proofreading to locate spelling errors in a rough draft
- Checking the spelling of unfamiliar words in a dictionary or a classroom chart

Teachers often give the traditional "sound it out" advice when young students ask how to spell an unfamiliar word, but they provide more useful information when they suggest a strategic "think it out" approach; this advice reminds students that spelling involves more than phonological information and encourages them to think about spelling patterns, inflectional endings, and what the word looks like.

DEVELOPMENTALLY APPROPRIATE INSTRUCTION.   Teachers provide explicit instruction on spelling concepts and strategies that are developmentally appropriate. Students who are Letter Name-Alphabetic spellers, for example, learn about consonant and short-vowel sounds because these are the concepts they're attempting to represent with letters. They're also ready to learn the "sound it out" strategy. Instruction on these topics wouldn't be appropriate for Stage 4 spellers because they've already learned these concepts. Figure 5–2 lists topics for developmentally appropriate spelling instruction. Sometimes teachers find that developmentally appropriate instruction conflicts with directives about focusing instruction on grade-level standards. **Differentiated instruction** is the best way to address students' needs while presenting lessons on grade-level topics.

DAILY READING AND WRITING OPPORTUNITIES.   Two of the most important ways that students learn to spell are through daily reading and writing activities. Students who are good readers tend to be good spellers, too: As they read, students visualize words—the shape of the word and the configuration of letters within it—and they use this knowledge to spell many words correctly and to recognize when a word

Figure 5–2 Developmentally Appropriate Spelling Instruction

STAGE	TOPICS	
Emergent Spelling	phonemic awareness	letters of the alphabet
	left-to-right progression of text	printing students' names
	concepts of "letter" and "word"	consonant sounds
Letter Name-Alphabetic Spelling	initial and final consonant sounds	short vowel sounds
	blending/segmenting sounds	"sound it out" spelling strategy
	initial/final consonant blends	high frequency words
Within-Word Pattern Spelling	consonant digraphs	vowel digraphs
	more complex consonant sounds	vowel diphthongs
	silent letters	r-controlled vowels
	more complex blends	"think it out" spelling strategy
	long-vowel spelling patterns	high frequency words
Syllables and Affixes Spelling	syllables	compound words
	schwa sound	contractions
	inflectional endings	homophones
	common prefixes and suffixes	dictionary use
Derivational Relations Spelling	Latin and greek root words	etymologies (word histories)
	prefixes and suffixes	

Teach Kids to Be Strategic!

Spelling Strategies

Teach students to use these strategies to spell words and to verify that words they've written are spelled correctly:

- Sound it out
- Spell by analogy
- Apply affixes
- Proofread
- Check a dictionary

Students learn to sound out spellings for phonetically regular words in kindergarten and first grade; later, they learn to think out spellings for longer words using a combination of spelling strategies. Teach minilessons and then monitor that students apply what they've learned during writing workshop. If students struggle, reteach developmentally appropriate strategies.

they've written doesn't look right. Through writing, of course, students gain valuable practice using the strategies they've learned for spelling words. And, as teachers work with students to proofread and edit their writing, they learn more about spelling and other writing conventions.

TEACHING HIGH FREQUENCY WORDS. High frequency words are common, frequently occurring words, including *the, me, said, can, to, was, like,* and *you,* that students need to be able to spell automatically. Fewer than half of the 100 most frequently used words in English are spelled phonetically, so it's essential that students learn to spell them correctly because writers use the words again and again. Of the eight high frequency words just listed as examples, only three—*can, me,* and *like*—are spelled phonetically.

When students are engaged in a spelling program that includes these components, there's evidence of their learning in their writing. Students make progressively fewer errors, but more importantly, the types of spelling errors change: They become more sophisticated. Students move from spelling phonetically to using morphological information and spelling rules.

Minilessons

Teachers regularly teach students about the English orthographic system through **minilessons** on phonics, phonograms, high frequency words, spelling strategies, spelling rules, and other spelling concepts. The following Minilesson shows how Mr. Cheng teaches his first graders to spell words using the -*at* phonogram or word family. In addition to teaching lessons to the whole class, teachers often differentiate instruction by teaching minilessons on developmentally appropriate topics to small groups of students, as Mrs. Zumwalt did in the vignette at the beginning of the chapter.

Word Walls

Teachers use two types of **word walls** in their classrooms. One type features "important" words from books students are reading or from thematic units. Words may be written on a large sheet of paper hanging in the classroom or on word cards and placed in a large pocket chart. Then students refer to these word walls when they're writing. Seeing the words posted on word walls and other charts in the classroom and using them in their writing helps students learn to spell the words. During a science unit on plants, for example, a first grade teacher wrote these 11 words on word cards and placed

Minilesson

TOPIC: Spelling -*at* Family Words
GRADE: First Grade
TIME: One 10-minute period

Mr. Cheng teaches phonics during guided reading lessons. He introduces, practices, and reviews phonics concepts using words from selections his first graders are reading. The students decode and spell words using letter and word cards, magnetic letters, and small whiteboards and pens.

1. **Introduce the Topic**
   Mr. Cheng holds up a copy of *At Home*, the small paperback Level E book the students read yesterday, and asks them to reread the title. Then he asks the students to identify the first word, *at*. After they read the word, he hands a card with the word *at* written on it to each of the six students in the guided reading group. "Who can read this word?" he asks. Several students recognize it immediately, and others carefully sound out the two-letter word.

2. **Share Examples**
   Mr. Cheng asks students to think about rhyming words: "Who knows what rhyming words are?" Mike answers that rhyming words sound alike at the end—for example, *Mike, bike*, and *like*. The teacher explains that there are many words in English that rhyme, and that today, they're going to read and write words that rhyme with *at*. "One rhyming word is *cat*," he explains. Students name rhyming words, including *hat, fat*, and *bat*. Mr. Cheng helps each student in the group to name at least three rhyming words.

3. **Provide Information**
   Mr. Cheng explains that students can spell these *at* words by adding a consonant in front of *at*. For example, he places the foam letter *c* in front of his *at* card, and the students blend *c* to *at* to read *cat*. Then he repeats the procedure by substituting other foam letters for the *c* to spell *bat, fat, hat, mat, pat, rat*, and *sat*. He continues the activity until every student successfully reads one of the words.

4. **Guide Practice**
   Mr. Cheng passes out small plastic trays with foam letters and asks the students to add one of the letters to their *at* cards to spell the words as he pronounces them. He continues the activity until students have had several opportunities to spell each word, and they can quickly choose the correct initial consonant to spell it. Then Mr. Cheng collects the *at* cards and trays with foam letters.

5. **Assess Learning**
   Mr. Cheng passes out small whiteboards and pens. He asks the first graders to write these words as he says each one aloud: *cat, hat, mat, pat, rat, sat, bat*, and *fat*. He carefully observes as each student segments the onset and rime to spell the word. The students hold up their boards to show him their spellings. Afterward, students erase the word and repeat the process, writing the next word. After students write all eight words, Mr. Cheng quickly jots a note about which students need additional practice with the -*at* word family before continuing with the guided reading lesson.

Figure 5–3 A Page From a First Grader's "All About Plants" Book

them in a pocket chart word wall: *seed, root, stem, leaf, leaves, flower, plant, grow, soil, water,* and *sunshine*. The first graders practiced reading the words and used them when they drew diagrams about how plants grow, drew pictures of favorite flowers, and wrote in their **learning logs**. As a culminating activity, the students wrote books about plants to demonstrate what they'd learned. They drew a picture and wrote a sentence on each page, often referring to the word wall to check the spelling of plant-related words. A page from one student's book is shown in Figure 5–3. It reads:

Plants need three things to grow big and strong.

Notice that the student used conventional spelling for the science words and high frequency words and invented spelling for other words.

The second type of word wall displays **high frequency words**. Researchers have identified the most commonly used words and recommend that students learn to spell 100 of these words because of their usefulness. The most frequently used words represent more than 50% of all the words students and adults write! Figure 5–4 lists the 100 most frequently used words.

Teachers plan a variety of activities to teach students how to read and spell high frequency words; more information about teaching students to read these words is provided in Chapter 6, "Developing Fluent Readers and Writers." As students learn to read the words, they're also learning to spell them. Because most of the words aren't spelled phonetically, students must memorize the spellings; constant repetition as they read and write the words is useful. Also, students develop a visual representation of the word so that when they write it, they can recognize that their spelling is too short or long, or that it lacks a "tall" letter. For instance, *litle* doesn't look right with only one *t*, does it? It's not long enough, and there aren't enough tall middle letters. Or, what about *houes*? Reversing the last two letters of *house* looks funny. Students learn to refer to the word wall to spell unfamiliar words when they're writing, and as they become more proficient writers, teachers should expect them to use the word wall and to spell high frequency words correctly.

MyLab Education
Video Example 5.3
Mrs. McNeal asks her first graders to use a high frequency word wall during writing workshop. How does she help her students learn to spell high frequency words?

Word Study Activities

Teachers provide hands-on activities for students to practice the spelling concepts they're learning. Concepts and strategies are usually introduced as whole-class activities, and then students have additional opportunities to practice them at centers. These

Figure 5–4 The 100 High Frequency Words

A	B	C	DE
a and	back	came	day do
about are	be	can	did don't
after around	because	could	didn't down
all as	but		
am at	by		
an			
FG	**H**	**IJ**	**KL**
for	had his	I is	know
from	have home	if it	like
get	he house	in just	little
got	her how	into	
	him		
MN	**O**	**PQR**	**S**
man no	of our	people	said she
me not	on out	put	saw so
mother now	one over		school some
my	or		see
T	**UV**	**WX**	**YZ**
that think	up	was when	you
the this	us	we who	your
them time	very	well will	
then to		went with	
there too		were would	
they two		what	
things			

activities expand students' spelling knowledge and help them move through the stages of spelling development.

MAKING WORDS. Teachers choose a five- to eight-letter word (or longer words for third and fourth graders) and prepare sets of letter cards for a **making words** activity (Cunningham & Cunningham, 1992). Then students use the cards to practice spelling words and to review spelling patterns and rules. They arrange and rearrange the cards to spell one-letter words, two-letter words, three-letter words, and so forth, until they use all the letters to spell the original word. Second graders, for example, can create these words using the letters in *weather*: *a, at, we, he, the, are, art, ear, eat, hat, her, hear, here, hate, heart, wheat, there*, and *where*. In addition, Mrs. Zumwalt's third graders participated in a making words activity using *grandfather* in the vignette at the beginning of the chapter.

WORD LADDERS. Students spell words and learn word meanings when they make **word ladders** (Rasinski, 2006). In this word-building game, teachers direct the whole class or a small group of students to write a word and then change it into another word by substituting, adding, deleting, or rearranging letters. For example, a first grade teacher used the word ladder game shown in Figure 5–5 to practice the short vowel sounds in CVC words. This word-building game is easy for teachers to adapt to almost any phonics or spelling concept.

WORD SORTS. Students use **word sorts** to explore, compare, and contrast word features as they sort a pack of word cards. Teachers prepare word cards for students to sort into two or more categories according to word families, spelling patterns, or other criteria (Bear et al., 2016). Sometimes teachers tell students what

Figure 5–5 CVC Word Ladder

The teacher says:	Students write:
Let's begin with a color word. The word is *red*. Write it now.	red
First, change one letter to spell the word for the piece of furniture you sleep on. What's the word?	bed
Change one letter to spell a word that is the opposite of *good*. What's the word?	bad
Change one letter to spell the word *mad*.	mad
Finally, change one letter to spell a word that means "wet dirt." What's the word?	mud

categories to use, which makes the sort a closed sort; when students determine the categories themselves, the sort is an open sort. Students can sort word cards and then return them to an envelope for future use, or they can glue the cards onto a sheet of paper.

INTERACTIVE WRITING. Teachers use **interactive writing** to teach spelling concepts as well as other concepts about written language. Because correct spelling and legible handwriting are courtesies for readers, teachers emphasize correct spelling as students take turns to collaboratively write a message. It's likely that students will misspell a few words as they write, so teachers take advantage of these "teachable moments" to clarify their misunderstandings. Through interactive writing, students learn to use a variety of resources to correct misspelled words, including classroom word walls, books, classmates, and the dictionary.

PROOFREADING. **Proofreading** is a special kind of reading that students use to locate misspelled words and other mechanical errors in rough drafts. As students learn about the writing process, they're introduced to proofreading in the editing stage. More in-depth instruction about how to use proofreading to locate spelling errors and then correct these misspelled words is part of spelling instruction (Cramer, 1998). Through a series of minilessons, students can learn to proofread sample student papers and mark misspelled words; then, working in pairs, they can correct the misspellings.

Teachers introduce proofreading in first grade through whole-class activities. They reread group writings to identify and correct errors, and through this experience, students learn that editing is an essential part of the writing process. In one first grade class, for example, students share daily news using interactive writing, but as they become more fluent writers, the activity becomes a proofreading exercise. One student writes his or her news independently and then shares it with classmates. An unedited sample is shown in the top part of Figure 5–6; this student wrote about her upcoming birthday. Everyone was interested in this news and asked questions about her party. Then the teacher, the student-writer, and her classmates proofread the rough draft to identify misspelled words, capitalization and punctuation errors, and missing words. They made corrections using interactive writing techniques, as shown in the bottom part of the figure. The teacher didn't correct every mistake, focusing instead on those that students noticed and those that reflected the concepts she'd taught. The rectangles represent correction tape used to cover errors. Through this exercise, the teacher modeled proofreading and took advantage of teachable moments to review spelling concepts.

DICTIONARY USE. Students need to learn to locate the spelling of unfamiliar words in the dictionary. Although it's relatively easy to find a known word in the dictionary, it's hard to locate unfamiliar words, and students need to learn what to do when they

---

Figure 5–6 A First Grader's Draft and Edited News

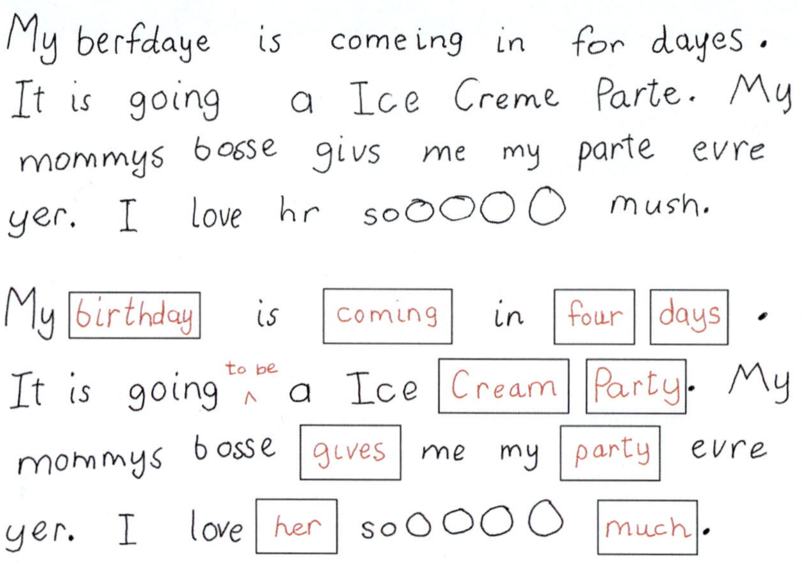

My berfdaye is comeing in for dayes.
It is going a Ice Creme Parte. My
mommys bosse givs me my parte evre
yer. I love hr soOOOO mush.

My [birthday] is [coming] in [four] [days] .
It is going ^to be a Ice [Cream] [Party]. My
mommys bosse [gives] me my [party] evre
yer. I love [her] soOOOO [much].

don't know how to spell a word. One approach is to predict possible spellings for unknown words, then check the most probable spellings in a dictionary.

Students should be encouraged to check the spelling of words in a dictionary as well as to use a dictionary to check multiple meanings or etymology. Too often, they consider consulting a dictionary to be a punishment; teachers must work to change this view. One way to do this is to appoint several students as dictionary checkers: These students keep dictionaries on their desks, and they're consulted whenever questions arise about spelling, a word's meaning, or word usage.

Weekly Spelling Tests

Many teachers question the usefulness of spelling tests because research on invented spelling suggests that spelling is best learned through reading and writing (Gentry & Gillet, 1993). In addition, teachers complain that lists of spelling words are unrelated to the words students are reading and writing and that the 30 minutes of valuable instructional time spent each day in completing spelling activities is excessive. Even so, parents and school board members value spelling tests as evidence that spelling is being taught. Weekly spelling tests, when they're used, should be individualized so that students learn to spell the words they need for writing.

In the individualized approach to spelling instruction, students choose the words they'll study, many of which are words they use in their writing projects. Students study 5 to 10 specific words during the week using a study strategy; this approach places more responsibility on students for their own learning. Teachers develop a weekly word list of 20 or more words of varying difficulty from which students select words to study. Words for the master list include high frequency words, words from the word wall related to literature focus units and thematic units, and words students needed for their writing projects during the previous week. Words from spelling programs can also be added to the list.

On Monday, the teacher administers a pretest using the master list of words, and students spell as many of the words as they can. Students correct their own pretests, and from the words they misspell, they create individual spelling lists. They make two copies of their study list, using the numbers on the master list to make it easier to take the final test on Friday. Students use one copy of the list for study activities, and the teacher keeps the second copy.

Students spend approximately 5 to 10 minutes studying the words on their study lists each day during the week. Research shows that instead of "busy-work" activities such as using their spelling words in sentences or gluing yarn in the shape of the words, it's more effective for students to use this study strategy:

1. Look at the word and say it to yourself.
2. Say each letter in the word to yourself.
3. Close your eyes and spell the word to yourself.
4. Write the word, and check that you spelled it correctly.
5. Write the word again, and check that you spelled it correctly.

This strategy focuses on the whole word rather than on breaking the word apart into sounds or syllables. Teachers explain how to use the strategy during a minilesson at the beginning of the school year and then post a copy of it in the classroom. In addition, students often trade word lists on Wednesday to give each other a practice test.

A final test is administered on Friday. The teacher reads the master list, and students write only those words they've practiced during the week. To make the test easier to administer, students first list on their test papers the numbers of the words they've practiced from their study lists. Any words that students misspell should be included on their lists the following week.

What's the Controversy About Spelling Instruction?

The press and concerned parent groups periodically raise questions about the "dangers" of invented spelling and the importance of weekly spelling tests so students learn the correct spelling of words. There's a misplaced public perception that today's students can't spell. These groups argue that if students are allowed to invent spellings, they'll never learn to spell words correctly. However, when students learn spelling strategies and developmentally appropriate spelling concepts, practice spelling high frequency words for spelling tests, and participate in daily reading and writing activities, they'll become conventional spellers. Researchers who have examined the types of errors students make have noted that the number of misspellings increases in grades one through four, as students write longer compositions, but that the percentage of errors decreases thereafter. The percentage continues to decline through middle school and high school, although students still make a few errors. In fact, most adults misspell a word or two every once in a while.

GO DIGITAL! Spelling Games

Students play spelling games at these websites. At several sites, teachers and students can create their own games to practice the words of the weekly spelling lists:

Houghton Mifflin's Spelling Games (http://www.eduplace.com). Go to the website's homepage, click on the "Students" tab, and then on the "Games" button to locate spelling games coordinated with Houghton Mifflin's spelling program. The games reinforce phonics and root words; they're useful for all students, not just those using this textbook program.

Kids Spell (http://www.kidsspell.com). This website offers a variety of spelling games, including Spellasaurus and Cast a Spell.

Puzzle Maker (http://www.puzzle-maker.com). Teachers and students can turn spelling lists into a variety of games at this free site.

Spelling City (http://www.spellingcity.com). This website allows teachers and students to type in spelling lists and use them to make spelling flash cards and word-search games. Students also take practice spelling tests at the site.

MyLab Education Self-Check 5.2
MyLab Education Application Exercise 5.1: Using Word Sorts to Study Words

Assessing Spelling

Teachers assess spelling by examining students' writing. The choices that students make as they misspell words are important indicators of their developmental level and their instructional priorities. For example, a student who spells phonetically might spell *money* as MUNE, and others who are experimenting with long vowels might spell the word as MONYE or MONIE. Teachers classify and analyze the words students misspell in their writing to gauge their level of spelling development and to plan for developmentally appropriate instruction.

Determining a Student's Stage of Spelling Development

The best way to determine a student's stage of spelling development is to examine how the student spells words in a writing sample. Teachers follow these steps to analyze the misspelled words and determine the student's developmental stage:

Assessment Snapshot

Spelling Analysis

I worked hard as a reasearcher. I took my time on pickers and handwriting. I read books too. After that I wrote the facks down on indecks cards. I laid them owt and then numberd them. My favorit part was when I figred owt I was stdying my first choyce.

Classification of Errors

Letter Name-Alphabetic	Within-Word Pattern	Syllables and Affixes	Derivational Relations
	pickers	reasearcher	
	facks	numberd	
	indecks	favorit	
	owt	figred	
	owt		
	stdying		
	choyce		

TEACHER'S NOTE

Tatum spelled 88% of the words correctly, and most errors were representative of the Within-Word Pattern stage. These errors indicate that she's investigating ways to spell complex consonant and vowel sounds. She also wrote 10 two- and three-syllable words and spelled three correctly. Tatum's moving into the Syllables and Affixes stage; her spelling development meets grade-level standards.

1. **Choose a writing sample.** Teachers choose a student's writing sample to analyze. It should total at least 50 words, and teachers must be able to decipher most words in the sample to analyze it.

2. **Identify spelling errors.** Teachers read the writing sample to note the errors and identify the words the student was trying to spell. If necessary, teachers check with the student to determine the intended word.

3. **Make a spelling analysis chart.** Teachers draw a chart with five columns, one for each stage of spelling development.

4. **Categorize the spelling errors.** Teachers classify the student's spelling errors according to stages of spelling development. They list each error in one of the stages, ignoring proper nouns, capitalization errors, and grammar errors. Teachers ignore poorly formed letters or reversed letterforms in kindergarten and first grade, but these errors are more significant when older students make them. To simplify the analysis, teachers write the intended word in parentheses after the student's error if the invented spelling isn't recognizable.

5. **Tally the errors.** Teachers count the errors in each column, and the one with the most errors indicates the student's current stage of development.

6. **Identify instructional priorities.** Teachers examine the student's errors to identify developmentally appropriate topics for instruction.

An analysis of a first grader's spelling development is shown in the Assessment Snapshot: Spelling Analysis. Tatum's writing sample was completed in April, and it shows that she's at the Within-Word Pattern stage, which meets grade-level standards.

Teachers also administer diagnostic tests to determine students' stage of spelling development. The Assessment Tools: Spelling feature lists quick and easy-to-administer tests that teachers use to screen the entire class at the beginning, middle, or end of the school year.

The Instruction–Assessment Cycle

Teachers integrate assessment with spelling instruction by providing developmentally appropriate instruction as well as addressing the Common Core State Standards for their grade level.

STEP 1: PLANNING.   Teachers plan developmentally appropriate instruction using their knowledge about students' current stage of spelling development, and they identify Common Core State Standards to teach.

STEP 2: MONITORING.   Teachers observe students' performance during minilessons and spelling games, and they analyze spelling errors to determine which spelling concepts, patterns, or rules students are misapplying. Based on their observations, teachers modify instruction or provide additional minilessons to personalize their teaching. They also examine students' spelling in their writing projects, especially during the editing stage of the writing process. Teachers often make a list of words that students misspell to use in future minilessons, games, and weekly spelling lists.

STEP 3: EVALUATING.   The most obvious way that teachers evaluate spelling is with weekly spelling tests, but grades may show only whether students did their homework. More importantly, teachers evaluate how well students apply their knowledge about English orthography in their writing because if they memorize words for weekly spelling tests but quickly forget how to spell the words, they haven't learned very much! Teachers also track students' growth in spelling, making sure that they're learning the spelling concepts that are appropriate for their stage of spelling development and that they're meeting grade-level expectations as they move through the stages.

STEP 4: REFLECTING.   Teachers use their evaluation of students' learning to judge the effectiveness of their instruction and decide how to adapt instruction to better

MyLab Education
Video Example 5.4

Ms. Smith has monitored her students' learning from early in the year. Why is monitoring literacy development an ongoing need?

Assessment Tools

Spelling

Teachers assess students' spelling development by examining misspelled words in the compositions that they write. They classify students' spelling errors according to the stages of spelling development and plan instruction based on their analysis. They also examine students' misspellings on weekly spelling tests and other tests. Here are three tests designed for classroom teachers to screen, monitor, diagnose, and document students' spelling development:

- **Developmental Spelling Analysis (DSA)**
  The DSA is a dictated spelling inventory with two components: a Screening Inventory for determining students' stage of spelling development and Feature Inventories to highlight students' knowledge of specific spelling concepts. The DSA with detailed guidelines is available in Ganske's book, *Word Journeys: Assessment-Guided Phonics, Spelling, and Vocabulary Instruction* (2000).

- **Phonological Awareness Literacy Screening (PALS) System: Spelling Subtest**
  This kindergarten-level battery of tests includes a brief spelling subtest in which students write the sounds they hear in CVC words. In the grades 1—3 tests, the spelling subtest includes words that exemplify phonics features that are appropriate for that grade level. Students receive credit for spelling the specific feature correctly and additional points for spelling the word correctly. The PALS test is available free for Virginia teachers from the University of Virginia, and it can be purchased by teachers in other states.

- **Qualitative Spelling Inventory (QSI)**
  The QSI includes 20 or 25 spelling words listed according to difficulty and can easily be administered to small groups or whole classes. The QSI is available in *Words Their Way: Word Study for Phonics, Vocabulary, and Spelling Instruction* (Bear et al., 2016).

Through these tests, teachers identify students' stages of spelling development and use this information to monitor their progress and plan for instruction.

serve students who are struggling. In addition, students reflect on their own spelling development: They reflect on their growth as spellers by examining the spelling errors in their writing as well as tracking their scores on weekly spelling tests. Use **My Teaching To-Do Checklist: Teaching Spelling** to review your responsibilities for teaching spelling.

MY TEACHING TO-DO CHECKLIST: Teaching Spelling

☐ I analyze the errors in students' writing to provide developmentally appropriate spelling instruction.

☐ I connect phonemic awareness, phonics, and spelling during minilessons by having students manipulate words orally and then read and write them.

☐ I guide students to use strategies to spell unfamiliar words.

☐ I teach students to spell high frequency words before less common ones.

☐ I post words on word walls and use them for a variety of spelling activities.

☐ I involve students in making words, word sorts, and other hands-on spelling activities.

☐ I consider spelling tests as only one part of an instructional program.

☐ I involve students in daily authentic reading and writing activities to apply their spelling knowledge.

☐ I integrate state standards into my instruction.

If Students Struggle . . .

Students who struggle with spelling often exhibit one or more of these problems:

High Frequency Words.   Students don't know how to spell high frequency words and don't refer to lists of these words that are posted in the classroom. When they don't know how to spell these common words, struggling spellers often rely on phonics, even though many high frequency words aren't phonetically regular. For example, they spell *was* as WUZ and *could* as CUD.

Phonics.   Students continue to depend on the first phonics skills they learned, spelling words phonetically without applying phonics and spelling rules. For example, they spell *soap* as SOP, *babies* as BABYS, and *running* as RUNING.

Handwriting.   Some struggling spellers don't write legibly, or they form letters carelessly or write so quickly that they leave out letters as they spell words. It appears that they're using poor handwriting to mask misspelled words.

It's crucial that teachers determine what's causing the students' spelling problems and intervene to get them back on track for success.

The first step is diagnosis. Teachers observe struggling spellers as they write and analyze several of their writing samples. For each student, teachers determine the student's stage of spelling development and examine both correctly spelled and misspelled words to identify specific problems. Teachers ask themselves these questions:

- Does the student spell most high frequency words correctly?
- Does the student apply the phonics concepts that have been taught to spelling?
- Does the student depend on phonics for spelling almost all words?
- Does the student refer to the word wall for thematic words?
- Does the student write legibly?
- Does the student write entire words or leave out letters?

Once teachers have diagnosed each student's spelling problems, they decide how to intervene and plan for instruction.

Teachers teach minilessons and provide one-on-one and small-group instruction to address the students' identified problems. They also involve the students in practice activities, including interactive writing, making words, word ladders, and word sorts. Quick and intensive intervention is the most effective way to assist struggling spellers; otherwise, they're likely to fall further behind.

Writing is another essential component of a spelling intervention program. Typically, students who struggle with spelling don't do much writing, but they need to participate in daily writing activities to break bad habits and apply what they're learning. At first, brief and informal activities work best. Students can write a sentence or two about a book the teacher is reading aloud or about a big idea in a thematic unit. They can also write entries in personal journals about events going on in their lives. Teachers supervise students as they write and provide assistance—spelling words, demonstrating how to form letters, and locating words on word walls, as needed. Although spelling isn't usually emphasized in informal writing activities, students are expected to correctly spell high frequency words they've been taught and words related to a book or unit that are posted on a word wall.

Teachers carefully monitor students' progress and reassess them every month or so to ensure that they're becoming more proficient spellers. If students continue to struggle, teachers repeat their diagnosis and adjust their instruction to meet students' needs.

MyLab Education Self-Check 5.3

Chapter Review

Teaching Spelling

- Teachers understand that learning to spell is a developmental process that involves five stages.

- Teachers analyze spelling errors in students' writing samples to identify their stage of spelling development and plan for instruction.

- Teachers assess each student's stage of spelling development as they plan for instruction.

Accountability Check

Visit the following assessment links to access quiz questions and instructional applications.

MyLab Education Application Exercise 5.2: Understanding Literacy Development
MyLab Education Application Exercise 5.3: Understanding Literacy Development
MyLab Education Application Exercise 5.4: Monitoring Literacy Development
MyLab Education Application Exercise 5.5: Measuring Literacy Development

References

Bear, D. R., Invernizzi, M., Templeton, S., & Johnston, F. (2016). *Words their way: Word study for phonics, vocabulary, and spelling instruction* (5th ed.). Boston: Allyn & Bacon/Pearson.

Cramer, R. L. (1998). *The spelling connection: Integrating reading, writing, and spelling instruction.* New York: Guilford Press.

Common core state standards for English language arts. (2010). Retrieved from http://www.corestandards.org/ELA-Literacy

Cunningham, P. M., & Cunningham, J. W. (1992). Making words: Enhancing the invented spelling-decoding connection. *The Reading Teacher, 46,* 106–115.

Ganske, K. (2000). *Word journeys: Assessment-guided phonics, spelling, and vocabulary instruction.* New York: Guilford Press.

Gentry, J. R., & Gillet, J. W. (1993). *Teaching kids to spell.* Portsmouth, NH: Heinemann.

Helman, L., Bear, D. R., Templeton, S., Invernizzi, M., & Johnston, F. (2012). Words their way with English learners: *Word study for phonics, vocabulary, and spelling* (2nd ed.). Upper Saddle River, NJ: Pearson Education.

Rasinski, T. (2006). Developing vocabulary through word building. In C. C. Block & J. N. Mangieri (Eds.), *The vocabulary-enriched classroom: Practices for improving the reading performance of all students in grades 3 and up* (pp. 36–53). New York: Scholastic.

Ray, K. W., & Glover, M. (2008). *Already ready: Nurturing writers in preschool and kindergarten.* Portsmouth, NH: Heinemann.

Read, C. (1975). *Children's categorization of speech sounds in English* (NCTE Research Report No. 17). Urbana, IL: National Council of Teachers of English.

Schickedanz, J. A., & Casbergue, R. M. (2009). *Writing in preschool: Learning to orchestrate meaning and marks* (2nd ed.). Newark, DE: International Reading Association.

Snow, C. E., Burns, M. S., & Griffin, P. (Eds.). (1998). *Preventing reading difficulties in young children.* Washington, DC: National Academy Press.

Chapter 6
Developing Fluent Readers and Writers

Learning Outcomes

After studying this chapter, you'll be prepared to:

6.1 Identify components of reading fluency and know how to teach for it.

6.2 Identify and explain the components of writing fluency and know how to teach for it.

6.3 Describe approaches to assessing reading and writing fluency.

Teaching High Frequency Words

Kzenon/Shutterstock

The focus in this chapter is fluency, that is, students' ability to read and write accurately, quickly, and with expression. Primary grade teachers, like Ms. Williams in this vignette, develop their young students' reading and writing fluency through instruction, guided practice, and independent reading and writing. As you read this vignette, identify the specific activities Ms. Williams uses to develop her students' reading and writing fluency, and ask yourself how she monitors their fluency development.

Ms. Williams's second graders are learning about hermit crabs and their tide pool environment. A plastic habitat box with a live hermit crab inside sits in the center of each group of desks, and as students learn how to care for their crustaceans, they study them. They've examined hermit crabs up close using magnifying glasses and identified their body parts. Ms. Williams helped them draw a diagram of a hermit crab on a large chart and label the body parts. They've also learned how to feed hermit crabs, how to get them to come out of their shells, and how they molt.

These students use reading and writing as tools for learning. Eric Carle's *A House for Hermit Crab* (2005) is the featured book for this unit. Ms. Williams has read it aloud several times, and she's also read *Moving Day* (Kaplan, 1996), *Hidden Hermit Crabs* (Doudna, 2007), and *Caring for Your Hermit Crab* (Richardson, 2006). Now the second graders are rereading these books independently or with buddies. Ms. Williams integrates many components of reading instruction into this literature focus unit, and she also conducts **guided reading** lessons using leveled books. Three of her second graders are fluent readers and writers; the others are at the beginning stage. They're learning high frequency words, increasing their reading and writing speed, and becoming more expressive readers and writers. Students also draw diagrams and write about them in **learning logs**. The Learning Log Entry shows one student's work.

To teach high frequency words, Ms. Williams uses a **word wall**, a brightly colored alphabet quilt with 26 letter blocks that's displayed permanently on one wall of the classroom. In September, Ms. Williams posted the 70 high frequency words that the students already knew on the wall; each word is written on a card in print that's large enough for everyone to read. Then each week, Ms. Williams adds three to five new words. First she chose words from her list of the 100 high frequency words; after finishing that list, she began choosing words from a list of the second 100 high frequency words. She doesn't introduce the words in the order they're presented in the list; instead, she chooses words that she can connect to literature focus units or phonics lessons, as well as words students misspell in their writing.

A Student's Learning Log Entry

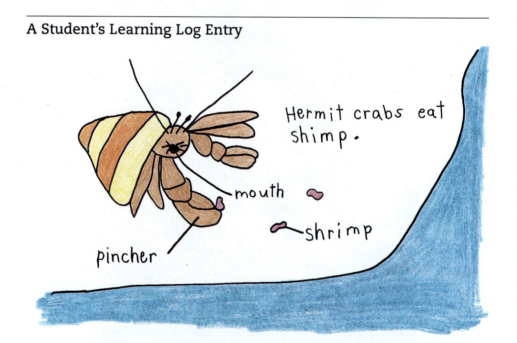

This week, Ms. Williams adds *soon, house, your*, and *you're* to the word wall. She chooses *soon* and *house* because these words are used in *A House for Hermit Crab* and because several students have recently asked her how to spell *house*. She chooses the homophones *your* and *you're* because the second graders are confusing these two words. She's also noticed that some students don't understand contractions, so she plans to review them using *you're* as an example.

The students sit on a rug in front of the word wall when Ms. Williams introduces new words. She explains that two of the new words—*house* and *soon*—are from *A House for Hermit Crab*. She uses a cookie sheet and large magnetic letters to introduce each new word, scrambling the letters at the bottom of the cookie sheet and slowly building the new word at the top as students make guesses. She begins with *h*, adds the *ou*, and several students call out "house." Ms. Williams continues adding letters, and when they're all in place, a chorus of voices cries, "house!" It's Kari's turn to write the new word card: She carefully writes *house* and places the card in the H square of the word wall. The students chant and clap as they say and spell the word. Ms. Williams begins, "House, house, h-o-u-s-e," and students echo her chant. Then she calls on Enrique to lead the chant, and students echo him. Afterward, Ms. Williams repeats the procedure with the three other new words.

The next day, Ms. Williams uses **interactive writing** to compose sentences with each of the new words. The students write these sentences and underline the new words:

> The hermit crab has a good shell for a <u>house</u>. He likes it but <u>soon</u> he will move. "<u>You're</u> too small for me," he says. "I have to move, but I will always be <u>your</u> friend."

During the week, the students practice reading and writing the words. They do a **cloze** activity by filling in the missing words on sentence strips that Ms. Williams has prepared and laminated, writing words from the sentences on whiteboards as Ms. Williams says them, and copying the sentences in their reading logs using their best handwriting. They also cut apart word cards, arrange the cards to create the sentences, and then glue them onto a sheet of construction paper.

Ms. Williams reviews contractions in a **minilesson**, explaining that *you're* is a contraction of *you* and *are* and that the apostrophe indicates that a letter's been omitted. Then students volunteer other contractions. Michael identifies three: *I'm, can't*, and *don't*; Miki offers *it's* and *won't*. They make a chart, listing the contractions and the two words that make up each one. Afterward, Ms. Williams puts the chart in the word work center so the students can use the information to make books about contractions.

After this practice with high frequency words, students participate in activities at literacy centers while Ms. Williams meets with guided reading groups. Most of the center activities integrate literacy activities with learning about hermit crabs, but students also practice reading and writing high frequency words at two centers. Ms. Williams's literacy centers are described here. Each morning, a sixth grade student-aide comes to the classroom to monitor the students, work at the centers. Ms. Williams worked with two sixth grade teachers to train 10 students to serve as aides, and they come to the classroom once every other week on a rotating basis.

As a culminating activity, the second graders write a retelling of *A House for Hermit Crab*. The students compose the text, and Ms. Williams uses the **Language Experience Approach** to write their draft on chart paper. The students revise their text, and then Ms. Williams types it and makes copies. Each student receives a copy of the five-page retelling to read and illustrate. Later, they'll take their booklets home to read to their families.

Ms. Wiliams's Literacy Centers

Center	Activity
Library	Students read books about hermit crabs and reread leveled books that they've read in guided reading groups.
Listening	Students use headphones to listen to *A House for Hermit Crab* (Carle, 2005) and *Hermit Crab's Home* (Halfmann, 2007) as they follow along in individual copies of the books.
Retelling	Students sequence pictures from *A House for Hermit Crab* and use them as a guide to retell the story.
Science	Students observe a hermit crab and write entries in learning logs about the crustacean's physical characteristics and eating habits.
Word Sort	Students sort vocabulary words from *A House for Hermit Crab* into categories, including ocean animals and plants.
Word Wall	Students practice reading the high frequency word wall using pointers. Then they copy familiar words from the word wall on a paper that's been divided into 10 sections with letters spelling *hermit crab* written in the sections.
Word Work	Students use magnetic letters to spell this week's high frequency words and the words from the last 2 weeks. They also make a book of contractions with picture and sentence examples.
Writing	Students write books about hermit crabs or "I Am a Hermit Crab" poems following the model posted at the center.

Ms. Williams reads their retelling aloud, and afterward, the students participate in **choral reading** activities; the numbers on the left side indicate which group reads each sentence. Everybody joins in for the last line. As students read, they're becoming more fluent readers. Here's the last section of the class's retelling:

1 Soon it was January again.

2 The big Hermit Crab moved out of his house and the little crab moved in.

3 Hermit Crab said, "Goodbye. Be good to my friends."

4 Soon Hermit Crab saw the next perfect house for him.

5 It was empty.

1 It was a little plain but Hermit Crab didn't care.

2 He will decorate it

3 with starfish,

4 with coral,

5 with sea anemones,

1 with sea urchins,

2 and with snails.

All: There are so many possibilities!

The underlined words are high frequency that are posted on the word wall in Ms. Williams's classroom; of the 75 words in this excerpt, 40 are high frequency words! Also, two of the new words for this week, *soon* and *house*, are used twice.

Fluency is reading and writing effortlessly and efficiently. Becoming fluent readers and writers is a developmental milestone. Most students reach the fluent stage during third grade through a combination of explicit instruction and lots of authentic reading and writing. This achievement is crucial because both readers and writers must be able to focus attention on meaning, not on decoding and spelling words.

The Common Core State Standards for English Language Arts (2010) address reading fluency as an essential foundational skill that students must develop no later than fourth grade to become proficient readers. The Standards focus on teaching students to use phonics and other word-identification strategies to decode unfamiliar words and on ensuring that students read fluently. The Common Core Standards box in this chapter provides additional information.

Reading Fluency

Reading **fluency** means reading quickly, accurately, with expression, and in a phrased way; to read fluently, students must recognize most words automatically and be able to identify unfamiliar words easily (Caldwell & Leslie, 2013). Fluent readers are better able to comprehend what they're reading because they automatically recognize most of the words and apply word-identification strategies to identify unfamiliar ones, and their reading is faster and more expressive (Kuhn, Rasinski & Zimmerman, 2014). Reading fluency involves these three components:

Automaticity.   Recognizing familiar words without conscious thought and identifying unfamiliar words almost as quickly, is called **automaticity**. It's crucial that students know most of the words they're reading because when they have to stop to decode words, their reading slows down. Students ought to be able to read a text after you have used it in instruction with 95% accuracy; that's 19 of every 20 words or 95 of every 100 words (Rodgers, D'Agostino, Kelly & Mikita, 2018). These are texts that you can then use to teach students fluently.

Speed.   Fluent readers read at least 100 words per minute; most students reach this speed by third grade, and their **reading rate** continues to grow each year. By eighth grade, most students read 150 words per minute, and many adults read 250 words per minute or more. In addition, fluent readers vary reading speed depending on the selection—its genre and level of difficulty—and their purpose for reading.

Prosody.   Reading with appropriate phrasing and intonation is called **prosody**. Paige and colleagues (2017) explain that reading with appropriate prosody contributes to comprehension. It seems that knowing how to group words together helps with understanding what you are reading, and vice versa, understanding what you

Common Core State Standards
Reading Fluency

The Reading Standards: Foundational Skills strand fosters K–4 students' understanding of the basic conventions of the English writing system so that they'll become proficient readers who can comprehend fiction and nonfiction texts. The Standards address these fluency requirements:

- Students know and apply grade-level phonics and word-analysis skills to decode words.
- Students read with sufficient accuracy and fluency to support comprehension.
- Students use word-identification strategies to decode unfamiliar words.

The Standards emphasize that foundational skills aren't an end in themselves, but they're essential for reading comprehension. They direct teachers to differentiate instruction because capable readers need less practice to become fluent than those who struggle. To learn more about the Standards, go to http://www.corestandards.org/ELA-Literacy, or check your state's educational standards website.

Figure 6–1 Characteristics of Fluent Readers

Component	Characteristics
Automaticity	Students recognize many high frequency words. Students apply phonics knowledge to decode words. Students decode words by analogy to familiar words. Students break longer words into syllables to decode them.
Speed	Students read at least 100 words per minute. Students vary their speed depending on their purpose for reading and the difficulty of the text.
Prosody	Students read expressively. Students chunk words into phrases. Students read smoothly, with few pauses or breakdowns. Students' reading pace approximates speech.

are reading helps you know how to group words. Why is this so? The meaning of a text can be said to reside in the phrases, or the way words are grouped together when reading.

Beginning readers may read word by word with little or no expression, but with teaching, they chunk words into phrases, attend to punctuation, and apply appropriate syntactic emphases. Once students become fluent readers, their oral reading approximates speech more closely.

Too often, reading quickly is equated with fluency; some assessment tools use speed as the only measure of fluency, but accurately identifying words and reading expressively are also critical components. Figure 6–1 presents an overview of the characteristics of fluent readers.

Automatic Reading

Students acquire a large stock of words that they recognize automatically and read correctly because it's impossible to analyze every word they encounter when reading. Through repeated reading and writing experiences, students develop automaticity—the ability to quickly recognize words (Samuels, 2013). The vital element in word recognition is learning each word's unique letter sequence.

HIGH FREQUENCY WORDS.   The most common words that readers use again and again are **high frequency words**. There have been numerous attempts to identify these words and to calculate their frequency in reading materials. Pinnell and Fountas (1998, p. 89) identified these 24 common words that kindergartners learn to read:

a	at	he	it	no	the
am	can	I	like	see	to
an	do	in	me	she	up
and	go	is	my	so	we

They also learn to write many of these words.

The words in this list are part of the 100 high frequency words, which account for more than half of the words people read and write. Eldredge (2005) has identified the 300 high frequency words that make up nearly three quarters of the words people read and write; these 300 words account for 72% of the words that beginning readers are able to read. Figure 6–2 presents Eldredge's list of 300 high frequency words; the 100 most common are in red. Most students learn the majority of the 100 highest frequency words in first grade and the rest of the words during second and third grades. If fourth graders don't know these words, it's essential that they learn them to become automatic and accurate readers and writers.

Figure 6–2 The 300 High Frequency Words

a	children	great	looking	ran	through
about	city	green	made	read	time
after	come	grow	make	red	to
again	could	had	man	ride	toad
all	couldn't	hand	many	right	together
along	cried	happy	may	road	told
always	dad	has	maybe	room	too
am	dark	hat	me	run	took
an	day	have	mom	said	top
and	did	he	more	sat	tree
animals	didn't	head	morning	saw	truck
another	do	hear	mother	say	try
any	does	heard	mouse	school	two
are	dog	help	Mr.	sea	under
around	don't	hen	Mrs.	see	until
as	door	her	much	she	up
asked	down	here	must	show	us
at	each	hill	my	sister	very
ate	eat	him	name	sky	wait
away	end	his	need	sleep	walk
baby	even	home	never	small	walked
back	ever	house	new	so	want
bad	every	how	next	some	wanted
ball	everyone	I	nice	something	was
be	eyes	I'll	night	soon	water
bear	far	I'm	no	started	way
because	fast	if	not	stay	we
bed	father	in	nothing	still	well
been	find	inside	now	stop	went
before	fine	into	of	stories	were
began	first	is	off	story	what
behind	fish	it	oh	sun	when
best	fly	it's	old	take	where
better	for	its	on	tell	while
big	found	jump	once	than	who
bird	fox	jumped	one	that	why
birds	friend	just	only	that's	will
blue	friends	keep	or	the	wind
book	frog	king	other	their	witch
books	from	know	our	them	with
box	fun	last	out	then	wizard
boy	garden	left	over	there	woman
brown	gave	let	people	these	words
but	get	let's	picture	they	work
by	girl	like	pig	thing	would
called	give	little	place	things	write
came	go	live	play	think	yes
can	going	long	pulled	this	you
can't	good	look	put	thought	your
cat	got	looked	rabbit	three	you're

From *Teach Decoding: Why and How* (2nd ed., pp. 119–120), by J. L. Eldredge, © 2005. Adapted by permission of Prentice Hall, Inc., Upper Saddle River, NJ.

The words in **red** are the first 100 most frequently used words, as shown in Figure 5–4 on p. 140.

Many high frequency words are tough to learn because they can't be easily decoded (Cunningham, 2014); try sounding out the words *to*, *what*, and *could* and you'll see how difficult they are. A further complication is that many of these words are function words, so they don't carry much meaning. It's easier to learn to recognize *whale* than *what*, because *whale* conjures up the image of the huge aquatic mammal, but *what* is abstract; however, *what* is used much more frequently, and students must learn to read and write it.

Teachers teach the high frequency words using explicit instruction. Each week they introduce three to five words, and then involve students in a variety of activities each day to practice reading and writing the words, as Ms. Williams did in the vignette at the beginning of the chapter. Even though the words are listed alphabetically in Figure 6–2, they aren't taught in that order; instead, teachers choose words that they can connect with literacy activities in the classroom or words that students are using but confusing.

Teachers create **word walls** with the high frequency words. They prepare word walls at the beginning of the school year and then add to them as they introduce new words. Kindergarten teachers begin by listing students' names and other common words (e.g., *love*, *Mom*) and then adding one or two per week of the 24 highest frequency words. First grade teachers begin with the 24 words introduced in kindergarten and add new words each week. In second grade, teachers begin with the easier half of the first 100 words and introduce 100 more words during the school year. Third grade teachers check students' knowledge of the 100 or 200 high frequency words at the beginning of the school year, add any words they don't know, and then teach the rest so that everyone learns most of the 300 high frequency words by the end of the year. Fourth grade teachers continue to use high frequency word walls if their students aren't fluent readers and writers; they test students' ability to read and write the 300 high frequency words and teach the ones they don't know.

> Check the Compendium of Instructional Procedures, which follows Chapter 12. These **green** terms also show a brief description of each procedure.

Teaching high frequency words isn't easy because many of them have little or no meaning when they're used in isolation. Cunningham (2014) recommends this chant-and-clap procedure to practice the words being placed on the word wall:

1. **Introduce the word in context.** Teachers introduce the new word using a familiar book or with pictures or objects.

2. **Have students chant and clap the word.** Teachers display the word card that will be placed on the word wall. They read and spell the word and have students read and spell it. Then they begin a chant, saying the word twice, spelling it, and then saying the word again; for the word *the*, teachers say, "The, the, t-h-e, the" as they clap their hands. The students repeat the chant several times.

3. **Involve students in practice activities.** Teachers provide daily opportunities for students to practice reading and writing the words:

   - Students search for the word in books they're reading and on charts posted in the classroom.

   - Students write a sentence using the word on a sentence strip, read it to classmates, and later cut the sentence apart and rearrange the words.

   - Students write the words on whiteboards.

   - Students use magnetic letters to spell the words.

   - Teachers lead students in some of these activities, and students do others at centers.

4. **Provide authentic reading and writing activities.** Students read and write the word during authentic literacy activities. During sharing sessions after independent reading and writing, teachers ask students to point where they read or wrote the word. Teachers also draw attention to the word during **interactive read-alouds**, **shared reading**, and **interactive writing** activities.

Using this chant-and-clap procedure, teachers highlight high frequency words, and easily confused words are clarified and practiced. A **minilesson** showing how a first grade teacher teaches high frequency words is presented in Minilesson.

WORD-IDENTIFICATION STRATEGIES.   Students use word-identification strategies to read unfamiliar words. Young students depend on phonics to sound out unfamiliar words, but beginning readers learn decoding by analogy and syllabic analysis as they become more fluent readers. These word-identification strategies are summarized in Figure 6–3.

Phonic Analysis.   Students apply what they've learned about phoneme–grapheme correspondences and phonics rules to decode words. Even though English isn't a perfectly phonetic language, phonic analysis is a very useful strategy because almost every word has some phonetically regular parts. Researchers report that the biggest difference between students who identify words effectively and those who don't is whether they notice almost all the letters in a word and analyze the letter sequences (Stanovich, 1992). Young students often try to decode a word by guessing at it based on the beginning sound. As you might imagine, their guesses are usually wrong; sometimes they don't even make sense in the sentence.

Decoding by Analogy.   Students identify some words by associating them with words they already know; this strategy is known as *decoding by analogy* (Cunningham, 2014). When readers come to *small*, for example, they might notice the phonogram *-all*, think of the word *ball*, and decode the word by analogy. Students learn to apply this strategy when they read and write "word families" using familiar phonograms, such as *-at, -ell, -ice, -own,* and *-unk*. Students must be familiar with consonant blends and digraphs and able manipulate sounds to apply this strategy. Using *-ill*, for example, students can read and spell these words: *bill, chill, fill, gill, grill, hill, kill, pill, spill, still,* and *will*. They can decode longer words, too, including *hills, chilly, killers, grilling, hilltop,* and *pillow*. Teachers also share picture books that include several words representing a particular phonogram (Caldwell & Leslie, 2013). In Fleming's *In the Tall, Tall Grass* (1995), for example, students can locate these *-um* words: *drum, hum, strum*. The Booklist in this chapter presents additional books with words representing common phonograms. Decoding by analogy is very useful, but it's a big step for students to move from a structured activity to using this strategy independently to identify unfamiliar words.

Figure 6–3 Word-Identification Strategies

Strategy	Description	Examples
Phonic Analysis	Students apply their knowledge of sound–symbol correspondences, phonics rules, and spelling patterns to read or write a word.	*blaze* *chin* *peach* *spring*
Decoding by Analogy	Students use their knowledge of phonograms to deduce the pronunciation or spelling of an unfamiliar word.	*claw* from *saw* *flat* from *cat* *stone* from *cone* *think* from *pink*
Syllabic Analysis	Students break a multisyllabic word into syllables and then use their knowledge of phonics and phonograms to decode the word, syllable by syllable.	*drag-on* *fa-mous* *mul-ti-ply* *vol-ca-no*
Morphemic Analysis	Students apply their knowledge of root words and affixes to read or write an unfamiliar word.	*astro-naut* *bi-cycle* *centi-pede* *trans-port*

Minilesson

TOPIC: Teaching High Frequency Words
GRADE: First Grade
TIME: One 15-minute period

Miss Shapiro's goal is for her first graders to learn at least 75 of the 100 high frequency words. She has a large word wall that's divided into sections for each letter. Each week, she introduces three new words and adds them to the word wall; she chooses words from the big book she's using for shared reading. On Monday, she introduces the new words, and over the next 4 days, she focuses on them and reviews those she's introduced previously. To make the word study more authentic, she often has the students hunt for the word in reading materials available in the classroom; sometimes they look in familiar big books, in small books they're rereading, on charts of familiar poems and songs, or on Language Experience and interactive writing charts. On other days, the students create sentences using the words, which the teacher writes on sentence strips and displays in the classroom.

1. **Introduce the Topic**
   "Let's read the D words on the word wall," Miss Shapiro says. As she points to the words, the class reads them aloud. "Which word is new this week?" she asks. The students respond, "do." Next, they read the H words and identify *here* as a new word, and then the M words and identify *my* as a new word. Miss Shapiro asks individual students to reread the D, H, and M words on the word wall.

2. **Share Examples**
   "Who can come up and point to our three new words for this week?" Miss Shapiro asks. Aaron eagerly comes to the word wall to point out *do, here,* and *my*. As he points to each word, Miss Shapiro writes it on the whiteboard, pronounces it, and spells it aloud. She and Aaron lead the class as they chant and clap the words: "Do, do, d-o, do!" "Here, here, h-e-r-e, here!" "My, my, m-y, my!"

3. **Provide Information**
   "Let's look for *do, here,* and *my* in these books," Miss Shapiro suggests as she passes out a familiar big book to the students at each table. In each group, the students reread the book, pointing out *do, here,* and *my* each time they occur. The teacher circulates around the classroom, checking that the students notice the words.

4. **Guide Practice**
   Miss Shapiro asks Aaron to choose three classmates to come to the whiteboard to spell the words with large magnetic letters; Daniel, Elizabeth, and Wills spell the words and read them aloud. Then Aaron passes out plastic bags with small magnetic letters and word cards to pairs of students; they read the word cards and spell the three words at their desks.

5. **Assess Learning**
   On Friday, Miss Shapiro works with the first graders in small groups, asking them to locate the words in sentences they've written and to read the words individually on word cards.

Booklist Books with Words Representing a Phonogram

Phonogram	Book
-ack	Shaw, N. E. (1996). *Sheep take a hike*.
-ail	Shaw, N. E. (1992). *Sheep on a ship*.
-are	Fleming, D. (1998). *In the small, small pond*.
-ash	Shaw, N. E. (2005). *Sheep eat out*.
-ay	Fleming, D. (1998). *In the small, small pond*.
-eep	Shaw, N. E. (1997). *Sheep in a jeep*.
-eet	Heiligman, D. (2005). *Fun dog, sun dog*.
-ip	Fleming, D. (1995). *In the tall, tall grass*.
-og	Wood, A. (1992). *Silly Sally*.
-oose	Numeroff, L. J. (1991). *If you give a moose a muffin*.
-op	Shaw, N. E. (2005). *Sheep eat out*.
-ouse	Hoberman, M. A. (2007). *A house is a house for me*.
-own	Wood, A. (1992). *Silly Sally*.
-uck	Root, R. (2003). *One duck stuck*.
-ug	Edwards, P. D. (1996). *Some smug slug*.
-um	Fleming, D. (1995). *In the tall, tall grass*.
-un	Heiligman, D. (2005). *Fun dog, sun dog*.

SYLLABIC ANALYSIS.   More experienced readers divide longer words, such as *angry*, *pioneer*, and *yogurt*, into syllables to identify them. There's one vowel sound in each syllable of a word, but sometimes there's more than one vowel letter in a syllable. Consider the two-syllable words *target* and *chimney*: *Target* has a single vowel letter representing a short vowel sound in each syllable; *chimney* has one vowel in the first syllable but two vowel letters (*ey*) representing a long vowel sound in the second syllable. The most common guidelines for dividing words into syllables are presented in Figure 6–4. The first rule about dividing syllables between two consonants is the easiest one; examples include *mer-maid* and *pic-nic*. The second rule deals with words where three consonants appear together, such as *ex-plore*: The word is divided between *x* and *p* to preserve the *pl* blend. The third and fourth rules involve the VCV pattern. Usually the syllable

Figure 6–4 Syllabication Rules

Rule	Examples	
When two consonants come between two vowels in a word, divide syllables between the consonants.	*mer-maid* *pic-nic*	*soc-cer* *win-dow*
When more than two consonants are together in a word, divide the syllables keeping the blends intact.	*bank-rupt* *con-trol*	*ex-plore* *mon-ster*
When one consonant comes between two vowels in a word, divide the syllables after the first vowel.	*bo-nus* *ho-tel*	*plu-ral* *shi-ny*
If following the previous rule doesn't make a recognizable word, divide the syllables after the consonant that comes between the vowels.	*doz-en* *ech-o*	*plan-et* *riv-er*
When there are two vowels together that don't represent a long vowel sound or a diphthong, divide the syllables between the vowels.	*li-ar* *li-on*	*po-em* *qui-et*

boundary comes after the first vowel, as in *ho-tel* and *shi-ny*; however, in words such as *riv-er*, the division comes after the consonant because *ri-ver* isn't a recognizable word. According to the fifth rule, syllables are divided between two vowels when they don't represent a digraph or diphthong; one example is *li-on*.

MORPHEMIC ANALYSIS. Students use morphemic analysis to identify multisyllabic words. They locate the root word by peeling off any affixes (prefixes or suffixes). A root word is a **morpheme**—the basic, most meaningful part of a word. **Prefixes** are added to the beginning of a root word, as in *replay*, and **suffixes** are added to the end, as in *playing*, *playful*, and *player*. Two types of suffixes are *inflectional* and *derivational*. Inflectional suffixes are endings that indicate verb tense, person, plurals, possession, and comparison:

the -s in *dogs*	the -ed in *walked*	the -er in *faster*
the -es in *beaches*	the -s in *eats*	the -est in *sunniest*
the -'s in *girl's*	the -ing in *singing*	

In contrast, derivational suffixes show the relationship of the word to its root word. Consider these words containing the root word *friend*: *friendly*, *friendship*, and *friendless*. When students recognize roots and affixes, they can more easily break apart multisyllabic words and identify them:

astronaut (astro = *star*; naut = *sailor*)

bicycle (bi = *two*; cycle = *wheels*)

microscope (micro = *small*; scope = *see*)

scribble (scrib = *write*)

synonym (syn = *same*; onym = *name*)

vitamin (vita = *life*)

In addition, knowing the meaning of word parts provides context and facilitates word identification.

Teaching word-identification strategies is an essential part of a balanced literacy program that helps students focus on words. Teachers choose words for minilessons from books students are reading, as Ms. Williams did in the vignette, or from thematic units.

Fluent readers recognize most words automatically and apply word-identification strategies effectively to decode unfamiliar words. Less fluent readers, in contrast, can't

Teach Kids to Be Strategic!

Word-Identification Strategies

Teach students to use these strategies to identify unfamiliar words when they're reading and writing:

- Phonic analysis
- Decode by analogy
- Divide into syllables
- Apply morphemic analysis

Students practice these strategies when they participate in guided reading lessons and during reading and writing workshop. Their choice of strategy depends on their knowledge about words and the complexity of the unfamiliar word. If students struggle, reteach the strategies in minilessons, demonstrate their use, and think aloud about their application.

Figure 6–5 Oral Reading Speeds

Grade	End of the Year
1	60–75 wcpm*
2	80–100
3	100–120
4	120–140

* wcpm = words correct per minute

read as many words or use as many strategies for decoding words. Researchers have concluded that students who don't become fluent readers depend on explicit instruction to learn how to identify words (Gaskins, Gaskins, & Gaskins, 1991).

Reading Speed

Students need to develop an adequate reading speed so they have the cognitive resources available to focus on meaning (Allington, McCuiston & Billen, 2015; Rasinski et al., 2017). Researchers have identified target reading speeds for each grade level, and they're shown in Figure 6–5; however, teachers should use these numbers cautiously because reading speed is affected by many factors. Fountas and Pinnell (2013) identified these factors that affect reading speed:

- Students who have background knowledge about the topic can read more quickly and connect the ideas they're reading to what they already know.

- Students who are knowledgeable about the genre, text structure, and text layout can anticipate what they're reading.

- Students who speak English fluently have an advantage in developing reading speed because they know more words, are familiar with English sentence structures, and recognize metaphors and other literary features.

Students become more strategic readers as they learn to use speed appropriately and vary their reading rate depending on the text.

Teachers provide daily practice opportunities to develop students' reading speed and stamina. To increase reading volume, teachers offer a combination of teacher-guided and independent reading practice:

Choral Reading.   Students work in small groups or together as a class for **choral reading**. They experiment with different ways to read poems and other short texts aloud (Rasinski & Young, 2017). More fluent classmates serve as models and set the reading speed.

Readers Theatre.   Students practice reading a story script to develop reading speed and expressiveness before performing it for classmates. Researchers have found that **readers theatre** sinificantly improves students' reading fluency (Martinez, Roser, & Strecker, 1998/1999).

Listening Centers.   Students read along in a book at their instructional reading level while listening to it being read aloud at a listening center (Kuhn & Stahl, 2013).

Partner Reading.   Classmates read or reread books together in pairs (Griffith & Rasinski, 2004). They choose a book that interests them and decide how they'll read it; they may read aloud in unison or take turns reading aloud while their buddy follows along.

To develop fluency through these practice activities, books must be appropriate; that is, students must be interested in the topics and be able to read them with 98 or 99% accuracy.

Once students become fluent readers, the focus shifts to helping them develop reading stamina so they can read for 30 minutes or more. Students develop this strength through daily opportunities to read independently for increasingly longer periods. When students' reading is limited to basal reader selections or leveled books that can be completed in 15 minutes or less, they won't develop the endurance they need. Teachers include extended opportunities each day for independent reading of self-selected texts, and students also benefit from doing additional independent reading at home.

Prosody

When students read expressively, they use their voices to add meaning to the words. Rasinski and Padak (2013) identified these components of prosody:

Expression.   Students read with enthusiasm and vary their expression to match their interpretation of the text.

Phrasing.   Students chunk words into phrases as they read and apply stress and intonation appropriately.

Volume.   Students vary the loudness of their voices to add meaning to the text.

Smoothness.   Students read with a smooth rhythm and quickly self-correct any breakdowns.

Pacing.   Students read at a conversational speed.

MyLab Education
Video Example 6.1

In this video, Mrs. Martin discusses strategies for reading expressively. What recommended practices did she use to engage her students?

Developmental Continuum Oral Reading Fluency

PreK	K	1	2	3	4
Four-year-olds begin to develop an understanding of fluency—accuracy, speed, and prosody—as they listen to teachers read aloud.	Students participate in fluent reading as they recite refrains while teachers read aloud big books and charts.	Students recognize many high frequency words and decode others; they read 50 wcpm.	Students' oral reading becomes more accurate, rapid, and expressive; they read 80 wcpm by the end of the year.	Most third graders read aloud 100 wcpm. with accuracy and expression the fluency milestone, where they accurately and expressively read aloud 100 wcpm.	Fluent fourth graders read most books successfully, but dysfluent readers struggle with grade level materials.

These components seem more related to oral reading, but prosody plays an important role during silent reading, too, because a student's internal voice affects comprehension.

Literacy Portraits

Most second graders move toward fluent reading, and Ms. Janusz spends a great deal of time talking about fluent reading, explaining its importance, teaching the components, and listening to her students read aloud to monitor their growth. Here, Ms. Janusz explains reading fluency during a guided reading lesson. Does she include all three components of fluency addressed in this chapter?

Rakie

Teachers emphasize prosody by modeling expressive reading every time they read aloud and using the **think-aloud** procedure to reflect on how they varied their expression, chunked words into phrases, modulated the loudness of their voice, or varied their pacing. They talk about the importance of prosody for both fluency and comprehension and show students how meaning is affected when they read in a monotone or slow down their reading speed.

Choral reading and **readers theatre** are two ways to develop prosody. In choral reading, students work together in small groups to read poems and other texts. They practice reading the text until they can read it smoothly, and they experiment with ways to read more expressively, including varying their intonation patterns, the loudness of their voices, and their pacing. In readers theatre, students assume the roles of characters and practice reading a script aloud without performing it; the emphasis is on reading smoothly at a conversational pace and using expression so their voices add meaning to the words.

MyLab Education Self-Check 6.1

MyLab Education Application Exercise 6.1: Adelia Reads Fluently

---

Writing Fluency

Fluent writers spell words automatically and write quickly so that they can focus on developing their ideas. Their writing seems to flow effortlessly, and it's distinctive. Fluent writing sounds like talking—it has "voice." Fluency is as crucial for writers as it is for readers, and the components are similar:

Automaticity.   Fluent writers write most words automatically, without having to stop and think about how to spell them. Students must know how to spell high frequency words and be able to apply strategies to spell other words; otherwise, they get so bogged down in spelling a word that they forget the sentence they're writing or the one that comes next.

Speed.   Students need to write quickly enough to keep pace with their thinking. Researchers have examined the number of words students write per minute, compared their speed to the quality of their compositions, and concluded that students need to write 10 words per minute to be considered fluent writers (Santangelo & Graham, 2016). Most third graders reach this rate, and because girls usually do more writing than boys do, it isn't surprising that they write one or two words per minute faster than boys. Sometimes legibility is an issue because students sacrifice neatness for speed: It doesn't do any good to write quickly if readers can't decipher students' writing.

Writer's Voice.   Writers develop distinctive voices that reflect their individuality (Spandel, 2012). Voice, which is similar to prosody, is the tone or emotional feeling of a piece of writing. Writers develop their voices through the words they choose and how they string words into sentences. Each student's voice is unique, and teachers can usually identify who wrote a composition according to its voice, just as many of us can identify books written by our favorite authors by their voice.

The characteristics of fluent writers are summarized in Figure 6–6.

Automatic Writing

To become fluent writers, students need to be able to spell most high frequency words automatically and apply spelling strategies to write other words. Teachers teach students to write high frequency words the same way they teach them to read the

Figure 6–6 Characteristics of Fluent Writers

Component	Characteristics
Automaticity	Students spell most high frequency words correctly.
	Students apply spelling patterns and rules to spell words correctly.
	Students' spelling becomes increasingly more conventional.
Speed	Students write quickly.
	Students write easily, without discomfort.
	Students write legibly.
	Students develop keyboarding skills to word process quickly.
Writer's Voice	Students' writing has a personal style.
	Students use distinctive vocabulary.
	Students incorporate particular sentence structures into their writing.

words. Each week they introduce five or six words and provide daily opportunities for students to practice reading and writing them through these activities:

- Students write the words and sentences they compose on whiteboards.
- Students use letter cards or magnetic letters to spell the words.
- Students write the words in interactive writing activities.

Teachers direct some of these activities, and students participate in others at literacy centers.

At first, students sound out the words they're trying to spell. They segment the word into sounds and write a letter for each sound they recognize. They might spell *baby* as *babe* or *house* as *hus*, for example, using their knowledge of phoneme–grapheme correspondences, but through phonics and spelling instruction and more experience with reading and writing, students spell words more accurately. They also learn to use the "think it out" strategy to spell words. Students apply their knowledge of phonics rules, spelling patterns, word families, syllables, and morphemes along with matching sounds to letters. They also develop a visual image of words they can read, and they're more likely to recognize when a spelling doesn't look right and ask a classmate, check a word wall, or consult a dictionary to get the correct spelling.

Writing Speed

For students to become fluent writers, their transcription of ideas onto paper must be automatic; that means they spell most words automatically and use legible handwriting without thinking about how to form letters or keyboard without hunting for letter keys.

Students need to know how to hold pencils comfortably, so their hands and arms don't hurt, and they need to learn how to form manuscript letters in kindergarten through second grade and cursive letters in third and fourth grades to improve their speed and legibility. Sometimes teachers require third and fourth graders to write only in cursive, but students should be allowed to use either form, as long as it's easy to read and can be written quickly for writing projects.

Left-handed writers face unique handwriting problems. The basic difference between right- and left-handed writers is physical orientation: Right-handed students pull their hand and arm away from the body, but left-handed students move their left hand across what has just been written, often covering it. Too often, students adopt a "hook" position to avoid covering what they've just written. To address that problem,

GO DIGITAL! Keyboarding.

Keyboarding is an essential 21st-century literacy skill; most schools use commercial tutorial programs to teach typing skills, beginning with the location of the home keys and correct fingering on the keyboard. Students like these software programs because they're fun and engaging:

- Ainsworth Keyboard Trainer
- All the Right Type
- Garfield's Typing Pal
- Type to Learn
- Typing Instructor for Kids
- Typing Quick and Easy
- Ultra Key

Students practice using the keys to write words and sentences in these programs, and they receive feedback about their accuracy and speed. Students usually learn keyboarding in third or fourth grade, and this instruction is critical, because when they don't know how to keyboard, they use the inefficient hunt-and-peck technique and their writing speed is very slow.

Students develop writing speed through practice. They need to use writing throughout the school day—for example, to contribute to class charts, to make entries in reading logs, to write words and sentences on whiteboards, to add pages to class books, to write books at the writing center or during writing workshop, and to create projects during literature focus units and thematic units. When students use writing three or four times a day or write for extended periods each day, their writing speed will increase.

left-handed writers should hold pencils and pens an inch or more farther back from the tip than right-handed writers do so they can see what they've just written. The tilt of their papers is a second issue: Left-handed students should tilt their papers slightly to the right, in contrast to right-handed writers, who tilt their papers to the left to more comfortably form letters. Slant is a third concern: Left-handed writers should slant their letters in a way that allows them to write comfortably. It's acceptable for them to write cursive letters vertically or even slightly backward, in contrast to right-handed students, who slant cursive letters to the right.

For students with legibility problems, teachers check that they know how to hold writing instruments and how to form manuscript or cursive letters. It may be necessary to have students slow down their writing at first, concentrating on forming letters carefully and including every letter in each word, before they try to increase their writing speed. **Interactive writing** is a useful procedure for examining young students' handwriting skills and demonstrating how to form letters legibly.

Writer's Voice

The writer's voice reflects the person doing the writing and it should be expressive, sounding natural, not stilted. Pulitzer prize–winning author and teacher Donald Murray (2003) says that a writer's voice is the person in the writing. As students gain experience as readers and writers, their writers' voices will emerge, especially when they're writing on topics they know well.

Developmental Continuum Writing Fluency

PreK	K	1	2	3	4
Four-year-olds experiment with writing, print their names, and learn about fluency by watching teachers write messages.	Kindergartners spell 10 high frequency words, develop legible handwriting skills, and write patterned sentences.	Students write 50 high frequency words, use phonics to spell other words, and increase writing speed.	Second grade writers become more self-reliant; they spell more words conventionally, write faster, and develop their "voice."	Many students reach fluency by writing 10 wcpm, spelling words automatically, and personalizing their writing style.	Fluent writers increase writing speed and refine their "voice"; dysfluent writers struggle or avoid writing.

As students develop their writers' voices, they learn to vary their tone to entertain, inform, or persuade. They also learn that some writing forms require a more informal or formal voice: Think about the difference when you're writing an email message and a business letter. Similarly, students' voices are more casual and relaxed when they're writing for classmates than when they're writing for unknown adults.

Doing lots of reading and writing helps students develop their voices. As they read books and listen to the teacher read aloud, students develop an awareness of the writer's voice. Teachers highlight the lyrical tone in *Owl Moon* (Yolen, 2007) and *My Mama Had a Dancing Heart* (Gray, 2001), the lively spirit in *Barn Dance!* (Martin & Archambault, 1988), and repetition in *The Napping House* (Wood & Wood, 2010) and *Alexander and the Terrible, Horrible, No Good, Very Bad Day* (Viorst, 2009). As students become aware of these techniques, they begin applying them in their own writing.

At the same time they're examining authors' voices in books they're reading, students do lots of informal writing to develop their own voices. They need to write every day to become fluent. Keeping a personal journal is a good way to begin, or they write in **reading logs** on topics they choose or on topics the teacher provides. They can try writing from varied viewpoints to experiment with voice. For example, if students were retelling "Goldilocks and the Three Bears" from Goldilocks's viewpoint, the tone would be different than if it were from Papa Bear's perspective.

MyLab Education Self-Check 6.2

Assessing Reading And Writing Fluency

Researchers have found that fluent readers comprehend what they're reading better than less fluent readers do (National Reading Panel, 2000). The same is true about writers: Fluent writers are more successful in crafting effective compositions than less fluent writers are. Teachers use several different approaches to assess fluency in reading and writing so that they can plan appropriate instruction to scaffold students' fluency.

Assessing Reading Fluency

Teachers informally monitor students' reading fluency by listening to them read aloud during guided reading lessons, reading workshop, or other reading activities. At the beginning of the school year and at the end of each month or quarter, teachers collect data about students' automaticity, speed, and prosody to document their progress and provide evidence of their growth over time:

Automaticity. Teachers check students' knowledge of high frequency words and their ability to use word-identification strategies to decode other words taken from

MyLab Education
Video Example 6.2

What do you need to consider when assessing students' reading fluency? Review what Dr. Elfrieda Hiebert shares regarding teachers' assessment of reading fluency.

grade-level texts. Kindergartners are expected to read 24 high frequency words, first graders 100 words, second graders 200 words, and third graders 300 words. In addition to the list of high frequency words presented in this chapter, teachers can use the Dolch list of 220 sight words and Fry's list of 300 and 600 instant words, both of which are available in *Assessment for Reading Instruction* (McKenna & Stahl, 2015) and online.

Speed.   Teachers time students as they read an instructional-level passage aloud and determine how many words they read correctly per minute. Teachers can use the speeds listed in Figure 6–5 to compare students' speeds to national norms.

Prosody.   Teachers choose excerpts for students to read from both familiar and unfamiliar instructional-level texts. As they listen, teachers judge whether students read with appropriate expression. The **rubric** in the Assessment Snapshot on the next page can be used to evaluate students' prosody.

This assessment information is also useful for teachers as they make instructional decisions.

Teachers use **running records**, informal reading inventories, and classroom tests to document students' reading fluency. The Assessment Tools feature for Reading Fluency lists the tests that evaluate students' oral reading fluency—their reading speed in particular. Until students become fluent readers, it's crucial that teachers regularly monitor their developing accuracy, speed, and prosody to ensure that they're making adequate progress and identify those who are struggling.

MyLab Education
Video Example 6.3

Ms. Sprague demonstrates how she monitors her student's fluency progress in this video. What does she measure and how often does she monitor student progress?

Assessing Writing Fluency

Teachers assess writing fluency as they observe students' writing and examine their compositions. They consider these questions:

- Do students spell most words automatically and accurately, or do they stop to figure out how to spell many words?

- Do students write quickly enough to complete the assignment, or do they write slowly or try to avoid writing?

- Do students write legibly?

- Do students write easily, or do they write laboriously, complaining that their hands hurt?

Assessment Snapshot

Fluency Rubric

	1	2	3	4
Expression	Monotone	Some expressiveness ✓	Reasonable expressiveness	Expression matches interpretation
Phrasing	Word-by-word reading	Choppy reading	Reasonable chunking and intonation ✓	Effective phrasing
Volume	Very quiet voice	Quiet voice ✓	Appropriate volume	Volume matches interpretation
Smoothness	Frequent extended pauses and breakdowns	Some pauses and breakdowns	A few pauses and breakdown ✓	Smooth rhythm
Pacing	Laborious reading	Slow reading	Uneven combination of fast and slow reading	Appropriate conversational pace ✓

TEACHER'S NOTE

Jesse is a second grader, and in the spring of the year, he's reading at grade level. On the fluency rubric, Jesse scored a 3, indicating that he's making good progress toward fluency. I plan to show Jesse how to read with more expression and encourage him to read a little louder.

These questions help teachers quickly identify students who aren't fluent writers. If their observation suggests that students are struggling, teachers conduct additional testing to diagnose fluency problems:

Automaticity.   Teachers assess students' ability to spell the high frequency words and use strategies to spell other words with spelling tests or by examining their writing samples. Fluent writers spell most words correctly, so it's essential that students know how to spell high frequency words automatically and efficiently figure out the spelling of most other words they want to write.

Speed.   Teachers time students as they write a paragraph or two to assess their writing speed. Students write for one to five minutes about a familiar topic, and then teachers count the number of words they've written and divide that total by the number of minutes to determine students' writing rates. For example, second grader Amie writes 43 words in 5 minutes; her speed is nearly 9 words per minute, and she's almost reached the threshold fluency rate of 10 words per minute. Teachers repeat this assessment several times a year using a different familiar topic; each topic must be accessible because the purpose of the assessment is to monitor students writing speed, not their knowledge about the topic. Teachers also carefully observe students as they write because their behavior may indicate handwriting problems.

Writer's Voice.   Teachers reread several compositions students have written to evaluate their unique style. There aren't standards to use in assessing voice, so teachers often compare one student's writing to that of his or her classmates to rate it as comparable, above, or below average.

Commercial tests aren't available to assess students' writing fluency, but several informal assessments are useful in diagnosing writers with fluency problems. Harmey and her colleagues (D'Agostino & Rodgers, 2018) developed and tested a four-point rubric to assess early writing. Their rubric includes a row to describe writing fluency on a four-point scale:

0 - Writing was slow and labored. Required high support to form letters or words.

1 - Writing was generally slow, but for known words or letters, pace picked up.

2 - Writing was mostly fast and fluent but faltered over formation of some letters or words.

3 - Transcription was fast.

Reading fluency typically precedes writing fluency, but the two are clearly linked. The more reading students do, the sooner they'll reach writing fluency; and the more writing students do, the sooner they'll achieve reading fluency.

If Students Struggle . . .

When students aren't making adequate progress toward becoming fluent readers, teachers pinpoint the problem and intervene to get students back on track. Most young struggling readers have difficulty reading words automatically; teachers analyze the data from running records, informal reading inventories, or classroom tests to figure out which words students have difficulty reading. For problems with high frequency words, teachers explicitly teach the words that students don't know and involve them in daily reading and writing activities to use the words. For problems with word-identification strategies, teachers use minilessons to teach phonic analysis, decoding by analogy, and syllabic analysis using words students are attempting to read and write. Accuracy problems often overlap with speed and prosody difficulties because students can't read quickly or expressively when they don't know the words they're trying to read.

If the problem is speed or prosody, teachers use choral reading, readers theatre, partner reading, listening centers, and other activities recommended in this chapter to develop fluency. They closely monitor students' progress and involve them in charting their own growth.

Fluency problems often reflect students' limited reading and writing experience. The amount of reading and writing that students do makes a critical difference in their literacy achievement. The most important recommendation for students who struggle with fluency is to dramatically increase the amount of reading and writing they do every day. Students need to spend at least 15 minutes reading books at their independent reading level in addition to their formal reading instruction and any intervention programs.

Assessment Tools

Oral Reading Fluency

Teachers use these assessment tools as well as running records and IRIs to monitor and document students' reading fluency:

- **AIMSweb**

  Teachers screen students' oral reading fluency at the beginning of the school year and periodically monitor their progress during the year using AIMSweb—an online assessment system. As students read a text aloud, teachers click on their errors on the online scoring sheet, and afterward the system automatically scores the test. This K–4 assessment system is available from Pearson Education.

- **Dynamic Indicators of Basic Early Literacy Skills (DIBELS): Oral Reading Fluency Subtest**

  The Oral Reading Fluency Subtest is a collection of graded passages used to measure first through third graders' reading speed. In this individually administered test, students read aloud for one minute, and teachers mark errors; students' speed is the number of words read correctly. This test is available on the DIBELS website.

- **Fluency Formula Kits**

  Teachers use these grade-level kits, developed by Scholastic, to quickly assess an individual student's reading fluency three times a year and interpret their scores using national norms. Each grade-level kit contains 3 benchmark passages, 24 progress-monitoring passages, an assessment handbook, a student timer, and progress charts. The progress-monitoring passages can be used weekly to monitor struggling students' growth, and the handbook offers guidance on setting instructional goals and differentiating instruction.

- **Observation Survey of Early Literacy Achievement (OS): Word Reading and Writing Vocabulary Subtests**

  These two OS subtests assess students' knowledge of high frequency words. In the Word Reading Subtest, students read 15 high frequency words, and in the Writing Vocabulary Subtest, they write all the words they know (with a 10-minute time limit). The tests and directions for administering and scoring them are included in *An Observation Survey of Early Literacy Achievement* (Clay, 2013), which is available from Heinemann.

- **Phonological Awareness Literacy Screening (PALS) System: Word Recognition in Isolation Subtest**

  The Word Recognition Subtest consists of graded word lists that students read aloud; the highest level at which students read 15 words correctly is their instructional level. First through third grade teachers use this subtest to monitor students' automatic word recognition. The PALS test is available free for Virginia teachers from the University of Virginia, and it can be purchased by schools in other states.

Although many of these tests use reading speed to measure fluency, it's important to remember that fluency also requires students to recognize high frequency words automatically, apply word-identification strategies to decode unfamiliar words, and read expressively.

If Students Struggle . . .

Most students become fluent writers by fourth grade, but if they aren't making adequate progress during the primary grades, teachers analyze assessment data to determine where the problem lies and then provide instruction and practice opportunities to resolve it. Students who aren't moving toward fluency may have problems in spelling words correctly, writing fast enough, or developing a distinctive voice.

If the problem is automaticity, teachers determine whether students know how to spell most high frequency words and whether they can apply strategies to spell other words. Depending on students' problems, teachers provide instruction on high frequency words or spelling strategies and increase the amount of reading and writing students do.

If students are slow writers, teachers observe them or conference with them to figure out the problem and decide how to address it. Some students are slow writers because they have handwriting problems, and others aren't writing because they don't know what to do or lack background knowledge about the topic. Perhaps the student is being distracted by a classmate, or the student spends too much time on the illustration and runs out of time to do much writing.

If students aren't developing their writers' voices, it's likely that they haven't done much reading or writing. The best solution is to drastically increase the amount of reading and writing these students are doing. In addition, they need to listen to more books read aloud and talk about authors and how they develop their writers' voices.

Students who struggle with fluency may have a single problem, such as slow reading speed or delayed spelling development, but more often they face obstacles in both reading and writing; in this case, providing a combination of reading and writing instruction and practice is often the best solution.

Teaching English Learners

Fluency

To become fluent readers, English learners need to read words automatically, quickly, and expressively, like native English speakers do; however, it's unlikely that they'll become fluent readers until they speak English fluently because their lack of oral language proficiency limits their recognition of high frequency words and use of word-identification strategies, and it interferes with their ability to understand word meanings, string words together into sentences, and read expressively (Peregoy & Boyle, 2013). It's also unlikely that ELs will become fluent writers before they develop oral language proficiency.

Students who are learning English are immersed in learning to read and write at the same time they're learning to speak English, and teachers help them to make connections between the oral and written language modes to accelerate their achievement and overcome the obstacles that get in the way of their becoming fluent readers and writers:

Automaticity.   Becoming automatic and accurate readers and writers is challenging for many English learners, and the process takes longer than it does for native English speakers. High frequency words are difficult to recognize because so many of them are abstract (*about, this, which*), and they're hard to spell because many violate spelling rules (*could, said, what, who*). Many ELs speak with a native-language accent, which makes phonic analysis more arduous, but their pronunciation differences needn't hamper their reading fluency. For example, even though some Hispanic students, especially more recent immigrants, pronounce *check* as /shĕk/ because the *ch* digraph doesn't exist in Spanish, they're reading the word accurately. Everyone has an accent, even native English speakers, so ELs shouldn't be expected to eliminate their accents to be considered fluent readers. Applying syllabic analysis to identify words that aren't in their speaking vocabularies can be a formidable task, especially if they're not familiar with cognates or related words in their native language.

Speed.   English learners' limited background knowledge and lack of English vocabulary affect their reading and writing speed. By building background knowledge and introducing new words beforehand, teachers can help ELs improve their reading speed. In addition, students need opportunities to reread familiar books. To develop their writing speed, ELs need to talk about topics before writing and have available lists of words related to a topic. In addition, if teachers are over concerned with grammatical correctness, students will stick with safe, grammatically correct sentences they already know how to write.

Expressiveness/Writer's Voice.   Students' knowledge of spoken English plays a critical role in developing prosody and a writer's voice. ELs' intonation patterns usually reflect their native language; this common problem is due to their limited knowledge of English syntax and to the fact that punctuation marks don't provide enough clues about how to group words (Allington, 2009). To remedy this problem, teachers teach about punctuation marks. They use **echo reading**, in which the teacher reads a sentence expressively and then students reread it, trying to imitate the teacher's prosody. Developing a writer's voice is just as challenging: Students need to learn to use varied sentence structures, idioms, and figurative language. Teachers highlight the authors' voices in books they're reading aloud, and ELs often use books they've read as models for their writing. For example, they can adapt the repetitive sentence structure from *Brown Bear, Brown Bear, What Do You See?* (Martin, 2010) or *If You Give a Mouse a Cookie* (Numeroff, 1985) for their writing. ELs develop expressiveness through lots of reading and writing practice.

English learners need to develop fluency because automaticity, accuracy, speed, and expressiveness are necessary to handle the demands of reading and writing in fourth grade and beyond. The same combination of explicit instruction and authentic practice activities that's recommended for native speakers works for English learners; however, ELs often require more time because they're learning to speak English at the same time they're learning to read and write.

Use the **"My Teaching To-Do Checklist: Reading and Writing Fluency"** to gauge your preparedness to teach reading and writing fluency to all students.

MyLab Education **Self-Check 6.3**

MY TEACHING TO-DO CHECKLIST: Reading and Writing Fluency

- ☐ I post the appropriate high frequency words for my grade level on a word wall.
- ☐ I teach my students to read and spell high frequency words.
- ☐ I have my students read and write every day using authentic literacy materials.
- ☐ I model for my students how to use word-identification strategies.
- ☐ I teach my students how to form letters and write legibly.
- ☐ I check my students' reading and writing speeds periodically.
- ☐ I encourage my students to develop prosody, or expressiveness in reading.
- ☐ I nurture students as they develop a distinctive writer's voice.
- ☐ I integrate state standards into my instruction.

Chapter Review

Reading and Writing Fluency

- Reading fluency is made up of three components—automaticity, speed, and prosody—and teachers work to improve each of these as part of their fluency instruction.

- Fluent writing is made up of three components—automaticity, speed, and writer's voice—and teachers use several approaches to scaffold each.

- Teachers are sure to assess fluency in both reading and writing in order to inform their instruction.

Accountability Check

Visit the following assessment links to access quiz questions and instructional applications.

> MyLab Education Application Exercise 6.2: Understanding Literacy Development
> MyLab Education Application Exercise 6.3: Understanding Literacy Development
> MyLab Education Application Exercise 6.4: Monitoring Literacy Development
> MyLab Education Application Exercise 6.5: Measuring Literacy Development

References

Allington, R. L. (2009). *What really matters in fluency: Research-based practices across the curriculum.* Allyn & Boston/Pearson.

Allington, R. L., McCuiston, K., & Billen, M. (2015). What research says about text complexity and learning to read. *The Reading Teacher, 68*(7), 491–501.

Caldwell, J. S., & Leslie, L. (2013). *Intervention strategies to follow informal reading inventory assessment: So what do I do now?* (3rd ed.). Boston: Pearson.

Carle, E. (2005). *A house for hermit crab.* New York: Aladdin Books.

Clay, M. M. (2013). *An observation survey of early literacy achievement* (rev. ed.). Portsmouth, NH: Heinemann.

Common Core state standards for English language arts. (2010). Retrieved from http://www.corestandards.org/ELA-Literacy/

Cunningham, P. M. (2014). *What really matters in vocabulary: Research-based practices across the curriculum* (2nd ed.). Boston: Pearson.

Doudna, K. (2007). *Hidden hermit crabs.* Edina, MN: ABDO.

Eldredge, J. L. (2005). *Teach decoding: Why and how* (2nd ed.). Upper Saddle River, NJ: Merrill/Prentice Hall.

Fleming, D. (1995). *In the tall, tall grass.* New York: Henry Holt.

Fountas, I. C., & Pinnell, G. S. (2013). *The Fountas and Pinnell leveled book list, K–8* (2013–2015 ed.). Portsmouth, NH: Heinemann.

Gaskins, R. W., Gaskins, J. W., & Gaskins, I. W. (1991). A decoding program for poor readers—and the rest of the class, too! *Language Arts, 68*, 213–225.

Gray, L. M. (2001). *My mama had a dancing heart.* New York: Scholastic.

Griffith, L. W., & Rasinski, T. V. (2004). A focus on fluency: How one teacher incorporated fluency with her reading curriculum. *The Reading Teacher, 58*, 126–137.

Harmey, S. J., D'Agostino, J. V. & Rodgers, E. M. (in press). Developing an observational rubric of writing: Preliminary reliability and validity evidence. *Journal of Early Childhood Literacy.* https://doi.org/10.1177/1468798417724862

Kaplan, R. (1996). *Moving day.* New York: Greenwillow.

Kuhn, M. R., & Stahl, S. A. (2013). Fluency: Developmental and remedial practices—revisited. In D. E. Alvermann, N. J. Unrau, & R. B. Ruddell (Eds.), *Theoretical models and processes of reading* (6th ed., pp. 385–411). Newark, DE: International Reading Association.

Kuhn, M., Rasinski, T., & Zimmerman, B. (2014). Integrated fluency instruction: Three approaches for working with struggling readers. *International Electronic Journal of Elementary Education*, 7(1), 71.

Martin, B., Jr. (2010). *Brown bear, brown bear, what do you see?* New York: Henry Holt.

Martin, B., Jr., & Archambault, J. (1988). *Barn dance!* New York: Henry Holt.

Martinez, M., Roser, N. L., & Strecker, S. (1998/1999). "I never thought I could be a star": A readers theatre ticket to fluency. *The Reading Teacher*, 52, 326–334.

McKenna, M. C., & Stahl, K. A. D. (2015). *Assessment for reading instruction*. Guilford Publications.

Murray, D. M. (2003). *A writer teaches writing* (2nd ed.). Belmont, CA: Wadsworth.

National Reading Panel. (2000). *Teaching children to read: An evidence-based assessment of the scientific research literature on reading and its implications for reading instruction*. Washington, DC: National Institute of Child Health and Human Development.

Numeroff, L. J. (1985). *If you give a mouse a cookie*. New York: HarperCollins.

Paige, D., Rupley, W., Smith, G., Rasinski, T., Nichols, W., & Magpuri-Lavell, T. (2017). Is prosodic reading a strategy for comprehension? *Journal for educational research online / journal für bildungsforschung online*, 9(2), 245–275. Retrieved from http://www.journal-for-educational-research-online.com/index.php/jero/article/view/774

Peregoy, S. F., & Boyle, O. F. (2013). *Reading, writing and learning in ESL: A resource book for K–12 teachers* (6th ed.). Boston: Pearson.

Pinnell, G. S., & Fountas, I. C. (1998). *Word matters: Teaching phonics and spelling in the reading/writing classroom*. Portsmouth, NH: Heinemann.

Rasinski, T. V., & Padak, N. D. (2013). *From phonics to fluency: Effective teaching of decoding and reading fluency in the elementary school* (3rd ed.). Boston: Allyn & Bacon.

Rasinski, T., & Young, C. (2017). Effective instruction for primary grade students who struggle with reading fluency. In *Inclusive Principles and Practices in Literacy Education* (pp. 143–157). Emerald Publishing Limited.

Rasinski, T., Paige, D., Rains, C., Stewart, F., Julovich, B., Prenkert, D., & Nichols, W. D. (2017). Effects of intensive fluency instruction on the reading proficiency of third-grade struggling readers. *Reading & Writing Quarterly*, 33(6), 519–532.

Richardson, A. (2006). *Caring for your hermit crab*. Mankato, MN: Capstone Press.

Rodgers, E., D'Agostino, J. V., Kelly, R. H., & Mikita, C. (2018). Oral reading accuracy: Findings and implications from recent research. *The Reading Teacher*. https://doi.org/10.1002/trtr.1686

Samuels, S. J. (2013). Toward a theory of automatic information processing in reading, revisited. In D. E. Alvermann, N. J. Unrau, & R. B. Ruddell (Eds.), *Theoretical models and processes of reading* (6th ed., pp. 698–718). Newark, DE: International Reading Association.

Santangelo, T., & Graham, S. (2016). A comprehensive meta-analysis of handwriting instruction. *Educational Psychology Review*, 28(2), 225-265.

Spandel, V. (2012). *Creating young writers: Using the six traits to enrich writing process in primary classrooms* (3rd ed.). Boston: Pearson.

Stanovich, K. E. (1992). Speculations on the causes and consequences of individual differences in early reading acquisition. In P. B. Gough, L. C. Ehri, & R. Treiman (Eds.), *Reading acquisition* (pp. 307–342). Hillsdale, NJ: Erlbaum.

Viorst, J. (2009). *Alexander and the terrible, horrible, no good, very bad day*. New York: Atheneum.

Wood, A., & Wood, D. (2010). *The napping house*. Boston: Harcourt.

Yolen, J. (2007). *Owl moon*. New York: Philomel.

Chapter 7
Building Students' Vocabulary

∨ Learning Outcomes

After studying this chapter, you'll be prepared to:

7.1 Explain what *academic vocabulary* means and cite some examples.

7.2 Define word-study and explain why it supports students' vocabulary development better than studying individual words.

7.3 Identify four components of vocabulary instruction and explain why they all go together in a balanced literacy classroom.

Mr. Wagner Teaches Vocabulary

Creativa Images/Shutterstock

It's Monday morning, and the 30 fourth graders in Mr. Wagner's classroom are reading the two-page introduction to this week's featured selection in their basal readers, "Happy Birthday, Dr. King!" Mr. Wagner reads aloud the introductory material about Martin Luther King Jr., Rosa Parks, and the Civil Rights Movement while the students follow along in their readers.

Afterward, Mr. Wagner asks, "What do you know about the Civil Rights Movement? Garrett offers, "Dr. King gave a famous speech in Washington, DC," and Dominique adds, "It was the 'I Have a Dream' speech." Madison says, "Black people and white people are equal, but some white people used to think they were more important." "We should respect everyone," Austin emphasizes. The discussion continues as students activate their background knowledge; they talk about the discrimination that African Americans faced and Dr. King's sit-ins and other nonviolent protests.

Next, Mr. Wagner distributes a collection of posters about the Civil Rights Movement to students sitting at each of the five table groups in the classroom. The students talk about the posters in table groups and then share them with the class, making connections with the introductory material in their basal readers. Then Mr. Wagner passes out this week's list of 10 vocabulary words and reads it aloud:

boycott	fare	protest	stupendous
civil rights	nuisance	requirement	tireless
commission	perspiration		

Most of the words come from this week's basal reader story, but a few are from the district's fourth grade vocabulary list.

The students use a study procedure to learn the words. They divide into groups of three, and each group studies one word. The students create a poster and an illustrative sentence with the word, and they provide a brief definition. Sometimes they locate the word in the story and copy the sentence containing it on the chart; at other times, they create their own sentence. To figure out the word's meaning, the fourth graders use what they've learned about root words and context clues to get an idea of the meaning, and then they check the definition in the basal reader's glossary or in a dictionary. Mr. Wagner circulates around the classroom, making sure that the fourth graders write useful sentences on their posters, spell words correctly, and choose the appropriate meaning when they check the glossary or dictionary.

Next, the students take turns sharing their posters and display them in the classroom. Aaron, Spencer, and Isabella share their word: *boycott*. They present their poster, which is shown here, and read aloud the sentence and the definition. Mr. Wagner explains, "This is an important word related to the Civil Rights Movement. Dr. King, Rosa Parks, and others were protesting when they boycotted and refused to ride in the back of buses or sit at blacks-only lunch counters. They were being treated unfairly." He also points out that *boycott* is an eponym, a word that developed from Charles Boycott's name; Mr. Boycott was a land manager in Ireland who charged unfair rents in the 1880s, which Irish tenants refused to pay.

VOCABULARY POSTER FOR *BOYCOTT*

WORD: boycott

SENTENCE: Dr. Martin Luther King, Jr. helped to organize a boycott.

DEFINITION: A refusal

As each group presents its chart, classmates write the word and its definition in their vocabulary journals; they use their notes to study for the Friday vocabulary test. The sharing takes about 10 minutes, and Mr. Wagner thinks that it's time well spent. The fourth graders agree: Ossanna says, "This activity helps me really learn the definitions and not just remember them for the test!"

On Tuesday, the students read the featured selection in their basal readers and confidently point out the vocabulary words they've studied. They continue with the textbook activities and workbook pages that are part of the basal reading program, and Mr. Wagner also sets out the text set of books about Martin Luther King Jr. and Rosa Parks that's shown here. The students read them during an independent reading time and mark this week's vocabulary words when they find them using small self-stick notes.

In this chapter, you'll learn how to expand students' academic vocabulary and to develop their word consciousness; that is, their interest in learning words. Teachers use a three-tier system to categorize words and identify the most important words to teach, and they also teach word-learning strategies. As you read this vignette, notice how Mr. Wagner develops his students' vocabulary knowledge through a combination of explicit instruction, word-study activities, and reading.

MR. WAGNER'S TEXT SET OF BOOKS

Farris, C. K. (2005). *My brother Martin: A sister remembers growing up with the Rev. Dr. Martin L. King, Jr.* New York: Aladdin Books.

Farris, C. K. (2008). *March on! The day my brother Martin changed the world.* New York: Scholastic.

Giovanni, N. (2007). *Rosa.* New York: Square Fish Books.

Johnson, A. (2007) *A sweet smell of roses.* New York: Simon & Schuster.

Parks, R., & Reed, G. J. (1997). *Dear Mrs. Parks.* New York: Lee & Low.

Pastan, A. (2004). *Martin Luther King, Jr.* New York: DK Children's Books.

Rappaport, d. (2007). *Martin's big words: The life of Dr. Martin Luther King, Jr.* New York: Jump at the Sun/Hyperion Books.

Ringgold, F. (1998). *My dream of Martin Luther King.* New York: Dragonfly Books.

Ringgold, F. (1999). *If a bus could talk: The story of Rosa Parks.* New York: Simon & Schuster.

During the week, Mr. Wagner teaches **minilessons** on a variety of literacy topics. This week, he teaches two vocabulary minilessons, using these words and others they studied earlier in the school year, on how suffixes change verbs into nouns: *move/movement, satisfy/satisfaction, wreck/wreckage, organize/organization, perspire/perspiration, require/requirement*, and *commit/commission*. He's taught other minilessons on how to write a good definition, how to choose the appropriate meaning, how to use context clues, how to identify root words, and how affixes change the meaning of words.

On Friday, the fourth graders take down their posters before the vocabulary test. The test format varies, but students usually match words and their definitions. Most of the fourth graders score 80% or higher on the test, and Mr. Wagner thinks that they do so well because of the vocabulary-learning routine they use. After they take the Friday test, the fourth graders ceremonially add the week's words to the large word wall in the classroom.

Mr. Wagner's Class Word Wall

AB	C	DE	FGH
ablaze	chamber	eager	horizon
ancestor	classical	etch	glare
attentively	conductor	experienced	fierce
bewildering	courageous	drought	flammable
blare	cordially	depot	honor
amplifier	consecutive	debut	homeland
abundance	charred	elegant	homage
aggressively	civil rights	ember	frontier
boycott	commission		fare

IJK	LMN	OP	QR
jazz	lure	petitioners	rugged
immense	long	oath	rhythm
jolt	landscape	persist	remind
	nervously	organization	renew
	miscalculate	plaque	reunion
	misunderstand	proud	referral
	modest	protest	requirement
	lurching	perspiration	
	nuisance		

S	T	UVW	XYZ
survivor	teeming	wreckage	
satchel	timid	voyage	
spawn	thermometer	unsinkable	
singe	temperature	worldwide	
shipwreck	tireless		
satisfaction	troublesome		
scavenger			
stride			
stupendous			

These fourth graders are interested in words. As they look at the class word wall, Isabella points to her favorite word, *rhythm*, explains that it means "a beat," and demonstrates by clapping a rhythm. Kaila and Erik agree that their favorite word is *bewildering*, which they say means "puzzling" or "confusing." One thing is certain: These fourth graders aren't bewildered by words!

Capable students' vocabularies grow at an astonishing rate—about 3,000 to 4,000 words a year, or roughly 8 to 10 new words every day. By the time they graduate from high school, their vocabularies reach 25,000 to 50,000 words or more. These students learn the meanings of words by being immersed in an environment that's rich with words, through lots of daily independent reading, teacher read-alouds, and explicit instruction. They learn most words incidentally through reading and family activities, but teachers expand students' vocabularies by teaching specific words and word-learning strategies and by fostering their interest in words (Graves, 2016). For example, kindergartners pick up pirate lingo as they listen to their teacher read aloud *How I Became a Pirate* (Long, 2003), about Jeremy Jacob's adventures with Braid Beard and his pirate crew:

Aargh

Ahoy, matey

Hey, ho, blow the man down

Shiver me timbers

Down the hatch

Aye, me laddies

Students repeat the phrases as they play in the blocks center, incorporate them into the **Language Experience Approach** stories that they dictate, and add talking balloons containing them to their drawings. They also learn words as they explore social studies and science topics during thematic units. At the same time, teachers reinforce students' learning in several important ways: They explicitly teach some words and word-learning strategies, and they foster students' interest in words, as Mr. Wagner did in the vignette.

Check the Compendium of Instructional Procedures, which follows Chapter 12. These green terms also show a brief description of each procedure.

Vocabulary knowledge and reading achievement are closely related: Students with larger vocabularies are more capable readers, and they know more strategies for figuring out the meanings of unfamiliar words than less capable readers do (Graves, 2006). One reason why capable readers have larger vocabularies is that they do more reading. This idea is known as the *Matthew effect*, which suggests that "the rich get richer and the poor get poorer" (Stanovich, 1986): Capable readers get better because they read more, and the books they read are more challenging, containing academic vocabulary words. The gulf between more capable and less capable readers grows each year because less capable readers do less reading and the books they read have fewer grade-level academic words.

Figure 7–1 Academic Vocabulary Words

Prek-Kindergarten	Grades 1-2	Grades 3-4
alphabet	atmosphere	agriculture
author	character	anecdote
calendar	condensation	bias
citizen	continent	colonial
count	fraction	gravity
environment	graph	hemisphere
forest	island	idiom
half	memorial	justify
measure	minus	metamorphosis
poem	noun	parallel
rhyme	paragraph	parasite
story	pattern	plateau
temperature	pledge	prey
week	sentence	semicolon
word	vote	symmetry

Vocabulary learning can't be left to chance because students' word knowledge affects whether they comprehend what they're listening to or what they're reading; it also affects the quality of their writing and how easily they learn content-area information (Stahl & Nagy, 2006). Students come to school with varying levels of word knowledge, both in the number of words they know and in the depth of their understanding. Students from low-income homes have less than half of the vocabulary that more affluent students possess, and some researchers estimate that they know only one quarter to one fifth of the words that their classmates do. To make matters worse, this gap widens every year (Cunningham, 2014). Therefore, it's essential that teachers recognize the impact of socioeconomic level on students' vocabulary knowledge, support all students' vocabulary growth, and emphasize word learning for students who know fewer words.

Academic Vocabulary

The words that are frequently used in language arts, social studies, science, and math are called **academic vocabulary** (Burke, 2008). These words—*circle, evaporation, citizen*, and *noun*, for instance—are found in books and textbooks that students read; teachers use

PreK Practices

Do you teach vocabulary to 4-year-olds?

Enriching students' vocabularies must be a priority, according to Bennett-Armistead, Duke, and Moses (2005), and the best way to do this is through daily read-alouds. As they listen, preschoolers learn many, many words they wouldn't encounter through conversation, and they're exposed to more complex sentence patterns and text structures. Teachers take time to talk about the key words as they read and encourage students to use the words themselves as they talk about the book, retell the story, and participate in other response activities. McGee (2007) also recommends that teachers describe what they're doing as they demonstrate a procedure, introduce new words (e.g., *whisk, cash register*) as they participate in literacy play centers, and share collections of objects related to books or thematic units.

them in minilessons and discussions, and students use them in classroom projects and are expected to understand them in high-stakes tests. Figure 7–1 shows examples of academic vocabulary at PreK-4 levels. Students' knowledge of academic vocabulary is part of their background knowledge, and it affects their school success (Marzano & Pickering, 2005).

Three Tiers of Words

Beck, McKeown, and Kucan (2017) have devised a tool to assist teachers in prioritizing words for instruction in which they recommend categorizing words into these three levels or tiers:

Tier 1: Basic Words.   These common words are used socially, in informal conversation at home and on the playground; examples include *tired, car, outside, spill*, and *water*. Native English speakers rarely require instruction on these words.

Tier 2: Academic Vocabulary.   These words have wide application in school contexts and are used more frequently in written than in oral language. Some are related to literacy concepts, such as *sentence, author, vowel, question mark, revise*, and *character*. Other words are related to familiar ones—antonyms and synonyms, for example. Most students know the Tier 1 word *bad* and its opposite, *good*, but related words, including *naughty, evil, dangerous, ill*, and *trouble*, are Tier 2 words because they're less familiar.

Tier 3: Specialized Terms.   These technical words are content specific and often abstract; examples include *fraction, explorer, chrysalis, healthy, amphibian*, and *equator*. They aren't used frequently enough to devote time to teaching them when they come up in texts students are reading, but they're the words that teachers explicitly teach during thematic units and math lessons.

As teachers choose words for instruction and word-study activities, they focus on Tier 2 words even though words representing all three levels are included on **word walls** and explained when necessary.

Teaching English Learners
Vocabulary

Young English learners often need more explicit vocabulary instruction than native English speakers do. Sometimes ELs only need to have a word translated; at other times, however, they're confused about a new meaning of a familiar word, or they don't know either the underlying concept or words that describe it, and instruction is necessary.

Tier 1 Words.   These words are easiest for ELs to learn because they often know the words in their native language; what they don't know are the equivalent words in English. If teachers speak students' native language, they translate the words and help students learn the English equivalents; English-speaking teachers can use pictures and pantomime to explain them. It's often helpful for teachers to put together collections of small objects and pictures to share during literature focus units and thematic units.

Tier 2 Words.   Teachers preteach some unfamiliar words, including essential Tier 2 words, before students listen to a book read aloud or read a book, and later, through explicit instruction and a variety of word-study activities, they teach other Tier 2 words. Calderón (2007) notes that, in addition, ELs need to understand transition words and phrases, such as *meanwhile* and *finally*; words with multiple meanings, such as *key, soft*, and *ready*; and English words with cognates. Teachers point out cognates—English words that are related to words in the students' first languages. Many Tier 2 words are Latin based, so it's important to teach English learners who speak Spanish, Portuguese,

Italian, and French to ask themselves whether an unfamiliar word is similar to a word in their native language. Examples of English/Spanish cognates include *syllable/sílaba*, *triangle/triángulo*, and *pioneer/pionero*.

Tier 3 Words.   It's less important to teach these technical words because of their limited usefulness, and only a few have cognates that ELs would know. Calderón (2007) recommends that teachers translate the words or briefly explain them. During thematic units, however, teachers do teach Tier 3 words that are essential to understanding the big ideas through a combination of explicit instruction and word-study activities.

The Development of Word Knowledge

Students develop knowledge about a word gradually through repeated exposure to it. They move from not knowing a word at all to recognizing that they've seen the word before, and then to a level of partial knowledge where they have a general sense of the word or know one meaning. Finally, students know the word fully: They know multiple meanings of the word and can use it in a variety of ways (Nagy, 1988). Here are the four levels:

Level 1: Unknown Word.   Students don't recognize the word.

Level 2: Initial Recognition.   Students have seen or heard the word or can pronounce it, but they don't know the meaning.

Level 3: Partial Word Knowledge.   Students know one meaning of the word and can use it in a sentence.

Level 4: Full Word Knowledge.   Students know more than one meaning of the word and can use it in several ways.

Once students reach the third level, they can generally understand the word in context. In fact, they don't reach the fourth level with every word they learn, but when they do develop full word knowledge, they're described as flexible word users because they understand the core meaning of a word and how it changes in different contexts (Stahl & Nagy, 2006).

Developmental Continuum Vocabulary

PreK	K	1	2	3	4
Children who have been read to and have developed good background knowledge possess vocabularies approaching 3,500 words; they know colors and animal names.	Kindergartners use book language to talk about stories and can name opposites for words, such as good, day, and little, and their vocabularies reach 5,000 words.	First graders literacy-related academic language, including consonant, sentence, predict, and question mark, as their vocabularies increase by 3,000 words.	Second graders expand their knowledge base and related words through thematic units and learn more antonyms and synonyms; their vocabularies reach 10,000 words.	Third graders' vocabularies grow by 3,000 words, and they develop word consciousness as they notice multiple meanings of words and figurative language.	The gulf between grade-level and struggling students' vocabularies widens and becomes more obvious as literacy and content-area demands increase.

Literacy Portraits

The second graders in Ms. Janusz's class vary widely in their vocabulary knowledge: Some students have limited background knowledge and words to express ideas, but others are interested in many topics and know lots of words. In February, Ms. Janusz holds a conference with Jimmy about a book he's reading during reading workshop; this informational book is about presidential elections. As they talk about the book, Jimmy uses sophisticated and technical vocabulary, including *democracy*, *electoral votes*, *snickering*, and *campaign slogan*, to discuss what he's learned. Most second graders aren't familiar with these concepts and don't use these words. How do you think Jimmy learned them? How does Ms. Janusz support his learning? Does his vocabulary knowledge correlate with his literacy level?

Jimmy

Word Consciousness

Students' interest in learning and using words is known as **word consciousness**. According to Scott and Nagy (2004), word consciousness is "essential for vocabulary growth and comprehending the language of schooling" (p. 201).

Students who have word consciousness exemplify these characteristics:

- Students use words skillfully, understanding the nuances of word meanings.
- Students gain a deep appreciation of words and value them.
- Students are aware of differences between social and academic, or school, language.
- Students understand the power of word choice.
- Students are motivated to learn the meaning of unfamiliar words.

Word consciousness is important because vocabulary knowledge is generative—that is, it transfers to and enhances students' learning of other words (Scott & Nagy, 2004).

As students develop word consciousness, they become more aware of words, manipulate them playfully, and appreciate their power. Teachers foster word consciousness in a variety of ways. Most importantly, they model interest in words and precise use of vocabulary (Graves, 2016). To encourage students' interest in words, teachers share books about words, including *Max's Words* (Banks, 2006), *Fancy Nancy's Favorite Fancy Words: From Accessories to Zany* (O'Connor, 2008), *Miss Alaineus: A Vocabulary Disaster* (Frasier, 2007), and *Baloney (Henry P.)* (Scieszka, 2005). Next, they call students' attention to words by highlighting words of the day, posting words on **word walls**, and having students collect words from books they're reading. They promote wordplay by sharing riddles, jokes, puns, songs, and poems and encouraging students to experiment with words and use them in new ways.

Vocabulary Knowledge and Reading Achievement

Vocabulary knowledge and reading achievement are closely related: Students with larger vocabularies are more capable readers (Graves, 2016). In the preschool years, students who listen to their parents and teachers read books aloud and talk about the books acquire larger vocabularies and are more prepared for reading instruction than students with fewer of these experiences. Then once students become fluent readers, reading widely is the most important way they learn new words; however, better readers do more reading, both in and out of school, and the books they read have more sophisticated words, so the gulf separating capable and less capable readers increases each year.

MyLab Education Self-Check 7.1

Word-Study Concepts

It's not enough to memorize one definition of a word; to develop full word knowledge, students need to learn more about a word (Stahl & Nagy, 2006). Consider the word *brave*: It can be used as an adjective, a noun, or a verb. It often means "showing no fear," but it can also mean an "American Indian warrior" or "to challenge or defy." These forms are related to the first meaning: *braver, bravest, bravely,* and *bravery*. Synonyms related to the first meaning include *bold, fearless,* and *daring*; antonyms are *cowardly* and *frightened*. As students learn about *brave*, they're better able to understand the word and use it orally and in writing.

A list of synonyms, antonyms, and homonyms that are appropriate for PreK–4 students is presented in Figure 7–2.

Synonyms

Words that have nearly the same meaning as other words are **synonyms**. These related words are useful because they're more precise. Think of all the synonyms for the word *cold*: *cool, chilly, frigid, icy, frosty,* and *freezing*. Each word has a different shade of meaning: *Cool* means "moderately cold," *chilly* is "uncomfortably cold," *frigid* is "intensely cold," *icy* means "very cold," *frosty* means "covered with frost," and *freezing* is "so cold that water changes into ice." English would be limited with only the word *cold*.

It's important to carefully articulate the differences among synonyms. Nagy (1988) emphasizes that teachers should focus on teaching concepts and related words, not just provide single-word definitions using synonyms. For example, to

Figure 7–2 Words for Word-Study Activities

Synonyms	Antonyms	Homonyms
angry–mad	add–subtract	ant–aunt
big–large	asleep–awake	ate–eight
build–construct	back–front	bare–bear
correct–right	big–little	be–bee
fast–quick	black–white	blew–blue
finish–end	boy–girl	brake–break
foolish–silly	clean–dirty	buy–by–bye
forgive–excuse	come–go	cent–scent–sent
funny–amusing	day–night	dear–deer
gift–present	dog–cat	eye–I
happy–glad	early–late	flew–flu
hard–difficult	fast–slow	flour–flower
hurry–rush	friend–enemy	hair–hare
joy–pleasure	go–stop	hear–here
know–understand	happy–sad	hoarse–horse
little–small	hot–cold	hole–whole
look–see	in–out	knew–new
mistake–error	laugh–cry	knight–night
ocean–sea	light–dark	made–maid
often–frequently	love–hate	mail–male
pain–ache	many–few	meat–meet
quiet–silent	morning–evening	one–won
rude–impolite	near–far	pair–pear
sad–unhappy	noisy–quiet	peace–piece
scare–frighten	off–on	plain–plane
sick–ill	open–close	read–red
smart–intelligent	play–work	right–write
smile–grin	remember–forget	road–rode
start–begin	rich–poor	sail–sale
steal–rob	smooth–rough	sea–see
talk–speak	strong–weak	son–sun
thin–slender	tight–loose	tail–tale
trash–garbage	truth–lie	their–there–they're
woman–lady	up–down	to–too–two
wrong–incorrect	wet–dry	wait–weight
yell–shout	young–old	wood–would

tell a student that *frigid* means *cold* provides only limited information. And, when a student says, "I want my sweater because it's frigid in here," it shows that he or she doesn't understand the different degrees of cold; there's a big difference between *chilly* and *frigid*.

Antonyms

Words that express opposite meanings are **antonyms**. For the word *loud*, antonyms include *soft, quiet, silent, dull,* and *colorless*. These antonyms express shades of meaning just as synonyms do, and some opposites are more appropriate for one meaning of *loud* than for another. When *loud* means *gaudy*, for instance, antonyms are *dull* and *colorless*; but when it means *noisy*, the opposites are *quiet* and *silent*. Antonyms are included in Figure 7–2.

Students learn to use a thesaurus to locate both synonyms and antonyms; *A First Thesaurus* (Wittels, 2001), *Scholastic Children's Thesaurus* (Bollard, 2006), and *The American Heritage Children's Thesaurus* (Hellweg, 2009) are excellent reference books. Students need to learn how to use these handy references to locate more effective words when they're revising their writing and during word-study activities.

Homonyms

Words that sound alike or are spelled alike are generally known as *homonyms*, but in fact there are three types. **Homophones** are the most common type: These words sound alike but are spelled differently, such as *ate–eight, hear–here,* and *to–too–two*. Sometimes students confuse the meanings of these words, but more often they mix up their spellings. A list of homophones is included in Figure 7–2. **Homographs** are the second type: These words are spelled alike but are pronounced differently. Examples include the noun and verb forms of *wind, bow, record,* and *present*; the present and past tenses of the verb *read*; and the noun and adjective forms of *minute*. **Homographic homophones** are the third type: These words sound alike and are spelled alike, such as *fly, water,* and *bark*. The following words have noun and verb forms that are pronounced and spelled the same way:

- A *fly* is a pesky insect. (noun)
- Most birds can *fly*. (verb)
- I like to drink *water*. (noun)
- Did you *water* the plants? (verb)
- This tree's *bark* is smooth. (noun)
- Dogs *bark* at squirrels. (verb)

Homographic homophones are like words with multiple meanings because the noun and verb forms have different definitions.

Many books of homonyms are available, including Gwynne's *The King Who Rained* (2006) and *A Chocolate Moose for Dinner* (2005), Barretta's *Dear Deer: A Book of Homophones* (2007), and *Eight Ate: A Feast of Homonym Riddles* (Terban, 2007a). Sharing these books with students helps to develop their understanding of homophones and homographs. Students also make posters, as shown in Figure 7–3, to contrast homophones and other homonyms. Displaying these posters in the classroom reminds students of the differences between the words.

MyLab Education
Video Example 7.1

This second grade teacher is teaching students about homophones. What follow-up activity might you engage students in after a similar lesson?

Multiple Meanings

Many, many words have more than one meaning. For some words, multiple meanings develop for the noun and verb forms, but sometimes meanings build in other ways, such as when new uses are created for words. The word *hot*, for example, usually means

Figure 7–3 A Second Grader's Homophone Poster

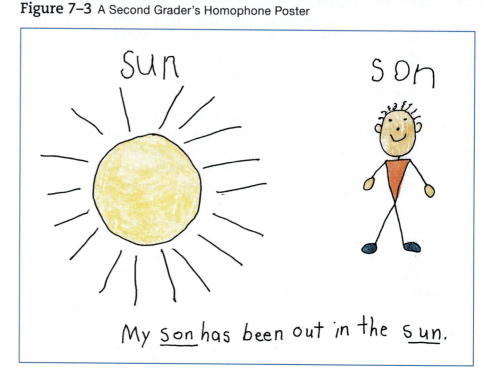

"having a high temperature" or "causing a sensation of heat," but it also has these meanings:

angry	fresh
bold (e.g., color)	feeling intense emotion
close to a solution	popular
current	radioactive
eager	recently stolen
extremely interested	spicy
fast	unusually lucky
fiery	violent

Figure 7–4 presents a list of common words with multiple meanings.

Students gradually acquire additional meanings for words, and they usually learn these new meanings through reading. For instance, when students read *Tough Cookie* (Wisniewski, 1999), a delicious spoof on detective stories, they encounter the phrase "hot on the trail" and learn that *hot* in this case means "close to a solution." When a familiar word is used in a new way, students often notice the new application and may be curious enough to check the meaning in a dictionary.

MyLab Education
Video Example 7.2

In this video, second grade teacher Angie Balterri helps her students practice multiple meanings of the word 'draw.' What kinds of activities help students learn multiple meanings of words?

Figure 7–4 Words with Multiple Meanings

band	fly	open	stamp
bar	good	out	star
break	high	part	strike
check	hot	pass	tie
color	house	pick	time
cross	keep	play	trip
cut	key	ride	turn
draw	make	right	up
dry	mind	ring	wear
eye	new	roll	
face	note	run	
fall	off	slip	

Figurative Meanings

Many words have both literal and figurative meanings: **Literal meanings** are the explicit, dictionary meanings, and **figurative meanings** are metaphorical. Two types of figurative expressions are idioms and comparisons. **Idioms** are groups of words, such as "in the dog house" and "raining cats and dogs," that must be interpreted figuratively. There are hundreds of idioms in English, which we use every day to create word pictures that make language more colorful. Because idioms are figurative sayings, many students—and especially English learners—have difficulty understanding them. It's crucial that teachers provide explicit instruction so that students move beyond their literal meanings of phrases. Students can examine books that explain idioms, including *My Teacher Likes to Say* (Brennan-Nelson, 2004), *There's a Frog in My Throat! 440 Animal Sayings a Little Bird Told Me* (Leedy & Street, 2003), *Raining Cats and Dogs* (Moses, 2008), and *Mad as a Wet Hen: And Other Funny Idioms* (Terban, 2007b).

Metaphors and similes are comparisons that liken something to something else. A **simile** is a comparison signaled by the use of *like* or *as*; "busy as a bee" and "roaring like a lion" are two examples. In contrast, a **metaphor** compares two things by implying that one is the other, without using *like* or *as*; "you are my sunshine" is an example. Metaphors are stronger comparisons, as these examples show:

Simile: The dead tree looked like a skeleton in the moonlight.

Metaphor: The dead tree was a skeleton in the moonlight.

Differentiating between the terms *simile* and *metaphor* is less important than understanding the meaning of comparisons in books students read and encouraging students to use comparisons to make their writing more vivid.

Students begin by learning traditional comparisons, such as "happy as a clam" and "butterflies in my stomach," and then they learn to notice and invent fresh, unexpected comparisons. Teachers often share these books to introduce comparisons: *Crazy Like a Fox: A Simile Story* (Leedy, 2009), *Quick as a Cricket* (Wood, 1997), *My Dog is as Smelly as Dirty Socks* (Piven, 2007), and *Skin Like Milk, Hair of Silk: What Are Similes and Metaphors?* (Cleary, 2009). Once they're familiar with metaphors and similes, students point them out in books they're reading and use them in their own writing.

MyLab Education Self-Check 7.2

Teaching Students About Words

Vocabulary instruction plays an important role in balanced literacy classrooms. Graves (2016) identified these components of vocabulary instruction:

- Immerse students in words through listening, talking, reading, and writing.
- Teach specific words through active involvement and multiple encounters.
- Teach word-learning strategies so students can figure out the meanings of unfamiliar words.
- Develop students' word consciousness.

Teachers address these components when they teach vocabulary. Too often, vocabulary instruction has emphasized only the second component—teaching specific words—without considering how to develop students' ability to learn words independently and use them effectively.

The Common Core State Standards for English Language Arts (2010) emphasize that learning grade-level academic vocabulary is essential. The Language Standards focus on teaching students to determine the meaning of unfamiliar words, understand figurative language, and acquire vocabulary needed for understanding books they're reading and for expressing ideas in talk and writing. The Common Core State Standards: Vocabulary box provides additional information.

Common Core State Standards

Vocabulary

The Common Core State Standards for English Language Arts (2010) emphasize that students are to build their academic vocabularies and learn to determine the meaning of unknown words. They address these requirements:

- Students choose the most appropriate meaning of words with multiple meanings.
- Students apply context clues.
- Students understand figurative language, word relationships, and nuances in word meanings.
- Students use strategies to determine the meaning of unknown words.

The Standards emphasize that vocabulary knowledge is inseparable from reading and writing instruction. To learn more about the vocabulary Standards, go to http://www.corestandards .org/ELA-Literacy, or check your state's educational standards website.

Word Walls

Teachers post **word walls** in the classroom; usually they're made from large sheets of butcher paper and divided into sections for each letter of the alphabet. Students and the teacher write interesting, confusing, and important words representing all three tiers on the word wall. Usually students choose the words to write on the word wall and may even do the writing themselves; teachers add other important words that students haven't chosen. Words are added to the word wall as they come up in books students are reading or during a thematic unit, not in advance. Allen (2009) says that word walls should be "a living part of the classroom with new words being added each day" (p. 120). Word walls are useful resources: Students locate words that they want to use during a **grand conversation** or check the spelling of a word they're writing, and teachers use the words for word-study activities.

Some teachers use large pocket charts and word cards instead of butcher paper for their word walls; this way, the word cards can easily be used for word-study activities, and they can be sorted and rearranged on the pocket chart. After the book or unit is completed, teachers punch holes in one end of the cards and hang them on a ring. Then the collection of word cards can be placed in the writing center for students to use when they're writing.

Students also make individual word walls by dividing a sheet of paper into 20–24 boxes and labeling the boxes with the letters of the alphabet; they can put several letters together in one box. Then students write important words and phrases in the boxes as they read and discuss a book. Figure 7–5 shows a third grader's word wall for *Molly's Pilgrim* (Cohen, 1999), a story about modern-day pilgrims.

Figure 7–5 A Third Grader's Word Wall for *Molly's Pilgrim*

AB	CD	EF	GH
apartment	clothespins	Elizabeth	homework
	dolls	freedom	God
		English	hot as fire
			holiday
IJ	**KL**	**MN**	**OPQ**
Jewish		Molly	pilgrim
		Miss Stickley	Plymouth
		Mama	peach
		modern	
RS	**TU**	**VW**	**XYZ**
Russia	Thanksgiving	Winter Hill	Yiddish
religious freedom	Tabernacles		

Even though 25, 50, or more words may be added to the word wall, not all of them are explicitly taught. As they plan, teachers create lists of words that will probably be written on word walls during the unit. From this list, teachers choose the words they teach—usually Tier 2 words that are critical to understanding the book or unit.

Explicit Instruction

Teachers explicitly teach students about specific words, usually Tier 2 words. McKeown and Beck (2004) emphasize that instruction should be rich, deep, and extended. This means that teachers provide multiple encounters with words; present a variety of information, including definitions, contexts, examples, and related words; and involve students in word-study activities so that they have multiple opportunities to interact with words. The procedure is time-consuming, but students are more successful at internalizing word meanings this way.

As teachers plan for instruction, they need to consider what students already know about a word. Sometimes the word is unfamiliar, or it represents a new concept. At other times, the word is familiar and students know one meaning, but they need to learn a new meaning. A word representing an unfamiliar concept usually takes the most time to teach, and a new meaning for a familiar word, the least.

Teachers use **minilessons** to teach specific words and other vocabulary concepts. They provide information about words, including both definitions and contextual information, and they engage students in activities to get them to think about and use words orally and in reading and writing. Sometimes teachers present minilessons before reading; at other times, they teach them afterward. The Minilesson that follows shows how a first grade teacher teaches vocabulary as part of a thematic unit on the four seasons; this explicit instruction is especially important for English learners.

Word-Study Activities

Students examine words, visualize word meanings, and think more deeply about them as they participate in word-study activities (Allen, 2009). In these activities, they create visual representations of words, categorize words, or investigate related words:

WORD POSTERS.   Students choose a word and write it on a small poster; then they draw and color a picture to illustrate the word and use it in a sentence. This is one way that students visualize the meaning of words.

WORD MAPS.   Students create a diagram to examine a word they're learning. They write the word, make a box around it, draw several lines from the box, and add information about the word in boxes they make at the end of each line. Three kinds of information typically included in a word map are a category for the word, examples, and characteristics or associations. Figure 7–6 shows a word map a first grader made after reading *Rosie's Walk* (Hutchins, 2005). For the examples section, he named stories he had read about foxes.

DRAMATIZING WORDS.   Students each choose a word and dramatize it for classmates, who then try to guess it. Sometimes an action explains a word more effectively than a verbal definition. For example, a teacher teaching a literature focus unit on *Chrysanthemum* (Henkes, 1996), the story of a little girl who didn't like her name, dramatized the word *wilted* for her second graders when they didn't understand how a girl could wilt. Other words in *Chrysanthemum* that can easily be acted out include *humorous, sprouted, dainty,* and *wildly.* Dramatization is an especially effective activity for English learners.

WORD SORTS.   Students sort a collection of words taken from the word wall into two or more categories in a **word sort** (Bear, Invernizzi, Templeton, & Johnston, 2016). Generally, students choose the categories they use for the sort, but sometimes the teacher chooses them. For example, words from a story might be sorted by character, or words

MyLab Education
Video Example 7.3

The fourth graders in this video are adding specialized terms to a word wall related to a thematic unit. What steps does Ms. Schietrum have her students follow to add content-area words to the word wall?

MyLab Education
Video Example 7.4

Dramatizing words can be particularly effective when working with English learners. How does first grade teacher Diane Leonard engage her English learners in expanding their knowledge of English vocabulary?

Minilesson

TOPIC: Word Sort
GRADE: First Grade
TIME: Two 30-minute periods

Mrs. Garcia's first graders are studying the four seasons. The teacher has read aloud several informational books about the seasons, and the students have added to the word wall more than 25 words that reflect the weather, holidays, clothes, plant and animal changes, and activities related to each season.

1. **Introduce the Topic**
   Mrs. Garcia brings her 19 first graders together on the rug near their weather word wall. She asks students to take turns identifying familiar words. "Who can name a *spring* word?" she asks. Anthony points to *tadpoles* and reads the word aloud. Other students name *summer, autumn,* and *winter*. Mrs. Garcia praises the students for including words representing all four seasons on their word wall.

2. **Share Examples**
   Mrs. Garcia hangs up four narrow pocket charts (each with 10 pockets) and labels each one with the name of a season. She writes the words the students have identified on word cards and asks other students to place them in the appropriate pocket charts; the words *tadpoles* and *rain* are added to the *Spring* pocket chart, *swimming* and *crops* are added to the *Summer* pocket chart, *Halloween* and *Thanksgiving* to the *Autumn* pocket chart, and *snow* and *Christmas* to the *Winter* pocket chart. The students also identify several other words representing each season from the word wall to add to the pocket charts.

3. **Provide Information**
   To locate additional words for each chart, the students suggest that they look in some of the books they've read or listened to Mrs. Garcia read aloud. Mrs. Garcia rereads an informational book about the seasons, and the students look through other familiar books. The teacher divides the students into four groups and asks each group to find words related to a particular season. The students identify new words, and these are written on word cards and placed in the appropriate chart.

4. **Guide Practice**
   During the second day of the lesson, Mrs. Garcia divides the class into groups of two or three students and gives each group a packet of small word cards and a large sheet of construction paper divided into four columns with the names of the seasons written at the top of the columns; the words on the small cards are the same as the ones on the larger cards used the previous day in the large-group part of the lesson. The students practice reading the cards and sorting them according to season. Mrs. Garcia moves around the classroom, providing assistance as needed and monitoring the students' work.

5. **Assess Learning**
   Mrs. Garcia puts several sets of the word cards and construction paper diagrams in the word work center for the students to practice reading and sorting during center time. Later, she'll have the students cut apart a list of the four seasons words and glue them in the appropriate columns on a construction paper diagram, and she'll assess these products.

Figure 7–6 A First Grader's Word Map on *Fox*

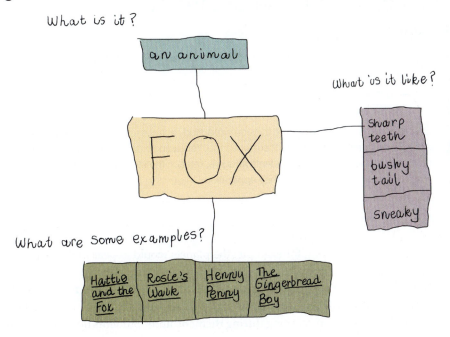

from a thematic unit on machines might be sorted according to type of machine. The words can be written on cards, and then students sort a pack of word cards into piles. Or, students can cut apart a list of words, sort them into categories, and then paste the grouped words together on a sheet of paper. Figure 7–7 presents a completed word sort for *Paul Bunyan* (Kellogg, 1985), a retelling of the American tall tale.

WORD CHAINS.   Students choose a word and then identify three or four words to sequence before or after it to make a chain. For example, the word *tadpole* can be chained this way: *egg, tadpole, frog;* and the word *aggravate* can be chained like this: *irritate, bother, aggravate, annoy.* Students can draw and write their word chains on a sheet of paper, or they can make a chain out of construction paper and write a word on each link.

SEMANTIC FEATURE ANALYSIS.   Students learn the meanings of conceptually related words by examining their characteristics in a **semantic feature analysis** (Rickelman & Taylor, 2006). Teachers create a grid in which they list a group of words related to a book or a thematic unit on the left and write distinguishing characteristics across the top. Students analyze the words, characteristic by characteristic, and place a plus or minus symbol in each cell to indicate whether a word represents a characteristic. In a semantic feature

Figure 7–7 A Word Sort Using Words from *Paul Bunyan*

Words Describing Paul Bunyan	Places Paul Bunyan Created	Places Paul Bunyan Visited	Words Describing Babe
strongest	St. Lawrence River	Maine	ox calf
smartest	Grand Canyon	Texas	blue
extremely helpful	Rocky Mountains	Arizona	depressed
colossal	Great Lakes	Great Plains	sturdy
legendary		California	unusual size
extraordinary		Pacific Ocean	
		Alaska	

Teach Kids to Be Strategic!

Word-Learning Strategies

Teach students to use these strategies to figure out the meaning of an unfamiliar word:

- Use context clues.
- Analyze word parts.
- Check a dictionary.

Students practice these strategies through word-study activities, such as word maps and word sorts. Look for students to apply them when they're reading independently and studying social studies and science topics. If students struggle, reteach the strategies, making sure to model their use, and think aloud about their application.

---

analysis on the solar system, for example, the planets would appear in the left column and characteristics such as "has a moon" and "life is possible" in the top row.

These word-study activities provide opportunities for students to deepen their understanding of words listed on word walls, other words related to books they're reading, and words they're learning during thematic units. Students develop concepts, learn one or more meanings of words, and make associations among words through these activities. None of them require students to simply write words and their definitions or to use the words in sentences or a contrived story.

Word-Learning Strategies

When students come across an unfamiliar word while reading, they can do several things to solve the problem: They can reread the sentence, sound out the word, look for context clues in the sentence, analyze the root word and affixes, check a dictionary, skip the word and keep reading, or ask the teacher for help, for example. Some techniques, however, work better than others. After studying the research on ways to deal with unfamiliar words, Graves (2016) identified these effective word-learning strategies:

- Using context clues
- Analyzing word parts
- Checking a dictionary

Teachers teach students to use these strategies to figure out the meanings of new words.

Students must learn what to do when they encounter an unfamiliar word. First, they notice when a word they're reading is unfamiliar and decide whether it's important to know its meaning. If it's unimportant to the text, students skip it and continue reading, but if it's important, they take action. Here's the procedure Graves (2016) recommends that students use to figure out the meaning of a new word:

1. Reread the sentence containing the word.
2. Use context clues to figure out the meaning, but if that doesn't work, go to the next step.
3. Examine the word parts, looking for familiar root words and affixes to aid in figuring out the meaning. If that's not successful, go to the next step.
4. Pronounce the word to see if you recognize it when you say it. If that doesn't work, go to the next step.
5. Check the word in a dictionary or ask the teacher for help.

This procedure has the greatest chance of success because it includes all three word-learning strategies.

USING CONTEXT CLUES.   The words and sentences that surround the new word offer **context clues**; some clues provide information about the meaning of the word. This contextual information helps students infer the word's meaning, and illustrations also provide useful information. The context clues that readers use are presented in Figure 7–8. Interestingly, two or three types of contextual information are often included in the same sentence.

Context clues rarely provide enough information to help students learn a word because typically it's only partial information, and it can be misleading. Nevertheless, Nagy, Anderson, and Herman (1987) found that grade-level readers have a 1 in 20 chance of learning the meaning of a word using context clues. Although that seems inconsequential, if students read 20,000 words a year and learn 1 of every 20 words through context, they'll learn 1,000 words, or one third of their annual vocabulary growth. That's significant! How long does it take to read 20,000 words? Nagy (1988) estimated that if teachers provide 30 minutes of daily reading time, students will learn an additional 1,000 words a year.

The best way to teach students about context clues is by modeling. When teachers read aloud, they should stop at a difficult word and talk with students about how they can use context clues to figure out its meaning. When the rest of the sentence or paragraph provides enough information, teachers use that information and continue reading, but when it doesn't, they use another strategy to figure out the meaning of the word.

ANALYZING WORD PARTS.   Students use their knowledge of prefixes, suffixes, and root words to unlock longer words when they understand how word parts function. For example, *omnivorous, carnivorous,* and *herbivorous* relate to the foods that animals eat; *omni* means "all," *carn* means "flesh," and *herb* means "vegetation." The common word part *vorous* comes from the Latin *vorare,* meaning "to swallow up." When students know *carnivorous* or *carnivore,* they use morphemic analysis to figure out the other words. Graves (2016) recommends that teachers teach morphemic analysis when non-English root words appear in books students are reading and during thematic units. Teachers

Figure 7–8 Six Types of Context Clues

Clue	Description	Sample Sentence
Definition	Readers use the definition in the sentence to understand the unknown word.	Some spiders spin silk with tiny organs called *spinnerets*.
Example-Illustration	Readers use an example or illustration to understand the unknown word.	Toads, frogs, and some birds are *predators* that hunt and eat spiders.
Contrast	Readers understand the unknown word because it's compared or contrasted with another word in the sentence.	Most spiders live for about one year, but *tarantulas* sometimes live for 20 years or more!
Logic	Readers think about the rest of the sentence to understand the unknown word.	An *exoskeleton* acts like a suit of armor to protect the spider.
Root Words and Affixes	Readers use their knowledge of root words and affixes to figure out the unknown word.	People who are terrified of spiders have *arachnophobia*.
Grammar	Readers use the word's function in the sentence or its part of speech to figure out the unknown word.	Most spiders *molt* five to ten times.

break apart the words and discuss the word parts when they're posted on the word wall and through minilessons.

CHECKING THE DICTIONARY.   Looking up unfamiliar words in the dictionary is often frustrating because the definitions don't provide enough useful information or because words used in the definition are forms of the word being defined. Sometimes the definition that students choose—usually the first one—is the wrong one or it doesn't make sense. For example, the word *pollution* is usually defined as "the act of polluting." Students could look for an entry for *polluting,* but they won't find it. They might notice an entry for *pollute,* where the first definition is "to make impure." The second definition is "to make unclean, especially with man-made waste," but it's difficult to understand. Because dictionary definitions are more useful when a reader is vaguely familiar with the word's meaning, teachers play an important role in dictionary work: They teach students how to read a dictionary entry and decide which definitions make sense, demonstrate the strategy when they're reading aloud and come across an unfamiliar word, and assist by explaining the definitions that students locate and comparing the word to related words.

Incidental Word Learning

Students learn words incidentally—without explicit instruction—all the time, and because students learn so many words this way, teachers know that they don't have to teach the meaning of every unfamiliar word in a book. Students learn words from many sources, but researchers report that reading is the single largest source of vocabulary growth for students, especially after third grade (Swanborn & de Glopper, 1999). In addition, the amount of time students spend reading independently is the best predictor of vocabulary growth between second and fifth grades.

INDEPENDENT READING.   Students need daily opportunities for independent reading in order to learn words, and they must read books at their independent reading levels. If the books are too easy or too hard, students learn very few new words. The best way to provide opportunities for independent reading is reading workshop. Students choose books they're interested in from age-appropriate and reading-level-suitable collections in their classroom libraries, and because they've chosen the books themselves, they're more likely to keep reading.

Sustained Silent Reading (SSR) is another way to encourage wide reading. All students in a classroom or in the school spend 10 to 30 minutes silently reading appropriate books that they've chosen themselves. Even the teacher takes time to read, in the process modeling how adults who enjoy reading make it part of their daily routine. Simply providing time for independent reading, however, doesn't guarantee that students will increase their vocabulary knowledge (Stahl & Nagy, 2006); to accomplish that task, students need to know how to figure out the meaning of unfamiliar words.

READING ALOUD TO STUDENTS.   Teachers also provide for incidental word learning when they read aloud stories, poems, and informational books. Daily read-aloud activities are important for students at all grade levels, prekindergarten through fourth grade. Teachers use the **interactive read-aloud** procedure and focus on a few key words in the book, model how to use context clues to understand new words, and talk about the words after reading. Teachers use **think-alouds** when they model using context clues and other word-identification strategies. Two recent studies found that teachers enhance students' vocabulary knowledge and their comprehension when they add a focus on vocabulary to their read-alouds (Santoro, Chard, Howard, & Baker, 2008).

Cunningham (2014) recommends that teachers choose one picture book each week to read aloud and teach key vocabulary. Teachers read the book aloud one time and then present three new words from the book, each written on a word card. During the second reading, students listen for the words, and the teacher takes time to talk about each word's meaning using information available in the text and in the illustrations. Later, the teacher encourages students to practice using the new words when they talk and write about the book.

Well-written books with rich vocabulary, figurative language, and wordplay are available for reading aloud to students at every grade level. *Hey, Al* (Yorinks, 1989), for example, is an award-winning story about a man named Al and his dog, Eddie, who leave their city apartment to find happiness on a tropical island paradise, only to learn that you make your own happiness and that things that sound too good to be true usually are. These words are included in the book:

aloft	ecstasy	gorgeous	shimmering
beady	exhausted	heartbroken	shrieked
blissfully	ferried	lush	squawked
cascaded	flitted	paradise	struggling
cooed	fortunately	plumed	talented
croaked	furiously	plunged	unbelievable

In addition to learning individual words as they listen to *Hey, Al* read aloud, students also hear language that's unique to stories—more complex sentence structures and more mature linguistic expressions. As teachers read *Hey, Al* and other stories and involve students in grand conversations and other response activities, they practice using some of these words and sentence structures.

The Booklist that you will see later in this chapter presents a list of read-aloud books with rich vocabulary. Some of these books are stories like *Hey, Al*, and others are informational books that expand students' background knowledge as well as build vocabulary. For example, as third graders listen to their teacher read aloud *The Magic School Bus Inside a Beehive* (Cole, 1996), they learn about bees and are introduced to, or deepen their understanding of, these words:

adult	hive	pollinate
antennae	honeycombs	pupa
beekeepers	insect	queen bee
cells	larvae	social
communicate	mate	sting
drones	metamorphosis	swarming
hexagon	nectar	worker bees

Students don't learn all of these words in a single reading, of course, but through repeated experiences with the words, their level of word knowledge deepens.

Although reading aloud is important for all students, it's especially important for struggling readers who typically read fewer books themselves, and because the books at their reading level have less sophisticated vocabulary words. Researchers report that students learn as many words incidentally while listening to teachers read aloud as they do by reading themselves (Stahl & Nagy, 2006). Use **My Teaching To-Do Checklist: Teaching Vocabulary** to ensure you are addressing students' needs with regard to vocabulary teaching.

Assessing Students' Word Knowledge

It's difficult to assess students' vocabulary knowledge because there aren't any grade-level standards to indicate which words students should know or even how many words they need to learn. Moreover, assessing vocabulary is complicated because students learn words gradually, moving to deeper levels of "knowing" a word. Teachers typically monitor students' independent reading and use informal measures to evaluate their word knowledge, but several tests are available to measure students' vocabulary knowledge; they're described later in the Assessment Tools feature.

MY TEACHING TO-DO CHECKLIST: Teaching Vocabulary

- ☐ I use word walls to highlight words from books students are reading and from thematic units.
- ☐ I encourage students to use new words as they talk about books they're reading and during thematic units.
- ☐ I choose Tier 2 words—academic vocabulary—for explicit instruction.
- ☐ I teach minilessons about individual words and word-learning strategies.
- ☐ I scaffold students as they develop full word knowledge by teaching synonyms, antonyms, multiple meanings, and figurative uses.
- ☐ I engage students in word-study activities, such as word posters, word maps, and word sorts, so they can deepen their understanding of specific words.
- ☐ I develop students' word consciousness by demonstrating curiosity about words, teaching about words, and involving them in wordplay activities.
- ☐ I provide opportunities for students to read independently for 15 minutes every day.
- ☐ I integrate state standards into my instruction.

Booklist Read-Aloud Books for Building Vocabulary

Grade	Books
PreK	Fleming, D. (1996). *Lunch*. Henkes, K. (2000). *Wemberly worried*. Himmelman, J. (2006). *Chickens to the rescue*. Martin, B., Jr., & Archambault, J. (2009). *Chicka chicka boom boom*. Schachner, J. (2005). *Skippyjon Jones*. Weatherford, C. B. (2006). *Jazz baby*. Willems, M. (2003). *Don't let the pigeon drive the bus!*
K	Bottner, B. (2003). *The scaredy cats*. Carle, E. (2004). *Mister seahorse*. Cronin, D. (2011). *Diary of a spider*. Frazee, M. (2006). *Roller coaster*. Long, M. (2003). *How I became a pirate*. Most, B. (1996). *Cock-a-doodle-moo!* O'Connor, J. (2005). *Fancy Nancy*. Wells, R. (1997). *McDuff comes home*.
1	Heller, R. (1992). *How to hide a butterfly*. Krull, K. (2000). *Wilma unlimited: How Wilma Rudolph became the world's fastest woman*. Lee, C. (2004). *Good dog, Paw!* Rathmann, P. (1995). *Officer Buckle and Gloria*. Schwartz, D. M. (2008). *How much is a million?* Simont, M. (2001). *The stray dog*. Yorinks, A. (1989). *Hey, Al*.
2	Choi, Y. (2001). *The name jar*. Cronin, D. (2011). *Click, clack, moo: Cows that type*. Demi. (1996). *The empty pot*. Dorros, A. (1991). *Abuela*. Levine, E. (2007). *Henry's freedom box*. Soto, G. (1993). *Too many tamales*. Yolen, J. (1987). *Owl moon*.
3	Barrett, J. (1985). *Cloudy with a chance of meatballs*. Cherry, L. (2000). *The great kapok tree*. Coerr, E. (1988). *Chang's paper pony*. Cohen, B. (1999). *Molly's pilgrim*. MacLachlan, P. (2005). *Sarah, plain and tall*. Scieszka, J. (1999). *The true story of the 3 little pigs!* Steig, W. (2010). *Sylvester and the magic pebble*. Zelinsky, P. O. (1996). *Rumpelstiltskin*.
4	Bunting, E. (1999). *Smoky night*. Dahl, R. (2007). *James and the giant peach*. Dillon, L., & Dillon, D. (2007). *Jazz on a Saturday night*. Polacco, P. (1994). *Pink and say*. Say, A. (2004). *Music for Alice*. Scieszka, J. (2005). *Baloney (Henry P.)*. Weatherford, C. B. (2007). *Freedom on the menu: The Greensboro sit-ins*. White, E. B. (2004). *Charlotte's web*.

Assessment Tools

Vocabulary

Both informal assessments and standardized tests can be used to measure students' vocabulary knowledge, but tests often equate word knowledge with recognizing or being able to state one definition of a word rather than assessing the depth of students' knowledge. Here are several norm-referenced vocabulary tests:

- **Peabody Picture Vocabulary Test-4 (PPVT-4)**

  The PPVT-4 (Dunn, Dunn, & Dunn, 2006) is an individually administered test to screen students' word knowledge. It can be used with PreK–4 students, but it's most commonly used with young students showing limited verbal fluency. The PPVT-4 measures receptive vocabulary: The teacher says a word and asks the student to identify one of four pictures that best illustrates the word's meaning. Unfortunately, this test takes 10 minutes to administer, making it too time-consuming for regular classroom use. The PPVT-4 is available from the American Guidance Service.

- **Expressive Vocabulary Test-2 (EVT-2)**

  The EVT-2 (Williams, 2006) is also an individual test that's used to screen PreK–4 students' knowledge of words. It's the expressive counterpart of the PPVT-4: The teacher points to a picture and asks the student to say a word that labels the picture or to provide a synonym for a word that's illustrated in the picture. This test, available from the American Guidance Service, is also very time-consuming for classroom teachers to use.

- **Informal Reading Inventories (IRIs)**

  Sometimes teachers in grades 2–4 use IRIs to assess students' vocabulary knowledge. One or two comprehension questions at each grade level focus on the meaning of words selected from the passage students have read. The usefulness of this assessment is limited, however, because so few questions deal with vocabulary and because students who read below grade level aren't tested on age-appropriate words.

Even though these tests aren't very useful in classroom settings, they're valuable in diagnosing students with limited word knowledge.

THE INSTRUCTION–ASSESSMENT CYCLE.   Teachers often choose authentic measures of students' vocabulary knowledge because they're more useful than formal tests (Bean & Swan, 2006). Informal assessment tools show whether students have learned the words and strategies being taught as well as the depth of their knowledge. Teachers use this instruction–assessment cycle:

Step 1: Planning.   As teachers plan for instruction, they take into account students' current level of word knowledge; consider using a variety of word-study activities, including word walls and word sorts; and coordinate instruction and assessment plans.

Step 2: Monitoring.   Teachers use these informal assessment tools to monitor students' progress:

- Teachers observe how students use new words during word-study activities, mini-lessons, and discussions.
- Teachers listen as students participate in **story retelling** activities to check that they're incorporating some of the vocabulary from the book in their version and using the words appropriately.

- Teachers talk with students in conferences about the words they've used in word-study activities and in their writing.
- Teachers include items about vocabulary on **rubrics** to emphasize its importance. For oral-presentation rubrics, teachers emphasize the use of technical words related to the topic, and for writing, they emphasize precise vocabulary.

Based on feedback, teachers make decisions about reteaching or using different activities to be more successful.

Step 3: Evaluating.   In addition to using informal assessments, teachers also create a variety of paper-and-pencil tests to monitor students' vocabulary knowledge. For example, they use the cloze procedure to create a passage and then have students fill in the missing words, write a paragraph about a word's meaning, create a word map, or draw a picture to represent a word's meaning.

Step 4: Reflecting.   Students reflect on their learning, sometimes by reading the words on the word wall to see how many words they've learned, and teachers reflect on the effectiveness of their instruction by determining the most valuable activities and examining how well students learned.

Informal assessments go beyond simply asking students to match words to definitions or to use a word in a sentence because students are using the words they're learning in meaningful ways.

If Students Struggle . . .

Most students pick up new words quickly. They understand their meaning and use the words in talk and writing. Some students, however, are less aware of words; they don't remember and use new words from books they're reading or from thematic units. When students aren't making adequate progress, teachers need to figure out why and provide an appropriate intervention. To begin, they usually talk with students about several of the words they're currently highlighting to identify the problem:

- Can students explain the meaning of these words?
- Can students locate the words on the word wall?
- Can students pronounce the words?
- Can students use the words in conversation?
- Can students use the words in writing?

Students need to understand the meaning of the words they're studying and use them expressively. They should also appreciate why it's important to learn and use new words.

Once teachers identify students' vocabulary problems, they identify intervention procedures and ways to differentiate instruction.

EMPHASIS ON VOCABULARY.   When students aren't aware of vocabulary words, teachers draw their attention to new vocabulary by seating them near the word wall and enlisting their assistance in posting new words on it. They also preteach new words to these students and have them use small self-stick notes to mark vocabulary words on **story boards** and in books.

WORD MEANINGS.   When students aren't learning word meanings, teachers preteach vocabulary, investigate the structure of words, make packs of word cards for practice activities, and involve them in interactive games, including **word ladders** and **word sorts**.

TALK ACTIVITIES.   When students can't use the words orally, teachers provide a variety of informal opportunities for them to use words in conversation: They talk with partners about specific words on the word wall, collaborate with classmates on semantic feature analysis charts, and participate in grand conversations and other discussions. Students also incorporate vocabulary words during story retelling activities and complete cloze activities orally before doing them in writing.

WRITING ACTIVITIES.   When students aren't using new words in writing, teachers have them use specific words as they draw and label pictures, write in **reading logs**, create word posters, and complete graphic organizers. To increase students' attention to words, teachers often have them use highlighter pens to mark vocabulary words in their writing.

Teachers can help students who struggle with vocabulary by preteaching new words and providing opportunities for them to play word games, talk about words, and incorporate words in writing activities.

MyLab Education **Self-Check 7.3**
MyLab Education **Application Exercise 7.1:** Word Mapping

Chapter Review

Vocabulary

- Teachers categorize unfamiliar words into three tiers—basic words, academic vocabulary, and specialized terms.

- Teachers support students' development of word-learning strategies.

- Teachers plan instruction to go beyond learning specific words and consider how to develop their students' ability to learn new words independently.

Accountability Check

Visit the following assessment links to access quiz questions and instructional applications.

MyLab Education **Application Exercise 7.2:** Understanding Literacy Development
MyLab Education **Application Exercise 7.3:** Understanding Literacy Development
MyLab Education **Application Exercise 7.4:** Monitoring Literacy Development
MyLab Education **Application Exercise 7.5:** Monitoring Literacy
Development

MyLab Education **Application Exercise 7.6:** Measuring Literacy
Development

References

Allen, J. (2009). *Inside words: Tools for teaching academic vocabulary, grades 4–12.* Portland, ME: Stenhouse.

Banks, K. (2006). *Max's words.* New York: Farrar, Straus & Giroux.

Barretta, G. (2007). *Dear deer: A book of homophones.* New York: Holt.

Bean, R. M., & Swan, A. (2006). Vocabulary assessment: A key to planning vocabulary instruction. In C. C. Block & J. N. Mangieri (Eds.), *The vocabulary-enriched classroom: Practices for improving the reading performance of all children in grades 3 and up* (pp. 164–187). New York: Scholastic.

Bear, D. R., Invernizzi, M., Templeton, S., & Johnston, F. (2016). *Words their way: Word study for phonics, vocabulary, and spelling instruction* (5th ed.). Upper Saddle River, NJ: Merrill/Pearson.

Beck, I. L., McKeown, M. G., & Kucan, L. (2017). *Bringing words to life: Robust vocabulary instruction.* New York: Guilford Press.

Bennett-Armistead, V. S., Duke, N. K., & Moses, A. M. (2005). *Literacy and the youngest learner: Best practices for educators of children from birth to 5.* New York: Scholastic.

Bollard, J. K. (2006). *Scholastic children's thesaurus.* New York: Scholastic.

Brennan-Nelson, D. (2004). *My teacher likes to say.* Chelsea, MI: Sleeping Bear Press.

Burke, J. (2008). *The English teacher's companion: A complete guide to classroom, curriculum, and the profession.* Portsmouth, NH: Heinemann.

Calderón, M. (2007). *Teaching reading to English language learners, grades 6–12.* Thousand Oaks, CA: Corwin Press.

Cleary, B. P. (2009). *Skin like milk, hair of silk: What are similes and metaphors?* Minneapolis: Millbrook Press.

Cohen, B. (1999). *Molly's pilgrim.* New York: Scholastic.

Cole, J. (1996). *The magic school bus inside a beehive.* New York: Scholastic.

Common core state standards for English language arts. (2010). Retrieved from http://www.corestandards.org/ELA-Literacy/

Cunningham, P. M. (2014). *What really matters in vocabulary: Research-based practices across the curriculum* (2nd ed.). Boston: Pearson.

Dunn, D. M., Dunn, L. W., & Dunn, L. M. (2006). *Peabody picture vocabulary test-4.* Bloomington, MN: American Guidance Service/Pearson.

Frasier, D. (2007). *Miss Alaineus: A vocabulary disaster.* New York: HarperCollins/Voyager.

Graves, M. F. (2016). *The vocabulary book: Learning and instruction.* New York: Teachers College Press.

Graves, M. F. (2016). *The vocabulary book: Learning and instruction.* New York: Teachers College Press

Gwynne, F. (2005). *A chocolate moose for dinner.* New York: Aladdin Books.

Gwynne, F. (2006). *The king who rained.* New York: Aladdin Books.

Hellweg, P. (2009). *The American Heritage children's thesaurus.* Boston: Houghton Mifflin.

Henkes, K. (1996). *Chrysanthemum.* New York: Harper Trophy.

Hutchins, P. (2005). *Rosie's walk.* New York: Aladdin Books.

Kellogg, S. (1985). *Paul Bunyan.* New York: HarperCollins.

Leedy, L. (2009). *Crazy like a fox: A simile story.* New York: Holiday House.

Leedy, L., & Street, P. (2003). *There's a frog in my throat! 440 animal sayings a little bird told me.* New York: Holiday House.

Long, M. (2003). *How I became a pirate.* Orlando: Harcourt.

Marzano, R. J., & Pickering, D. J. (2005). *Building academic vocabulary: Teacher's manual.* Alexandria, VA: Association for Supervision and Curriculum Development.

McGee, L. M. (2007). *Transforming literacy practices in preschool: Research-based practices that give all children the opportunity to reach their potential as learners.* New York: Scholastic.

McKeown, M. G., & Beck, I. L. (2004). Direct and rich vocabulary instruction. In J. F. Baumann & E. J. Kame'enui (Eds.), *Vocabulary instruction: Research to practice* (pp. 13–27). New York: Guilford Press.

Moses, W. (2008). *Raining cats and dogs.* New York: Philomel.

Nagy, W. E. (1988). *Teaching vocabulary to improve reading comprehension.* Urbana, IL: ERIC Clearinghouse on Reading and Communication Skills and the National Council of Teachers of English and the International Reading Association.

Nagy, W. E., Anderson, R. C., & Herman, P. A. (1987). Learning word meanings from context during normal reading. *American Educational Research Journal, 24,* 237–270.

O'Connor, J. (2008). *Fancy Nancy's favorite fancy words: From accessories to zany.* New York: HarperCollins.

Piven, H. (2007). *My dog is as smelly as dirty socks.* New York: Schwartz & Wade.

Rickelman, R. J., & Taylor, D. B. (2006). Teaching vocabulary by learning content-area words. In C. C. Block & J. N. Mangieri (Eds.), *The vocabulary-enriched classroom: Practices for improving the reading performance of all students in grades 3 and up* (pp. 54–73). New York: Scholastic.

Santoro, L. E., Chard, D. J., Howard, L., & Baker, S. K. (2008). Making the very most of classroom read-alouds to promote comprehension and vocabulary. *The Reading Teacher, 61*, 396–408.

Scieszka, J. (2005). *Baloney (Henry P.)*. New York: Puffin Books.

Scott, J. A., & Nagy, W. E. (2004). Developing word consciousness. In J. F. Baumann & E. J. Kame'enui (Eds.), *Vocabulary instruction: Theory to practice* (pp. 210–217). New York: Guilford Press.

Stahl, S. A., & Nagy, W. E. (2006). *Teaching word meanings*. Mahwah, NJ: Erlbaum.

Stanovich, K. E. (1986). Matthew effects in reading: Some consequences of individual differences in the acquisition of literacy. *Reading Research Quarterly, 21*, 360–406.

Swanborn, M. S. W., & de Glopper, K. (1999). Incidental word learning while reading: A meta-analysis. *Review of Educational Research, 69*, 261–285.

Terban, M. (2007a). *Eight ate: A feast of homonym riddles*. New York: Clarion Books.

Terban, M. (2007b). *Mad as a wet hen!: And other funny idioms*. New York: Sandpiper.

Williams, K. T. (2006). *Expressive vocabulary test-2*. Bloomington, MN: American Guidance Service/ Pearson.

Wisniewski, D. (1999). *Tough cookie*. New York: Lothrop, Lee & Shepard.

Wittels, H. (2001). *A first thesaurus*. New York: Golden Books.

Wood, A. (1997). *Quick as a cricket*. London: Child's Play.

Yorinks, A. (1989). *Hey, Al*. New York: Farrar, Straus & Giroux.

Chapter 8
Teaching Comprehension: Reader Factors

After studying this chapter, you'll be prepared to:

8.1 Define comprehension in terms of reader and text factors and identify three prerequisites that support a reader's comprehension of a text.

8.2 List 12 comprehension strategies that readers use during reading, and explain how they support comprehension.

8.3 Discuss how teachers can teach comprehension strategies.

Becoming Strategic Readers

It's reading workshop time in Mrs. Chase's third grade classroom. The students are reading books they've selected themselves from the classroom library. Twenty small boxes of books are set up across the counter under the windows that run the length of the classroom. Some books are arranged by reading level; others are grouped by topics such as space and the rain forest; favorite authors; and series, including Amber Brown, Magic School Bus, Lemony Snicket, and A to Z Mysteries. In addition, four crates are filled with *Cobblestones*, *National Geographic Kids*, and other magazines. As students choose reading materials, they clip a clothespin with their name on it to the crate so Mrs. Chase can easily monitor what they're reading.

The students know their reading levels and how to choose appropriate books. Aaron is reading *Flat Stanley* (Brown, 2003a) (Level N), and his friend Henry is reading *Stanley in Space* (Brown, 2003b) (Level N); these two boys read at about the same level, and they like to read related books so they can talk about them. Tanner is reading *Horrible Harry's Secret* (Kline, 1998) (Level L), which his friend Connor read recently and recommended. Jordan is reading every book in Paula Danziger's popular Amber Brown series; currently, she's reading *Amber Brown Is Green With Envy* (2004) (Level N), and she thinks it's the best one yet. Madison is reading *The Borrowers Aloft* (Norton, 2003b) (Level S), a sequel Mrs. Chase recommended after Madison enjoyed *The Borrowers* (Norton, 2003a).

Mrs. Chase conferences with the students sitting in one table group each day while the others are reading. Today, she meets with Jordan, Ava, Jack, William, and Grace. After the students talk briefly about the books they're reading, Mrs. Chase asks them to tell her about the strategies they're using to comprehend. Jack says, "I'm making awesome text-to-self connections because the characters are a lot like me. They do what I do—stuff like going to school, telling jokes, and riding bikes. And they get in trouble just like me, too." Jordan, who's reading the books in the Amber Brown series, says, "I'm making connections, too, but lots of mine are text-to-text connections because I'm noticing things that are the same in each book." William shares, "Predicting is my strategy. I'm wicked good at predicting what's going to happen. I'm reading faster and faster because I have to know if I'm right. That's what's different about my reading this year: I'm thinking and reading at the same time!" Grace talks about the visualizing strategy: "I'm sort of dreaming the story in my brain as I read it, and it seems like it's happening for real." After the other group members talk about their strategy use, Mrs. Chase reviews the following chart on the types of comprehension strategies that the class made at the beginning of the school year.

The third graders learned about the comprehension strategies in first and second grades, so Mrs. Chase quickly reviewed them at the beginning of the school year. The students could identify the strategies and use them one at a time when they were directed to do so, but they weren't using them when they were reading independently. Now the teacher is focusing on how the students can use the strategies purposefully to improve their comprehension.

The third graders spend 100 minutes in three reading workshop activities: reading independently, participating in a **minilesson**, and listening to Mrs. Chase read aloud. Mrs. Chase also conducts guided reading lessons where she focuses her instruction to accommodate students' specific needs. After the reading workshop, the third graders

In this chapter, you'll read how students learn to apply predicting, connecting, visualizing, monitoring, evaluating, and other comprehension strategies to improve their understanding of complex texts. These strategies help readers to engage with, and think about, what they're reading. As you read this vignette, notice how Mrs. Chase demonstrates a strategy, and then her students apply it, first with teacher guidance and later as they read independently.

Comprehension Strategies Chart

Strategy	What Readers Do
Predicting	Readers predict what will happen next.
Connecting	Readers think about what they already know about the topic.
Visualizing	Readers make a movie in their heads.
Questioning	Readers ask questions about things that don't make sense.
Identifying Big Ideas	Readers think about the big ideas.
Summarizing	Readers combine the big ideas in a summary.
Monitoring	Readers check that they are understanding and take action if they're confused.
Evaluating	Readers reflect on the book and think about how well they read.

Third Graders' Connections With Open Wide: Tooth School Inside

Text-to-Self	Text-to-World	Text-to-Text
I'm thinking about all the ways tooth school is like our school.	It's like my dentist told me about tooth decay.	It's a very funny book like The Scrambled States of America [Keller, 1998].
This book reminds me to take good care of my teeth.	I think all dentists should have this book.	
The book made me think about when I believed in the tooth fairy.	There's a model of a tooth of my dentist's that's just like a picture in this book.	This book reminds me of Miss Alaineus [Frasier, 2007] because the pages are crowded with little pictures and lots of words and details.
My great-grandma has false teeth because she didn't take care of her teeth when she was a girl.	I know there's a chemical called fluoride in our water that keeps our teeth strong.	I'm thinking about a book called Dear Tooth Fairy [Durant, 2004] that my grandma gave me.
I started thinking that my dentist would like to read this book.		
This book gives good advice about brushing teeth just like my dad does.		

participate in a writing workshop where they learn to use writing strategies and write books on self-selected topics.

After 15 minutes of independent reading time, Mrs. Chase brings the class together for a minilesson on the connecting strategy. "What do you remember about making connections?" Mrs. Chase begins. "It's when you connect what you know to what you're reading," Aiden answers. "There are three kinds of connections: text-to-self, text-to-world, and text-to-text," Katie continues. Students take turns explaining each type of connection. Connor explains, "Text-to-self connections are personal. You think of things in your own life that are like in the book." Madison describes text-to-world connections: "You think about what's happening in your town, what you see on the TV news, and what you know about the world; then you make connections. Sometimes they're sort of hard for me." "Text-to-text connections," Tanner says, "are connections from one book to another one that you've read." "Or one author makes you think of another author," Katie adds. Then Mrs. Chase reviews the three types of connections using the chart they made several weeks ago after reading *Open Wide: Tooth School Inside* (Keller, 2003), a hilarious picture book about tooth care. See the class chart Third Graders' Connections with Open Wide: Tooth School Inside.

Mrs. Chase uses examples in her minilessons from the book she's reading aloud. Yesterday, she read aloud the first chapter of Beverly Cleary's *Henry Huggins* (2000), a classic story about the adventures of a boy and his dog; so for today's minilesson, she's copied several paragraphs from that chapter on chart paper for everyone to reread. The first paragraph is about Henry and his new dog, Ribsy, causing an uproar as they ride home on a bus. After she reads it aloud to the class, Mrs. Chase models how she uses the connecting strategy:

This paragraph is confusing, and the word "lurch" is a new one. I think I can make some connections to help me understand it better. I've ridden on buses, and I remember that a ride on a bus isn't as smooth as in a car. Sometimes I have to hold on, so I don't slide off the seat. I'm making a text-to-self connection: I can imagine that Henry had a very hard time holding on to the box with Ribsy in it, and I'm not surprised that the frightened dog wiggled out of the box and got away from Henry.

Mrs. Chase writes about her text-to-self connection on a self-stick note. Then she places the note on the chart paper and reads it aloud: "T-S: I know buses lurch and you have to hold on."

Next, the teacher flips the page of chart paper and reads aloud a second paragraph; this one is about Henry and Ribsy being ordered off the bus. "What connections can you make to understand what's happening in this paragraph?" Mrs. Chase asks. Ava responds this way:

> *I'm not surprised that the bus driver ordered them off the bus. If I was him, that's what I'd do, but I don't understand why everyone is laughing. It's not funny; it's a big mess. Now I'm making a text-to-self connection. I remember when my dad and my brother made a big mess when they were cleaning out the garage. First my mom came outside and saw the mess, and she looked real mad. Then she started laughing. I don't know why she laughed, but I think that's what the man was doing.*

Mrs. Chase suggests that laughter releases tension, and she compliments Ava on her text-to-self connection. She hands Ava a self-stick note and a marking pen to write a note about her connection. Ava writes the note, places it on the chart paper, and reads it aloud to the class: "T-S: My mom was mad and then she laughed."

Mrs. Chase shares the third paragraph, and Tanner talks about the connection he can make to understand it better and then writes his connection on a self-stick note. Then Mrs. Chase asks, "Why does making connections help you comprehend better?" Katie responds this way: "If a part is confusing you, and you think about what you know, it will help you figure it out." And Henry says, "Well, if your name is the same as the main character's name, like mine is, you think the story is about you, and you think about what you would do in that situation."

At the end of the minilesson, the third graders return to their desks to continue reading in self-selected books. Mrs. Chase asks them to use the connecting strategy they practiced in the minilesson as they're reading on their own and to add small self-stick notes to show how the connection helped them understand better. While most of the students continue with independent reading, the teacher conducts guided reading lessons with small groups of students.

Sharing time is next, and Mrs. Chase brings the students together to talk about the books they've been reading. They explain the connections they've made and share the notes they've written. Aiden goes first: "I'm reading *Toliver's Secret* (Brady, 2000), and it's about the Revolutionary War. I made a text-to-world connection to what I know because I know a lot about wars. Here's my note: 'T-W: I'm thinking about wars.'" Gillian jumps into the conversation and adds: "I'm doing it, too. My book is *Phoebe the Spy* (Griffin, 2002), and it's about the American Revolution. I'm making text-to-world connections because I know about wars, too. My note says 'T-W: I'm thinking about cannons and stuff.'" "I'm making text-to-text connections," Jack adds. "First I read all of the Marvin Redpost books; next I read *Sideways Stories From Wayside School* (Sachar, 2004); and now I'm reading *There's a Boy in the Girls' Bathroom* (Sachar, 1988). You can tell that the same man wrote all of these wacky stories. I really like this author!" Mrs. Chase asks about his note, and Jack reads, "T-T: This wacky book is by the great Louis Sachar!"

At 9:40, the third graders go to a 30-minute physical education class, and when they return, Mrs. Chase reads aloud while they eat a snack. Today, she's reading the second chapter in *Henry Huggins* (Cleary, 2000) using the **interactive read-aloud** procedure. As she picks up the book, she points out that this is the 50th anniversary edition, and the students are impressed that this story is still so popular. As they review the first chapter, Jerry shares that he'd been confused about something: "I thought it was weird that Henry only had 25 cents to buy an ice cream and ride the bus home. I know that ice cream costs more, and so does a bus ride. I was confused because I was making text-to-world connections, but if this book is 50 years old, I'm thinking that people way back then could buy ice cream and ride the bus for 25 cents." The teacher congratulates Jerry for making connections and using them to figure out a confusing part.

After Mrs. Chase asks the students to predict what might happen in the second chapter, "Gallons of Guppies," she reads about Henry's trip to the pet store to buy fish. When she pauses partway through the chapter, Jerry points out that the book says a fishbowl, guppies, and fish food cost 79 cents, but he knows that at Bailey's Pets—the pet store where he bought his goldfish—it would cost more than five dollars. The students agree with him, and several share their fish-buying experiences. Toward the end of the chapter, Mrs. Chase pauses again so that the students can speculate on how the chapter will end. "What will Henry do with all the baby guppies?" she asks. Ava suggests that Henry will give them away, but others think he'll sell them. Mrs. Chase reads to the end of the chapter, and the students are pleased with the conclusion: Henry takes the guppies to the pet store and trades them for a fish tank and some tropical fish. As they talk about the chapter, several students say that they plan to write about their pets during writing workshop.

MyLab Education

Video Example 8.1

The National Reading Panel conducted numerous studies on reading comprehension that have important implications for literacy instruction. What have you learned about teaching reading from this video?

Comprehension is the goal of reading instruction; it's the reason why people read. Readers must comprehend the text to learn from the experience; they must make sense of their reading to maintain interest; and they must enjoy reading to become lifelong readers. Decoding words is a relatively straightforward procedure compared to the complexity of constructing meaning after the words have been recognized (Sweet & Snow, 2003). Readers activate background knowledge and think about what they're reading; they apply cognitive and metacognitive strategies to understand the text. In the vignette, Mrs. Chase was teaching her third graders to use comprehension strategies because strategic readers are more likely to understand what they're reading.

Readers use four levels of thinking—literal, inferential, critical, and evaluative—as they comprehend. The most basic level is **literal comprehension,** in which readers pick out the big ideas, sequence details, notice similarities and differences, and identify explicitly stated reasons. The higher levels differ from this kind of thinking because readers integrate their own knowledge with the information presented in the text. In **inferential comprehension,** readers use clues they notice in the text, implied information, and their background knowledge to draw inferences. They make predictions, recognize cause and effect, and determine the author's purpose. **Critical comprehension** is the third level: Readers analyze symbolic meanings, distinguish fact from opinion, and draw conclusions. The most sophisticated level is **evaluative comprehension:** Readers judge the quality of texts. These levels point out the range of thinking students can do.

Developmental Continuum Comprehension: Reader Factors

PreK	K	1	2	3	4
Young children actively engage with literature as teachers read aloud and respond through talk, drama, and drawing.	Kindergartners use strategies, including predicting and connecting, to comprehend books that teachers read aloud.	First graders transfer listening strategies they've learned to reading and use repairing to solve reading problems.	Students learn additional comprehension strategies, including questioning, visualizing, summarizing, and repairing.	Students vary how they use comprehension strategies to read and respond to stories, informational books, and poems.	Fourth graders become more adept at drawing inferences and thinking critically to understand books they're reading.

What Is Comprehension?

Comprehension is a creative, multifaceted process in which students engage with, and think about, the text (Tierney, 1990). The comprehension process begins as students activate their background knowledge, and it develops as they read or listen to a book read aloud and then respond to it. Readers construct a mental "picture" or representation of the text through the comprehension process (Van den Broek & Kremer, 2000).

Judith Irwin (2007) defines comprehension as a reader's process of using prior experiences and the author's text to construct meaning that's useful to that reader for a specific purpose. This definition emphasizes that comprehension depends on two factors: the *reader* and the *text* that's being read. Whether comprehension is successful, according to Sweet and Snow (2003), depends on the interaction of reader factors and text factors.

Reader and Text Factors

Students actively engage with the text as they read or listen to it read aloud. For example, they do the following:

- Activate background knowledge
- Examine the text to uncover its organization
- Make predictions
- Connect to their own experiences
- Create mental images
- Monitor their understanding
- Solve problems that interfere with comprehension

These activities can be categorized as reader and text factors (National Reading Panel, 2000). **Reader factors** include the background knowledge students bring to the reading process, the strategies they use while reading, and their engagement in the reading experience. **Text factors** include the author's ideas, the words the author uses to express those ideas, and the organization of ideas. Students apply reader and text factors as they read, and their understanding of these factors determines whether they'll be successful. Figure 8–1 presents an overview of these two factors. This chapter focuses on reader factors, and Chapter 9 addresses text factors.

Figure 8–1 The Comprehension Factors

Type	Factors	Role in Comprehension
Reader	Background Knowledge	Students activate their world and literary knowledge to link what they know to what they're reading.
	Vocabulary	Students recognize the meaning of familiar words and apply word-learning strategies to understand what they're reading.
	Fluency	Fluent readers have cognitive resources available to understand what they're reading.
	Comprehension Strategies	Students actively direct their reading, monitor their understanding, and troubleshoot comprehension problems when they occur.
	Comprehension skills	Students automatically note details that support big ideas, sequence events, and use other skills.
	Engagement	Students who meet the prerequisites for comprehension and apply comprehension strategies are more likely to be engaged with the text.
Text	Genres	Students knowledge of the characteristics of genres provides a scaffold for comprehension.
	Text Structures	Students recognize the big ideas more easily when they understand how authors organize text.
	Text Features	Students apply their knowledge of literary devices to deepen their understanding and appreciate the author's use of language.

Text Complexity

Text complexity is a new way of examining reader and text factors to determine the comprehension demands of books or, more specifically, how well readers can complete an assigned task with a particular text (Fisher, Frey, & Lapp, 2012). Traditionally, teachers have identified students' independent, instructional, and frustration levels, and matched books to students using **readability formulas,** but the Common Core State Standards movement has drawn new attention to the topic due to the 10th reading Standard specification that students will read and comprehend challenging fiction and nonfiction texts independently and proficiently at each grade level. This Standard emphasizes two goals: First, students read books at their grade-level placements, and second, they learn to read and understand these books on their own, without teachers leading them through comprehension activities or reading the books aloud. Examples of fiction and nonfiction texts from the Common Core State Standards document are shown in the Booklist that follows.

A number of factors affect text complexity, which the Common Core State Standards group into these three components:

Qualitative Dimensions.   Teachers make informed judgments about a book's grade appropriateness by examining its layout, text structure, language features, purpose and meaning, and the demands placed on readers' background knowledge. These dimensions are difficult to evaluate because they can't easily be quantified.

Quantitative Measures.   Teachers use readability formulas or other scores to determine a book's grade appropriateness by calculating word length, word frequency, word difficulty, sentence length, text length, and other quantitative features. They often rely on computer software to determine reading levels, such as Lexile scores.

Reader and Task Considerations.   Teachers reflect on how they expect students to interact with the book, students' literary knowledge and strategy use, as well as their motivation and interests. With instruction, students grow in their understanding of how to read complex texts, and they learn to think about ideas and information in different ways. For instance, younger students are often asked to examine the theme in one story, but older students are asked to investigate how the point of view in two stories influences the theme.

Teachers analyze these components to determine a book's text complexity for their students. Unfortunately, there's no easy formula for figuring out the complexity level of a book.

Booklist Books With Complex Texts

Grades	Fiction	Nonfiction
PreK–K	Pinkney, J. (2013). *The tortoise and the hare.* Reynolds, A. (2012). *Creepy carrots!* Shannon, D. (2006). *Good boy, Fergus!*	Aliki. (1989). *My five senses.* Jenkins, S., & Page, R. (2003). *What do you do with a tail like this?* Pfeffer, W. (2004). *From seed to pumpkin.*
1–2	Allard, H. G. (1985). *Miss Nelson is missing!* Rathmann, P. (1995). *Officer Buckle and Gloria.* Yolen, J. (1985). *Owl moon.*	Roth, S. L. (2011). *The mangrove tree: Planting trees to feed families.* Schwartz, D. M. (2004). *How much is a million?* Smith, L. (2006). *John, Paul, George, and Ben.*
3–4	MacLachlan, P. (2005). *Sarah, plain and tall.* Ryan, P. M. (2002). *Esperanza rising.* White, E. B. (2006). *Charlotte's web.*	Ruurs, M. (2005). *My librarian is a camel: How books are brought to students around the world.* Spengler, K. T. (2011). *An illustrated timeline of inventions and inventors.* Thimmesh, C. (2006). *Team moon.*

Before Reading: Reader Factors to Consider

For students to comprehend a text, they must have several prerequisites in place: adequate background knowledge, understanding most of the words in the text, and the ability to read it fluently. When any of these prerequisites for comprehension are lacking, students aren't likely to understand what they're reading. Teachers can ameliorate students' difficulties through differentiated instruction, carefully matching readers to books, and using **interactive read-alouds** to share books with students.

BACKGROUND KNOWLEDGE. Students' world and literary knowledge provides a bridge to a new text (Braunger & Lewis, 2006). World knowledge includes what students know about grocery stores, hermit crabs, deserts, and Martin Luther King Jr., for example; Recognizing the beginning, middle, and end of stories, differentiating between stories and biographies, knowing how to arrange a poem on a page, and making connections are examples of literary knowledge. For example, four- and five-year-olds need to understand the sequential structure of *First the Egg* (Seeger, 2007) to appreciate this award-winning concept book; third graders who aren't familiar with mysteries and the clipped sentences that detectives use will have trouble understanding *Tough Cookie* (Wisniewski, 1999), an absurd crime drama that's set in a cookie jar; and fourth graders need to know about the Underground Railroad to understand *Henry's Freedom Box* (Levine, 2007), the unforgettable story of a slave's escape to freedom.

To build background knowledge, teachers determine whether readers lack world or literary knowledge and then provide experiences, visual representations, and lecture to build the concepts they need for a specific book. Authentic experiences such as taking field trips, participating in dramatizations, and examining artifacts are the most effective; but photos and pictures, picture books, videos, and other visual representations also work. Lecture is often the least effective way, especially for English learners, but sometimes explaining a concept or describing the characteristics of a genre provides enough information.

VOCABULARY. Students' knowledge of words plays a tremendous role in comprehension because it's difficult to decode and comprehend a text that's loaded with unfamiliar words. When they don't know many words related to a topic, it's usually a sign that students don't have adequate background knowledge, either. For example, students who listen to their teacher read aloud a book on plants, such as *Jack's Garden* (Cole, 1995), *Planting a Rainbow* (Ehlert, 1992), or *From Seed to Plant* (Gibbons, 1993), must be familiar with some of these words: *blossom, bloom, bud, petals, pistil, pollination, roots, seedlings, soil, sprout, stamen,* and *stem.* Those who know more of the words are more likely to understand than those who recognize fewer words.

Blachowicz and Fisher (2015) recommend creating a word-rich classroom environment to immerse students in words, organizing vocabulary instruction into concepts, and teaching word-learning strategies so readers can figure out the meaning of new words. Because of the link between background knowledge and vocabulary, teachers introduce key words at the same time they're building background knowledge. To reinforce the new vocabulary words, teachers also read some books aloud and use **shared reading** for others before students read them.

FLUENCY. Fluent readers read quickly and efficiently. Because they recognize most words automatically, their cognitive resources aren't consumed by decoding unfamiliar words, and they can devote their attention to comprehension. Developing reading fluency is an important component of reading instruction in the primary grades because students need to recognize words automatically so that they can concentrate their attention on comprehending what they're reading (Rasinski & Samuels, 2011).

Teachers, like Mrs. Chase in the vignette at the beginning of the chapter, often teach comprehension using the books they're reading aloud so that fluency isn't an issue. The interest-level-appropriate books that teachers read aloud provide more opportunities

Check the Compendium of Instructional Procedures, which follows Chapter 12. These **green** terms also show a brief description of each procedure.

for students to practice higher level thinking than predictable books and easy-to-read books do. Teachers also ensure that the books students read independently fit their reading level so they have cognitive resources available to apply what they're learning about comprehension.

MyLab Education **Self-Check 8.1**

Comprehension Strategies That Readers Use While Reading

Comprehension strategies are thoughtful behaviors that readers use to facilitate their understanding while they are reading (Afflerbach, Pearson, & Paris, 2008). They apply these strategies to deepen their understanding, determine whether they're comprehending, and solve problems as they arise during reading. Some strategies are *cognitive*—they involve thinking, or cognition; others are *metacognitive*—they require reflection. For example, readers make predictions about a story when they begin reading: They wonder what will happen to the characters and whether they'll enjoy the story. Predicting is a cognitive strategy because it involves thinking. Readers also monitor their reading which is a metacognitive strategy that means thinking about how well you're understanding while reading. Skilled readers who monitor their comprehension and notice they have lost their understanding, then take action to solve the problem. We say that students are monitoring their reading when they're alert to the possibility of getting confused, and they know several ways to solve the problem (Pressley, 2002b).

Teachers teach students to apply these cognitive and metacognitive strategies while reading to ensure that they are comprehending:

- Activating background knowledge
- Connecting
- Determining importance
- Drawing inferences
- Evaluating
- Monitoring
- Predicting
- Questioning
- Repairing
- Setting a purpose
- Summarizing
- Visualizing

Students use these comprehension strategies not only to understand what they're reading, but also to understand books teachers are reading aloud. Figure 8–2 presents an overview of the comprehension strategies and explains how readers use them.

Even preschoolers use many of these comprehension strategies as they listen to books being read aloud. For example, four-year-olds listening to Mo Willems cautionary tale, *Knuffle Bunny* (2004), about a beloved stuffed animal that's left behind at the laundromat, use these strategies:

Activating Background Knowledge. Students who live in cities recognize the book's setting and know what laundromats are, but others wonder why Trixie's parents can't wash their clothes at home.

Literacy Portraits

Ms. Janusz regularly teaches her second graders about comprehension strategies, including predicting, connecting, visualizing, asking questions, and repairing. She introduces a strategy and demonstrates how to use it in a minilesson; next, she encourages the students to practice using it as she reads books aloud. Then students start using the strategy themselves during guided reading lessons and reading workshop. Ms. Janusz monitors their strategy use as she conferences with them. Listen to Rakie, Rhiannon, and Jimmy talk about comprehension strategies and their ability to use them: Which strategies do they seem most confident about using?

Rakie

Rhiannon

Jimmy

Connecting.   Students make personal connections as they think about errands they've run with their fathers, remember their favorite stuffed animals, and recall when younger brothers and sisters were learning to talk.

Drawing Inferences.   Students make these three inferences: First, they infer that Trixie and her daddy's errand was to take their dirty clothes to the laundromat. In the middle of the story, students infer that Trixie's temper tantrum occurred when she realized that her stuffed animal was lost. Finally, they infer that Trixie's parents are running to the laundromat to find Knuffle Bunny quickly.

Figure 8–2 Comprehension Strategies

Strategy	What Readers Do	How It Aids Comprehension
Activating Background Knowledge	Readers make connections between what they already know and the information in the text.	Readers use their background knowledge to fill in gaps in the text and enhance their comprehension.
Connecting	Readers make text-to-self, text-to-world, and text-to-text links.	Readers personalize their reading by relating what they're reading to their background knowledge.
Determining Importance	Readers notice the big ideas in the text and the relationships among them.	Readers focus on the big ideas so they don't become overwhelmed with details.
Drawing Inferences	Readers use background knowledge and clues in the text to "read between the lines."	Readers move beyond literal thinking to grasp meaning that isn't explicitly stated in the text.
Evaluating	Readers evaluate both the text itself and their reading experience.	Readers assume responsibility for their own strategy use.
Monitoring	Readers supervise their reading experience, checking that they're understanding the text.	Readers expect the text to make sense, and they recognize when it doesn't so they can take action.
Predicting	Readers make thoughtful "guesses" about what will happen and then read to confirm their predictions.	Readers become more engaged in the reading experience and want to continue reading.
Questioning	Readers ask themselves literal and higher level questions about the text.	Readers use questions to direct their reading, clarify confusions, and make inferences.
Repairing	Readers identify a problem interfering with comprehension and then solve it.	Readers solve problems to regain comprehension and continue reading.
Setting a Purpose	Readers identify a broad focus to direct their reading through the text.	Readers focus their attention as they read according to the purpose they've set.
Summarizing	Readers paraphrase the big ideas to create a concise statement.	Readers have better recall of the big ideas when they summarize.
Visualizing	Readers create mental images of what they're reading.	Readers use the mental images to make the text more memorable.

Teach Kids to Be Strategic!
Comprehension Strategies

Teach students to apply these strategies (presented here in alphabetical order):

- Activate background knowledge
- Connect
- Determine importance
- Draw inferences
- Evaluate
- Monitor
- Predict
- Question
- Repair
- Set a purpose
- Summarize
- Visualize

Students learn to use each strategy and make posters to highlight their new knowledge. They apply strategies as they read and use self-stick notes to record their strategy use. Monitor students' growing use of strategies during independent reading activities, and if they struggle, reteach the strategies, making sure to name them and model their use.

Predicting. At the beginning of the story, students predict that Trixie and her daddy will have fun together, and in the middle, they predict that Knuffle Bunny will go into the washing machine by mistake. Finally, they predict that Trixie and her parents will find the lost stuffed animal.

Questioning. Students ask several questions about events in the story, including why Trixie's daddy wasn't more careful with Knuffle Bunny and why he didn't understand what Trixie meant when she was trying to tell him that her stuffed animal was lost.

Teachers nurture students' use of comprehension strategies by stopping occasionally while they're reading to ask questions and by rereading books so that students can delve more deeply into them.

ACTIVATING BACKGROUND KNOWLEDGE. Readers bring their background knowledge to every reading experience; in fact, they read a text differently depending on their prior experiences. Zimmermann and Hutchins (2003) explain that "the meaning you get from a piece is intertwined with the meaning you bring to it" (p. 45). Readers think about the topic before they begin reading and call up relevant information and related vocabulary to use while reading. The more background knowledge and prior experiences readers have about a topic, the more likely they are to comprehend what they're reading (Harvey & Goudvis, 2007).

Teachers rarely pick up a book and just start reading because it's essential to activate students' background knowledge first. They use a variety of prereading activities to help activate and build students' background knowledge, such as creating **KWL charts**, examining artifacts, and viewing pictures and videos. Through these activities, students think about the topic, use vocabulary related to the topic, and get interested in reading the text.

CONNECTING. Readers make three types of connections between a text and their background knowledge: text-to-self, text-to-world, and text-to-text connections (Harvey & Goudvis, 2007):

Text-to-Self Connections. Students link the ideas they're reading about to experiences in their own lives; these are personal connections. A story event or character may remind

MyLab Education
Video Example 8.2

Teachers teach comprehension strategies throughout the reading process. Some are taught during prereading, before students begin to read. Some are modeled during reading. How do these strategies aid comprehension?

them of something or someone in their own lives, and the facts in an informational book may remind them of a past experience or something a family member taught them.

Text-to-World Connections.   Students move beyond personal experience to relate what they're reading to their "world" knowledge, learned both in and out of school. For example, students who are reading a story about a stranded whale may recall a recent TV news report about a similar situation, or students reading an informational book about insects may make a connection to an animated movie they've seen about bugs.

Text-to-Text Connections.   Students link the text to another book they've read or to a familiar film, video, or television program. Readers often compare different versions of familiar folktales, books by the same author, and books in a series, such as Barbara Park's Junie B. Jones stories, James Preller's Jigsaw Jones mysteries, or Paula Danziger's Amber Brown chapter-book series. Text-to-text connections are often the most difficult, especially for students who know less about literature.

One way that teachers teach this strategy is by making a connection chart with three columns labeled *text-to-self*, *text-to-world*, and *text-to-text*; then students write connections that they've made on small self-stick notes and post them in the correct column of the chart. A second grade connections chart created after reading *The Moon Over Star* (Aston, 2008), a 40th-anniversary tribute to the first moon landing, is shown in Figure 8–3. Students can also make connection charts in their **reading logs** and write their connections in each column. Later in the reading process, they make connections as they assume the role of a character and sit on the **hot seat** to be interviewed by classmates, create **open-mind portraits** to share the character's thinking, write a letter or a diary entry from the viewpoint of a character, or participate in other activities that clarify connections.

DETERMINING IMPORTANCE.   Readers sift through the text to identify the important ideas as they read because it isn't possible to remember everything (Harvey & Goudvis, 2007; Keene & Zimmermann, 2007). Students learn the difference between the big ideas and the details and to recognize the more important ideas as they read and talk about the books they've read. This comprehension strategy is important because students need to be able to identify the big ideas in order to understand and summarize a story's theme.

Teachers often direct students' attention to the big ideas when they encourage them to make predictions, and the way teachers introduce the text also influences students' thinking about what's important in a book. When students read stories, they make diagrams about the plot, characters, and setting, and these graphic organizers emphasize the big ideas. Similarly, they make diagrams that reflect the structure of the text when they read informational books. Teachers usually provide the diagrams with the big ideas highlighted, but sometimes students analyze the text to determine its structure and then develop their own graphic organizers.

Figure 8–3 A Connections Chart About *The Moon Over Star*

Text-to-Self-Connections	Text-to-World-Connections	Text-to-Text-Connections
I've been thinking about being an astronaut. It would be an exciting job.	It's true that on July 20, 1969 the astronauts landed on the moon.	I'm reading a book called Spacebusters. It's about the moon landing, too.
Me and my friends have built spaceships and pretended that we were astronauts going to the moon.	Now everybody knows the words that Neil Armstrong said, "that's one small step for man, one giant leap for mankind."	This book is like Team Moon because they're both about how Apollo 11 changed people but one book is fiction and the other is nonfiction.
My grandma was alive then and she remembers watching the moon landing on TV.	This is a fact: the moon is 240,000 miles away from earth.	
	Both John Kennedy and Walter Cronkite are dead now, but the 3 astronauts are still alive.	

DRAWING INFERENCES. Readers seem to "read between the lines" to draw inferences, but what they actually do is synthesize their background knowledge with the author's clues to ask questions that point toward inferences. Keene and Zimmermann (2007) explain that when readers draw inferences, they have "an opportunity to sense a meaning not explicit in the text, but which derives or flows from it" (p. 145). Readers make both conscious and unconscious inferences about characters in a story and its theme, the big ideas in an informational book, and the author's purpose in a poem (Pressley, 2002a).

Students often have to read or listen to a story two or three times to draw inferences because they focus on literal comprehension at first, which has to precede higher level thinking. Sometimes they draw inferences when prompted by the teacher, but it's important to teach them how to draw inferences so that they can think more deeply when they read independently. Teachers begin by explaining what inferences are, how they differ from literal thinking, and why they're important. Then they teach these steps in drawing inferences:

1. **Activate background knowledge.** Teachers support readers as they think about topics related to the text.

2. **Look for clues.** Students notice the author's clues—unexpected information in the text—as they read.

3. **Ask questions.** Readers tie together background knowledge and the author's clues as they think of things that puzzle them about the text.

4. **Reach conclusions.** Readers draw inferences by answering the questions they posed.

Teachers comment on clues, express puzzlement, and ask "why" questions to encourage students to draw inferences.

Teachers can create inference charts to make the steps more visible as students practice drawing inferences, and readers can make their own charts to answer an inferential question. For example, after reading and discussing *The Garden of Abdul Gasazi* (Van Allsburg, 1994), the story of a magician who turns a misbehaving dog into a duck, fourth graders worked in pairs to make the inference chart shown in Figure 8–4 to answer this question: What happened to the dog? By thinking about their background knowledge, looking for clues in the story, and asking questions, the students concluded that the magician's spell didn't last long, and that after the duck flew home, it changed back into a dog.

Although drawing inferences is a difficult strategy because it requires higher level thinking, even young students are capable of using it with teacher guidance. As teachers read aloud, they encourage preschoolers and kindergartners to use their background knowledge, clues in the illustrations, and the words in the text to grasp the author's meaning. When preschoolers listen to David Shannon's hilarious autobiographical story, *No, David!* (1998), for example, they draw inferences on almost every page. The illustrations show a mischievous little boy tracking dirt into the house, eating with his mouth open, and letting his bath water overflow the tub, and the very brief text says "No, David, no!" "That's enough, David," "No! No! No!" and other reprimands. Students grasp the meaning and can explain the inferences.

EVALUATING. Readers reflect on their reading experience and evaluate the text and what they're learning (Owocki, 2003). As with the other comprehension strategies, students use the evaluating strategy throughout the reading process. They monitor their interest in the text from the moment they pick up the book, and they judge their success in solving reading problems each time one arises. They evaluate their reading experience, including these aspects:

- Their ease in reading the text

- The adequacy of their background knowledge

Figure 8–4 Inference Chart About *The Garden of Abdul Gasazi*

Title **The Garden of Abdul Gasazi** Author **Chris Van Allsburg**

BACKGROUND KNOWLEDGE	QUESTIONS
Magicians do tricks. This story is a fantasy so magic can happen. Sometimes dogs don't behave.	Did the magician do it? How did Fritz get home? Why was Alan's hat in Miss Hester's yard?

CLUES FROM THE STORY	INFERENCES
Only time can change Fritz back into a dog. The duck was like Fritz because he took Alan's hat. Fritz the dog has Alan's hat at the end.	The magician did cast a spell and make the dog into a duck. The spell didn't last very long.

- Their use of comprehension strategies
- How they solved reading problems
- Their interest and attention in the text

They also consider the text:

- Their assessment of the text's quality
- Their opinions about the author
- The knowledge they gained
- How they'll apply what they're learning

Students usually write about their reflections in reading log entries and talk about their evaluations in **grand conversations** and other discussions and conferences. Evaluating is important because it helps students assume more responsibility for their own learning.

MONITORING.   Readers monitor their understanding as they read, although they may be aware that they're using this strategy only when their comprehension breaks down and they have to take action to solve their problem. Harvey and Goudvis (2007) describe monitoring as the inner conversation that students carry on in their minds with the text as they read—expressing wonder, making connections, asking questions, reacting to information, drawing conclusions, and noticing confusions, for example.

Monitoring involves regulating reader and text factors at the same time. Readers often ask themselves these questions:

- What's my purpose for reading?
- Is this book too difficult for me to read on my own?

MyLab Education

Video Example 8.3

Monitoring requires students to apply their knowledge of reader and text factors as they check their understanding of the text they're reading. How do students monitor their reading comprehension?

- Do I need to read the entire book or only parts of it?
- What's special about the genre of this book?
- How does the author use text structure?
- What is the author's viewpoint?
- Do I understand the meaning of the words I'm reading? (Pressley, 2002b)

Once students detect a problem, they shift into problem-solving mode to repair their comprehension.

PREDICTING.   Readers make thoughtful "guesses" or predictions about what will happen or what they'll learn in the book they're reading. These guesses are based on what students already know about the topic and genre or on what they've read thus far. Students often make a prediction before beginning to read and several others at pivotal points in a text—no matter whether they're reading stories, informational books, or poems—and then as they read, they either confirm or revise their predictions. Predictions about nonfiction are different than for fictional stories and poems; here students are generating questions about the topic that they would like to find answers to as they read.

When teachers read big books using shared reading, they prompt students to make predictions at the beginning of the book and again at key points during the reading. They model how to make reasonable predictions and use **think-alouds** to explain their thinking. When third and fourth graders are reading novels, they often write their predictions on small self-stick notes while they're reading and place them in their books to share with classmates afterward.

QUESTIONING.   Readers ask themselves questions about the text as they read (Duke, Pearson, Strachan, & Billman, 2011). They ask questions out of curiosity, and in the process, they become more engaged with the text and want to keep reading to find the answers (Harvey & Goudvis, 2007). These questions often lead to making predictions and drawing inferences. Students also ask themselves questions to clarify misunderstandings as they read. They use this strategy throughout the reading process—to activate background knowledge and make predictions before reading, to engage with the text and clarify confusions during reading, and to evaluate and reflect on the text and the characters' experiences after reading.

Traditionally, teachers have been the question-askers and students the question-answerers, but when students learn to generate questions about the text, their comprehension improves. In fact, students comprehend better when they generate their own questions than when teachers ask questions (Duke et al., 2011). Many students don't know how to ask questions to guide their reading, so it's important that teachers guide them in learning how. They model generating questions and then encourage students to do the same. Tovani (2000) suggests having students brainstorm a list of "I wonder" questions on a topic because they need to learn how to generate questions.

The questions students ask shape their comprehension: If they ask literal "what" and "who" questions, their comprehension will be more literal, but if students generate inferential "how" and "why" questions, their comprehension will be higher level.

REPAIRING.   Readers use repairing to fix comprehension problems that arise while reading (Zimmermann & Hutchins, 2003). When students use the monitoring strategy and notice that they're confused or bored, they can't remember what they just read, or they're not asking questions, they need to use repairing (Tovani, 2000). This strategy involves figuring out the problem and taking action to solve it. Sometimes students go back and reread or skip ahead and read; sometimes they try visualizing, questioning, or another strategy that might help; and at other times, they check the meaning of an unfamiliar word, examine the structure of a confusing sentence, use picture clues, learn more about an unfamiliar topic related to the text, or ask a classmate or the teacher for assistance. These solutions are referred to as *fix-up strategies*, and teachers often post lists of these strategies in the classroom.

SETTING A PURPOSE.   Readers read for different reasons—for entertainment, to learn about a topic, for directions to accomplish a task, or to find the answer to a specific question, for instance—and the purposes they set direct their attention during reading (Tovani, 2000). Setting a purpose activates a mental blueprint to use while reading, which aids in determining how readers focus their attention and how they sort relevant from irrelevant information as they read (Blanton, Wood, & Moorman, 1990). Before they begin to read, students identify a single, fairly broad purpose that they sustain while reading the entire text; it must fit both their reason for reading and the text. Students can ask themselves "Why am I going to read this text?" or "What do I need to learn from this book?" to help them set a purpose. It's important that they have a purpose when they read, because readers vary how they read and what they remember according to their purpose. When students don't set useful purposes, they misdirect their attention and remember unimportant ideas.

SUMMARIZING.   Readers pick out the most important ideas and the relationships among them and briefly restate them so they can be remembered (Harvey & Goudvis, 2007). It's crucial that students determine which ideas are the most important because if they focus on tangential ideas or details, their comprehension is compromised. To create effective summaries, students need to paraphrase, or restate ideas in their own words.

Summarizing is a difficult task, but instruction and practice improve students' ability to summarize as well as their overall comprehension (Duke et al., 2011). One way to teach students to summarize folktales and other brief stories is by using the Somebody-Wanted-But-So (Macon, Bewell, & Vogt, 1991) summarizing frame. Students create a sentence or two to identify who wanted something, what they wanted, the problem that arose, and how it was resolved. Figure 8–5 shows how a first grade teacher used this frame to create a summary of "The 3 Billy Goats Gruff."

VISUALIZING.   Readers use the visualizing strategy when they create mental images of what they're reading (Harvey & Goudvis, 2007; Keene & Zimmermann, 2007). They often place themselves in the images they create, becoming a character in the story they're reading, traveling to that setting, or facing the conflict situations the characters face. Sometimes teachers ask students to close their eyes to help visualize the story or to draw pictures of the scenes and characters they visualize. A second grader's poster about the visualizing strategy is shown in Figure 8–6. How well students use visualization often becomes clear when they view film versions of books they've read: Those who are good visualizers are usually disappointed with the film version and the actors who portray the characters; however, students who don't visualize are often amazed by the film and prefer it to the book.

MyLab Education
Video Example 8.4

Students continue to apply comprehension strategies after reading as well as earlier in the reading process. Which strategies do students use after reading?

MyLab Education Self-Check 8.2

MyLab Education Application Exercise 8.1: Do Readers Monitor Their Comprehension?

MyLab Education Application Exercise 8.2: Comprehension Strategies Readers Use While Reading

Figure 8–5 The Somebody-Wanted-But-So Summarizing Frame

Frame	Question	Example
Somebody	Who is the character?	the 3 billy goats gruff
Wanted	What does the character want?	to eat grass up on the hill
But	What is the problem?	the mean troll wouldn't let them cross the bridge
So	How does the character solve it?	the biggest goat attacked and killed him

Figure 8–6 A Visualization Poster

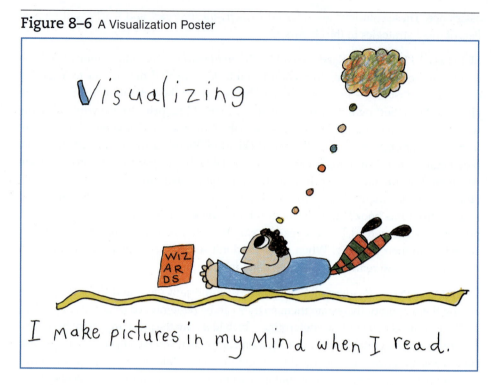

GO DIGITAL! Online Comprehension Strategies.
Websites are dynamic learning contexts that create new challenges for readers because online texts differ from print texts in significant ways (Castek, Bevans-Mangelson, & Goldstone, 2006): Print texts are linear and unchanging, with a finite number of pages and with information arranged in predictable narrative, nonfiction, and poetic genres; online texts, in contrast, are multilayered, with unlimited multimodal information accessed through hypertext links.

Students use these traditional comprehension strategies to read Web-based texts, but they use them in new ways (Coiro & Dobler, 2007):

Activating Background Knowledge.   Readers need to know about websites and how to navigate search engines to locate useful ones.

Predicting.   Students predict which links will be useful; otherwise, they get distracted or waste time finding their way back from unproductive links.

Evaluating.   Students determine the accuracy, objectivity, relevance, and quality of information on websites, because some information may be erroneous or biased.

Monitoring.   Students monitor their navigational choices and decide whether the links they've reached are useful.

Repairing.   Students use the repairing strategy to correct poor navigational choices.

Students also learn comprehension strategies that address the unique characteristics and complex applications of online texts (Coiro, 2003). Coauthoring is a comprehension strategy that readers use to impose an organization on online texts (Leu, Kinzer, Coiro, Castek & Laurie, 2013). Students make a series of decisions as they move from one link to another, searching for information, and they plan, predict, monitor, and evaluate with each navigational choice.

It's essential that teachers prepare students to use 21st-century technology. Students need to understand how print and Web-based texts differ so they can adjust how they apply traditional comprehension strategies and learn ones to use for Internet texts.

Teaching Comprehension Strategies

Comprehension instruction involves teaching students about comprehension and the strategies readers use to understand what they're reading, and then providing opportunities for students to practice what they're learning using authentic books (Duke et al., 2011). Researchers emphasize the need to establish the expectation that the books students read will make sense (Duke et al., 2011; Owocki, 2003). Teachers create an expectation of comprehension in these ways:

- Involving students in authentic reading activities every day
- Providing students access to well-stocked classroom libraries
- Teaching students to use comprehension strategies
- Ensuring that students become fluent readers
- Providing opportunities for students to talk about the books they read
- Linking vocabulary instruction to underlying concepts

Teachers can't assume that students will learn to comprehend simply by doing lots of reading; instead, students develop an understanding of comprehension and what readers do to be successful through a combination of instruction, opportunities for authentic reading, and comprehension activities (Almasi & Hart, 2015). Use **My Teaching To-Do Checklist Comprehension: Readier Factors** to examine the effectiveness of your comprehension instruction.

The Common Core State Standards for English Language Arts (2010) emphasize the importance of comprehension: They focus on having students read increasingly complex texts through the grades and teaching them how to comprehend the author's message. Students learn to understand precisely what authors say, but also to question authors' assumptions and assess the veracity of their claims. The document identifies these reader factors:

Key Ideas and Details.   Students demonstrate their understanding of a text, ask and answer both literal and inferential questions, and explain relationships among ideas.

Integration of Knowledge and Ideas.   Students analyze visual and multimedia elements, use reasons and evidence to support ideas, and make comparisons between two texts.

Range of Reading.   Students read and understand grade-level fiction and nonfiction texts independently and proficiently.

Level of Text Complexity.   Students learn how to read increasingly challenging texts.

MY TEACHING TO-DO CHECKLIST Comprehension: Reader Factors

☐ I teach students to attend to both reader and text factors as they read.

☐ I teach comprehension strategies using a combination of explanations, demonstrations, think-alouds, and practice activities.

☐ I expect students to apply the strategies they've learned when they're reading independently.

☐ I have students apply comprehension strategies in literacy activities as well as in thematic units.

☐ I display student-made charts about the strategies in the classroom.

☐ I have students read and analyze increasingly complex texts.

☐ I have students read grade-appropriate fiction and nonfiction texts.

☐ I integrate state standards into my instruction

Common Core State Standards

Comprehension: Reader Factors

The Common Core State Standards for English Language Arts emphasize that students are expected to read a broad range of high-quality and increasingly challenging texts. Students must understand precisely what authors say and make interpretations based on textual evidence. The Standards specify these comprehension requirements:

- Students determine the central ideas of a text and analyze their development.
- Students make connections with background knowledge and other texts.
- Students draw inferences from the textual evidence.
- Students cite textual evidence that supports an analysis of what the text states explicitly.
- Students comprehend grade-level stories, informational books, and other texts independently and proficiently.

The Standards emphasize that students use reader factors to comprehend increasingly complex fiction and nonfiction texts. To learn more about the Standards, go to http://www.corestandards.org/ELA-Literacy, or check your state's educational standards website.

The Common Core State Standards challenge teachers to provide a balance of instruction and scaffolding so students learn to read and comprehend complex texts. In the vignette, Mrs. Chase demonstrated how teachers teach students about challenging texts and then gradually release responsibility to them to apply what they've learned about comprehension when they're reading independently. For more information, check the Common Core State Standards box.

Using Explicit Instruction

The fact that comprehension is an invisible mental process makes it difficult to teach; however, through explicit instruction, teachers can make it more visible. They explain what comprehension is and why it's important, and they model how to do it. When teachers are reading aloud or doing **shared reading**, they use the **think-aloud** procedure to talk about their predictions, connections, and use of other strategies.

Teachers teach individual comprehension strategies and then show students how to integrate several strategies (Block & Pressley, 2007). They introduce each comprehension strategy in a series of **minilessons** in which they describe the strategy, model it as they read a book aloud, use it collaboratively with students, and then provide opportunities for guided and independent practice (Duke et al., 2011). The Minilesson, Teaching Students to Ask Self-Questions shows how Mrs. Macadangdang teaches her third graders to use the questioning strategy.

To teach comprehension strategies, teachers use stories they're reading aloud, books being featured in literature focus units, chapter books students are reading in literature circles, and leveled books students are reading in guided reading lessons. Almost any book can be used to teach at least several comprehension strategies. Figure 8–7 illustrates how *Officer Buckle and Gloria* (Rathmann, 1995), an award-winning story about a police officer and his dog who work as a team, can be used to teach any comprehension strategy, even though teachers wouldn't use the same book to teach more than one or two strategies. Other recommended books for teaching comprehension strategies are presented in this chapter's Booklist.

Teaching for Comprehension During Reading

Students reinforce their awareness that reading is a meaning-making process, and they refine their ability to apply comprehension strategies when they read books at their

Figure 8–7 Teaching Comprehension Strategies Using *Officer Buckle and Gloria*

Strategy	Activity
Activating Background Knowledge	Teachers talk about how police officers protect people, and sometimes they invite a police officer to visit the class and talk about safety.
Connecting	Students talk about their connections to their experiences with police officers, safety rules, dogs, and school assemblies. They also make text-to-text connections by comparing this book to *Make Way for Ducklings* (McCloskey, 2004), another story involving a police officer.
Determining Importance	Teachers use discussion and make graphic organizers to help students identify the characters, organize the story into the beginning-middle-end, and deduce the story's message or theme.
Drawing Inferences	Teachers scaffold students' thinking about whether Officer Buckle will appreciate Gloria's antics and about the story's message concerning teamwork.
Evaluating	Students evaluate the quality of the story and its award-winning illustrations as well as their comprehension of the story and its theme.
Monitoring	Teachers use think-alouds to demonstrate how they monitor their understanding of the story, and they invite one or two students to share their thinking.
Predicting	Teachers encourage students to make predictions about whether Gloria will make a good partner and what Officer Buckle will do once he learns about Gloria's antics.
Questioning	Teachers have students brainstorm questions after reading each page or two to demonstrate engagement, suggest predictions, and clarify any confusions.
Repairing	Teachers normally share this book using the interactive read-aloud procedure so students don't use fix-up strategies; however, they do monitor their understanding and ask questions when they're confused.
Setting a Purpose	This complex story can be approached in different ways: Teachers might ask students to focus on the safety lessons Officer Buckle teaches, consider how Officer Buckle faces his problems, or examine Gloria's role as a sidekick.
Summarizing	Students summarize the story by making a story map and drawing a picture or writing a sentence about the beginning, middle, and end. They also sequence story boards and use them to briefly retell the story.
Visualizing	Teachers focus on the characters, especially at the high point, when Officer Buckle learns about Gloria's antics. Students can role-play the characters or draw pictures to show each character's thoughts at specific points in the story.

reading level and listen to teachers read aloud grade-appropriate stories, informational books, and poems that they can't read themselves. They practice the comprehension strategies that they're learning and use higher levels of thinking to make predictions, notice clues in the text, draw inferences, and evaluate the book's quality. Teachers provide a combination of independent, small-group, and whole-class reading opportunities every day.

Booklist Books to Use in Teaching Comprehension Strategies

Grades	Books
PreK–K	Galdone, P. (2008). *The gingerbread boy.* Henkes, K. (1996). *Lilly's purple plastic purse.* Long, M. (2003). *How I became a pirate.* McCloskey, R. (2004). *Make way for ducklings.* Pinkney, J. (2009). *The lion and the mouse.* Willems, M. (2004). *Knuffle bunny.*
1–2	Cronin, D. (2011). *Click, clack, moo: Cows that type.* Henkes, K. (1996). *Chrysanthemum.* Scieszka, J. (1999). *The true story of the 3 little pigs!* Steig, W. (2010). *Sylvester and the magic pebble.* Woodson, J. (2001). *The other side.* Yorinks, A. (1989). *Hey, Al.*
3–4	Bunting, E. (1999). *Smoky night.* Demi. (1996). *The empty pot.* Kajikawa, K. (2009). *Tsunami!* Steig, W. (1990). *Doctor De Soto.* Van Allsburg, C. (1986). *The stranger.* Van Allsburg, C. (1991). *The wretched stone.*

Minilesson

TOPIC: Teaching Students to Ask Self-Questions
GRADE: Third Grade
TIME: Three 30-minute periods

Mrs. Macadangdang (the students call her Mrs. Mac) introduced questioning by talking about why people ask questions and by asking questions about stories the third graders were reading. She encouraged them to ask questions, too. They made a list of questions for each chapter of *Chang's Paper Pony* (Coerr, 1993)—a story set in the California gold rush era—as she read it aloud, and then they evaluated their questions, choosing the ones that focus on the big ideas and that helped them to understand the story better. Now all of her students can generate questions, so she's ready to introduce the questioning strategy.

1. **Introduce the Topic**
   Mrs. Mac reads the list posted in the classroom of comprehension strategies that they've learned to use and explains, "Today, we're going to learn a new thinking strategy—questioning. Readers ask themselves questions while they're reading to help them think about the book." She adds "Questioning" to the list.

2. **Share Examples**
   The teacher introduces *The Josefina Story Quilt* (Coerr, 1989), the story of a pioneer family going to California in a covered wagon. She reads aloud the first chapter, thinking aloud and generating questions about the story. Each time she says a question, she places a sentence strip with the question on it in a pocket chart. Here are the questions: Why is Faith excited? Why are they going in a covered wagon? Who is Josefina? Can a chicken be a pet? Can Josefina do anything useful? Why is Faith crying?

3. **Provide Information**
   Mrs. Mac explains, "Questions really turn your thinking on! I know it's important to think while I'm reading because it helps me understand. I like to ask questions about things I think are important and things that don't make sense to me." They reread the questions in the pocket chart and talk about the most helpful ones. Many students thought the question about the covered wagon was important, but as they continue reading, they'll learn that Josefina does, indeed, do something useful—she turns out to be a "humdinger of a watch dog" (p. 54)! Then Mrs. Mac reads aloud the second chapter, stopping often for students to generate questions. They write their questions on sentence strips and add them to the pocket chart.

4. **Guide Practice**
   The following day, Mrs. Mac reviews the questioning strategy and students reread the questions for Chapters 1 and 2. Then the students form pairs, get copies of the book, and read the next two chapters of *The Josefina Story Quilt* together, generating questions as they read. They write their questions on small self-stick notes and place them in the book. Mrs. Mac monitors students, noticing which ones need additional practice. Then the class comes together to share their questions and talk about the chapters they've read. On the third day, they read the last two chapters and generate more questions.

5. **Assess Learning**
   As she monitored the students, Mrs. Mac made a list of students who needed more practice generating questions, and she'll work with them as they read another book together.

PreK Practices

How do four-year-olds learn to comprehend?

Teachers nurture young students' comprehension by sharing picture books using interactive read-alouds and big books using shared reading (Morrow, Freitag, & Gambrell, 2009). As they read, teachers emphasize concepts about written language; build students' background knowledge and vocabulary; and model how to use comprehension strategies, including activating background knowledge, predicting what will happen next, and making connections to their own lives. Students listen attentively and engage in the reading experience, repeating refrains, clapping or pointing as the teacher directs, and talking about the book. They participate in response activities, such as using puppets to retell stories and drawing pictures to share information. Students demonstrate their budding knowledge about comprehension as they do "pretend reading," talk about books, and retell stories.

INDEPENDENT READING. Students need to spend lots of time reading authentic texts independently and talking about their reading with classmates and teachers. Having students read interesting books written at their reading level is the best way for them to apply comprehension strategies. As they read and discuss their reading, students are practicing what they're learning about comprehension. Reading a selection in a basal textbook each week isn't enough; instead, students need to read many, many books representing a range of genres during reading workshop or another daily independent reading time.

INTERACTIVE READ-ALOUDS. Teachers read books aloud using the interactive read-aloud procedure every day, even after students have learned to read. They share high-quality, grade-appropriate books that interest students and challenge them to think. As they listen, students build background knowledge and expand their vocabulary, watch their teacher demonstrate comprehension strategies, and practice the strategies they're learning. Afterward, they talk about the book in a **grand conversation** and other discussions, using comprehension strategies to ask questions, make connections, draw inferences, and evaluate the book.

SHARED READING. As teachers read big books aloud using **shared reading**, they demonstrate how to use comprehension strategies and provide opportunities for students to practice activating background knowledge, predicting, connecting, questioning, and other strategies. Because students can see the text in big books, teachers can also demonstrate how to monitor their reading, use the repairing strategy, and decode unfamiliar words more effectively than when they're reading regular-size books to students.

Activities That Promote Comprehension

Teachers use a variety of activities to support students' comprehension of stories and other books they're reading. Figure 8–8 presents a list of activities for each comprehension strategy. Second graders practice questioning by asking questions instead of giving answers during a **grand conversation**, for example, and fourth graders practice connecting when they write favorite quotes in one column of a **reading logs** and then explain in the second column why each quote is meaningful. These activities help students review story events, clarify misconceptions, and deepen their comprehension.

Figure 8–8 Ways to Teach the Comprehension Strategies

Strategy	Instructional Procedures
Activating Background Knowledge	• Students develop a KWL chart. • Students listen to teachers read aloud books related to the topic.
Connecting	• Students add text-to-self, text-to-world, and text-to-text connections to a class chart. • Students become a character and participate in a hot seat activity.
Determining Importance	• Students create graphic organizers. • Students make posters highlighting the big ideas.
Drawing Inferences	• Students use small self-stick notes to mark clues in the text. • Students contribute to class charts with the author's clues, questions, and inferences.
Evaluating	• Students conference with the teacher about a book they've read. • Students write reflections in reading logs.
Monitoring	• Students think aloud to demonstrate how they monitor their reading. • Students write about their strategy use on small self-stick notes and in reading logs.
Predicting	• Students share their predictions during read-alouds. • Teachers have Students make predictions during guided reading lessons.
Questioning	• Students brainstorm questions before reading. • Students ask questions during grand conversations and other discussions.
Repairing	• Students make personal charts of the ways they solve comprehension problems. • Students think aloud to demonstrate how they use the repairing strategy.
Setting a Purpose	• Students identify their purpose in a discussion before beginning to read. • Students write about their purpose in a reading log entry before beginning to read.
Summarizing	• Students create visual summaries on charts using words, diagrams, and pictures. • Students write a summary using interactive writing.
Visualizing	• Students create open-mind portraits of characters. • Students draw pictures of events from a book they're reading.

Teaching English Learners
Comprehension And Reader Factors

Comprehension is often very difficult for English learners for a number of reasons (Bouchard, 2005). ELs often lack one or more of the three prerequisites for comprehension—background knowledge, vocabulary, and fluency. Many students who haven't had middle-class American experiences or who lack mainstream cultural knowledge can be at a disadvantage when they read or listen to a book read aloud because they don't have crucial background knowledge. First graders who listen to *Ira Sleeps Over* (Waber, 2008), for example, but who have never stayed overnight at a friend's house, will have difficulty comprehending this story, and fourth graders who read *Molly's Pilgrim* (Cohen, 1999), but don't know about the Pilgrims who came to America in 1620 or about European Jewish immigrants, will have difficulty grasping the story's theme.

ELs' limited background knowledge is typically reflected in their lack of familiarity with Tier 2 vocabulary. It isn't surprising that students have difficulty identifying and understanding words when they aren't familiar with a topic. Even if students seem to be aware of a topic, however, they may have difficulty with the vocabulary. For example, second graders who seem to know about football may have difficulty reading and comprehending *Kick, Pass, and Run!* (Kessler, 1996) because they don't understand the sports lingo, even though the book is at their reading level. Even when students are familiar with a topic, they can become so overwhelmed while trying to wade through unfamiliar Tier 2 vocabulary words in nearly every sentence that they don't understand what they're reading.

There can be a mismatch, too, between students' English proficiency and the book's reading level. Books with sophisticated sentence structures, including poetry, books with a great deal of dialogue, and books with unusual page layouts, are more difficult. Like all readers, ELs can't read fluently and won't comprehend what they're reading if the book is too difficult.

CHOOSING BOOKS.   When teachers choose books for English learners, they consider the three prerequisites for comprehension and the students' level of English language development. They ask themselves these questions:

- **Topic.** Do students have adequate background knowledge about the topic?
- **Vocabulary.** Do students know the meanings of most of the words related to the topic?
- **Linguistic Style.** Are the book's sentence patterns and language features familiar?
- **Page Layout.** Does the book have an unusual or confusing format?
- **Reading Level.** Is the book's reading level appropriate?

Teachers address these concerns by choosing books that are suitable for students at their level of English proficiency, and by providing extra support. They commonly build background knowledge and introduce key vocabulary words before students read; they can also read aloud part or all of the book before students read it, if the linguistic style is unfamiliar, or demonstrate how to read the first few pages, if the format is unusual.

TEACHING COMPREHENSION STRATEGIES.   English learners use the same comprehension strategies that native English speakers do, and they learn them the same way (Garcia, 2003). Teachers provide explicit instruction, and during the lessons, they demonstrate a strategy and explain how and when to use it and why it will help students become better readers. Teachers use creativity to make strategies—invisible thought processes—more concrete; for example, some teachers put on hats they call "thinking caps," and others draw quick sketches of their thinking. They spend more time modeling how to apply the strategy and doing **think-alouds** to share their thoughts as they read big books using shared reading and during **interactive read-alouds.** Next, teachers provide guided practice, often in guided reading groups, with students working with partners and in small groups, and they guide students as they apply the strategy. Teachers often have students mark codes on small self-stick notes and place them next to the text that prompted their strategy use in the books they're reading. Once students understand how and when to use a strategy, they read independently, applying the strategy as they read.

ACTIVE ENGAGEMENT WITH BOOKS.   Peregoy and Boyle (2013) point out that many ELs read texts passively, as if they were waiting for the information to organize itself and highlight the big ideas. To help these students become more active readers and thinkers, teachers use these activities:

- Share objects related to the book to introduce it
- Read the book using the interactive read-aloud procedure
- Provide puppets and other props for students to use for story retelling
- Guide students as they dramatize a story
- Encourage students to retell stories with a series of drawings or in writing
- Have students draw pictures about the book and share them with classmates
- Take students' dictation about the book using the Language Experience Approach
- Encourage students to use story boards to explore a picture book or retell it
- Have students create a story board for each chapter in a novel
- Prepare a graphic organizer about the book for students to complete

- Make a class poster about the book using interactive writing
- Have students construct open-mind portraits
- Add important words from the book to the word wall
- Do a word sort using words from the word wall
- Have students reread familiar books with partners or at the listening center
- Use choral reading to reread a pattern book or a poem

These activities nurture students' ability to use higher level thinking and apply the comprehension strategies they're learning.

Assessing Students' Knowledge of Reader Factors

Teachers use a combination of diagnostic tests as well as an integrated instruction–assessment approach to ensure that students are growing in their ability to understand complex texts and using increasingly more sophisticated strategies to deepen comprehension.

DIAGNOSTIC ASSESSMENT. Teachers also use diagnostic assessment tools to screen the entire class for comprehension problems or to measure struggling students' comprehension and plan for intervention. The Assessment Tools feature on the next page presents more information about comprehension tests used in the primary grades.

THE INSTRUCTION–ASSESSMENT CYCLE. Teachers follow the four-step instruction–assessment cycle to monitor students' learning and the effectiveness of their teaching. They use these steps:

Step 1: Planning.   Teachers make decisions about how they'll teach comprehension strategies and other reader factor concepts, and they decide how to monitor students' progress during instruction and evaluate it afterward.

Step 2: Monitoring.   Teachers assess students' comprehension informally every day; for example, they listen to the comments students make during **grand conversations**, confer with students about books they're reading, and examine their entries in reading logs. Students' interest in a book is sometimes an indicator, too: When students dismiss a book as "boring," they may mean that it's confusing or too difficult.

Teachers use these informal assessment procedures to monitor students' use of comprehension strategies and their understanding of books they're reading:

- **Cloze Procedure.** Teachers examine students' understanding of a text using the **cloze procedure**, in which students supply the deleted words in a passage taken from a book they've read. Although filling in the blanks may seem like a simple activity, it isn't, because students need to consider the content of the passage, vocabulary words, and sentence structure to choose the exact word that was deleted.

- **Story Retellings.** Teachers often have students retell stories they've read or listened to read aloud to assess their literal comprehension (Morrow, 2002). Students' **story retellings** should be coherent and well organized and should include the big ideas and important details. When teachers prompt students with questions and encourage them to "tell me more," they're known as *aided retellings*; otherwise, they're *unaided retellings*. Teachers often use checklists and rubrics to score students' story retellings.

- **Running Records.** Teachers use **running records** (Clay, 2007) to examine students' oral reading behaviors, analyze their comprehension, and determine their reading levels. Students read a book aloud, and afterward they retell it orally. Teachers encourage students to recall as much detail as possible, asking questions to prompt

Assessment Tools

Comprehension

Teachers use a combination of informal assessment procedures, including story retellings and think-alouds, and commercially available tests to measure students' comprehension. These tests are often used in PreK through fourth grade classrooms:

- **Comprehension Thinking Strategies Assessment**

  The Comprehension Thinking Strategies Assessment (Keene, 2006) examines first through eighth graders' ability to use these strategies to think about fiction and nonfiction texts: activating background knowledge, determining importance, drawing inferences, noticing text structure, questioning, setting a purpose, and visualizing. As students read a passage, they pause and reflect on their strategy use. Teachers score students' responses using a rubric. This 30-minute test can be administered to individuals or to the class, depending on whether students' responses are oral or written. This flexible assessment tool can be used to evaluate students' learning after teaching a strategy, to survey progress at the beginning of the school year, or to document achievement at the end of the year. It's available online from Shell Education.

- **Developmental Reading Assessment (DRA2)**

  Teachers use the K–3 or 4–8 DRA2 kit (Beaver, 2006; Beaver & Carter, 2005) to determine students' reading levels, assess their strengths and weaknesses in fluency and comprehension, and make instructional decisions. Students read a leveled book and then retell what they've read. Their retellings are scored using a 4-point rubric. Both DRA2 test kits are available from Pearson at https://www.pearsonassessments.com/.

- **Informal Reading Inventories (IRIs)**

  Teachers use individually administered IRIs to assess students' comprehension of narrative and informational texts. Comprehension is measured by students' ability to retell what they've read and to answer questions about the passage. The questions examine how well students use literal and higher-level thinking and their knowledge about word meanings. A number of commercially published IRIs are available:

  Analytical Reading Inventory (Woods & Moe, 2011)
  Critical Reading Inventory (Applegate, Quinn, & Applegate, 2008)
  Qualitative Reading Inventory-4 (Leslie & Caldwell, 2011)

  These IRIs can be purchased from Pearson; others accompany basal reading series. IRIs are typically designed for the elementary grades, but first and second grade teachers often find that running records provide more useful information about beginning readers.

These tests provide valuable information about whether students meet grade-level comprehension standards.

their recall when necessary, and sometimes posing other questions to probe the depth of their understanding. Finally, they evaluate the completeness of the retelling.

- **Think-Alouds.** Teachers assess students' ability to apply comprehension strategies by having them think aloud and share their thinking as they read a passage (Wilhelm, 2001). Students usually think aloud orally, but they can also write their thoughts on small self-stick notes that they place beside sections of text or write entries in reading logs.

Step 3: Evaluating. Teachers assess students' knowledge about reading strategies and other reader factor concepts using many of the same ways that they monitor students' progress. For example, they often ask students to think aloud about the strategies they're applying as they read a book or to talk about their use of a specific strategy or other concept.

Step 4: Reflecting. Students reflect on what they've learned about reader factors through conferences with the teacher, and they also write entries in their reading logs about the strategies they've learned and can use independently. Teachers also reflect on the effectiveness of their instruction and how they might improve it.

If Students Struggle . . .

The most important reason why students struggle with comprehension is that they don't apply comprehension strategies. Again and again, researchers have concluded that struggling readers don't read strategically (Cooper, Chard, & Kiger, 2006). These students read passively, without using comprehension strategies to think about the words they're reading. Sometimes students simply need to transfer the strategies they use for listening to reading, but more often they haven't learned to use comprehension strategies to think about what they're reading, or they're ignoring the strategies they've been taught. These students must understand how essential strategic reading is and learn to actively engage in reading; otherwise, it's unlikely that their comprehension will improve very much. The good news is that teachers can help students become more thoughtful readers by teaching them how and why to use comprehension strategies (Allington, 2012).

The second reason why students struggle with comprehension is that they lack one or more of the three prerequisites for comprehension—background knowledge, vocabulary, and fluency. Teachers take these prerequisites into account as they plan for reading instruction. They match students to books by choosing suitable books whenever they can, and they differentiate instruction and provide scaffolding so students can be successful. Students, too, need to learn how to choose appropriate books for independent reading, because when they regularly read books that are too easy or too difficult, they don't become capable and confident readers.

> **MyLab Education** Self-Check 8.3

Chapter Review

Comprehension: Reader Factors

- Teachers recognize that comprehension is a process involving both reader and text factors and they ensure that students have adequate background knowledge, academic vocabulary, and reading fluency so they can comprehend what they're reading.

- Teachers can identify comprehension strategies that readers use while reading to support their understanding.

- Teachers teach students how to use comprehension strategies.

Accountability Check

Visit the following assessment links to access quiz questions and instructional applications.

MyLab Education Application Exercise 8.3: Understanding Literacy Development
MyLab Education Application Exercise 8.4: Understanding Literacy Development
MyLab Education Application Exercise 8.5: Monitoring Literacy Development
MyLab Education Application Exercise 8.6: Measuring Literacy Development

References

Afflerbach, P., Pearson, P. D., & Paris, S. G. (2008). Clarifying differences between reading skills and strategies. *The Reading Teacher, 61,* 364–373.

Allington, R. L. (2012). *What really matters for struggling readers: Designing research-based programs* (3rd ed.). Boston: Allyn & Bacon/Pearson.

Almasi, J., & Hart, S. (2015). Best practices in narrative text comprehension instruction. In L. B. Gambrell & L. M. Morrow (Eds.), *Best practices in literacy instruction* (5th ed., pp. 223–248). New York: Guilford Press.

Applegate, M. D., Quinn, K. B., & Applegate, A. J. (2008). *The critical reading inventory: Assessing students' reading and thinking* (2nd ed.). Upper Saddle River, NJ: Merrill/Prentice Hall.

Aston, D. H. (2008). *The moon over star.* New York: Dial Books.

Beaver, J. (2006). *Developmental reading assessment, grades K–3* (2nd ed.). Upper Saddle River, NJ: Celebration Press/Pearson.

Beaver, J., & Carter, M. (2005). *Developmental reading assessment, grades 4–8* (2nd ed.). Upper Saddle River, NJ: Celebration Press/Pearson.

Blachowicz, C. L. Z., & Fisher, P. J. (2015). Best practices in vocabulary instruction. In L. M. Morrow & L. B. Gambrell (Eds.), *Best practices in literacy instruction* (5th ed., pp. 195–222). New York: Guilford Press.

Blanton, W. E., Wood, K. D., & Moorman, G. B. (1990). The role of purpose in reading instruction. *The Reading Teacher, 43,* 486–493.

Block, C.C., & Pressley, M. (2007). Best practices in teaching comprehension. In L.B. Gambrell, L.M. Morrow, & M. Pressley (Eds.), *Best practices in literacy instruction* (3rd ed., pp. 220-242), New York: Guilford Press.

Bouchard, M. (2005). *Comprehension strategies for English language learners.* New York: Scholastic.

Brady, E. W. (2000). *Toliver's secret.* New York: Yearling.

Braunger, J., & Lewis, J. P. (2006). *Building a knowledge base in reading* (2nd ed.). Newark, DE: International Reading Association/National Council of Teachers of English.

Brown, J. (2003a). *Flat Stanley.* New York: HarperCollins.

Brown, J. (2003b). *Stanley in space.* New York: HarperCollins.

Castek, J., Bevans-Mangelson, J., & Goldstone, B. (2006). Reading adventures online: Five ways to introduce the new literacies of the Internet through students' literature. *The Reading Teacher, 59,* 714–728.

Clay, M. M. (2007). *An observation survey of early literacy achievement* (rev. ed.). Portsmouth, NH: Heinemann.

Cleary, B. (2000). *Henry Huggins* (50th anniversary ed.). New York: HarperCollins.

Coerr, E. (1989). *The Josefina story quilt.* New York: HarperCollins.

Coerr, E. (1993). *Chang's paper pony.* New York: HarperCollins.

Cohen, B. (1999). *Molly's pilgrim.* New York: Scholastic.

Coiro, J. (2003). Reading comprehension on the Internet: Expanding our understanding of reading comprehension to encompass new literacies. *The Reading Teacher, 56,* 458–464.

Coiro, J., & Dobler, E. (2007). Exploring the online reading comprehension strategies used by sixth-grade skilled readers to search for and locate information on the Internet. *Reading Research Quarterly, 42,* 214–257.

Cole, H. (1995). *Jack's garden.* New York: Greenwillow.

Common core state standards for English language arts. (2010). Retrieved from http://www.corestandards.org/ELA-Literacy/

Cooper, J. D., Chard, D. J., & Kiger, N. D. (2006). *The struggling reader: Interventions that work.* New York: Scholastic.

Danziger, P. (2004). *Amber Brown is green with envy.* New York: Scholastic.

Duke, N. K., & Pearson, P. D. (2002). Effective practices for developing reading comprehension. In A. E. Farstrup & S. J. Samuels (Eds.), *What research has to say about reading instruction* (3rd ed., pp. 205–242). Newark, DE: International Reading Association.

Duke, N. K., Pearson, P. D., Strachan, S. L., & Billman, A. K. (2011). Effective practices for developing reading comprehension. In S. J. Samuels & A. E. Farstrup (Eds.), *What research has to say about reading instruction* (3rd ed., pp. 51–93). Newark, DE: International Reading Association.

Durant, A. (2004). *Dear tooth fairy*. Cambridge, MA: Candlewick Press.

Ehlert, L. (1992). *Planting a rainbow*. Orlando: Voyager.

Fisher, D., Frey, N., & Lapp, D. (2012). *Text complexity: Raising rigor in reading*. Newark, DE: International Reading Association.

Garcia, G. E. (2003). Comprehension development and instruction of English-language learners. In A. P. Sweet & C. E. Snow (Eds.), *Rethinking reading comprehension* (pp. 30–50). New York: Guilford Press.

Gibbons, G. (1993). *From seed to plant*. New York: Holiday House.

Griffin, J. B. (2002). *Phoebe the spy*. New York: Putnam.

Harvey, S., & Goudvis, A. (2007). *Strategies that work: Teaching comprehension for understanding and engagement* (2nd ed.). Portland, ME: Stenhouse.

Irwin, J. W. (2007). *Teaching reading comprehension processes* (3rd ed.). Boston: Allyn & Bacon.

Keene, E. (2006). *Assessing comprehension thinking strategies*. Huntington Beach, CA: Shell Education.

Keene, E. O., & Zimmermann, S. (2007). *Mosaic of thought: The power of comprehension strategy instruction* (2nd ed.). Portsmouth, NH: Heinemann.

Keller, L. (2003). *Open wide: Tooth school inside*. New York: Owlet.

Kessler, L. (1996). *Kick, pass, and run!* New York: HarperCollins.

Kline, S. (1998). *Horrible Harry's secret*. New York: Puffin Books.

Leslie, L. & Caldwell, J. (2011). *Qualitative reading inventory* (5th ed.). Boston: Allyn & Bacon/Pearson.

Leu, D. J., Kinzer, C. K., Coiro, J., Castek, J. & Henry, L.A. (2013) New literacies: A dual-level theory of the changing nature of literacy, instruction, and assessment. In: D. E. Alvermann, N. Unrau, and R. B. Ruddell (Eds.), *Theoretical models and processes of reading* (6th ed., pp. 1150–1181). Newark, DE: International Reading Association.

Levine, E. (2007). *Henry's freedom box*. New York: Scholastic.

Macon, J. M., Bewell, D., & Vogt, M. E. (1991). *Responses to literature*. Newark, DE: International Reading Association.

Morrow, L. M. (2002). *Organizing and managing the language arts block*. New York: Guilford Press.

Morrow, L. M., Freitag, E., & Gambrell, L. B. (2009). *Using students' literature in preschool to develop comprehension* (2nd ed.). Newark, DE: International Reading Association.

National Reading Panel. (2000). *Teaching students to read: An evidence-based assessment of the scientific research literature on reading and its implications for reading instruction*. Washington, DC: National Institute of Child Health and Human Development.

Norton, M. (2003a). *The borrowers*. New York: Sandpiper.

Norton, M. (2003b). *The borrowers aloft*. New York: Sandpiper.

Owocki, G. (2003). *Comprehension: Strategic instruction for K–3 students*. Portsmouth, NH: Heinemann.

Peregoy, S. F., & Boyle, O. F. (2013). *Reading, writing and learning in ESL: A resource book for K–12 teachers* (6th ed.). Boston: Pearson.

Pressley, M. (2002a). Comprehension strategies instruction: A turn-of-the-century status report. In C. C. Block & M. Pressley (Eds.), *Comprehension instruction: Research-based best practices* (pp. 11–27). New York: Guilford Press.

Pressley, M. (2002b). Metacognition and self-regulated comprehension. In A. E. Farstrup & S. J. Samuels (Eds.), *What research has to say about reading instruction* (3rd ed., pp. 291–309). Newark, DE: International Reading Association.

Rasinski, T., & Samuels, S. J. (2011). Reading fluency: What it is and what it is not. In S. J. Samuels & A. E. Farstrup (Eds.), *What research has to say about reading instruction* (3rd ed., pp. 94–114). Newark, DE: International Reading Association.

Rathmann, P. (1995). *Officer Buckle and Gloria*. New York: Putnam.

Sachar, L. (1988). *There's a boy in the girls' bathroom*. New York: Yearling.

Sachar, L. (2004). *Sideways stories from Wayside School*. New York: HarperCollins.

Seeger, L. V. (2007). *First the egg*. New York: Roaring Brook Press.

Shannon, D. (1998). *No, David!* New York: Blue Sky Press.

Sweet, A. P., & Snow, C. E. (2003). Reading for comprehension. In A. P. Sweet & C. E. Snow (Eds.), *Rethinking reading comprehension* (pp. 1–11). New York: Guilford Press.

Tierney, R. J. (1990). Redefining reading comprehension. *Educational Leadership, 47*, 37–42.

Tovani, C. (2000). *I read it, but I don't get it: Comprehension strategies for adolescent readers*. Portland, ME: Stenhouse.

Van Allsburg, C. (1994). *The garden of Abdul Gasazi*. Boston: Houghton Mifflin.

Van den Broek, P., & Kremer, K. E. (2000). The mind in action: What it means to comprehend during reading. In B. M. Taylor, M. F. Graves, & P. Van den Broek (Eds.), *Reading for meaning: Fostering comprehension in the middle grades* (pp. 1–31). New York: Teachers College Press.

Waber, B. (2008). *Ira sleeps over*. New York: Sandpiper.

Wilhelm, J. D. (2001). *Improving comprehension with think-aloud strategies*. New York: Scholastic.

Willems, M. (2004). *Knuffle bunny: A cautionary tale*. New York: Hyperion Books.

Wisniewski, D. (1999). *Tough cookie*. New York: Lothrop, Lee & Shepard.

Woods, M. L., & Moe, A. J. (2011). *Analytical reading inventory* (9th ed.). Boston: Allyn & Bacon/Pearson.

Zimmermann, S., & Hutchins, C. (2003). *Seven keys to comprehension: How to help your kids read it and get it!* New York: Three Rivers Press.

Chapter 9
Facilitating Students' Comprehension: Text Factors

Learning Outcomes

After studying this chapter, you'll be prepared to:

9.1 Discuss the text factors of stories.

9.2 Discuss the text factors of informational books.

9.3 Discuss the text factors of poems.

9.4 Explain how to teach students about text factors.

Learning About Frogs

Monkey Business Images/Shutterstock

The fourth graders in Mr. Abrams's class are studying frogs. They began by making a class **KWL chart** (Ogle, 1986), listing what they already know about frogs in the "K: What We Know" column and things they want to learn in the "W: What We Wonder" column. At the end of the unit, the students will finish the chart by listing what they've learned in the "L: What We Have Learned" column. The fourth graders want to know how frogs and toads are different and if it's true that you get warts from frogs. Mr. Abrams assures them that they'll learn the answers to many of their questions and makes a mental note to find the answer to their question about warts.

Aquariums with frogs and frog spawn are arranged in one area in the classroom. Mr. Abrams has brought in five aquariums and filled them with frogs he collected in his backyard and others he "rented" from a local pet store. He has also brought in frog

In this chapter, you'll learn about the text factors in stories, nonfiction, and poetry and how they affect students' comprehension. Three types of text factors are *genres, text structures,* and *text features.* As you read this vignette, notice how Mr. Abrams integrates what the fourth graders are learning about text factors with the thematic unit he's teaching on frogs. He integrates reading and writing as the students expand their science knowledge.

spawn from a nearby pond. The fourth graders are observing the frogs and the frog spawn daily and drawing diagrams and making notes in their **learning logs**.

Mr. Abrams sets out a collection of books about frogs representing the three genres—stories, informational books, and poetry—on a special shelf in the classroom library. He reads many of the books aloud to the class. When he begins, he reads the title and shows the students several pages and asks them whether the book is a story, an informational book, or a poem. After determining the genre, they talk about their purpose for listening. For an informational book, the teacher writes a question or two on the whiteboard to guide their listening. After reading, the students answer the questions as part of their discussion. They also read and reread many of these books during an independent reading time.

Mr. Abrams also has a class set of *Amazing Frogs and Toads* (Clarke, 1990), a nonfiction book with striking photographs and well-organized presentations of information. He reads it once with the whole class using **shared reading**, and they discuss the interesting information in the book. He then divides the class into small groups, and each group chooses a question about frogs to research. The students reread the book, hunting for the answer to their question. Mr. Abrams has already taught the class to use the table of contents and the index to locate facts in an informational book. After the students locate and reread the information, they use the writing process to develop a poster to answer their question and share what they've learned. The teacher meets with each group to help them organize their posters and revise and edit their writing.

From the vast amount of information in *Amazing Frogs and Toads*, Mr. Abrams chooses nine questions, which he designs to address some of the questions on the "W: What We Wonder" section of the KWL chart to highlight important information in the text and to focus on the five expository text structures—the organizational patterns used for nonfiction texts. He's teaching the fourth graders that informational books, like stories, have special organizational elements. Here are his questions organized according to the five expository text structures:

What are amphibians? (description)

What do frogs look like? (description)

What is the life cycle of a frog? (sequence)

How do frogs eat? (sequence)

How are frogs and toads alike and different? (comparison)

Why do frogs hibernate? (cause and effect)

How do frogs croak? (cause and effect)

How do frogs use their eyes and eyelids? (problem and solution)

How do frogs escape from their enemies? (problem and solution)

After the students complete their posters, they share them with the class through brief presentations, and the posters are displayed in the classroom. Two of the posters are shown here; the life-cycle poster emphasizes the sequence structure, and the "Frogs Have Big Eyes" poster explains that the frog's eyes help it solve problems—finding food, hiding from enemies, and seeing underwater.

Mr. Abrams's students use the information in the posters to write books about frogs: They choose three posters and write one- to three-paragraph chapters to report the information from them. They meet in revising groups to revise their rough drafts and then edit them with a classmate and with Mr. Abrams. Finally, students word process their final copies and add illustrations, a title page, and a table of contents. Then they compile their books and "publish" them by sharing them with classmates from the author's chair.

Armin wrote this chapter on "Hibernation" in his book:

Hibernation means that an animal sleeps all winter long. Frogs hibernate because they are cold blooded and they might freeze to death if they didn't.

Two Posters About Frogs

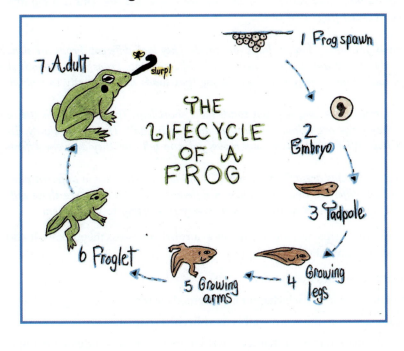

They find a good place to sleep like a hole in the ground, or in a log, or under some leaves. They go to sleep and they do not eat, or drink, or go to the bathroom. They sleep all winter and when they wake up it is spring. They are very, very hungry and they want to eat a lot of food. Their blood warms up when it is spring because the temperature warms up and when they are warm they want to be awake and eat. They are awake in the spring and in the summer, and then in the fall they start to think about hibernating again.

Jessica wrote this chapter on "The Differences Between Frogs and Toads" for her book:

You might think that frogs and toads are the same but you would be wrong. They are really different but they are both amphibians. I am going to tell you three ways they are different.

First of all, frogs really love water so they stay in the water or pretty close to it. Toads don't love water. They usually live where it is dry. This is a big difference between frogs and toads.

Second, you should look at frogs and toads. They look different. Frogs are slender and thin but toads are fat. Their skin is different, too. Frogs have smooth skin and toads have bumpy skin. I would say that toads are not pretty to look at.

Third, frogs have long legs but toads have short legs. That probably is the reason why frogs are wonderful jumpers and toads can't. They move slowly. They just hop. When you watch them move, you can tell that they are very different.

Frogs and toads are different kinds of amphibians. They live in different places, they look different, and they move in different ways. You can see these differences when you look at them and it is very interesting to study them.

Mr. Abrams helps his students develop a **rubric** to assess their books. It addresses the following points about the chapters:

- The title describes the chapter.
- The information in each chapter is presented clearly.
- Vocabulary from the **word wall** is used in each chapter.
- The information in each chapter is written in one or more indented paragraphs.
- The information in each chapter has very few spelling, capitalization, and punctuation errors.
- Each chapter has a useful illustration.

Other points on the rubric consider the book as a whole:

- The title page lists the title and the author's name.
- All pages in the book are numbered.
- The table of contents lists the chapters and the pages for each chapter.
- The title is written on the cover of the book.
- The illustrations on the cover of the book relate to frogs.

The students evaluate their books using a four-point scale; Mr. Abrams also uses the rubric to assess their writing. He conferences with students and shares his scoring with them. Also, he helps them set goals for their next writing project.

To end the unit, the students finish the **KWL chart**. In the third column, "L: What We Have Learned," they list some of the information they've learned:

Tadpoles breathe through gills, but frogs breathe through lungs.

Tadpoles are vegetarians, but frogs eat worms and insects.

Snakes, rats, birds, and foxes are the frogs' enemies.

Some frogs in the rainforest are brightly colored and poisonous, too.

Some frogs are hard to see because they have camouflage coloring.

Male frogs puff up their air sacs to croak and make sounds.

Frogs have teeth, but they swallow their food whole.

Frogs have two sets of eyelids, and one set is clear so frogs can see when they are underwater.

Frogs can jump ten times their body length, but toads can't—they're hoppers.

Mr. Abrams stands back to reread the fourth graders' comments. "I can tell how much you've learned when I read the detailed information you've added in the L column," he remarks with a smile. He knows that one reason why his students are successful is because he taught them to use text structure as a tool for learning.

Why readers know and do during reading has a tremendous impact on how well they comprehend, but comprehension involves more than just reader factors: It also involves **text factors** (Valencia, Wixson & Pearson 2014). Stories, informational books, and poems can be easier or more difficult to read depending on factors that are inherent in them (Harvey & Goudvis, 2007). These three types of text factors are the most important:

Genres.   The three broad categories of literature are stories, informational books or nonfiction, and poetry, and there are subgenres within each category. For example, folktales, fantasies, and historical fiction are subgenres of stories.

Text Structures.   Authors use structures or patterns to organize texts and emphasize the big ideas. Sequence, comparison, and cause and effect, for example, are internal patterns used to organize nonfiction texts.

Text Features.   Authors use text features to achieve a particular effect in their writing. Narrative devices include foreshadowing and dialogue in stories; headings and indexes are nonfiction features in informational books; repetition and rhyme are poetic devices.

When students understand how authors organize and present their ideas in texts, this knowledge about text factors serves as a scaffold, making comprehension easier (Meyer & Poon, 2004; Sweet & Snow, 2003). Text factors make a similar contribution to writing: Students apply what they've learned about genres, text structures, and text features when they're writing (Mooney, 2001).

Text Factors of Stories

Stories are narratives about characters trying to overcome problems or deal with difficulties. They've been described as "waking dreams" that people use to find meaning in their lives. Students develop an understanding of what constitutes a story beginning in the preschool years when their parents read aloud to them, and they refine and expand their understanding through literacy instruction at school (Applebee, 1978). They learn about the subgenres of stories and read stories representing each one, examine the structural patterns that authors use to organize stories, and point out the narrative devices that authors use to breathe life into their stories.

Formats of Stories

Stories are available in picture-book and chapter-book formats. Picture books have brief texts, usually spread over 32 pages, in which text and illustrations combine to tell a story. The text is minimal, and the illustrations extend the sparse text. These popular picture books illustrate a variety of artistic styles and media:

Smoky Night (Bunting, 1999)

Kitten's First Full Moon (Henkes, 2004)

Officer Buckle and Gloria (Rathmann, 1995)

The House in the Night (Swanson, 2008)

Knuffle Bunny: A Cautionary Tale (Willems, 2004)

Owl Moon (Yolen, 2007)

Each year, the American Library Association honors the best illustrated children's book with its Caldecott Medal; the books just listed either received this prestigious award or were designated as Honor Books.

In some books, the illustrations tell the story without any text; these books are called wordless picture books. Some are appropriate for preschoolers and kindergartners, such as *Have You Seen My Cat?* (Carle, 1997) and *Freight Train* (Crews, 2008); some for first and second graders, such as *Hogwash* (Geisert, 2008) and *The Red Book* (Lehman, 2004); and others for third and fourth graders, such as *Time Flies* (Rohmann, 1997) and *Flotsam* (Wiesner, 2006).

Developmental Continuum Comprehension: Text Factor

PreK	K	1	2	3	4
Four-year-olds know that texts differ by genre, and they can identify examples of stories, informational books, and poems.	Kindergartners tell well-organized stories, identify big ideas in nonfiction books, and notice poetic devices in poems.	First graders apply what they've learned about text factors when crafting brief stories, informational books, and poems.	Students classify books by sub-genre and pick out examples of text structures and text features in books they're reading.	Students draw diagrams to highlight story elements and expository text structures, and they identify poetic forms or devices.	Fourth graders analyze story elements, use expository text structures in writing, and apply poetic forms in poems they write.

Novels are longer stories organized into chapters. They have only a few illustrations because pictures don't play an integral role in the story. Some of the choices of first novels for beginning readers include Barbara Park's Junie B. Jones stories about the antics of a sassy primary grade student, Marc Brown's chapter-book stories of a lovable aardvark named Arthur, and Dan Greenburg's adventure series, The Zack Files. Popular novels for third and fourth graders include *Flat Stanley* (Brown, 2003), *Sideways Stories From Wayside School* (Sachar, 2004), *Tales of a Fourth Grade Nothing* (Blume, 2007), and *Because of Winn-Dixie* (DiCamillo, 2009).

Narrative Genres

Stories can be categorized in different ways, one of which is according to **genre** (Buss & Karnowski, 2000). Three general categories are folklore, fantasies, and realistic fiction. Figure 9–1 presents an overview of these narrative genres.

FOLKLORE.   Stories that began hundreds of years ago and were passed down from generation to generation by storytellers before being written down are *folk literature*. These stories,

Figure 9–1 Narrative Genres

Category	Genres	Description
Folklore	Fables	Brief tales told to point out a moral. For example: Town Mouse, Country Mouse (Brett, 2003) and The Boy Who Cried Wolf (Hennessy, 2006).
	Folktales	Stories in which heroes demonstrate virtues to triumph over adversity. For example: Goldilocks and the Three Bears (Marshall, 1998) and Rumpelstiltskin (Zelinsky, 1996).
	Myths	Stories created by ancient peoples to explain natural phenomena. For example: Why Mosquitoes Buzz in People's Ears (Aardema, 2004) and Raven (McDermott, 2001).
	Legends	Stories, including hero tales and tall tales, that recount the courageous deeds of people who struggled against each other or against gods and monsters. For example: John Henry (J. Lester, 1999) and Johnny Appleseed (Kellogg, 1988).
Fantasy	Modern Literary Tales	Stories written by modern authors that are similar to folktales. For example: The Ugly Duckling (Mitchell, 2007) and Sylvester and the Magic Pebble (Steig, 2010).
	Fantastic Stories	Imaginative stories that explore alternate realities and contain elements not found in the natural world. For example: Inkheart (Funke, 2003) and Poppy (Avi, 2005).
	Science Fiction	Stories that explore scientific possibilities. For example: Moo Cow Kaboom! (Hurd, 2003) and Commander Toad in Space (Yolen, 1996).
	High Fantasy	Stories that focus on the conflict between good and evil and often involve quests. For example: the Harry Potter series.
Realistic Fiction	Contemporary Stories	Stories that portray today's society. For example: Going Home (Bunting, 1998) and Because of Winn-Dixie (DiCamillo, 2009).
	Historical Stories	Realistic stories set in the past. For example: Sarah, Plain and Tall (MacLachlan, 2005) and Henry's Freedom Box (Levine, 2007).

Literacy Portraits

Ms. Janusz's classroom is filled with stories and informational books. She uses these books for instructional purposes, and plenty of books are available for students to read independently. These second graders know about genres. They can identify books representing each genre and talk about the differences between them. Ms. Janusz teaches minilessons on genres and points out the genre of books she's reading aloud. She also shares informational books with the students and the elements of nonfiction books. Ms. Janusz has the students distinguish these story structures in their writing. Listen to Rakie identify what parts of her story are fiction and what is nonfiction. As you listen, think about the information provided in this chapter. What conclusions can you draw about what Ms. Janusz has taught about text factors?

Rakie

including fables, folktales, and myths, are an important part of our cultural heritage. *Fables* are brief narratives designed to teach a moral. The story format makes the lesson easier to understand, and the moral is usually stated at the end. Fables exemplify these characteristics:

- They are short, often less than a page long.
- The characters are usually animals.
- The characters are one-dimensional: strong or weak, wise or foolish.
- The setting is barely sketched; the stories could take place anywhere.
- The theme is usually stated as a moral at the end of the story.

The best known fables, including "The Hare and the Tortoise" and "The Ant and the Grasshopper," are believed to have been written by a Greek slave named Aesop in the sixth century B.C.E. Individual fables have been retold as picture-book stories, including *The Hare and the Tortoise* (Ward, 1999) and *The Lion and the Rat* (Wildsmith, 2007).

Folktales began as oral stories, told and retold by medieval storytellers as they traveled from town to town. The problem in a folktale usually revolves around one of four situations: a journey from home to perform a task, a journey to confront a monster, the miraculous change from a harsh home to a secure home, or a confrontation between a wise beast and a foolish beast. Here are other characteristics:

- The story often begins with the phrase "Once upon a time . . . "
- The setting is generalized and could be located anywhere.
- The plot structure is simple and straightforward.
- Characters are one-dimensional: good or bad, stupid or clever, industrious or lazy.
- The end is happy, and everyone lives "happily ever after."

Some folktales are cumulative tales, such as *The Gingerbread Boy* (Galdone, 2008); these stories are built around the repetition of words and events. Others are talking animal stories; in these stories, such as *The Three Little Pigs* (Kellogg, 2002), animals act and talk like humans. The best known folktales are fairy tales: They have motifs or small recurring elements, including magical powers, transformations, enchantments, magical objects, trickery, and wishes that are granted; and they feature witches, giants, fairy godmothers, and other fantastic characters. Well-known examples are *Cinderella* (Ehrlich, 2004) and *Jack and the Beanstalk* (Kellogg, 1997).

People around the world have created myths to explain natural phenomena. Some explain the seasons, the sun, the moon, and the constellations, and others tell how the mountains and other physical features of the earth were created. Ancient peoples used myths to explain many things that have since been explained by scientific investigations. Myths exemplify these characteristics:

- Myths explain creations.
- Characters are often heroes with supernatural powers.
- The setting is barely sketched.
- Magical powers are required.

For example, the Native American myth *The Legend of the Bluebonnet* (dePaola, 1996) recounts how these flowers came to beautify the countryside. Other myths tell how animals came to be or why they look the way they do. *Legends* are myths about heroes such as Robin Hood and King Arthur, who have done things important enough to be remembered in a story; they may have some basis in history but aren't verifiable. American legends about Johnny Appleseed, Paul Bunyan, and Pecos Bill are known as *tall tales*.

FANTASIES.   *Fantasies* are imaginative stories. Authors create new worlds for their characters, but these worlds must be based in reality so that readers will believe they exist. One of the most beloved fantasies is *Charlotte's Web* (White, 2006). Fantasies include modern literary tales, fantastic stories, science fiction, and high fantasy.

Modern literary tales are related to folktales and fairy tales because they often incorporate many characteristics and conventions of traditional literature, but they've been written more recently and have identifiable authors. The best known author of modern literary tales is Hans Christian Andersen, a Danish writer of the 1800s who wrote *The Snow Queen* (Ehrlich, 2006) and *The Ugly Duckling* (Mitchell, 2007). Other examples of modern literary tales include *Alexander and the Wind-Up Mouse* (Lionni, 2006) and *The Wolf's Chicken Stew* (Kasza, 1996).

Fantastic stories are realistic in most details, but some events require readers to suspend disbelief. They exemplify these characteristics:

- The events in the story could not happen in today's world.
- The setting is realistic.
- Main characters are people or personified animals.
- Themes often deal with the conflict between good and evil.

Some are animal fantasies, such as *Babe: The Gallant Pig* (King-Smith, 2005). The main characters in these stories are animals endowed with human traits. Readers often realize that the animals symbolize human beings and that these stories explore human relationships. Some are toy fantasies, such as *The Miraculous Journey of Edward Tulane* (DiCamillo, 2008). Toy fantasies are similar to animal fantasies except that the main characters are talking toys, usually stuffed animals or dolls. Other fantasies involve enchanted journeys during which wondrous things happen. The journey must have a purpose, but it's usually overshadowed by the thrill and delight of the fantastic world, as in Roald Dahl's *Charlie and the Chocolate Factory* (2007).

In science fiction stories, authors create a world in which science interacts with society. Many stories involve traveling through space to distant galaxies or meeting alien societies. Authors hypothesize scientific advancements and imagine technology of the future to create the plot. Science fiction exemplifies these characteristics:

- The story is set in the future.
- Conflict is usually between the characters and natural or mechanical forces.
- The characters believe in the advanced technology.
- A detailed description of scientific facts is provided.

Time-warp stories in which the characters move forward and back in time are also classified as science fiction. Jon Scieszka's Time Warp Trio stories, including *Knights of the Kitchen Table* (2004), are popular with third and fourth graders.

Heroes confront evil for the good of humanity in high fantasy. The primary characteristic is the focus on the conflict between good and evil, as in C. S. Lewis's *The Lion, the Witch and the Wardrobe* (2005) and J. K. Rowling's Harry Potter stories. High fantasy is related to folk literature in that it's characterized by motifs and themes. Most stories include magical kingdoms, quests, tests of courage, magical powers, and superhuman characters.

REALISTIC FICTION. These stories are lifelike and believable. The outcome is reasonable, and the story is a representation of action that seems truthful. Realistic fiction helps students discover that their problems aren't unique and that they aren't alone in experiencing certain feelings and situations. Realistic fiction also broadens students' horizons and allows them to experience new adventures. Two types are contemporary stories and historical stories.

Readers identify with characters who are their own age and have similar interests and problems in contemporary stories. In Paula Danziger's *Amber Brown Is Not a Crayon* (2006) and other books in the series, students read about a feisty girl with a colorful name who adjusts to contemporary life changes as her best friend since preschool moves away, her parents divorce, and her mom remarries. Here are the characteristics of contemporary fiction:

- Characters act like real people or like real animals.
- The setting is in the world as we know it today.
- Stories deal with everyday occurrences or "relevant subjects."

Other contemporary stories include *Knuffle Bunny: A Cautionary Tale* (Willems, 2004) and *Ramona the Pest* (Cleary, 1992).

In contrast, historical stories are set in the past. Details about food, clothing, and culture must be typical of the era in which the story is set because the setting influences the plot. These are the characteristics of this genre:

- The setting is historically accurate.
- Conflict is often between characters or between a character and society.
- The language is appropriate to the setting.
- Themes are universal, both for the historical period of the book and for today.

Examples of historical fiction include *Chang's Paper Pony* (Coerr, 1993) and *Follow the Drinking Gourd* (Winter, 2008). In these stories, readers are immersed in historical events, they appreciate the contributions of people who have lived before them, and they learn about human relationships.

Elements of Story Structure

Stories have unique structural elements that distinguish them from other genres. The most important story elements are plot, characters, setting, point of view, and theme. They work together to structure a story, and authors manipulate them to develop their stories.

PLOT. *Plot* is the sequence of events involving characters in conflict situations. It's based on the goals of one or more characters and the processes they go through to attain them (Lukens, Smith, & Miller Coffel, 2012). The main characters want to achieve the goal, and other characters are introduced to prevent them from being successful. The story events are set in motion by characters as they attempt to overcome conflict and solve their problems. See the Booklist: Elements of Story Structure for examples of stories with well-developed plots and other elements of story structure.

The most basic aspect of plot is the division of the main events into the beginning, middle, and end. In *The Tale of Peter Rabbit* (Potter, 2006), for instance, the three story parts are easy to pick out. As the story begins, Mrs. Rabbit sends her children out to

Figure 9–2 A Beginning-Middle-End Story Map for *The Tale of Peter Rabbit*

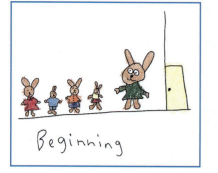

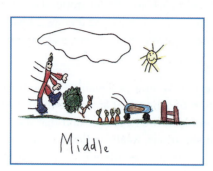

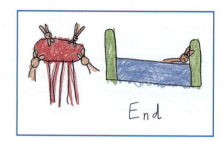

play after warning them not to go into Mr. McGregor's garden. In the middle, Peter goes into Mr. McGregor's garden and is almost caught. Then Peter finds his way out of the garden and gets home safely—the end of the story. Students can make a beginning-middle-end story map using words and pictures, as the story map for *The Tale of Peter Rabbit* in Figure 9–2 shows.

Specific types of information are included in each part. In the beginning, the author introduces the characters, describes the setting, and presents a problem; together, the characters, setting, and events develop the plot and sustain the theme through the story. In the middle, the plot unfolds, with each event preparing readers for what follows. Conflict heightens as the characters face roadblocks that keep them from solving their problems; how the characters tackle these problems adds suspense to keep readers interested. In the end, all is reconciled, and readers learn whether the characters' struggles are successful.

Booklist Elements of Story Structure*

Element	Books
Plot	Fleming, D. (2003). *Buster*. (PreK–1) Marshall, J. (1998). *Goldilocks and the three bears*. (PreK–1) Rathmann, P. (1995). *Officer Buckle and Gloria*. (K–2) Steig, W. (2010). *Sylvester and the magic pebble*. (1–3) Willems, M. (2004). *Knuffle bunny: A cautionary tale*. (PreK–1)
Characters	Cleary, B. (1992). *Ramona the pest*. (3–4) Dahl, R. (2007). *James and the giant peach*. (3–4) Henkes, K. (1996). *Lilly's purple plastic purse*. (K–2) Levine, E. (2007). *Henry's freedom box*. (3–4) Shannon, D. (2006). *Good boy, Fergus!* (1–2)
Setting	Bunting, E. (2006). *Pop's bridge*. (1–3) Coerr, E. (1993). *Chang's paper pony*. (3–4) DiCamillo, K. (2009). *Because of Winn-Dixie*. (3–4) Hurd, T. (2003). *Moo cow kaboom!* (K–2) Yorinks, A. (1989). *Hey, Al*. (K–2)
Point of View	Bunting, E. (2006). *One green apple*. (2–3) Long, M. (2003). *How I became a pirate*. (K–2) MacLachlan, P. (2005). *Sarah, plain and tall*. (3–4) Pinkney, J. (2006). *The little red hen*. (K–1) Scieszka, J. (1999). *The true story of the 3 little pigs!* (1–3)
Theme	Bunting, E. (1999). *Smoky night*. (2–4) DiCamillo, K. (2008). *The miraculous journey of Edward Tulane*. (3–4) Henkes, K. (1996). *Lilly's purple plastic purse*. (K–2) Naylor, P. R. (2000). *Shiloh*. (3–4) Woodson, J. (2001). *The other side*. (K–1)

* Grade level designations provided.

Conflict is the tension or opposition between forces in the plot, and is what interests readers enough to continue reading the story (Lukens et al., 2012). Conflict occurs in these four ways:

Between a Character and Nature.   Conflict between a character and nature occurs in stories in which severe weather plays an important role and in stories set in isolated geographic locations.

Between a Character and Society.   Sometimes the main character's activities and beliefs differ from those of others, and conflict arises between the character and society.

Between Characters.   In this most common type of conflict, characters with different goals interact as the story progresses, and tension grows.

Within a Character.   The main character struggles to overcome challenges in his or her own life.

Plot is developed through conflict that's introduced at the beginning, expanded in the middle, and finally resolved at the end. The development of the plot involves these components:

- A problem that introduces conflict is presented at the beginning of the story.
- Characters face roadblocks in attempting to solve the problem in the middle.
- The high point in the action occurs when the problem is about to be solved. This high point separates the middle and the end.
- The problem is solved and the roadblocks are overcome at the end of the story.

Figure 9–3 presents a plot diagram shaped like a mountain that incorporates these four components, which fourth graders completed after reading *Esperanza Rising* (Ryan, 2002). The problem in *Esperanza Rising* is that Esperanza and her mother must create a new life for themselves in California because they can't remain at their Mexican ranch home any longer.

Figure 9–3 A Plot Diagram for *Esperanza Rising*

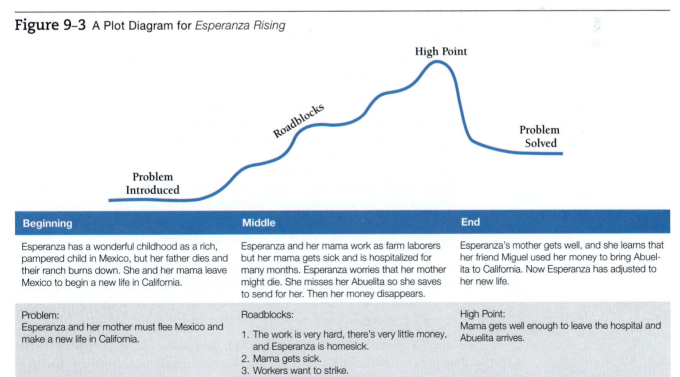

Beginning	Middle	End
Esperanza has a wonderful childhood as a rich, pampered child in Mexico, but her father dies and their ranch burns down. She and her mama leave Mexico to begin a new life in California.	Esperanza and her mama work as farm laborers but her mama gets sick and is hospitalized for many months. Esperanza worries that her mother might die. She misses her Abuelita so she saves to send for her. Then her money disappears.	Esperanza's mother gets well, and she learns that her friend Miguel used her money to bring Abuelita to California. Now Esperanza has adjusted to her new life.
Problem: Esperanza and her mother must flee Mexico and make a new life in California.	Roadblocks: 1. The work is very hard, there's very little money, and Esperanza is homesick. 2. Mama gets sick. 3. Workers want to strike. 4. Esperanza's money is missing.	High Point: Mama gets well enough to leave the hospital and Abuelita arrives.

Certainly, there's conflict between characters here and conflict with society, too, but the most important conflict is within Esperanza as she leaves her comfortable life in Mexico to become a migrant laborer in California. She and her mother face many roadblocks. They become farm laborers, and the work is very hard. Esperanza wants to bring her grandmother to join them, but they don't have enough money for her travel expenses. Then Esperanza's mother becomes ill, and Esperanza takes over her mother's work. Finally, Esperanza saves enough to bring her grandmother to California, but her money disappears. The high point of the action occurs when Esperanza's mother recovers enough to return to the farm labor camp, and it turns out that her money wasn't stolen after all: Esperanza's friend Miguel used it to bring her grandmother to California. As the story ends, the problem is solved: Esperanza adjusts to her new life in California with her mother and grandmother. *Esperanza* means "hope" in Spanish, and readers have reason to be optimistic that the girl and her family will create a good life for themselves.

CHARACTERS.   *Characters* are the people or personified animals in the story. They're the most important structural element when stories are centered on a character or group of characters. Main characters have many personality traits, both good and bad; that is to say, they have all the characteristics of real people. Inferring a character's traits is an important part of comprehension: Through character traits, readers get to know a character well, and the character seems to come to life. A list of stories with fully developed main characters is included in the Booklist: Elements of Story Structure. Characters are developed in four ways:

Appearance.   Readers learn about characters by the description of their facial features, body shapes, habits of dress, mannerisms, and gestures.

Action.   The best way to learn about characters is through their actions.

Dialogue.   Authors use dialogue to breathe life into characters, develop their personalities, and spark reader interest. Also, dialogue is an effective way to move a story forward.

Monologue.   Authors provide insight into characters by revealing their thoughts. Authors often use more than one of these techniques to develop their characters.

SETTING.   The *setting* is generally thought of as the location where the story takes place, but that's only one of four aspects of setting:

Location.   Many stories take place in predictable settings that don't contribute to a story's effectiveness, but sometimes the location is integral.

Weather.   Severe weather, such as a blizzard, rainstorm, or tornado, is crucial in some stories, but in others, the weather isn't mentioned because it doesn't affect the outcome of the story. Many stories take place on warm, sunny days.

Time Period.   For stories set in the past or in the future, the time period is important. If *Riding Freedom* (Ryan, 1999) and *The Bracelet* (Uchida, 1996) were set in different eras, for example, they would lose much of their impact: Today, young women in the United States don't have to masquerade as men to work or vote, and Japanese Americans aren't sent to internment camps.

Time.   This dimension involves both the time of day and the passage of time. Most stories take place during the day, except for scary stories that are set after dark. Many stories span a brief period of time, but others span as much as a year—long enough for the main character to grow to maturity.

In some stories, the setting is barely sketched; these are called *backdrop settings*. The setting in many folktales, for instance, is relatively unimportant, and the convention "Once upon a time . . . " is enough to set the stage. In other stories, the setting is elaborated and essential to the story's effectiveness; these settings are called *integral settings*

Figure 9–4 A Second Grader's Story Map for *Tulip Sees America*

(Lukens et al., 2012). Stories with integral settings also are included in the Booklist: Elements of Story Structure.

Students can draw maps to show the setting of a story; these maps might show the path a character traveled or the passage of time in a story. Figure 9–4 shows a map for *Tulip Sees America* (Rylant, 1998); in this story, a man and his dog, named Tulip, take a trip across the United States and decide to stay in Oregon, where they can see the Pacific Ocean.

POINT OF VIEW.   Stories are written from a particular viewpoint, and this perspective determines, to a great extent, readers' understanding of the characters and events of the story (Lukens et al., 2012). Stories written from different viewpoints are presented in the Booklist: Expository Book Structures. Here are the points of view:

First-Person Viewpoint.   This point of view is used to tell a story through the eyes of one character using the first-person pronoun "I." The narrator, usually the main character, speaks as an eyewitness and a participant in the events.

Omniscient Viewpoint.   The author is godlike, seeing and knowing all. The author tells readers about the thought processes of each character without worrying about how the information is obtained.

Limited Omniscient Viewpoint.   This viewpoint is used so that readers know the thoughts of one character. It's told in third person, and the author concentrates on

MyLab Education
Video Example 9.1

Second grade teacher Linda Gall engages her students in a lively activity to compare the story structure of two stories about exploration. Why do you think these second graders are so absorbed in this activity? What additional activities might you have students do to help them understand story structure?

the thoughts, feelings, and experiences of the main character or another important character.

Objective Viewpoint.   Readers are eyewitnesses to the story and are confined to the immediate scene. They learn only what's visible and audible and aren't aware of what any characters think. Most fairy tales are told from the objective viewpoint. The focus is on recounting events, not on developing the personalities of the characters.

THEME.   *Theme* is the underlying meaning of a story; it embodies general truths about human nature (Lukens et al., 2012). Themes usually deal with the characters' emotions and values, and can be stated either explicitly or implicitly: Explicit themes are expressed clearly in the story, but implicit themes must be inferred. In a fable, the theme is often stated explicitly at the end, but in most stories, the theme emerges through the thoughts, speech, and actions of the characters as they try to overcome the obstacles that prevent them from reaching their goals. In *A Chair for My Mother* (Williams, 1993), for example, a young girl demonstrates the importance of sacrificing personal wants for her family's welfare as she and her mother collect money to buy a new chair after losing all of their belongings in a fire.

Stories usually have more than one theme, and the themes generally can't be articulated with a single word. *Charlotte's Web* (White, 2006), for example, has several "friendship" themes, one explicitly stated and others that must be inferred. Friendship is a multidimensional theme—qualities of a good friend, unlikely friends, and sacrificing for a friend, for instance. Teachers probe students' thinking as they work to construct a theme and move beyond simplistic one-word labels.

Narrative Devices

Authors use narrative devices to make their writing more vivid and memorable (Lukens et al., 2012):

* **Dialogue.**   Written conversations in which characters speak to each other
* **Flashbacks.**   An interruption, often taking readers back to the beginning of the story
* **Foreshadowing.**   Hints about events to come later in the story to build readers' expectations
* **Imagery.**   Descriptive words and phrases used to create a picture in readers' minds
* **Suspense.**   An excited uncertainty about the outcome of conflict in a story
* **Symbol.**   A person, place, or thing used to represent something else, such as a lion to imply courage

Flashbacks, for example, are commonly used in stories, such as Jon Scieszka's Time Warp Trio series and Mary Pope Osborne's Magic Tree House series, where readers travel back in time for adventures.

Examining Text Factors in a Story

Jan Brett's *The Mitten* (2009) is an adaptation of a Ukrainian folktale. While walking through a snowy forest, a boy named Nicki unknowingly drops one of the new white mittens his grandmother knitted for him. A mole discovers it and crawls inside. One by one, a rabbit, a badger, and other woodland animals crawl inside, too, each bigger than the one before. Even a brown bear squeezes in, and everyone sleeps snugly in the mitten until a tiny mouse joins them, curling up on the bear's nose. The mouse tickles the bear's nose, and the bear sneezes, causing the mitten to shoot up into the air. The animals scatter, and Nicki sees a white shape in the distance floating to the ground—it's his lost mitten, stretched out of shape.

This story is a cumulative tale that's built through the repetition of events—animals crawling into the white mitten. It's similar in structure to other folktales, such as "The Little Red Hen" and "The Three Little Pigs," and the repetitive structure makes it easy for students to retell, especially when they're using **story boards** or stuffed animals. The plot is simple and straightforward: In the beginning, Nicki loses the mitten; in the middle, animals crawl into it; and at the end, Nicki recovers his stretched-out mitten. Nicki and the other characters are one-dimensional, and the story's told from the objective viewpoint. *The Mitten* is most appropriate for prekindergartners through first graders.

Jan Brett is a talented author-illustrator; her distinctive style is what makes this picture book special. Her illustrations are inspired by Ukrainian folk art, and they create the story's mood. Jan Brett incorporates border illustrations in most of her books, and here she creates mitten-shaped windows at the edge of each page. On left-facing pages, readers look through the windows to see Nicki walking through the woods, unaware of the woodland animals crawling into his mitten, and the windows on right-facing pages provide hints about what will happen next. She uses foreshadowing very effectively, and students quickly learn to check the mitten-shaped windows on each page.

Check the Compendium of Instructional Procedures, which follows Chapter 12. These **green** terms also show a brief description of each procedure.

MyLab Education **Self-Check 9.1**
MyLab Education **Application Exercise 9.1:** Identifying Text Factors of Stories

---

Text Factors of Informational Books

Stories have been the principal genre for reading and writing instruction in prekindergarten to fourth grade because it's been assumed that constructing stories is a fundamental way of learning; however, many students prefer to read informational books (Stead & Duke, 2005). Certainly, students are interested in learning about their world—about the difference between dolphins and whales, how a road is built, threats to the environment, or the Apollo 11 moon landing—and informational books provide this knowledge.

Nonfiction Genres

Informational books provide facts on just about any topic you can think of. Consider, for example: *Flick a Switch: How Electricity Gets to Your Home* (Seuling, 2003), *Taj Mahal* (Arnold & Comora, 2007), *Martin's Big Words: The Life of Dr. Martin Luther King, Jr.* (Rappaport, 2007), *Saguaro Moon: A Desert Journal* (Pratt-Serafini, 2002), and *Groundhog Day!* (Gibbons, 2007). These books are picture books that use a combination of text and illustrations to present information.

Other books present information within a story context; the Magic School Bus series is perhaps the best known. In *The Magic School Bus and the Science Fair Expedition* (Cole, 2006), for example, Ms. Frizzle and her class travel through time to learn how scientific thinking developed. The page layout is innovative, with charts and reports containing factual information presented at the outside edges of most pages.

ALPHABET BOOKS. Many alphabet books are designed for young students who are learning to identify the letters of the alphabet. Some are predictable, featuring a letter and an illustration of a familiar object on each page, but others, such as *Alphabet Adventure* (Wood, 2001), *The Alphabet Room* (Pinto, 2003), and *Fancy Nancy's Favorite Fancy Words: From Accessories to Zany* (O'Connor, 2008), are more imaginative presentations. In these books, words representing each letter are highlighted and sometimes used in sentences.

BIOGRAPHIES. Students read biographies to learn about a person's life. A wide range of biographies are available for students today, such as *Neil Armstrong* (Rau, 2003), *Marco Polo* (Demi, 2008), and *Wilma Unlimited: How Wilma Rudolph Became the World's*

MyLab Education
Video Example 9.2
Informational texts build students' background knowledge and boost their vocabulary. Why might reading these kinds of books also be especially beneficial to struggling readers?

Fastest Woman (Krull, 2000). Only a few autobiographies are available for students, but the Meet the Author series of autobiographies for kindergarten through fourth grade students from Richard C. Owen Publishers, Inc. is interesting to students who have read these authors' books. These autobiographies of contemporary authors, including Laura Numeroff's *If You Give an Author a Pencil* (2003) and Eve Bunting's *Once Upon a Time* (1995), include information about their lives and insights into their writing.

Expository Text Structures

Informational books are organized in particular ways known as **expository text structures** (McGee & Richgels, 1985). Figure 9–5 describes these patterns, presents sample passages and cue words that signal the use of each pattern, and suggests a graphic organizer for each structure. When readers are aware of these patterns, it's easier to

Figure 9–5 The Five Nonfiction Text Structures

Pattern	Graphic Organizer	Sample Passage
Description The author describes a topic by listing characteristics and examples. Cue words include for example and characteristics are.		The Olympic symbol consists of five interlocking rings. The rings represent the five continents from which athletes come to compete in the games. The rings are colored black, blue, green, red, and yellow. At least one of these colors is found in the flag of every country sending athletes to compete in the Olympic games.
Sequence The author lists items or events in numerical or chronological order. Cue words include first, second, third, next, then, and finally.	1. ___ 2. ___ 3. ___ 4. ___ 5. ___	The Olympic games began as athletic festivals to honor the Greek gods. The most important festival honored Zeus, the king of the gods, and this festival became the Olympic games in 776 B.C. They ended in A.D. 394, and no games were held for more than 1,500 years. Then the modern Olympics began in 1896. Almost 300 male athletes competed in the first modern Olympics. In the 1900 games, female athletes also competed. The games have continued every four years since 1896 except during World War II.
Comparison The author explains how two or more things are alike and/or how they're different. Cue words include different, in contrast, alike, same as, and on the other hand.	Alike / Different	The modern Olympics is very different than the ancient games. While there were no swimming races, for example, there were chariot races. There were no female contestants, and all athletes competed in the nude. Of course, the ancient and modern Olympics are also alike in many ways. Some events, such as the javelin and discus throws, are the same. Some people say that cheating, professionalism, and nationalism in the modern games are a disgrace to the Olympic tradition, but according to ancient Greek writers, cheating, nationalism, and professionalism existed in their Olympics, too.
Cause and Effect The author lists one or more causes and the resulting effect or effects. Cue words include reasons why, if . . . then, as a result, therefore, and because.	Cause → Effect #1, Effect #2, Effect #3	There are several reasons why so many people attend the Olympic games or watch them on television. One reason is tradition. The name Olympics and the torch and flame remind people of the ancient games. People escape the ordinariness of daily life by attending or watching the Olympics. They like to identify with someone else's accomplishment. National pride is another reason, and an athlete's hard-earned victory becomes a nation's victory. There are national medal counts, and people keep track of how many medals their country's team has won.
Problem and Solution The author states a problem and lists one or more solutions. A variation is the question-and-answer format. Cue words include problem is, dilemma is, puzzle is, solved, and question . . . answer.	Problem → Solution	One problem with the modern Olympics games is that they're very expensive to operate. A stadium, pools, and playing fields must be built for the athletic events, and housing is needed for the athletes. And these facilities are used for only 2 weeks! In 1984, Los Angeles solved these problems by charging a fee for companies to be official sponsors. Many buildings that were already built in the Los Angeles area were also used. The Coliseum where the 1932 games were held was used again, and many local colleges became playing and living sites.

Booklist Expository Text Structures

Structure	Books
Description	Crews, D. (2008). *Freight train*. (PreK) Gibbons, G. (2007). *Groundhog day!* (K–2)
Sequence	Cole, J. (2006). *The magic school bus and the science fair expedition*. (2–4) Kelly, I. (2007). *It's a butterfly's life*. (K–3) Minor, W. (2006). *Yankee Doodle America: The spirit of 1776 from A to Z*. (3–4) Royston, A. (2006). *The life and times of a drop of water: The water cycle*. (1–4)
Comparison	Bidner, J. (2007). *Is my cat a tiger? How your cat compares to its wild cousins*. (2–4) Thomas, I. (2006). *Scorpion vs. tarantula*. (3–4)
Cause-Effect	Brown, C. L. (2006). *The day the dinosaurs died*. (1–3) Collins, A. (2006). *Violent weather: Thunderstorms, tornadoes, and hurricanes*. (3–4) Rockwell, A. (2006). *Why are the ice caps melting? The dangers of global warming*. (1–4)
Problem-Solution	Berger, M., & Berger, G. (1999). *Do stars have points?* New York: Scholastic. (2–4) Calmenson, S. (2007). *May I pet your dog? The how-to guide for kids meeting dogs (and dogs meeting kids)*. (1–4) Morrison, M. (2006). *Mysteries of the sea: How divers explore the ocean depths*. (2–4) Thimmesh, C. (2006). *Team moon: How 400,000 people landed Apollo 11 on the moon*. (3–4)

understand what they're reading, and when writers use these structures to organize their writing, it's easier for the reader to understand. Sometimes the pattern is signaled through the title, a topic sentence, or cue words, but sometimes it isn't. These are the most common expository text structures:

Description.   The author describes a topic by listing characteristics, features, and examples. Phrases such as *for example* and *characteristics are* cue this structure. When students delineate any topic, such as reptiles or the solar system, they use description.

Sequence.   The author lists or explains items or events in numerical, chronological, or alphabetical order. Cue words for sequence include *first, second, third, next, then,* and *finally*. Students use this pattern to write directions for completing a math problem or the stages in an animal's life cycle. The events in a biography are often written in the sequence pattern, too.

Comparison.   The author compares two or more things. *Different, in contrast, alike,* and *on the other hand* are cue words and phrases that signal this structure. When students compare and contrast book and movie versions of a story about reptiles and amphibians, they use this organizational pattern.

Cause and Effect.   The author explains one or more causes and the resulting effect or effects. *Reasons why, if . . . then, as a result, therefore,* and *because* are words and

PreK Practices

Do preschoolers recognize different genres?

When you think about the best books for young students, you probably think of stories, but four-year-olds also enjoy nonfiction and poetry, and they do notice differences among genres (Bennett-Armistead, Duke, & Moses, 2005). As PreK teachers share books during interactive read-alouds, it's important to identify the genre and talk about how it differs from other genres. Prekindergarten literacy standards state that young students should learn to identify genres, recognize their differences, and understand basic text structures. For instance, four-year-olds apply beginning-middle-end to organize the stories they tell, use sequence to structure the information they share, and incorporate rhyme in the ditties they sing (Vukelich & Christie, 2009).

phrases that cue this structure. Explanations of why dinosaurs became extinct or the effects of pollution use this pattern.

Problem and Solution. The author states a problem and offers one or more solutions. A variation is the question-and-answer format, in which the writer poses a question and then answers it. Cue words and phrases include *the problem is, the puzzle is, solve,* and *question . . . answer.* Students use this structure when they write about why money was invented or why endangered animals should be saved.

The Booklist: Expository Text Structures presents books exemplifying each of the expository text structures.

Nonfiction Features

Informational books have unique text features that stories and books of poetry normally don't have, such as margin notes and glossaries. The purpose of these features is to make text easier to read and to facilitate students' comprehension. Here's a list of nonfiction text features:

- Headings and subheadings to direct readers' attention to the big ideas
- Photographs and drawings to illustrate the big ideas
- Figures, maps, and tables to provide detailed information visually
- Margin notes that provide supplemental information or direct readers to additional information on a topic
- Highlighted vocabulary words to identify key terms
- A glossary to assist readers in pronouncing and defining key terms
- An index to assist readers in locating specific information

It's important that students understand these nonfiction text features so they can use them to make their reading more effective and improve their comprehension (Harvey & Goudvis, 2007).

MyLab Education
Video Example 9.3
Fourth graders are generally familiar with text structures for stories. What features of nonfiction books help them engage in doing research?

Examining Text Factors in an Informational Book

What Do You Do With a Tail Like This? (Jenkins & Page, 2008) is a stunning informational book that was named a Caldecott Honor Book in recognition of its vibrant cut-paper collage illustrations. The book teaches that animals use their eyes, mouths, feet, and other body parts in very different ways. It's organized around these six questions:

What do you do with a nose like this?

What do you do with ears like this?

What do you do with a tail like this?

What do you do with eyes like this?

What do you do with feet like this?

What do you do with a mouth like this?

Each question is presented on a double-page spread with pictures of that feature belonging to five animals. Readers turn the page to see pictures of entire animals with sentence-long explanations of how each animal uses the feature. Each explanation predictably begins, "If you're a . . . " and shows a tail, ears, feet, or other body part. Then, when the page is turned, there's a picture of the whole animal with a sentence explaining how the animal uses that body part.

This question-and-answer book uses a problem-solution structure, and the predictable format and limited text make it appropriate for K–3 students. At the back of the book, there's a special section, like a glossary, that provides more detailed information about each animal's special adaptation. The interactive quality makes this book unique: Students try to identify the animals based on picture clues and eagerly turn the page to learn amazing facts about alligators, skunks, hyenas, scorpions, monkeys, pelicans, snakes, and other animals.

Text Factors of Poetry

It's easy to recognize a poem because the text looks different from a page in a story or an informational book. Layout, or the arrangement of words on a page, is an important text factor. Poems are written in a variety of poetic forms, ranging from free verse to haiku, and poets use poetic devices to make their writing more effective. Janeczko (2003) explains that it's important to point out poetic forms and devices to establish a common vocabulary for talking about poems, and because poems are shorter than other types of text, it's often easier for students to examine the text, notice differences in poetic forms, and find examples of poetic devices that authors have used.

Formats of Poetry Books

Three types of poetry books are published for students. Picture-book versions of *The Midnight Ride of Paul Revere* (Longfellow, 2001) and other classic poems are one type. In these books, each line or stanza is presented and illustrated on a page. Others are specialized collections of poems, either written by a single poet or related to a single theme, such as *Tour America: A Journey Through Poems and Art* (Siebert, 2006). Comprehensive anthologies are the third type, and these books feature 50 to 500 or more poems arranged by category. One of the best is Jack Prelutsky's *The Random House Book of Poetry for Students* (1983). The Booklist: Collections of Poetry presents examples of poetry books in each format.

Poetic Forms

Poets who write for students employ a variety of poetic forms; some are conventional, but others are innovative. These are the more commonly used poetic forms:

Booklist Collections of Poetry

Category	Books
Picture-Book Versions of Single Poems	Bates, K. L. (2002). *America the beautiful*. (1–4) Hoberman, M. A. (2004). *Eensy-weensy spider*. (PreK–K) Scholastic. (2001). *The pledge of allegiance*. (K–2) Westcott, N. B. (2003). *The lady with the alligator purse*. (PreK–1)
Specialized Collections	Elliott, D. (2012). *In the sea*. (PreK) Florian, D. (2012). *Shiver me timbers! Pirate poems and paintings*. (K–3) Havill, J. (2006). *I heard it from Alice Zucchini: Poems about the garden*. (K–3) Hoberman, M. A. (Sel.) (2012). *Forget-me-nots: Poems to learn by heart*. (PreK–3) Hopkins, L. B. (2012). *Nasty bugs*. (2–4) Katz, S. (2012). *The president's stuck in the bathtub: Poems about the presidents*. (1–4) Prelutsky, J. (2005). *It's raining pigs and noodles*. (2–4) Yolen, J., & Peters, A. F. (2007). *Here's a little poem: A very first book of poetry*. (PreK–K)
Comprehensive Anthologies	Martin, B., Jr., & Sampson, M. (Sels.). (2008). *The Bill Martin Jr. big book of poetry*. (All) Paschen, E., & Raccah, D. (Sels.). (2005). *Poetry speaks to students*. (2–4) Prelutsky, J. (Sel.). (1983). *The Random House book of poetry for students*. (All) Rosen, M. (Sel.). (1993). *Poems for the very young*. (PreK–1)

RHYMED VERSE.   The most common type of poetry is rhymed verse, as in *My Parents Think I'm Sleeping* (Prelutsky, 2007) and *Today at the Bluebird Café: A Branchful of Birds* (Ruddell, 2007). Poets use various rhyme schemes, including limericks, and the effect of the rhyming words is a poem that's fun to read and listen to when it's read aloud.

Narrative Poems.   Poems that tell a story are *narrative poems*. Perhaps our best known narrative poem is Clement Moore's classic, "The Night Before Christmas."

Haiku.   *Haiku* is a Japanese poetic form that contains just 17 syllables arranged in three lines of 5, 7, and 5 syllables. It's a concise form, much like a telegram, and the poems normally deal with nature, presenting a single clear image. Books of haiku to share with students include *Dogku* (Clements, 2007) and *Cool Melons—Turn to Frogs! The Life and Poems of Issa* (Gollub, 2004). The artwork in these picture books may give students ideas for illustrating their own haiku poems.

Free Verse.   Unrhymed poetry is *free verse*. Word choice and visual images take on greater importance in free verse, and rhythm is less important than in other types of poetry. *The Friendly Four* (Greenfield, 2006) and *Next Stop Grand Central* (Kalman, 2001) are two collections of free verse. Poems for two voices are a unique form of free verse written in two side-by-side columns, and the columns are read simultaneously by two readers. The best known collection is Paul Fleischman's Newbery Award–winning *Joyful Noise: Poems for Two Voices* (2004).

Concrete Poems.   The words and lines in concrete poems are arranged on the page to help convey the meaning. When the words and lines form a picture or outline the objects they describe, they're called *shape poems*. Sometimes the layout of words, lines, and stanzas is spread across a page or two to emphasize the meaning. *A Dazzling Display of Dogs* (Franco, 2011) is a delightful cacophony of words and brightly colored pictures; students will collect many ideas for their own concrete poems from this book.

To learn about other poetic forms, check *Handbook of Poetic Forms* (Padgett, 2007). Students use some of these forms when they write their own poems, including concrete poems.

Poetic Devices

Poetic devices are especially important tools because poets express their ideas very concisely. Every word counts! Here are some of the poetic devices they use:

Alliteration.   Repetition of sounds in nearby words

Imagery.   Words and phrases that appeal to the senses and evoke mental pictures

Metaphor.   A comparison between two unlikely things, without using *like* or *as*

Onomatopoeia.   Words that imitate sounds

Repetition.   Words, phrases, or lines that are repeated for special effect

Rhyme.   Words ending with similar sounds used at the end of the lines

Rhythm.   The internal beat in a poem that's felt when poetry is read aloud

Simile.   A comparison incorporating the word *like* or *as*

Narrative and poetic devices are similar, and many of them, such as imagery and metaphor, are important in both genres.

Poets use other conventions, too. Capitalization and punctuation are used differently: Poets choose where to use capital letters and whether or when to add punctuation marks. They think about the meaning they're conveying and the rhythm of their writing as they decide how to break poems into lines and whether to divide the lines into stanzas. Layout is another consideration: The arrangement of lines on the page is especially important in concrete poems, but it matters for all poems.

Examining Text Factors in a Book of Poetry

Poetry Speaks to Students (Paschen & Raccah, 2005) is a comprehensive anthology for second through fourth graders that's accompanied by a CD of poets reading their poems. This richly illustrated picture book makes poetry fun and accessible. The anthology contains 95 classic and contemporary poems written by 73 poets on topics ranging from silly to serious: Nikki Giovanni tells why she likes chocolate, Billy Collins remembers turning 10, Ogden Nash recounts the story of brave little Isabel, and X. J. Kennedy reveals the secret of how to stay up late. Although most classic poems were written by white men, the contemporary poets contribute multicultural voices—Janet S. Wong, Naomi Shihab Nye, Gwendolyn Brooks, and Sandra Cisneros, for example.

The hour-long CD presents 50 poems read by 34 readers, many of them poets reading their own work. Several are slightly scratchy archival recordings, including Robert Frost reading his "Stopping by Woods on a Snowy Evening" and Basil Rathbone sharing Edgar Allan Poe's "The Raven." The readers display a variety of voices with unique accents, including James Berry, who speaks with a Jamaican-British lilt. For each poem that's included on the CD, the track number is shown next to the poem in the book.

Rhymed verse, narrative poems, and free-verse forms are represented in *Poetry Speaks to Students*. Lewis Carroll's "Jabberwocky" and Karla Kuskin's "Knitted Things" are rhymed verse, and Roald Dahl's "The Dentist and the Crocodile" and Ernest Thayer's "Casey at the Bat" are narrative poems. Contemporary poets often use free verse, and in this collection, James Berry's "Okay, Brown Girl, Okay," Sandra Cisneros's "Good Hot Dogs," and James Stevenson's "Why?" are written in free verse.

Rhyme is the most commonly used poetic device: X. J. Kennedy's "Flashlight," Jane Yolen's "Dinosaur Diet," and John Ciardi's "About the Teeth of Sharks" are examples. Gwendolyn Brooks uses rhyme, alliteration, and repetition in "The Tiger Who Wore White Gloves, or, What You Are You Are." Other poets use repetition, too: David McCord repeats the title in "Every Time I Climb a Tree," and Mary Ann Hoberman repeats the word *bit* in "Rabbit." Most of the poems are formatted in stanzas, but Nikki Giovanni's "Knoxville, Tennessee," a poem that explains why she likes summer, is formatted as a list without any punctuation or capitalization.

MyLab Education Self-Check 9.3

Teaching about Text Factors

Researchers have documented that when teachers teach about text factors, students' comprehension increases (Fisher & Frey, 2015; Shanahan, Fisher & Frey, 2016). In addition, when students are familiar with the genres, organizational patterns, and text features in books they're reading, they're better able to create those text factors in their own writing (Buss & Karnowski, 2002). It's not enough to focus on stories, however; students need to learn about a variety of genres. In the vignette at the beginning of the chapter, Mr. Abrams used text factors to scaffold his students' learning about frogs. He taught them about the unique characteristics of informational books, emphasized text structures through the questions he asked, and used graphic organizers to help students visualize big ideas. **My Teaching To-Do Checklist Comprehension: Text Factors** emphasizes that teachers need to teach students about the unique text factors of all genres—stories, nonfiction, and poetry.

The Common Core State Standards for English Language Arts (2010) emphasize that at each grade level, students grow in their ability to use text factors to comprehend stories and nonfiction texts, particularly complex texts, more effectively. Teachers teach about genres, structural patterns, and literary devices so students can accomplish these tasks:

MY TEACHING TO-DO CHECKLIST Comprehension: Text Factors

☐ I teach students how to identify the genres of books they read.

☐ I teach students how to identify plot, characters, and other structural elements of stories.

☐ I teach students how to recognize imagery, flashbacks, symbolism, and other narrative devices.

☐ I expect students to explain how authors use expository text structures to organize nonfiction texts.

☐ I teach students how to use headings and other nonfiction features to improve their comprehension of textbooks and other nonfiction books.

☐ I teach students how to recognize poetic forms of the poems they read.

☐ I teach students how to apply poetic formulas in the poems they write.

☐ I teach students how to recognize and use alliteration and other poetic devices.

☐ I expect students to apply what they've learned about text factors when they read and write.

☐ I integrate state standards into my instruction.

- Noticing how plot and other elements of story structure shape the content and style of stories
- Making connections among big ideas and details
- Integrating information presented visually and through media
- Examining sentences and paragraphs to see how they relate to each other and the whole text
- Analyzing texts to draw conclusions
- Citing textual evidence to support conclusions

After instruction and guided practice, students need to be able to apply their knowledge about text factors when they read grade-level texts independently. To learn more about the Standards, check the Common Core State Standards: Comprehension Text Factors box.

Minilessons

Teachers teach about text factors directly—often through **minilessons** (Simon, 2005). They highlight a genre, explain its characteristics, and then read aloud books representing that genre, modeling their thinking about text factors. Later, students make charts of the information they're learning and hang them in the classroom. Similarly, teachers introduce structural patterns and have students examine how authors use them to organize a book or an excerpt from a book they're reading.

Common Core State Standards

Comprehension: Text Factors

The Common Core State Standards for English Language Arts emphasize that students need to apply their knowledge of text factors to comprehend the texts they're reading. The Reading Standards for narrative and nonfiction texts address these requirements:

- Students identify the genres of texts.
- Students describe the overall structure of stories and nonfiction texts.
- Students explain how the structure of a text contributes to its meaning and style.
- Students analyze how visual and multimedia elements contribute to a text.

These Standards specify that students must be able to use text factors to comprehend complex grade-level texts. To learn more about the Standards, go to http://www.corestandards .org/ELA-Literacy, or check your state's educational standards website

Students often create graphic organizers to visualize the structure of informational books they're reading and appreciate how the organization emphasizes the big ideas (Opitz, Ford, & Zbaracki, 2006). Teachers also focus on the literary devices that authors use to make their writing more vivid and the conventions that make a text more reader-friendly. Students often collect sentences with narrative devices from stories they're reading and lines of poetry with poetic devices from poems to share with classmates, and they create charts with nonfiction features they've found in books to incorporate in reports they're writing. The Minilesson: The Middle of a Story shows how Ms. Tomas teaches her first graders about the beginning, middle, and end of stories.

Comprehension Strategies

It's not enough that students can name the characteristics of a myth, identify cue words that signal expository text structures, or define *metaphor* or *assonance*; the goal is for them to actually use what they've learned about text factors when they're reading and writing. The comprehension strategy they use to apply what they've learned is called *noticing text factors*; it involves considering genre, recognizing text structure, and attending to literary devices. Lattimer (2003) explains the strategy this way: Students need to think about "what to expect from a text, how to approach it, and what to take away from it" (p. 12). Teachers teach about text factors through minilessons and other activities, but the last step is to help students internalize the information and apply it when they're reading and writing. One way teachers do this is by demonstrating how they use the strategy as they read books aloud using **think-alouds** (Harvey & Goudvis, 2007). Teachers also use the think-aloud procedure to demonstrate this strategy as they do modeled and shared writing.

Reading and Writing Activities

Instructional activities provide opportunities for students to examine text genres, text structures, and text features in the stories, informational books, and poems they're reading. These activities offer guided practice where students apply what they've learned through minilessons and deepen their comprehension, often in collaboration with classmates and with teacher guidance. Many teachers use these activities to differentiate instruction.

STORIES Students examine text factors as they participate in **grand conversations** and write and draw entries in **reading logs**, and they also learn more about stories as they participate in these oral, dramatic, and visual activities:

Story Boards. Students manipulate **story boards**, the cut-apart pages of a picture-book story, for a variety of activities. They can sequence story events, explore characters or setting, reread dialogue, and locate examples of other narrative devices. Teachers often have students line up around the classroom to sequence the pages, retell their page, or group themselves in the beginning, middle, and end parts.

Hot Seat. Students assume the role of a character and participate in a **hot seat** activity where they talk about the story from the character's point of view and answer classmates' questions. Sometimes several characters from a story get together to talk, sharing their perspectives and asking each other questions. This comprehension activity deepens students' understanding of the story as well as their awareness of plot, characters, and point of view and often leads to writing journal entries and letters from the character's perspective.

Drawings and Diagrams. As they analyze story elements, students draw pictures of the beginning, middle, and end of stories, design plot diagrams and setting maps, and make posters about the characteristics of an element of story structure or charts about the text factors used in a particular story. These visual

Minilesson

TOPIC: **The Middle of a Story**
GRADE: **First Grade**
TIME: **One 30-minute period**

Ms. Tomas is teaching a series of minilessons to her first grade class about the characteristics of the beginning, middle, and end of stories. Several days ago, she taught a lesson about story beginnings, and the students analyzed the beginnings of several familiar stories. In this minilesson, Ms. Tomas uses the same stories to analyze the characteristics of story middles.

1. **Introduce the Topic**

   Ms. Tomas begins by asking her first graders to name the three parts of a story, and they respond "beginning, middle, and end" in unison. She invites Kevin to read aloud the chart about the characteristics of story beginnings that they made previously. Then Ms. Tomas explains that in today's minilesson, they'll examine the middle part of a story.

2. **Share Examples**

   Ms. Tomas shows the students three familiar books: *Hey, Al* (Yorinks, 1989), *The Wolf's Chicken Stew* (Kasza, 1996), and *Tacky the Penguin* (Lester, 2008). She reminds them that several days ago, she read aloud the beginnings of these stories and explains that today she'll read aloud the middle parts. She briefly summarizes *Hey, Al* and reads the middle part aloud; then she repeats the procedure with the other two stories.

3. **Provide Information**

   The teacher asks the students to think about the middle of the stories. Alexi replies that the problem is getting worse in the middle of each story: "It looks like the hunters will get the penguins in *Tacky the Penguin,* and the wolf looks like he is getting ready to eat the little chicks in *The Wolf's Chicken Stew,* and something bad is happening to Al and Eddie in *Hey, Al.*" Ms. Tomas explains that authors add roadblocks to keep characters from solving their problems too quickly. The first graders identify the roadblocks in each story. Jack mentions another characteristic of story middles: "You meet other characters." Clara offers still another characteristic: "I think it's important that you get a little hint about how the story is going to end. I mean, Mr. Wolf is beginning to like the little chicks—you can tell." The teacher also points out that the middle is the longest part of the story, and students count the pages to assure themselves that she's right.

4. **Guide Practice**

   Ms. Tomas uses interactive writing to develop a chart about the middle of stories. Their chart lists these characteristics:

   1. The problem gets worse.

   2. There are roadblocks.

   3. You meet new characters.

   4. You get a hint about the ending.

   5. It is the longest part.

5. **Assess Learning**

   After Ms. Tomas teaches a minilesson on the end of stories, she'll read *Martha Speaks* (Meddaugh, 1995). Afterward, the students will make flip booklets and retell the beginning on the first page, the middle on the second page, and the end on the third page. Ms. Tomas will monitor their understanding of beginning, middle, and end through their retellings.

Teach Kids to Be Strategic!

Comprehension Strategies

Teach students how to recognize and analyze text factors using these strategies so they can increase their comprehension of complex texts:

- Consider genre
- Recognize text structure
- Attend to literary devices

Introduce these strategies in minilessons and have students practice using them as they read books and listen to books read aloud. If students struggle, reteach the strategies, model their use, and think aloud about their application.

representations highlight important concepts about stories and reinforce students' learning.

Story Retelling.   Students retell stories, often using puppets, story boards, or collections of objects related to the story. As they participate in a **story retelling** activity, students apply their knowledge of plot, especially beginning-middle-end, and other elements of story structure, and they experiment with foreshadowing, dialogue, and other narrative devices. Sometimes students pretend to be a character and retell a story from that character's point of view; for example, they can retell *Officer Buckle and Gloria* (Rathmann, 1995), the story of a police officer and his dog who learn to work as a team, from an objective viewpoint or from either Officer Buckle's or Gloria's perspective. As students retell stories from different points of view, they learn that a character's perspective influences the story and its theme.

Open-Mind Portraits.   Students create multipage **open-mind portraits** to explore a character's appearance and thoughts. They use the information that the author provides about the character's appearance for the "portrait" page, and on the "thinking" pages they infer the character's thoughts at pivotal points in the story and represent his or her thinking using words and pictures. This activity helps students grapple with theme—the most difficult story element—because the character's thoughts as the story ends often address theme.

Through these activities, teachers have opportunities to emphasize the importance of text factors in comprehending stories.

NONFICTION.   After students read informational books, they explore them through the following activities that emphasize both the information students are learning and the books' unique text factors:

Semantic Feature Analysis.   When students do a **semantic feature analysis**, they're examining a big idea in a thematic unit and applying what they know about nonfiction, especially expository text structures. As they complete the semantic feature analysis chart, they think about relationships among the components listed in the left column. **Word sorts** are a similar classification activity, and as students organize words into categories, they're emphasizing relationships among the concepts represented by the words.

Story Boards.   Teachers also cut apart nonfiction picture books to make **story boards** for students to examine; however, to avoid confusion about genres, it might be better to call these cut-apart picture books "information" or "nonfiction" boards. In addition to locating the big ideas and key vocabulary words, students notice cue words the author used to emphasize the text structure and pick out text features, including headings, margin notes, illustrations, and highlighted vocabulary. Once students are aware of these features, they begin to insert them into the informational books they write.

Writing Informational Books.   As students write informational books to share what they've learned in a thematic unit, they incorporate what they know about the nonfiction genre, expository text structures, and nonfiction features into their books to make them more reader-friendly. They create alphabet books, counting books, and question-and-answer books and use other formats that are similar to those in books they've read. They organize their writing into one-page chapters, and the chapter titles often hint at the structural patterns they're using. For example, second graders writing about plants used these chapter titles:

The Parts of a Plant   (description)

A Plant's Life Cycle   (sequence)

Is It a Plant?   (comparison)

What Plants Need to Grow   (cause and effect)

Why People Need Plants   (problem and solution)

Students also add a table of contents, illustrations and diagrams, margin notes, a glossary, an index, and other nonfiction features to their books.

Through these activities, students apply what they're learning about nonfiction in meaningful ways.

POETRY.   Students deepen their understanding of poetry text factors as they read poems and listen to poems being read aloud, talk about poems, examine individual lines in a poem, and write their own poetry:

Interactive Read-Alouds.   As teachers encourage students to participate in the reading experience by repeating lines, echoing rhyming words, or adding sound effects during **interactive read-alouds**, they're emphasizing the poem's text factors, and students develop an implicit understanding of poetic forms and devices that teachers can build on during minilessons.

Choral Reading.   Students apply what they're learning about text features as they arrange poems and participate in **choral reading** activities. The power of the poet's words becomes clearer as students experiment with different ways of reading a poem. Not surprisingly, the most effective choral readings highlight the poem's structure and the poetic devices the poet used; rhyming verse, for example, is read differently than free verse or poems with repeated lines or a refrain.

Poetry Picture Books.   Students create picture-book versions to celebrate favorite poems. Each student chooses one line to write on a page and illustrate. Then the pages are compiled and made into a book, and the published book is placed in the classroom library for students to read. As they copy their line and draw their illustration, students think about the words and the images the poet has created. This close examination of one line and how it contributes to the entire poem provides an opportunity for students to think about text factors.

Writing Poems.   Students write poems imitating the form of poems they've read, and they experiment with poetic devices, including alliteration, rhyme, and repetition, in their poems. For example, third grader Jeremy wrote this poem, titled "Jeremy's Favorite Pizza," using poems from Georgia Heard's *Falling Down the Page: A Book of List Poems* (2009) as his model:

crispy crust

tomato sauce

Italian seasoning

pepperoni slices

sausage meatballs

mushrooms—OK

NO olives

mozzarella cheese

PIPING HOT!

Jeremy proudly pointed out that each of the lines in his poem has exactly two words, and he used capital letters to indicate which words should be emphasized when the poem is read aloud. Teachers often use these comprehension activities to provide guided practice as part of literature focus units and thematic units.

Assessing Students' Knowledge of Text Factors

Even though there aren't formal tests to assess students' knowledge of text factors, the Common Core State Standards expect teachers to teach students about three types of text factors, and expects students to apply what they've learned to enhance their comprehension when they're reading stories, poems, and informational books. Students also apply what they know about text factors when they write—especially during district and state writing assessments. Teachers use the instruction–assessment cycle with these four steps to evaluate students' developing knowledge about text factors:

Step 1: Planning.   Teachers plan how to assess students' knowledge of text factors as they design instruction. They decide how to incorporate the remaining steps of the cycle into their lesson plans.

Step 2: Monitoring.   Teachers monitor students' learning informally as they talk with them about genre characteristics in **book talks** and grand conversations, and ask them to apply their understanding of story elements as they write entries in reading logs. Students also document their understanding of text structures as they make graphic organizers, and choose sentences with literary devices when asked to share favorite sentences with the class from a book they're reading. These assessments are typically an ongoing part of classroom interaction, and it's up to teachers to notice how well students are applying their knowledge about text factors and to find fresh ways for them to share their understanding.

Step 3: Evaluating.   Teachers evaluate students' learning through the reading and writing projects they create. They often ask students to incorporate genres, text structures, and text features in their own writing; for example, first grade teachers often ask students to write stories that are modeled on a predictable book they've read. Students also apply their knowledge of text factors when they respond to prompts as part of district and state writing assessments.

Step 4: Reflecting.   Teachers ask students to reflect on what they've learned about text factors. Some teachers use class discussions at the end of a genre study or an author unit, and others ask students to evaluate themselves by writing letters to the teacher.

Embedding assessment into instruction makes it easier for teachers to notice students who are struggling with text factors so they can modify their instruction to improve these students' comprehension.

If Students Struggle . . .

There's a good chance that students who are struggling to understand text factors don't have adequate background knowledge about literature. Daily experiences with books—reading and listening to stories, nonfiction, and poems—are essential for building students' familiarity with books; otherwise, they can't relate information about text factors to their background knowledge. Teachers intervene to expand students' knowledge about literature in these ways:

- Increase read-aloud experiences using both new and familiar books
- Provide opportunities for students to read both new and familiar books independently
- Invite students to talk about books in grand conversations, other discussions, and conferences
- Encourage students to use *genre, poem*, and other academic vocabulary related to text factors as they talk and write about books they're reading
- Ask students to compare books they're reading with others they've read previously

Reading new books and rereading familiar books are both worthwhile activities because struggling readers need to broaden their experiential base and dig deeper into familiar books. Students focus on the plot in the first reading, but they examine text factors through repeated readings.

Teachers intervene to teach students about text factors through minilessons and during guided reading lessons. They follow these guidelines:

- Use very familiar books to teach about text factors
- Incorporate academic vocabulary about text factors, including *genre, setting, expository text structures, sequence*, and *alliteration*, into lessons
- Have students create charts about text factors to display in the classroom

Most struggling readers benefit from additional explicit instruction.

When students aren't learning about text factors, teachers assess their teaching to ensure that they're providing enough attention to genres, text structures, and text features, because students' ability to comprehend depends on both reader and text factors. For example, they ask themselves which text factors they've taught during literature focus units: Have they taught genre units or chosen books for literature circles according to genre? They also check that they're talking about text factors as they do interactive read-alouds and are asking students to reflect on the author's use of text structures and narrative devices during grand conversations.

> **MyLab Education** Self-Check 9.4

Chapter Review

Comprehension: Text Factors

- Teachers teach students that stories have unique text factors: narrative genres, story elements, and narrative devices.
- Teachers teach students that informational books have unique text factors: nonfiction genres, nonfiction text structures, and nonfiction features.

- Teachers teach students that poems have unique text factors: book formats, poetic forms, and poetic devices.
- Teachers encourage students to apply their knowledge of text factors when they're reading and writing.

Accountability Check!

Visit the following assessment links to access quiz questions and instructional applications.

> **MyLab Education** Application Exercise 9.2: Understanding Literacy Development
> **MyLab Education** Application Exercise 9.3: Understanding Literacy Development
> **MyLab Education** Application Exercise 9.4: Understanding Literacy Development
> **MyLab Education** Application Exercise 9.5: Monitoring Literacy Development
> **MyLab Education** Application Exercise 9.6: Measuring Literacy Development

References

Applebee, A. N. (1978). *Child's concept of story: Ages 2–17.* Chicago: University of Chicago Press.

Arnold, C., & Comora, M. (2007). *Taj Mahal.* Minneapolis: Carolrhoda.

Bennett-Armistead, V. S., Duke, N. K., & Moses, A. M. (2005). *Literacy and the youngest learner: Best practices for educators of students from birth to 5.* New York: Scholastic.

Blume, J. (2007). *Tales of a fourth grade nothing.* New York: Puffin Books.

Brett, J. (2009). *The mitten* (20th anniversary ed.). New York: Putnam.

Brown, J. (2003). *Flat Stanley.* New York: HarperCollins.

Bunting, E. (1995). *Once upon a time.* Katonah, NY: Richard C. Owen.

Bunting, E. (1999). *Smoky night.* San Diego: Voyager.

Buss, K., & Karnowski, L. (2000). *Reading and writing literary genres.* Newark, DE: International Reading Association.

Buss, K., & Karnowski, L. (2002). *Reading and writing expository genres.* Newark, DE: International Reading Association.

Carle, E. (1997). *Have you seen my cat?* New York: Aladdin Books.

Clarke, B. (1990). *Amazing frogs and toads.* New York: Knopf.

Cleary, B. (1992). *Ramona the pest.* New York: HarperCollins.

Clements, A. (2007). *Dogku.* New York: Simon & Schuster.

Coerr, E. (1993). *Chang's paper pony.* New York: HarperCollins.

Cole, J. (2006). *The magic school bus and the science fair expedition.* New York: Scholastic.

Common core state standards for English language arts. (2010). Retrieved from http://www.corestandards.org/ELA-Literacy/

Crews, D. (2008). *Freight train.* New York: Greenwillow.

Dahl, R. (2007). *Charlie and the chocolate factory.* New York: Puffin Books.

Danziger, P. (2006). *Amber Brown is not a crayon.* New York: Scholastic.

Demi. (2008). *Marco Polo.* Tarrytown, NY: Marshall Cavendish.

dePaola, T. (1996). *The legend of the bluebonnet.* New York: Putnam.

DiCamillo, K. (2008). *The miraculous journey of Edward Tulane.* New York: Walker.

DiCamillo, K. (2009). *Because of Winn-Dixie.* Cambridge, MA: Candlewick Press.

Ehrlich, A. (2004). *Cinderella.* New York: Dutton.

Ehrlich, A. (2006). *The snow queen.* New York: Dutton.

Fisher, D., & Frey, N. (2015). Teacher modeling using complex informational texts. *The Reading Teacher, 69*(1), 63–69.

Fleischman, P. (2004). *Joyful noise: Poems for two voices.* New York: HarperCollins.

Franco, B. (2011). *A dazzling display of dogs.* Berkeley, CA: Tricycle Press.

Galdone, P. (2008). *The gingerbread boy.* New York: Clarion Books.

Geisert, A. (2008). *Hogwash.* Boston: Houghton Mifflin.

Gibbons, G. (2007). *Groundhog Day!* New York: Holiday House.

Gollub, M. (2004). *Cool melons—turn to frogs! The life and poems of Issa.* New York: Lee & Low.

Greenfield, E. (2006). *The friendly four.* New York: HarperCollins.

Harvey, S., & Goudvis, A. (2007). *Strategies that work: Teaching comprehension for understanding and engagement* (2nd ed.). Portland, ME: Stenhouse.

Heard, G. (Ed.). (2009). *Falling down the page: A book of list poems.* New York: Roaring Brook Press.

Henkes, K. (2004). *Kitten's first full moon.* New York: Greenwillow.

Janeczko, P. B. (2003). *Opening a door: Reading poetry in the middle school classroom.* New York: Scholastic.

Jenkins, S., & Page, R. (2008). *What do you do with a tail like this?* New York: Sandpiper.

Kalman, M. (2001). *Next stop Grand Central.* New York: Putnam.

Kasza, K. (1996). *The wolf's chicken stew.* New York: Putnam.

Kellogg, S. (1997). *Jack and the beanstalk.* New York: Harper Trophy.

Kellogg, S. (2002). *The three little pigs.* New York: Harper Trophy.

King-Smith, D. (2005). *Babe: The gallant pig.* New York: Knopf.

Krull, K. (2000). *Wilma unlimited: How Wilma Rudolph became the world's fastest woman.* New York: Sandpiper.

Lattimer, H. (2003). *Thinking through genre.* Portland, ME: Stenhouse.

Lehman, B. (2004). *The red book.* Boston: Houghton Mifflin.

Lester, H. (2008). *Tacky the penguin.* New York: Houghton Mifflin.

Lewis, C. S. (2005). *The lion, the witch and the wardrobe.* New York: HarperCollins.

Lionni, L. (2006). *Alexander and the wind-up mouse.* New York: Knopf.

Longfellow, H. W. (2001). *The midnight ride of Paul Revere* (C. Bing, Illus.). Brooklyn, NY: Handprint Books.

Lukens, R. J., Smith, J. J., & Miller Coffel, C. (2012). *A critical handbook of students' literature* (9th ed.). Boston: Allyn & Bacon.

McGee, L. M., & Richgels, D. J. (1985). Teaching expository text structures to elementary students. *The Reading Teacher, 38,* 739–745.

Meddaugh, S. (1995). *Martha speaks.* Boston: Houghton Mifflin.

Meyer, B. J. F., & Poon, L. W. (2004). Effects of structure strategy training and signaling on recall of text. In R. B. Ruddell & N. J. Unrau (Eds.), *Theoretical models and processes of reading* (5th ed., pp. 810–850). Newark, DE: International Reading Association.

Mitchell, S. (2007). *The ugly duckling.* Cambridge, MA: Candlewick Press.

Mooney, M. E. (2001). *Text forms and features: A resource for intentional teaching.* Katonah, NY: Richard C. Owen.

Numeroff, L. J. (2003). *If you give an author a pencil.* Katonah, NY: Richard C. Owen.

O'Connor, J. (2008). *Fancy Nancy's favorite fancy words: From accessories to zany.* New York: HarperCollins.

Ogle, D. M. (1986). K-W-L: A teaching model that develops active reading of expository text. *The Reading Teacher, 39,* 564–570.

Opitz, M. F., Ford, M. P., & Zbaracki, M. D. (2006). *Books and beyond: New ways to reach readers.* Portsmouth, NH: Heinemann.

Padgett, R. (2007). *Handbook of poetic forms* (2nd ed.). New York: Teachers & Writers Collaborative.

Paschen, E., & Raccah, D. (Sels.). (2005). *Poetry speaks to students.* Naperville, IL: Sourcebooks MediaFusion.

Pinto, S. (2003). *The alphabet room.* New York: Bloomsbury.

Potter, B. (2006). *The tale of Peter Rabbit.* New York: Warne.

Pratt-Serafini, K. J. (2002). *Saguaro moon: A desert journal.* Nevada City, CA: Dawn.

Prelutsky, J. (Sel.). (1983). *The Random House book of poetry for students.* New York: Random House.

Prelutsky, J. (2007). *My parents think I'm sleeping.* New York: Greenwillow.

Rappaport, D. (2007). *Martin's big words: The life of Dr. Martin Luther King, Jr.* New York: Hyperion Books.

Rathmann, P. (1995). *Officer Buckle and Gloria.* New York: Putnam.

Rau, D. M. (2003). *Neil Armstrong.* Chicago: Students' Press.

Rohmann, E. (1997). *Time flies.* New York: Dragonfly.

Ruddell, D. (2007). *Today at the Bluebird Café: A branchful of birds.* New York: McElderry.

Ryan, P. M. (1999). *Riding Freedom.* New York: Scholastic.

Ryan, P. M. (2002). *Esperanza rising.* New York: Scholastic/Blue Sky Press.

Rylant, C. (1998). *Tulip sees America.* New York: Blue Sky Press.

Sachar, L. (2004). *Sideways stories from Wayside School.* New York: HarperCollins.

Scieszka, J. (2004). *Knights of the kitchen table.* New York: Puffin Books.

Seuling, B. (2003). *Flick a switch: How electricity gets to your home.* New York: Holiday House.

Siebert, D. (2006). *Tour America: A journey through poems and art.* San Francisco: Chronicle Books.

Simon, L. (2005). *Write as an expert: Explicit teaching of genres.* Portsmouth, NH: Heinemann.

Shanahan, T., Fisher, D., & Frey, N. (2016). The challenge of challenging text. In M. Scherer (Ed.) *On developing readers: Readings from educational leadership (EL Essentials)* (pp. 100–110). Alexandria, VA: ASCD.

Stead, T., & Duke, N. K. (2005). *Reality checks: Teaching reading comprehension with nonfiction, K–5.* York, ME: Stenhouse.

Swanson, S. M. (2008). *The house in the night.* Boston: Houghton Mifflin.

Sweet, A. P., & Snow, C. E. (2003). Reading for comprehension. In A. P. Sweet & C. E. Snow (Eds.), *Rethinking reading comprehension* (pp. 1–11). New York: Guilford Press.

Uchida, Y. (1996). *The bracelet.* New York: Putnam.

Valencia, S. W., Wixson, K. K., & Pearson, P. D. (2014). Putting text complexity in context: Refocusing on comprehension of complex text. *The Elementary School Journal, 115*(2), 270–289.

Vukelich, C., & Christie, J. (2009). *Building a foundation for preschool literacy* (2nd ed.). Newark, DE: International Reading Association.

Ward, C. (1999). *The hare and the tortoise*. New York: Millbrook Press.

White, E. B. (2006). *Charlotte's web*. New York: HarperCollins.

Wiesner, D. (2006). *Flotsam*. New York: Clarion Books.

Wildsmith, B. (2007). *The lion and the rat*. New York: Oxford University Press.

Willems, M. (2004). *Knuffle bunny: A cautionary tale.* New York: Hyperion Books.

Williams, V. B. (1993). *A chair for my mother*. New York: Harper Trophy.

Winter, J. (2008). *Follow the drinking gourd.* New York: Knopf.

Wood, A. (2001). *Alphabet adventure*. New York: Blue Sky Press.

Yolen, J. (2007). *Owl moon*. New York: Philomel.

Yorinks, A. (1989). *Hey, Al*. New York: Farrar, Straus & Giroux.

Chapter 10
Scaffolding Students' Reading Development

 Learning Outcomes

After studying this chapter, you'll be prepared to:

10.1 Describe the five stages of the reading process.

10.2 Explain the difference between strategies and skills.

10.3 Identify the five commonly used instructional programs and discuss the strengths and weaknesses of each one.

Using the Reading Process

Anna Nahabed/Shutterstock

Mrs. Ogata's students are reading "The Great Kapok Tree," a selection in their basal readers. This story, set in the Amazon rain forest, was originally published as a trade book. In the basal reader version, the text is unabridged, but because text from several pages has been printed on a single page, the text appears dense and some illustrations from the original version have been deleted.

The third graders spend a week reading "The Great Kapok Tree" and participating in related literacy activities. Mrs. Ogata's language arts block lasts two and a half hours. During the first hour, she works with reading groups while other students work independently at centers. During the second hour, she teaches spelling, grammar, and writing. The last half hour is independent reading time, when students read books from the classroom library.

The skills that Mrs. Ogata teaches each week are determined by the basal reading program. She'll focus on cause and effect as students read and think about the selection. The vocabulary words she'll highlight are *community, depend, environment, generations, hesitated, ruins, silent,* and *squawking.* The third graders will learn about persuasive writing, and they'll write a persuasive letter to their parents. Mrs. Ogata will teach **minilessons** on irregular past-tense verbs, and students will study the list of spelling words the basal reading program provides.

Mrs. Ogata's class is divided into four reading groups, and all but the group reading at the first grade level can read the basal reader with her support. Her district's policy is that, in addition to reading books at their instructional level, all students should be exposed to the grade-level textbooks. Mrs. Ogata involves all students in most instructional activities, but she reads the story to the students in the lowest group, and then these students read instructional-level books using the **guided reading** approach.

To choose names for the groups at the beginning of the school year, Mrs. Ogata put crayons into a basket; a student from each group chose a crayon, and the crayon's name became the name of the group. The students who read at or almost at grade level are heterogeneously grouped into the Wild Watermelon, Electric Lime, and Blizzard Blue groups, and the six remaining students form the Atomic Tangerine group.

On Monday, Mrs. Ogata begins the reading process with the first stage, *prereading.* She builds the students' background knowledge about the rain forest by reading aloud *Nature's Green Umbrella* (Gibbons, 1997). Students talk about rain forests and together compile a list of information they've learned, including the fact that each year, more than 200 inches of rain fall in the rain forest. Next, she introduces the selection of the week and students "picture walk" through it, looking at the illustrations, connecting with what they already know about rain forests, and predicting what the story is about.

The second stage is *reading.* Most of the third graders read the story with buddies, but the Atomic Tangerine group reads the selection with Mrs. Ogata; these students join her at the reading group table, and she uses **shared reading**. She reads the story aloud while they follow along in their books. The teacher stops periodically to explain a word, invite predictions, clarify confusions, and **think aloud** about the story.

Responding is the third stage. After everyone finishes reading the selection, students come together to talk about the story in a **grand conversation**. They talk about why the rain forests must be preserved. Ashley explains, "I know why the author wrote the story. On page 71, it tells about her. Her name is Lynne Cherry and it says that she wants to 'try to make the world a better place.' That's the message of this story." Then Katrina compares this story to *Miss Rumphius* (Cooney, 1985), the selection they read the previous week: "I think this story is just like the one we read before. It was about making the world more beautiful with flowers, and that's almost the same."

Mrs. Ogata asks what would happen if there were no more rain forests. Students mention that animals in the rain forest might become extinct because they wouldn't have homes, and that there would be more air pollution because the trees wouldn't be able to clean the air. Then Mrs. Ogata introduces a basket of foods, spices, and other products that come from the rain forest, including chocolate, coffee, tea, bananas, cashews, cinnamon, ginger, vanilla, bamboo, and rubber. The students are amazed at the variety of things that come from the rain forest.

Mrs. Ogata moves on to the fourth stage, *exploring,* and introduces the grammar skill of the week: the past tense of irregular verbs. As directed in the teacher's guide, she has prepared 10 sentence strips with sentences about "The Great Kapok Tree," leaving blanks for the past-tense verbs. On separate cards, she's written correct and incorrect verb forms on each side; for example, *The birds comed/came down from their trees.* She puts the sentence strips and the verb cards in a pocket chart. She begins by talking about the past-tense form of regular verbs. The students understand that *-ed* marks the past tense, as in this sentence: *The man walked into the rain forest.* Other verbs, she explains, have different forms for present and past tense; for example, *The man sleeps/slept in the rain forest.* Then students read the sentences in the pocket chart and choose the correct form of each irregular verb.

Next, she explains that many irregular verbs have three forms—present tense, past tense, and past participle—as in *sing–sang–sung.* She puts word cards with these

In this chapter, you'll read about five ways to organize reading instruction: Teachers use a combination of guided reading lessons, basal readers, literature focus units, literature circles, reading workshop, and other approaches to create a balanced literacy program. As you read this vignette, notice how Mrs. Ogata integrates these approaches: She combines explicit instruction with authentic reading and writing activities to develop students' reading fluency and comprehension.

10 present-tense forms in another pocket chart: *go, give, come, begin, run, do, eat, grow, see,* and *sing*. Then she passes out additional word cards listing the two past-tense forms of each verb. As they talk about each verb, students holding word cards with the past-tense forms add them to the pocket chart.

For the last 20 minutes of the language arts block, Mrs. Ogata introduces this week's literacy centers and explains what to do at each one:

Comprehension Center.   Students write a letter to Mrs. Ogata in response to a question posted at the center or complete page 108 in their Practice Book.

Computer Center.   Students play a phonics game on *r*-controlled vowels.

Grammar Center.   Students sort word cards, putting present, past, and past-participle forms of a verb together, and then complete page 56 in their Grammar Practice Book.

Listening Center.   Students listen to "The Great Kapok Tree" or another of Lynne Cherry's books.

Reading Center.   Students read books from the text set on rain forests.

Spelling Center.   Students complete page 86 in their Spelling Activity Book.

Vocabulary Center.   Students complete a word sort using words about rain forests.

These centers are arranged next to bulletin boards, on tables, or in corners of the classroom.

During the rest of the week, Mrs. Ogata meets with reading groups during the first hour of the language arts block while other students work at centers. She meets with each group several times during the week and uses guided reading procedures as students reread the selection and supplemental or other leveled books. She also teaches vocabulary and comprehension as directed in the teacher's guide.

Mrs. Ogata likes to begin with the Atomic Tangerine group each morning because she believes that it gets them off to a more successful start. She teaches guided reading lessons to these students. They begin by rereading several familiar leveled books, and Mrs. Ogata listens to the students as they read. Next, she reviews one- and two-syllable words with *ar*, and they decode these words: *car, carpet, mark, bookmark, sharp, sharpest,* and *sharks*. Mrs. Ogata introduces their new book, *Hungry, Hungry Sharks* (Cole, 1986). Students text walk through the first 11 pages, looking at illustrations and making predictions, and they put a bookmark at page 11 to remember where to stop reading. Mrs. Ogata asks them to read to find out if sharks are dinosaurs, and they eagerly begin. Students mumble-read so that the teacher can listen to them read. When students don't know a word, Mrs. Ogata helps them sound it out or, if necessary, pronounces it for them. She writes the words on cards to review after reading. As soon as they finish, students discuss possible answers to her question: Several believe that sharks were dinosaurs, but others disagree. So, Mrs. Ogata rereads page 10, which says, "There are no more dinosaurs left on earth. But there are plenty of sharks." After they agree that sharks aren't dinosaurs, they practice reading the word cards that Mrs. Ogata prepared while they were reading.

Next, the students compose this sentence using **interactive writing**: *There are more than three hundred kinds of sharks*. Students write on individual whiteboards as they take turns writing on chart paper. Then they reread the five sentences they wrote last week. During the rest of the week, students in the Atomic Tangerine group will continue reading *Hungry, Hungry Sharks* and participate in phonics, spelling, vocabulary, and writing activities.

Mrs. Ogata meets with the Wild Watermelon group to reread "The Great Kapok Tree." The students read silently, but Mrs. Ogata asks individual students to read a page aloud so that she can conduct **running records** to check their fluency. Afterward, the students talk about what the man might have been thinking as he walked away from the kapok tree on the last page of the story.

Next, she focuses on cause and effect. She asks what's causing a problem in the story, and the students respond that cutting down the rain forest is the problem. When she asks about the effects of cutting down the trees, students mention several, including air pollution and destroying animal habitats. Then she passes out cards, each with a picture of an animal from the story, and asks students to scan the story to find the effect each animal told the sleeping man. Students reread and then share what they found.

Then Mrs. Ogata repeats these activities with the other two reading groups. On the fourth and fifth days, she focuses on vocabulary words from the selection with the three grade-level reading groups.

In the second hour, Mrs. Ogata begins a persuasive writing project. She explains that people read and write for three purposes—to entertain, to inform, and to persuade. "Which purpose," she asks, "do you think Lynne Cherry had for writing 'The Great Kapok Tree'?" The students respond that she had all three purposes, but that perhaps the most important purpose was to persuade. Then Mrs. Ogata explains that in persuasive writing, authors use cause and effect. They explain a problem and tell how to solve it; they also provide reasons why it must be solved and tell what will happen if it isn't.

The fifth stage of the reading process is *applying*, and in this stage, readers create projects to extend their learning. The students talk about environmental problems in their community and decide to write letters to their parents and grandparents urging them to take good care of the environment. This is the format they'll use:

Sentence 1: Urge their parents to conserve and recycle.

Sentence 2: Tell how to conserve and recycle.

Sentence 3: Tell another way.

Sentence 4: Tell why it's important.

Sentence 5: Urge their parents to conserve and recycle.

Mrs. Ogata and the third graders brainstorm many ideas and words on the whiteboard before they begin to write their rough drafts. On Wednesday and Thursday, they revise and edit their letters, and Mrs. Ogata meets with students to work on them. By Friday, most students are writing their final copies and addressing envelopes so their letters can be mailed. Before they begin recopying, Mrs. Ogata reviews the friendly letter form so students will be sure to format their letters correctly. Rachel's letter to her grandparents is shown here.

A Third Grader's Persuasive Letter

Dear Nana and Pappa,

    I want you to take very good care of the earth and it a more beautiful place. I want you to recyle paper. Like old newspapper and cardboard and bags from Savemart. You shuold put it in the blue [RECYCLE] can and it will be made into new paper. Don't burn it!! That means more air pollution. I love you and you love me so help me to have a good life on a healthy planet.

               Love,
               Rachel

Mrs. Ogata ends the language arts block on Friday by showing the video version of "The Great Kapok Tree," which appeared on PBS's Reading Rainbow series. Afterward, the students make a Venn diagram comparing the two versions of the story.

Teachers use the reading process for literacy instruction. The reading process involves a series of stages during which readers develop their comprehension of a text by reading, responding to, and applying what they've read. The term **text** refers to all reading materials—stories, text messages, maps, cereal boxes, magazines, textbooks, email, and so on; it's not limited to basal reading textbooks. In the vignette, Mrs. Ogata guided her third graders through the reading process to scaffold their comprehension. Her instruction demonstrated that she knows that meaning doesn't exist on the pages of a book; instead, readers create comprehension through their interaction with the texts they're reading.

Teachers use a variety of programs for reading instruction; five of the most common are guided reading lessons, basal reading programs, literature focus units, literature circles, and reading workshop. Each one incorporates the reading process. In the **balanced approach**, teachers typically combine two or three programs or supplement one program with additional literacy activities. No matter which programs teachers use, their goal is to provide a combination of explicit instruction, guided practice, and authentic application, often incorporating technology.

The Reading Process

Reading is a constructive process of creating meaning that involves the reader, the text, and the purpose within social and cultural contexts. The goal is comprehension, understanding the text and being able to use it for the intended purpose. Readers don't simply look at the words on a page and grasp the meaning; rather, it's a complex process involving these essential components:

Phonemic Awareness and Phonics.   As they read, students use their knowledge about the **phonological system**, including how to manipulate sounds in spoken words and apply phoneme–grapheme correspondences and phonics rules. They develop these abilities through phonemic awareness and phonics instruction.

Word Identification.   Students recognize high-frequency words automatically and use their knowledge of phonics and word parts to decode unfamiliar words. Until students can recognize most of the words they're reading, they're slow, word-by-word readers.

Fluency.   Students become fluent readers once they recognize most words automatically and read quickly and with expression. This is a milestone because students have limited cognitive resources to devote to reading, and beginning readers use most of this energy to decode words. Fluent readers, in contrast, devote most of their cognitive resources to comprehension.

Vocabulary.   Students think about the meaning of words they're reading, choosing appropriate meanings, recognizing figurative uses, and relating them to their background knowledge. Knowing the meaning of words influences comprehension because it's difficult to understand when the words being read don't make sense.

Comprehension.   Students use a combination of reader and text factors to understand what they're reading. They predict, connect, monitor, repair, and use other comprehension strategies as well as their knowledge of genres, organizational patterns, and literary devices to create meaning.

These components are supported by scientifically based reading research (National Reading Panel, 2000).

Teachers use the reading process to involve students in activities to teach, practice, and apply these components. The reading process is organized into five stages: *prereading, reading, responding, exploring,* and *applying.* This process is used, no matter which instructional program teachers have chosen, even though some of the activities at each stage differ. Figure 10–1 presents an overview of the reading process.

Stage 1: Prereading

The reading process begins before readers even open a book: The first stage, *prereading,* occurs as readers prepare to read. In the vignette, Mrs. Ogata developed her students' background knowledge and stimulated their interest in "The Great Kapok Tree" as they learned about the rain forest. As readers get ready to read, they activate background knowledge, set purposes, and make plans for reading.

ACTIVATING BACKGROUND KNOWLEDGE.   Students have both world and literary background knowledge (Braunger & Lewis, 2006). *World knowledge* is what students have acquired through life experiences and learning in their home communities and at school; in contrast, *literary knowledge* is the information about reading, genres, and text structures that students need to read and comprehend a text. Students activate their world and literary background knowledge in this stage, but when they lack the knowledge to read a text, teachers must build their knowledge base; otherwise, students won't be successful.

Teachers build students' knowledge about a topic by sharing a text set of related books, engaging students in discussions, sharing artifacts, and introducing key vocabulary words. Sometimes they collect objects related to the book and create a book box to

---

Figure 10–1 Key Features of the Reading Process

Stage 1: Prereading
- Activate or build background knowledge and related vocabulary
- Set purposes
- Introduce key vocabulary words
- Make predictions
- Do a picture walk to preview the text

Stage 2: Reading
- Read independently, with a partner, or using shared reading; or listen to the text read aloud
- Apply reading strategies and skills
- Examine illustrations, charts, and diagrams

Stage 3: Responding
- Write and draw pictures in reading logs
- Participate in grand conversations or other discussions

Stage 4: Exploring
- Reread all or part of the text
- Learn new vocabulary words
- Participate in minilessons on reading strategies and skills
- Examine the writer's craft

Stage 5: Applying
- Construct projects
- Read related books
- Use information in thematic units
- Value the reading experience

use in introducing it. In the vignette, Mrs. Ogata collected rain forest products to share with her third graders to build their background knowledge and engage them in the selection. Once students pick up a book, they think about its title, look at the illustration on the cover, and take a "picture walk" through the book to trigger this activation. Those who read novels often read the first paragraph or two to activate their world knowledge.

Teachers build students' literary knowledge by teaching about reading strategies and skills and studying different genres. Students read books representing a genre, examine structural patterns, and chart the characteristics. Through these activities, they learn how to vary their reading according to genre. It's not enough just to build students' knowledge about the topic; literary knowledge is also essential!

SETTING PURPOSES. The purpose guides students' reading: It provides motivation and direction for reading, as well as a mechanism for students to monitor their reading to see if they're fulfilling their purpose. Sustaining a single purpose is more effective than presenting students with a series of purposes (Blanton, Wood, & Moorman, 1990). Teachers often set purposes for reading, but students also need to set their own purposes. In literature circles and reading workshop, for example, readers choose texts they want to read and set their own purposes. With lots of small-group and independent reading experiences, students become more effective at choosing books and setting their own purposes.

PLANNING FOR READING. Once students activate their background knowledge and identify their purpose, they plan for reading. They vary how they make plans according to the type of selection they're preparing to read; for stories, for example, they make predictions about the characters and events in the story, often basing them on the book's title or the cover illustration. If students have read other stories by the same author or in the same genre, they also use this information in making their predictions. Young students usually share their predictions orally, but more experienced readers write predictions in **reading logs**.

When students are preparing to read informational books, they preview the selection by flipping through the pages and noting section headings, illustrations, and diagrams. Sometimes they examine the table of contents to see how the book is organized, or they consult the index to locate specific information they want to read. They also notice highlighted terminology, which often triggers their background knowledge.

Stage 2: Reading

Students read the book or other selection during the reading stage using one of these types of reading:

- Independent reading
- Partner reading
- Shared reading
- Teacher read-alouds

These types of reading vary in the amount of teacher scaffolding: Teachers provide very little support during independent reading and the most support when they read aloud. As they decide which type of reading to use, teachers consider the purpose, students' reading levels, and the number of available copies of the text.

INDEPENDENT READING. When students read independently, they read quietly, by themselves, at their own pace, and often for their own purposes. Fluent readers usually read silently, but emergent and beginning readers typically read aloud softly to themselves. Because students generally choose the books they want to read independently, they need to learn how to choose books at an appropriate

Check the Compendium of Instructional Procedures, which follows Chapter 12. These **green** terms also show a brief description of each procedure.

MyLab Education
Video Example 10.1
Teachers use discussions to scaffold learning, reminding students of the strategies they engage in when they are reading. How do teachers remind students to use strategies when they read independently?

level of difficulty. Ohlhausen and Jepsen (1992) developed a procedure for choosing books that they called the **Goldilocks Strategy**. These teachers created three categories—"too easy" books, "too hard" books, and "just right" books—using "The Three Bears" folktale as their model. The books in the "too easy" category are those students have read before or books without any unknown words; books in the "too hard" category are unfamiliar and confusing; and books in the "just right" category are interesting with just a few new words. Figure 10–2 presents a Goldilocks Strategy chart made by a third grade class. Students at every grade level can develop their own charts, using similar characteristics.

Independent reading is an important part of a balanced reading program because it's the most authentic type of reading. It's the way students develop a love of reading and come to think of themselves as readers. The reading selection, however, must be at an appropriate level of difficulty so that students can read it independently; otherwise, teachers use another type of reading to scaffold students and make it possible for them to be successful.

PARTNER READING.   Students read or reread a selection with a classmate or sometimes with an older "buddy" (Friedland & Truesdell, 2004). Partner reading is an enjoyable social activity, and students can often read selections together that neither one could read individually. It's a good alternative to independent reading, and by working together, students are often able to figure out unfamiliar words and talk out confusions.

Figure 10–2 Third Graders' Goldilocks Strategy Chart

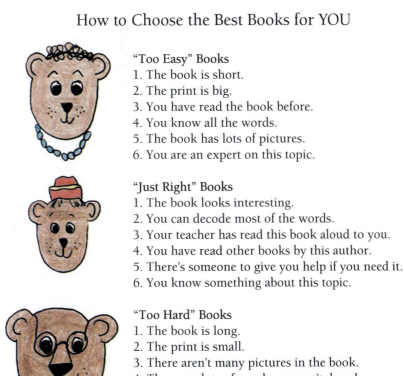

How to Choose the Best Books for YOU

"Too Easy" Books
1. The book is short.
2. The print is big.
3. You have read the book before.
4. You know all the words.
5. The book has lots of pictures.
6. You are an expert on this topic.

"Just Right" Books
1. The book looks interesting.
2. You can decode most of the words.
3. Your teacher has read this book aloud to you.
4. You have read other books by this author.
5. There's someone to give you help if you need it.
6. You know something about this topic.

"Too Hard" Books
1. The book is long.
2. The print is small.
3. There aren't many pictures in the book.
4. There are lots of words you can't decode.
5. There's no one to help you read this book.
6. You don't know much about this topic.

As teachers introduce partner reading, they show students how to read together and how to support each other. Students take turns reading aloud to each other or read in unison. They often stop and help each other identify an unfamiliar word or take a minute or two at the end of each page to talk about what they've read. Partner reading is a valuable way of providing the practice that beginning readers need to become fluent; it's also an effective way to work with students with special learning needs. However, unless the teacher has explained the technique and taught students how to work collaboratively, partner reading often deteriorates into the stronger of the two students reading aloud to the other student.

Teachers often organize cross-age partner reading programs with upper grade students. The older students pair up with younger students and read books aloud or listen to the younger students read. Teachers prepare upper grade students by teaching them how to choose books, read aloud, encourage students to make predictions and connections, and respond to books. The effectiveness of cross-age reading programs is supported by research, and teachers report that both younger and older students' reading improves; these activities have social benefits, too (Whang, Samway, & Pippitt, 1995).

Another way to encourage partner reading is with traveling bags of books. Teachers collect text sets with three or four books on a particular topic for students to take home and read with their parents (Reutzel & Fawson, 1990). For example, teachers might collect copies of *Good Dog, Paw!* (Lee, 2004), *Martha Speaks* (Meddaugh, 1995), and *McDuff's Wild Romp* (Wells, 2005) for a traveling bag of dog stories. Then students and their parents read the books and write a response in a reading log that's included in the bag. Students keep the bag at home for a week and then return it to school so that another student can borrow it. Teachers often add small toys or stuffed animals to the bags. If students are English learners whose parents don't read English, teachers send home small cassette-tape players with audiotapes of the books.

SHARED READING. Teachers use **shared reading** to read aloud texts that are appropriate for students' interest level but too difficult for them to read on their own (Holdaway, 1979; Parkes, 2000). They use enlarged picture books, known as *big books,* so that students can see the text and read along. As they read, teachers model what fluent readers do (Fountas & Pinnell, 2016). After reading the book several times, teachers use it to teach phonics, high-frequency words, and other literacy concepts. Students can also read small versions of the book independently or with partners and use the text's pattern or structure for writing activities.

Predictable books are often used for shared reading because these books have rhyme, repetition, and patterns that enable young students to read them more easily. For example, preschoolers can remember and read the repeated questions and answers in *Where's Spot?* (Hill, 2003) and the circular structure of *This Is the House That Jack Built* (Taback, 2004), and the repetitive sentence patterns make this book easier for beginning readers to read. These and other predictable books are presented in the Booklist: Predictable Books.

Shared reading is best known as part of a balanced literacy program in kindergarten and first grade classrooms. It differs from reading aloud because students view the text as the teacher reads, and they often join in the reading of predictable refrains and rhyming words. After listening to the text read several times, they often remember enough of it to read along with the teacher.

TEACHER READ-ALOUDS. Teachers use the **interactive read-aloud** procedure as they read aloud books that are developmentally appropriate but written above students' reading levels (Fisher, Flood, Lapp, & Frey, 2011). As they read, teachers engage students in the experience rather than postponing their involvement until after reading. Students become active participants as they make predictions, repeat refrains, ask

PreK Practices

Which reading activities are best for young students?

Interactive read-alouds are the single most important reading activity for young students (McClure & Fullerton, 2017). As teachers read aloud picture books and involve students in a variety of participation activities, they model what good readers do. The students acquire positive attitudes about reading, develop concepts about written language, build background knowledge, and expand their vocabularies. In addition to reading aloud at least twice daily, teachers read big books using shared reading procedures; encourage students to look at books that have been read aloud; and have them read calendars, signs, students' names, and other environmental print in the classroom.

questions, identify big ideas, and make connections. In addition, when teachers read aloud, they model how good readers use reading strategies and **think-aloud** about their use of reading strategies (Cappellini, 2005).

Read-alouds are an important component of literacy instruction at all grade levels, not just for emergent readers who can't read many books on their own. Teachers read books aloud during literature focus units, reading and writing workshop, and thematic units. There are many benefits of reading aloud: introducing vocabulary, modeling comprehension strategies, and increasing students' motivation (Rasinski, 2003).

Booklist Predictable Books

Type	Books
Rhymes Rhyming words and refrains are repeated.	Kuskin, K. (2005). *So, what's it like to be a cat?* Martin, B., Jr., & Archambault, J. (2009). *Chicka chicka boom boom.* Seuss, Dr. (1963). *Hop on pop.* Shaw, N. (1997). *Sheep in a jeep.*
Repetitive Sentences A sentence is repeated throughout the book.	Carle, E. (1991). *Have you seen my cat?* Ho, M. (2000). *Hush! A Thai lullaby.* Rathmann, P. (2000). *Good night, gorilla.* Rosen, M. (2004). *We're going on a bear hunt.*
Sequential Patterns The book is organized using numbers, days of the week, or other familiar patterns.	Carle, E. (1997). *Today is Monday.* Christelow, E. (1998). *Five little monkeys jumping on the bed.* Moss, L. (2000). *Zin! Zin! Zin! A violin.* Peek, M. (1991). *Roll over: A counting song.*
Pattern Stories Episodes are repeated with new characters or other variations.	Brett, J. (2009). *The mitten.* Carle, E. (1987). *A house for hermit crab.* Carle, E. (1996). *The grouchy ladybug.* Taback, S. (1997). *There was an old lady who swallowed a fly.*
Circular Stories The plot is organized so that the end leads back to the beginning.	Aardema, V. (1992). *Why mosquitoes buzz in people's ears.* Numeroff, L. J. (1987). *If you give a mouse a cookie.* Wood, A., & Wood, D. (2010). *The napping house.*
Cumulative Stories As each new episode is introduced, the previous episodes are repeated.	Cole, H. (1997). *Jack's garden.* Dunphy, M. (1995). *Here is the southwestern desert.* Taback, S. (2004). *This is the house that Jack built.* West, C. (1996). *"Buzz, buzz, buzz," went bumblebee.*
Questions and Answers The same question is repeated on each page.	Guarino, D. (1989). *Is your mama a llama?* Hill, E. (2003). *Where's Spot?* Martin, B., Jr. (2010). *Brown bear, brown bear, what do you see?*
Songs Familiar songs with repetitive patterns are presented with one line or verse on each page.	Cabrera, J. (2005). *If you're happy and you know it!* Galdone, P. (1988). *Cat goes fiddle-i-fee.* Raffi. (1988). *Wheels on the bus.* Westcott, N. B. (2003). *The lady with the alligator purse.*

Figure 10–3 Types of Reading

Type	Strengths	Limitations
Independent Reading Students read a text on their own, without teacher scaffolding.	Students develop responsibility. Students learn to select texts. Experience is authentic.	Students may not choose texts that they can read independently. Teacher has little involvement or control.
Partner Reading Two students take turns as they read a text together.	Students collaborate and assist each other. Students become more fluent readers. Students talk to develop comprehension.	One student may simply read to the other. Teacher has little involvement or control.
Shared Reading Teacher reads aloud while students follow along using a big book or individual copies.	Teacher teaches concepts about print. Teacher models fluent reading and reading strategies. Students become a community of readers.	Big books or a class set of books are needed. Text may not be appropriate for everyone.
Teacher Read-Alouds Teacher reads aloud and provides opportunities for students to be actively involved in the experience.	Students have access to books they can't read themselves. Teacher models fluent reading and reading strategies. Students build background knowledge and vocabulary.	Students have no opportunity to read. Students may not be interested in the text.

The types of reading are compared in Figure 10–3. As teachers plan their instructional programs, they include reading aloud to students, teacher-led reading lessons, and independent reading each day.

Stage 3: Responding

Students respond to what they've read and continue to negotiate the meaning after reading. This stage reflects Rosenblatt's (2005) **transactional theory**. Two ways that students make tentative and exploratory comments immediately after reading are by writing in reading logs and participating in grand conversations or other discussions.

READING LOGS.   Students write and draw their thoughts and feelings about what they've read in **reading logs**. As they write about what they've read, they unravel their thinking and elaborate on and clarify their responses. Students usually write in reading logs when they're reading stories and poems; sometimes they also do so when they're reading informational books, but during thematic units, they make notes of important information or draw charts and diagrams in **learning logs**.

GRAND CONVERSATIONS AND OTHER DISCUSSIONS.   Students also talk about stories and poems with classmates in **grand conversations** and have other discussions about informational books. Peterson and Eeds (2007) explain that in grand conversations, students share their personal responses and tell what they liked about the text. After sharing personal reactions, they shift the focus to "puzzle over what the author has written and . . . share what it is they find revealed" (p. 61). Often students make connections between the text and their own lives or between the text and other literature they've read. If they're reading a novel, they also make predictions about what might happen in the next chapter.

Teachers often share their ideas in grand conversations, but they act as interested participants, not leaders. The talk is primarily among the students, but teachers ask questions regarding things they're genuinely interested in learning more about and share information in response to questions that students ask. In the past, many discussions were "gentle inquisitions" during which students recited answers to factual questions that teachers asked to determine whether students read and understood an assignment. Although teachers can still judge comprehension, the focus in grand conversations is on deepening students' understanding of the story they've read.

Teachers and students also have discussions after reading informational books. Students talk about what interested them and what they learned about the topic, but teachers also focus their attention on the big ideas, ask clarifying questions, share information, and reread brief excerpts to explore an idea.

These discussions can be held with the whole class or with small groups. Young students usually meet as a class, but older students often prefer to talk in small groups. When students meet as a class, there's a feeling of community, and the teacher can be part of the group. When students meet in small groups, they have more opportunities to share their interpretations, but fewer viewpoints are expressed in each group and teachers move around, spending only a few minutes with each group. Teachers often compromise by having students begin their discussions in small groups and then come together as a class so that the groups can share what they discussed.

Stage 4: Exploring

Students go back into the text to examine it more analytically. This stage is more teacher directed than the others; it reflects the teacher-centered theory. Students reread the selection or excerpts from it, examine the writer's craft, and focus on words and sentences from the text. Teachers also teach minilessons on strategies and skills.

REREADING THE SELECTION.   As students reread the selection or excerpts from it, they think about what they've read. Each time they reread a selection, students benefit in specific ways (Yaden, 1988): They deepen their comprehension by moving beyond their initial focus on the events, the big ideas to understanding the theme of a story, or the relationships among the big ideas in a nonfiction text.

EXAMINING THE WRITER'S CRAFT.   Teachers plan exploring activities to focus students' attention on the genres, text structures, and literary devices that authors use. For example, they have students use **story boards** to sequence the events in the story or make graphic organizers to highlight the plot, characters, and other elements of story structure. Students also learn about the structure of stories and informational books by writing books based on the selection they've read.

Teachers share information about the author of the featured selection and introduce other books by the same author. Sometimes students read and compare several books by the same author. To focus on literary devices, students often reread excerpts to locate examples of onomatopoeia, similes and metaphors, and other types of figurative language.

FOCUSING ON WORDS AND SENTENCES.   Teachers and students add "important" words to the **word wall** posted in the classroom. Students refer to it when they write and use the words in word-study activities, including drawing word clusters and posters to highlight particular words and doing **word sorts** to categorize words. Students also locate "important" sentences in books they read; these sentences are worthy of examination because they contain figurative language, employ an interesting sentence structure, express a theme, or illustrate a character trait. Students often copy the sentences onto sentence strips to display in the classroom, and sometimes they copy them in their reading logs and use them to begin their entries.

TEACHING MINILESSONS.   Teachers present **minilessons** on procedures, concepts, strategies, and skills (Angelillo, 2008). They introduce the topic and make connections between the topic and examples in the featured selection the students have read.

Stage 5: Applying

Readers extend their comprehension, reflect on their understanding, and value the reading experience in this final stage. Often, they create projects to apply what they've learned; these projects take many forms, including **open-mind portraits**, **readers**

MyLab Education
Video Example 10.2
Mrs. Schietrum's fourth graders have read informational books on forests and deserts. How does an instructional conversation help students respond to what they have read and prepare them for writing about those topics?

MyLab Education
Video Example 10.3
Here, Mrs. Martin discusses a character's thoughts, feelings, and actions with her third graders. What was the purpose of the minilesson Mrs. Martin taught her students?

Figure 10–4 Application Projects

Type	Projects
Digital	• Create a PowerPoint presentation about the book. • Write a book review and post it online. • Investigate an author's website and share information from it with classmates. • Create a multimodal project about the book using text, images, and sounds. • Search the Web for information on a topic related to the book and share the results with classmates.
Talk and Drama	• Give a readers theatre presentation of an excerpt from a book. • Create a choral reading using an excerpt from a book and have classmates present it. • Dress as a book character and sit on the "hot seat" to answer classmates' questions. • Present a rap, song, or poem about a book.
Visual	• Design a graphic organizer or model about a book. • Create a collage to represent the theme in a story or the big ideas in a nonfiction book. • Prepare illustrations of a story's events to use in retelling the story. • Make a book box and fill it with objects and pictures representing the book. • Construct a paper quilt about a book. • Create an open-mind portrait to probe the thoughts of a character.
Writing	• Rewrite a story from a different point of view. • Create a new version of a predictable or patterned story. • Write another episode or a sequel for a book. • Write text messages or postcards from one character to another. • Create a found poem using words and phrases from a book. • Write a poem on a topic related to a book. • Keep a journal from one character's viewpoint. • Create a multigenre project about a book.

theatre performances, and PowerPoint presentations. A list of projects is presented in Figure 10–4. Usually students choose which project they want to pursue and work independently, with a classmate, or in a small group, but sometimes the class decides to work together on a project.

> **MyLab Education** Self-Check 10.1

Reading Strategies and Skills

Reading is a complex process involving both strategies and skills. **Strategies** represent the thinking that readers do as they read; in contrast, **skills** are quick, automatic behaviors that don't require any thought. For example, readers use the connecting strategy to compare the story they're reading to their own lives, the world around them, and other books they've read; they're actively thinking as they make connections. In contrast, noticing quotation marks that signal a character's dialogue is a skill; students don't have to think about what these punctuation marks show because they recognize their meaning automatically. The terms *strategy* and *skill* can be confusing; sometimes they're considered synonyms, but they're not. It's important to clarify the distinctions between the two.

Strategies

Strategies are deliberate, goal-directed actions (Afflerbach, Pearson, & Paris, 2011). Readers exercise control in choosing appropriate strategies, using them flexibly, and monitoring their effectiveness. Strategies are linked with motivation: Afflerbach and his colleagues explain that "strategic readers feel confident that they can monitor and improve their own reading so they have both knowledge and motivation to succeed" (p. 370). Most strategies are **cognitive strategies** because they focus on students' thinking about what they're reading—activating background knowledge, visualizing, and drawing inferences, for instance. Others are **metacognitive strategies**, and they involve students' thinking about whether they're successful and understanding what they're reading. When students realize that they're not understanding, they use monitoring, repairing, or another metacognitive strategy to solve the problem in order to continue reading.

Strategies reflect information-processing theory. In contrast, skills are automatic actions that occur without deliberate control or conscious awareness; the emphasis is on their effortless and accurate use. Skills reflect the behavioral theory, and they're always used in the same way, no matter the reading situation. It's crucial that students become both strategic and skilled readers.

TYPES OF STRATEGIES.   Comprehension strategies are probably the best known type, but readers use strategies throughout the reading process:

Phonemic Awareness Strategies.   Students manipulate sounds in words using the blending and segmenting strategies.

Word-Identification Strategies.   Students use strategies such as decoding by analogy to decode unfamiliar words.

Word-Learning Strategies.   Students apply strategies such as context clues to figure out the meaning of unfamiliar words.

Comprehension Strategies.   Students make predictions, draw inferences, monitor their progress, and use other strategies to understand what they're reading.

Learning about strategies begins when students are preschoolers: They learn to blend and segment sounds in words and to make predictions about stories teachers are reading to them. During the primary grades, students continue to learn more complex strategies, including drawing inferences and syllabic analysis.

Students need explicit instruction about reading strategies because they don't acquire the knowledge through reading (Dowhower, 1999). For them to learn to use a strategy, teachers need to provide three types of information about it:

- **Declarative knowledge**   —what the strategy does
- **Procedural knowledge**   —how to use the strategy
- **Conditional knowledge**   —when to use the strategy

For example, let's examine the declarative, procedural, and conditional knowledge for questioning, a comprehension strategy that students use to ask themselves questions while they're reading. They apply it to direct their reading, monitor whether they're understanding, and construct meaning (declarative knowledge). They ask themselves questions such as "What's going to happen next?" "How does this relate to what I know about _____?" and "Does this make sense?" (procedural knowledge). Students use this strategy again and again while they're reading (conditional knowledge).

USING MINILESSONS TO TEACH STRATEGIES.   Teachers use **minilessons** to teach students about strategies. They explain the strategy and model its use, and then students practice with teacher guidance and supervision before using it independently. Through this instruction, students develop metacognitive awareness—their ability to think about how they use cognitive and metacognitive strategies. Use My Teaching To-Do Checklist: Strategy Instruction to assess your knowledge of strategy use.

Teachers demonstrate the thought processes readers use as they read by doing **think-alouds** (Wilhelm, 2001). Teachers think aloud or explain what they're thinking while they're reading so that students become more aware of how capable readers

MyLab Education
Video Example 10.4
In this video, the teacher shares strategies for developing vocabulary. What explicit and implicit strategies can help students develop their vocabulary through reading?

think. In the process, students also learn to think aloud about their use of strategies: They set a purpose for reading, predict what will happen next, make connections, ask questions, summarize what's happened so far, draw inferences, evaluate the text, and make other comments that reflect their thinking. Think-alouds are valuable both when teachers model them for students and when students engage in them themselves. When students use think-alouds, they're more thoughtful, strategic readers who improve the way they monitor their comprehension.

Students often record their strategy use with small self-stick notes. Teachers distribute pads of notes and explain how to use them. Students can focus on applying a single strategy or integrating a group of strategies. They write comments about their thinking on the self-stick notes while they're reading and place them in the margins of the pages so they can locate them when the book is closed. Afterward, students share their notes and talk about the strategies they used in a discussion with classmates.

SKILLS Students also learn skills that they use when they're reading. Phonics skills are probably the best known type, but a variety are used throughout the reading process. Skills can be grouped into much the same categories as reading strategies:

Phonemic Awareness Skills. Students break one-syllable words into onsets and rimes; identify beginning, middle, and ending sounds in words; and notice rhyming words.

Phonics Skills. Students use their knowledge of sound–symbol correspondences and phonics rules to decode words.

Word-Identification Skills. Students apply their knowledge of phonics, word families, syllabication rules, and root words and affixes to identify unfamiliar words.

Word-Learning Skills. Students identify synonyms, recognize metaphors and similes, and notice capital letters signaling proper nouns and adjectives as clues to the meaning of words.

Comprehension Skills. Students recognize details and connect them to main ideas, separate fact and opinion, and use other comprehension skills. They often use these skills in connection with strategies; the big difference is that strategies are used thoughtfully and skills are automatic.

MyLab Education Self-Check 10.2
MyLab Education Application Exercise 10.1: Reading Strategies and Skills

---

MY TEACHING TO-DO CHECKLIST: Strategy Instruction

☐ I teach strategies in minilessons, using explanations, demonstrations, think-alouds, and practice activities.

☐ I provide step-by-step explanations and modeling so that students understand what the strategy does, and how and when to use it.

☐ I offer both guided and independent practice opportunities so that students can apply the strategy in new situations.

☐ My students apply the strategy in thematic unit activities as well as in literacy activities.

☐ I encourage students to refer to the strategy charts hanging in the classroom when reading and writing.

☐ My students reflect on their use of strategies.

☐ I differentiate between the terms *strategies* and *skills* so students understand that strategies are problem-solving tactics and skills are automatic behaviors.

☐ I integrate state standards into my instruction.

Organizing for Instruction: Five Approaches

There's no one best way to teach reading; instead, teachers create a balanced literacy approach using two or more instructional programs. Five commonly used literacy programs for prekindergarten through fourth grade are *guided reading lessons, basal readers, literature focus units, literature circles*, and *reading workshop*. By combining several approaches, teachers ensure that students receive explicit instruction to meet grade-level standards, differentiated instruction to meet their instructional needs, and opportunities for authentic literacy experiences. In the vignette, Mrs. Ogata used the district's adopted basal reading program and added components from other programs to enrich her third graders' literacy learning and meet the third grade Common Core State Standards. Use **My Teaching To-Do Checklist: Instructional Approaches** to judge the effectiveness of your literacy instruction.

The purpose of the Common Core State Standards for English Language Arts (2010) is to delineate what students are expected to know and be able to do at each grade level in reading and writing, but they don't prescribe how teachers are to teach reading or which instructional program to use. The Standards organize their reading achievement expectations for K–4 students into these four categories:

Reading: Foundational Skills.   Students develop written language concepts, phonemic awareness, phonics and word recognition, and fluency.

Reading: Literature.   Students comprehend stories, interpret word choice, analyze the structure of stories, evaluate media presentations of stories, and compare stories with similar themes.

Reading: Informational Text.   Students comprehend nonfiction texts, use evidence in the text to support their conclusions, analyze the structure of text, assess how the author's viewpoint affects a text, evaluate arguments, and compare how several texts deal with a similar topic.

Range of Reading.   Students read and comprehend complex grade-appropriate stories, poems, and informational texts. In kindergarten and through second grade, teachers are expected to scaffold students by reading text aloud and asking questions to prompt their thinking, but starting in third grade, students are expected to read and comprehend challenging texts independently.

MY TEACHING TO-DO CHECKLIST: Instructional Approaches

- ☐ I combine several instructional programs to meet my students' needs.
- ☐ I use texts at my students' instructional level for reading instruction.
- ☐ My students read and respond to award-winning grade-appropriate books.
- ☐ I provide explicit instruction on reading and writing strategies and skills.
- ☐ I incorporate whole-class, small-group, and independent activities.
- ☐ My students have daily opportunities to read books independently.
- ☐ My students participate in authentic reading and writing activities.
- ☐ My students use the Goldilocks Strategy to select appropriate books.
- ☐ I regularly monitor and assess my students' progress.
- ☐ I intervene and modify instruction when my students struggle.
- ☐ I integrate state standards into my instruction.

The Standards document does make several important points about instruction. First, teachers should differentiate instruction to increase opportunities for all students to be successful. Next, the Standards aren't taught separately; instead, teachers should integrate reading and writing so that most literacy activities address several Standards. Third—across the curriculum—connections to reading instruction are crucial; teachers should incorporate reading instruction using a text set of stories, informational books, media, and digital texts organized into thematic units. Mrs. Ogata demonstrated these guidelines in the vignette. The Common Core State Standards box that follows reviews these recommendations.

1. Guided Reading Lessons

Teachers use guided reading lessons to teach reading to small groups of four to six students who read at the same level. They use books written at the students' instructional level and support students use of reading strategies (Fountas & Pinnell, 2016). Students do the actual reading themselves, although the teacher often reads the first page aloud to get the group off to a successful start. Beginning readers mumble-read the words, which helps the teacher keep track of students' knowledge of high-frequency words and use of decoding and other reading strategies; more fluent readers read silently. This instructional program is typically used in kindergarten through third grade, but it can also be used with older students, especially struggling readers. An overview of this instructional approach is presented below.

COMPONENTS OF A GUIDED READING LESSON. Guided reading lessons last approximately 20 minutes. To begin, students reread, either individually or with a partner, familiar books they've already read during previous lessons. Then teachers introduce a new book and guide students as they read it. Beginning readers generally read brief picture books at one sitting, but more fluent readers take several days to a week to read chapter books.

To introduce the new book, teachers activate and build students' background knowledge, build their interest, and take the students on a "walk" through the book, talking about the illustrations and the text. Teachers also set a purpose for reading. Next, students read the entire book, with the teacher providing assistance when needed. They read softly to themselves while the teacher monitors each student's progress by listening in as the student reads, stops to decode unfamiliar words, and rereads confusing passages. An Overview of the Instructional Approach: Guided Reading Lessons is presented for your review.

Common Core State Standards
Reading

The Common Core State Standards focus on what students are expected to learn, not how teachers should teach. K–4 students are expected to become fluent readers, capable of reading and comprehending complex, grade-appropriate literature and informational texts. Teachers scaffold young students, but beginning in third grade, students are expected to read and comprehend the texts independently. The Standards specify these teaching recommendations:

- Teachers differentiate instruction.
- Teachers integrate reading and writing instruction.
- Teachers incorporate reading instruction into thematic units.

To learn more about the reading Standards, go to http://www.corestandards.org/ELA-Literacy, or check your state's educational standards website.

Overview of the Instructional Approach Guided Reading Lessons

Topic	Description
Purpose	To develop independent readers who use strategies flexibly to decode unfamiliar words, read fluently, and comprehend what they're reading.
Components	Guided reading lessons begin with students rereading a familiar leveled book, and then the teacher introduces a new leveled book for that day's lesson and students read it independently. Afterward, the students discuss the selection and the teacher uses the book for phonics, vocabulary, and strategy lessons. Sometimes students extend their reading by doing a writing project.
Theory Base	Guided reading lessons reflect the constructivist and information-processing theories because teachers use reading groups to differentiate instruction, and they teach reading strategies.
Applications	Teachers often use guided reading lessons in conjunction with literature focus units or reading and writing workshop so students have opportunities to apply the reading strategies they're learning and integrate reading and writing.
Strengths	• Students read books at their instructional reading levels. • Teachers teach reading strategies. • Teachers differentiate instruction to address students' needs. • Teachers supervise students as they read to provide assistance when needed.
Limitations	• Teachers often feel a loss of control, because while they work with a small group, the other students work at centers. • Teachers must locate multiple copies of appropriate leveled books for each group.

Once everyone in the group has finished reading, the students talk about the book in a **grand conversation**—sharing ideas, making connections, asking clarifying questions, and reading from the text to make a point. Teachers also use words from the book to teach and practice phonics, new vocabulary words, and reading strategies.

Sometimes students extend the reading experience through writing. Teachers design projects based on the book: Sometimes students write about a personal experience that's related to the book's events, or they write their own pattern book using a sentence stem from the book. Students also use interactive writing to create a group project. Figure 10–5 shows how guided reading lessons apply the reading process.

READING STRATEGIES.   The goal of this instructional program is to develop independent readers, and students who read independently are strategic: They can read fluently, monitor their progress, and solve problems as they arise. Students learn to use these reading strategies through guided reading lessons:

- Self-monitoring
- Checking predictions
- Decoding unfamiliar words
- Determining if a word makes sense
- Checking that the word is appropriate in the syntax of the sentence
- Using all sources of information
- Chunking phrases to read more fluently

Figure 10–5 How Guided Reading Lessons Apply the Reading Process

Stage	Activities
Prereading	Teachers build students' background knowledge, introduce vocabulary, and preview the book.
Reading	students read the entire book independently while the teacher listens to them read to monitor their progress.
Responding	students talk about the book in discussions similar to grand conversations, sharing ideas, asking questions, and making connections.
Exploring	students use the book to teach phonics, vocabulary, and reading strategies.
Applying	Sometimes students create writing projects related to the book they've read.

Teachers observe students as they read. They spend a minute or two with each reader, sitting either in front of or beside the student and watching for evidence that the student is using strategies to identify words and solve reading problems. Teachers take notes about their observations and use the information when choosing the next book for that student to read.

INSTRUCTIONAL MATERIALS.   Teachers choose leveled books for guided reading lessons that match their students' instructional reading levels. Many schools purchase grade-level kits of leveled books, such as Scholastic's Guided Reading Book Collections; these kits typically include six copies of a fiction and nonfiction book at each level. Or, teachers put together their own kits using books they've leveled themselves.

MANAGING GUIDED READING LESSONS.   Teachers organize the small-group lessons so that they work with each group three to five times a week; students who are struggling meet with the teacher more often than those reading at grade level do. The groupings are flexible because whenever teachers observe a student who's struggling or one who's moving ahead of other group members, they move that student into a more appropriate group.

While teachers are involved in guided reading lessons, the rest of the students in the classroom are involved in other literacy activities. Most teachers have students work at literacy centers that have been set up around the classroom. These centers are inviting, and students know how to work independently or cooperatively in small groups at the centers using all sorts of literacy materials, including media, books, and games. Teachers set up sign-in sheets at the centers or another accounting system to monitor students' work. Whenever possible, they enlist parents, teachers' aides, or older students to supervise the centers so they can focus on the guided reading lessons they're teaching.

2. Basal Reading Programs

Commercial reading programs, commonly called **basal readers**, have been a staple in reading instruction for 150 years starting with McGuffey Readers developed by William Holmes McGuffey in the mid-1800's. Much like today's basals, the McGuffey Readers were a series of books arranged along a gradient of difficulty designed for each grade level. The lessons featured selections that emphasized religious and patriotic values; students used phonics to sound out words, studied vocabulary words in the context of stories, and practiced proper enunciation as they read aloud to classmates. These books were widely used until the beginning of the 20th century.

The Scott Foresman reading program, introduced in 1930 and used through the 1960s, is probably the most famous basal series; the first grade textbooks featured stories about two students named Dick and Jane; their little sister, Sally; their pets, Puff and Spot; and their parents. To practice reading words, the texts relied on the repetition of words in contrived sentences such as "See Jane. See Sally. See Jane and Sally." Students were expected to memorize words rather than use phonics to decode them; this whole-word method was known as "look and say." The Scott Foresman program, which is no longer used, has been criticized for its lack of phonics instruction as well as for centering stories on an "ideal" middle-class white family.

Today's basal readers include more literature selections, celebrate diverse cultures, and emphasize an organized presentation of strategies and skills, especially phonics. Walsh (2003) reviewed five widely used series and found that they all present visually stimulating artwork to engage students' interest, employ similar methods of teaching decoding and comprehension, and provide detailed lesson plans in the teacher's guide. She also uncovered a common problem: None of the programs provide for the sustained development of background knowledge. Ignoring background knowledge is a problem, because beginning in fourth grade, students who don't have a strong foundation of world and literary knowledge have difficulty reading and understanding conceptually demanding books; this drop in achievement is known as the "fourth grade slump." Students from economically disadvantaged families are more likely to fall behind their classmates because they often have less background knowledge and are less proficient readers (Chall, Jacobs, & Baldwin, 1991).

Publishers of basal reading programs tout their textbooks as complete literacy programs containing all the materials needed for students to become successful readers. The accessibility of reading materials is one advantage: Teachers have copies of grade-level textbooks for every student. Another plus is that the instructional program is already planned: Teachers follow step-by-step directions to teach reading and assign practice materials found in workbooks that accompany the textbook. It's unrealistic, however, to assume that a textbook could be a complete literacy program. Students who read above or below grade level need reading materials at their level. In addition, students need many more opportunities to listen to books read aloud and to read and reread books than are provided in a basal reading program. An Overview of the Instructional Approach: Basal Reading Programs is presented for your review.

Teachers usually have strong feelings about textbooks—they either love or hate them. Advocates highlight these benefits:

- Instructional materials and lesson plans are supplied, which makes the teacher's job easier.
- The program is closely aligned with grade-level literacy standards.
- Students are prepared for high-stakes achievement tests because instruction focuses on grade-level standards.

Overview of the Instructional Approach Basal Reading Programs

Topic	Description
Purpose	To teach the strategies and skills that successful readers need using an organized program that includes grade-level reading selections, workbook practice assignments, and frequent testing.
Components	Basal reading programs involve five components: reading the selections in the grade-level textbook, instruction on strategies and skills, workbook assignments, independent reading opportunities, and a management plan that includes flexible grouping and regular assessment.
Theory Base	Basal reading programs are based on behaviorism because teachers provide explicit instruction and students are passive, rather than active, learners.
Applications	Basal reading programs organize instruction into units with week-long lessons that include reading, strategy and skill instruction, and workbook activities. They should be used with other instructional approaches to ensure that students read books at their instructional levels and have opportunities to participate in authentic writing activities.
Strengths	• Textbooks are aligned with grade-level standards. • Students read selections at their grade level. • Teachers teach strategies and skills sequentially, and students practice them through reading and workbook assignments. • The teacher's guide provides detailed instructions for teaching reading. • Assessment materials are included in the program.
Limitations	• Selections may be too difficult for some students and too easy for others. • Selections may lack the authenticity of good literature or may not include a variety of genres. • Programs include many workbook assignments. • Most instruction is presented to the whole class.

- Strategies and skills are clearly identified to make them easier to teach, test, and reteach.
- These programs are especially beneficial for inexperienced teachers, who are less familiar with state standards and grade-level instructional materials and procedures.

What some people tout as benefits, however, others criticize as drawbacks. Detractors argue these points:

- The instructional materials are less authentic than trade books.
- Students aren't as engaged in reading textbook selections as they are in reading trade books.
- Textbook programs don't produce in-depth learning or an appreciation of literature.
- Instruction focuses on teaching isolated strategies and skills.
- Students often spend more time completing worksheets than reading.
- Textbooks aren't appropriate for all students.

Despite these criticisms, many teachers like Mrs. Ogata use textbooks as part of their literacy programs.

Basal reading programs attempt to incorporate the reading process, although detractors point out some of the issues. For example, instruction in this approach focuses on teaching isolated strategies and skills, and workbook assignments are a poor substitute for authentic response activities. Despite this and other problems, it's possible to identify each of the five stages of the reading process, as shown in Figure 10–6.

COMPONENTS OF BASAL READING PROGRAMS.   Basal readers are recognized for their strong skills component: Teachers teach skills in a predetermined sequence, and students apply what they're learning as they read textbook selections and complete workbook assignments. They have these components:

Selections.   Basal reading programs are organized into units on topics such as challenges, folktales, and friends. Each unit consists of four to six week-long lessons, each with a featured selection. The selections in first grade textbooks contain decodable text so students can apply the phonics skills they're learning, but as students become fluent readers, textbooks transition to literature selections that were originally published as trade books. Everyone reads the same selection, no matter their reading level; publishers argue that all students should be exposed to grade-level instruction because minority students have been denied equal access in the past.

Instruction.   Teachers use basal reading programs to deliver explicit and systematic instruction that's aligned with state literacy standards. Most textbooks include instruction in phonemic awareness, phonics, high-frequency words, word-identification skills,

Figure 10–6 How Basal Reading Programs Apply the Reading Process

Stage	Activities
Prereading	Teachers activate students' background knowledge, introduce vocabulary, and preview the selection.
Reading	Students read the selection; if it's too difficult, teachers read it aloud before students read it themselves.
Responding	Teachers ask comprehension questions, and students complete workbook assignments that focus on vocabulary and comprehension.
Exploring	Teachers teach phonics, spelling, and grammar skills, and students practice skills by completing additional workbook assignments.
Applying	Students read related selections in the basal reader or in supplemental books.

spelling, grammar, and writing mechanics (capitalization and punctuation). The programs also emphasize comprehension strategies, including predicting, questioning, summarizing, and monitoring. These programs claim that it's their explicit, systematic instruction that ensures success.

Workbook Assignments.   For each selection, students complete workbook assignments before, during, and after reading to reinforce instruction; 10 to 12 workbook pages that focus on phonics, vocabulary, comprehension, grammar, spelling, and writing accompany each selection. On these pages, students write words, letters, or sentences; match words and sentences; or complete graphic organizers as they apply the concepts, strategies, and skills they're learning. Teachers vary how they use the workbook pages. Once students know how to complete a workbook page, such as those that focus on practicing spelling words, they work independently or with partners. For more challenging assignments, however, such as those dealing with a comprehension strategy or a newly introduced skill, teachers guide students as the whole class works together.

Books for Independent Reading.   Most basal reading programs include a collection of easy, on-grade-level, and challenging paperback books for students to read independently. Multiple copies of each book are available, and teachers set out some of these books for students to read after finishing each selection. Certain books, especially in the primary grades, have been written to reinforce phonics skills and vocabulary words, but others are trade books. The goal is for the collection to meet the needs of all students, but sometimes teachers still need to supplement with easier books for English learners or struggling readers.

Assessment Tools.   Basal reading programs provide a battery of tests that are aligned with state literacy standards. The tests include selection tests, unit tests, skill tests, and spelling tests that teachers administer to track students' achievement, diagnose reading problems, and report to parents and administrators. Increasingly, basal reading programs are using Web-based testing and reporting systems where teachers retrieve tests from the program's online test library and generate customized tests. Students can take these tests online, and teachers receive immediate results, pinpointing standards that students have achieved and those requiring reteaching.

PROGRAM MATERIALS.   At the center of a basal reading program is the student textbook. It's colorful and inviting, often featuring fanciful pictures of students and exciting images of animals on the cover. The selections are grouped into units, and each unit presents stories, poems, and informational articles. Many multicultural selections have been included, and illustrations usually feature ethnically diverse people. Information about authors and illustrators is provided for many selections.

Commercial reading programs provide a variety of materials to support students' learning. Consumable workbooks are well known; students write letters, words, and sentences to practice phonics, comprehension, and vocabulary strategies and skills. Big books and kits with letter and word cards, wall charts, and manipulatives are available for preschool, kindergarten, and first grade classrooms. CDs, DVDs, and online resources are included, and some programs offer online versions of their textbooks. First and second grade collections of paperback books have decodable text to provide practice on phonics skills and high-frequency words; supplemental paperbacks for third and fourth grades are related to unit topics.

Teachers receive multiple management tools along with basal reading programs. The teacher's guide is an oversize instructional manual that provides comprehensive information about how to plan lessons, teach the selections, differentiate instruction, and assess students' progress. The selections are shown in reduced size in the guidebook, and background information about each selection, instructions for reading it, and ideas for coordinating skill and strategy instruction are included. Online lesson planners are available that teachers download and use to develop schedules, organize instruction, and coordinate their lessons with state standards. Most programs include handbooks that provide in-depth information about differentiating instruction, strengthening home–school connections, and teaching test-taking skills. In addition, publishers of basal reading programs provide in-service training for teachers.

MANAGING A BASAL READING PROGRAM.   Many teachers find that basal reading programs make teaching easier because detailed lesson plans are available in the teacher's guide, and assessment is less time-consuming because of the tests available at the publisher's website. Teachers use online lesson planners to plan for instruction and coordinate their daily lessons with grade-level literacy standards. They check the teacher's guide for suggestions about pacing each unit, ideas for flexible grouping, and ways to monitor students' learning. Some teachers, however, are frustrated with basal readers because they provide few opportunities to customize instruction and because they reflect a teacher-centered approach to instruction.

3. Literature Focus Units

Teachers teach **literature focus units** featuring popular and award-winning stories, informational books, or books of poetry. Some literature focus units feature a single book, but others feature several books for an author study or a genre unit. Teachers guide students through the reading process as they read and respond to a book; Figure 10–7 shows how this instructional approach applies the reading process. The emphasis in literature focus units is on teaching students about literature, but teachers include lessons on vocabulary and comprehension in the unit. An overview of literature focus units is presented here.

DEVELOPING A UNIT.   Teachers develop a literature focus unit through a series of steps, beginning with choosing the literature and setting goals; then identifying and scheduling activities; and, finally, deciding how to assess students' learning. Effective teachers don't simply follow directions in literature focus unit planning guides available in school supply stores; rather, they do the planning themselves because they're the ones who are most knowledgeable about their students, the time available, the strategies and skills they need to teach, and the activities they want to develop. Teachers follow these steps:

Step 1: Select the literature.   Teachers select the book—a story, an informational book, or a book of poetry—for the unit and collect copies for each student. Many schools have class sets of books available; however, sometimes teachers must ask administrators to purchase multiple copies or buy books themselves. They collect one or two copies of 10 or more related books for the text set, too, including different versions of the story,

Figure 10–7 How Literature Focus Units Apply the Reading Process

Stage	Activities
Prereading	Teachers involve students in activities to build background knowledge and interest them in reading the book.
Reading	Students read the book independently or with a partner, or the teacher reads it aloud or uses shared reading.
Responding	Students participate in grand conversations to talk about the book and write entries in reading logs.
Exploring	Teachers teach vocabulary, phonics, and comprehension in minilessons. Students also research the book's author or related topics.
Applying	Students create oral and written projects and share them with their classmates.

sequels, additional books by the same author, or other books in the same genre, and place them on a special shelf in the classroom library. Teachers introduce the text set and then provide opportunities for students to read the books. In addition, they assemble book boxes of artifacts to use in introducing the featured book, information about the author and the illustrator, and other supplemental materials. Teachers also locate multimedia resources, including CDs of the featured selection, DVDs to provide background knowledge, and author and illustrator websites.

Step 2: Set goals.   Teachers decide what they want students to learn during the unit, and they connect their goals with Common Core State Standards or other literacy standards.

Step 3: Develop a unit plan.   Teachers read the selected book and choose the focus for the unit—for example, an element of story structure, the author or genre, or a related topic, such as weather or desert life. Next, teachers choose activities to use at each stage, often jotting notes on a chart divided into sections for the corresponding stage; then they use the ideas they've brainstormed as they plan the unit. Generally, not all activities will be used, but teachers select the most appropriate ones according to their focus and the available time.

Step 4: Differentiate instruction.   Teachers think about the activities they'll use to teach the unit and how to adapt them to ensure that every student can be successful. They decide how to use grouping, tiered activities, centers, and projects to accommodate students' learning differences.

Step 5: Create a time schedule.   Teachers create a schedule that provides sufficient time for students to move through the reading process and to complete the activities planned for the unit. They also plan **minilessons** to teach the strategies and skills identified in their goals and those needed for students to be successful. Teachers usually have a set time for minilessons in their weekly schedule, but sometimes they arrange their schedules to teach minilessons just before they introduce specific activities.

Step 6: Assess students' learning.   Teachers often distribute unit folders in which students store all their work; keeping all the materials together makes the unit easier for both students and teachers to manage. Teachers also plan ways to document students' learning and assign grades. One type of record keeping is an assignment checklist, which is developed with students and distributed at the beginning of the unit. Students keep track of their work, and sometimes negotiate to change the checklist as the unit evolves. They file the checklists in their unit folders and mark off each item as it's completed. At the end of the unit, students turn in their assignment checklist and other completed work. Although this list doesn't include every activity, it identifies those that will be graded. Review the Overview of the Instructional Approach: Literature Focus Units to see how it differs from other literacy programs.

UNITS FEATURING A BOOK.   Teachers choose award-winning and other high-quality books for literature focus units. Young students read predictable picture books or books with very little text, such as *Rosie's Walk* (Hutchins, 2005), a humorous story about a hen who walks leisurely around the barnyard, unwittingly leading the fox who is following her into one mishap after another. Other students read more sophisticated picture-book stories and novels, such as *Train to Somewhere* (Bunting, 2000), a story about an orphan train taking children to adoptive families in the West in the late 1800s, and *Bunnicula: A Rabbit-Tale of Mystery* (Howe & Howe, 2006), a hilarious story about a bunny that might be a vampire.

Overview of the Instructional Approach Literature Focus Units

Topic	Description
Purpose	To teach reading through literature, using high-quality, grade-appropriate trade books.
Components	Teachers involve students in three activities: Students read and respond to a book together as a class; the teacher teaches mini-lessons on phonics, vocabulary, and comprehension using the book they're reading; and students create projects to extend their understanding.
Theory Base	Literature focus units represent a transition between teacher-centered and student-centered learning, because the teacher guides students as they read a book. This approach reflects information-processing theory because teachers develop students' background knowledge, read aloud when students can't read fluently, and teach vocabulary and comprehension. It also reflects both Rosenblatt's (2005) transactional theory, because students participate in grand conversations and write in reading logs, and her critical literacy theory, because issues of social justice often arise in trade books.
Applications	Teachers teach units featuring a trade book, generally using books on a district-approved list, or units featuring a genre or author. Literature focus units are often alternated with another approach where students read books at their own reading levels.
Strengths	• Teachers select award-winning literature for these units. • Teachers scaffold students' comprehension as they read with the class or small groups. • Teachers teach minilessons on reading strategies and skills. • Students learn vocabulary through word walls and other activities. • Students learn about genres, story structure, and literary devices.
Limitations	• All students read the same book even if they don't like it and regardless of whether it's at their reading level. • Many activities are teacher directed.

UNITS FEATURING A GENRE OR AN AUTHOR.   Teachers teach about a particular genre, such as folktales, science fiction, or biographies, in a genre unit. Students read several books illustrating the genre, participate in a variety of activities to deepen their knowledge about the genre's text factors, and sometimes apply what they've learned through a writing project. For example, after reading and comparing Cinderella tales from around the world, third graders often create picture books to retell their favorite version.

During an author study, students learn about an author's life and read one or more books he or she has written. Most contemporary authors have set up websites to share information about themselves and their books, and each year more authors are writing autobiographies. As students learn about authors, they develop a concept of "author"; this awareness is important so that students will think of them as real people who eat breakfast, ride bikes, and take out the garbage, just as they do. When students think of authors as real people, they view reading in a more personal way. This awareness also carries over to their writing: Students gain a new perspective as they realize that they, too, can write books. Figure 10–8 presents a list of recommended authors for author studies; the list is divided into grade levels, but many authors write books that are appropriate for students at more than one level.

Figure 10–8 Recommended Authors for Author Studies

Prek and Kindergarten	First and Second Grades	Third and Fourth Grades
Ashley Bryan	Jan Brett	Eve Bunting
Eric Carle	Doreen Cronin	Joanna Cole
Donald Crews	Denise Fleming	Gail Gibbons
Tomie dePaola	Steven Kellogg	Patricia MacLachlan
Arthur Dorros	Patricia McKissack	Mary Pope Osborne
Dr. Seuss	Barbara Park	Jack Prelutsky
Lois Ehlert	Patricia Polacco	Pam Muñoz Ryan
Denise Fleming	Jon Scieszka	Jon Scieszka
Kevin Henkes	Janet Stevens	Chris Van Allsburg
Mo Willems	Jane Yolen	David Wiesner

MANAGING A LITERATURE FOCUS UNIT.   Although many teachers love teaching their favorite books in literature focus units, this instructional approach requires them to invest time and energy to plan the unit. Teachers read and analyze the books they've chosen and plan for instruction, including minilessons, vocabulary activities, and writing assignments. They need to connect what they're teaching to grade-level standards and differentiate instruction so that all students can be successful.

Timing is another issue. Usually literature focus units featuring a picture book are completed in one week, and those featuring a chapter book are completed in two or three weeks. Genre and author units often last three or four weeks. Rarely, if ever, do literature focus units continue for more than a month; when teachers drag out a unit, they risk killing students' interest in that particular book or, worse yet, their interest in literature and reading.

In addition, teachers must decide how to balance teaching literature with teaching reading, especially if some students can't read the books selected for the units. Teachers often hold daily guided reading lessons during a literature focus unit so that students receive instruction and have opportunities to read books at their level.

4. Literature Circles

One of the best ways to nurture students' love of reading and ensure that they become lifelong readers is through literature circles—small, student-led book-discussion groups that meet regularly in the classroom (Daniels, 2002). The reading materials are quality books of students' literature, including stories, poems, biographies, and other informational books; what matters most is that students are reading something that interests them and is manageable. Students choose the books to read and form temporary groups. Next, they set a reading and discussion schedule. Then they read independently or with partners and come together to talk about their reading in discussions that are like **grand conversations**. Generally, the group meets independently, but sometimes the teacher meets with the group. A literature circle on one book may last from several days to a week or two, depending on the length of the book and the age of the students. Students use all five stages in the reading process; Figure 10–9 shows how this instructional approach incorporates the reading process.

MyLab Education
Video Example 10.5
First grade teacher Michelle Kern completes a literature focus unit on Gail Gibbon's book, *Deserts*. What culminating activity did Ms. Kern ask students to engage in to complete the unit?

FEATURES OF LITERATURE CIRCLES.   The key features of literature circles are *choice*, *literature*, and *response*:

Choice.   Students make many choices in literature circles. They choose the books they'll read and the groups they'll participate in. They share in setting the schedule for reading and discussing the book, and they choose the roles they assume in the discussions. They also choose how they'll share the book with classmates. Teachers structure

Figure 10–9 How Literature Circles Apply the Reading Process

Stage	Activities
Prereading	Students choose books to read, form groups, and get ready to read by making schedules and choosing roles.
Reading	Students read the book independently or with a partner according to the schedule, and prepare for the group meetings.
Responding	Students complete their role assignments and participate actively in discussions about the book.
Exploring	Teachers teach minilessons about literature circle procedures and reader and text factors.
Applying	Students give brief presentations to the class about the books they've read.

literature circles so that students have these opportunities, but even more important, they prepare students for making choices by creating a community of learners in their classrooms in which students assume responsibility for their learning and can work collaboratively with classmates.

Literature. The books chosen for literature circles should be interesting to students and at their reading level. The books must seem manageable, especially during students' first literature circles. Samway and Whang (1996) recommend choosing shorter books or picture books at first so that students don't become bogged down. It's also important that teachers have read and liked the books, because otherwise, they won't be able to do convincing **book talks** when they introduce them. In addition, they won't be able to contribute to the book discussions.

Response. Students meet to discuss the book. Through these discussions, students summarize their reading, make connections, learn vocabulary, and explore the author's use of text factors. They learn that comprehension develops in layers. From an initial comprehension gained during reading, students deepen their understanding through the subsequent discussions. They learn to return to the text to reread sentences and paragraphs in order to clarify a point or state an opinion. Literature circles are effective because of these three key features. As students read and discuss books with classmates, they often become more engaged in reading and literature than they do in more teacher-directed approaches. Use the Overview of the Instructional Approach: Literature Circles to compare literature focus units or other literacy programs.

DISCUSSION ROLES. Sometimes teachers have students assume roles and complete assignments in preparation for discussion group meetings (Daniels, 2002). One student is the discussion director; he or she assumes the leadership role and directs the discussion, choosing topics and formulating questions to guide the group. The other students prepare by selecting a passage to read aloud, drawing a picture or making a graphic related to the book, or investigating a topic connected to the book. The roles are detailed in Figure 10–10. Although having students assume specific roles may seem artificial, it teaches them about the ways they can respond to literature.

Figure 10–10 Roles Students' Play in Literature Circles

Role	Responsibilities
Discussion Director	The discussion director guides the group's discussion and keeps the group on task. To get the discussion started or to redirect it, the student may ask: • What did the reading make you think of? • What questions do you have about the reading? • What do you predict will happen next?
Passage Master	The passage master focuses on the literary merits of the book. This student chooses several memorable passages to share with the group and tells why each one was chosen.
Word Wizard	The word wizard focuses on vocabulary. This student identifies several important or unfamiliar words from the reading, checks their meaning in a dictionary, and shares the information about the words with the group.
Connector	The connector makes links between the book and group members' lives, school and neighborhood happenings, historical events, or other books by the same author or on the same topic.
Summarizer	The summarizer prepares a brief summary of the reading to convey the big ideas. This student often begins the discussion by reading the summary aloud to the group.
Illustrator	The illustrator draws a picture or diagram related to the reading and shares it with the group.
Investigator	The investigator locates some information about the book, the author, or a related topic to share with the group

Overview of the Instructional Approach Literature Circles

Topic	Description
Purpose	To provide students with opportunities for authentic reading and response.
Components	Students form literature circles to read and discuss books that they choose themselves. They often assume roles for the book discussions.
Theory Base	Literature circles reflect sociolinguistic, transactional, and critical literacy theories: Students work in small, supportive groups to read and discuss books, and the books they read often involve cultural and social issues that require students to think critically.
Applications	Teachers often use literature circles in conjunction with a basal reading program or with literature focus units so students have opportunities to do independent reading.
Strengths	• Books are available at a variety of reading levels.
	• Students are more strongly motivated because they choose the books they read.
	• Students have opportunities to work with their classmates.
	• Students participate in authentic literacy experiences.
	• Students learn how to respond to literature.
	• Teachers may participate in discussions to help students clarify misunderstandings and think more critically about the book.
Limitations	• Teachers often feel a loss of control because students are reading different books.
	• Students must be task oriented and use time wisely to be successful.
	• Sometimes students choose books that are too difficult or too easy for them.

IMPLEMENTING LITERATURE CIRCLES.   Teachers organize literature circles using a six-step series of activities:

Step 1: Select books.   Teachers prepare text sets with five or six related titles and collect copies of each book. They give a brief book talk to introduce the books, and then students sign up for the one they want to read. Students need time to preview the books, and then they decide what to read after considering the topic and the difficulty level.

Step 2: Form literature circles.   Students get together to read each book; usually no more than four to six participate in a group. They begin by setting a schedule for reading and discussing the book within the time limits set by the teacher. Students also choose discussion roles so that they can prepare for the discussion after reading.

Step 3: Read the book.   Students read all or part of the book independently or with a partner, depending on the book's reading level. Afterward, they prepare for the discussion by doing the assignment for the role they assumed.

Step 4: Participate in a discussion.   Students meet to talk about the book; these discussions usually last about 15 to 20 minutes. The discussion director or another student who's been chosen as the leader begins the discussion, and then classmates continue as they do in grand conversations. The talk is meaningful because students talk about what interests them in the book, and they share their responses according to their roles.

Step 5: Teach minilessons.   Teachers teach minilessons before or after group meetings on various topics, including asking insightful questions, completing role sheets, using comprehension strategies, and examining text factors (Daniels & Steineke, 2004).

Step 6: Share with the class.   Students in each literature circle share the book they've read with their classmates through a book talk or another presentation.

USING LITERATURE CIRCLES WITH YOUNG STUDENTS.   First and second graders can meet in small groups to read and discuss books just as older, more experienced readers do (Frank, Dixon, & Brandts, 2001; Marriott, 2002; Martinez-Roldan & Lopez-Robertson, 1999/2000). These young students choose books at their reading levels, listen to the teacher read a book aloud, or participate in a **shared reading** activity. They benefit from listening to a book read aloud two times or reading it themselves several times before participating in the discussion. In preparation for the literature circle, students often draw or write reading log entries to share with the group. Students meet with the teacher to talk about a book; the teacher guides the discussion at first and models how to share ideas and to participate in a discussion. The talk is meaningful because students share what interests them in the book; make text-to-self, text-to-world, and text-to-text connections; point out illustrations and other book features; ask questions; and discuss themes. Young students don't usually assume roles as older students do, but second and third graders are often ready to take on leadership roles. While one literature circle meets with the teacher, the other students in the classroom are usually reading books or preparing for their upcoming literature circle meeting with the teacher.

MANAGING LITERATURE CIRCLES.   When teachers introduce literature circles, they teach students how to participate in small-group discussions and respond to literature. At first, many teachers participate in discussions, but they step back as students become comfortable with the procedures and engaged in the discussions. Unfortunately, groups don't always work well: Sometimes conversations get off track because students are disruptive, monopolize the discussion, or exclude certain classmates. If this happens, teachers must work to develop positive relationships among group members and build more effective discussion skills. Study the Overview of the Instructional Approach: Literature Circles and compare it to overviews of other literacy programs.

5. Reading Workshop

Nancie Atwell introduced reading workshop in 1987 as an alternative to traditional reading instruction. Students do authentic and independent reading, and teachers present minilessons on reading concepts, strategies, and procedures during reading workshop (Atwell, 1998). This approach represented a change in what teachers believe about how students learn and how literature should be used in the classroom: Traditional reading programs emphasized dependence on a teacher's guide to determine how and when particular strategies and skills should be taught, but reading workshop is an individualized reading program. Atwell developed reading workshop with her middle school students, but it's been adapted and used successfully in first through fourth grades. An Overview of the Instructional Approach: Reading Workshop is shown here. Compare it to other literacy programs.

Overview of the Instructional Approach Reading Workshop

Topic	Description
Purpose	To provide students with opportunities for authentic reading activities.
Components	Reading workshop involves reading, responding, sharing, teaching minilessons, and reading aloud to students.
Theory Base	The workshop approach reflects sociolinguistic and information-processing theories: Students participate in authentic activities that encourage them to become lifelong readers.
Applications	Teachers often use reading workshop in conjunction with a basal reading program or with literature focus units so students have opportunities to do independent reading.
Strengths	• Students read books at their reading levels. • Students choose books that they want to read. • Activities are authentic and student-directed. • Teachers have opportunities to work individually with students.
Limitations	• Teachers often feel a loss of control because students are reading different books. • Teachers have to design and teach minilessons on strategies and skills. • Students must be task oriented and use time wisely to be successful.

Reading workshop fosters real reading of self-selected books using the reading process; Figure 10–11 shows how this instructional approach applies the reading process. Students read hundreds of books during reading workshop. At the first grade level, students might read or reread three or four books each day, totaling close to a thousand books during the school year; older students read fewer, longer books. Even so, fourth grade teachers report that their students read 20 to 25 books during the school year. Kindergarten teachers can also implement reading workshop in their classrooms (Cunningham & Shagoury, 2005); even though they do more of the reading themselves, teachers involve five-year-olds in authentic literacy experiences and teach them about comprehension strategies and text factors.

COMPONENTS OF READING WORKSHOP. There are several versions of reading workshop, but all of them contain five components—*reading, responding, sharing, minilessons,* and *teacher read-alouds*:

Reading.   Students spend 30 to 60 minutes independently reading books. They choose the books they read, often reading series books or using recommendations from classmates. It's crucial that students be able to read the books they choose.

Responding.   Students keep reading logs in which they write their initial impressions about the books they're reading. Sometimes they dialogue with the teacher about their book; journals allow for ongoing written conversation between the teacher and individual students. Responses often demonstrate students' reading strategies and offer insights into their thinking about literature; seeing how students think about their reading helps teachers guide their learning. Teachers collect students' reading logs periodically to monitor their entries. They write back and forth with students; however, because responding to students' journals is very time-consuming, teachers keep their responses brief and don't respond to every entry.

Sharing.   For the last 15 minutes of reading workshop, the class gathers together to discuss books they've finished reading. Students talk about a book and why they liked it. Sometimes they read a brief excerpt aloud or pass the book to a classmate who wants to read it. Sharing is important because it helps students become a community to value and celebrate each other's accomplishments.

Minilessons.   The teacher also spends 5 to 15 minutes teaching minilessons on reading workshop procedures, comprehension strategies, and text factors. Sometimes minilessons are taught to the whole class, and at other times, they're taught to small groups. At the beginning of the school year, teachers teach minilessons to the whole class on

Figure 10–11 How Reading Workshop Applies the Reading Process

Stage	Activities
Prereading	Students choose books at their reading level and activate background knowledge by examining the cover or thinking about what they know about the author.
Reading	Students read the book independently, at their own pace, while classmates are reading independently, too.
Responding	Students talk about the book they're reading in conferences with the teacher, and sometimes they write in reading logs.
Exploring	Teachers teach minilessons about reader and text factors.
Applying	Sometimes students celebrate having completed the book by giving a book talk to a group of classmates and then pass the book off to a classmate who's interested in reading it.

choosing books to read and other reading workshop procedures; later in the year, they teach minilessons on drawing inferences and other comprehension strategies and text factors. Teachers teach minilessons on particular authors when they introduce their books to the whole class, and on literary genres when they set out collections of books representing a genre in the classroom library.

Teacher Read-Alouds.   Teachers use the **interactive read-aloud** procedure to read picture books and chapter books to the class as part of reading workshop. They choose high-quality literature that students might not be able to read themselves, award-winning books that they believe every student should be exposed to, or books that relate to a thematic unit. After reading, students talk about the book and share the reading experience. This activity is important because students listen to a book read aloud and respond to it together as a community of learners, not as individuals.

MANAGING A WORKSHOP CLASSROOM.   Teachers establish the workshop environment in their classrooms, beginning on the first day of the school year. They provide time for students to read and teach them how to choose and respond to books. Through their interactions with students, the respect they show them, and the way they model reading, teachers establish a community of learners.

Teachers develop a schedule for reading workshop with time allocated for each component, as shown in Figure 10–12. In their schedules, teachers allot as much time as possible for students to read. After developing the schedule, teachers post it in the classroom and talk with students about the activities and their expectations. They teach the workshop procedures and continue to model them until students become comfortable with the routines. As students gain experience with the workshop approach, their enthusiasm grows and the workshop is successful.

Teachers take time during reading workshop to observe students as they work together in small groups. Researchers report that some students, even as young as first graders, are excluded from group activities because of their sex, gender, ethnicity, or economic status (Henkin, 1995). Teachers should work to foster a classroom environment where students treat each other equitably.

MyLab Education Self-Check 10.3

Figure 10–12 Schedules for Reading Workshop

First Grade	
10 min.	The teacher rereads several familiar big books and then reads aloud a new big book.
15 min.	Students read matching small books independently and reread other familiar books.
10 min.	Students choose one of the books they've read or reread during independent reading to draw and write about.
10 min.	
15 min.	Several students share their favorite book.
	The teacher teaches a minilesson.

Second Grade	
30 min.	Students read self-selected books and respond to them in reading logs.
10 min.	Students share with classmates books they've finished reading and do informal book talks about
20 min.	them. They often pass the "good" books to classmates who want to read them next.
30 min.	The teacher teaches a minilesson.
	The teacher reads aloud, and afterward, Students participate in a grand conversation.

Fourth Grade	
20 min.	Students read self-selected books independently.
20 min.	The teacher reads a novel aloud, and students talk about it in a grand conversation.
10 min.	The teacher teaches a minilesson using the read-aloud book as a mentor text.
20 min.	Students read self-selected books independently, applying the strategy or skill the teacher taught in
10 min.	the minilesson.
	Students talk about the books they're reading and how they used the strategy or skill taught in the minilesson.

Chapter Review

Scaffolding Students' Reading Development

- Teachers use the reading process—*prereading, reading, responding, exploring,* and *applying*—to ensure that students comprehend the books they read.

- Teachers teach reading strategies and skills to ensure that students become capable readers.

- Teachers use a combination of instructional approaches to provide effective literacy instruction, because they understand that no single approach is a complete program.

Accountability Check

Visit the following assessment links to access quiz questions and instructional applications.

MyLab Education Application Exercise 10.2: Understanding Literacy Development
MyLab Education Application Education 10.3: Understanding Literacy Development
MyLab Education Application Education 10.4: Understanding Literacy Development
MyLab Education Application Exercise 10.5: Monitoring Literacy Development
MyLab Education Application Exercise 10.6: Measuring Literacy Development

References

Afflerbach, P., Pearson, P. D., & Paris, S. G. (2011). Clarifying differences between reading skills and strategies. *The Reading Teacher, 61,* 364–373.

Angelillo, J. (2008). *Whole-class teaching: Minilessons and more.* Portsmouth, NH: Heinemann.

Atwell, N. (1998). *In the middle: New understandings about reading and writing with adolescents* (2nd ed.). Upper Montclair, NJ: Boynton/Cook.

Blanton, W. E., Wood, K. D., & Moorman, G. B. (1990). The role of purpose in reading instruction. *The Reading Teacher, 43,* 486–493.

Braunger, J., & Lewis, J. P. (2006). *Building a knowledge base in reading* (2nd ed.). Newark, DE: International Reading Association/National Council of Teachers of English.

Bunting, E. (2000). *Train to somewhere.* New York: Clarion Books.

Cappellini, M. (2005). *Balancing reading and language learning: A resource for teaching English language learners, K–5.* York, ME: Stenhouse.

Chall, J. S., Jacobs, V. A., & Baldwin, L. E. (1991). *The reading crisis: Why poor children fall behind.* Cambridge, MA: Harvard University Press.

Cole, J. (1986). *Hungry, hungry sharks.* New York: Random House.

Common core state standards for English language arts. (2010). Retrieved from http://www.corestandards.org/ELA-Literacy/

Cooney, B. (1985). *Miss Rumphius.* New York: Puffin Books.

Cunningham, A., & Shagoury, R. (2005). *Starting with comprehension: Reading strategies for the youngest learners.* Portland, ME: Stenhouse.

Daniels, H. (2002). *Literature circles: Voice and choice in book clubs and reading groups.* York, ME: Stenhouse.

Daniels, H., & Steineke, N. (2004). *Mini-lessons for literature circles.* Portsmouth, NH: Heinemann.

Dowhower, S. L. (1999). Supporting a strategic stance in the classroom: A comprehension framework for helping teachers help students' to be strategic. *The Reading Teacher, 52,* 672–688.

Fisher, D., Flood, J., Lapp, D., & Frey, N. (2011). Interactive read-alouds: Is there a common set of implementation practices? *The Reading Teacher, 58,* 8–17.

Fountas, I. C., & Pinnell, G. S. (2016). *Guided reading: Good first teaching for all children.* Portsmouth, NH: Heinemann.

Frank, C. R., Dixon, C. N., & Brandts, L. R. (2001). Bears, trolls, and pagemasters: Learning about learners in book clubs. *The Reading Teacher, 54,* 448–462.

Friedland, E. S., & Truesdell, K. S. (2004). Kids reading together. *The Reading Teacher, 58,* 76–83.

Gibbons, G. (1997). *Nature's green umbrella.* New York: HarperCollins.

Henkin, R. (1995). Insiders and outsiders in first-grade writing workshops: Gender and equity issues. *Language Arts, 72,* 429–434.

Hill, E. (2003). *Where's Spot?* New York: Puffin Books.

Holdaway, D. (1979). *The foundations of literacy.* Portsmouth, NH: Heinemann.

Howe, D., & Howe, J. (2006). *Bunnicula: A rabbit-tale of mystery.* New York: Aladdin Books.

Hutchins, P. (2005). *Rosie's walk.* New York: Aladdin Books.

Lee, C. (2004). *Good dog, Paw!* Cambridge, MA: Candlewick Press.

Marriott, D. (2002). *Comprehension right from the start: How to organize and manage book clubs for young readers.* Portsmouth, NH: Heinemann.

Martinez-Roldan, C. M., & Lopez-Robertson, J. M. (1999/2000). Initiating literature circles in a first grade bilingual classroom. *The Reading Teacher, 53,* 270–281.

McClure, E. L., & Fullerton, S. K. (2017). Instructional interactions: Supporting students' reading development through interactive read-alouds of informational texts. *The Reading Teacher, 71*(1), 51–59.

Meddaugh, S. (1995). *Martha speaks.* Boston: Houghton Mifflin.

National Reading Panel. (2000). *Teaching children to read: An evidence-based assessment of the scientific research literature on reading and its implications for reading instruction.* Washington, DC: National Institute of Child Health and Human Development.

Ohlhausen, M. M., & Jepsen, M. (1992). Lessons from Goldilocks: "Somebody's been choosing my books but I can make my own choices now!" *The New Advocate, 5,* 31–46.

Parkes, B. (2000). *Read it again! Revisiting shared reading.* Portland, ME: Stenhouse.

Peterson, R., & Eeds, M. (2007). *Grand conversations: Literature groups in action.* New York: Scholastic.

Rasinski, T. V. (2003). *The fluent reader.* New York: Scholastic.

Reutzel, D. R., & Fawson, P. C. (1990). Traveling tales: Connecting parents and students' in writing. *The Reading Teacher, 44,* 222–227.

Rosenblatt, L. (2005). *Making meaning with texts: Selected essays.* Portsmouth, NH: Heinemann.

Samway, K. D., & Whang, G. (1996). *Literature study circles in a multicultural classroom.* York, ME: Stenhouse.

Taback, S. (2004). *This is the house that Jack built.* New York: Puffin Books.

Walsh, K. (2003, Spring). Basal readers: The lost opportunity to build the knowledge that propels comprehension. *American Educator, 27,* 24–27.

Wells, R. (2005). *McDuff's wild romp.* New York: Hyperion Books.

Whang, G., Samway, K. D., & Pippitt, M. (1995). *Buddy reading: Cross-age tutoring in a multicultural school.* Portsmouth, NH: Heinemann.

Wilhelm, J. D. (2001). *Improving comprehension with think-aloud strategies.* New York: Scholastic.

Yaden, D. B., Jr. (1988). Understanding stories through repeated read-alouds: How many does it take? *The Reading Teacher, 41,* 556–560.

Chapter 11
Scaffolding Students' Writing Development

⌄ Learning Outcomes

After studying this chapter, you'll be prepared to:

11.1 Describe the five stages in the writing process.

11.2 Discuss how to teach writing using the six traits.

11.3 Explain how to assess students' writing development.

11.4 Describe three ways to implement the writing process in classrooms.

Participating in Writing Workshop

Wavebreakmedia/Shutterstock

The 20 first graders in Mrs. Albers' class participate in writing workshop from 10:20 to 11:30. Here's the schedule:

> 10:20–10:40 Shared reading/minilesson
>
> 10:40–11:15 Writing and conferencing with Mrs. Albers
>
> 11:15–11:30 Author's chair

Mrs. Albers devotes more than an hour each morning to writing workshop because she wants her students to have time to talk about their experiences, extend their vocabulary, and manipulate basic English syntactic patterns through writing and talking. Many of these five- and six-year-olds are English learners whose parents or grandparents immigrated to the United States from Southeast Asia and who speak Hmong, Khmer, or Lao at home; they're learning to speak English as they learn to read and write in English.

Writing workshop begins with a 20-minute whole-class meeting. Mrs. Albers either reads a big book using the **shared reading** procedures or teaches a **minilesson**, often using as an example something from the big book she has read previously. Yesterday, Mrs. Albers read *An Egg Is an Egg* (Weiss, 1990), an informational book about egg-laying animals. After reading the big book twice, Mrs. Albers and the students talked about animals that lay eggs and those that don't.

Today, Mrs. Albers rereads *An Egg Is an Egg*, and the students join in to read familiar words. Afterward, she reads the book again, asking the students to look for words on each page with *ou* and *ow* spellings. In a previous minilesson, Mrs. Albers explained that usually these spellings are pronounced /ou/ as in *ouch*, but sometimes *ow* is pronounced /ō/ as in *snow*, and they began a chart of words with each spelling or pronunciation. The first graders locate several more words and write them on their chart. After they add the new words from the big book, Boupha (bo-fa) writes *hour* and Leticia writes *found*, words they noticed in books they were reading. The students practice reading the lists of words together, and Beso reads the lists by himself. He smiles proudly as his classmates clap. Now the chart looks like this:

ou	ow	ow (long o)
loud	clown	low
sound	brown	blowing
cloud	down	tow
outside	town	slowly
flour	flower	sown
around	tower	snows
shout	now	
hour		
found		

In this chapter, you'll read about the writing process. Like the reading process, this essential process has five stages. As you read this vignette, notice how Mrs. Albers uses the writing process as her first graders participate in writing workshop. Try to pick out the stages: *prewriting, drafting, revising, editing,* and *publishing.*

Mrs. Albers quickly reviews the class's guidelines for writing because two students have recently joined the class, and she has noticed that some of the other students aren't on task during the writing and conferencing period. The class's guidelines for writing are posted on a chart that the students wrote using **interactive writing** earlier in the school year. Mrs. Albers rereads each guideline and then asks a student to explain it in his or her own words. Here's the class's list:

1. **Think about your story.**
2. **Draw pictures on a storyboard.**
3. **Write words by the pictures.**
4. **Tell your story to one editor.**
5. **Write your story.**
6. **Read your story to two editors.**
7. **Illustrate your story.**
8. **Publish your story.**

The second part of writing workshop is writing and conferencing. The students use a process approach to write personal narratives, stories about their families and pets, and events in their lives. To begin, the students plan their stories using storyboards, sheets of paper divided into four, six, or eight blocks. (Note that these are different from **story boards**, described in the Compendium.) They sketch a drawing in each numbered block and then add a word or two to describe the picture. Next, they use their storyboards to tell their stories to one of five first graders serving as editors that day; today's editors are Pauline, Lily, Mai, Destiny, and Khammala. It's easy to recognize the editors in Mrs. Albers's classroom because they're wearing neon-colored plastic visors with the word "Editor" printed on them.

Check Your Work!

Does the story make sense?	☑	☑
Punctuation marks	☑	☑
Capital letters	☑	☑
Spelling	☑	☑

My editors are:

Lily _____   Mai _____

After this rehearsal, the students write their stories using one sheet of paper for each block on their planning sheets. Next, they read their writing to two editors, who often ask the student to add more detail or to insert a word or phrase that has been omitted. Then the students draw and color a picture to complement and extend the words on each page. Sometimes they add a cover and title page and staple their stories together, and at other times, they turn in their drafts for the bilingual aide in the classroom to word process.

Students complete an editing sheet when they share their writing with the two classmates who are serving as editors; a copy of the editing sheet is shown here. The author writes his or her name and the title of the story at the top of the sheet. The editors check off each box as they read their classmate's story and then sign their names at the bottom of the page. Mrs. Albers often calls herself their third editor, and the students know that they must complete this editing sheet with two classmates before they ask her to review their writing.

Mrs. Albers has divided the class into five conference groups, and she meets with one group each day while the other students are working on their stories. The students bring their writing folders to the conference table and talk with Mrs. Albers about their work. They're working at different stages of the writing process.

The teacher begins by asking the students to each explain what they're writing about and where they are in the writing process. Then she examines each student's storyboard or writing and offers compliments, asks questions, and provides feedback about the student's work. She also makes notes about each student's progress.

Today, she's meeting with Lily, Beso, Dalany, and Matthew. Lily begins by showing Mrs. Albers her storyboard for a story about her cousin's birthday. She has developed eight blocks for her story, and she talks about each one, working to express her ideas in a sentence or two. Mrs. Albers praises Lily for tackling such a long story and for including a beginning, middle, and end. She encourages Lily to begin writing, and a week later, Lily completes her book and shares it with her classmates. Here is Lily's published story, "My Cousin's Birthday":

Page 1 **This is my cousin's birthday.**

Page 2 **I bought her a present.**

Page 3 **I have clothes for her present.**

Page 4 **She makes a wish on her birthday cake.**

Page 5 **We eat cake.**

Page 6 **We play games.**

Page 7 **My cousin is happy.**

Page 8 **We went to sleep.**

Next, Mrs. Albers turns to Beso, who says that he's working on a storyboard for a story about his grandmother's cat, but he can't find it. Mrs. Albers checks her notes and recalls that Beso couldn't find his storyboard for the same story last week, so she asks him to get a new storyboard and start again. They talk out the story together. Beso wants to describe what his grandmother's cat looks like and then tell all the things that she can do. He begins drawing a picture in the first block while Mrs. Albers watches. After he draws the picture, Mrs. Albers will help him add one or two key words in the block, then she'll help him do a second block. Mrs. Albers plans to keep Beso close to her for a few days to ensure that he completes the storyboard and writes his story.

Next, Mrs. Albers turns her attention to Matthew, who's finishing his ninth book, "The Soccer Game." He reads it to Mrs. Albers:

Page 1 **Me and my friends play soccr.**

Page 2 **I won a trophe.**

Page 3 **I won another point.**

Page 4 **I played at the soccr field.**

Page 5 **I won again.**

Page 6 **I went home.**

Then they read it over again, and Mrs. Albers helps him correct the spelling of *trophy* and *soccer* and correct several letters that were printed backward. He also shows her his editing sheet, which indicates that he had already edited his story with Pauline and Sammy serving as his editors. Matthew says that he wants to finish the book today so that he can share it at the author's chair. Mrs. Albers sends him over to write his name on the sharing list posted beside the author's chair.

Dalany is next. She reminds Mrs. Albers that she finished her book, "The Apple Tree," last week, and she's waiting for it to be word processed. Mrs. Albers tells her that it's done and gives her the word processed copy. They read it over together, and Dalany returns to her desk to draw the illustrations. Here's Dalany's book, "The Apple Tree":

Page 1 **I see the apple tree.**

Page 2 **I picked the apple up.**

Page 3 **I ate the apple.**

Page 4 **I see another girl pick up the apple.**

Page 5 **The girl ate the apple.**

Page 6 **We are friends.**

The fifth page from Dalany's word processed book with hand-drawn illustrations is shown.

After the students write their stories, an aide word processes them in Standard English, adding a title page, a dedication page, and a "Readers' Comments" page. The

The girl ate the apple.

student draws an illustration on each page. Then Mrs. Albers laminates the title page and adds a back cover and the student staples the book together. The author shares the book at that day's author's chair, and then it's placed in the classroom library. Students take turns reading each other's books and adding comments on the back page; they take great pride in reading their classmates' comments in their books. Mrs. Albers and the first graders have written these comments in Matthew's book about playing soccer:

I have tropy. Michael

I like Matthew play soccer. Pauline

You are a good soccer player! Mrs. Albers

Nice story. Rosemary

You god sucr ply. Jesse

Do you win and win? Lily

I lik play soccr. Beso

Although not all comments are grammatically correct or spelled correctly, Matthew can read them, and he has walked around and thanked each person for his or her comment. It's important to him that lots of friends read his book and write comments.

The third part of writing workshop is author's chair. Each day, three students sit in the author's chair and share their published stories. After students read their stories, their classmates offer comments and ask clarifying questions. Then they clap for the author, and the published book is ceremonially placed in a special section of the classroom library for everyone to read.

The writing process, like the reading process, involves a series of five recursive stages. Students participate in a variety of activities as they gather and organize ideas, draft their compositions, revise and edit their drafts, and finally, publish their writings (Dorn & Soffos, 2001). Some teachers have thought that young students weren't ready for writing, but the first graders in Mrs. Albers's class demonstrated that beginning writers—even English learners—can learn about the writing process and move beyond single-draft compositions.

Reading and writing have been thought of as opposites: Readers decoded or deciphered written language, and writers encoded or produced written language. Then researchers began to notice similarities between reading and writing and talked of both of them as processes (Hayes, 2004; Kintsch, 2013; Rumelhart, 2013). Now reading and writing are viewed as parallel processes of meaning construction, and we understand that readers and writers use similar strategies for making meaning with text.

The Writing Process

The focus in the **writing process** is on what students think about and do as they write. The five stages are *prewriting, drafting, revising, editing,* and *publishing*. The labeling and numbering of the stages don't mean that the writing process is a linear series of neatly packaged categories; rather, the process involves recurring cycles, and labeling is simply an aid for identifying and discussing writing activities. In the classroom, the stages merge and recur as students write. The key features of each stage are shown in Figure 11–1.

Stage 1: Prewriting

Prewriting is the "getting ready to write" stage. The traditional notion that writers have a topic completely thought out and ready to flow onto the page is ridiculous: If writers wait for ideas to fully develop, they may wait forever. Instead, writers begin tentatively—talking, reading, writing—to see what they know and in what direction they want to go. Prewriting has probably been the most neglected stage in the writing process; however, it's as crucial to writers as a warm-up is to athletes. Murray (1982) believes that at least 70% of writing time should be spent in prewriting. During the prewriting stage, students choose a topic, consider purpose and form, and gather and organize ideas for writing.

MyLab Education
Video Example 11.1
Young students learn the key features of the writing process. Why is engaging students in the stages of the writing process a valued practice?

Figure 11–1 Key Features of the Writing Process

STAGE 1: PREWRITING
- Choose a topic
- Consider the purpose for writing
- Identify the genre the writing will take
- Gather and organize ideas using words, pictures, diagrams, and talk

STAGE 2: DRAFTING
- Write a rough draft
- Emphasize ideas rather than mechanical correctness

STAGE 3: REVISING
- Reread the rough draft
- Share writing in revising groups
- Make substantive changes that reflect classmates' comments
- Conference with the teacher

STAGE 4: EDITING
- Proofread the revised rough draft
- Identify and correct spelling, capitalization, punctuation, and grammar errors
- Conference with the teacher

STAGE 5: PUBLISHING
- Make the final copy
- Share the writing with an authentic audience

CHOOSING A TOPIC.   Students should choose their own topics for writing—topics that they're interested in and know about—so that they'll be more engaged, but that isn't always possible: Sometimes teachers provide the topics, especially in connection with literature focus units and content-area units. It's best when teacher-selected topics are broad so students can narrow them in the way that's best for them. Asking students to choose their own topics for writing doesn't mean that teachers do not provide guidance; teachers still provide general guidelines. They may specify the writing form, and at other times they may establish the function, but students should choose their own content.

CONSIDERING PURPOSE.   As students prepare to write, they need to think about the purpose of their writing: Are they writing to entertain? to inform? to persuade? Setting the purpose for writing is just as important as setting the purpose for reading because purpose influences decisions students make about form.

CONSIDERING GENRE.   Students make decisions about the genre or form their writing will take: a story? a letter? a poem? a report? Figure 11–2 describes the genres that students learn to use. The genre they choose relates to their purpose for writing: If they're writing to share information, a report might be the most appropriate genre, but if they're writing to convince someone about something, a persuasive letter may be the best choice.

REHEARSAL ACTIVITIES.   Students engage in a variety of activities to gather and organize ideas for writing. They brainstorm words, draw pictures, and talk with classmates as they gather ideas, and they create graphic organizers to visually display their words and images. Their choice of diagram varies according to genre; for example, students often draw a series of three boxes for the beginning, middle, and end when they're planning a story, and use a Venn diagram to compare two ideas.

Stage 2: Drafting

Students get their ideas down on paper and write a first draft of their compositions in this stage. Because they don't start writing with their pieces already composed in their minds, writers begin tentatively with the ideas they've developed through prewriting activities. Their drafts are usually messy, reflecting the outpouring of ideas with cross-outs, lines, and arrows as they think of better ways to express ideas. Students write quickly, with little concern about legible handwriting, correct spelling, or careful use of capitalization and punctuation.

Figure 11–2 Writing Genres

Genre	Purpose	Activities
Descriptive Writing	Students use this genre to paint vivid pictures of people, places, events, and things. They use sensory details to breathe life into their writing.	descriptive paragraphs descriptive sentences poems
Expository Writing	Students use this genre to present information. They use expository text structures to organize their presentation of information and cue words to guide readers.	alphabet books directions posters
Journals and Letters	Students use this genre for personal writing. They share news and explore new ideas. They also learn the special formats that letters and envelopes require.	email messages friendly letters learning logs
Narrative Writing	Students use this genre to present accounts of experiences, either true or imaginary. They create a world for readers to imagine, tell a story, and explain why it's memorable.	innovations personal narratives retellings of stories
Persuasive Writing	Students use this genre to win someone to their viewpoint. They state their position and support it with examples and evidence.	advertisements book and movie reviews persuasive letters
Poetry Writing	Students use this genre to create word pictures and evoke emotional responses. They use figurative language, poetic forms, and poetic devices to make their poems more powerful.	acrostics color poems "I Am . . ." poems

When they write rough drafts, students skip every other line to leave space for revisions and write only on one side of a sheet of paper. Wide spacing between lines is crucial. At first, teachers make small *x*'s on every other line as a reminder to skip lines, but once students understand the importance of leaving space, they skip lines automatically. Students write *Rough Draft* on their drafts; this label indicates to classmates, parents, and administrators that the emphasis is on content, not mechanics. It also explains why the draft hasn't been graded.

Instead of writing drafts by hand, many students, even kindergartners and first graders, use computers to compose rough drafts, polish their writing, and print out final copies. There are many benefits of using computers for word processing. Students are often more motivated to write, and they tend to write longer pieces. Their writing looks neater, and they use spell-check programs to identify and correct misspelled words.

Stage 3: Revising

MyLab Education
Video Example 11.2
Students can learn to be good writers, but they're often influenced by what their teachers think is important in writing. As you read through this chapter, consider what you will emphasize during writing instruction.

After writers have completed their rough drafts, they work to refine their presentation of ideas. Students often break the writing process cycle as soon as they complete a draft, believing that once they've jotted down their ideas, the writing task is complete. Experienced writers, however, know they must turn to others for reactions and revise on the basis of these comments. Revision is not just polishing; it's meeting the needs of readers by adding, substituting, deleting, and rearranging material. *Revision* means "seeing again," and in this stage, writers see their compositions again with the help of classmates and the teacher. Revising consists of three activities: rereading the rough draft, sharing the rough draft with classmates, and revising on the basis of feedback.

REREADING THE ROUGH DRAFT.   Writers need to distance themselves from their rough drafts for a day or two and then reread them from a fresh perspective, as a reader might. As they reread, students make changes—adding, substituting, deleting, and moving words, sentences, and paragraphs—and place question marks by sections that need work; students ask for help with these trouble spots when they meet with classmates in revising groups.

REVISING GROUPS.   Students meet in small revising groups to share their rough drafts with classmates, who respond and suggest possible revisions. Sometimes teachers participate in these groups, and sometimes they meet separately with students, as Mrs. Albers did in the vignette at the beginning of the chapter. Revising groups provide a scaffold in which teachers and classmates talk about plans and strategies for writing and revising.

In some classrooms, revising groups form whenever four or five students finish their rough drafts and want to get feedback. The students gather around a conference table or sit on the floor in a corner of the classroom and take turns reading their rough drafts aloud; classmates listen and respond, offering compliments and revision suggestions. But in other classrooms, revising groups are assigned, and students get together when everyone in the group has finished writing and is ready to share. Sometimes the teacher participates in the group; however, if the teacher is involved in something else, students work independently and conference with the teacher afterward.

MAKING REVISIONS.   Students make four types of changes as they revise their drafts:

Additions.   Writers insert words and sentences to provide additional information and improve the flow of ideas. Students like to use the caret symbol (^) to indicate where they're inserting new words and sentences.

Substitutions.   Writers replace words and sentences to express their ideas more effectively. As students learn about synonyms, alternatives for tired words such as *good* and *said*, and how to use a thesaurus, they become more interested in making substitutions.

Literacy Portraits

Michael and his classmates are confident writers who willingly share their rough drafts and revise their writing. Compare Michael's work with his writing in February, when Ms. Janusz taught a minilesson on writing effective endings and then conferenced with Michael about how he planned to end the story he was writing. You might also check Rhiannon's April video clip of her writing conference with Ms. Janusz. Because Rhiannon's writing is a challenge to read, Ms. Janusz usually combines revising and editing when she works with her. Ideas are born so quickly in Rhiannon's imagination that she forgets about inserting punctuation when she writes, and her abbreviated phonetic spellings are difficult to decipher. Getting students to revise isn't easy. What do you notice in these video clips to suggest why these second graders are so successful?

Michael in May

Rhiannon in April

Deletions.   Writers cross out redundant, unnecessary, or inappropriate words and sentences. Deletions are particularly difficult for writers to make, especially those who think longer compositions are better than shorter ones.

Moves.   Writers change the location of words and sentences to improve their presentation of ideas or heighten the lyrical quality of their writing. This is the most sophisticated type of revision, and students make fewer moves than additions, substitutions, or deletions. (Faigley & Witte, 1981)

Students often use a blue pen to cross out words, draw arrows, and write between the double-spaced lines of their rough drafts so that revisions will show clearly; this way, teachers can easily check the types of revisions they make. Revisions are an important gauge of students' growth as writers.

REVISING CENTERS.   Teachers often set up revising centers to give students revision options: They can talk with a classmate about the ideas in their rough draft, examine the organization of their writing, consider their word choice, or check that they've included all required components in the composition. A list of revising centers is shown in Figure 11–3. Teachers introduce these centers as they teach about the writing process, and then students work at them before or after participating in a writing group. Teachers usually provide a checklist of center options that students put in their writing folders, and then they check off the centers that they complete. Through these center activities, students develop a repertoire of revising strategies and personalize their writing process.

Stage 4: Editing

Editing is putting the piece of writing into its final form. Until this stage, the focus has been primarily on ideas. Now the focus changes to mechanics, and students polish their writing by correcting spelling mistakes and other mechanical errors. **Mechanics** are the commonly accepted conventions of written Standard English; they consist of capitalization, punctuation, spelling, sentence structure, usage, and formatting considerations specific to poems, scripts, letters, and other writing genres. The use of these commonly accepted conventions is a courtesy to those who'll read the composition.

Students are more efficient editors if they set the composition aside for a few days before beginning to edit. After working so closely with a piece of writing during drafting

Figure 11–3 Revising and Editing Centers

Type	Centers	Activities
Revising	Rereading	Students reread their rough drafts with a partner, who offers compliments and asks questions.
	Word Choice	Students choose three to five words in their rough drafts and look for more specific or more powerful synonyms using a thesaurus, word walls in the classroom, or suggestions from classmates.
	Graphic Organizer	Students draw a chart or diagram to illustrate the organization of their compositions, and they revise their rough drafts if the organization isn't effective or the writing isn't complete.
	Sentence Combining	Students choose a section of their drafts with too many short sentences and combine some of them to improve the flow of their writing.
Editing	Spelling	Students work with a partner to proofread their writing. They locate misspelled words and use a dictionary to correct them. Students may also check for specific errors in their application of recently taught skills.
	Homonyms	Students check their rough drafts for homonym errors, and after consulting a chart posted in the center, they correct the errors.
	Punctuation	Students proofread their writing to check for punctuation marks. They make corrections as needed and then highlight all punctuation marks in their drafts.
	Capitalization	Students check that each sentence begins with a capital letter, the word *I* is capitalized, and proper nouns and adjectives are capitalized. After the errors are corrected, students highlight all capital letters in their drafts.

and revising, they're too familiar with it to notice many mechanical errors; but with the distance gained by waiting a few days, students are better able to approach editing with a fresh perspective and gather the enthusiasm necessary to finish the writing process. Then students move through two activities in the editing stage: proofreading to locate errors and correcting the ones they find.

PROOFREADING. Students proofread their compositions to locate and mark possible errors. **Proofreading** is a unique type of reading in which students read word by word, hunting for errors rather than reading for meaning. Errors are highlighted with special proofreader's marks; students enjoy using these marks—the same as those used by adult authors and editors. Figure 11–4 presents a list of proofreaders' marks that students use when they're proofreading their writing. Concentrating on mechanics is difficult because of our natural inclination to read for meaning; even experienced proofreaders often find themselves focusing on comprehension and thus overlook errors that don't inhibit meaning. It's important, therefore, to take time to explain proofreading and demonstrate how it differs from regular reading.

To demonstrate proofreading, teachers copy a piece of writing on the whiteboard or display it on an overhead projector. The teacher reads it aloud several times, each time hunting for a particular type of error, such as spelling, capitalization, or paragraph indentation. During each reading, the teacher reads the composition slowly, softly pronouncing each word and touching it with a pen to focus attention on it. The teacher marks possible errors as they're located.

Editing checklists help students focus on particular types of errors. Teachers develop checklists with two to six items that are appropriate for their grade level. A first grade checklist, for example, might have only two items—perhaps one about capital letters at the beginnings of sentences and a second about periods at the ends. In contrast, a fourth grade checklist might contain items such as using commas in a series, indenting paragraphs, and spelling homonyms correctly. Teachers revise the checklist during the school year to focus attention on skills that have recently been taught.

Figure 11–4 Proofreaders' Marks

Correction	Mark	Example
Delete	ℒ	Most whales are big and huge creatures.
Insert	∧	A baby whale is a calf. called
Indent paragraph	¶	¶Whales look a lot like fish, but the two are quite different.
Capitalize	≡	In the United states it is illegal to hunt whales.
Change to lower case	/	Why do beached Whales die?
Add period	⊙	Baleen whales do not have any teeth ⊙
Add comma	∧	Some baleen whales are blue whales ∧ gray whales and humpback whales.
Add apostrophe	∨	People are the whales only enemy.

The Assessment Snapshot shows a third grade editing checklist. Classmates work as partners to edit their drafts. First, students proofread their own compositions, searching for errors in each category on the checklist, and after proofreading, check off the item. After completing the checklist, students sign their names and then trade checklists and compositions; they now become editors and complete each other's checklist. Having both the writer and the editor sign the checklist helps them take the activity seriously.

Assessment Snapshot
A Third Grade Editing Checklist

Author Editor

Author	Editor	
✓	✓	1. I have circled the words that might be misspelled.
✓	✓	2. I have checked that all sentences begin with capital letters.
✓	✓	3. I have checked that all sentences end with punctuation marks.
✓	✓	4. I have checked that all proper nouns begin with a capital letter.

Signatures:

Author: _Jessie_   Editor: _Alex_

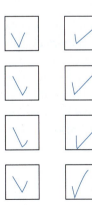

TEACHER'S NOTE
Jessie is getting better at checking her own work before showing it to me, and she's found that Alex is a very helpful proofreader. I found only six errors—mainly proper nouns. She doesn't capitalize days of the week, but does capitalize third grade, boys, girls, and school. She needs more practice to learn which words to capitalize.

CORRECTING ERRORS.   After students proofread their compositions and locate as many errors as they can, they use red pens to correct the errors independently or with an editor's assistance. Some errors are easy to correct, some require a dictionary, and others involve instruction from the teacher. It's unrealistic to expect students to locate and correct every mechanical error in their compositions; published books aren't always error-free! Once in a while, students may change a correct spelling or punctuation mark and make it incorrect, but they catch far more errors than they create.

Students work at editing centers to check for and correct specific types of errors; a list of editing centers is also shown in Figure 11–3. Teachers often vary the activities at a center to reflect the types of errors students are making. For example, students who continue to misspell common words can check for these words on a chart posted in the center, or after a series of lessons on contractions or punctuation marks, one or more centers can focus on applying the newly taught skill.

Editing can end after students and their editors correct as many mechanical errors as possible, or after students meet with the teacher for a final editing conference; when mechanical correctness is crucial, this conference is important. Teachers proofread the composition with the student, and they identify and make the remaining corrections together, or the teacher makes checkmarks in the margin to note errors for the student to correct independently.

Stage 5: Publishing

When students publish their compositions, they bring their writing to life. They make the final copy and share it orally with a real audience of classmates, parents, and others; in this way, students come to think of themselves as authors. Publication is a powerful motivator: Students want to continue writing and to improve the quality of their writing through revising and editing (Weber, 2002).

MAKING BOOKS.   The most popular way for students to publish their writing is by making books. Simple booklets can be made by folding a sheet of paper into quarters, like a greeting card; students write the title on the front and use the three remaining sides for their composition. They can also construct booklets by stapling sheets of writing paper together and adding covers made out of construction paper. Sheets of wallpaper cut from old sample books also make sturdy covers. These stapled booklets can be cut into various shapes, too. Students can make more sophisticated books by wrapping cardboard covers with contact paper, wallpaper samples, or cloth. Pages are sewn or stapled together, and the first and last pages (endpapers) are glued to the cardboard covers to hold the book together.

SHARING WRITING.   Students share their writing by sitting in a special chair called the *Author's Chair* and reading their writing aloud to classmates. Afterward, classmates ask questions, offer compliments, and celebrate the completion of the writing project. Sharing writing is a social activity that helps writers develop sensitivity to their audience and confidence in themselves as authors. Beyond just providing the opportunity for students to share writing, teachers need to teach students how to make appropriate comments as they respond to their classmates' writing. Teachers also serve as a model for responding to students' writing without dominating the sharing.

Students also share their writing in these ways:

- Read it to their families
- Share it at a back-to-school event
- Place it in the class library
- Post it on the class website
- Display it at a school or community event
- Submit it to a student's literary magazine

Through this sharing, students communicate with genuine audiences who respond to their writing in meaningful ways.

Adapting the Writing Process for Young Students

Young students do learn to use the five-stage writing process, but at first, teachers often simplify it by abbreviating the revising and editing stages. Students' revising is limited to reading the text to themselves or to the teacher to check that they've written all that they wanted to say. Revising becomes more elaborate as students learn about audience and decide to "add more" or "fix" their writing to make it appeal to their classmates. Some emergent and beginning writers ignore editing altogether—as soon as they've dashed off their drafts, they're ready to publish or share their writing. Others, however, change a spelling, fix a poorly written letter, or add a period to the end of the text as they read over their writing. When students begin writing, teachers accept their work as it's written and focus on the message. Then as students gain experience with writing, teachers encourage them to fix more and more of their errors.

MyLab Education Self-Check 11.1
MyLab Education Application Exercise 11.1: The Five Stages of the Writing Process

---

Teaching Writing

The Common Core State Standards for English Language Arts (2010) specify that students are expected to develop a range of writing strategies, skills, and applications to meet grade-level expectations. The Standards integrate reading and writing with social studies, science, and other content areas. They address these components:

Genres or Text Types. The Standards emphasize these three text types: persuasive, informational, and narrative writing. Students learn to vary their writing according to genre, purpose, and audience. These genres are introduced in kindergarten, where students use a combination of drawing, dictating, and writing to present their ideas, and as they become more proficient writers, they do the writing themselves.

Writing Process. Although the term *writing process* isn't mentioned in the Standards document, students are expected to produce writing where they develop ideas, get feedback from classmates and the teacher, refine and polish their drafts based on the feedback, and finally publish their compositions. Students at all grade levels are expected to explore digital tools for drafting and publishing compositions.

Research. Students conduct short research on topics related to thematic units to build knowledge, and then they present what they've learned to interested audiences. Young students work together as a whole class, and with more experience, they work in small groups and, finally, individually. By the end of fourth grade, students should be able to investigate topics, gather information from print and digital sources, take notes, organize information, and make lists of sources.

Range of Writing. Beginning in third grade, students are expected to be regularly involved in a combination of short- and long-term writing and research projects, usually in connection with thematic units. This Standard emphasizes the importance of having students develop writing fluency as they apply their knowledge of writing genres, the writing process, and research procedures to complete projects.

Check the Compendium of Instructional Procedures, which follows Chapter 12. These green terms also show a brief description of each procedure.

Teachers teach the writing process; present **minilessons** on writing strategies, the six traits, and other skills; and use a variety of instructional procedures to ensure that their students meet grade-level standards. This Common Core State Standards: Writing box presents additional information about the writing Standards.

Teachers use an apprenticeship approach to writing, where they cultivate a community of writers, teach students to use the writing process, and present **minilessons** that address the Common Core State Standards topics. Like Mrs. Albers, they combine explicit instruction with authentic practice as students apply what they're learning about writing strategies, the traits of effective writing, and genres in their own compositions.

Writing Strategies and Skills

Writing strategies are like reading strategies: They're tools that students use deliberately to craft effective compositions. Students apply many of the same strategies for both reading and writing, such as activating background knowledge, questioning, repairing, and evaluating, and they also use some strategies that are specific to writing. They use strategies purposefully as they plan, revise, and edit their writing. Writers also draw on other, more specific strategies at each stage of the writing process and for varied types of writing activities (Dean, 2006). Students learn to apply these writing strategies:

Elaborating.   Writers expand their ideas by adding details, examples, and quotes; it's the opposite of *narrowing*. Sometimes students brainstorm additional words and ideas; at other times, however, they have to do more research to elaborate their ideas.

Formatting.   Writers design the layout of the final copies of their compositions. Formatting plays a more important role in some genres than in others; for example, students spend a great deal of time formatting the poems they write and digital compositions of information, including PowerPoint presentations.

Generating.   Writers brainstorm ideas and the words to express them. Sometimes they activate their background knowledge and brainstorm lists, but at other times, they read books or research a topic.

Common Core State Standards
Writing

The Common Core State Standards focus on having students learn writing strategies and skills that they apply through extended writing projects; many of the projects integrate writing with thematic units. Students use the writing process to develop and refine their writing, and they learn to use research procedures to build and present knowledge. The Standards emphasize these points:

- Students write persuasive, informational, and narrative texts for varied purposes and audiences.
- Students use a process to develop a topic, write a rough draft, get feedback, refine the composition, and publish the final copy.
- Students participate in research projects in connection with thematic units.
- Students participate in a wide range of writing projects on literacy and content-area topics.

To learn more about the writing Standards, go o http://www.corestandards.org/ELA-Literacy, or check your state's educational standards website.

Teach Kids to Be Strategic!

Writing Strategies

Teach students to use these strategies as they learn to use the writing process:

- Elaborate
- Format
- Generate
- Narrow
- Organize
- Proofread
- Reread
- Revise

Students practice these strategies as they participate in writing workshop and other writing activities. They use different strategies during various stages of the writing process; in drafting, for instance, they often use *generate, elaborate, organize*, and *reread*. If students struggle, reteach the strategies in minilessons, demonstrate their use, and think aloud about their application.

Narrowing.   Writers limit the scope of their topic to make it more manageable. When students attempt to write about a broad topic, they're often so overwhelmed with information that they can't complete the composition.

Organizing.   Writers impose an order on their presentation of ideas using their knowledge of narrative elements, expository structures, or poetic forms. Outlining is the traditional form of organizing, but clusters and other graphic organizers are usually more effective.

Proofreading.   Writers proofread to identify mechanical errors in their compositions, including spelling, capitalization, punctuation, and grammar mistakes.

Rereading.   Writers often stop writing to read what they've written. They use this strategy for a number of reasons: to check that they're achieving their purpose, to monitor their flow of ideas, or to appreciate the voice they're creating. After a break, students reread to remember where they left off so they can begin to write again.

Revising.   Revising isn't just a stage in the writing process; it's also a strategy writers use to improve the quality of their compositions. The four most important aspects are adding, deleting, substituting, and moving words, sentences, and longer pieces of text. For example, students add dialogue, delete redundant sentences, substitute more vivid verbs, or move paragraphs to improve the organization.

Students use these writing strategies purposefully as they draft and refine their writing.

In contrast, writing skills are knowledge-based, automatic actions that students learn to apply during the writing process. Writers use these skills:

Content Skills.   Students apply skills such as crafting topic sentences to arrange information into paragraphs. These skills are most important during the drafting and revising stages.

Word Skills.   Students use skills such as adding synonyms and figurative language during drafting and revising to make their writing clearer.

Sentence Skills.   Students apply skills such as varying the type of sentences to make their writing more interesting. They use these skills during drafting and revising.

Grammar Skills.   Students use skills such as monitoring subject–verb agreement to correct any nonstandard English errors during editing.

Mechanical Skills.   Students apply spelling, capitalization, and punctuation skills to make their compositions more readable, especially during the editing stage.

Teachers use **minilessons** with demonstrations and **think-alouds** to teach writing strategies and skills, and then students apply what they're learning during guided practice and independent writing projects. These strategies and skills are often reflected in **rubrics** that teachers and students use to assess writing.

The Six Traits

Specific techniques that writers use to capture readers' attention and convey meaning are referred to as the *writer's craft*. Establishing a clear voice, incorporating a useful organization, choosing precise words, and fashioning effective sentences are often mentioned as essential components of the writer's craft. More than 20 years ago, researchers at Education Northwest identified six writer's craft techniques, which they called *traits*: *ideas, organization, voice, word choice, sentence fluency*, and *conventions*. Later *presentation* was added as the seventh trait, but these qualities are still referred to as "the six traits" or "the six traits plus one." Two of the researchers who developed the traits—Ruth Culham (2003, 2005) and Vicki Spandel (2008)—continue to design instruction and assessment procedures and share them with teachers. Students, even in the primary grades, learn to incorporate these traits into their writing:

Ideas.   The ideas are the essence of a composition. Students choose an interesting idea during prewriting, and as they draft and revise, they narrow and develop it using main ideas and details.

Organization.   The organization is the skeleton of the composition. Students hook the reader in the beginning, identify the purpose, present ideas logically, provide transitions between ideas, and end with a satisfying conclusion so that the important questions are answered. Students organize their writing during prewriting and follow their plans as they draft.

Voice.   The writer's distinctive style is *voice*; it's what breathes life into a piece of writing. Culham (2003) calls voice "the writer's music coming out through the words" (p. 102). During the drafting and revising stages, students create voice in their writing through the words they choose, the sentences they craft, and the tone they adopt.

Word Choice.   Careful word choice makes the meaning clear and the composition more interesting to read. Students learn to choose lively verbs and specific nouns, create word pictures, and use idiomatic expressions as they craft their pieces. They focus on word choice as they draft and revise their writing.

Sentence Fluency.   Sentence fluency is the rhythm and flow of language. Students vary the length and structure of their writing so that it has a natural cadence and is easy to read aloud. They develop sentence fluency as they draft, revise, and edit their writing.

Conventions.   In the editing stage, students proofread their compositions to make sure they have used the conventions (or rules) of writing correctly: that means checking spelling, punctuation, capitalization, and grammar. When students correctly use the

Booklist The Six Traits

Trait	Books
Ideas	Baylor, B. (1995). *I'm in charge of celebrations.* Shannon, D. (2006). *Good boy, Fergus!* Willems, M. (2004). *Knuffle bunny.*
Organization	Fleming, D. (2006). *The cow who clucked.* Ryan, P. M. (2001). *Mice and beans.* Smith, R. (1993). *The hat book.*
Voice	Biedrycki, D. (2005). *Ace Lacewing, bug detective.* Raschka, C. (2007). *Yo! Yes?* Schachner, J. (2003). *Skippyjon Jones.*
Word Choice	Henkes, K. (2008). *Chrysanthemum.* Scieszka, J. (2005). *Baloney (Henry P.).* Steig, W. (2009). *Amos & Boris.*
Sentence Fluency	Aylesworth, J. (1995). *Old black fly.* MacLachlan, P. (1994). *All the places to love.* Yolen, J. (1987). *Owl moon.*
Mechanics	Donohue, M. R. (2008). *Penny and the punctuation bee.* Pattison, D. (2003). *The journey of Oliver K. Woodman.* Pulver, R. (2003). *Punctuation takes a vacation.*

conventions of writing, the reader does not have to stop to figure out the intended message.

As students learn about these traits, they apply their knowledge and find ways to make their writing more effective.

TEACHING PROCEDURE.   Teachers teach a series of **minilessons** about each trait. They explain the trait, share examples from books they've read aloud and from students' own writing, involve students in activities to investigate and experiment with the trait, and have students apply what they've learned in their own writing. The Booklist: The Six Traits presents books and activities that teachers can use in teaching the six traits.

As students study the six traits, they internalize what good writers do. They learn to recognize good writing, develop a vocabulary for talking about writing, get better at evaluating their own writing, and acquire strategies to improve the quality of their writing.

Writing Genres

The forms of writing are called **genres**. That's the same term used for the types of literature, and some literature and writing genres are the same, such as poetry, but others are different. Students learn to use a variety of writing genres, and they're often expected to apply their knowledge of writing genres on state- and district-mandated writing assessments. Through reading and examining writing samples, students become knowledgeable about these genres and how they're structured (Donovan & Smolkin, 2002).

DESCRIPTIVE WRITING.   Students describe something by painting a word picture. They use sensory words and comparisons so that readers can imagine people, places, and things; they don't explain or tell a story about it. Sometimes writers add descriptive words and sentences to their writing, but they also do descriptive writing—including descriptive sentences and paragraphs—and poems. Teachers teach descriptive writing by having students examine something—an apple or a maple tree, for instance—or look at a photo or a piece of art, and brainstorm lists of words about the object or picture using each of the five senses. Later, students use the words they've collected for a writing project.

EXPOSITORY WRITING.   Students use expository writing to explain something, present information, or specify how to make or do something. They use the writing process to draft and refine alphabet books, informational books, and other types of reports to share information they've learned during thematic units and about their hobbies and special interests.

JOURNALS AND LETTERS.   Young students compose daily entries about themselves and topics that interest them in personal journals; this type of journal is especially beneficial for emergent and beginning writers who are learning to print letters, spell high-frequency words, and develop writing fluency. Students also write entries in **reading logs** to explore books they're reading and in **learning logs** to examine big ideas they're studying in thematic units. In addition, students learn the format used in letters and write friendly letters, courtesy letters (thank you notes, invitations, get well cards), and email messages.

NARRATIVE WRITING.   Students write stories about true and imaginary experiences, focusing on a single event and applying what they've learned about story elements and narrative devices. In particular, they organize their stories into three parts—beginning, middle, and end. Students often write about events in their own lives; these stories are called *personal narratives*. They also write innovations that are modeled on books they've read and retellings of familiar stories, often from a different viewpoint.

PERSUASIVE/ARGUMENTATIVE WRITING.   Students use persuasive writing to make claims and persuade others to agree with them. They make posters and advertisements, write letters, and prepare book and movie reviews. When students write persuasively, they use logical arguments: They clearly state their position and support it with examples and evidence. Older students also identify and refute opposing viewpoints.

POETRY.   Poetry is a unique genre: Poets create word pictures, powerful images, and stirring stories using very few words. Poetry is meant to be read aloud so that readers and listeners can appreciate the sounds of language as well as its meaning. Students use poetic forms to structure their poems and choose their words carefully, often using wordplay and poetic devices. They organize the words they write into lines, not sentences, and arrange the lines creatively on the page to visually enhance the meaning. Some students use capitalization and punctuation, but others ignore these conventions.

Students often write powerful poems, especially when they use poetic forms to structure their writing. Here are four poetic forms that students use successfully:

Color Poems.   Students begin each line or every other line of their poems with a color; the same color may be repeated, or different colors may be used (Koch, 2000). For example, kindergartners dictated this poem about America's colors:

Red, white, and blue are America's colors.

Red is for love:

We love America.

We say, "America is the best!"

White is for patriotism:

We salute the flag.

We say the Pledge of Allegiance.

Blue is for honor:

We honor our brave soldiers.

We say, "thank you!"

Hurray for the red, white, and blue!

The repetition of colors and beginning the two lines that follow with *we* provide the structure for the poem.

"I Am . . ." Poems.   Students assume the perspective of another person and repeat the "I am . . ." line at the beginning and end of each stanza. They begin the other lines with *I* followed by an active-voice verb, not a form of "to be." Fourth grader Madison wrote this poem about Neil Armstrong:

I am the First Man to walk on the moon.

I flew in a landing craft named Eagle.

I landed in the Sea of Tranquility.

I climbed down the ladder.

I put my left foot on the ground.

I said some famous words—

"That's one small step for a man,

one giant leap for mankind."

I collected soil samples.

I planted the American flag.

I am Neil Armstrong.

Madison repeats the *I* pattern to recount the events of the astronaut's famous moon walk.

"If I Were . . ." Poems.   As in "I Am . . ." poems, students write from the perspective of other people or things (Koch, 2000). In this poem, second grader David writes about what he would do if he were a giant:

If I were a giant

I would drink up the seas

and I would touch the sun.

I would eat the world

and stick my head in space.

Students can also write poems from the perspective of characters in books they're reading, historical personalities, or things related to thematic units, such as a whale or a saguaro cactus.

List Poems.   Students brainstorm a list about a topic, with each line following the same structure (Heard, 2009); the last line presents a twist or sums up the poem. You can read a list poem about a pizza in Chapter 9 and one about life at the aquarium in Chapter 12.

Students use the writing process to draft and refine their poems. During revising, they learn to "unwrite," or delete unnecessary words in the poems, and as they make their final copies, students decide how to arrange the lines in their poems and how to use capitalization and punctuation.

Teaching English Learners
Writing Development

Writing can be a daunting task for English learners. Students need to know English vocabulary, sentence structure, and spelling to communicate effectively in writing, but Mrs. Albers's first graders in the vignette at the beginning of the chapter showed that young English learners can become good writers when their teacher sets high expectations, teaches them how to write, and involves them in daily writing activities.

Teachers must be mindful of the increased linguistic demands placed on English learners and take into account these considerations as they teach writing:

Topics.   At first, students write about personal topics—their families, after-school activities, friends, and family trips, for example—but with experience, they move on to writing about books they're reading and topics they're learning in thematic units. To nudge ELs toward new writing topics, teachers offer suggestions about content-related topics, demonstrate how to write a book on a topic related to a book or unit, and create a collaborative book where each student contributes a page. Making this switch is especially important because English learners need to take advantage of writing as a tool for learning academic vocabulary and understanding the big ideas they're studying.

Talk.   All students need to talk before they begin writing to activate background knowledge and develop ideas, but conversation is even more important for English learners because they're learning English vocabulary and sentence structures, too. Teachers often make a list of academic words that they call a _word bank_ as they talk with ELs during prewriting so the students will have the words available when they're writing. Sometimes teachers include a few phrases they've practiced for students to use when they're writing.

Models.   English learners often use a pattern book as a model for their writing. Pattern books help students move beyond personal writing, and they're useful in teaching new sentence structures. For example, students learn to write questions and answers as they make their own versions or innovations of Bill Martin Jr.'s _Brown Bear, Brown Bear, What Do You See?_ (2010) and three of his other books that follow the same pattern: _Panda Bear, Panda Bear, What Do You See?_ (2007b), about endangered animals; _Baby Bear, Baby Bear, What Do You See?_ (2007a), about animal babies; and _Polar Bear, Polar Bear, What Do You Hear?_ (1992), about animal sounds. Students write innovations using _If You Give a Mouse a Cookie_ (Numeroff, 1985), _The Cow Who Clucked_ (Fleming, 2006), and other pattern books, too.

Focus on Ideas.   Many young writers value correctly spelled words and neat handwriting over the clear communication of ideas; but as they learn to use the writing process, most students gradually understand that the focus is on developing ideas before they reach the editing stage, and that messy rough drafts are a good thing because they reflect thoughtful drafting and revising. English learners, however, often struggle to accept the notion that developing ideas precedes mechanical correctness. Teachers demonstrate the writing process using interactive writing to nurture ELs' appreciation of the concept that writers often make their papers messy as they improve them.

If teachers address these considerations, ELs are better able to grow as writers along with their classmates.

Teachers also vary the instructional procedures they use with emergent, beginning, and fluent EL writers. Teachers use the **Language Experience Approach** to demonstrate how speech is recorded (Rothenberg & Fisher, 2007). They help students organize their ideas into words and into one or more sentences, write the sentences, saying each word as they write it, and read the sentences. Later, students often copy the text underneath the teacher's writing and practice rereading it.

Beginning writers learn writing strategies and skills through **interactive writing**. As students take turns doing the writing, they learn to form letters correctly, spell high-frequency words and phonetically regular words, capitalize words, and add punctuation marks correctly. Teachers guide students, help them correct errors, and take advantage of teachable moments to provide instruction when students are most likely to learn from it. Students often practice what they've seen demonstrated when they're writing at writing centers or during writing workshop.

Once students become fluent writers, they still benefit from teacher scaffolding because they're continuing to deal with their limited knowledge of English vocabulary and linguistic structures. Teachers provide assistance by meeting with these students during prewriting and by conferencing with them while they're revising and editing their writing.

MyLab Education Self-Check 11.2

Assessing Students' Writing

Teachers use the instruction–assessment cycle to assess both the process students use as they write and the quality of their compositions. They observe as students use the writing process to develop their compositions and conference with students as they revise and edit their writing. Teachers notice, for example, whether students use writing strategies to organize ideas for writing and whether they take into account feedback from classmates when they revise. So that students can document their writing process activities, teachers also have them keep all drafts, checklists, and rubrics in writing folders.

THE INSTRUCTION–ASSESSMENT CYCLE   Teachers integrate writing instruction with assessment by providing developmentally appropriate instruction and addressing the Common Core State Standards for their grade level. They follow these steps:

Step 1: Planning.   Teachers plan developmentally appropriate instruction using their knowledge about students' current stage of writing development, and they identify Common Core State Standards to teach.

Step 2: Monitoring.   Teachers monitor students' progress through regularly scheduled writing conferences. They read students' rough drafts, talk with them about their successes and struggles, and set goals to achieve before their next conference.

Step 3: Evaluating. Teachers evaluate students' writing using rubrics, and sometimes students also use rubrics to evaluate their own compositions. Rubrics may include items that are developmentally appropriate, items reflecting concepts that have recently been taught, and items reflecting Common Core State Standards.

Step 4: Reflecting. Teachers use their evaluation of students' learning to judge the effectiveness of their instruction and decide how to adapt instruction to better serve struggling students. In addition, students reflect on their own writing development. They reflect on their growth as writers by noting their accomplishments and setting goals for the next writing experience.

RUBRICS. Teachers develop **rubrics**, or scoring guides, to assess the quality of students' writing (Farr & Tone, 1994). Rubrics make the analysis of writing simpler and the assessment process more reliable and consistent. They may have four, five, or six levels, with descriptors related to ideas, organization, language, and mechanics at each level. Some rubrics are general and are appropriate for almost any writing assignment, and others are designed for a specific writing assignment. The Assessment Snapshot presents a kindergarten writing rubric used to document Emmy's growth. For more information about locating rubrics online, check the Assessment Tools feature in this chapter.

Students, too, can learn to create rubrics to assess the quality of their writing. To be successful, they need to analyze examples of other students' writing and determine the qualities that demonstrate strong, average, and weak papers; teachers need to model how to address the qualities at each level in the rubric. Skillings and Ferrell (2000) taught second and third graders to develop the criteria for evaluating their writing, and the students moved from using the rubrics their teachers prepared to creating their own three-level rubrics, which they labeled as the "very best" level, the "okay" level, and the "not so good" level. Perhaps the most important outcome of teaching students to create rubrics, according to Skillings and Ferrell, is that they develop metacognitive strategies and the ability to think about themselves as writers.

ON-DEMAND WRITING TESTS. In most school districts, students take on-demand writing tests every year, and most states have implemented writing assessments, beginning in third or fourth grade. These writing tests present a prompt for students to respond to within a set time period, and they're scored using a four- or six-point scale. Good writing instruction is the best way to prepare students for on-demand writing assessments (Angelillo, 2005). Students who use writing strategies and skills, apply the six traits, and vary their writing according to genre will do well on almost any type of writing assignment. Nevertheless, writing tests place additional demands on students:

The Prompt. Students need to know how to read and interpret the prompt. They must identify the genre and the audience and look for clue words, such as *describe* and *convince*, to figure out what they're expected to do. Prompts usually have several parts, so students must consider the entire prompt carefully without jumping to conclusions.

The Topic. Students need to get used to writing on assigned topics that may not interest them, because they're accustomed to choosing their own.

Time Restrictions. Students need to practice writing under test conditions so they'll know how to allocate their time for planning, writing, and proofreading.

Teachers teach students about prompts, model how to write in response to a prompt, and have students practice taking writing tests.

Assessment Snapshot

Kindergarten Writing Rubric

4   *Exceptional Writer*
- Writes several complete sentences or one sophisticated sentence.
- Spaces between words and sentences consistently.
- Spells some high-frequency words correctly.
- Spells some consonant-vowel-consonant words correctly.
- Uses capital letters to begin some sentences.
- Uses periods and other punctuation marks to end some sentences.

3   *Developing Writer*
- Writes a complete sentence.
- Spaces between some words.
- Spells one or more high-frequency words correctly.
- Spells beginning and ending sounds in most words.
- Uses both upper- and lowercase letters.

2   *Beginning Writer*
- Writes from left to right and top to bottom.
- Spells one or more words using one or more letters that represent beginning or other sounds in the word.
- Rereads the writing with one-to-one matching of words.

1   *Emergent Writer*
- Uses random letters that do not correspond to sounds.
- Uses scribbles to represent writing.
- Draws a picture instead of writing.
- Dictates words or sentences.

TEACHER'S NOTE

Emmy is a developing writer. She's making very good progress. She writes long pieces that include several sentences. She spells the, go, in, I, you, see, and other high frequency words correctly, and most of her writing is easy to decipher. She uses phonics to sound out beginning and ending sounds in many phonetically regular words.

Teachers use a four-step procedure to help students practice for on-demand writing tests:

1. **Analyze the prompt.**   Students read and analyze the prompt to determine what it's really asking them to do.

2. **Develop ideas.**   Students brainstorm a list of ideas about the topic.

3. **Plan their writing.**   Students create a graphic organizer with their plan for writing.

4. **Proofread.**   Students take a minute or two at the end of the writing time to proofread their compositions and correct errors in spelling, capitalization, punctuation, and grammar.

Through these steps, students become familiar with the test-taking procedure. Shelton and Fu (2004) describe how a fourth grade teacher interrupted her students' writing workshop to provide an intensive six-week test preparation before the state on-demand writing assessment. During the preparation, students learned to read prompts, studied the two genres that might be tested, and practiced writing under test conditions. These fourth graders scored higher than the state average, but even though they did well, they disliked writing for the test and eagerly returned to writing workshop, where they chose their own topics, collaborated with classmates, and didn't have to adhere to time restrictions.

Assessment Tools

Rubrics

Teachers use rubrics to assess students' writing. Sometimes they create their own rubrics, but at other times, they use rubrics developed by the school district or state department of education. These rubrics are often used for yearly or quarterly mandated writing assessments. Basal reading programs and supplemental writing programs also provide rubrics.

In addition, teachers access writing rubrics that are posted online. They often use Google or another search engine to locate an online rubric that's appropriate for their grade level or for a specific writing assignment. They also check these websites that offer collections of rubrics:

- **Education Northwest**
  https://educationnorthwest.org Scoring guides or rubrics to assess the 6 + 1 traits are available from Education Northwest, the group that developed this approach to writing instruction and assessment.

- **RubiStar**
  http://rubistar.4teachers.org/index.php. Use RubiStar to create your own rubric in English or Spanish.

- **Rubrician.com**
  http://www.rubrician.com This website has links to hundreds of writing rubrics at all grade levels.

- **Writing With Writers**
  http://teacher.scholastic.com

Scholastic provides genre-related writing rubrics, including descriptive writing, biography, and poetry scoring guides.

Before they use any writing rubric, teachers should examine it, checking that it addresses the characteristics or qualities they've taught, varies the achievement of characteristics at each level, and is written in student-friendly language.

If Students Struggle . . .

When students aren't making adequate progress in writing, teachers step in to determine the problem and then intervene to address it. Emergent, beginning, and fluent writers exhibit different problems that reflect what they know about writing, so teachers start by identifying students' stage of writing development. They observe students as they write independently and with classmates, examine samples of students' writing, and talk with students about their writing as they analyze their problems.

When the students are emergent writers, teachers ask themselves these questions:

- Do students use pencils to print letters and letterlike forms?
- Do students print their names and other letters of the alphabet?
- Do students demonstrate an awareness of concepts about written language, including the direction of print on a page?
- Do students dictate words and sentences for the teacher to write?
- Do students write a few high-frequency words?
- Do students choose letters to represent words according to beginning sound?

Some students struggle because they don't understand how written language works and haven't developed concepts about print. Some aren't focusing on letters and words, and others aren't applying phonemic awareness and phonics concepts they're being taught to represent words with letters signifying beginning sounds. Teachers use **shared reading** and the **Language Experience Approach** in their interventions, and they also provide daily opportunities for students to write independently and with teacher guidance.

When students are beginning writers, teachers consider these questions:

- Do students write single-draft, multisentence compositions on a topic?
- Do students reread their writing and try to make it better?
- Do students sit in the author's chair to share their writing?
- Do students spell some high-frequency words correctly?
- Do students apply phonics and spelling strategies to spell other words?
- Do students use capitalization and punctuation?
- Do students use legible handwriting?

Beginning writers who struggle have developed concepts about written language, but they aren't aware of audience and haven't learned to develop ideas, spell words conventionally, and write legibly. Teachers design interventions that include using **minilessons** and **interactive writing** to teach writing strategies and skills, introduce the writing process, and provide daily guided and independent writing opportunities.

Once students are fluent writers, teachers ask themselves these questions:

- Do students use the writing process to draft and refine their writing?
- Do students use writing strategies to solve problems?
- Do students apply their knowledge of the six traits when they revise their writing?
- Do students vary their writing according to genre?

Fluent writers' problems are difficult to identify and solve because as students get older, their problems become more complex. Teachers usually begin with the writing process and observe as students complete a writing project. Many struggling writers don't spend enough time gathering and organizing ideas before they begin writing, and they revise only superficially, if at all. Editing is another stumbling point because many struggling writers are poor spellers who can't catch the words they've misspelled during proofreading. Ensuring that students understand and use the writing process goes a long way toward improving their writing. Teachers also provide time every day for these struggling students to write with teacher guidance and independently.

MyLab Education Self-Check 11.3

The Writing Process In Action

Teachers use an apprenticeship model of writing where they cultivate a community of writers, and students use the writing process to draft and refine their writing, as the first graders in Mrs. Albers's classroom did in the vignette. Teachers use interactive writing to model how to apply the writing process, and they use writing centers and writing workshop to provide opportunities for students to do their own writing.

Interactive Writing

Students and the teacher create a text together in **interactive writing** and "share the pen" as they write it on chart paper (Button, Johnson, & Furgerson, 1996; McCarrier, Pinnell, & Fountas, 2000). The teacher guides students as they write the words and sentences on chart paper, taking advantage of opportunities to demonstrate how to form letters and think aloud about remembering the sentence they're writing. The teacher also explains about capitalizing names, using apostrophes in contractions, and adding quotation marks. As students learn more about written language, the teacher releases more and more responsibility to them, and they write longer texts.

Teachers use interactive writing to write class news, predictions before reading, retellings of stories, thank-you letters, math story problems, and many other group writings (Tompkins & Collom, 2004). An interactive writing sample written by a

MyLab Education
Video Example 11.3
Ms. McCloskey teaches in a multilingual K–3 classroom. She engages her first graders in interactive writing. Most of these students are English learners. How does Ms. McCloskey reinforce skills during the lesson?

Figure 11–5 An Interactive Writing Sample

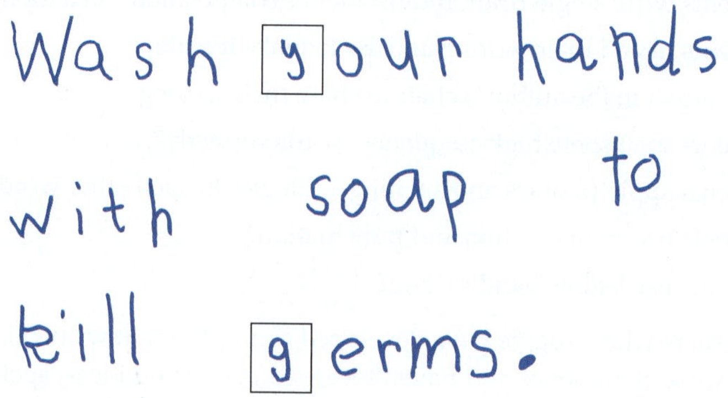

Wash your hands with soap to kill germs.

kindergarten class during a health unit is shown in Figure 11–5. Students took turns writing individual letters. The boxes drawn around some of the letters represent correction tape that was used to correct misspellings or poorly formed letters.

Teachers help students spell all words conventionally. They teach high-frequency words, assist students in segmenting sounds and syllables in other words, point out unusual spelling patterns, and teach other conventions of print. Whenever students misspell a word or form a letter incorrectly, teachers use correction tape to cover the mistake and help them make the correction. Teachers emphasize the importance of using conventional spelling as a courtesy to readers; in contrast to the emphasis on conventional spelling in interactive writing, students are encouraged to use invented spelling when writing independently at writing centers or during writing workshop.

Writing Centers

Teachers set up writing centers in preschool and kindergarten classrooms so that students have a special place to write. The center should be located at a table with chairs and equipped with a box of supplies containing pencils, crayons, a date stamp, different kinds of paper, journal notebooks, a stapler, blank books, notepaper, and envelopes. The alphabet, printed in upper- and lowercase letters, should be available for students to refer to as they write. In addition, a crate with files for each student is needed so writers can store their work. They also send their completed writings to classmates using the classroom mail delivery system. Writers often place their messages in a box or bag at the center, and each day one student delivers the mail.

When students come to the writing center, they draw and write in journals, compile books, and write messages to classmates. At first, they write single-draft compositions, but the social interaction that's part of life at a center encourages students to consider their audience and make revisions and editing changes. Teachers should be available to encourage and assist students at the center. They can observe students as they invent spellings and can provide information about letters, words, and sentences, as needed. If the teacher can't be at the writing center, perhaps an aide, a parent volunteer, or an older student might be able to assist.

Young students also make books at the writing center modeled on books they've read. For example, they use the same patterns in *Polar Bear, Polar Bear, What Do You Hear?* (Martin, 1992); *The Very Hungry Caterpillar* (Carle, 2002); *No David!* (Shannon, 1998); and *Is Your Mama a Llama?* (Guarino, 2004) to create innovations. Figure 11–6 shows Benji's response to *If You Give a Mouse a Cookie* (Numeroff, 1985). This emergent writer read his writing this way: "I love chocolate chip cookies." Not surprisingly, the four-year-old focused on the cookie theme, not the "if . . . then" structure of the book.

Figure 11–6 An Emergent Writer's Sample

With more literacy experiences, Benji will learn to incorporate the structure of the book he's using as a model.

Writing Workshop

Writing workshop is the best way to implement the writing process (Fletcher & Portalupi, 2007). Students write on topics that they choose themselves and assume ownership of their writing. At the same time, the teacher's role changes from provider of knowledge to guide, and the classroom becomes a community of writers who write and share their writing.

Students have writing folders in which they keep all papers related to the writing project they're working on. Different kinds of paper, some lined and some unlined, are available, as are writing instruments, including pencils and red and blue pens. Students also have access to the classroom library because their writing often grows out of books they've read; they may write a pattern story or retell a story from a different viewpoint, for example.

As they write, students sit at desks or tables arranged in small groups. The teacher circulates, conferencing briefly with everyone, and the classroom atmosphere is free enough that students converse quietly with classmates and move around to assist each other or share ideas. There's space for students to meet for revising groups, and often

PreK Practices

Can four-year-olds learn to write?

Preschoolers aren't too young to be writers (Schickedanz & Casbergue, 2009). They understand that print carries a message and that it's different from drawing. Many four-year-olds incorporate writing into play activities; for example, they create signs for block constructions and write grocery lists in the housekeeping center. Others staple together booklets of paper and write books using a combination of drawing and scribbles to convey a message (Ray & Glover, 2008). Sometimes they remember the text long enough to reread it; at other times, however, it's forgotten as quickly as it's written. Once they learn to write their names, preschoolers acquire a stock of familiar letters to use in writing other words, and they begin to write simple messages that adults can decipher.

MyLab Education
Video Example 11.4
Mrs. Ockey is engaging her second graders in a minilesson on using multiple paragraphs. Which of the six writing traits is Mrs. Ockey teaching her students?

a sign-up sheet for revising groups is posted in the classroom. A table is available for the teacher to meet with individual students or small groups for conferences, revising groups, proofreading, and **minilessons**.

Writing workshop is a 60-minute period scheduled each day. During this time, students are involved in three components: writing, sharing, and minilessons. Sometimes teacher interactive **read-alouds** are added when they're not used in conjunction with reading workshop.

MINILESSONS. Teachers teach minilessons on writing workshop procedures; writing strategies and skills, such as organizing ideas, proofreading, and using quotation marks; the six traits; and writing genres (Fletcher & Portalupi, 2007). Teachers often display an anonymous piece of writing (from a student in another class or from a previous year) for students to read and use it in teaching the lesson. Teachers also select excerpts from read-aloud books and mentor texts to show how published authors use writing strategies and skills.

WRITING. Students spend 30 minutes or longer working on writing projects. Just as students in reading workshop read at their own pace, in writing workshop, they usually work independently on writing projects they've chosen themselves. They move through the writing process as they plan, draft, revise, edit, and finally, publish their writing:

Prewriting. Students choose topics and set their own purposes for writing. Then they gather and organize ideas, often drawing pictures, making graphic organizers, or talking out their ideas with classmates.

Drafting. Students work independently to write rough drafts using the ideas they developed during prewriting.

Revising. Students participate in small groups to share their rough drafts and get feedback to help them revise their writing.

Editing. Students work with classmates to proofread and correct mechanical errors in their writing, and they also meet with the teacher for a final editing.

Publishing. Students prepare a final copy of their writing, and they sit in the author's chair to share it with classmates.

Overview Of The Instructional Approach Writing Workshop

Topic	Description
Purpose	To provide students with opportunities for authentic writing activities.
Components	Writing workshop consists of writing, sharing, teaching minilessons, and teacher read-alouds to students.
Theory Base	The workshop approach reflects sociolinguistic and information-processing theories, because students participate in authentic activities that encourage them to enjoy writing.
Applications	Teachers often add writing workshop to other instructional approaches so students have opportunities to use the writing process to develop and refine compositions.
Strengths	• Students learn to work through the stages of the writing process. • Activities are student directed, and students work at their own pace. • Teachers have opportunities to work individually with students during conferences.
Limitations	• Teachers often feel a loss of control because students are working at different stages of the writing process. • Teachers have the responsibility to teach minilessons on strategies and skills, both to the whole class and to students working in small groups. • Students must learn to be task oriented and to use time wisely to be successful.

At first, students may use an abbreviated writing process, but once they've learned to revise and edit, they move through all five stages of the writing process.

Teachers conference with students as they write. Many teachers prefer moving around the classroom to meet with students rather than having writers come to a table to meet with them: Too often, a line forms, and students lose precious writing time. Some teachers move around the classroom in a regular pattern, meeting with one fifth of the class each day so that they're sure to conference with everyone during the week.

Other teachers spend the first 15 minutes of writing time stopping briefly to check on 10 or more students. Many use a zigzag pattern to reach all areas of the classroom each day. These teachers often kneel down beside each student, sit on the edge of the student's chair, or carry their own stool around to each student's desk. During the one- or two-minute conferences, teachers ask students what they're writing, listen to them read a paragraph or a page or two, and ask what they plan to do next. Then these teachers use the remaining time to conference more formally with students who are revising and editing their compositions. They identify strengths in students' writing, ask questions, and discover possibilities during revising conferences. Some teachers like to read the pieces themselves, and others like to listen to students read their drafts aloud. As they interact with students, teachers model the kinds of responses that students are learning to give to each other.

Students work with classmates to revise and edit their writing. They share their rough drafts in revising groups composed of three or four classmates. Sometimes teachers join in, but students normally run the groups themselves. They take turns reading their rough drafts to each other and listen as classmates offer compliments and suggestions for revision. Students also participate in revising and editing centers. They know how to work at each center and understand the importance of working with classmates to make their writing better.

After proofreading their drafts with a classmate and then meeting with the teacher for a final editing, students make the final copy of their writing. They often want to word process their writing so that it looks professional. Many times, students compile their final copies to make books, but sometimes they attach their writing to artwork, make posters, write letters that will be mailed, or perform scripts. Not every piece is necessarily published; sometimes students decide not to continue with a piece of writing, and they file that piece in their writing folders and start something new.

SHARING. For the last 10 minutes, students share their new publications (Mermelstein, 2007). They take turns sitting in the author's chair to read their published writing aloud. After each sharing, classmates clap and offer compliments; they may also make other comments and suggestions, but the focus is on celebrating completed writing projects, not on revising them.

MANAGING WRITING WORKSHOP. It takes time to implement the workshop approach because students have to learn how to use the writing process to develop and refine a piece of writing and other workshop procedures (Gillet & Beverly, 2001). Some students expect to write single-draft compositions because that's what they're used to doing, or they complain that they don't know what to write about because they're used to having their teachers supply the topics. But with careful instruction and clear guidelines, even young students can learn to use writing workshop, as Mrs. Albers's first graders demonstrated in the vignette.

Teachers develop a schedule for writing workshop, allocating as much time as possible for writing. The writing workshop schedule in first and second grade classrooms often looks like this:

8:45–9:05 Minilesson

9:05–9:35 Writing

9:35–9:45 Sharing

After developing the schedule, teachers post it in the classroom and talk to students about the activities and their expectations. Teachers teach the workshop procedures and continue to model them until students become comfortable with the routines. As students gain experience with the workshop approach, their enthusiasm grows and the workshop approach is successful.

Teachers monitor students' progress on their writing projects using a classroom chart that Nancie Atwell (1998) calls "status of the class"; a third grade class chart is shown in the Assessment Snapshot: Status of the Class Chart. At the beginning of each writing workshop session, students identify the stage of the writing process they're involved in and write it on the chart; if they move to another stage during the writing period, they also write in that number. This chart provides a quick way for teachers to assess whether students are moving through the writing process at a reasonable pace, determine if anyone is "stuck," decide who's ready for a revising or editing conference, and choose students to sit in the author's chair to share their writing.

As you engage in writing instruction use **My Teaching To-Do Checklist: Writing Instruction** to reflect on the effectiveness of your teaching.

Assessment Snapshot
Status of the Class Chart

Names	Dates 3/17	3/18	3/19	3/20	3/21	3/24	3/25	3/26
Antonio	4	5	5	5	1	1	1	2
Bella	2	2	2	3	2	3	3	4
Charlie	3	3	1	2	2	3	3	1
Dina	5	5	5	1	1	1	1	2
Dustin	3	3	4	4	4	5	5	1
Eddie	2	3	2	4	5	1	1	2
Elizabeth	2	3	3	4	4	4	5	1
Elsa	1	2	2	3	4	5	5	1

Code: 1 = Prewriting 2 = Drafting 3 = Revising 4 = Editing 5 = Publishing

TEACHER'S NOTE

Most of my students are making good progress using the writing process in writing workshop, but several are struggling. Charlie gets stuck during revising and then abandons his drafts. Dina works very slowly. Eddie rushes through the process, and his writing reflects this. Elsa works quickly, too, but her writing is strong.

MY TEACHING TO-DO CHECKLIST: Writing Instruction

- ☐ I cultivate a community of writers.
- ☐ I provide daily opportunities for my students to write.
- ☐ I guide students as they apply the writing process, with particular emphasis on revising.
- ☐ I model and teach writing strategies and skills.
- ☐ I teach the six traits so students can incorporate these qualities into their own writing.
- ☐ My students participate regularly in writing workshop.
- ☐ I train my students to use rubrics to assess their own writing.
- ☐ I collect my students' writing in portfolios.
- ☐ I integrate state standards into my instruction.

Chapter Review

Scaffolding Students' Writing Development

- Teachers teach the five stages in the writing process—*prewriting, drafting, revising, editing,* and *publishing*—so that students can write and refine their compositions.

- Teachers teach students about the six traits of effective writing—*ideas, organization, voice, word choice, sentence fluency,* and *mechanics.*

- Teachers assess students' writing development using rubrics and on-demand writing tests.

- Teachers use interactive writing, writing centers and writing workshop to teach the writing process.

Accountability Check

Visit the following assessment links to access quiz questions and instructional applications.

MyLab Education Application Exercise 11.2: Understanding Literacy Development
MyLab Education Application Exercise 11.3: Understanding Literacy Development
MyLab Education Application Exercise 11.4: Understanding Literacy Development
MyLab Education Application Exercise 11.5: Monitoring Literacy Development
MyLab Education Application Exercise 11.6: Measuring Literacy Development

References

Angelillo, J. (2005). *Making revision matter.* New York: Scholastic.

Atwell, N. (1998). *In the middle: New understandings about writing, reading, and learning.* Boynton/Cook: Portsmouth, NH.

Button, K., Johnson, M. J., & Furgerson, P. (1996). Interactive writing in a primary classroom. *The Reading Teacher, 49,* 446–454.

Carle, E. (2002). *The very hungry caterpillar.* New York: Puffin Books.

Common core state standards for English language arts. (2010). Retrieved from http://www.corestandards.org/ELA-Literacy/

Culham, R. (2003). *6 + 1 traits of writing, grades 3 and up.* New York: Scholastic.

Culham, R. (2005). *6 + 1 traits of writing: The complete guide for the primary grades.* New York: Scholastic.

Dean, D. (2006). *Strategic writing: The writing process and beyond in the secondary English classroom.* Urbana, IL: National Council of Teachers of English.

Donovan, C. A., & Smolkin, L. B. (2002). Children's genre knowledge: An examination of K–5 children's performance on multiple tasks providing differing levels of scaffolding. *Reading Research Quarterly 37,* 428–465.

Dorn, L. J., & Soffos, C. (2001). *Shaping literate minds: Developing self-regulated learners.* York, ME: Stenhouse.

Faigley, L., & Witte, S. (1981). Analyzing revision. *College Composition and Communication, 32,* 400–410.

Farr, R., & Tone, B. (1994). *Portfolio and performance assessment.* Orlando: Harcourt Brace.

Fleming, D. (2006). *The cow who clucked.* New York: Henry Holt.

Fletcher, R., & Portalupi, J. (2007). *Craft lessons: Teaching writing K–8* (2nd ed.). York, ME: Stenhouse.

Gillet, J. W., & Beverly, L. (2001). *Directing the writing workshop: An elementary teacher's handbook.* New York: Guilford Press.

Guarino, D. (2004). *Is your mama a llama?* New York: Scholastic.

Hayes, J. R. (2004). A new framework for understanding cognition and affect in writing. In R. B. Ruddell & N. J. Unrau (Eds.), *Theoretical models and processes of reading* (5th ed., pp. 1399–1430). Newark, DE: International Reading Association.

Heard, G. (Ed.). (2009). *Falling down the page: A book of list poems.* New York: Roaring Brook Press.

Kintsch, W. (2013). Revisiting the construction-integration model and its implications for instruction. In D. E. Alvermann, N. J. Unrau, & R. B. Ruddell (Eds.), *Theoretical models and processes of reading* (6th ed., pp. 807–839). Newark, DE: International Reading Association.

Koch, K. (2000). *Wishes, lies, and dreams: Teaching children to write poetry.* New York: HarperCollins.

Martin, B., Jr. (1992). *Polar bear, polar bear, what do you hear?* New York: Henry Holt.

Martin, B., Jr. (2007a). *Baby bear, baby bear, what do you see?* New York: Henry Holt.

Martin, B., Jr. (2007b). *Panda bear, panda bear, what do you see?* New York: Henry Holt.

Martin, B., Jr. (2010). *Brown bear, brown bear, what do you see?* New York: Holt.

McCarrier, A., Pinnell, G. S., & Fountas, I. C. (2000). *Interactive writing: How language and literacy come together, K–2.* Portsmouth, NH: Heinemann.

Mermelstein, L. (2007). *Don't forget to share: The crucial last step in the writing workshop.* Portsmouth, NH: Heinemann.

Murray, D. M. (1982). *Learning by teaching.* Montclair, NJ: Boynton/Cook.

Numeroff, L. J. (1985). *If you give a mouse a cookie.* New York: HarperCollins.

Ray, K. W., & Glover, M. (2008). *Already ready: Nurturing writers in preschool and kindergarten.* Portsmouth, NH: Heinemann.

Rothenberg, C., & Fisher, D. (2007). *Teaching English language learners: A differentiated approach.* Upper Saddle River, NJ: Merrill/Prentice Hall.

Rumelhart, D. E. (2013). Toward an interactive model of reading. In D. E. Alvermann, N. J. Unrau, & R. B. Ruddell (Eds.), *Theoretical models and processes of reading* (6th ed., pp. 719–747). Newark, DE: International Reading Association.

Schickedanz, J. A., & Casbergue, R. M. (2009). *Writing in preschool: Learning to orchestrate meaning and marks* (2nd ed.). Newark, DE: International Reading Association.

Shannon, D. (1998). *No, David!* New York: Blue Sky Press.

Shelton, N. R., & Fu, D. (2004). Creating space for teaching writing and for test preparation. *Language Arts, 82,* 120–128.

Skillings, M. J., & Ferrell, R. (2000). Student-generated rubrics: Bringing children into the assessment process. *The Reading Teacher, 53,* 452–455.

Spandel, V. (2008). *Creating young writers: Using the 6 traits to enrich the writing process in primary classrooms* (2nd ed.). Boston: Allyn & Bacon/Pearson.

Tompkins, G. E., & Collom, S. (Eds.). (2004). *Sharing the pen: Interactive writing with young children.* Upper Saddle River, NJ: Merrill/Prentice Hall.

Weber, C. (2002). *Publishing with students: A comprehensive guide.* Portsmouth, NH: Heinemann.

Weiss, N. (1990). *An egg is an egg.* New York: Putnam.

Chapter 12
Integrating Literacy Into Thematic Units

Learning Outcomes

After studying this chapter, you'll be prepared to:

12.1 Describe how reading and writing are used as learning tools.

12.2 Discuss how students create projects rather than take tests to demonstrate their learning.

12.3 Explain how to develop a thematic unit.

Creating Multigenre Projects

Dolgachov/123RF

Mrs. Zumwalt's third graders are studying ocean animals, and her focus is adaptation: How do animals adapt to survive in the ocean? As the students learn about ocean life, they take special notice of how individual animals adapt. For example, Alyssa learns that whelks have hard shells to protect them, Aidan knows that some small fish travel together in schools, Cody reports that clams burrow into the sand to be safe, and Christopher read that sea otters have thick fur to keep them warm in cold ocean water. Students add what they learn about adaptation to a chart in the classroom.

A month ago, Mrs. Zumwalt began the unit by passing out informational books from the text set on ocean animals for students to examine. After they looked at the books for 30 minutes or so, she brought them together to begin a **KWL chart**. This chart covers half of the back wall of the classroom; three sheets of poster paper hang vertically, side by side. The first sheet is labeled "K—What We Know About Ocean Animals," the middle one is labeled "W—What We Wonder About Ocean Animals," and the one on the right is labeled "L—What We've Learned About Ocean Animals." Mrs. Zumwalt asked students what they already knew about ocean animals; they offered many facts, including "sea stars can grow a lot of arms," "sharks have three rows of teeth," and "jellyfish and puffer fish are poisonous," which she recorded in the K column. They also asked questions, including "How can an animal live inside a jellyfish?" "Is it true that father seahorses give birth?" and "How do some fish light up?" which the teacher wrote in the W column. The students continued to think of questions for several days, and Mrs. Zumwalt added them to the W column. At the end of the unit, they'll complete the L column.

Mrs. Zumwalt talked about the six ocean habitats—seashore, open ocean, deep ocean, seabed, coral reefs, and polar seas—and the animals living in each one. She began with the seashore, and the class took a field trip to the Monterey Bay Aquarium to learn about animals that live at the seashore. She focused on several animals in each habitat, reading books aloud and emphasizing how animals have adapted. For each habitat, they made a class chart about it, and students recorded information in their **learning logs**. They hung the charts in the classroom, and after all six habitats were introduced, Mrs. Zumwalt set out a pack of cards with names of animals and pictures of them for students to sort according to habitat. This **word sort** is shown here in the Ocean Habitat Sort.

Students have **learning logs** with 20 sheets of lined paper for writing, 10 sheets of unlined paper for drawing and charting, and 15 information sheets about ocean animals. There's also a page for a personal word wall that's divided into nine boxes and labeled with letters of the alphabet; students record words from the class **word wall** on their personal word walls. Mrs. Zumwalt introduces new words during her presentations and as she reads aloud books from the text set on ocean animals; then she adds them to the word wall.

Several of Mrs. Zumwalt's third graders come from homes where Spanish is spoken, and these students struggle with oral and written English. Mrs. Zumwalt brings them together most days for an extra lesson while their classmates work on other activities; she either previews the next lesson she'll teach or the next book she'll read, or she reviews her last lesson or the last book she read. In this small-group setting, students talk about what they're learning, ask questions, examine artifacts and pictures, and practice vocabulary. They often create **interactive writing** charts to share what they've discussed with their classmates. Here's their chart about schools of fish:

There are two kinds of schools. Kids go to school to get smart and little fish travel in groups that are called "schools." Fish are safer when they stick together in schools.

In this chapter, you'll learn how to integrate literacy instruction with content-area study. Teachers develop thematic units in which students read nonfiction articles and books and participate in a combination of "writing to learn" and "writing to demonstrate learning" activities. As you read this vignette, notice how Mrs. Zumwalt uses reading and writing as learning tools, and how her students create multigenre reports to share what they've learned about ocean animals.

OCEAN HABITAT SORT

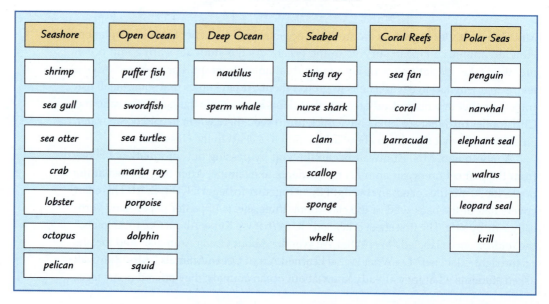

Seashore	Open Ocean	Deep Ocean	Seabed	Coral Reefs	Polar Seas
shrimp	puffer fish	nautilus	sting ray	sea fan	penguin
sea gull	swordfish	sperm whale	nurse shark	coral	narwhal
sea otter	sea turtles		clam	barracuda	elephant seal
crab	manta ray		scallop		walrus
lobster	porpoise		sponge		leopard seal
octopus	dolphin		whelk		krill
pelican	squid				

Once the class became familiar with a variety of ocean animals, each student picked an animal to study; they chose sting rays, dolphins, squids, sea anemones, sand dollars, great white sharks, seals, penguins, sea turtles, jellyfish, octopuses, seahorses, pelicans, killer whales, barracudas, tunas, electric eels, lobsters, manatees, and squid. They researched their animals using books in the text set and online resources.

After they became experts, Mrs. Zumwalt introduced the idea of developing multigenre projects about the animals they'd studied. For this multigenre project, students will create items representing different genres and package them in a box. Earlier in the year, the students worked collaboratively to develop a class multigenre project, so they were familiar with the procedure and the format.

The students decided to create four items for their multigenre projects: an informational book with chapters about their animal's physical traits, diet, habitat, and enemies and three other items. Possible items included an adaptation poster, a lifecycle chart, a poem, an alliterative sentence, a diagram of the animal, and a pack of true/false cards about the animal. They plan to package their projects in cereal boxes brought from home and decorated with pictures, interesting information, and a big-idea statement about how that animal has adapted to ocean life.

The third graders used the writing process to develop their informational books. For prewriting, they used large, multicolored index cards to jot notes: green for "Physical Traits," yellow for "Diet," blue for "Habitat," purple for "Enemies," and pink for "Other Interesting Information." After they took notes using book and online resources, they shared the information they'd gathered one-on-one with classmates, who asked questions about things that confused them and encouraged the students to add more information about incomplete topics. Next, students wrote rough drafts and shared them with the partners they worked with earlier. Then they met in revising groups with Mrs. Zumwalt and several classmates and refined their drafts using the feedback they received from their group.

Now students are proofreading and correcting their revised drafts and publishing their books. Once they correct the mechanical errors and meet with Mrs. Zumwalt for an editing conference, they recopy their drafts in their best handwriting, add illustrations,

CHRISTIAN'S BOOK ABOUT PELICANS

Chapter 1—Introduction
Pelicans are birds that live on the seashore. They have web feet for walking on sand and swimming. They can dive underwater to catch their food. That's how they live near the ocean.

Chapter 2—Physical Traits
Pelicans have some interesting physical traits. The pelican is easy to identify. They have big pouches and you can tell them by their big necks and plump bodies. The pelican has big legs and colors brown and white.

Chapter 3—Diet
Diet is what an animal eats. The pelican swallows a lot of fish. Pelicans gobble up meat. Pelicans attack sea stars and they chomp on seahorses.

Chapter 4—Habitat
A habitat is where an animal lives. The pelican lives in many countries. Pelicans are found where there's air and where it's warm. Some pelicans are now living in Monterey. Pelicans live by water, too.

Chapter 5—Enemies
Most animals are both prey and predator. That means animals are usually both the hunted and the hunter. The pelican eats seahorses and sea stars. Pelicans are hunted by sharks and people. Why do people hurt these birds? People dump waste into the water and it kills the fishes that the pelicans eat!

Chapter 6—Conclusion
I hope pelicans will always live in Monterey Bay but they could die if people dump pollution into the ocean and that would be very sad.

and compile the pages into a hardbound book. They're also preparing their boxes and the other items for their multigenre projects.

Christian researched pelicans; his informational book is shown here. In addition, he drew a life-cycle chart showing a pelican egg, a newly hatched bird in the nest, a young adult bird flapping its wings, and an older adult diving into the ocean for food; he made a Venn diagram comparing white and brown pelicans; and he wrote an alliterative sentence about pelicans using only words that begin with *p*. His multigenre project box is decorated with pictures of pelicans and interesting information he collected, including "their wings are nine feet long" and "pelicans can live to be 25 years old." The adaptation statement on his multigenre box reads, "Pelicans have web feet and they can dive underwater to catch their food to eat. That's how they can survive at the seashore."

Today, the students finish the **KWL chart** by adding comments about what they've learned about ocean animals: Cody offers that "octopuses can change shape and color to camouflage themselves," Hernan reports that "dolphins' tails go up and down and fishes' tails go side to side," and Carlos adds that "jellyfish are related to sea anemones because neither one has teeth."

Next Monday afternoon, the third graders will share their completed multigenre boxes one-on-one with second graders, and that evening, they'll share them with their parents at back-to-school night. To prepare, the students have been sharing their projects in the classroom; each day, three students sit in the author's chair to explain their projects and read their books aloud to the class.

Students read and write all through the school day as they learn science, social studies, and other content areas in thematic units. Just as Mrs. Zumwalt's third graders learned about ocean animals through reading and writing, students at all grade levels—even kindergartners and first graders—use reading and writing as tools to learn about insects, the water cycle, pioneers, space, the rain forest, and other topics. Teachers integrate the curriculum, breaking down barriers between subjects to make learning more meaningful, and organize content-area study into thematic units (Bredekamp, 1990). They identify big ideas to investigate, because teachers can't try to cover every topic; if they do, students will learn very little. Units are time-consuming because student-centered learning takes time (Harvey, 1998). Teachers must make careful choices as they plan units, because only a relatively few topics can be presented in depth during a school year.

During thematic units, students have authentic opportunities to question, discuss, explore, and apply what they're learning. They use talking, reading, and writing as tools for learning and to demonstrate their learning as they give oral reports, create posters, write books, and develop projects. Thematic units are an important part of balanced literacy programs because they provide opportunities for real-world application of what students are learning about reading and writing.

Connecting Reading and Writing

The Common Core State Standards for English Language Arts (Common Core State Standards for English Language Arts, 2010) emphasize the importance of teaching students to read and write nonfiction texts, even in the primary grades. By fourth grade, students are expected to balance their reading between fiction and nonfiction texts. Students who master the Standards build strong content knowledge by reading nonfiction purposefully to gain knowledge, using research, and sharing their knowledge through speaking and writing. Specific Standards address reading nonfiction texts and writing reports and other nonfiction compositions to develop these abilities:

- Students integrate and evaluate information presented in diverse media and formats.
- Students analyze how two or more texts address a topic.
- Students conduct research to build and present knowledge.
- Students write informative texts to examine and convey complex ideas.

These competencies are drawn from the Reading Standards for Informational Text and the Writing Standards. Check the Common Core State Standards: Content-area learning box in this chapter to read more about how the Standards emphasize reading and writing in the content areas.

Reading and writing should be connected because reading has a powerful impact on writing, and vice versa (Harmey & Rodgers, 2017): When students read about a topic before writing, their writing is enhanced because of what they learn about the topic, and when they write about the ideas in a book they're reading, their comprehension is deepened because they're exploring big ideas and the relationships among them. Making this connection is especially important when students are learning content-area information because of the added challenges that unfamiliar topics and technical vocabulary present.

There are other reasons for connecting reading and writing, too. Making meaning is the goal of both reading and writing: Students activate background knowledge, set purposes, and use many of the same strategies for reading and writing. In addition, the reading and writing processes are remarkably similar.

Reading to Learn

A wide variety of high-quality picture books and chapter books are available today for teachers to use in teaching thematic units. Two outstanding science-related trade books, for example, are *Team Moon: How 400,000 People Landed Apollo 11 on the Moon* (Thimmesh, 2006)—a stunning book that highlights the contributions of the people working behind the scenes on that space mission—and *Owen and Mzee: The True Story of a Remarkable Friendship* (Hatkoff, Hatkoff, & Kahumbu, 2006)—a photo essay about a friendship between a giant tortoise and a baby hippo orphaned during a tsunami. Two notable trade books on social studies topics are *Freedom on the Menu: The Greensboro Sit-Ins* (Weatherford, 2007)—a powerful book that tells the story of desegregation through the eyes of an 8-year-old—and *One Thousand Tracings: Healing the Wounds of World War II* (Judge, 2007)—a moving picture-book story of an American family who started a relief effort that reached 3,000 people in war-ravaged Europe. Other informational books, such as *Martin's Big Words: The Life of Martin Luther King, Jr.* (Rappaport, 2007), *Through Georgia's Eyes* (Rodriguez, 2006), and *Wilma Unlimited: How Wilma Rudolph Became the World's Fastest Woman* (Krull, 2000), are biographies. These books are entertaining and informative, and the authors' engaging writing styles and formats keep readers interested. They're relevant, too, because many students make connections to their own life experiences and background knowledge as they read these books, and teachers use them to build students' background knowledge at the beginning of a thematic unit.

Teachers share these trade books in many ways. They use **interactive read-alouds** to share some books that are too difficult for students to read on their own, and they feature others in literature focus units. They use related books at a range of reading levels for literature circles, and others for students to read independently during reading workshop. Because many books on social studies and science topics are available at a range of reading levels, teachers can find good books—many at their students' reading levels—to use in teaching in the content areas.

Check the Compendium of Instructional Procedures, which follows Chapter 12. These **green** terms also show a brief description of each procedure.

TEXT SETS. Teachers collect text sets of books and other reading materials on topics to use in teaching thematic units, as Mrs. Zumwalt did in the vignette at the beginning of the chapter. Materials for text sets are carefully chosen to incorporate different genres,

Common Core State Standards

Content-Area Learning

The English Language Arts Standards link content-area study and literacy learning; they emphasize that students need to learn to read both fiction and nonfiction texts; research content-area topics; and write to explain, persuade, and convey real experiences. They address these content-area learning requirements:

- Students integrate information from several texts on the same topic.
- Students read and comprehend grade-level nonfiction texts.
- Students participate in research and writing projects.
- Students use digital media and visual displays to share information.

The Standards emphasize the significance of nonfiction reading and writing beginning in kindergarten, and this importance increases so that by eighth grade, nonfiction takes precedence over fiction. To learn more about the Standards, go to http://www.corestandards.org/ELA-Literacy, or check your state's educational standards website.

MyLab Education
Video Example 12.1
Third grade teacher, Mr. Tucker, is engaging his students in a multigenre project on discrimination and prejudice. He put together a text set of multicultural literature. How do the books chosen provide his students opportunities to interact in meaningful text discussions?

a range of reading levels to meet the needs of all students in the class, and multimedia resources that present a variety of perspectives. It's especially important to include plenty of books and other materials that English learners and struggling readers can read (Robb, 2003).

Teachers collect as many types of materials as possible, for example:

- artifacts and models
- informational books
- magazines
- maps
- photographs
- poems and songs
- reference books
- stories
- videos and DVDs
- websites

Too often, teachers don't think about using magazines to teach social studies and science concepts, but excellent magazines are available, including *Click* and *National Geographic Explorer*. Some magazines are also available online, including *Time for Kids*. Figure 12–1 presents a list of print and online magazines.

MENTOR TEXTS. Teachers use stories, informational books, and poems that students are familiar with to model the writer's craft (Dorfman & Cappelli, 2009). Picture books are especially useful mentor texts because they're short enough to be reread quickly. Teachers begin by rereading a mentor text and pointing out a specific feature, such as using a repetitive pattern, adding punch with strong verbs, or writing from a different perspective. Then students imitate the feature in brief collaborative compositions and in their own writing so that they have opportunities to experiment with literary devices, imitate sentence and book structures, try out new genres, or explore different page arrangements.

Nonfiction books are often used as mentor texts to teach students about new genres, organizational structures, and page formats. One excellent mentor text is Margaret Wise Brown's classic, *The Important Book* (Brown, 1990), which describes significant associations with common words. Students use Brown's text pattern to describe associations related to words and concepts they're learning. For example, a kindergarten class studying frogs dictated this description, "The Important Things About Frogs":

Figure 12–1 Children's Magazines

FORMAT	MAGAZINES
Print	*Click* (science) (PreK–2)
	Faces: People, Places, and Cultures (multicultural) (3–4)
	Kids Discover (science and history) (2–4)
	Ladybug (stories, poems, and songs) (PreK–K)
	National Geographic Explorer (social studies) (3–4)
	Odyssey (science) (3–4)
	Ranger Rick (nature) (1–4)
	Spider (stories and poems) (K–3)
	Ranger Rick Jr. (nature) (PreK–1)
Online	*Odyssey,* http://www.odysseymagazine.com (science) (3–4)
	National Geographic Kids, http://kids.nationalgeographic.com (social studies) (3–4)
	Time for Kids, http://www.timeforkids.com (current events) (K–4)
	Ranger Rick, http://www.nwf.org/rangerrick (nature) (1–4)
	Ranger Rick Jr., http://www.nwf.org/kidzone (nature) (PreK–1)

The most important thing about frogs

is that they're amphibians.

Frogs are cold blooded,

and they hibernate during the winter.

Frogs eat insects,

and they're strong jumpers.

But the most important thing about frogs

is that they're amphibians—

First they live in the water

and then they live on land.

Another nonfiction mentor text is *Gone Wild: An Endangered Animal Alphabet* (McLimans, 2006)—a graphic masterpiece in which letters of the alphabet are transformed into vulnerable animals, and text boxes accompanying each letter provide information about the animal. Students can use this format to write a class alphabet book during a science or social studies unit.

Teachers use mentor texts in **minilessons** to teach students how to make their writing more powerful, and students use these books as springboards for writing as part of thematic units. Dorfman and Cappelli (2017) explain that "mentor texts serve as snapshots into the future. They help students envision the kind of writers they can become" (p. 3).

Writing as a Learning Tool

Students use writing as a tool for learning during thematic units to record information, categorize ideas, draw graphic organizers, and write summaries. The focus is on using writing to help students think and learn, not on spelling every word correctly. Nevertheless, students should use classroom resources, such as word walls, to spell most words correctly and write as neatly as possible so that they can reread their own writing. Armbruster, McCarthey, and Cummins (2005) point out that writing to learn serves two other purposes as well: When students write about what they're learning, it helps them become better writers, and teachers can use students' writing to assess their learning.

LEARNING LOGS.   Students use **learning logs** to record and react to what they're learning. Robb (2003) explains that learning logs are "a place to think on paper" (p. 60). Students write in these journals to discover gaps in their knowledge and to explore relationships between what they're learning and their past experiences: They make and label diagrams, write notes about important concepts, and practice using new academic vocabulary and technical terms.

Figure 12–2 Two Pages from a Second Grader's Learning Log

Teachers also have students keep observation logs in which they make daily entries to track the growth of plants or animals. A class of second graders took a walk in the woods wearing old socks over their shoes to collect seeds, in much the same way that animals pick up seeds on their fur coats and transport them. To simulate winter, the teacher placed the students' socks in the freezer for several weeks. Then they "planted" one student's sock in the class terrarium and watched it each day as they waited for the seeds to sprout. Two pages from a student's log documenting the experiment are presented in Figure 12–2. In the left entry, the student wrote, "No plants so far and still dirt!" In the second entry, he wrote, "I see a leaf with a point on it."

QUICKWRITING.   Students use quickwriting to review what they're learning. This type of impromptu writing was popularized by Peter Elbow (1998) as a way to help students focus on content rather than mechanics. Students choose a topic and reflect on paper on what they're learning about the topic. They generate ideas and the words to express them, make connections among ideas, and draw conclusions. Emergent writers often do "quickdraws" in which they draw pictures and add a few words. During a thematic unit on the solar system, for example, fourth graders each chose a word from the word wall for a quickwrite. One student wrote about the red planet:

> *Mars is known as the red planet. Mars is Earth's neighbor. Mars is a lot like Earth. On Mars one day lasts 24 hours. It is the fourth planet in the solar system. Mars may have life forms. Two Viking ships landed on Mars. It has a dusty and rocky surface. The Viking ships found no life forms. Mars' surface shows signs of water from long ago. It has no water now. And Mars has no rings either.*

Quickwrites take only 5–10 minutes to complete, and they provide a good way of checking on what students are learning.

GRAPHIC ORGANIZERS.   Students make charts called *graphic organizers* to arrange information to highlight big ideas and relationships among them. These charts take

Figure 12–3 A Second Grader's Chart About Penguins

many forms, and the form reflects the information being provided: When students chronicle the life cycle of a penguin, for example, they make a circle flow chart; when they compare penguins with other birds, they make a Venn diagram; when they identify a penguin's body parts, they draw and label a picture; when they brainstorm what makes a penguin unique, they make a cluster; and when they research penguins and other animals that live in Antarctica, they use a data chart to record information. Figure 12–3 presents a second grader's chart about penguins. The chart shows that penguins have three enemies—leopard seals, skua gulls, and people. Sometimes teachers want to prepare the diagram for students to fill in, but it's important that students learn to choose the most appropriate format for themselves. Students in the primary grades need to learn to recognize text structures and how to represent them in charts.

MyLab Education **Self-Check 12.1**

Demonstrating Learning

Students use writing and talking to demonstrate their learning when they write books and poems and make oral presentations to their classmates. Through these demonstrations, they synthesize their knowledge and apply it in new ways. In addition, students celebrate and bring closure to their study during a thematic unit.

Writing Projects

Students research topics and then use writing to demonstrate their learning. Because this writing is more formal, students use the writing process to revise and edit their rough drafts before making a final copy. They demonstrate learning by making reports, poems, and multigenre projects.

REPORTS.   Reports are the best known type of writing to demonstrate learning; students write many types of reports, ranging from posters to collaborative books and individual reports. Too often, students aren't exposed to report writing until they're faced with writing a term paper in high school, and then they're overwhelmed with learning how to take notes on note cards, organize information, write the paper, and compile a bibliography. There's no reason to postpone report writing; early, successful experiences with nonfiction reinforce students' learning about content-area topics as well as enhance their writing abilities (Tompkins, 2019). Students often prepare these type of reports:

Posters. Students combine visual and verbal elements when they make posters (Moline, 2012). They draw pictures and diagrams and write labels and commentary. For example, students draw diagrams of the inner and outer planets in the solar system, identify the parts of a complex machine, label the parts of a covered wagon and the essential provisions pioneers carried, identify important events of a person's life on a timeline, or chart the explorers' voyages to America and around the world on a map. Students plan the information they want to include in the poster and consider how to devise an attention-getting display using headings, illustrations, captions, boxes, and rules. They prepare a rough draft of their posters, section by section, and then revise and edit each section. Then they make a final copy of each section, glue the sections onto a sheet of poster board, and share their posters with classmates in the same way they would share finished pieces of writing.

"All About . . ." Books. The first reports that young students write are "All About . . ." books, in which they provide information about familiar topics such as "Going to the Beach" and "Meat-Eating Dinosaurs." Young students write an entire booklet on a single topic; usually one piece of information and an illustration appear on each page. A page from a first grader's "All About Penguins" book is shown in Figure 12–4. Rosa drew a picture at the top of the page and wrote a sentence explaining it underneath.

Alphabet Books. Students use the letters of the alphabet to organize the information they want to share in an alphabet book. These collaborative books incorporate the sequence structure, because the pages are arranged in alphabetical order. Alphabet books such as *Z Is for Zamboni: A Hockey Alphabet* (Napier, 2002) can be used as models. Students begin by brainstorming information related to the topic being studied and identify a word or fact for each letter of the alphabet. Then they work individually, in pairs, or in small groups to compose pages for the book. The format for the pages is similar to the one used in alphabet books written by professional authors: Students write the letter in one corner of the page, draw an illustration, and write a sentence or paragraph to describe the word or fact. The text usually begins "is for," and then a sentence or paragraph description follows. In a fourth grade class's alphabet book on the California missions, for instance, Ramon wrote the *"U Is for Unbearable"* page:

> *Life was UNBEARABLE at the missions for many Indians because they couldn't hunt or do the things they used to. They had to stay at the mission and obey the padres. Sometimes the padres even beat them if they tried to go home to see their families.*

Class Collaborations. Students work together to write **collaborative books**. Sometimes they each write one page for the report, or they can work together in small groups to write chapters. Students create collaborative reports on almost any science or social studies topic. For example, they write collaborative biographies where each student or small group writes about one event or accomplishment in the subject's life, and then the pages are assembled in chronological order. Or, students work in small groups to write chapters for a report on the planets in the solar system or the Oregon Trail.

Individual Reports. Students write their own reports during thematic units. They do "authentic" research, in which they explore topics that interest them or hunt for answers to questions that puzzle them (Harvey, 1998; Stead, 2002). Students read books and

Figure 12–4 A Page From a First Grader's "All About Penguins" Book

> Penguins lay eggs and keep them worm with ther feets and ther stomech s.

interview people with special knowledge to learn about their topics, and increasingly they're turning to the Internet for information. After learning about their topics, they write reports to share their new knowledge.

POETRY PROJECTS. Student often write poems to demonstrate their learning; They write formula poems by beginning each line or stanza with a particular word or line; they create free-form poems; and they follow the structure of model poems as they create their own poems. Students use these poetry forms to demonstrate content-area learning:

"I Am . . . " Poems. Students assume the role of a person and write a poem from that person's viewpoint. They begin and end the poem (or each stanza) with "I am _____" and begin all the other lines with "I." For example, a second grader wrote this "I Am . . . " poem about Rosa Parks:

I am Rosa Parks.

I didn't obey the bus driver.

I didn't want to sit in the back of the bus.

I said, "It's not fair!"

I want equal rights for everybody.

I am Rosa Parks.

List Poems. Students create a poem from a brainstormed list, following the models in Georgia Heard's (2009) book of list poems. Second graders collaborated on this list poem, "At the Aquarium," after a field trip; they worked with partners and in small groups to craft their lines, incorporating descriptive words and powerful verbs, and the teacher contributed the last two lines:

Gooey jellyfish floating by.

A blue lobster waving at us.

Seahorses holding tails.

Lionfish gobbling up shrimp.

Sharks circling round and round.

Electric eels shocking their prey.

A giant octopus changing colors.

Harbor seals catching fish.

Dolphins playing with their trainers.

Sea turtles swimming in slow motion.

Silly crabs walking sideways.

Kids pressing their faces against the glass,

wishing they were aquarists!

Found Poems. Students create poems by culling words and phrases from a book they're reading and arranging them into a free-form poem. Fourth graders created this poem about a saguaro cactus after reading *Cactus Hotel* (Guiberson, 2007):

A young cactus sprouts up.

After 10 years only four inches high,

after 25 years two feet tall,

after 50 years 10 feet tall.

A welcoming signal across the desert.

A Gila woodpecker,

a white-winged dove,

an elf owl

decide to stay.

After 60 years an arm grows,

the cactus hotel is 18 feet tall.

After 150 years 7 long branches

and holes of every size

in the cactus hotel.

Oral Presentations

Teachers often have students develop and give brief oral presentations to demonstrate their learning. A good first oral presentation is to draw a picture to illustrate an important fact and share it with classmates. As students talk about the picture, teachers encourage them to use content-related vocabulary and to articulate the important facts. During a unit on the solar system, for example, students can draw a picture of a planet and then share their pictures with the class, pointing out several features of the planet that they included in their drawings.

A second quick and easy oral presentation is the question-and-answer report: Teachers and students generate a list of questions related to a unit, and then students develop very brief reports to answer the questions. For example, a student might prepare a report to answer one of these questions about the solar system: Is the sun a planet? What are the inner planets? Are there people living on other planets? A variation of the question-and-answer report is the true-false report: A student prepares a statement that could be either true or false, shares it with the class, tells whether it's true or false, and then gives a couple of reasons for his or her answer.

Another type of beginning presentation is the "three-things-I-know" report: Students choose a topic and develop a brief presentation to share three things that they know about it. For example, a first grader might share these three things about the moon:

The moon is the earth's satellite.

The moon reflects the sun's light.

Astronauts have walked on the moon.

When students give a three-things report, they often hold up three fingers and point to one finger as they talk about each thing.

As they gain experience, students develop the poise and confidence to give longer, more sophisticated oral reports. For these presentations, students follow several steps that are similar to the stages of the writing process. First, they focus their topics. For example, a presentation on the solar system is too broad, but one on whether life is possible on each planet is more specific and more interesting. Next, students identify several big ideas, gather information about each one, and decide how to organize the presentation. Third, students create a visual to support their presentation, such as a poster listing their big ideas, a chart with a diagram to help listeners visualize some information, or an illustration about their topic. Sometimes they also collect artifacts or prepare a costume to wear. Fourth, they rehearse their presentation, thinking about how they'll share the information they've gathered succinctly and incorporate important vocabulary words. Finally, they give the presentation to their classmates.

Sometimes students give individual oral presentations, and at other times, they work in small groups and share the presentation. In a group presentation, each student is responsible for one part. For a presentation on whether life is possible on each planet, for instance, one student could delineate the qualities necessary for life and other students could explain whether each planet exhibits these qualities. In this way, students can tackle complex topics because they're sharing the responsibility.

Classmates who are the listeners also play an important role in successful oral presentations: Students should be attentive, listen to the speaker, ask questions, and applaud afterward. Young students are better listeners when they understand what's expected of them, when the presentations are brief and supported by visuals, and when only one or two are presented at a time.

Multigenre Projects

Students explore a science or social studies topic through several genres in a multigenre project (Allen, 2001), combining content-area study with writing in significant and meaningful ways. Romano (2000) explains that the benefit of this approach is that each genre offers ways of learning and understanding that the others don't; students gain different understandings, for example, by writing a simulated diary entry, an alphabet book, and a timeline. Teachers or students identify a **repetend**—a common thread or unifying feature for the project—which helps students move beyond the level of remembering facts to a higher, more analytical level of understanding. In the vignette,

Mrs. Zumwalt's repetend was adaptation, and in their multigenre projects, her students highlighted how the animal they studied adapted to life in the ocean.

Depending on the information they want to present and their repetend, students use a variety of genres such as these for their projects:

alphabet books	questions and answers
artifacts	quotes
biographical sketches	reports
books	riddles
journals	slide shows
letters	songs
life lines	timelines
maps	Venn diagrams
poems	videos
postcards	websites
posters	word clouds
PowerPoint presentations	word sorts

Students generally use three or more genres in a multigenre project and include both textual and visual genres. What matters most is that the genres extend and amplify the repetend.

Not only can students create multigenre projects, but some authors use the technique in trade books; *The Magic School Bus and the Electric Field Trip* (Cole, 1999) and others in the Magic School Bus series are examples of multigenre books. Each book features a story about Ms. Frizzle and her students on a fantastic science adventure; and on the side panels of pages, a variety of explanations, charts, diagrams, and essays are presented. Together, the story and informational side panels present a more complete, multigenre presentation or project.

MyLab Education Self-Check 12.2

Thematic Units

Thematic units are interdisciplinary units that integrate reading and writing with social studies, science, and other curricular areas. Students explore topics that interest them and find answers to questions they've posed and are genuinely interested in answering. Then they share their learning at the end of the unit, as Mrs. Zumwalt's students did in the vignette. They're assessed on what they've learned as well as on the processes they used in learning and working in the classroom.

How to Develop a Thematic Unit

To begin planning a thematic unit, teachers choose the general topic and determine the instructional focus using literacy and content-area standards. Next, they identify the resources they have available and develop their teaching plan, integrating content-area study with reading and writing activities. Teachers work through these steps in developing a thematic unit:

1. **Determine the focus.** Teachers identify three or four big ideas to emphasize in the unit, because the goal isn't to teach a collection of facts but to help students grapple

with several big understandings. Teachers also choose which Common Core State Standards to teach during the unit.

2. **Collect a text set of books.** Teachers collect stories, informational books, and poems on topics related to the unit for the text set and place them in a special area in the classroom library. They'll read some books aloud, and students will read others independently or in small groups. Other books are used for minilessons or as models or patterns for writing projects.

3. **Locate Internet, digital, and other multimedia materials.** Teachers locate websites, DVDs, maps, models, artifacts, and other materials for the unit; some materials are used to build students' background knowledge, and others to teach the big ideas. Also, students create multimedia materials to display in the classroom.

4. **Plan instructional activities.** Teachers think about ways to teach the unit using reading and writing as learning tools, brainstorm possible activities, and then develop a unit plan with possible activities. They also make decisions about coordinating the thematic unit with a literature focus unit using one book related to the unit, literature circles featuring books from the text set, or reading and writing workshop.

5. **Identify topics for minilessons.** Teachers plan minilessons to teach strategies and skills related to reading and writing nonfiction as well as content-area topics related to the unit, based on state standards and on needs they've identified from students' work.

6. **Devise ways to differentiate instruction.** Teachers devise ways to use flexible grouping to adjust instruction to meet students' developmental and language proficiency levels, provide appropriate books and other instructional materials for all students, and scaffold struggling students while challenging high achievers with tiered activities and projects.

7. **Brainstorm possible projects.** Teachers think about projects students can develop to apply and personalize their learning at the end of the unit. They often use the **RAFT** procedure to design tiered projects so students have alternative ways to demonstrate their learning. This planning makes it possible for teachers to collect needed supplies and have suggestions ready for students who need assistance in choosing a project. Students usually work independently or in small groups, but sometimes the whole class works together on a project.

8. **Plan for assessment.** Teachers use the instruction–assessment cycle to decide how they'll monitor students' progress and evaluate learning at the end of the unit. This way, they can explain to students at the beginning of the unit how they'll be evaluated and check to see that their assessment emphasizes students' learning of the big ideas.

After considering unit goals, standards to teach, the available resources, and possible activities, teachers are prepared to develop a time schedule, write lesson plans, and create rubrics and other assessment tools.

Teaching English Learners
Integrating Literacy Into Thematic Units

Teachers have two goals in mind as they consider how to accommodate English learners' instructional needs when they develop thematic units: to maximize students' opportunities to learn English and to develop content-area knowledge. They have to consider the instructional challenges facing ELs and how to adjust instruction and assessment to meet their needs (Peregoy & Boyle, 2017).

CHALLENGES IN LEARNING CONTENT-AREA INFORMATION. English learners often have more difficulty learning during thematic units than during literacy instruction because of the additional language demands of unfamiliar topics, vocabulary words, and informational books (Rothenberg & Fisher, 2007). Here are the most important challenges:

English Language Proficiency.   Students' ability to understand and communicate in English has an obvious effect on their learning; teachers address this challenge by teaching English and content-area information together. They use artifacts and visual materials to support students' understanding of the topics they're teaching and simplify the language, when necessary, in their explanations of the big ideas. They consider the reading levels of the stories and informational books they're using, and when students can't read these books themselves, they read them aloud. If the books are still too difficult, they find others to use instead. Teachers also provide frequent opportunities for ELs to use the new vocabulary as they talk informally about the topics they're learning.

Background Knowledge.   English learners often lack the necessary background knowledge about content-area topics, so teachers need to take time to expand students' knowledge base using artifacts, photos, models, picture books, videos, and field trips. They also need to make clear links between the topics and students' past experiences and previous thematic units; otherwise, the instruction won't be meaningful. Finding time to preteach this information isn't easy, but without it, English learners aren't likely to learn much during the unit. Teachers also involve all students, including ELs, in activities to activate their background knowledge.

Vocabulary.   English learners are often unfamiliar with content-area vocabulary because these words aren't used in everyday conversation; they're technical terms, such as *pioneer, democracy, scavenger,* and *amphibian*. Because some words, such as *democracy,* are cognates, students who speak Spanish or another Latin-based language at home may be familiar with them, but other Tier 3 words entered English from other languages. Teachers address this challenge by preteaching key vocabulary words, posting words (with picture clues, if needed) on **word walls**, and using artifacts, photos, and picture books to introduce the words. They also involve students in vocabulary activities, including making words posters and doing **word sorts**.

Reading.   Informational books are different from stories: Authors organize facts differently, incorporate special features, and use more sophisticated sentence structures. In addition, nonfiction text is dense—packed with facts and technical vocabulary. Teachers address the challenge of an unfamiliar genre in three ways. First, they teach students about informational books, including the expository text structures and distinctive text features of this genre. Next, they teach the strategies that readers use to comprehend informational books, including determining the big ideas and summarizing. Third, they teach ELs to make graphic organizers to highlight the big ideas and the relationships among them. Through this instruction, English learners are equipped with the necessary tools to read informational books more effectively.

Writing.   Writing is difficult for English learners because it reflects their English proficiency, but it also supports their learning of content knowledge and English. All students should use writing as a tool for learning during thematic units. As they draw graphic organizers, make charts, and write in learning logs, they're grappling with the big ideas and the vocabulary they're learning. Students also use writing to demonstrate learning. This more formal writing is much harder for English learners because of increased language demands, so teachers choose projects that require less writing or have students work with partners or in small groups.

These challenges are primarily the result of the students' limited knowledge of English, and when teachers differentiate instruction, ELs are more likely to be successful in learning content-area information and developing English language proficiency.

ADJUSTING INSTRUCTION.   Teachers differentiate instruction to maximize students' learning. They encourage students' participation in instructional activities because many ELs avoid interacting with mainstream classmates or fear asking questions in class (Peregoy & Boyle, 2017; Rothenberg & Fisher, 2007). Teachers adjust their instruction in these ways:

- Use visuals and manipulatives, including artifacts, videos, photographs, and models
- Preteach big ideas and key vocabulary
- Teach students about expository text structures
- Use graphic organizers to highlight relationships among big ideas
- Organize students to work in small collaborative groups and with partners
- Include frequent opportunities for students to talk informally about big ideas
- Provide opportunities for students to use oral language, reading, and writing
- Collect text sets, including picture books and online resources
- Review big ideas and key vocabulary

These suggestions take into account students' levels of English development, their limited background knowledge and vocabulary about many topics, and their reading and writing levels.

CHOOSING ALTERNATIVE ASSESSMENTS.   Teachers monitor English learners' progress by observing them and asking questions. Too often, teachers ask ELs if they understand, but that usually isn't effective, because they tend to respond positively, even when they're confused. It's more productive to interact with students, talking with them about the activity they're involved in or asking questions about the book they're reading.

Teachers also devise alternative assessments to learn more about English learners' achievement when they have difficulty on regular evaluations (Rothenberg & Fisher, 2007). For example, instead of writing compositions, students can draw pictures or graphic organizers about the big ideas and label them with words from the word wall to demonstrate their learning, or they can talk about what they've learned in a conference. When it's important to have English learners create written projects, they'll be more successful if they work with partners and in small groups. Portfolios are especially useful in documenting ELs' achievement. Students place work samples in their portfolios to show what they've learned about content-area topics and how their English proficiency has developed.

Topics for Thematic Units

Teachers develop thematic units on a variety of topics. Figure 12–5 lists possible topics for thematic units at each grade level. The units teachers develop are organized to provide opportunities for students to apply what they're learning about reading and writing as well as to meet grade-level standards.

A FIRST GRADE UNIT ON TREES.   A four-week unit plan on trees is shown in this chapter. In this unit, first graders learn about trees and their importance to people and animals. Students observe trees in their community and learn to identify the parts of a tree and types of trees. Teachers use the **interactive read-aloud** procedure to share books from the text set and list important words on the word wall. A collection of leaves, photos of trees, pictures of animals that live in trees, and products that come from trees is displayed in the classroom, and students learn about categorizing as they sort types of leaves, shapes of trees, foods that grow on trees and those that don't, and animals

MyLab Education
Video Example 12.2

PreK programs may have a bit more flexibility than typical classrooms for curriculum planning and activities. What valuable lessons can you learn from this PreK thematic unit on birds?

Figure 12–5 Topics for Thematic Units

PREKINDERGARTEN	KINDERGARTEN	FIRST GRADE
Caring for Pets	Zoo Animals	Animals Around the World
Comparing Animals and Plants	Plants	How Plants Grow
Farm Animals	Water	Solids, Liquids, and Gases
Floating and Sinking	Being a Scientist	Energy
All About Me	Five Senses	Weather
My Family	Being Healthy	Trees
Celebrations and Traditions	My School	My Neighborhood
Houses	We Are Americans	Traditions
	Foods Around the World	Homes Around the World

SECOND GRADE	THIRD GRADE	FOURTH GRADE
Animal Life Cycles	Ecosystems (Deserts, Ponds, Oceans, Rain Forests)	Food Chains
Motion		Electricity
Sound	Types of Animals (Mammals, Birds, Fish, Reptiles, Amphibians, Insects)	Light
Water Cycle		Solar System
The Earth's Surface		Rocks and Minerals
People Grow and Change	Properties of Matter	Ecology
Nutrition	My County	Archeology
My Town or City	American Indians	My State
Inventors and Inventions	Pioneers	Immigrants
Patriotism		Famous Americans

that live in trees and those that don't. Students learn how to use writing as a tool for learning as they make entries in learning logs, and teachers use **interactive writing** to make charts about the big ideas. They also view information on bookmarked websites to learn more about trees. As a culminating activity, students plant a tree at their school or participate in a community tree-planting campaign.

In this unit, teachers differentiate instruction in several ways. First, they include books in the text set that match students' reading levels; if they can't find books for emergent readers, they collaborate with these young students to make pattern books that they can read. One adaptable pattern is "I see tree":

- Students use the pattern to make a number book.

  I see 1 tree.

  I see 2 trees.

  I see 3 trees.

- Students add color words.

  I see a green tree.

  I see a purple tree.

  I see an orange tree.

- Students combine a number and a color on each page.

  I see 3 brown trees.

  I see 4 yellow trees.

  I see 5 red trees.

- Students name different species of trees.

  I see a maple tree.

  I see a pine tree.

  I see a dogwood tree.

- Students incorporate a more complex sentence pattern.

  I see a bird in a little tree.

I see a squirrel in a big tree.

I see 3 bees in an apple tree.

They illustrate the pages, usually with drawings, but for the tree species book, they use photos taken during a field trip.

Second, teachers vary the grouping patterns: Some instruction is presented to the whole class, but students are organized into small groups and pairs for other activities. Teachers use small groups for **shared reading** and interactive writing activities, and students read books from the text set and make posters with partners if they're more successful working with a classmate. Students also examine tree artifacts, read books, and write books independently.

Third, teachers adapt activities to accommodate students' instructional needs, checking their background knowledge at the beginning of the unit and adjusting instruction accordingly. They focus their instruction on the big ideas using a combination of oral, visual, written, and digital activities; for example, students listen to books read aloud, participate in discussions, make charts and diagrams, post words on the **word wall**, participate in interactive writing, and visit websites as they learn about trees.

Teachers also differentiate students' culminating projects about trees. Some projects involve the whole class, and students work with partners or individually on others. The tree-planting project that grew out of a student's suggestion involves the whole class; students work together to make multigenre projects and class scrapbooks and work individually or with partners to write "All About Trees" books. Teachers recognize that students' books will vary, because some first graders write three-page books with one sentence on each page, some craft seven- or eight-page books with several sentences and informative diagrams on each page, and others dictate a sentence or two that the teacher writes for them.

Teachers link assessment with instruction in this thematic unit. At the beginning of the unit, they survey students' background knowledge using a **KWL chart**. During the unit, teachers monitor students' progress as they observe them, listening to their comments during discussions and watching them participating in activities. At the end of the unit, teachers evaluate students' learning without using tests; instead, they ask students to demonstrate what they've learned by drawing and labeling a picture about one of the big ideas they've studied, or they examine the information that students include in their "All About Trees" books. Teachers also gauge students' learning as they finish the last column of the KWL chart.

A FOURTH GRADE UNIT ON THE DESERT ECOSYSTEM. A three-week plan for a unit on desert life is also presented in this chapter. In this unit, students investigate the plants, animals, and people that live in the desert and learn how they support each other. They write entries in learning logs to take notes, draw diagrams, record words they're learning, and write reactions to books they're reading. Students divide into book clubs during the first week to read books about the desert. During the second week, they participate in an author study of Byrd Baylor—a woman who lives in the desert and writes about desert life—and they read many of her books. During the third week, students participate in reading workshop to read other desert books and reread favorites. To apply their learning, students create projects, including writing desert riddles, making a chart of the desert ecosystem, and drawing a desert mural. Together, as a class, students create a desert alphabet book.

Teachers differentiate instruction in this unit to allow for individual learning differences. They include books in the text set that match students' reading levels so everyone can participate in literature circles and reading workshop, and they emphasize learning in small groups through center activities, book clubs, and collaborative projects. Teachers include oral, visual, written, and computer activities in the

MyLab Education
Video Example 12.3

Word sorting can be used to have students demonstrate their understanding of word meaning. How did Ms. Koch instruct her students to categorize these words as a way to ensure they have learned the vocabulary for a project on plants?

Planning Guide A First Grade Unit on Trees

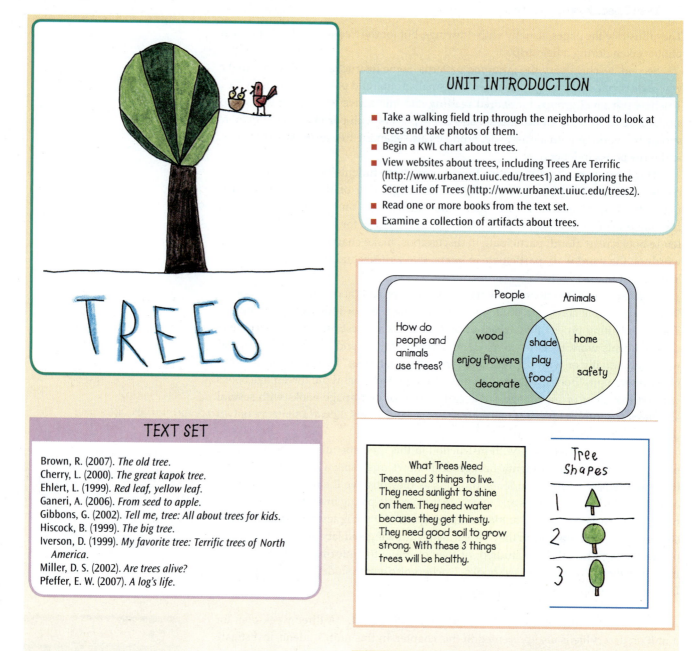

TEXT SET

Brown, R. (2007). *The old tree.*
Cherry, L. (2000). *The great kapok tree.*
Ehlert, L. (1999). *Red leaf, yellow leaf.*
Ganeri, A. (2006). *From seed to apple.*
Gibbons, G. (2002). *Tell me, tree: All about trees for kids.*
Hiscock, B. (1999). *The big tree.*
Iverson, D. (1999). *My favorite tree: Terrific trees of North America.*
Miller, D. S. (2002). *Are trees alive?*
Pfeffer, E. W. (2007). *A log's life.*

UNIT INTRODUCTION

■ Take a walking field trip through the neighborhood to look at trees and take photos of them.
■ Begin a KWL chart about trees.
■ View websites about trees, including Trees Are Terrific (http://www.urbanext.uiuc.edu/trees1) and Exploring the Secret Life of Trees (http://www.urbanext.uiuc.edu/trees2).
■ Read one or more books from the text set.
■ Examine a collection of artifacts about trees.

How do people and animals use trees?

People | Animals
wood | home
enjoy flowers | shade play food | safety
decorate

What Trees Need
Trees need 3 things to live. They need sunlight to shine on them. They need water because they get thirsty. They need good soil to grow strong. With these 3 things trees will be healthy.

Tree Shapes
1
2
3

USING THE TEXT SET

■ Read books using interactive read-alouds.
■ Use shared reading to read big books.
■ Do book talks to interest students in looking at or reading some of the books.
■ Have students read those books at their reading level at the reading center.
■ Examine nonfiction text factors in informational books.
■ Use books as mentor texts or models for writing.

DIGGING INTO THE BIG IDEAS

■ Use interactive writing to create charts about the parts of a tree, how we use trees, or what trees need to live.
■ Write a big book about the foods that come from trees.
■ Do a semantic feature analysis to classify animals that live in trees.
■ Draw a Venn diagram to compare the ways people and animals use trees.
■ Create a poster about the shapes of trees or features of leaves.

WORD WALL

AB	CDEFGH	IJKLM
bark	fruit	leaf
branch	flower	leaves
birds	evergreen	kapok
acorn	chocolate	jagged
apples		maple syrup
beaver		

NO	PQR	STUVWYZ
nest	root	trunk
oak	paper	smooth
needle	rough	wood
nuts	palm	seed
owl	pine	squirrel
oxygen	rain forest	shade
		vein

VOCABULARY ACTIVITIES

- Add new words to the word wall.
- Make word posters.
- Highlight words in books students are reading and around the classroom.
- Do word sorts.
- Have students label pictures they draw using words on the word wall.

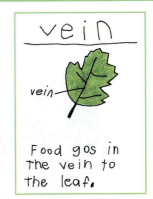

DIFFERENTIATION

- **Books:** Include books at students' reading levels in the text set.
- **Grouping:** Incorporate small-group, partner, individual, and whole-class activities into the unit.
- **Activities:** Use the Language Experience Approach and interactive writing to support emergent writers, and shared reading for emergent readers.
- **Projects:** Have students create collaborative projects.

ASSESSMENT

- **Plan.** Check students' background knowledge about trees using the K column of the KWL chart.
- **Monitor.** Ask students to choose one word from the word wall to talk, draw, or write about, and observe them as they participate in activities.
- **Evaluate.** Have students draw and label a picture about one big idea to demonstrate learning, check the information students include in their "All About Trees" books, and complete the KWL chart.
- **Reflect.** Invite students to create posters to highlight the most important thing they learned. At the same time, reflect on the thematic unit and how to better meet all students' needs.

CULMINATING PROJECTS

- Plant a tree at school or join with a community group to plant a tree in the neighborhood.
- Write "All About Trees" books.
- Develop a class multigenre project about trees.
- Make a class scrapbook of tree photos taken at the beginning of the unit with sentences to describe each one.

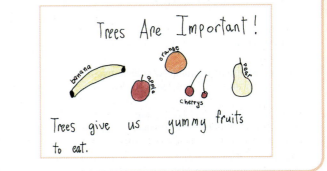

CENTERS

- **Reading:** Read books from the text set.
- **Listening:** Listen to a book from the text set.
- **Word Sort:** Do word sorts using vocabulary from the word wall.
- **Learning Logs:** Draw and write about trees in learning logs.
- **Art:** Paint a picture of a tree in each season, dictate or write a descriptive sentence to describe each one, and compile the pages to make a book.
- **Science:** Examine and sort leaves, bark, nuts, plastic fruits, and other artifacts related to trees.
- **Writing:** Write poems and riddles about trees.
- **Computers:** View bookmarked websites about trees.

Planning Guide A Fourth Grade Unit on the Desert Ecosystem

DIFFERENTIATION

- **Books:** Include books at all students' reading levels in the text set.
- **Grouping:** Make available small-group and partner activities, including at centers, and provide small-group instruction.
- **Activities:** Include oral and visual activities, and provide plenty of opportunities for active involvement in activities.
- **Projects:** Design tiered projects and collaborative projects.

CENTERS

- **Data chart:** Record information about desert biomes on the ecosystem chart.
- **Listening:** Listen to a book from the text set.
- **Word sort:** Sort words from the word wall.
- **Visual literacy:** Create tabletop dioramas about various desert biomes.
- **Writing:** Prepare a page for the class alphabet book about deserts.

UNIT INTRODUCTION

- Begin a KWL chart about the desert ecosystem.
- Share one or more books from the text set.
- Have students participate in a tea party activity.
- Visit theme-related websites, including Desert Biomes (http://www.desertusa.com) and A Virtual Museum of the Mojave Desert (http://score.rims.k12.ca.us/activity/Mojave).

DIGGING INTO THE BIG IDEAS

- Create posters and graphic organizers about big ideas and relationships among them.
- Complete a semantic feature analysis comparing the desert to other ecosystems.
- Record information and explore ideas about deserts in learning logs.
- Research topics related to this ecosystem and share information in multigenre reports and other projects.

ASSESSMENT

- **Plan.** Begin a KWL chart or have students write in learning logs about what they already know about this ecosystem.
- **Monitor.** Have students complete graphic organizers about big ideas and write entries in learning logs.
- **Evaluate.** Use rubrics to evaluate students' projects, and have students complete the L column of the KWL chart individually or with partners.
- **Reflect.** Ask students several questions to help them reflect on their learning by writing letters to the teacher. At the same time, reflect on the unit and how to adapt activities and projects to meet the needs of all students.

USING THE TEXT SET

- Use for interactive read-alouds.
- Read these books during reading workshop.
- Participate in literature circles using books from the text set.
- Do book talks to encourage independent reading.
- Use books in minilessons about genres, expository text structures, and nonfiction features.
- Use books as models or mentor texts for writing projects.

TEXT SET ON THE DESERT ECOSYSTEM

Bash, B. (2002). *Desert giant*.
Baylor, B. (1987). *The desert is theirs*.
Baylor, B. (1993). *Desert voices*.
George, J. C. (1996). *One day in the desert*.
Gibbons, G. (1999). *Deserts*.
Guiberson, B. Z. (2007). *Cactus hotel*.
Jablonsky, A. (1994). *100 questions about desert life*.
Mora, P. (2008). *The desert is my mother*.
Pratt-Serafini, K. J. (2002). *Saguaro moon: A desert journal*.
Siebert, D. (1992). *Mojave*.
Simon, S. (1990). *Deserts*.
Taylor, B. (1998). *Desert life*.
Wright-Frierson, V. (2002). *A desert scrapbook*.

VOCABULARY ACTIVITIES

- Post words on a word wall.
- Make posters and diagrams to learn about key Tier 3 vocabulary.
- Use quickwrites to explore meanings of words.
- Do a word sort using words from the word wall.
- Create a class alphabet book about the desert using words from the word wall.

AUTHOR STUDY

- Share information about author Byrd Baylor, who lives in the Arizona desert.
- Read Byrd Baylor's books about the desert, including *The Desert Is Theirs* (Baylor, 1987) and *Desert Voices* (Baylor, 1993).
- Write "I Am . . ." poems based on *Desert Voices*.
- Create a multigenre project about the author and her books.

DESERT WORD WALL

ABC	DEFGH	IJKL
biome	ecosystem	kangaroo rat
cactus	fragile	king snake
adaptation	gila monster	jackrabbit
coyote	dunes	Joshua tree
coral snake	endangered	lizard
camouflage	exoskeleton	javelina
burrow	hamster	
coyote	hawk	

MNO	PQRS	TUVWXYZ
Mojave Desert	Sahara Desert	water
oasis	scorpion	tortoise
owl	Sonoran Desert	toad
	roadrunner	yucca
	sandgrouse	
	spiny	
	saguaro	
	sidewinder	

CULMINATING PROJECTS

- Create a class multigenre project on deserts.
- Write a collaborative report about the desert ecosystem.
- Research a desert animal or plant and give an oral presentation about it.
- Design a chart to compare the desert ecosystem with another ecosystem.
- Develop a museum or online virtual museum about this ecosystem.

unit. Students listen to **book talks**, participate in tea parties where they share cards about the desert ecosystem with classmates, do **word sorts**, complete **semantic feature analysis** charts, conduct research, write in learning logs, and view websites about deserts. Teachers also have students create culminating projects to share the results of their research about desert plants and animals; they incorporate individual, small-group, and whole-class projects, including multigenre projects, oral presentations, and virtual museums.

Assessment using the instruction–assessment cycle is an integral part of the desert ecosystem unit: Teachers survey students' knowledge about deserts when they start the unit, monitor their progress each week, and at the end, evaluate their understanding of the big ideas they've studied. To begin, teachers survey students' background knowledge by creating a **KWL chart** and completing the K column. They monitor students' progress by listening to their comments during discussions, reading their learning log entries, and reviewing the graphic organizers they complete. Teachers use **rubrics** to evaluate projects, and they have students use them to self-assess their own work. They also bring closure to the unit by completing the L column of the KWL chart.

MyLab Education Self-Check 12.3
MyLab Education Application Exercise 12.1: Developing Thematic Units

Chapter Review

Integrating Literacy Into Thematic Units

- Teachers have students use reading and writing as learning tools.

- Teachers provide opportunities for students to create projects to demonstrate learning.

- Teachers organize content-area instruction into thematic units.

Accountability Check

Visit the following assessment links to access quiz questions and instructional applications

MyLab Education Application Exercise 12.2: Understanding Literacy Development

MyLab Education Application Exercise 12.3: Monitoring Literacy Development

MyLab Education Application Exercise 12.4: Measuring Literacy Development

References

Allen, C. A. (2001). *The multigenre research paper: Voice, passion, and discovery in grades 4–6.* Portsmouth, NH: Heinemann.

Armbruster, B. B., McCarthey, S. J., & Cummins, S. (2005). Writing to learn in elementary classrooms. In R. Indrisano & J. R. Paratore (Eds.), *Learning to write, writing to learn: Theory and research in practice* (pp. 71–96). Newark, DE: International Reading Association.

Baylor, B. (1987). *The desert is theirs.* New York: Aladdin Books.

Baylor, B. (1993). *Desert voices.* New York: Scribner.

Bredekamp, S. (Ed.). (1990). *Developmentally appropriate practice in early childhood programs serving children from birth through age 8.* Washington, DC: National Association for the Education of Young Children.

Brown, M. W. (1990). *The important book.* New York: HarperCollins.

Cole, J. (1999). *The magic school bus and the electric field trip.* New York: Scholastic.

Common core state standards for English language arts. (2010). Retrieved from http://www.corestandards.org/ELA-Literacy/

Dorfman, L. R., & Cappelli, R. (2017). *Mentor texts: Teaching writing through children's literature, K–6.* (2nd ed.). Portland, ME: Stenhouse.

Dorfman, L. R., & Cappelli, R. (2009). *Nonfiction mentor texts.* Portland, ME: Stenhouse.

Elbow, P. (1998). *Writing without teachers* (2nd ed.). New York: Oxford University Press.

Harvey, S. (1998). *Nonfiction matters: Reading, writing, and research in grades 3–8.* York, ME: Stenhouse.

Hatkoff, I., Hatkoff, C., & Kahumbu, P. (2006). *Owen and Mzee: The true story of a remarkable friendship.* New York: Scholastic.

Heard, G. (Ed.). (2009). *Falling down the page: A book of list poems.* New York: Roaring Brook Press.

Guiberson, B. Z. (2007). *Cactus hotel.* New York: Henry Holt.

Harmey, S. J., & Rodgers, E. M. (2017). Differences in the Early Writing Development of Struggling Children Who Beat the Odds and Those Who Did Not. *Journal of Education for Students Placed at Risk (JESPAR),* 22(3), 157–177.

Judge, L. (2007). *One thousand tracings: Healing the wounds of World War II.* New York: Hyperion Books.

Krull, K. (2000). *Wilma unlimited: How Wilma Rudolph became the world's fastest woman.* New York: Sandpiper.

McLimans, D. (2006). *Gone wild: An endangered animal alphabet.* New York: Walker.

Moline, S. (2012). *I see what you mean: Visual literacy, K-8.* (2nd ed.). York, ME: Stenhouse.

Napier, M. (2002). *Z is for Zamboni: A hockey alphabet.* Chelsea, MI: Sleeping Bear Press.

Peregoy, S. F., & Boyle, O. F. (2017). *Reading, writing and learning in ESL: A resource book for K–12 teachers.* (7th ed.). Boston: Pearson.

Rappaport, D. (2007). *Martin's big words: The life of Dr. Martin Luther King, Jr.* New York: Hyperion Books.

Robb, L. (2003). *Teaching reading in social studies, science, and math.* New York: Scholastic.

Rodriguez, R. V. (2006). *Through Georgia's eyes.* New York: Henry Holt.

Romano, T. (2000). *Blending genre, alternating style: Writing multiple genre papers.* Portsmouth, NH: Heinemann/Boynton/Cook.

Rothenberg, C., & Fisher, D. (2007). *Teaching English language learners: A differentiated approach.* Upper Saddle River, NJ: Merrill/Prentice Hall.

Stead, T. (2002). *Is that a fact? Teaching nonfiction writing K–3.* Portland, ME: Stenhouse.

Thimmesh, C. (2006). *Team moon: How 400,000 people landed Apollo 11 on the moon.* Boston: Houghton Mifflin.

Tompkins, G. E. (2019). *Teaching writing: Balancing process and product.* (7th ed.). Boston: Allyn & Bacon/Pearson.

Weatherford, C. B. (2007). *Freedom on the menu: The Greensboro sit-ins.* New York: Dial Books.

Compendium of Instructional Procedures

- Book Talks
- Choral Reading
- Cloze Procedure
- Collaborative Books
- Grand Conversations
- Hot Seat
- Interactive Read-Alouds
- Interactive Writing
- KWL Charts
- Language Experience Approach
- Learning Logs
- Making Words
- Minilessons
- Open-Mind Portraits

- RAFT
- Readers Theatre
- Reading Logs
- Revising Groups
- Rubrics
- Running Records
- Semantic Feature Analysis
- Shared Reading
- Story Boards
- Story Retelling
- Think-Alouds
- Word Ladders
- Word Sorts
- Word Walls

Book Talks

Book talks are brief teasers that teachers give to introduce books and interest students in reading them. Teachers show the book, summarize it without giving away the ending, and read a short excerpt aloud to hook students' interest. Then they pass the book off to an interested reader or place it in the classroom library. Students use the same steps when they give book talks to share the books they've read during reading workshop. This transcript shows a third grader's book talk about Paula Danziger's *Amber Brown Is Not a Crayon* (2006):

> This is my book: Amber Brown Is Not a Crayon. It's about these two kids—
> Amber Brown, who is a girl, and Justin Daniels, who is a boy. See? Here is
> their picture. They are in third grade, too, and their teacher—his name is Mr.
> Cohen—pretends to take them on airplane trips to the places they study. They
> move their chairs so that it is like they are on an airplane and Amber and Justin
> always put their chairs side by side. I'm going to read you the very beginning of
> the book. [She reads the first three pages aloud to the class.] This story is really
> funny, and when you are reading you think the author is telling you the story
> instead of you reading it. And there are more stories about Amber Brown. This
> is the one I'm reading now—You Can't Eat Your Chicken Pox, Amber Brown.

This student and others in her class are so successful in giving book talks because their teacher modeled how to give a book talk, and students are reading books that they've chosen—books they really like. In addition, they're experienced in talking with their classmates about books.

PROCEDURE. Teachers follow these steps in conducting a book talk:

1. *Select a book to share.* Teachers choose a new book to introduce to students or a book that students haven't shown much interest in. They familiarize themselves with the book by reading or rereading it.

2. *Plan a brief presentation.* Teachers plan how they'll present the book to interest students in reading it. They usually begin with the title and author of the book, and they mention the genre or topic and briefly summarize the plot without giving away the ending. Teachers also decide why they liked the book and think about why students might be interested in it. Sometimes they choose a short excerpt to read and an illustration to show.

3. *Present the book talk.* Teachers present the planned book talk while showing the book. Their comments are usually enough so that at least one student will ask to borrow the book to read.

Teachers use book talks to introduce students to books in the classroom library. At the beginning of the school year, they take time to introduce many of the books in the library, and during the year, they introduce new books as they're added. They also introduce the books selected for a literature circle or a text set for a thematic unit.

Choral Reading

Students use choral reading to orally share poems and other brief texts. This group reading activity provides students, especially struggling readers, with valuable oral reading practice, in which they learn to read more expressively and increase their reading fluency. In addition, it's a great activity for English learners because they practice reading aloud with classmates in a nonthreatening group setting; as they read with English-speaking classmates, they hear and practice English pronunciation, phrasing of words in a sentence, and intonation patterns.

Many arrangements for choral reading are possible: Students read the text together as a class, divide it and read sections in small groups, or individual students read particular lines or stanzas while the class reads the rest of the text. Here are four arrangements:

Echo Reading.   A leader reads each line, and the group repeats it.

Leader and Chorus Reading.   A leader reads the main part, and the group reads the refrain in unison.

Small-Group Reading.   The class divides into two or more groups, and each group reads part of the text.

Cumulative Reading.   One student reads the first line or stanza, and another student joins in as each line or stanza is read to create a cumulative effect.

Students read the text aloud several times, experimenting with different arrangements until they decide which one conveys the meaning most effectively.

PROCEDURE.   Teachers follow this procedure:

1. *Select a text.* Teachers choose a poem or other short text and copy it onto a chart or make multiple copies for students to read.

2. *Arrange the text.* Teachers work with students to decide how to arrange the text. They add marks to the chart, or they have students mark individual copies so that they can follow the arrangement.

3. *Rehearse the text.* Students practice reading the text several times at natural speed, pronouncing words carefully.

4. *Read the text aloud.* Students read the text aloud, pronouncing words clearly and reading with expression. Teachers can tape-record students' reading so they can

hear their choral reading; sometimes they want to rearrange the choral reading after hearing the recording.

Many poems can easily be arranged for choral reading. Poems such as these, with repetitions, echoes, refrains, or questions and answers, work well:

"My Parents Think I'm Sleeping," by Jack Prelutsky (2007)
"I Woke Up This Morning," by Karla Kuskin (2003)
"Ode to La Tortilla," by Gary Soto (2005)
"The New Kid on the Block," by Jack Prelutsky (1983)
"A Circle of Sun," by Rebecca Kai Dotlich (Yolen & Peters, 2007)

Poems written specifically for two readers lend themselves to choral reading, including the book-length poem *I Am the Dog/I Am the Cat* (Hall, 1994). In addition, songs, such as Woody Guthrie's *This Land Is Your Land* (2002), are very effective.

Cloze Procedure

The cloze procedure is an informal diagnostic assessment that teachers use to gather information about readers' ability to deal with the complexity of texts they're reading (Taylor, 1953). Teachers construct a cloze passage by selecting an excerpt from a story or a nonfiction book that students have read and deleting every fifth word in the passage; the deleted words are replaced with blanks. Then students read the passage and fill in the missing words, using their knowledge of syntax and semantics to successfully predict the missing words in the text passage. Only the exact word is considered a correct answer.

This cloze passage is about wolves:

> The leaders of a wolf pack are called the alpha wolves. There is an _____ male and an alpha _____. They are usually the _____ and the strongest wolves _____ the pack. An alpha _____ fight any wolf that _____ to take over the _____. When the alpha looks _____ other wolf in the _____, the other wolf crouches _____ and tucks its tail _____ its hind legs. Sometimes _____ rolls over and licks _____ alpha wolf's face as _____ to say, "You are _____ boss."

The missing words are *alpha, female, largest, in, will, tries, pack, eye, down, between, it, the, if,* and *the.*

The cloze procedure assesses sentence-level comprehension (Tierney & Readence, 2005). It's a useful classroom tool for determining which texts are at students' instructional levels. A caution, however: Cloze doesn't measure comprehension globally; it only assesses students' ability to use syntax and semantics within individual sentences and paragraphs.

PROCEDURE. Teachers follow these steps:

1. *Select a passage.* Teachers select a passage from a book and retype it. The first sentence is typed exactly as it appears in the original text, and beginning with the second sentence, one of the first five words is deleted and replaced with a blank. Then every fifth word in the remainder of the passage is deleted and replaced with a blank.

2. *Complete the cloze activity.* Students read the passage all the way through once silently and then reread it and predict or "guess" the word that goes in each blank. They write the deleted words in the blanks.

3. *Score students' work.* Teachers award one point each time the missing word is identified. The percentage of correct answers is determined by dividing the number

of points by the number of blanks. If students score more than 60% correct replacements, the text is likely at their independent reading level; if they score 40%–59% correct replacements, the text is probably at their instructional level; and if they score less than 40% correct replacements, the text is likely at their frustration level.

This assessment procedure can also be used to judge whether a particular book is appropriate for classroom instruction. Teachers prepare a cloze passage and have students predict the missing words, then they score the predictions. If students correctly predict more than 50% of the deleted words, the text is easy reading, but if they predict less than 30%, it's too difficult for classroom instruction. The instructional range is 30%–50% correct predictions (Reutzel & Cooter, 2008).

Collaborative Books

Students work together in small groups to make collaborative books; they each contribute one page or work with a classmate to write a page or a section of the book. Younger students prepare their pages in a single draft, but older students use the writing process to fine-tune their pages. Teachers often use class collaborations as a first bookmaking project and to introduce the writing process. Students write collaborative books to retell a favorite story, illustrate a poem with one line or stanza on each page, or write a nonfiction book or biography.

PROCEDURE.   Teachers follow these steps:

1. *Choose a topic.* Teachers choose a topic related to a literature focus unit or thematic unit. Then students choose specific topics or pages to prepare.
2. *Introduce the organization.* Teachers explain how students are to organize their writing and where to place drawings on the page or in the section. They often write one page or section of the book together as a class before students begin working on their pages.
3. *Prepare the pages.* Students create their pages following the teacher's organizational design. Older students use the writing process and share their rough drafts in revising groups, incorporate classmates' feedback in their drafts, proofread with partners, and then make their final copies.
4. *Compile the pages.* Students hand in their pages and arrange them for the book. They also add a title page and a cover. Older students also prepare a table of contents, an introduction, a conclusion, and a bibliography for nonfiction books.

The benefit of collaborative books is that students share the work, so the books are completed much more quickly and easily than individual books. Because they write only one page or section, it takes less time for teachers to conference with students and assist them with time-consuming revising and editing.

Grand Conversations

Grand conversations are discussions about stories in which students explore the big ideas, deepen their comprehension, and reflect on their feelings (Peterson & Eeds, 2007). They're different from traditional discussions because they're student centered: Students do most of the talking as they voice their opinions and support their views with examples from the story. They talk about what puzzles them, what they find interesting, and their connections to the story. Students usually don't raise their hands to be called on by the teacher; instead, they take turns and speak when no one else is speaking, much as adults do when they talk with friends. They also encourage their classmates to contribute to the conversation. Even though teachers participate, the talk is primarily among the students.

Grand conversations have two parts. The first part is open-ended: Students talk about their reactions to the book, and their comments determine the direction of the conversation; teachers share their responses, ask questions, and provide information. Later, teachers focus students' attention on one or two topics that they didn't talk about in the first part of the conversation.

PROCEDURE.   Teachers follow these steps in using this instructional procedure:

1. *Read the book.* Students read a story or part of a story, or they listen to the teacher read it aloud.

2. *Think about the story.* Students think about the story by drawing pictures or writing in reading logs. This step is especially important when students don't talk much, because with this preparation, they're more likely to have ideas to share with classmates.

3. *Begin the conversation.* Students form a circle for the class conversation so that everyone can see each other. Teachers begin by asking, "Who would like to begin?" or "What are you thinking about?" One student makes a comment, and classmates take turns talking about the idea the first student introduced.

4. *Continue the conversation.* A student introduces a new idea and classmates talk about it, sharing ideas, asking questions, and reading excerpts to make a point. Students limit their comments to the idea being discussed, and after they finish discussing this idea, a new one is introduced. To ensure that everyone participates, teachers often ask that each student make no more than three comments until everyone has spoken at least once.

5. *Ask questions.* Teachers ask questions to direct students to aspects of the story that have been missed; for example, they might focus on an element of story structure or the writer's craft. Or they may ask students to compare the book to others by the same author.

6. *Conclude the conversation.* After exploring all of the big ideas, teachers end the conversation by summarizing and drawing conclusions about the story.

Young students usually meet as a class for grand conversations, but when they're participating in literature circles, they meet in small groups because they're reading different books. The benefit of whole-class conversations is the feeling of community that's established, and when they meet in small groups, students have more opportunities to talk and share their ideas.

Hot Seat

Hot seat is a role-playing activity that builds students' comprehension. Students assume the persona of a character from a story, the featured person from a biography they're reading, or an author whose books they've read, and they sit in a chair designated as the "hot seat" to be interviewed by classmates. It's called "hot seat" because students have to think quickly to respond to their classmates' questions and comments. Students aren't intimidated by performing for classmates; in fact, in most classrooms, the activity is very popular. Students often wear a costume they've created when they assume the character's persona and share objects they've collected and artifacts they've made.

PROCEDURE.   Here are the steps in the hot seat activity:

1. *Learn about the character.* Students prepare for the hot seat activity by reading a story or a biography to learn about the character they'll impersonate.

2. *Create a costume.* Students design a costume appropriate for their character. In addition, they often collect objects or create artifacts to use in their presentations.

3. *Prepare opening remarks.* Students think about the most important things they'd like to share about the character and plan what they'll say at the beginning of the activity.

4. *Introduce the character.* One student sits in front of classmates in a chair designated as the "hot seat," tells a little about the character he or she is role-playing using a first-person viewpoint (e.g., "I said, 'One small step for man, one giant leap for humankind'"), and shares artifacts.

5. *Ask questions and make comments.* Classmates ask questions to learn more about the character and offer advice, and the student remains in the role to respond to them.

6. *Summarize the ideas.* The student doing the role-play selects a classmate to summarize the important ideas that were presented about the character. The student on the hot seat clarifies any misunderstandings and adds any big ideas that classmates don't mention.

When students participate in the hot seat activity, they deepen their understanding of the book they're reading: They explore the characters, analyze story events, draw inferences, and try out different interpretations.

Interactive Read-Alouds

Teachers use interactive read-alouds to share books with students. The focus is on enhancing students' comprehension by engaging them in the reading process before, during, and after reading. Teachers introduce the book and activate students' background knowledge before beginning to read. Next, they include students during reading through conversation and other activities. Afterward, students respond to the book. What's most important is how teachers engage students while they're reading aloud (Fisher, Flood, Lapp, & Frey, 2004).

Teachers often involve students by pausing periodically to talk about what's just been read. The timing is crucial: When reading stories, it's more effective to stop where students can make predictions and connections, after episodes that students might find confusing, and just before the ending becomes clear. When reading informational books, teachers stop to talk about big ideas as they're presented, briefly explain technical terms, and emphasize connections between the ideas. Teachers often read a poem from beginning to end once, and then stop as they're rereading it for students to play with words, notice poetic devices, and repeat favorite words and lines. Review the Interactive Techniques box. Deciding how often to pause for an activity and knowing when to continue reading develops through practice and varies from one group of students to another.

Interactive Techniques

GENRE	ACTIVITIES
Stories	• Make and revise predictions at pivotal points • Share personal, world, and literary connections • Draw a picture of a character or an event • Assume the persona of a character and share the character's thoughts • Reenact a scene from the story
Informational Books	• Ask questions or share information • Raise hands when specific information is read • Restate the headings as questions • Take notes • Complete graphic organizers
Poetry	• Add sound effects • Mumble-read along with the teacher • Repeat lines after the teacher • Clap when rhyming words, alliteration, or other poetic devices are heard

PROCEDURE.   Teachers follow these steps to conduct interactive read-alouds:

1. *Pick a book.* Teachers choose award-winning and other high-quality books that are appropriate for students and that fit into their instructional programs.

2. *Prepare to share the book.* Teachers practice reading the book to ensure that they can read it fluently and to decide where to pause and engage students with the text; they write prompts on self-stick notes to mark these pages. Teachers also think about how they'll introduce the book and highlight difficult vocabulary words.

3. *Introduce the book.* Teachers activate students' background knowledge, set a clear purpose for listening, and preview the text.

4. *Read the book interactively.* Teachers read the book aloud, modeling fluent reading. They stop periodically to ask questions to focus students' attention on specific points in the text and involve them in other activities.

5. *Participate in after-reading activities.* Students participate in discussions and other response activities.

Teachers use this instructional procedure whenever they're reading aloud, no matter whether it's an after-lunch read-aloud period or during a literature focus unit or a thematic unit. Reading aloud has always been an important activity in preschool and kindergarten classrooms. While some teachers think they should read to students only until they learn to read, reading aloud to share the excitement of books, especially those that students can't yet read themselves, should remain an important part of the literacy program at all grade levels.

Interactive Writing

Teachers use interactive writing to compose a message with students and write it on chart paper (Button, Johnson, & Furgerson, 1996). The text is created by the group, and the teacher guides students as they write it word by word. Students take turns writing known letters and familiar words, adding punctuation marks, and marking spaces between words. As students participate in creating and writing the text on chart paper, they also write it on small whiteboards. Afterward, they read and reread the text using shared reading at first, and then reading it independently.

Interactive writing is used to demonstrate how writing works and show students how to construct words using their knowledge of sound–symbol correspondences and spelling patterns. It's also a powerful instructional procedure to use with English learners, no matter their age (Tompkins & Collom, 2004). It was developed by the well-known British educator Moira McKenzie, who based it on Don Holdaway's work in **shared reading** (Fountas & Pinnell, 1996).

PROCEDURE.   Teachers follow these steps to do interactive writing with small groups or the entire class:

1. *Collect materials.* Teachers collect chart paper, colored marking pens, white correction tape, an alphabet chart, magnetic letters or letter cards, and a pointer. They also collect small whiteboards, pens, and erasers for individual students to use when writing.

2. *Pass out writing supplies.* Teachers distribute individual whiteboards, pens, and erasers for students to use to write the text individually as it's being written on chart paper. They periodically ask students to hold their boards up to check their work.

3. *Set a purpose.* Teachers present a stimulus activity. Often, they read or reread a trade book, but students also share daily news or summarize information they're learning during a thematic unit.

4. *Choose a sentence to write.* Teachers negotiate the text—often a sentence or two—with students. Students repeat the sentence several times and segment it into words.

5. *Write the first sentence.* The teacher and students slowly pronounce the first word of the sentence, "stretching" it out; students identify the sounds and the letters that represent them, and they write the letters on chart paper. The teacher chooses students to write letters and words, depending on their knowledge of phonics and spelling. They use a colored pen, and the teacher uses another color to write the words students can't spell to keep track of how much writing students are able to do. Teachers have an alphabet poster with upper- and lowercase letters available for students to refer to when they're unsure how to form a letter, and white correction tape (sometimes called "boo-boo" tape) is available for students to correct poorly formed letters and misspellings. After each word is written, one student serves as the "spacer" and uses his or her hand to mark the space between words. This procedure is repeated to write each word in the sentence, and students reread the sentence from the beginning after each new word is completed. When appropriate, teachers point out capital letters, punctuation marks, and other conventions of print.

6. *Write additional sentences.* Teachers repeat the fifth step to write the remaining sentences.

7. *Display the completed text.* After completing the message, teachers post the chart in the classroom and have students reread it, first using shared reading and then independent reading. Students often reread interactive charts when they "read the room," and teachers use the charts in teaching high-frequency words and phonics concepts.

When teachers introduce interactive writing in preschool or kindergarten, they ask students to write both letters to represent the beginning sounds in familiar words such as *the*, *a*, and *is*. As students learn more about phoneme–grapheme correspondences, they do more of the writing. The featured box, First Graders' Prediction About *Rosie's Walk* Written Interactively, shows a class's prediction about what will happen to a hen named Rosie that was written before reading *Rosie's Walk* (Hutchins, 2005). The students wrote the red letters and the teacher wrote blue ones; the rectangles represent correction tape used to cover errors. Once students write words fluently, they do interactive writing in small groups. Each group member uses a different colored pen and takes turns writing words. They also sign their names in their color on the page so that the teacher can track who wrote each word.

First Graders' Prediction about *Rosie's Walk* Written Interactively

We think the fox will
catch Rosie the hen.

KWL Charts

Teachers use KWL charts during thematic units to activate students' background knowledge about a topic and to scaffold them as they ask questions and organize the information they're learning (Ogle, 1986). Teachers create a KWL chart by hanging

Second Grade KWL Chart on the Water Cycle

K	W	L
WHAT WE KNOW	**WHAT WE WONDER**	**WHAT WE LEARNED**
Water is very important. Animals and plants need water to drink. People need water, too. Water comes from the water pipes and the faucet in the kitchen. Water comes from oceans and rivers and ponds. We get water from the rain. Water sinks into the ground when it rains.	Where does water come from? Is snow like rain? How does rain get in the clouds? Why are clouds white? What is the water cycle? Why does it rain? What would happen if it never rained?	Water goes up into the air and makes clouds. The water cycle happens over and over. Water vapor goes up into the clouds. Another word for rain is precipitation. Water goes up, makes a cloud, comes down, and it starts all over. Evaporation is when water changes from a liquid to a gas. Condensation is the opposite of evaporation. Condensation is when water vapor changes into a liquid—water.

up three sheets of butcher paper and labeling them *K, W,* and *L*; the letters stand for "What We **K**now," "What We **W**onder," and "What We **L**earned." Review the KWL chart, Second Grader KWL Chart on the Water Cycle, developed by a second grade class as they were studying Earth's Systems. The teacher did the actual writing on the chart, but the students generated the ideas and questions. It often takes several weeks to complete this activity because teachers introduce the KWL chart at the beginning of a unit and use it to identify what students already know and what they want to learn. At the end of the unit, students complete the last section of the chart, listing what they've learned.

PROCEDURE. Teachers follow these steps to create KWL charts:

1. *Post a KWL chart.* Teachers post a large chart on the classroom wall, divide it into three columns, and label them *K* (What We **K**now), *W* (What We **W**onder), and *L* (What We Learned).

2. *Complete the K column.* At the beginning of a thematic unit, teachers ask students to brainstorm what they know about the topic and write this information in the K column. Sometimes students suggest information that isn't correct; these statements are turned into questions and added to the W column.

3. *Complete the W column.* Teachers write the questions that students suggest in the W column. They continue to add questions during the unit.

4. *Complete the L column.* At the end of the unit, students reflect on what they've learned, and teachers record this information in the L column.

Students also make individual KWL charts by folding a legal-size sheet of paper in half, lengthwise, cutting the top flap into thirds, and labeling the flaps *K, W,* and *L.* Then students lift the flaps to write in each column, as shown on the next page. Checking how students complete their L columns is a good way to monitor their learning. Inspect the example of an individual student's KWL chart in the featured box, A Fourth Grader's Flip Chart on Spiders.

Language Experience Approach

The Language Experience Approach (LEA) is a reading and writing procedure that's based on students' language and experiences (Ashton-Warner, 1986). A student dictates words and sentences about an experience, and the teacher writes them; as the words

A Fourth Grader's Flip Chart On Spiders

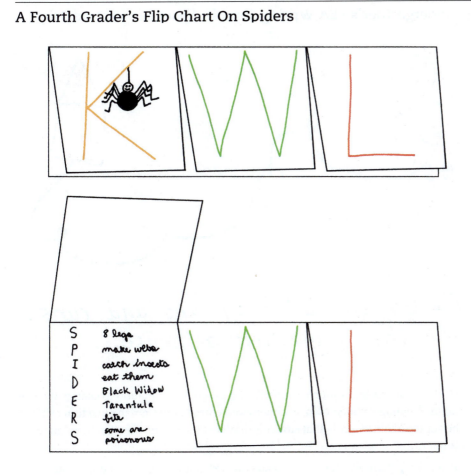

and sentences are written, the teacher models how written language works, and the text becomes the students' reading material. Because the language comes from the student and the content is based on his or her experiences, the student is usually able to read the text. A kindergartner's LEA writing is shown in the featured box, A Kindergartner's LEA Writing Sample About *Gingerbread Baby*. The student drew this picture and dictated the accompanying sentence after listening to her teacher read Jan Brett's *Gingerbread Baby* (1999), a version of "The Gingerbread Man" story. This shared reading activity is an effective way to help students begin reading; even those who haven't been successful with other reading activities can read what they've dictated.

PROCEDURE. This flexible procedure can be used with the entire class, with small groups, and with individual students, depending on the teacher's purpose. Teachers follow these steps when working with individual students:

1. *Provide an experience.* The writing stimulus can be an experience shared in school, a book read aloud, a field trip, or something else, such as having a pet or playing in the snow.

2. *Talk about the experience.* The teacher and the student talk about the experience to review it and generate words so that the students' dictation will be more complete. Teachers often begin with an open-ended question, such as "What are we going to write about?" The student talks about the experience to clarify and organize ideas and use more specific vocabulary.

3. *Record the students' dictation.* The teacher takes the students' dictation. If the student hesitates, the teacher rereads what's been written and encourages him or her to continue. Teachers print neatly and spell words correctly, but they preserve

A Kindergartner's LEA Writing Sample About *Gingerbread Baby*

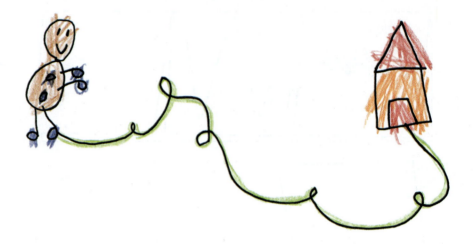

The Gingerbread Baby runs and runs into the gingerbread house.

students' language as much as possible. It's a great temptation to change the students' language to their own, in either word choice or grammar, but editing should be kept to a minimum so that students don't get the impression that their language is inferior or inadequate.

4. *Read the text aloud.* The teacher reads the text aloud, pointing at each word as it's read; this reading reminds the student of the content and demonstrates how to read the text aloud with appropriate intonation. Then the student reads along with the teacher, and after several joint readings, he or she reads it alone.

5. *Make sentence strips.* The teacher rewrites the text on sentence strips that the student keeps in an envelope attached to the back of the paper. The student reads and sequences the sentence strips, and once he or she can read them smoothly, the student cuts the strips into individual words and arranges the words into the familiar sentence. Later, the student creates new sentences with the word cards.

6. *Add word cards to a word bank.* The student adds the word cards to his or her word bank (a small box that holds the word cards) after working with this text. These word cards can be used for a variety of activities.

LEA is often used to create texts students can read and use as a resource for writing. For example, during a thematic unit on insects, first and second graders learned about ladybugs and created a big book with this dictated text:

Part 1: What Ladybugs Do

Ladybugs are helper insects. They help people because they eat aphids. They make the earth pretty. They are red and they have 7 black spots. Ladybugs keep their wings under the red wing cases. Their wings are transparent and they fly with these wings. Ladybugs love to eat aphids. They love them so much that they can eat 50 aphids in one day!

Part 2: How Ladybugs Grow

Ladybugs live on leaves in bushes and in tree trunks. They lay eggs that are sticky and yellow on a leaf. The eggs hatch and out come tiny and black larvae. They like to eat aphids, too. Next the larva becomes a pupa and then it changes into a ladybug. When *the ladybugs first come out of the pupa, they are yellow but they change into red and their spots appear. Then they can fly.*

Part 3: Ladybugs Are Smart

Ladybugs have a good trick so that the birds won't eat them. If a bird starts to attack, the ladybug turns over on her back and squeezes a stinky liquid from her legs. It smells terrible and makes the bird fly away.

Each part was written on a poster, and they were bound into a book. After reading the book, students each chose a sentence to be written on a sentence strip; some wrote their own sentences, and the teacher wrote them for others. After they practiced reading their sentences, they cut them apart and rearranged the words. Finally, they used the sentences in writing their own "All About Ladybugs" books.

Learning Logs

Students write in learning logs during thematic units. Like other journals, *learning logs* are booklets in which students record information, write questions, summarize big ideas, draw diagrams, and reflect on their learning. Their writing is impromptu, and the emphasis is on using writing as a learning tool rather than creating polished products. Even so, students work carefully and spell content-related words posted on the word wall correctly. As teachers monitor learning logs, they quickly see how well the students understand the big ideas they're learning.

PROCEDURE.   Students construct learning logs at the beginning of a thematic unit and then write entries in them. Here are the steps:

1. *Prepare learning logs.* Students construct learning logs using a combination of lined and unlined paper that's stapled into booklets with cardboard or laminated construction paper covers.

2. *Make entries.* Students make entries in their learning logs by taking notes, drawing diagrams and illustrations, listing vocabulary words, and writing summaries.

3. *Monitor students' entries.* Teachers read students' entries, answer their questions, and sometimes write responses.

4. *Write reflections.* Teachers often have students review their entries at the end of the unit and write a reflection about what they've learned.

Students use writing as a tool for learning as they write entries, and these journals document students' learning during thematic units.

Making Words

Making words is a teacher-directed spelling activity in which students arrange letter cards to spell words (Cunningham & Cunningham, 1992). Teachers choose a key word from a book students are reading and then prepare a set of letter cards that students manipulate to spell words. The teacher leads students as they create a variety of words using the letters. For example, after reading *Diary of a Spider* (Cronin, 2011), a group of first graders built these short-*i* and long-*i* words using the letters in the word *spider*: *is, sip, rip, dip, drip, side, ride,* and *ripe*. After spelling these words, students used all of the letters to spell the key word—*spider*. As students make words, they're practicing what they know about phoneme–grapheme correspondences and spelling patterns, and teachers get feedback on what students understand, correct confusions, and review phonics and spelling concepts when necessary.

Teachers often use this activity with small groups of English learners to practice spelling strategies and skills. It's effective because ELs collaborate with classmates, and the activity is both nonthreatening and hands-on. Sometimes teachers bring together a group of ELs to do a making words activity as a preview before doing it with the whole class (or afterward as a review), and sometimes a different word is used to reinforce a spelling pattern that they're learning.

PROCEDURE. Here are the steps in making words:

1. *Make letter cards.* Teachers prepare a set of small letter cards with multiple copies of each letter, especially common letters such as *a, e, i, r, s,* and *t,* printing the lowercase letterform on one side and the uppercase form on the reverse. They package the cards by letter in small plastic bags or partitioned plastic boxes.

2. *Choose a word.* Teachers choose a word to use in the word-making activity, and without disclosing it, have a student distribute the needed letter cards to classmates.

3. *Name the letter cards.* Teachers ask students to name the letter cards and arrange them on their desks, with consonants in one group and vowels in another.

4. *Make words.* Students use the letter cards to spell words containing two, three, four, five, six, or more letters, and they list the words they can spell on a chart. Teachers monitor students' work and encourage them to fix any misspelled words.

5. *Share words.* Teachers have students identify two-letter words they made with the letter cards and continue to report longer and longer words until they identify the chosen word made using every letter card. After students share all of the words, teachers suggest any words they missed and point out recently taught spelling patterns.

Teachers choose words for word-making lessons from books students are reading. For additional ideas, they can check the collection of grade-level word-making books by Patricia Cunningham and Dorothy Hall (2008a, 2008b, 2008c, 2008d, 2008e).

Minilessons

Teachers teach short, focused lessons called *minilessons* on literacy strategies and skills (Hoyt, 2000). Topics include how to write an entry in a reading log, make connections, insert quotation marks, and add inflectional endings. Teachers introduce a topic and connect it to the reading or writing students are involved in, provide information, and supervise as students practice the topic. Minilessons usually last 15 to 30 minutes, and sometimes teachers extend the lesson over several days as students apply the topic in reading and writing activities. It's not enough to simply explain strategies and skills or remind students to use them.

Minilessons are an effective way to teach strategies and skills so that students actually learn to use them. Teachers must actively engage students, encourage and scaffold them while they're learning, and then gradually withdraw their support.

PROCEDURE. Teachers follow these steps to teach minilessons to small groups and to the whole class:

1. *Introduce the topic.* Teachers introduce the strategy or skill by naming it and making a connection between the topic and ongoing classroom activities.

2. *Share examples.* Teachers explain how to use the topic with examples from students' writing or from books students are reading.

3. *Provide information.* Teachers provide information about the topic and demonstrate how they use the strategy or skill.

4. *Supervise practice.* Students practice applying the strategy or skill with teacher supervision.

5. *Assess learning.* Teachers monitor students' progress and evaluate their use of newly learned strategies or skills.

Teachers teach minilessons on literacy strategies and skills as a part of literature focus units, reading and writing workshop, and other instructional approaches. Other minilessons focus on instructional procedures, such as how to use a dictionary or share writing from the author's chair, and concepts, such as homophones or adjectives.

Open-Mind Portraits

Students draw open-mind portraits to help them think more deeply about a character, reflect on story events from the character's viewpoint, and analyze the theme (McLaughlin & Allen, 2001). The portraits have two parts: the character's face on the top, "portrait" page, and several "thinking" pages revealing the character's thoughts at pivotal points in the story. The two pages of a second grader's open-mind portrait depicting the piglet who tells a hilarious tale about how she outwits a big, bad wolf in *Hog-Eye* (Meddaugh, 1998) is shown in the featured box, An Open-Mind Portrait of the Piglet Hog-Eye.

PROCEDURE. Students follow these steps to make open-mind portraits while they're reading a story or immediately afterward:

1. *Draw a portrait.* Students draw and color a large portrait of the head and neck of a character in a story they're reading.

2. *Cut out the "portrait" and "thinking" pages.* Students cut out the portrait and attach it with a brad or staple on top of several more sheets of drawing paper. It's important that students place the fastener at the top of the portrait so that there's space available to draw and write on the "thinking" pages.

3. *Design "thinking" pages.* Students lift the portrait page and draw and write about the character's thoughts at key points in the story.

An Open-Mind Portrait of the Piglet in *Hog-Eye*

Portrait Page   Thinking Page

4. *Share the completed open-mind portraits.* Students share their portraits with classmates and talk about the words and pictures they chose to include on the "thinking" pages.

Students create open-mind portraits to think more deeply about a character in a story they're reading in literature focus units and literature circles. They often reread parts of the story to recall specific details about the character's appearance before they draw the portrait, and they write several entries in a simulated journal to start thinking from that character's viewpoint before making the "thinking" pages. In addition to using this activity with stories, students can make open-mind portraits of historical figures as part of social studies units.

RAFT

Teachers use RAFT to create project topics and other assignments to enhance students' comprehension of stories they're reading and information they're learning in thematic units (Buehl, 2014; Holston & Santa, 1985). *RAFT* is an acronym for *role, audience, format,* and *topic,* and teachers consider these four dimensions as they design projects:

Role.   Students assume the *role* of a person or the voice of a group of people for this project. Sometimes they take on the role of a book character or a historical figure, but at other times, they remain themselves.

Audience.   The *audience* is the person or people who'll read or view the project, including classmates, teachers, parents, or community members; students may also have simulated audiences, such as book characters and historical personalities.

Format.   The *format* is the genre or activity that students create; it might be a letter, brochure, cartoon, journal, poster, speech, or digital scrapbook.

Topic.   The *topic* is the subject of the project; it may be an issue related to the text, an essential question, or something of personal interest.

When students develop projects, they process ideas and information in different ways as they assume varied viewpoints and complete projects directed to specific audiences. Their thinking is imaginative and interpretive; in contrast, students' comprehension tends to be more literal when they do more traditional assignments, such as writing answers to questions.

PROCEDURE.   Teachers follow these steps to create projects:

1. *Establish a purpose.* Teachers reflect on what they want students to learn through this activity and consider how it can enhance their comprehension of a book they're reading or a thematic unit they're studying.

2. *Prepare a RAFT chart.* Teachers prepare a RAFT chart of possible projects by brainstorming roles, choosing audiences, identifying genres and other formats for projects, and listing topics.

3. *Read the book or study the topic.* Students read and discuss a book or learn about a social studies or science topic before they create RAFT projects.

4. *Choose projects.* Sometimes teachers assign the same project for groups of students, but at other times, they let students choose a project from the RAFT chart.

5. *Create projects.* Students prepare their oral, written, or multimedia projects and get feedback from the teacher as they work.

6. *Share completed projects.* Students share their projects with small groups or the whole class and other appropriate audiences.

RAFT is an effective way to differentiate instruction by providing tiered activities; projects on the same text or topic can be adjusted according to students' achievement

RAFT On *Officer Buckle and Gloria*

ROLE	AUDIENCE	FORMAT	TOPIC
Officer Buckle	Gloria	conversation	Students pretend to be Officer Buckle and apologize to Gloria for his behavior.
Gloria	students	book	Students become Gloria and write a book of safety rules.
students	Officer Buckle	letter	Students write a letter to Officer Buckle telling him what they learned about safety.
chief of police	Officer Buckle	conversation	Students assume the role of the chief and talk to Officer Buckle about the requirements of his safety job.
TV news reporter	community members	oral report	Students become a TV news reporter and video a report about Officer Buckle and Gloria on-site at the elementary school.
parents	Officer Buckle	interview	Students assume the role of parents and interview Officer Buckle about safety.
students	principal	persuasive writing	Students write a persuasive letter to their principal asking that a police officer come to their school for safety lessons.

levels, English proficiency, and interests. For example, a teacher of first and second grades developed the chart of RAFT ideas for *Officer Buckle and Gloria* (Rathmann, 1995), an award-winning story of a police officer and his talented dog who visit schools and teach students how to be safe. The details can be found in the featured box entitled RAFT on *Officer Buckle and Gloria*.

Readers Theatre

Readers theatre is a dramatic performance of a script by a group of readers (Black & Stave, 2007). Students assume parts, rehearse by reading their characters' lines in the script, and then do a performance for their classmates. Students interpret the story with their voices, without using much action. Readers theatre is an effective instructional procedure because students have opportunities to read good literature, and through this procedure they engage with text, interpret characters, and bring the text to life (Keehn, Martinez, & Roser, 2005). Moreover, English learners and readers who aren't fluent gain valuable oral reading practice in a relaxed small-group setting. The Booklist: Readers Theatre Scripts presents books of narrative and informational scripts for primary grade students.

PROCEDURE. Teachers follow these steps as they work with a small group or the whole class:

1. *Select a script.* Students select a script and then read and discuss it as they would any story. Afterward, they volunteer to read each part.

2. *Rehearse the reading.* Students decide how to use their voice, gestures, and facial expressions to interpret the characters they're reading. They read the script several times, striving for accurate pronunciation, voice projection, and appropriate inflections. Less rehearsal is needed for an informal, in-class presentation than for a more formal production; nevertheless, interpretations should always be developed as fully as possible.

3. *Stage the reading.* Readers theatre can be presented on a stage or in a corner of the classroom. Students stand or sit in a row and read their lines. They stay in position through the production or enter and leave according to the characters' appearances "onstage." If readers are sitting, they stand to read their lines; if they're standing, they step forward to read. The emphasis isn't on production quality; rather, it's on

BOOKLIST

Readers Theatre Scripts

Barchers, S. I. (1997). *50 fabulous fables: Beginning readers theatre*. Portsmouth, NH: Teacher Ideas Press.

Barchers, S. I., & Pfeffinger, C. R. (2006). *More readers theatre for beginning readers*. Portsmouth, NH: Teacher Ideas Press.

Fredericks, A. D. (2007). *Nonfiction readers theatre for beginning readers*. Portsmouth, NH: Teacher Ideas Press.

Laughlin, M. K., Black, P. T., & Loberg, M. K. (1991). *Social studies readers theatre for children: Scripts and script development*. Portsmouth, NH: Teacher Ideas Press.

Martin, J. M. (2002). *12 fabulously funny fairy tale plays*. New York: Scholastic.

Pugliano-Martin, C. (1999). *25 just-right plays for emergent readers*. New York: Scholastic.

Shepard, A. (2007). *Stories on stage: Scripts for reader's theater*. Olympia, WA: Shepard.

Wolf, J. M. (2002). *Cinderella outgrows the glass slipper and other zany fractured fairy tale plays*. New York: Scholastic.

Wolfman, J. (2004). *How and why stories for readers theatre*. Portsmouth, NH: Teacher Ideas Press.

Worthy, J. (2005). *Readers theatre for building fluency: Strategies and scripts for making the most of this highly effective, motivating, and research-based approach to oral reading*. New York: Scholastic.

the interpretive quality of readers' voices and expressions. Costumes and props aren't necessary; however, adding a few small props enhances interest as long as they don't interfere with the interpretive quality of the reading.

Readers theatre avoids many of the restrictions inherent in theatrical productions: Students don't memorize their parts or spend long hours rehearsing, and elaborate props, costumes, and backdrops aren't needed.

Reading Logs

Reading logs are journals in which students write their reactions to books they're reading or listening to the teacher read aloud. In these entries, students clarify misunderstandings, explore ideas, and deepen their comprehension (Hancock, 2008). They also add diagrams about story elements and information about authors and genres. Students usually write single entries after reading picture books, but they write after reading every chapter or two when they're reading novels. They often write a series of entries about a collection of books written by the same author or about versions of the same folktale.

Sometimes students choose topics for entries, and at other times, they respond to questions or prompts that teachers have prepared. Both student-choice and teacher-directed entries are useful: When students choose their own topics, they delve into their own ideas, sharing what's important to them, and when teachers provide prompts, they direct students' thinking to topics that they might otherwise miss.

PROCEDURE.   Students follow these steps as they write in reading logs:

1. *Prepare reading logs.* Students make reading logs by stapling paper into booklets and write the title of the book on the cover.

2. *Write entries.* Students write their reactions and reflections, make diagrams, and draw illustrations. Sometimes they choose their own topics, and at other times, teachers provide topics. Students also jot down memorable quotes, and take notes about characters, plot, or other story elements.

3. *Share entries.* Teachers monitor students' work by reading and responding to their entries. They ask questions and write comments back to students.

Students write and draw reading log entries to help them understand stories they're reading and those the teacher is reading aloud during literature focus units and literature circles (Daniels, 2001).

Revising Groups

During the revising stage of the writing process, students meet in revising groups to share their rough drafts and get feedback on how well they're communicating (Tompkins, 2012). Revising group members offer compliments about things writers have done well and make suggestions for improvement. Their comments reflect these topics and other aspects of the writer's craft:

leads	word choice	voice
dialogue	sentences	rhyme
endings	character development	sequence
description	point of view	flashbacks
ideas	organization	alliterations

These topics are used for both compliments and suggestions. When students are offering a compliment, they might say, "I liked your lead. It grabbed me and made me keep listening," and when they're making a suggestion, they might say, "I wonder if you could start with a question to make your lead more interesting. Maybe you could say, 'Have you ever ridden in a police car? Well, that's what happened to me!'"

Teaching students how to share their rough drafts and offer constructive feedback isn't easy. When teachers introduce revision, they model appropriate responses because students may not know how to offer specific and meaningful comments tactfully. Teachers and students can brainstorm a list of appropriate compliments and suggestions and post it in the classroom to refer to. Comments should usually begin with "I," not "you." Notice the difference in tone in these two sentence stems: "I wonder if . . . " versus "You need to . . . " Here are some ways to begin compliments:

I like the part where . . .
I learned how . . .
I like the way you described . . .
I like how you organized the information because . . .

Students also offer suggestions about how classmates can revise their writing, and it's important that they phrase what they say in helpful ways. Writers often begin suggestions this way:

I got confused in the part about . . .
I wonder if you need a closing . . .
I'd like you to add more about . . .
I wonder if these paragraphs are in the right order . . .
I think you might want to combine these sentences . . .

Students also ask classmates for help with specific problems they've identified; looking to classmates for feedback is a big step in learning to revise. Writers ask questions such as these:

What do you want to know more about?
Is there a part that I should throw away?
What details can I add?
What do you think is the best part of my writing?
Are there some words I need to change?

Revising groups work effectively once students understand how to support and help their classmates by offering compliments, making suggestions, and asking questions.

Revising is the most difficult part of the writing process because it's hard for students to stand back and evaluate their writing objectively in order to make changes to communicate more effectively. As they participate in revising groups, they learn how to accept compliments and suggestions and to provide useful feedback to classmates.

Teachers teach students how to use this instructional procedure so that they can then work in small groups to get ideas for revising their writing. Here are the steps:

1. *Read drafts aloud.* Students take turns reading their rough drafts aloud to the group. Everyone listens politely, thinking about compliments and suggestions they'll make after the writer finishes reading. Only the writer looks at the composition because when classmates look at it, they quickly notice and comment on mechanical errors, even though the emphasis during revising is on content. Listening to the writing read aloud keeps the focus on content.

2. *Offer compliments.* After listening to the rough draft read aloud, classmates in the revising group tell the writer what they liked about the composition. These positive comments should be specific, focusing on strengths, rather than the often-heard "I liked it" or "It was good"; even though these are positive comments, they don't provide effective feedback.

3. *Ask clarifying questions.* Writers ask for assistance with trouble spots they identified earlier when rereading their writing, or they may ask questions that reflect more general concerns about how well they're communicating.

4. *Offer other revision suggestions.* Group members ask questions about things that were unclear to them and make suggestions about how to revise the rough draft.

5. *Repeat the process.* Members of the revising group repeat the first four steps so that all students can share their rough drafts.

6. *Make plans for revision.* Each student makes a commitment to revise their writing based on the comments and suggestions of the group members. The final decision on what to revise always rests with the writers themselves, but with the understanding that their rough drafts aren't perfect comes the realization that some revision will be necessary. When students verbalize their planned revisions, they're more likely to complete the revision stage.

Students meet in revising groups whenever they're using the writing process. Once they've written a rough draft, students are ready to share their writing and get some feedback from classmates. They often meet with the same revising group throughout the school year, or students can form groups when they're ready to get feedback about their rough drafts. Many teachers have students sign up on the whiteboard; this way, whenever four are ready, they form a group. Both established and spontaneously formed groups can be effective. What matters most is that students get feedback about their writing when they need it.

Rubrics

Rubrics are scoring guides that teachers use to assess students' achievement (Spandel, 2009). These guides usually have levels, ranging from high to low, with assessment criteria at each level. Rubrics are distributed when students begin a project so that they know what's expected and how they'll be assessed. Teachers mark the assessment criteria either while they're reading or examining the project or immediately afterward and then determine the overall score. The assessment criteria on some rubrics describe the traits or qualities students are expected to demonstrate. No matter which assessment criteria are used, the same criteria are addressed at each level.

Rubrics can be constructed with any number of levels, but it's easier to show growth when the rubric has more levels: Much more improvement is needed to move to the next level if the rubric has 4 levels than if it has 6 levels. A rubric with 10 levels would be even more sensitive, but rubrics with many levels are harder to construct and more time-consuming to use. Researchers recommend that teachers use rubrics with 4 or 6 levels so that there's no middle score—each level is either above or below the middle—because teachers are inclined to rely on the middle level when there is one. Rubrics are often used for determining proficiency levels and assigning grades. The level that's above the midpoint is usually designated as "proficient" or "passing"— that's a 3 on a 4-point rubric and a 4 on a 5- or 6-point rubric. The levels on a 6-point rubric can be described this way:

1 = minimal level	4 = proficient level
2 = beginning level	5 = excellent level
3 = developing level	6 = superior level

Teachers also equate levels to letter grades.

Scoring guides help students become better speakers, readers, and writers because they lay out the qualities that constitute excellence and clarify teachers' expectations so students understand how their projects will be assessed. Students, too, use rubrics to improve their work: When they're involved in a small-group multigenre writing project, for instance, students each examine their rough drafts and then turn to the group to decide how to revise to make each piece in their group project more effective.

PROCEDURE.   Teachers follow these steps:

1. *Choose a rubric.* Teachers choose a rubric that's appropriate to the project or create one that reflects the assignment.

2. *Introduce the rubric.* Teachers distribute copies of the rubric and talk about the criteria used at each level, focusing on the requirements at the proficient level.

3. *Self-assess the project.* Students use the rubric to self-assess their work. They highlight phrases in the rubric or check off items that best describe their achievement. Then they determine which level has the most highlighted words or checkmarks; that level is the overall score, and students circle it.

4. *Assess students' projects.* Teachers assess students' projects by highlighting phrases in the rubric or checking off items that best describe the work. Then they assign the overall score by determining which level has the most highlighted words or checkmarks and circle it.

5. *Conference with students.* Teachers talk with students about the assessment, identifying strengths and weaknesses. Then students set goals for the next project.

Many commercially prepared rubrics are currently available, especially for writing. State departments of education post rubrics for mandated writing tests on their websites, and school districts hire teams of teachers to develop writing rubrics. Spandel (2009) provides rubrics that assess the six traits; rubrics accompany basal reading programs; and still others are available on the Internet. Even though ready-to-use rubrics are convenient, they're not appropriate for all students or every project: Rubrics may have only 4 levels when 6 would be better, or they may have been written for teachers, not in kid-friendly language. Because of these limitations, teachers often adapt commercial rubrics or develop their own.

Running Records

In this reading-stage activity, teachers observe individual students as they read aloud and record information to analyze their reading fluency (Clay, 2000c). They calculate the percentage of words the student reads correctly and then analyze the errors.

How to Mark Errors

ERROR	EXPLANATION	MARKING
Incorrect word	If the student reads a word incorrectly, the teacher writes the incorrect word above the correct word.	take / taken
Self-correction	If the student self-corrects an error, the teacher writes SC (for "self-correction") following the incorrect word.	for SC / from
Unsuccessful attempt	If the student attempts to pronounce a word, the teacher records each attempt above the correct text.	be-bēf-before / before
Skipped word	If the student skips a word, the teacher marks the error with a dash.	— / the
Inserted word	If the student says words that aren't in the text, the teacher writes an insertion symbol (caret) where the student made the error and records the inserted words.	out / go ‸ for a walk
Supplied word	If the student can't identify a word, the teacher supplies it and writes T above the word.	T / which
Repetition	If the student repeats a word or phrase, it isn't scored as an error, but the teacher notes it by making a checkmark for each repetition.	✓✓✓ / so

Teachers mark a copy of the text as the student reads to indicate which words are read correctly and which the student can't identify. Inspect the featured box, How to Mark Errors.

PROCEDURE. Teachers conduct running records with individual students using these steps:

1. *Choose a book.* Teachers have the student read aloud a leveled book or other text.

2. *Take the running record.* As the student reads aloud, the teacher makes a checkmark on a copy of the text above each word read correctly, and uses other marks to indicate words that the student mispronounces or doesn't know. The How to Mark Errors box shows the method for marking student errors.

3. *Calculate the percentage of errors.* Teachers calculate the percentage of errors by dividing the number of errors by the total number of words read. When the student makes 5% errors or less, the book's considered to be at his or her independent level. When there are 6%–10% errors, the book is at the students' instructional level, and when there are more than 10% errors, it's too difficult—the students' frustration level.

4. *Analyze the errors.* Teachers look for patterns in the errors to determine how the student is growing as a reader and what strategies and skills should be taught next.

Many teachers conduct running records on all students at the beginning of the school year and at the end of each grading period. In addition, they do running records more often during guided reading lessons and with students who aren't making expected progress in order to diagnose their reading problems and make instructional decisions.

Semantic Feature Analysis

Teachers create a semantic feature analysis to help students examine the characteristics of content-area concepts (Rickelman & Taylor, 2006). They draw a grid for the analysis with characteristics or components of the concept listed on one axis and examples listed on the other. Students reading a novel, for example, can do a semantic feature analysis with vocabulary words listed on one axis and the characters' names on the other; they decide which words relate to which characters and use pluses and minuses to mark the relationships on the grid. Teachers often do a semantic feature analysis with the whole class, but students can work in small groups or individually to complete the grid. The examination should be done as a whole-class activity, however, so that students can share their insights.

PROCEDURE. Teachers follow these steps to do a semantic feature analysis:

1. *Create a grid.* Teachers create a grid with characteristics or components of the concept listed on the horizontal axis and examples on the vertical axis.

2. *Complete the grid.* Students complete the grid, cell by cell, by considering the relationship between each item on the vertical axis and the items on the horizontal axis. Then they mark the cell with a plus to indicate a relationship, a minus to indicate no relationship, and a question mark when they're unsure.

3. *Examine the grid.* Students and the teacher examine the grid for patterns and then draw conclusions based on the patterns.

Students do a semantic feature analysis as part of literature focus units and thematic units. For example, during a unit on ecosystems, students completed the Semantic Feature Analysis on Pond Life, shown here. By doing this semantic feature analysis, the students learned that animals living in or near ponds are food consumers, and that aquatic plants are food producers and they oxygenate the water.

Semantic Feature Analysis on Pond Life

Type	Lives on or in water	Lives near water	Is a food consumer	Is a plant	Produces oxygen
algae	+	−	−	+	+
catfish	+	−	+	−	−
cattail	+	−	−	+	+
crayfish	+	−	+	−	−
dragonfly	?	?	+	−	−
duckweed	+	−	−	+	+
frog	?	?	+	−	−
great blue heron	−	+	+	−	−
mallard duck	−	+	+	−	−
mosquito	?	?	+	−	−
mussel	+	−	+	−	−
pond skater	+	−	+	−	−
pond snail	+	−	+	−	−
raccoon	−	+	+	−	−
salamander	?	?	+	−	−
snapping turtle	?	?	+	−	−
water boatman	+	−	+	−	−
waterlily	+	−	−	+	+

Code: + = yes; − = no; ? = don't know

Shared Reading

Teachers use shared reading to read authentic literature with students who can't read those books independently (Holdaway, 1979). Teachers read the book aloud, modeling fluent reading, and then they read the book again and again for several days. The focus for the first reading is students' enjoyment; during the next couple of readings, teachers draw students' attention to concepts about print, comprehension, and interesting words and sentences. Finally, students focus on decoding particular words during the last reading or two.

Students are actively involved in shared reading. Teachers encourage them to make predictions and to chime in on reading repeated words and phrases. Individual students or small groups take turns reading brief parts once they begin to recognize words and phrases. Students examine interesting features that they notice in the book—punctuation marks, illustrations, and table of contents, for example—and teachers point out others. They also talk about the book, both while they're reading and afterward. Shared reading builds on students' experience listening to their parents read bedtime stories (Fisher & Medvic, 2000).

PROCEDURE.   Teachers follow these steps to use shared reading with the whole class or small groups of students:

1. *Introduce the text.* Teachers talk about the book or other text by activating or building background knowledge on topics related to the book and by reading the title and the author's name aloud.

2. *Read the text aloud.* Teachers read the story aloud to students, using a pointer (a dowel rod with a pencil eraser on the end) to track the text as they read. They invite students to be actively involved by making predictions and by joining in the reading if the story is repetitive.

3. *Have a grand conversation.* Students talk about the story, ask questions, and share their responses.

4. *Reread the story.* Students take turns using the pointer to track the reading and turning pages. Teachers invite students to join in reading familiar and predictable words. Also, they take opportunities to teach and use graphophonic cues and reading strategies while reading. Depending on students' reading expertise, teachers vary the support that they provide.

5. *Continue the process.* Teachers continue to reread the story with students over a period of several days, again having them turn pages and take turns using the pointer to track the text while reading. They encourage students who can read the text to read along with them.

6. *Read independently.* After students become familiar with the text, teachers distribute individual copies for students to read independently and use for a variety of activities.

Teachers use shared reading during literature focus units, literature circles, and thematic units. They usually choose big books for shared reading but they also use poems written on charts, **Language Experience** stories, and **interactive writing** charts so that students can see the text and read along.

Story Boards

Story boards are cards on which the illustrations and text from a picture book have been attached. Teachers make story boards by cutting apart two copies of a picture book and gluing the pages on pieces of cardboard. The most important use of story boards is to sequence the events of a story by lining the cards up on a whiteboard marker tray or hanging them on a clothesline. Once the pages have been laid out, students visualize the story and its structure in new ways and examine the illustrations more closely. For example, they arrange story boards from *How I Became a Pirate* (Long, 2003) to retell the story and pick out the beginning, middle, and end. They use story boards to identify the dream sequences in the middle of *Abuela* (Dorros, 1997) and compare versions of folktales, such as *The Mitten* (Brett, 2009; Tresselt, 1989) and *The Woodcutter's Mitten* (Koopmans, 1995).

Teachers use this instructional procedure because it allows students to manipulate and sequence stories and examine illustrations more carefully. Story boards are especially useful tools for English learners, who use them to preview a story before reading or to review the events in a story after reading. ELs also draw story boards because they can often share their understanding better through art than through language. In addition, story boards present many opportunities for teaching comprehension when only one copy of a picture book is available.

PROCEDURE.   Teachers generally use story boards with a small group of students or with the whole class, but individual students can reexamine them as part of center activities. Here are the steps:

1. *Collect two copies of a book.* Teachers use two copies of a picture book for the story boards; paperback copies are preferable because they're less expensive. In a few picture books, all the illustrations are on right-hand or left-hand pages, so only one copy is needed.

2. *Cut the books apart.* Teachers remove the covers and separate the pages, evening out the cut edges.

3. *Attach the pages to pieces of cardboard.* Teachers glue each page or double-page spread to a piece of cardboard, making sure that pages are alternated so that each illustration is included.

4. *Laminate the cards.* Teachers laminate the cards so that they can withstand use by students.

5. *Use the cards in sequencing activities.* Teachers use the story board cards for a number of activities, including sequencing, story structure, rereading, and word-study activities.

Students use story boards for a variety of activities during literature focus units. For a sequencing activity, teachers pass out the cards in random order, and students line up around the classroom to sequence the story events. Story boards can also be used when only a few copies of a picture book are available so that students can identify words for the **word wall**, notice literary language, examine an element of story structure, or study the illustrations.

Story Retelling

Teachers use story retelling to monitor students' comprehension (Morrow, 1985). They sit one-on-one with individual students and ask them to retell a story they've just read or listened to read aloud; students organize the information they remember to provide a personalized summary that reveals their level of comprehension (Hoyt, 1999). Teachers can't assume that students already know how to retell stories, even though many do. Through explanations and demonstrations of the retelling procedure, students learn what's expected of them. They also need to practice retelling stories before they'll be good at it.

Once teachers begin listening to students retell stories, they notice that those who understand a story retell it differently than those who don't. Good comprehenders' retellings make sense: They reflect the organization of the story and include all of the important story events. In contrast, weak comprehenders often recall events haphazardly or omit important events, especially those in the middle of the story.

PROCEDURE. Teachers follow these steps to have students retell a story:

1. *Introduce the story.* Teachers introduce the story by reading the title, examining the cover of the book, or talking about a topic related to the story. They also explain that students will be asked to retell the story afterward.

2. *Read and discuss the story.* Students read the story or listen to it read aloud; when they're reading the story themselves, it's essential that the story is at their reading level. Afterward, they talk about the story, sharing ideas and clarifying confusions.

3. *Create a graphic organizer.* Students create a graphic organizer or a series of drawings to guide their retelling. (This step is optional, but it's especially helpful for students who have difficulty retelling stories.)

4. *Retell the story.* Teachers ask students to individually retell the story in their own words, asking questions, if necessary, to elicit more information:

   Who was the story about?

   What happened next?

   Where did the story take place?

   What did the character do next?

   How did the story end?

5. *Mark the scoring guide.* Teachers mark a scoring guide as the student retells the story; the scoring guide lists important information about characters and events in the story, usually organized into beginning, middle, and end sections. As they listen to the retelling, teachers place checkmarks by each piece of information that the student recalls. If the student omits important information, teachers ask questions to prompt his or her recall, and they write *P* beside information that was recalled with prompting.

Retelling is an instructional tool as well as an assessment tool. McKenna and Stahl (2003) explain that through story retelling, students expand their oral language, enhance their use of comprehension strategies, and deepen their knowledge of story structure. When they participate regularly in retelling activities, their comprehension improves as they learn to focus on the big ideas in the story, and their oral language abilities are enhanced as they incorporate sentence patterns, vocabulary, and phrases from stories into their own talk.

Think-Alouds

Teachers use the think-aloud procedure to teach students how to direct and monitor their thinking during reading (Wilhelm, 2001). By making their thinking explicit, teachers are demonstrating what capable readers do implicitly (Keene & Zimmerman, 2007). After they watch teachers think aloud, students practice the procedure by thinking aloud about the literacy strategies they're learning. As they think aloud, students respond to the text, identify big ideas, ask self-questions, make connections, figure out how to solve problems that arise, and reflect on their use of strategies. This procedure is valuable because students learn to be more active readers: They learn how to think metacognitively and to regulate their own cognitive processes.

PROCEDURE. Teachers use these steps to teach students to think aloud:

1. *Choose a book.* Teachers choose a text, often a big book, that students are familiar with to demonstrate how to think aloud.

2. *Plan the think-aloud.* Teachers decide which strategy they want to demonstrate, where they'll pause, and the kinds of thinking they want to share.

3. *Demonstrate the think-aloud.* Teachers read the text—pausing to think aloud—explaining what they're thinking and how they're using a strategy or solving a reading problem. They often use these "I" sentence starters to talk about their thinking:

> I wondered if . . .
>
> I was confused by . . .
>
> I didn't understand why . . .
>
> I think the big idea is . . .
>
> I reread this part because . . .

4. *Annotate the text.* Teachers write a small self-stick note about their thinking and attach it next to the text that prompted the think-aloud. They often use a word or phrase, such as *picture in my mind* or *reread*, to quickly document their thinking.

5. *Continue thinking aloud.* Teachers continue reading the book—pausing to think aloud again—and annotate the text with additional notes about their thinking.

6. *Reflect on the procedure.* Teachers review their annotations, talk about their strategy use, and reflect on the usefulness of think-alouds as a tool for comprehending what they're reading.

7. *Repeat the procedure.* Teachers read another book and have students take turns thinking aloud and annotating the text. Once students are familiar with the procedure, they practice doing think-alouds in small groups and with partners.

After students know how to think aloud, teachers can use this procedure as an assessment tool. During student–teacher conferences, students reflect on their reading and evaluate how well they use particular strategies, and they think about what they could do differently to comprehend more effectively. They can also refer to their annotations and write reflections about their use of particular strategies.

Word Ladders

Word ladders are games where students change one word into another through a series of steps, altering one letter at each step; the goal is to use as few steps as possible to change the first word into the last word. This type of puzzle was invented by Lewis Carroll, author of *Alice in Wonderland*. Typically, the first and last words are related in some way, such as *fall–down, slow–fast,* and *trick–treat,* and all the middle words must be real words. A well-known word ladder, shown here, is *cat–dog,* and it can be solved in three steps: *cat–cot–dot–dog.*

Teachers can create a variation of word ladders to practice phonics, spelling, and vocabulary skills (Rasinski, 2006), guiding students to build a series of words as they

A Cat–Dog Word Ladder

THE TEACHER SAYS:	STUDENTS WRITE:
Begin with the word *cat*.	cat
Change the vowel to form another word for *bed*, sometimes the kind of bed you use when you're camping.	cot
Change one letter to form a word that means "a tiny, round mark."	dot
Finally, change the final consonant to make a word that goes with the first word, *cat*.	dog

An OO Word Ladder

THE TEACHER SAYS:	STUDENTS WRITE:
Write the word *good*. We're practicing words with *oo* today.	good
Change the beginning sound to write the past tense of *stand*. The word is *stood*.	stood
Change the ending sound to write a word that means "a seat without arms or a back."	stool
Change the beginning sound to write a word that means the opposite of *warm*.	cool
Add two letters—one before and one after the *c*—to spell where we are right now.	school
Change the beginning sound to spell *tool*.	tool
Drop a letter to make a word that means *also*.	too
Change the first letter to write a word that means "a place where people can go to see wild animals."	zoo
Add a letter to *zoo* to spell the sound a car makes.	zoom
Change the beginning sound—use two letters for this blend—to spell something we use for sweeping.	broom
Change one letter to spell a word that means *creek*.	brook
Change the beginning sound to make a word that means "a dishonest person."	crook

provide graphophonemic and semantic clues about the words. As for traditional word ladder puzzles, each word comes from the previous one, but students may be asked to add, delete, or change one or more letters to make the next word. Students write the words in a list so they can see what they've written. Teachers make their own word ladders to reinforce the phonics concepts and spelling patterns; in this case, it's not necessary to relate the first and last words as in traditional word ladders. A word ladder to practice words with the short and long sounds of *oo* is shown here. Inspect the featured box, An *OO* Word Ladder.

PROCEDURE.   Here's the procedure for using word ladders:

1. *Create the word ladder.* Teachers create a word ladder with 5 to 15 words—choosing words from spelling lists or phonics lessons—and they write clues for each word, incorporating a combination of graphophonemic and semantic clues.

2. *Pass out supplies.* Teachers often have students use whiteboards and marking pens for this activity, but they can also use blank paper or papers with word ladders already drawn on them.

3. *Do the word ladder.* Teachers read the clues they've prepared and have students write the words. Students take turns identifying the words and spelling them correctly. When necessary, teachers provide additional clues and explain any unfamiliar words, phonics rules, or spelling patterns.

4. *Review the completed ladder.* Once students complete the word ladder, they reread the words and talk about any that they had difficulty writing. They also volunteer other words they can write using these letters.

Word ladders are a fun way for students to practice the phonics and spelling skills they're learning and, at the same time, think about the meanings of words. The activity's gamelike format makes it engaging for both students and teachers. To inspect more word ladders, check Rasinski's (2005a, 2005b) books of word ladder games for second through fourth graders; other word ladder games are also available on the Internet.

Word Sorts

Students use word sorts to examine and categorize words according to their meanings, phoneme–grapheme correspondences, or spelling patterns (Bear, Invernizzi, Templeton, & Johnston, 2012). The purpose of word sorts is to help students focus on conceptual and phonological features of words and identify recurring patterns. For example, as students sort cards with words such as *stopping, eating, hugging, running,* and *raining,* they discover the rule for doubling the final consonant in short-vowel words before adding an inflectional ending.

Word sorts are effective for English learners because students build skills to understand how English differs from their native language, and they develop knowledge to help them predict meaning through spelling (Helman, Bear, Templeton, Invernizzi, & Johnston, 2012). Because word sorts can be done in small groups, teachers can choose words for the sorts that are appropriate for students' developmental levels.

PROCEDURE.   Here are the steps for conducting a word sort:

1. *Choose a topic.* Teachers choose a language skill or content-area topic for the word sort and decide whether it'll be an open or closed sort. In an open sort, students determine the categories themselves based on the words they're sorting, and in a closed sort, teachers present the categories as they introduce the sorting activity.

2. *Compile a list of words.* Teachers compile a list of 6 to 20 words, depending on grade level, that exemplify particular categories, and they write the words on small cards. Or, small picture cards can be used.

3. *Introduce the sorting activity.* If it's a closed sort, teachers present the categories and have students sort word cards into these categories. If it's an open sort, students identify the words and look for possible categories. Students arrange and rearrange the cards until they're satisfied with the sorting. Then they add category labels.

4. *Make a permanent record.* Students make a permanent record of their sort by gluing the word cards onto a large sheet of construction paper or poster board or by writing the words on a sheet of paper.

5. *Share word sorts.* Students share their word sorts with classmates, explaining the categories they used (for open sorts).

Teachers use word sorts to teach phonics, spelling, and vocabulary. During literature focus units, students sort vocabulary words according to the beginning, middle, or end of the story or according to character. During thematic units, they sort vocabulary words according to big ideas.

Word Walls

Word walls are collections of words posted in the classroom that students use for word-study activities and refer to when they're writing (Wagstaff, 1999). Teachers make word walls using sheets of construction paper or butcher paper that have been divided into alphabetized sections. For one type of word wall, students and the teacher write important words from books they're reading or about big ideas they're learning during thematic units. Usually students choose the words to write on the word wall, and they may even do the writing themselves, but teachers add any Tier 2 words that students haven't chosen. These word walls are taken down after each book or unit is completed.

A second type of word wall features high-frequency words students are learning. Teachers hang large sheets of construction paper—one for each letter of the alphabet—on a wall of the classroom, and then post high-frequency words as they're introduced (Cunningham, 2013; Lynch, 2005). This word wall remains on display all year, and additional words are added during the year. In kindergarten classrooms, teachers begin the school year by placing word cards with students' names on the wall chart and add common environmental print, such as *Walmart* and *McDonald's*. Later in the year, they add words such as *I, love, the, you, Mom, Dad, good*, and other words that students want to read and write.

PROCEDURE. Teachers usually create word walls with the whole class, and they follow these steps:

1. *Prepare the word wall.* Teachers prepare a blank word wall in the classroom from sheets of construction paper or butcher paper, dividing it into 12 to 24 boxes and labeling the boxes with letters of the alphabet.

2. *Introduce the word wall.* Teachers introduce the word wall and write several key words on it when they're beginning a new book or a thematic unit.

3. *Add words to the word wall.* Students suggest "important" words for the word wall as they're reading a book or participating in thematic-unit activities. Students and the teacher write the words in the alphabetized blocks, making sure to write large enough so the words are visible. If a word is misspelled, it's corrected, because students will be using the words in various activities. Sometimes the teacher adds a small picture or writes a synonym for a difficult word, puts a box around the root word, or writes the plural form or other related words nearby.

4. *Use the word wall.* Teachers use the word wall for a variety of word-study activities, and students refer to the word wall when they're writing.

Teachers use word walls during literature focus units and thematic units, and to teach high-frequency words. They involve students in a variety of word-study activities, including **making words**, **word ladders**, and **word sorts**. In addition, teachers use words from high-frequency word walls for word-study activities. One example is a popular word hunt game: Teachers distribute small whiteboards and have students identify and write words from the word wall on their boards according to the clues they provide. For example, depending on what students are learning, teachers say, "Find the word that begins like _____," "Look for the word that rhymes with _____," "Find the word that alphabetically follows _____," or "Think of the word that means the opposite of _____." Students read and reread the words, apply phonics and word-study concepts, and practice spelling high-frequency words as they play this game.

Readers Theatre Scripts

Barchers, S. I. (1997). *50 fabulous fables: Beginning readers theatre*. Portsmouth, NH: Teacher Ideas Press.

Barchers, S. I., & Pfeffinger, C. R. (2006). *More readers theatre for beginning readers*. Portsmouth, NH: Teacher Ideas Press.

Fredericks, A. D. (2007). *Nonfiction readers theatre for beginning readers*. Portsmouth, NH: Teacher Ideas Press.

Laughlin, M. K., Black, P. T., & Loberg, M. K. (1991). *Social studies readers theatre for children: Scripts and script development*. Portsmouth, NH: Teacher Ideas Press.

Martin, J. M. (2002). *12 fabulously funny fairy tale plays*. New York: Scholastic.

Pugliano-Martin, C. (1999). *25 just-right plays for emergent readers*. New York: Scholastic.

Shepard, A. (2007). *Stories on stage: Scripts for reader's theater*. Olympia, WA: Shepard.

Wolf, J. M. (2002). *Cinderella outgrows the glass slipper and other zany fractured fairy tale plays*. New York: Scholastic.

Wolfman, J. (2004). *How and why stories for readers theatre*. Portsmouth, NH: Teacher Ideas Press.

Worthy, J. (2005). *Readers theatre for building fluency: Strategies and scripts for making the most of this highly effective, motivating, and research-based approach to oral reading*. New York: Scholastic.

References

Ashton-Warner, S. (1986). *Teacher*. New York: Simon & Schuster.

Bear, D. R., Invernizzi, M., Templeton, S., & Johnston, F. (2012). *Words their way: Word study for phonics, vocabulary, and spelling instruction* (5th ed.). Upper Saddle River, NJ: Merrill/Prentice Hall.

Black, A., & Stave, A. M. (2007). *A comprehensive guide to readers theatre: Enhancing fluency and comprehension in middle school and beyond*. Newark, DE: International Reading Association.

Brett, J. (1999). *Gingerbread baby*. New York: Putnam.

Brett, J. (2009). *The mitten* (20th anniversary ed.). New York: Putnam.

Buehl, D. (2014). *Classroom strategies for interactive learning* (4th ed.). Newark, DE: International Reading Association.

Button, K., Johnson, M. J., & Furgerson, P. (1996). Interactive writing in a primary classroom. *The Reading Teacher, 49*, 446–454.

Clay, M. M. (2000c). *Running records for classroom teachers*. Portsmouth, NH: Heinemann.

Cronin, D. (2011). *Diary of a spider*. New York: Scholastic.

Cunningham, P. M. (2013). *Phonics they use: Words for reading and writing* (6th ed.). New York: HarperCollins.

Cunningham, P. M., & Allington, R. L. (2010). *Classrooms that work: They can all read and write* (5th ed.). Boston: Allyn & Bacon/Pearson.

Cunningham, P. M., & Cunningham, J. W. (1992). Making words: Enhancing the invented spelling-decoding connection. *The Reading Teacher, 46*, 106–115.

Cunningham, P. M., & Hall, D. P. (2008a). *Making words: First grade*. Boston: Allyn & Bacon/Pearson.

Cunningham, P. M., & Hall, D. P. (2008b). *Making words: Fourth grade*. Boston: Allyn & Bacon/Pearson.

Cunningham, P. M., & Hall, D. P. (2008c). *Making words: Kindergarten*. Boston: Allyn & Bacon/Pearson.

Cunningham, P. M., & Hall, D. P. (2008d). *Making words: Second grade*. Boston: Allyn & Bacon/Pearson.

Cunningham, P. M., & Hall, D. P. (2008e). *Making words: Third grade*. Boston: Allyn & Bacon/Pearson.

Daniels, H. (2001). *Literature circles: Voice and choice in book clubs and reading groups*. York, ME: Stenhouse.

Danziger, P. (1995). *You can't eat your chicken pox, Amber Brown*. New York: Putnam.

Danziger, P. (2006). *Amber Brown is not a crayon*. New York: Scholastic.

Dorros, A. (1997). *Abuela*. New York: Puffin Books.

Fisher, B., & Medvic, E. F. (2000). *Perspectives on shared reading: Planning and practice*. Portsmouth, NH: Heinemann.

Fisher, D., Flood, J., Lapp, D., & Frey, N. (2004). Interactive read-alouds: Is there a common set of implementation practices? *The Reading Teacher, 58*, 8–17.

Fountas, I. C., & Pinnell, G. S. (1996). *Guided reading: Good first teaching for all children*. Portsmouth, NH: Heinemann.

Guthrie, W. (2002). *This land is your land*. Boston: Little, Brown.

Hall, D. (1994). *I am the dog/I am the cat*. New York: Dial Books.

Hancock, M. R. (2008). *A celebration of literature and response: children, books, and teachers in K–8 classrooms* (3rd ed.). Upper Saddle River, NJ: Merrill/Prentice Hall.

Helman, L., Bear, D., Templeton, S., Invernizzi, M., & Johnston, F. (2012). *Words their way with English learners: Word study for phonics, vocabulary, and spelling* (2nd ed.). Upper Saddle River, NJ: Merrill/Prentice Hall.

Holdaway, D. (1979). *The foundations of literacy*. Portsmouth, NH: Heinemann.

Holston, V., & Santa, C. (1985). RAFT: A method of writing across the curriculum that works. *Journal of Reading, 28*, 456–457.

Hoyt, L. (1999). *Revisit, reflect, retell: Strategies for improving reading comprehension*. Portsmouth, NH: Heinemann.

Hoyt, L. (2000). *Snapshots*. Portsmouth, NH: Heinemann.

Hutchins, P. (2005). *Rosie's walk*. New York: Aladdin Books.

Keehn, S., Martinez, M. G., & Roser, N. L. (2005). Exploring character through readers theatre. In N. L. Roser & M. G. Martinez (Eds.), *What a character! Character study as a guide to literary meaning making in grades K–8* (pp. 96–110). Newark, DE: International Reading Association.

Keene, E. O., & Zimmermann, S. (2007). *Mosaic of thought: The power of comprehension strategy instruction* (2nd ed.). Portsmouth, NH: Heinemann.

Koopmans, L. (1995). *The woodcutter's mitten*. New York: Crocodile Books.

Kuskin, K. (2003). *Moon, have you met my mother? The collected poems of Karla Kuskin*. New York: HarperCollins.

Long, M. (2003). *How I became a pirate*. Orlando: Harcourt.

Lynch, J. (2005). *High frequency word walls*. New York: Scholastic.

McKenna, M. C., & Stahl, S. A. (2003). *Assessment for reading instruction*. New York: Guilford Press.

McLaughlin, M., & Allen, M. B. (2001). *Guided comprehension: A teaching model for grades 3–8*. Newark, DE: International Reading Association.

Meddaugh, S. (1998). *Hog-eye*. New York: Sandpiper.

Morrow, L. M. (1985). Retelling stories: A strategy for improving students' comprehension, concept of story structure, and oral language complexity. *Elementary School Journal, 85,* 647–661.

Ogle, D. M. (1986). KWL: A teaching model that develops active reading of expository text. *The Reading Teacher, 39,* 564–570.

Peterson, R., & Eeds, M. (2007). *Grand conversations: Literature groups in action*. New York: Scholastic.

Prelutsky, J. (Sel.). (1983). *The Random House book of poetry for children*. New York: Random House.

Prelutsky, J. (2007). *My parents think I'm sleeping*. New York: Greenwillow.

Rasinski, T. (2005a). *Daily word ladders: Grades 2–3*. New York: Scholastic.

Rasinski, T. (2005b). *Daily word ladders: Grades 4–6*. New York: Scholastic.

Rasinski, T. (2006). Developing vocabulary through word building. In C. C. Block & J. N. Mangieri (Eds.), *The vocabulary-enriched classroom: Practices for improving the reading performance of all students in grades 3 and up* (pp. 36–53). New York: Scholastic.

Rathmann, P. (1995). *Officer Buckle and Gloria*. New York: Putnam.

Reutzel, D. R., & Cooter, R. B., Jr. (2008). *Teaching children to read: From basals to books* (5th ed.). Upper Saddle River, NJ: Merrill/Prentice Hall.

Rickelman, R. J., & Taylor, D. B. (2006). Teaching vocabulary by learning content-area words. In C. C. Block & J. N. Mangieri (Eds.), *The vocabulary-enriched classroom: Practices for improving the reading performance of all students in grades 3 and up* (pp. 54–73). New York: Scholastic.

Soto, G. (2005). *Neighborhood odes*. San Diego: Harcourt.

Spandel, V. (2009). *Creating writers through 6-trait writing assessment and instruction* (5th ed.). Boston: Allyn & Bacon/Pearson.

Taylor, W. L. (1953). "Cloze procedure": A new tool for measuring readability. *Journalism Quarterly, 30,* 415–433.

Tierney, R. J., & Readence, J. E. (2005). *Reading strategies and practices: A compendium* (6th ed.). Boston: Allyn & Bacon.

Tompkins, G. E. (2012). *Teaching writing: Balancing process and product* (6th ed.). Boston: Allyn & Bacon.

Tompkins, G. E., & Collom, S. (Eds.). (2004). *Sharing the pen: Interactive writing with young children*. Upper Saddle River, NJ: Merrill/Prentice Hall.

Tresselt, A. (1989). *The mitten*. New York: Harper Trophy.

Wagstaff, J. (1999). *Teaching reading and writing with word walls*. New York: Scholastic.

Wilhelm, J. D. (2001). *Improving comprehension with think-aloud strategies*. New York: Scholastic.

Yolen, J., & Peters, A. F. (Eds.). (2007). *Here's a little poem*. Cambridge, MA: Candlewick Press.

Glossary

academic vocabulary   Words that are critical to understanding what's taught at school, including school-related words and directions (e.g., *explain, compare,* and *list*), more sophisticated terms for familiar words (e.g., *see—observe*), and content-specific vocabulary (e.g., *amphibian, divide, vowel, paragraph,* and *citizen*).

accommodation   A Piagetian process in which learners create schemas because of new information or experiences.

affix   A syllable that's added to the beginning (prefix) or end (suffix) of a word to change the word's meaning (e.g., *il-* in *illiterate* and *-al* in *national*).

alphabetic principle   The assumption underlying alphabetical language systems that each sound has a corresponding graphic representation (or letter).

antonyms   Words with opposite meanings (e.g., *good—bad*).

assessment   An approach to measuring students' learning that's process-oriented, ongoing, and positive; in contrast to evaluation, which is product-oriented and judgmental. The goal of assessment is to document students' growth, provide feedback, modify instruction when needed, and plan for future instruction.

assimilation   A Piagetian process in which learners modify or incorporate new information and experiences into existing schemas.

automaticity   A component of fluency in which readers identify words accurately and quickly when reading, and writers spell words efficiently to continue writing.

balanced approach   An approach to literacy instruction in which teachers integrate instruction with authentic reading and writing experiences.

basal readers   Reading textbooks that are leveled according to grade.

Basic Interpersonal Communicative Skills (BICS)   Social English skills that children use every day to communicate successfully in home and community situations, in contrast to **Cognitive Academic Language Proficiency** language skills. English learners usually learn social English skills within 2 years after they arrive in the United States.

cloze   An activity in which children replace words that have been deleted from a text.

Cognitive Academic Language Proficiency (CALP)   Academic English skills that children use to communicate successfully in school situations; in contrast to **Basic Interpersonal Communicative Skills**. Academic English skills, including school language and content-area vocabulary, are cognitively more challenging to learn than everyday social skills. English learners often take 7 years or more to catch up with native English speakers.

cognitive strategy   A learning process that requires thinking, such as predicting, inferring, and revising.

compound word   A new word formed with two or more words that has its own meaning; it can be spelled as one word, joined with a hyphen, or spelled as separate words (e.g., *makeup, newspaper, upside-down, mother-in-law, high school, police officer*).

comprehension   The process of constructing meaning using both the author's text and the reader's background knowledge for a specific purpose.

Concepts of Print (CAP)   Assesses young students concepts of written language; book orientation, directionality of print, and letter and word concepts.

consonant   A speech sound characterized by friction or stoppage of the airflow as it passes through the vocal tract; usually any letter except *a, e, i, o,* and *u*.

consonant blend   Two or three adjacent consonants that represent a single, distinguishable sound (e.g., bl-blue, sl-slide, cr-crib, dr--drum, sm--small, sp-space, str-straw).

consonant digraph   Two adjacent consonants that represent a sound not represented by either consonant alone (e.g., *th—this, ch–chin, sh–wash, ph–telephone*).

context clue   Information from the words or sentences surrounding an unfamiliar word that helps to clarify the word's meaning.

critical comprehension   The third level of comprehension; readers analyze symbolic meanings, distinguish between facts and opinions, and draw conclusions.

cueing systems   The phonological, semantic, syntactic, and pragmatic information that children rely on as they read.

dialect   A variety of language, typically representing different social classes or geographic locations.

differentiated instruction   Procedures for assisting children in learning, providing options, challenging them, and matching books to readers to maximize their learning.

diphthong   A sound produced when the tongue glides from one sound to another; it's represented by two vowels (e.g., *oy–boy, ou–house, ow–how*).

echo reading   The teacher or another reader reads a sentence and a group of children reread or "echo" what was read.

editing   The fourth stage of the writing process, in which writers proofread to identify and correct spelling, capitalization, punctuation, and grammar errors.

Elkonin boxes   A procedure for segmenting sounds in a word that involves drawing a box to represent each sound.

emergent literacy   Children's early reading and writing development before conventional reading and writing.

environmental print   Signs, labels, and other print found in the community.

etymology   The study of word origins and how the meaning and spelling of words have evolved through history.

evaluation   Summative assessment that teachers conduct after teaching.

evaluative comprehension   The fourth and most sophisticated level of comprehension; readers judge the value of the text they're reading.

expository text structures   The organizational patterns of nonfiction texts—description, comparison, sequence, cause-effect, and problem-solution.

figurative meaning   An idea that's expressed in an imaginative way, often using a metaphor or simile. For example, the figurative meaning of the phrase *a piece of cake* is "easy." In contrast, the **literal meaning** is factual.

fluency   Reading and writing smoothly, quickly, and with expression.

formative assessment   Informal assessment procedures that teachers use during the learning process.

frustration reading level   The level of reading material that's too difficult for a child to read successfully; accuracy level is less than 90%.

genre A category of literature, such as folklore, science fiction, biography, or historical fiction, or a writing form.

Goldilocks Strategy A technique for choosing "just right" books.

grammar The structure of language; that is, how words combine to form sentences.

grapheme A written representation of a sound using one or more letters.

graphophonemic A phonics term that refers to sound–symbol relationships.

guided reading An instructional approach in which children work in small groups to read as independently as possible a text selected and introduced by the teacher.

high frequency word A common English word, usually a word among the 100 or 300 most common words (e.g., *the, see, go, with*).

high-stakes tests Standardized achievement texts that are administered with the knowledge that important decisions about funding, placement, graduation, or tenure are riding on the result.

homographic homophones Words that sound alike and are spelled alike but have different meanings (e.g., baseball *bat* and the animal *bat*).

homographs Words that are spelled alike but are pronounced differently (e.g., a *present* and to *present*).

homophones Words that sound alike but are spelled differently (e.g., *there–their–they're*); also called *homonyms*.

idioms Expressions that mean something different from the literal meanings of the individual words (e.g., "kick the bucket," "a piece of cake," "hold your horses").

independent reading level The level of reading material that a child can read independently with high comprehension and an accuracy level of 95%–100%.

inferential comprehension The second level of comprehension; readers draw inferences using clues in the text, implied information, and their own background knowledge.

inflectional endings Suffixes that express plurality or possession when added to a noun (e.g., *girls, girl's*), tense when added to a verb (e.g., *walked, walking*), or comparison when added to an adjective (e.g., *happier, happiest*).

informal reading inventory (IRI) An individually administered reading test used to determine children's independent, instructional, and frustration levels and listening capacity level.

instructional reading level The level of reading material that a child can read with teacher support and instruction with 90%–94% accuracy.

invented spelling Children's attempts to spell words that reflect their developing knowledge about the spelling system.

Lexile scores A method of estimating the difficulty level of a text.

literal comprehension The most basic level of comprehension; readers pick out main ideas, sequence details, and notice similarities and differences to understand what's explicitly stated in a text.

literal meaning The meaning of a word or phrase that's straightforward and factual; it's the dictionary definition. The literal meaning of the phrase *a piece of cake* refers to cake, not to whether something is easy.

literature circle An approach to reading instruction in which children meet in small groups to read and respond to a book.

literature focus unit An approach to reading instruction in which the whole class reads and responds to a piece of literature.

mechanics Conventions of writing, including spelling, capitalization, punctuation, and grammar.

metacognition Children's awareness of their own thought and learning processes.

metacognitive strategy A learning process that requires reflection, such as monitoring or evaluating.

metaphor A comparison expressed directly, without using *like* or *as*.

minilesson Explicit instruction about literacy procedures, concepts, strategies, and skills that is taught to small groups or the whole class.

morpheme The smallest meaningful part of a word; sometimes it's a word (e.g., *cup, hope*), and sometimes it's not a whole word (e.g., *-ly, bi-*).

onset The part of a syllable (or one-syllable word) that comes before the vowel (e.g., *str* in *string*).

orthography The spelling system.

phoneme A sound; it's represented in print with slashes (e.g., /s/ and /th/).

phoneme–grapheme correspondence The relationships between sounds and the letters that represent them.

phonemic awareness The ability to manipulate the sounds in words orally.

phonics Predictable relationships between phonemes and graphemes.

phonogram A rime used for word-family decoding and spelling activities.

phonological awareness The ability to identify and manipulate phonemes, onsets and rimes, and syllables; it includes phonemic awareness.

phonology The sound system of language.

phonological system The way sounds in a language are organized. Our sound system in English is organized around these kinds of sounds: syllables, onset-rimes, and phonemes. By contrast, the phonological system of Chinese languages includes tones ranging from a low pitch to a high pitch. To understand Chinese languages, you would need to develop an awareness of the tones you hear.

prefix A syllable added to the beginning of a word to change the word's meaning (e.g., *re-* in *reread*).

prewriting The first stage of the writing process, in which writers gather and organize ideas for writing.

proofreading Reading a composition to identify spelling and other mechanical errors.

prosody The ability to orally read sentences expressively, with appropriate phrasing and intonation.

readability formula A method of estimating the difficulty level of a text.

reader factors The factors that children bring to the reading process that influence their success, including background knowledge, ability to apply comprehension strategies, and engagement with the task.

reading rate Reading speed, usually reported as the average number of words read correctly in 1 minute.

repetend The theme of a multigenre project.

rime The part of a syllable (or one-syllable word) that begins with the vowel (e.g., *ing* in *string*).

rubric A guide listing specific criteria for evaluating children's work; it includes levels of achievement and is scored numerically.

schema A cognitive structure or mental file.

self-efficacy Children's belief in their capability to succeed and reach their goals; children who have self-efficacy are more likely to be higher achieving readers and writers.

shared reading   The teacher reads a book aloud, often a big book, as a group of children follow along in the text.

simile   A figure of speech that compares two things using *like* or *as*, for example, "as snug as a bug in a rug," "as blind as a bat," and "stand out like a sore thumb."

skill   An automatic processing behavior that children use in reading and writing, such as sounding out words, recognizing antonyms, and capitalizing proper nouns.

strategy   A problem-solving behavior that children use in reading and writing, such as predicting, monitoring, visualizing, and summarizing.

suffix   A syllable added to the end of a word to change the word's meaning (e.g., *-y* in *hairy*, *-ful* in *careful*).

summative assessment   Formal assessment procedures used after learning to judge the children's achievement and the effectiveness of instruction.

synonyms   Words that mean nearly the same thing (e.g., *road–street*).

text factors   Children's knowledge of genres, text structures, and text features that affects their comprehension of stories, nonfiction, and poems.

think-aloud (think-it-out strategy)   A procedure in which teachers or students verbalize their thoughts while reading or writing to describe their use of strategies.

transactional theory   The view that meaning does not reside in the text itself but is something created between the reader and the text during reading. This theory explains why two people can read the same text but come away from it with slightly different understandings.

vowel   A voiced speech sound made without friction or stoppage of the airflow as it passes through the vocal tract; the letters *a, e, i, o, u,* and sometimes *w* and *y*.

vowel digraph   Two or more adjacent vowels in a syllable that represent a single sound (e.g., *bread, eight, pain, saw*).

word consciousness   Children's interest in and awareness of words and their meanings.

word sort   A word-study activity in which children group words into categories.

word wall   An alphabetized chart posted in the classroom listing words children are learning.

writing process   The process in which children use prewriting, drafting, revising, editing, and publishing to develop and refine a composition.

zone of proximal development   The distance between a child's actual developmental level and his or her potential level that can be reached with teacher scaffolding.

Index

Note: Page numbers followed by *f* represent figures.